Severe and Mild Depression

THE PSYCHOTHERAPEUTIC
APPROACH

SEVERE
AND MILD
DEPRESSION

The Psychotherapeutic
Approach

SILVANO ARIETI, M.D.
&
JULES BEMPORAD, M.D.

Basic Books, Inc., Publishers

NEW YORK

Library of Congress Cataloging in Publication Data

Arieti, Silvano.
    Severe and mild depression.

    Bibliography: p. 431
    Includes index.
    1. Depression, Mental. I. Bemporad, Jules, joint
author. II. Title. [DNLM: 1. Depression—Therapy.
WM171 A698s]
RC537.A73   616.8'52   78-53811
ISBN: 0-465-07693-9

To Vana and Enrico

aunt and uncle of Silvano Arieti

mother and father of Jules Bemporad

CONTENTS

PART FOUR

Sociological and Literary Aspects of Depression

PART FIVE

Further Analysis of Cognition and Depression

PREFACE

The abnormal state of the psyche called depression has been known since biblical and Homeric times, but the present decade has seen an unusual intensification of interest in this disorder. The condition is very common and affects many people in various degrees, ranging from relatively mild disturbances to the most severe types of suffering.

Recent interest has focused on the study of depression as a metabolic disorder, to be treated exclusively or predominantly with drug therapy. This book is the effort of two authors who belong to what is today a minority, but a vocal minority which wants to be heard as widely as possible, for its exponents feel they have important things to say, even to psychiatrists who follow a basically different approach.

With the present work, we wish to illustrate the importance of psychological factors in both the etiology and the therapy of depression. We attempt to clarify how these factors came to be and how their effects can be corrected or resolved. These psychological factors may not be the only ones involved in every case of depression, but we believe they are necessary; they are always there to be found if we know how to search for them, and we must account for them, unless we settle for a superficial and symptomatic recovery which may relapse at any time. Even a therapist who treats depressed patients mainly with tricyclics and monoamine oxidase (MAO) inhibitors cannot help practicing some kind of psychotherapy, cannot help inquiring about the dynamics of the patient's anguish and conflict, cannot refrain from interpreting the patient's past history and what goes on in the therapeutic situation.

After reviewing the major theories of depression and describing the clinical symptomatology of its various forms, we examine the psychodynamics and psychotherapy of this condition in adults, children, and adolescents. Special chapters are devoted to the depressions occurring postpartum and in the middle years. One of the early chapters deals with the psychobiology of sadness—a knowledge of which is a prerequisite to the understanding of depression. One of the last chapters deals with the sociocultural factors which may be intimately involved in the engendering of depression.

The field of depression is vast, and no single psychiatrist can master it in its entirety. Each of us has written the sections of the book that deal with the areas of his respective competence. One of us, Silvano Arieti, prepared the chapters on severe depressions in adults, as well as one on the questions of the psychological approach: chapters 1, 3, 5, 6, 9, 10, 11, and 12. The other, Jules Bemporad, prepared the chapters on mild depression in adults and those on depression in children and adolescents, as well as a chapter on the major concepts of depression: chapters 2, 4, 7, 8, 13, 14, 15, 17, and 18. Chapter 16, which deals with sociocultural factors, is divided into two parts: the first is written by Silvano Arieti, and the second is by Jules Bemporad.

Although both of us conceived this work in its general content, policy, and major points of view, no page of the book (with the exception of this preface) has been written in collaboration. In each chapter the respective author is indicated.

We hope that the detailed case reports presented in chapters 10, 11, 12, and 14 will illustrate at a practical level the nature of our work and will clarify the theoretical premises reported in other chapters.

Those who look for confirmation from statistics gathered from studying large numbers of patients will not find what they seek in this book. This statistical type of study is incompatible with an in-depth and thorough psychodynamic investigation which limits the number of individuals who can be studied. Although we feel that we have covered a vast panorama of depression from childhood to maturity, depth has been our prime concern and not the number of patients treated.

If the reading of this book succeeds in convincing our colleagues that this approach is effective and not at all difficult to follow once the therapist has overcome his first hesitations and reservations, we shall feel fulfilled in our effort. We shall renew our hopes that many others will pursue and further explore this promising type of research and therapy.

Silvano Arieti, M.D.
Jules Bemporad, M.D.

PART ONE

Basic Notions and
Manifest Symptomatology

[I]

THE BASIC QUESTIONS AND
THE PSYCHOLOGICAL APPROACH

Common is the sorrow that visits the human being when an adverse event hits his precarious existence or when the discrepancy between the way life is and the way it possibly could be becomes the center of his fervid reflection. In some people this sorrow comes and goes repeatedly, and in some others, only from time to time. It is painful, delays actions, and generally heals, often but not always after deepening its host's understanding and hastening his maturation.

Less common—but frequent enough to constitute a major psychiatric concern—is the sorrow that does not abate with the passage of time, that seems exaggerated in relation to the supposed precipitating event, or inappropriate, or unrelated to any discernible cause, or replacing a more congruous emotion. This sorrow slows down, interrupts, or disrupts one's actions; it spreads a sense of anguish which may become difficult to contain; at times it tends to expand relentlessly into a psyche which seems endless in its capacity to experience mental pain; often it recurs even after appearing to be healed. This emotional state is generally called depression.

Is it just a feeling? Is it a syndrome? Is it a disease? It is a feeling but, contrary to common sorrow and sadness, it is also a syndrome insofar as it brings about severe alterations of psychological and some somatic functions. Whether or not it is a disease depends on the definition given to the term disease. If "disease" means a condition that causes a dysfunction of the organism, irrespective of evidence of cellular pathology and irrespective of the nature of the cause which determined it, we can certainly call depression a disease. Again, we must carefully differentiate depression from sadness and normal sorrow, which is a topic we shall take into con-

This chapter was written by Silvano Arieti.

sideration in chapter 5. Depression thus implies deviation from the normal way of experiencing some emotions, including sadness and sorrow.

One of the basic and most frequently asked questions is whether this deviation from the normal is *dependent upon external circumstances.* Many authors have emphatically stressed that depression is not dependent upon external circumstances; at times a dependency seems to exist, but it is illusory. An unpleasant event which would elicit only temporary sadness or sorrow in the normal person, brings about in the patient a psychiatric illness that soon reveals an autonomous process. This psychiatric illness is at first difficult to distinguish from normal sadness, but eventually it is accompanied by agitation and restlessness or by severe retardation, inhibition, reduction in responsiveness to external stimuli, and recurrent sequences of gloomy and pessimistic thoughts. In some cases —those labeled manic-depressive—this psychiatric picture alternates with periods of euphoria and motor excitement.

If this condition is an illness or a medical entity, and if it is not found to be connected with external circumstances and has an autonomous development, then the conclusion drawn by many is that it is an endogenous condition; that is, originating within the organism itself.

When such a position is taken, research along certain lines of inquiry receives momentum. Inasmuch as neuropathological research proved to be completely useless since the time of Kraepelin (1921), the major fields investigated have been the genetic and the biochemical. It is not within the scope of this book to cover these two vast fields. We shall mention only that several authors have found evidence that at least in biphasic manic-depressive psychosis (a disorder characterized by both depressive and manic attacks) there is a genetic factor. (See Mendels, 1974; Cadoret and Tanna, 1977.) Perris (1966) also reached the conclusion that patients who suffer from both manic and depressive episodes are to be genetically distinguished from those who suffer only from depressive attacks. In a subsequent article, Perris (1976) reached the moderate conclusion that "the combined results of clinical and biological studies of affective disorders support the hypothesis that genetic factors are of some importance for the occurrence of at least some groups of these disorders" (especially those presenting both the manic and the depressive phases).

Contrasting with quite a large number of authors who have concluded that a genetic factor may be involved in the typical biphasic manic-depressive disorder is the work of Odegard (1963), which showed no genetic difference between psychotic and neurotic forms of depression. In summary, a genetic factor seems to have been almost convincingly demonstrated only in typical cases of manic-depressive psychosis. In them, too, however, it seems to be in the nature of a predisposition, and not a factor sufficient in itself to bring about the clinical condition.

If studies on heredity are far from conclusive, biochemical studies are even more so. The most promising line of research has followed the catecholamine hypothesis, according to which depression may be connected with decreased activity of some amine synaptic neurotransmitters, probably norepinephrine and dopamine. Conversely, in manic states there would be increased activity of these amines. This hypothesis and others have not gone beyond the hypothetical stage. (See Mendels, Stern, and Frazer, 1976.)

Another issue which to my knowledge has not been investigated is that the biological predisposition may consist of a greater facility to activate specific neuronal spatio-temporal patterns in the brain. These spatio-temporal patterns ultimately would engage more intensively than usual those parts of the limbic system or other parts of the brain that mediate the phenomenon of depression.

I am not in a position to say whether these altered patterns ultimately could be subsumed in the category of altered biochemical events. But it seems to me that we should not bypass in a cavalier fashion a level of investigation which has been followed in the studies of other functions— for instance, language. Obviously we cannot believe that there is a center of sadness and depression which is similar to language centers or even to the pleasure center that the experiments by Olds and Milner (1954) suggest. If areas which mediate sadness and depression do exist, they probably consist of many cerebral areas, not contiguous, but working together through neuronal associations and constituting what Luria (1966, 1973) called a functional system.

In contrast with my hesitation in taking any position about the previous matter is the security with which I can make the following affirmation: in the several decades spent in psychiatric practice and research, I have never treated for a considerable length of time a case of depression about which I could say that there was no psychological factor involved. I have never seen a patient about whom I could say that his depression was unrelated to a prior anguish, or about whom I could say that his depression came from nowhere and its origin had to be sought exclusively in a metabolic disorder. And yet I want to stress that my experience deals predominantly with cases of severe depression that many authors call endogenous. Bemporad (who is not the author of this chapter), joins me in asserting that in the mild cases of depression which he has treated there was always some psychological factor involved.

Does this mean that the position taken in this book is that every case of depression is a *reactive* depression? Not at all, at least in the sense in which the word reaction is used by many psychiatrists. The concept of psychiatric illness as a reaction is attributed by some to Karl Bonhoeffer, who described what he called "exogenous reactions" (1910). However, Bonhoeffer referred to diseases of the brain caused by external toxic agents. He interpreted mental illness as a reaction to a physical alteration.

In the United States the concept of depression as a reaction derives from the works and teachings of Adolph Meyer. Although Meyer was much more interested in schizophrenia, he also enunciated for depression some principles that followed his general psychiatric orientation. He spoke of patients who "are apt to *react* with a peculiar depressive reaction where others get along with fair balance" (1908*a*). (Italics mine.) In the same article Meyer stated, ". . . the etiology thus involves (1) constitutional make-up and (2) a precipitating factor; and in our eagerness we cut out the latter and only speak of the heredity or constitutional make-up. It is my contention that we must use *both* facts and that of the two, for *prevention* and for special characterization of the make-up, the precipitating factor is of the greater importance because it alone gives us an idea of the actual defect and a suggestion as to how to strengthen the person that he may become resistive." (Italics in the original.)

Adolph Meyer's words, written in 1908, retain their poignancy today. Meyer stressed that both factors have to be considered. He italicized "both" but not "reaction." Although Meyer referred to the precipitating factor as being important "because it alone gives us an idea of the actual defect," American psychiatry subsequently gave the emphasis to the concept of reaction. But what was the nature of the defect to which Meyer referred? We know from his other works and especially from his studies on schizophrenia that he felt both the "actual defect" and the reaction were the result of the total life experience of the patient as well as of his biological endowment (the psychobiologic set). However, if Meyer was not able to penetrate sufficiently into the depth psychology of the schizophrenic, even though he studied him longitudinally, he was even less able to do so with the depressed patient. Although Meyer very correctly stressed that "the reaction" would not occur in psychiatric patients if they had not been prepared for it, he investigated this preparation in a vague and unsatisfactory way; namely as "substitutive activity" (Meyer, 1908*b*). As a result of Meyer's influence, American psychiatrists could be divided into two groups: the group who gave importance only to the reaction and saw the patient as a passive entity dominated by the external event; and the group who retained the old conception that the patient was suffering from an endogenous disease and therefore was to be viewed as an organism at the mercy of its chromosomic or metabolic destiny.

It is not the aim of this book to demonstrate or deny the existence of constitutional or biochemical factors. Whether such factors exist is not of major relevance to our theme, according to which other factors— psychological factors—must exist or at least coexist. Inasmuch as every psychological event requires neurophysiological and biochemical mechanism for its occurrence, in this book the existence of such mechanisms is reaffirmed but not studied.

Although the authors of this book give major importance to psychological factors, they do not subscribe to the usual concept of reaction. When the authors use the word "reaction" to describe some forms of depression in which the precipitating event seems of major importance (for instance, in the so-called reactive depression), they follow a commonly adopted terminology in order to prevent possible confusion.

The reason that does not permit us to embrace the concept of reaction, even in cases where the precipitating event exists and is likely to be of the greatest importance, is the conclusion drawn from our studies that such an event would not have become a precipitating factor unless it had a special meaning for the patient, and consequently an assumed pathogenetic power. Thus the environment and the patient both contribute to the transformation of the event into a cause: the environment, by offering the contingency of the event; the patient, by attributing either consciously or unconsciously a special meaning to the event. Furthermore, the event would not be given such a meaning and would not be endowed with such power if the patient had not integrated his past life experiences and personality in specific ways.

For many years I have indicated (and Bemporad, through clinical work, has also confirmed) that a preceding ideology prepares the ground for depression. The ideology is responsible for the special meaning given to the precipitating event and for the way the patient deals with that event. When there is no recognizable precipitating event, there is nevertheless a special preexisting ideology which to some extent consciously, and to a much larger extent unconsciously, has prepared the ground for the depressive outcome. The ideology, which had an integrative function in the life of the patient and was used as a defense, now makes him experience a state of partial or total loss, helplessness, or hopelessness which is accompanied by depression. Whereas the depression generally remains as a subjective and conscious phenomenon, the cognitive substratum may become partially or totally unconscious.

In this book we shall illustrate how this ideology came to be. In many cases its origin can be traced to childhood events. However, it will be apparent to the reader that although we consider childhood experiences very important, in agreement with classic Freudian tenets, we do not consider them the exclusive determinants of a psychopathological course of events as it unfolds in the life history of the patient.

In the terminology of general systems theory, the psyche is not a closed system but a system open to continuous influences from factors occurring outside the system (Bertalanffy, 1956). Psychopathological structures are also open systems. They are states of various degrees of improbability that are maintained by negative psychological entropy coming from outside the original system. An open system such as the psyche follows the principle of equifinality; the final state is not unequivocally determined by the initial condition. Each stage of life is under the influence of the previous stages, but not in rigid or ineluctable ways. Other factors intervene. Early experiences participate in causing depression only when, together with other factors, they facilitate the formation of an ideology which will lead to unfavorable patterns of living.

Several issues emerge from the foregoing. Even though we speak of patterns of living and of specific behavior throughout this book, we do not focus on the external behavior, but on the ideology and subsequent mechanisms that lead to the formation of these patterns. It is for this reason that our approach is called cognitive. Although I have done psychiatric research on cognition since 1946, my first writings on cognition in reference to depression appeared in 1959 and 1962. Since 1963 Aaron Beck has also stressed the cognitive approach to depression. The approach that I have proposed and to which Bemporad has added a number of original contributions differs from Beck's in that our approach is longitudinal and dynamic. It does not stress the point that the patient is depressed because he has depressive thoughts, but it puts in evidence a cognitive history whose existence was to a considerable extent unconscious. Many people experience reluctance to accept a cognitive approach lest the affective life and especially motivation, conscious and unconscious, be disregarded or not recognized in its full role. This apprehension particularly is felt in connection with the study and treatment of affective disorders, in which the major deviation from the normal involves affects.

A prevailing cultural anti-intellectualism has caused misapprehensions and distortions even in the fields of psychiatry and psychoanalysis. A cognitive approach stresses a fact which is very seldom acknowledged in psychiatry and psychoanalysis: at a human level most emotions do not exist without a cognitive substratum. The expansion of the neocortex and consequently of our cognitive functions also has permitted an expansion of our affective life. In a classic paper published in 1937, Papez demonstrated that several parts of the rhinencephalon and archipallium (included now after MacLean, 1959, in the limbic system) are not used for olfactory functions in the human being, but for experiencing emotion. In spite of the diminished importance of olfaction, these areas have expanded rather than decreased in man, and have become associated with vast neocortical areas. Elsewhere (Arieti, 1967) I have shown that in the human being elementary emotions, which can exist without or with relatively little cognitive counterpart—such as tension, fear, and rage—are changed into higher emotions (anxiety, anger, depression, hate, and so forth) through the intervention of complicated cognitive mechanisms. It is because of these connections with a potentially infinite realm of symbolic cognition that the emotional life of the human being also becomes immense and potentially infinite. In chapter 5 I shall illustrate how cognitive elements can give rise to sadness and depression.

At the beginning of this century, Bleuler and Jung introduced into psychiatry the concept of "complex." According to Laplanche and Pontalis (1973) a complex is an "organized group of ideas and memories of great affective force which are either partly or totally unconscious. Complexes are constituted on the basis of the interpersonal relationships of childhood history; they may serve to structure all levels of the psyche: emotions, attitudes, adapted behavior."

The concept of complex was embraced immediately by classic psychoanalysts, but Freud soon found it to be an unsatisfactory theoretical notion (Jones, 1955). Since then it has lost popularity in psychoanalytic and psychiatric circles, although gaining great popularity in common parlance. A complex is referred to in this book as a cognitive construct or as a system of constructs. The old term "complex" has lost value in professional circles because not enough importance was given to its cognitive components. It is understood that when we refer to a construct we do not connote something static, but something potentially capable of changing throughout the life of the individual; something which is altered by life events and at the same time is a promoter of other life events.

Although it is important to study the transformation from the cognitive to the affective components of the psyche, it is equally important to study why in our psychiatric cases it is so difficult for the patient to free himself from the intense feeling of depression. Often he cannot escape from the feeling of having lost what was most valuable to him, either something specific or something very vague, undefinable, or impossible to express with words. In serious cases the patient mourns the most profound loss, the loss of life's meaning—an experience which reflects in magnified form an original loss or a series of factual or symbolic losses. In these very serious cases the patient feels or acts as if he had reached an inevitable conclusion that his life is meaningless and worthless. The intense depression that accompanies this apparent conclusion actually betrays the patient's attachment to and love for life, and his inherent premise that life is meaningful and should be worthwhile. There is thus something psychologically positive even in this deep depression. In his inner self the patient is not one of those people who consider the events of the cosmos to be due to random collisions of atoms, transformed by chance into organized unities, and completely independent from the needs of the human heart.

Outside the realm of pathology, is there anything similar to this deep depression which implies the inevitability of what is dreaded most? Yes: the *tragic* situation. The relation between depression and tragedy will be studied in chapter 16.

Before proceeding to discuss further the cognitive approach, I must mention that the other psychological interpretations of depression are reviewed by Bemporad in chapter 2. In chapter 16 the relation between depression and some ideologies to which the patient is exposed in his sociocultural environment also are described and discussed.

The major themes of this book will be, however, the psychopathology and psychotherapy of the individual patient—child, adolescent, and adult. When we go beyond the study of manifest symptomatology and make our first acquaintance with the history of the depressed patient, we feel as if an invisible force, running throughout his life, has brought him to his present predicament. One of the main aims of this book is to make visible that invisible force, by showing how it came into existence and sustained itself on many facts, internal and external, individual and socio-cultural; most of them unconscious and others conscious, but with unconscious ramifications.

Another purpose of this book is to illustrate in detail our psychotherapeutic approach. The psychotherapist intends to affect the psychological etiological factors and mechanisms to such an extent that even when biological mechanisms enter into the picture, by themselves they will not be able to maintain the disorder, at least with the same degree of intensity. A successful psychotherapy also will make much less likely the recurrence of the disorder. We hope that our case reports will support our optimism. We have come to the conclusion that most cases of depression, ranging from mild to severe, benefit from psychotherapy. We do not object to the use of other types of treatment in some cases, but we feel that for many patients the psychotherapeutic approach will prove very rewarding, even when other types of therapy have failed. Combined forms of treatment also can be used in a few selected cases.

Although the patient is by far our major concern, we should not omit considering that the psychotherapeutic approach also is rewarding for the therapist, who learns in greater depth some dimensions of human existence. As I wrote elsewhere (1976), when we successfully treat a patient who has been severely depressed we experience a burst of joy because we have helped a person who is happy to have known us. But we also feel a secret joy because we have come to know the patient, and in knowing him we know more of ourselves. There is always a resonance in our heart for the anguish of the depressed which does not seem to us completely unfounded, but similar to ours, and containing a partial truth based on the human predicament.

This study of the depressed person will show how we ourselves can contribute to our own sorrow with the strange ways in which we mix and give meaning to our ideas and feelings. We shall learn that the study of life circumstances is important, but that even more important is the study of our ideas about these circumstances, our ideals and what we do with them, and how we use them to create feelings. This study will explore, and we hope to some extent enlighten, not just our pathology but our so-called normality; not just our despair but our confident expectation; not just our loneliness but also our ways of helping each other and reinforcing the human bond.

[2]

CRITICAL REVIEW OF THE

MAJOR CONCEPTS OF DEPRESSION

Melancholia is one of the great words of psychiatry. Suffering many mutations, at one time the guardian of outworn
schemes or errant theories, presently misused, cavilled at, dis-
possessed, it has endured into our own times, a part of medical terminology no less than of common sense.

Sir Aubrey Lewis

Introduction

Depression, perhaps unlike any other disorder in psychiatry or in medicine in general, traces its history to the first written records of mankind. Various characters of ancient myths or protagonists in the Bible are depicted as manifesting symptoms which today would be classified as typical of depressive illness. The first objective clinical description of depression was made by Hippocrates, who coined the term "melancholia," intending to call attention to the surfeit of black bile in the depressed individual.

The significance of the early records, as noted by Zilboorg (1944), is that they demonstrate that the symptoms of affective illness have remained essentially the same for twenty-five centuries. Despite this historical consistency of symptom description, the proposed causes and treatments of depression have been revised consistently, reflecting the etiological and theoretical fashions of the day. Therefore any comprehensive summary of the history of depression amounts to a documentation of the evolution of psychiatric thought. In consideration of this enormous literature, I will discuss only those authors who were either pioneers in advancing novel ideas on depression or whose thoughts on depression continue to exert a considerable influence on current conceptualizations.*

This chapter was written by Jules Bemporad.
* The reader is referred to the excellent reviews by Lewis (1934), Jellife (1931), and Zilboorg (1941) for a more exhaustive account of the early psychiatric studies of depression.

The Delineation of a Syndrome

Hippocrates, who is said to have lived in the fourth century BC, gave the first medical description of depression, which he called melancholia, believing it to be caused by an excess of black bile in the brain. He concluded that melancholia was closely related to epilepsy and categorized it with mania, phrenitis, and paranoia as one of the four major types of psychiatric illness. Although Hippocrates may claim priority as the first to describe the disorder, it was Aretaeus of Cappadocia who in the second century AD wrote the most complete, and remarkably modern, depiction of depression. Aretaeus proposed that depression was caused by purely psychological factors and it had little to do with either bile, phlegm, or humours. Aretaeus also seems to have antedated Kraepelin by seventeen centuries in associating mania with depression in certain cases and by considering both conditions as part of a single disease entity. He may even have given a more accurate prognosis than Kraepelin, noting that the illness recurred despite remissions, and recovery from one episode did not ensure cure (Arieti, 1974). Finally, Aretaeus appreciated the significance of interpersonal relationships in the course of depression, reporting the case of a severely disturbed patient who recovered when he fell in love.

We may further appreciate his contributions in the description below, which is remarkably similar to our own contemporary textbooks:

"The characteristic appearances, then, are not obscure; for the patients are dull or stern, dejected or unreasonably torpid, without any manifest cause: such is the commencement of melancholy. And they also become peevish, dispirited, sleepless and start up from a disturbed sleep . . . . They are prone to change their minds readily; to become bossy, mean-spirited, illiberal, and in a little time, perhaps, simple, extravagant, munificent, not from any virtue of soul, but from the changeableness of the disease. But if the illness becomes more urgent, hatred, avoidance of the haunts of men, vain lamentations are seen; they complain of life and desire to die." (Quoted in Lewis, 1934.)

This promising work on depression initiated by Aretaeus (and also by Celsus, who wrote insightful descriptions of depression) was unfortunately not continued by his immediate successors. Galen in the second century also developed a theory of mental illness based on alleged humours. His theory remained doctrine throughout the Middle Ages. It was not until the Renaissance that a renewed interest in depression and an original approach to its causes appeared. This was especially true in Elizabethan England, where an apparent epidemic of melancholia seems to have occurred, as evident from the number of works devoted to this disorder in that short period of history. Timothy Bright published his *Treatise on Melancholia* in 1586 and twenty years later Thomas Walkington's *Optick Glass of Humours* appeared, which dealt extensively with the "melancholick complexion" resulting from humours and the effect of the planets (Veith, 1970). Finally, in 1621 Robert Burton finished his massive *Anatomy of Melancholy* which is still available today. This immense, meandering work is as much a reflection on life as a tome on depression. Despite its encyclopedic comprehensiveness and erudition, it is difficult to distill a central theme on depression in terms of either cause or treatment. Physicians on the continent were discovering again that melancholia and mania often alternate in the same individuals. Bonet in 1684, Schact in 1747, and Herchel in 1768 all associated the two conditions as part of one diagnostic entity.

With the spread of the scientific revolution, psychiatric investigators began to look upon mental illness as caused physiologically rather than by demonic possession. However, there was little overall order in their discoveries; each investigator claimed to have found a new syndrome on the basis of a few patients. It was a time of extremely detailed delineation of pathological states, sanctified by Latin terminology for each diagnostic entity. Falret in 1851 differentiated between ordinary melancholia and the episodic variety, and three years later Baillarger made a similar observation. Falret also coined the term "folie circulaire" and described in some patients the occurrence of healthy intervals, which contrasted with gradual but definite degeneration in other individuals. Falret's other significant contributions were his observations that recurrent depression seemed to be familial and females were more frequently affected. However, the state of the art was actually one of confusion; there was little correspondence between the diagnostic divisions made by different psychiatrists. One general theme that did emerge was the preoccupation with the outcome of a disorder, which then was used to certify its diagnosis. Greisinger in the mid-nineteenth century divided "insanity" into two broad categories: recoverable and incurable. Perhaps the interest in prognosis resulted from a lack of suitable treatment methods, so that studying the course of an illness and then classifying it was the best that could be done.

This state of affairs may help to explain the tremendous contribution of Kraepelin, who revolutionized psychiatry by establishing a nosological system that continues to be used today. Kraepelin sifted out the common elements from the confusion of individualistic syndromes and consolidated these into three major categories of illness: dementia praecox, paraphrenia, and manic-depressive psychosis. He based his classifications on both the similarity of symptoms and the eventual outcome of the disorder.

Kraepelin included a variety of depressive disorders under the larger category of manic-depressive psychosis. He reasoned that this group of disorders shared common symptoms despite superficial differences, that different symptoms might replace one another in the same patient, and that there was a uniformly benign prognosis (Arieti, 1974). In Kraepelin's nosological system, the following mental states were included under manic-depressive psychosis: intermittent psychosis, simple mania, some cases of confusion, most cases of melancholia, and certain cases of mild mood disorders that were prodromal of a more severe condition. Overall, he distinguished four major subgroups: depressive states, manic states, mixed states, and fundamental states, that is, disorders of mood experienced between, before, or as replacing manic-depressive attacks (Braceland, 1957).

Kraepelin's great contribution to psychiatry was in imposing order on the nosological chaos that had existed before him. According to Braceland (1957), when Kraepelin entered psychiatry "workers were floundering helplessly around in a morass of symptoms for which they were unable to find any common denominators" (p. 872). In his attempt at a workable system of classification, Kraepelin followed the medical model; he viewed psychiatric disorders as having an (as yet) unidentified but certain organic cause, a characteristic course, and a predictable outcome.

In keeping with this set of criteria, he differentiated manic-depressive psychosis from dementia praecox, in that the former condition was remitting and normal health returned despite severe derangement during clinical episodes. In a sense Kraepelin created a psychiatry of end results, utilizing prognosis as a major diagnostic criterion.

Although Kraepelin's system was widely adopted and hailed as a major progressive step, it also had its critics. It was argued that in view of the great number of influences (from without and within) acting on any individual, a strictly deterministic prognosis could not be maintained with certainty. In his later writings, Kraepelin conceded the validity of this criticism and admitted that a certain percentage of cases did not follow the prescribed course. However, Kraepelin's critics were not so much concerned with his clinical data as with his fatalistic view of illness and his use of outcome (which could not be known for a single patient) in making a diagnosis.

One of Kraepelin's most vocal critics was Adolf Meyer, whose own system of classification in contrast was based on a broader catagory of reaction types. Meyer had initially welcomed and employed the new Kraepelinian system but he eventually grew skeptical of it because it relied too heavily on outcome. Meyer began to treat psychiatric disorders as influenced by life events rather than by strictly organic conditions that progress regardless of environmental factors. Meyer eventually discarded the disease model entirely, preferring to view psychiatric disorders as an individual's specific reactions to a succession of life events. In 1904 Meyer argued against the term melancholia, stating that it gave a stamp of certainty to a vague condition of which little sure knowledge existed. He suggested that the disorder be called depression, at least until positive evidence of disease (such as brain pathology) could be demonstrated.

Probably Meyer was reflecting a growing mood within psychiatry; that mental illness was to be explained and integrated within a growing knowledge of normal behavior, rather than considered simply as another form of physical illness whose symptoms could be taken at face value and tabulated as if for inventory. He undoubtedly was influenced by the exciting new disclosures of psychoanalysis, whose adherents purported to penetrate beneath the surface manifestations of illness to the hidden core of pathology which then could be understood in psychological terms.

To his death, Kraepelin remained a meticulous and objective observer, unwilling to go beyond the mandate of clinical data. Even when psychoanalysis was already luring the attention of the most promising psychiatrists, he wrote: "As I am accustomed to walk on the sure foundations of direct experience, my Philistine conscience of natural science stumbles at every step on objections, considerations and doubts, over which the lightly soaring power of imagination of Freud's disciples carries them without difficulty." (Cited in Braceland, 1957.)

Kraepelin remains the paragon of the objective scientist who refuses to allow his intuitive hunches to interfere with his carefully documented observations. This imposition of order on the chaos that preceded him may be considered the true beginning of modern psychiatry.

The Search for Causes

One of the great appeals that psychoanalysis held for psychiatrists was its insistence that mental illness was not simply the outward manifestation of cerebral pathology, but that its symptoms were psychological in origin and had meaning. Psychoanalysis offered a way of divining that meaning. Kraepelin essentially had disregarded the actual content of his patients' presentations of illness, relying instead on the formal structure of their illness. For Freud, what a patient said and did had meaning and, if one knew how to investigate these behaviors or symptoms, they revealed a sense of logic that could be understood. Beyond Freud's theory of human nature, his formulations of the unconscious, the elaboration of ego defenses, the prepotency of childhood traumas, and the general theory of drives and their derivatives, there is a monumental attempt to seek out the causes of illness. Whether or not any modern student of psychopathology adopts the orthodox viewpoint, it cannot be doubted that he will be influenced by the psychoanalytic search for the hidden motives of behavior.

It was because of this need to prove the existence of disguised motivation that the early psychoanalysts dealt with disorders such as hysteria or obsessive compulsive neurosis, which they believed could demonstrate more readily evidence of unconscious conflicts. Depression, which does not manifest dramatic symptoms that can be interpreted as symbolic of deeper problems, was initially ignored. It was only after Freud had investigated hysteria, obsessions, dreams, parapraxes, jokes, childhood sexuality, and paranoia that he turned his attention to depressive states. When he and his followers did interest themselves in depressive states, their formulations were no less imaginative or revolutionary. The influence of these early psychoanalytic investigations on subsequent psychiatric attitudes toward affective disorders cannot be emphasized strongly enough and consequently will be presented here in rather meticulous detail.

ABRAHAM'S EARLY CONTRIBUTIONS

In 1911 Karl Abraham published what may be considered the first psychoanalytic investigation of depression. This pioneer paper must be understood retrospectively within the then prevailing psychoanalytic formulations. In 1911 psychoneurosis was interpreted as a result of repression of libido, so that in this early paper Abraham compares depression to anxiety, which also was believed to be the result of repressed drives. Abraham differentiates between these two states: while anxiety arises when repression prevents the attainment of desired gratification that may still be possible, depression arises when the individual has given up the hope of satisfying his libidinal strivings. Furthermore, in depression the striving toward libidinal satisfaction is so deeply repressed that the individual is unable to feel loved or able to love, despairing of ever achieving emotional intimacy. Thus Abraham applies the basic doctrine of excessive repression of libido to depression and goes on to confirm this formulation by describing six depressed patients that he treated. These case studies remain classics of description in the psychoanalytic literature.

In discussing these patients, Abraham first draws attention to the similarity between depressed and obsessive patients, a relationship that occurs repeatedly in Abraham's works. In both conditions, Abraham finds a profound ambivalence toward others, in which the striving toward love is blocked by strong feelings of hatred which in turn are repressed because the individual cannot acknowledge his extreme hostility. As with the obsessive, the depressive cannot develop adequately because his feelings of hatred and love constantly interfere with each other. The depressive's interpersonal relations illustrate this repressed hatred which is rooted in blocked libido.

Although the ability to love others is blocked in both conditions because of repression of libido, depressives and obsessives differ radically in the way the blocked impulses find substitutive expression. In the obsessive, repetitive rituals replace the original unacceptable sexual desires. For the depressive, Abraham postulates a peculiar process of projection which he appears to have modeled after the explanation of paranoia that

Freud had recently formulated. The internal dynamic processes of the depressive are that he basically feels, "I cannot love people; I have to hate them." This acknowledgement of hatred is unacceptable and must be repressed. Then the hostility is projected onto others and conscious thought is transformed into, "People do not love me; they hate me." This formulation is acceptable and further bolstered by the rationalization that being hated is justified because of some imagined inborn defect.

Abraham goes on to explain other significant aspects of depression on the basis of repression. In a surprisingly modern observation, he states that the massive guilt of the depressive is due to his actual destructive wishes which are kept unconscious. This repressed hostility is clearly manifested in dreams, parapraxes, and other symbolic acts. Abraham asserts that some patients take pride in their sense of guilt, wishing "to be a criminal of the deepest dye, to have more guilt than anyone else put together" (1911, p. 146). He also notes that some depressives appear to enjoy their self-reproaches and to take pleasure in suffering because it allows them to center all of their thoughts on themselves. This self-involvement accounts for the delusions of impoverishment which are symbolic of the emotional deprivation that results from the withdrawal of libido from one's surroundings.

The remainder of Abraham's early contribution concerns itself with mania and with the suitability of depressed individuals for psychoanalytic therapy. Mania is considered to be the overt manifestation of what was repressed during the depressed phase. The blatant expression of love and hate, aptly termed "a frenzy of freedom," which is seen in the manic phase is interpreted as a return to the phase of childhood before the repression of emotion took place. He observes that interviewing a manic adult is much like talking to a five-year old. Abraham admits that he is at a loss to explain why this lifting of repression should occur in some cases and not in others.

The significance of this pioneering work lies in its attempt to bring the affective disorders within the realm of psychoanalytic understanding. In so doing, Abraham limits himself to the formulations available at that time, such as repression and projection. Yet even in this early paper Abraham identifies significant aspects of depressive illness that were missed by previous investigators. He perceives the depressive's ambivalence and his inability to truly love others. He also touches on the depressive's excessive self-concern and his utilization of guilt to draw attention to himself. Finally, Abraham notes the basic hostility which blocks proper emotional growth. In retrospect, what may be lacking here is an appreciation of the role others play in the etiology and maintenance of a depressive episode. The significance of object loss, which later is to become the cardinal event in depression, is not mentioned. Rather, Abraham speculates that affective disorders develop as a result of feelings of being incapable to face the responsibilities of an adult role in society. Ironically, these conclusions were later reached by Adler and others who repudiated much of Freudian theory.

Five years later Abraham published his second contribution to affective disorders, a paper entitled "The First Pregenital Stage of the Libido." The very title of this work indicates the shift that had taken place since the appearance of the preceding paper. In the opening sentences Abraham expresses his intention to give clinical support to the theories Freud had expounded in the third edition of his *Three Essays on the Theory of Sexuality*, which appeared in 1915. Thus Abraham undertakes the task of demonstrating how depression can be integrated into the formulation of regression to a particular libidinal stage of development.

Abraham believes that depression can be understood as a regression to the first psychosexual or oral phase. The similarity between the oral phase and depression is to be found in the mode of libidinal discharge as well as in a characteristic form of object relations. Freud indicated that the orally fixated individual's dominant mode of unconscious relationships was characterized by introjection. Abraham believes that the depressive goes beyond incorporating the psychic object: "In the depths of his unconscious there is a tendency to devour and demolish the object." (1916, p. 276.) It is this unconscious desire to destroy the object orally that accounts for two of the major symptoms of depression: the refusal to take food (that is, equating food with the love object that the individual fears he will destroy) and the fear of starvation (again resulting from a fear of realizing the oral-destructive wishes). Abraham also argues for a seeming antithetical situation; that in some depressives taking food relieves the feeling of depression. However, even in this instance Abraham notes the relationship between depression and orality.

In this contribution the reader begins to detect a drifting away from empirical observation and a subtle yet persistent tendency to force clinical data to fit pre-existing theory. Furthermore, the theory itself becomes more distant from actual observation and thus more difficult to validate empirically. The formulation that depression is an unconscious regression to the first pregenital stage of libido, entailing cannibalistic fantasies as well as defenses against the wishes, is a highly complex formulation that reflects the growing speculative and convoluted nature of psychoanalytic theory. This paper is noteworthy, however, in postulating the role of introjection in depression, which anticipates Freud's later contribution to this subject. Perhaps of greater heuristic value is Abraham's broadening of the libidinal stages to include modes of object relations rather than simply modes of libidinal gratification. In this sense, the pregenital stages become more psychological and less biological, eventually culminating in the work of Sullivan, Fairbairn, and the ego psychologists.

In his third contribution on depression, which appeared in 1924, Abraham continued to trace the origins of the disorder to fixation at the oral stage, although Freud by this time had published his own views on melancholia. Although he again tries to find confirmation for Freud's theories, in this particular publication Abraham seems primarily intent on organizing a typology of illness based on fixations at particular libidinal stages. As before, Abraham begins with the similarity between obsessives and melancholics. Both form ambivalent relationships and show aberrant character traits, such as excessive orderliness and overconcern about money. Abraham speculates that the depressive is actually obsessional during his healthy intervals. He then proposes that both types regress to early pregenital stages; but while the obsessive appears to be satisfied with an unconscious control of the love object, the depressive actually destroys the internalized psychic object. In order to account for this difference, Abraham postulates two subphases of the anal stage: a later phase characterized by witholding, and an earlier phase characterized by expulsion. Abraham suggests that in later life the individual treats his internalized love object the way he originally treated his "earliest piece of private property," namely his feces. He stipulates that the obsessive regresses to the later anal stage, thus maintaining the object; and the depressive regresses to the earlier anal phase, unconsciously expelling and losing the love object. He believes that the obsessive is able to mobilize defenses against further regression that the depressive cannot muster. As a result, the depressive's loss of the internalized love object leaves him with a sense of inner emptiness that he desperately tries to rectify by oral incorporation. Abraham renews his emphasis on oral symptoms in depression: this time he interprets them as efforts to reincorporate the destroyed love object. As proof of his hypothesis, Abraham cites the frequency of coprophilic fantasies in depression, which he interprets not as attempts at self-debasement, but as an unconscious wish to incorporate the anally expelled object by oral means.

Although much of Abraham's effort in this contribution appears to define further the fixation points for later psychopathology, he also strives to integrate the latest of Freud's theories; in this case the essay *Mourning and Melancholia*, which will be discussed in detail. For the present, it is sufficient to note briefly that Abraham does associate a reparative incorporation of the love object, which is subsequent to loss in depression, with a later ambivalent relationship to this introjected object. This aspect of Freud's theory clearly coincides with Abraham's own contributions. He further agrees that the lost object is treated as part of the ego, so that there is an ambivalent regard toward one's own self, as exemplified by the contrasting self-recriminations during depression and the depressive's feeling superiority during healthy intervals.

Thus having interwoven his own research with current Freudian thinking, Abraham moves on to etiological considerations, in which on clinical grounds his observations again are outstanding. He notes the frequent correlation between the onset of depression and a disappointment in love.

Analysis of these cases "invariably" shows that the rejection had a great pathogenic effect because it was sensed in the unconscious to be a repetition of childhood loss of a love object. This early traumatic experience is a potent etiological predisposer to later depressions following any loss. In line with this theory of libidinal development, Abraham states that the childhood disappointment must occur prior to the Oedipal stage when the child's libido is still "narcissistic." That is, object love is tinged with bringing the mental representation of the love object into one's unconscious and treating it as part of one's own self, as well as wishing to destroy it (as described previously). Significant for later theory is Abraham's conclusion, as a result of these theoretical speculations, that since the trauma occurred so early in life it must have been the result of inadequate mothering rather than Oedipal rivalry.

In the last part of this paper, Abraham gives a summary of all three of his contributions on depression and considers various predisposing factors, which are: (1) A constitutional factor in regard to an overaccentuation of oral-eroticism. (2) A special fixation of the libido at the oral level, manifested by disproportionate grievance at frustration and an over-utilization of oral activities (sucking, eating, etc.) in everyday life. (3) A severe injury to infantile narcissism brought about by successive disappointments in love, leading to the childhood prototype of depression called "primal parathymia." (4) The occurrence of the first important disappointment in love before the Oedipal wishes have been overcome. (5) The repetition of the primary disappointment in later life. Throughout, Abraham stresses the importance of ambivalence, be it toward others or toward the incorporated object.

Abraham's final position on depression may be summarized by the following quotation: "When melancholic persons suffer an unbearable disappointment from their love-object they tend to expel that object as though it were feces and to destroy it. They thereupon accomplish the act of introjecting and devouring it—an act which is a specifically melancholic form of narcissistic identification. Their sadistic thirst for vengeance now finds its satisfaction in tormenting the ego—an activity which is in part pleasurable." (1924, p. 469)

In conclusion, Abraham may well be remembered as the person who initiated the psychoanalytic study of depression. He wrote at a time when psychoanalytic theory was fairly uncomplicated, when all psychological illness could be conceived as regression to particular libidinal fixation points.* However, in addition to carefully delineating and defining the specific fixations in depression, he stressed the important role of ambivalence, the theory of childhood disappointment in love relationships, and the notion that depression is an adult recapitulation of a childhood

---

* It may be of interest that Freud criticized Abraham as placing too much importance on libidinal stages and ignoring the other aspects of the personality. (See Jones, 1955, Vol. II.)

trauma. Therefore, even while formulating a somewhat mechanistic metapsychology of melancholia, his clinical acumen allowed him to perceive the powerful interpersonal and psychological aspects of depression.

MOURNING AND MELANCHOLIA

It may be no understatement that Freud's short essay, *Mourning and Melancholia* (1917), changed the course of psychoanalysis. This work stands out because it is the first time that Freud postulates any pathological mechanisms in which the thwarting of sexuality does not play a role. Furthermore, in this paper Freud talks about "object relations" rather than repression, sketches out an agency that later was to become the superego, and also enlarges the role of the ego in pathology. The whole British school of psychoanalysis appears to have its roots in this seminal work in which Freud alters the content of the unconscious to include objects (i.e., mental representations of others) as well as affects and ideas. With this paper, the "mature" works of Freud begin. There is now an appreciation of guilt and aggression as primary motivations, at the expense of blocked erotic expression.

According to Jones (1955), Freud expressed an interest in depression as early as 1914, possibly stimulated by the work of Abraham and Tausk. He wrote *Mourning and Melancholia* in 1915, but it did not appear until 1917 because of the war. The paper is barely twenty pages in length, yet its effect was remarkable; it continues to influence views on depression half a century later, and to reorient much of the course of psychoanalytic investigation. The paper demonstrates flashes of Freud's genius—his ability to see clinical manifestation from a startling new perspective and his power of insightful logical argument.

Freud begins this essay by expressing concern over writing about melancholia, since ultimately this diagnosis may characterize a group of disorders. He further warns the reader that he is basing his findings on a small group of patients who may not warrant generalization.

Freud then compares melancholia with the phenomenon of mourning, noting numerous similarities as well as some critical differences: both share a sense of painful dejection over a loss, a lack of interest in the outside world, the loss of the capacity to love, and an inhibition in activity. However, only melancholia exhibits lowering of self-regard to the extent that there are utterances of self-reproach and an irrational expectation of punishment. Additionally, the melancholic is vague about the nature of his loss, and he is not aware of what has given rise to his dejection. Even when aware of whom he has lost, he is not clear "what it is he has lost in them." This finding leads Freud to believe the loss is internal and unconscious. The loss of self-esteem also points to an internal impoverishment. "In grief," states Freud, "the world has become poor and empty; in melancholia it is the ego itself." How then does Freud account for this inner sense of loss in depression?

He picks up his cue from the inappropriate self-reproaches which (1) are usually moral in content, (2) are grossly unjustified, and (3) are publicly and shamelessly declared. According to Freud this is due to a split in the melancholic's ego, in which one part sets itself over and against the other, judges it critically, and looks upon it as an external object.* From these clinical data, Freud speculates that the self-reproaches are not really directed at the self at all, but at some person whom the patient loves, has loved, or ought to have loved. The key to the clinical picture is that the self-reproaches are actually reproaches against a loved object that have been shifted onto the patient's own ego. Therefore the melancholic need have no shame over these reproaches, since they are intended for someone else. Freud shrewdly adds that the melancholic does not really act like a worthless person, despite his protestations, but constantly takes offense as if he had been treated with great injustice. How does this intrapsychic process of shifting an object onto the ego develop?

Freud postulates that in childhood the future melancholic formed an intense object relationship which was undermined because of a disappointment with the loved person. A withdrawal of libidinal investment followed the rupture of the relationship, but the freed libido was not transferred to another object, possibly because of a basically narcissistic type of relating. Instead this libido was withdrawn into the ego. However, an identification was made between part of the ego and the forsaken object, and this ego identification absorbs the libido. Freud describes this process with his famous and dramatic words: "Thus the shadow of the object fell upon the ego, so that the latter could henceforth be criticized by a special mental faculty like an object, like the forsaken object." Therefore the internalized effigy of the lost object becomes subject to the ambivalent feelings of the individual and is subject to the scorn and hatred that would have been directed at the lost object. This, then, is the intrapsychic predisposition to melancholia.

Later losses reactivate the primal loss and cause the patient's fury to be vented at the original disappointing object, which has been fused with part of the patient's own ego. In extreme cases, the sadism is so virulent that the individual wishes to destroy the internal effigy of the object totally and commits suicide. For most melancholics, sufficient gratification is obtained by vilifying the effigy, which clinically appears as self-reproachment. When this fury has been spent or the object effigy abandoned as being no longer of value, the illnesses passes until another loss reinitiates the entire process. In some patients there is a sudden release of libido from the internal effigy and this surplus of energy is expended in manic behavior. In mania, the ego has mastered this inter-

---

* At this point, this judgmental part of the ego is called the conscience but clearly it later becomes the superego with the revision brought about by the structural theory.

nalized rage and thrust the problem aside; in melancholia, the ego is beaten by the critical agency and continues to be subjected to its anger.

In conclusion, Freud stipulates three conditioning factors in melancholia: the loss of the object, a high degree of ambivalence, and a regression of libido into the ego. While all three are necessary, only the last is specific to melancholia.

In retrospect, Freud's short essay is a masterpiece of clinical investigation and logical deduction. Yet it may have raised more difficulties than it resolved. The essay proposed an entirely new model of illness: the expression of affect toward an incorporated object (although Abraham, in his investigation of depression along the lines of libidinal regression, gave a similar description).* This formulation has become increasingly difficult to prove or corroborate by clinical evidence. Therapists for decades have induced their depressed patients, with little success, to express anger so as to deflect it from the internalized effigy. Some depressives have not evidenced the crucial self-reproaches. Depressed individuals do not uniformly present a history of past or current loss. Therefore Freud's bold and imaginative formulation does not appear to have survived the test of time.

The formulation has also had its problems from a theoretical standpoint. The critical agency has become the superego which vents its anger at the ego in all neurotic disorders, not just in melancholia. The concept of the introjection of the disappointing object has gained wider application, especially in the work of the Kleinians, so that it also is no longer specific for melancholia. Later orthodox formulations on depression, which will be discussed below, have essentially discarded the introject hypothesis in favor of one viewing depression as a result of a felt disparity between the ego ideal and the actual self.

Nevertheless *Mourning and Melancholia* remains a classic in psychoanalytic literature. Freud was able to see that in depression one person has deeply affected the mental state of another, and that the loss of this person results in an *internal* loss for the depressive. He thus recognized the interpersonal nature of the disorder and the close relationship between maintenance of self-esteem and maintenance of a successful relationship. He also attempted to show that depressives are predisposed to their disorder by childhood events, usually prior disappointments with significant

---

* An interesting historical finding is that in 1920 George Carver, an English psychiatrist, independently arrived at conclusions very similar to those espoused by Freud in an analysis of a depressed patient. Carver emphasized his patient's unconscious anger against her dead husband for having abandoned her, but went on further to speak of an "identification of the self with a beloved person who is blamed for having caused the deprivation." Carver wrote that the major mechanism in the case "seems to be a displacement of the reproach from the environment, including the husband, to the self; analysis showing the abuse which the patient heaped so lavishly upon herself was really intended for the former" (Carver, 1921; cited in Mendelson, 1974).

others which lead to a pervasive ambivalence in all their relationships. Finally, in his insightful way he managed to see through the specious self-reproaches of some depressives, noting that in the end they also punish the external, loved other by becoming ill.

FURTHER TRADITIONAL DEVELOPMENTS

Freud did not devote another complete work to depression, but he did allude to it in a number of his later writings. In his book *Group Psychology and the Analysis of Ego* (1921), in which Freud discusses the forces that account for the cohesion of a group, he also briefly recapitulates his formulation on melancholia. Freud examines the relationships of the ego to the ego ideal, as well as to idealized others. Here he describes mania as a fusion of the ego and the ego ideal so that the former is free of criticism from the latter. In melancholia the ego, having identified with the disappointing object, is subject to the ego ideal's attacks. It becomes clear that the ego ideal soon will be recast as the superego.

Finally in *The Ego and the Id* (1922), which outlines the major revision of the structural theory, Freud returns to the mechanism of introjection or identification with a cathected object. He states that introjection is a much more general process than he had previously considered it to be. The mechanism of incorporating a frustrating object may in fact be the manner by which the child's ego gradually develops its specific character, as a "precipitate" of abandoned, internalized objects. Therefore, identification or incorporation becomes the major mechanism for dealing with objects that are lost, abandoned, or frustrating. This internalization becomes the manner through which a loss is undone in the unconscious.

Having shown that an ego ideal (or superego) is ubiquitous, as is the process of internalizing abandoned objects, Freud now proposes that melancholia results from an extreme discord between the superego and the ego, with the superego venting its rage against a seemingly helpless ego. As for why the melancholic should have such a harsh and powerful superego, Freud relies on his newly formulated hypothesis of the death instinct and also notes that if aggression is not expressed outwardly, it will be turned against the self.

Freud's final revision of his theory of melancholia in *The Ego and the Id* is of crucial importance, for it essentially negates much of what had been written earlier in *Mourning and Melancholia*. Yet Freud's later statement is often ignored and the earlier work later taken as his last word on depression. Freud dramatically restates this later view of melancholia in his *New Introduction Lectures* (1933): "No sooner have we got used to the idea of the superego . . . then we are faced with a clinical picture which throws into strong relief the severity, and even cruelty, of this function, and the vicissitudes through which its relations with the ego may pass. I refer to the condition of melancholia" (1933, p. 87).

The Impact of the Structural Theory

The revision of psychoanalytic theory that was brought about by the effect of the structural theory on psychodynamics was most thoroughly and creatively described by Sandar Rado. In a highly influential paper (1928), Rado considered depression and mania in terms of the interlocking relationships between the ego, the superego, and the love object. Rado observed that prior to the onset of an episode of depression, the individual goes through a period of arrogant and embittered rebellion. Rado explained that this phase of affective disorder is easily overlooked in that it passes quickly and is soon overshadowed by more blatant melancholic symptomatology. This phase is typical—although an exaggeration—of the depressive manner of treating the love object during healthy intervals. As soon as the depressive is sure of the other's love, he treats his beloved with a "sublime nonchalance," gradually progressing to a domineering and tyrannical control of the love object. This behavior may ultimately push away the loved other, who will not tolerate this mistreatment any longer. When and if this loss occurs, the individual lapses into depression.

The reason for this response to object loss resides in the peculiar personality structure of the depression-prone individual. Although he bullies and tests the love object, the depressive desperately needs the other's constant nurturance. He needs to be showered with love and admiration and will not tolerate frustration of this need. This type of individual appears inordinately reliant on others for narcissistic gratification and for maintaining self-esteem. Even trivial disappointments appear to cause an upset in the depressive's self-regard and to result in his immediate effort to relieve subsequent discomfort. To quote Rado, "They have a sense of security and comfort only when they feel themselves loved, esteemed, and encouraged. Even when they display an approximately normal activity in the gratification of their instincts and succeed in realizing their aims and ideals, the self-esteem largely depends on whether they do or do not meet with approbation and recognition" (1928). As a result of this need, the depressive become exquisitely skillful in extracting demonstration of love from others. However, as just described, he will push the test of love to the limits of tolerance in any relationship during periods of security and relative health. During periods of depression which occur after the object have been driven away, the individual resorts to a different method of coercion. He becomes remorseful and contrite, begging for forgiveness, and hopes to regain the lost object through inducing pity and guilt.

This pattern of hostility–guilt–contrition is explained by Rado as arising in early childhood when the child learned that he could win forgiveness and regain the all-meaningful love of the mother by appropriate remorseful behavior. This guilt–atonement sequence is traced by Rado to an earlier progression of rage–hunger–drinking at the mother's breast. Rado strongly emphasizes that the desire to be nursed at the mother's breast is at the core of melancholia and its unconscious persistence into adult life accounts for both the oral fixation described by Abraham and the need for external emotional nurturance. Ultimately the depressive's desires to be passive are satisfied by an all-giving other whom he can control and tyrannize.

If the depressive cannot win back the love of the lost object, he progresses to a more malignant form of melancholia in which the interpersonal drama is replaced by an intrapsychic struggle. Here Rado shows the influence of the structural theory by postulating that in severe (possibly psychotic) depression, external objects are given up and the ego seeks forgiveness from the superego which has replaced the love object. Therefore the self-reproaches of the severe melancholic are understandable in terms of the ego's hoping to attain the love of the superego by appropriate repentive behavior.

Rado believes that this intrapsychic stage of depression is an extension of the basic psychodynamics but at a different level; he assumes that both ego and superego were originally formed by incorporation of aspects of a love object, and the ego now seeks love and forgiveness from an internalized rather than external love object. He postulates that in childhood, when self-esteem was primarily derived from positive parental responses, the child gradually internalized this esteem-giving parent into an intrapsychic agency—namely, the superego. However, Rado speculates that there was actually a double introjection. Due to the immature cognitive abilities of the child, the parent was experienced as totally good (when giving pleasure) or totally bad (when frustrating needs), and not as a complete person who could be good and bad at the same time. Rado believes that the good object, whose love was strongly desired, was incorporated into the superego, while the bad, frustrating object was internalized into the ego which became the "whipping boy" of the good object. The depressive continues to desire the love of the good internalized object, and the outward manifestations of the ego's attempt to gain the love through contrition and atonement make up the clinical manifestations of melancholia. Through self-denial and self-punishment, the ego eventually regains the love of the superego and the episode of depression resolves itself with a resulting rise in the self-esteem and a renewed interest in external objects.

The significant aspects of Rado's theory are that depression represents a process of repair and a period of atonement for having driven away the needed object. At first there is an attempt to coerce an external object into granting forgiveness and love. If this interpersonal maneuver fails, the disorder progresses to an intrapsychic level where the struggle takes place between the ego and superego. The influence of Abraham's notion of controlling and losing the object is evident, as well as Freud's ideas of a harsh superego and anger turned toward an object that has been introjected into the ego. Rado transforms these previous formulations to fit the concepts of the structural theory, but he also adds much original thought, such as the depressive's need of others to bolster his self-esteem and the repetition of a childhood pattern of rage–atonement. Rado further tries to place degrees of severity of depression on a continuum with the same basic causative mechanisms. He brings his formulation closer to clinical data by demonstrating how the melancholic episode eventually clears by itself by gaining atonement from the superego or by reinstating a relationship with the love object. The weaknesses of Rado's theory appear to be his basic speculation of a double introjection in childhood, and his treatment of the intrapsychic structural agencies in a rather anthropomorphic manner.

Almost a quarter of a century later, Rado (1951) returned to the study of depression after he had reformulated psychoanalysis from the standpoint of psychobiological adaptation to the environment. In this later personal view, he conceived of psychopathology as the inappropriate persistence of infantile adaptive patterns into adult life. With particular reference to depression, Rado still maintained that the depressive manifestations are attempts to restore a sense of being cared for which is analogous to the security that the infant feels at its mother's breast. The symptoms of the adult melancholic were interpreted as patterned after the infant's "loud cry for help." For example, the depressive's fear of impoverishment, and his hypochondriasis and gastro-intestinal complaints, were equated with the infant's fear of not getting sufficient nutrients. In addition, Rado still interpreted the whole purpose of depression as an unconscious expiation which aims at restoring the lost love object. At this point Rado recapitulated his earlier exposition of pushing the love object to the limits of tolerance and then punishing oneself for the loss. However, Rado added some new dimensions to his 1928 theory. He now believed that the depressive may despise himself because of his own weakness and because he cannot get his own way through anger. The dilemma of the melancholic is to be torn between coercive rage and submissive fear. In a manner reminiscent of Abraham's emphasis on ambivalence, Rado declared that the depressive wishes to express tremendous anger at the love object, but he is prevented from overt manifestations of hostility because of his dependency on the love object. When this balance is upset and the depressive loses the object, he is said to vent his rage on himself and simultaneously revert to the old pattern of atonement in the hopes of winning back the love object.

Rado calls this reaction to loss "a process of miscarried repair." For the healthy person, the experience of loss is a challenge which marshalls his resources to continue life without the needed object or to take appropriate steps to rectify the loss. In the depressive individual, a loss "presses the obsolete adaptive pattern of alimentary maternal dependence into service and by this regressive move, it incapacitates the patient still more." Therefore depression from the standpoint of adaptational psychodynamics is a persistent but no longer effective mode of reaction to the loss of love.

Finally, Rado adds that he is less impressed with the role of actual environmental loss. At times the loss may be insignificant, but it is exaggerated by the patient. At other times the loss may be totally unconscious and outside the awareness of the individual. And, like Sullivan, he believes that in some cases no loss occurs but the patient invents a precipitating event to rationalize becoming depressed. Rado concludes that depression can be brought on by whatever succeeds in arousing guilty fear and regressive dependency—i.e., the maladaptive repair sequence. Melancholia is significant as a pathological reparative process and not for what may elicit it. By 1951 Rado's interests had clearly shifted from classical psychodynamics to describing both healthy and pathological responses to stress in which adaptive, appropriate, and mature patterns were the criteria of health, and maladaptive, anachronistic, and childhood patterns were the criteria of pathology.

Depression and Ego Psychology

When Fenichel's encyclopedic summary of psychoanalysis appeared in 1945, he devoted a chapter to depression in which he discussed the current psychoanalytic views on the disorder. In this work Fenichel drew upon the works of others in enumerating the various factors in depression. He mentioned the "pathognomic introject" formulation initiated by Freud, the oral fixation as postulated by Abraham, and the incessant need for love as described by Rado. In this last regard, Fenichel referred to depressives as love addicts who insist on a constant flow of benevolence and care little for the actual personality or needs of the bestower of this love. Fenichel also agreed with Rado's differentiation of neurotic depression as a state where love from an external object is sought, from psychotic depression as a state where external objects have been renounced and love is demanded from an internal agency. However, he believed this difference to be less absolute in that neurotic depressives try to appease the superego, and severe melancholics have not totally withdrawn from the object world but hope that an all-giving other will fulfill their craving for love. In reviewing all of these theories in detail, Fenichel strongly emphasized another aspect of depression which was to greatly influence the course of later psychoanalytic thinking.

This aspect that Fenichel conceived to be central to the whole problem of depression was the fall in self-esteem. Previous authors had alluded to a lowering of self-regard as present in depression, but Fenichel appeared to make the fall in self-esteem the key factor. Fenichel wrote: "A person who is fixated on the state where his self-esteem is regulated by external supplies or a person whose guilt feelings motivate him to regress to this state vitally needs these supplies. He goes through this world in a condition of perpetual greediness. If his narcissistic needs are not satisfied, his self-esteem diminishes to a danger point" (1945, p. 387).

The centrality of the regulation of self-esteem and its relationship to depression has redirected the line of psychoanalytic investigation into affective disorders. The subsequent importance of the ego can be appreciated when it is understood that it is the ego that allegedly gauges self-esteem by measuring the discrepancy between the actual state of self and a desired ego ideal. Self-esteem is believed to be the felt expression of this disparity.

This approach to depression has been taken by three theorists: Jacobson, Bibring, and Sandler. Their views continue to influence current thinking on depression strongly. Although proposing quite different overall systems of thought, each selected self-esteem regulation as central to depression and also roughly equated self-esteem as the felt discrepancy between the actual self and a desired ideal state.

The first of these theorists to be considered is Edith Jacobson, who has written extensively on depression and whose interest in severely disturbed manicdepressive patients extends over half a century. Her writings are very complex and her explanation of depression is embedded in her own theory of psychological development. Briefly, Jacobson (1954) postulates that the mind develops out of an undifferentiated matrix by the gradual formation on self and object representations, roughly meaning the internalized image of oneself and other individuals. Each of these representations can be cathected by libido, aggressive, or neutralized energy. These "cathectic shifts" account for one's feeling about oneself and others, depending on which representation is the recipient of each type of energy. In infancy a devaluation of others (an aggressive cathexis of the object representation) due to frustration is said to result also in a devaluation of the self, since the self still is fused with the representation of others. In an early paper (1946) Jacobson describes the effect of early disappointments on the belief in parental omnipotence, and the subsequent devaluation of parental images. This disappointment leads to a concurrent devaluation of the self and a primary childhood depression which is reactivated by adult disillusionments. Similarly, the infant's alleged grandiosity is said to be a result of self-representation being fused with an idealized (libidinally cathected) object representation.

Other more traditional constructs utilized by Jacobson are the ego ideal and the superego. The former is defined as the residual of narcissistic strivings in the child which the ego constantly seeks to measure up to in terms of standards. The latter is defined as a system that regulates the libidinous and aggressive cathexis to the self-representations, independent of the outside world. In healthy individuals the superego develops into an abstract, depersonified agency, but in pathology the superego is not well formed, still being tied to persons from the past and apt to be confused with objects in the outside world. This lack of differentiation of the superego interferes with appropriate cathexis of the self-representation and also affects self-esteem.

In depression there is an aggressive cathexis of the self, with a poor differentiation of the superego and a lack of adequate separation of object representations from the childhood parental ideal. In this sense depression can be seen economically as a problem of cathectic investment, and structurally as a lack of differentiation. For Jacobson the basic conflict in all affective disorders is as follows: When frustration is encountered, rage is aroused and leads to hostile attempts to gain the desired gratification. However, if the ego is unable (for external or internal reasons) to achieve this goal, aggression is turned to the self-image (1971, p. 183). This deflation of the self-image causes a greater disparity between it and the ideal self-image, leading to a feeling of low self-esteem. The depressed individual then may defensively try to fuse with an omnipotent object (mania) or turn to a new object to replenish libidinal supplies in order to raise self-esteem.

In describing a severely depressed patient, Jacobson states: "His self-representations retained the infantile conception of a helpless self drawing its strength from a powerful, ideal love object. He tried to keep the image of this love object hypercathected, by constantly depriving the self-image of its libidinal cathexis and pouring it on the object image. He then had to bolster his self-image again by a reflux of libido from the image of his love object" (1971, p. 235). In this passage, Jacobson is describing how the patient needed to relate to an overvalued other to maintain self-esteem. The text is quoted to give the reader a sense of her insistence on utilizing drive theory in describing clinical pathology. Jacobson has, in fact, criticized other theorists for their neglect of the economic aspects of psychoanalytic theory in their formulations.

She continues to rely on drive dynamics in describing the further course of depression. According to Jacobson, if the depressive fails to find a new love object that can replenish libidinal supplies to his self-image, he then will turn to a powerful but sadistic love object in the hope of gaining strength, if not love. If this last-ditch effort also fails, she postulates that the individual will retreat from relationships with the outside world and will reanimate an internal primitive and powerful image from the past. This powerful, internal object-representation merges with the superego, which becomes personified, and the true object representations, which have become deflated, merge with the self-representation. In this manner the last step in the depressive progression is the familiar retreat from the world of objects and the reconstitution of the love object in the superego. Thus while Jacobson follows the traditional view of psychotic depression as characterized (in contrast to neurotic depression) by a shifting from external relationships to strictly intrapsychic cathexes, she also believes that an as yet undiscovered neurological defect is necessary for the development of psychotic depression.

These few words cannot do justice to the complexity of Jacobson's views on the regulation of moods and self-esteem. Her system is an attempt at a "purification" of psychoanalytic constructs which she has elaborately defined and differentiated. However, in describing her clinical work, doubts arise as to her own ability to adhere to her strict definitions and many of the concepts become anthropomorphized. Significant about her formulations may be her attempt to assimilate ego psychology and drive theory together with her own brand of an objects-relations approach. It may well be that this synthesis is not possible in every detail when applied to actual clinical experience as opposed to purely theoretical speculation. Nevertheless Jacobson presents a comprehensive analysis of depression built on cathectic shifts of aggressive energy and libido between self and object representations, as well as on the fusion of intrapsychic structures—all the while considering the regulation of self-esteem to be the major problem of depression. In summary, Jacobson should be read as both a clinician and a metapsychologist. In her clinical work her insights are remarkable, and her work on the therapy of depression is outstanding. As for her metapsychology, it remains a theoretical attempt to reduce clinical data to speculative hypothetical constructs. It is almost as if she were describing two theories, the clinical and the hypothetical, and the reader is free to follow her formulations as far as they coincide with his own convictions.

In contrast to Jacobson's complicated metapsychology, Bibring's (1953) theory is a paradigm of simplicity and clarity. He presents brief vignettes of patients who were depressed following a variety of life events. Despite differences in circumstances and secondary symptomatology, all of these individuals presented a basic common pattern. All felt helpless in the face of superior powers or were unavoidably confronted with the sense of being a failure, and all had suffered a blow to self-esteem. Bibring concludes: "From this point of view, depression can be defined as the emotional expression (indication) of a state of helplessness and powerlessness of the ego, irrespective of what may have caused the breakdown of the mechanisms which established his self-esteem" (1953, p. 24). Further central features of depression, according to Bibring, are the ego's acute awareness of its actual or imaginary helplessness and its strong narcissistic aspirations which it cannot fulfill.

While these two factors—the sense of helplessness and the discrepancy between one's actual situation and a wished for set of ideal circumstances —have been mentioned by others, Bibring's originality is that he views this combination of events as resulting in a tension within the ego itself and not in an intersystemic conflict (for example, between ego and super-ego) or in a conflict between the ego and the environment. For Bibring, depression is the emotional correlate of a particular state of the ego. By considering depression in this light, Bibring compares it with anxiety and concludes that both are primary experiences which cannot be broken down any further. Although it seems a somewhat simple observation, this view of depression has far-reaching consequences: it unites normal, neu-rotic, and psychotic depressions as being due to the same basic mecha-nism. Furthermore, by viewing depression as a primary ego state that is possible in everyone, this formulation shifts the importance from the internal structure of depression to the environmental and characterologi-cal factors that facilitate the depressive response. Therefore Bibring men-tions that some individuals are predisposed to depression because of unrealistic aspirations which cannot be fulfilled or because of excessive past experiences of feeling, and perhaps being, helpless. Finally, if depres-sion is a simple, basic experiential state like anxiety, it is to be expected that individuals may form certain defenses against it or even that it may serve a useful purpose (again, like anxiety) when experienced in mild forms. Therefore the symptoms of depression itself are not reparative (as postulated by Rado and others), but other symptoms developed in re-action to depression may well be so.

Sandler and Joffe (1965) have reached conclusions similar to Bibring's as a result of clinical work with disturbed children, and from theoretical investigations of the meaning of some psychoanalytic concepts such as the superego and the ego ideal. They also view depression to be a basic affect (like anxiety) that is experienced when an individual believes he has lost something that was essential to his state of well-being and he feels unable to undo this loss. Sandler and Joffee further postulate that what is lost in depression is a feeling of narcissistic integrity, and not any specific "object." They state, "When a love-object is lost, what is really lost, we believe, is the state of well-being implicit, both psychologically and biologically, in the relationship with the object" (1965, p. 91). While acknowledging their debt to Bibring, Sandler and Joffe believe that "loss of self-esteem" is too elaborate and intellectual a concept to indicate the primal nature of this reaction which, for example, can be seen in children. Rather, they conceive of depression as the feeling of having been deprived of an ideal state, the vehicle of which was often but not exclusively a relationship with another person.

Sandler and Joffe also differentiate between depression as a basic psychobiological response that automatically results from the situations described, and clinical depression which is a further elaboration or ab-normal persistence of the basic unpleasant reaction. The initial response is analogous to a sort of "mental pain," which reflects a discrepancy between the actual state of the self and an ideal state of psychological well-being. If the individual feels helpless, resigned, or impotent in the face of the painful situation, then he experiences the affective response of depression. In regard to the hypothesis of depression as anger turned toward the self, they suggest that the initial loss generates rage; but this hostility is not allowed expression or is directed against a self which is disliked for its lack of effectiveness. Therefore there is blocked aggression in depressed individuals, according to Sandler and Joffe, but this finding does not necessarily conform to the Freudian introject formulation. Finally, like Bibring, Sandler and Joffe perceive that the initial psychobiological depressive reaction elicits defenses and does not uniformly proceed to a clinical depressive episode. It may also have a salutary effect in the manner that Freud proposed for signal anxiety.

Ego psychology has altered the traditional psychoanalytic thinking on depression, stressing that the ego's awareness of painful discrepancies is central to depression and its cardinal feature is a fall in self-esteem. Jacobson has incorporated this view into a complex system that relies heavily on metaphysical constructs and drive theory. Bibring, Sandler, and Joffee, on the other hand, have utilized the insights of ego psychology to simplify the traditional view of depression and reduce it to a basic psychobiological experiential state that cannot be explained by or further reduced to intersystemic conflicts.

While this shift in orientation appears to be closely aligned to clinical data, questions arise as to its adequacy in explaining or describing a depressive episode. Numerous authors outside the orthodox camp, such as Sullivan or Horney, for decades have postulated a fall in self-esteem to be basic to almost all psychopathology, so that the ego psychologists have actually just come around to a previously well-documented position. If this view is correct, then poor self-esteem regulation is a necessary but not sufficient explanation for depression since it occurs in other disorders. Rather, what appears necessary is an explanation of how depression differs from other syndromes that are also a reaction to low self-esteem. Jacobson has attempted such an explanation with her utilization of the concept of an aggressive cathexis of the self-representation. However, as stated earlier, her system requires accepting an elaborate metapsychology which does not always appear to fit clinical observations. Nevertheless, the "self-esteem regulation" approach to depression does allow for this disorder to be compared to other states of pathology that result from a fall in self-esteem and for the utilization of specific mechanisms that produce depression in certain individuals to be investigated.

The Contributions of Melanie Klein

Although Melanie Klein considered her contributions to be a logical extension of orthodox psychoanalysis, it has become clear over the years that
she was an innovative thinker who originated a unique system of psychodynamic interpretation that ultimately crystallized into a separate group
of disciples loosely called the British school of psychoanalysis. Her major
concerns, which grew out of her first-hand clinical experience with severely disturbed children and her personal exposure to the thinking of
Karl Abraham, were the earliest stages of psychic life and the predominant role of ambivalence in psychopathology. Her contributions to depression can be understood only in the context of her general system,
so a cursory sketch of it is presented here.[*]

Klein postulates two basic developmental stages in the first year of
life which she calls "positions." The first is the schizo-paranoid position,
and it is characterized by a particular perception of part-objects rather
than of realistic whole objects. For example, the infant during this stage
of development is said to conceive of the breast as separate from the
mother. In addition, the "good" feeding breast is perceived to be a
different object than the "bad" nongiving breast. In this manner, the child
resolves the problem of ambivalence by "splitting" the whole object into
separate good and bad part objects that do not belong to the same person.
In addition to sensing that these good and bad objects exist in the
external world, the infant internalizes the objects (because of poor self-
environment differentiation) so that they become "internal objects" within
the psyche. According to Klein, the infant is frightened that the bad
internalized objects will destroy the good internalized objects. He resolves
this conflict by projecting the bad objects back into the environment in
order to safeguard his inner sense of goodness. In this manner, the child
senses danger from without, called "persecutory anxiety," although the
child has himself projected the bad inner objects into the environment:
hence the term "paranoid position." Initially Klein believed that the
danger to the good objects came from the child's own innate aggression
which was a deflection of the death instinct, and this struggle to ward
off the bad objects was independent of environmental factors. Subsequent
theorists have taken a less nativistic view; they believe that the quality
of maternal care affects the balance of good and bad objects.

The second position is called the "depressive position." It is said to
occur at about four to five months of age, when the infant's cognitive
abilities mature sufficiently and he can begin to perceive realistic whole
objects. At this stage the child realizes that the good and bad breasts both

---

[*] The interested reader may find a summary of Klein's system in Hannah Segal's
excellent book (1964).

belong to the same mother, and he has to deal with the conflict of external figures being the sources of both pain and pleasure. Similarly he must deal with his own ambivalence and can no longer project his hostility onto the environment. The crisis at this stage is the child's fear that his aggression, which he now recognizes as his own, will destroy the good objects both external and internal. Thus the major dread is called "depressive" anxiety; it relates to the child's fear that he himself has caused the loss or destruction of his sense of well-being (good objects).

There are a variety of ways in which the child can deal with the depressive position. One is to become inhibited, depressed, and fearful of action lest he destroy the good objects. Another is to deny the value of the good objects and to insist that he needs no other object than himself (the so-called manic defense). Finally, the healthy resolution is for the child to realize that although his actions or wishes may have temporarily caused the loss of the good objects, these can be reinstated by appropriate restitutive maneuvers. In this way the individual acknowledges his responsibilities for his hostile feelings (he does not project them onto others), and at the same time he has the assurance that his hostility is not so massively destructive, that through appropriate behavior he can regain a good feeling about himself (i.e., the inner good objects). Kleinians have gone as far as speculating that most, if not all, adult creative endeavors are symbolic reparative productions for childhood destructive wishes.

This brief summary does not do justice to the complexity of the Kleinian system, but it may allow an appreciation of her conceptualization of depression. For Klein, depression holds a central place in psychopathology because it is seen as underlying many other clinical entities. As such, her position is similar to Sandler and to Bibring in viewing depression as an almost basic state which has to be defended against in either an abnormal or healthy fashion. However, in Klein's system depression takes on a new and less specific meaning; it is a normal stage of development, a specific form of anxiety, and the "depressive conflict" can be seen as underlying most neurotic illness (in contrast to the schizoparanoid position, which appears to describe schizophrenic states). Winnicott has, in fact, considered the depressive position as a developmental achievement in that the individual accepts responsibility for his anger and is able to tolerate ambivalence.

Klein (1940) did attempt to relate the symptoms of clinical depression to her system, proposing that in the "internal warfare" of inner objects, depression is experienced when the ego identifies itself with the sufferings of the good objects subjected to the attacks of bad objects and the id. She also relates the suffering of the adult melancholic to the nursing child's feelings of guilt and remorse over experiencing conflict between love and uncontrollable hatred toward its good objects. The most significant predisposition to melancholia, according to Klein, is the failure of the infant to establish its loved, good object with the ego. This accounts for a lifelong feeling of "badness" which is not projected outward, but which is incorporated into the self-image.

Klein's system has been rightly accused of extreme reification; that is, the hypothetical internal objects are talked of as actual concrete entities. There have also been criticisms that she ascribes all sorts of sophisticated abilities to the young infant, that she stresses pathology too much in everyday behavior, and that she fits all the patient's therapeutic productions in her system in a procrustean fashion. Finally, she has been accused of totally ignoring the environment and focusing only on the innate unfolding of instinctual processes and later on the inner battle between internalized objects. As for this last criticism, her followers—especially Fairbairn, Winnicott, and Guntrip—have increasingly taken cognizance of environmental factors so that the term "object relations" refers to external as well as internal objects. Lately Kleinian formulations have surprisingly found favor with family therapists who have expanded them to account for interactions between family members. In this regard, Slipp (1976) has combined family transactional theory with Kleinian psychodynamics in a comprehensive exposition of the development of the melancholic patient. Slipp enumerates various roles that are forced on the child according to the parental introject that the parents project onto the child. These projected parental introjects are often contradictory so that the child grows up in a conflict over his own behavior. For example, the child is pressured to succeed in order to salvage the family's image, yet his successes are sabotaged because the parents fear the child's ultimate independence from them. Slipp further elaborates how the child gradually evolves a depressive character and specific defenses in reaction to these parental interactions. He describes the adult depressive's main struggle as turning the bad parental introject into a good introject so that he can feel worthwhile.

In summary, Klein advanced the study of depression by stressing the fear of action for loss of needed objects, the lack of early incorporation of good objects, and the important role of guilt and hostility rather than libidinal transformation. However, she continued to be locked within the intrapsychic world (as have been most of the other authors considered so far), and to virtually ignore the real impact of interchange with significant others in the predisposition to depression. Attention will now be directed to an appreciation of these interpersonal and cultural factors.

The Interpersonal and Cultural Schools

Since Freud's fateful decision to treat his patients' reminiscences as childhood fantasies rather than as true—albeit distorted—memories, traditional psychoanalysis has taken a specific perspective on human behavior, considering mainly the intrapsychic at the expense of cultural and interpersonal influences. Freud was obviously aware of the importance of human interaction in the regulation of psychic functioning, but he preferred to deal with relationships in terms of object representations within the mind which were subject to instinctual cathexes either in harmony or in battle with other internal structures. He chose to conceptualize both pathological and normal development as the unfolding of innate forces and to give minimal regard to societal or interpersonal influences. An exception was made for experiences in childhood because they fit into his prearranged psychosexual stages which, however, were conceived of as means of obtaining gratification rather than as ways of relating to others. Another obvious exception was the boy's identification with his father at the termination of the Oedipal conflict.

In a similar unilateral perspective, Freud saw adult problems as clear repetitions of childhood events without giving appropriate weight to the individual's current situation, the actual effect of life vicissitudes on adult experience as independent of past history, and—most important—the effect of the patient's behavior, including his illness, on those around him. In reaction to Freud's intrapsychic, biological, and mechanistic metapyschology, opposing points of view became organized into various schools, each stressing a particular objection. Some of these reactions may loosely be called the interpersonal, the cultural, and the existential psychoanalytic schools of thought. While many of these schools rejected orthodox psychoanalysis completely, others attempted a synthesis of Freudian doctrine with other points of view. Finally, even within the orthodox psychoanalytic circles there has been a gradual evolution toward these newer formulations which originally were considered deviant and radical.

The first comprehensive works which dealt extensively with nonintrapsychic factors in the study of depression were the two publications on manic-depressives by Cohen and her co-workers (1949, 1954), undertaken by the Washington School of Psychiatry, and utilizing a predominantly Sullivanian orientation. These studies are noteworthy; they consider the family atmosphere in which the future depressive grows up, the effect of the patient on others, and the overall depressive personality.

In terms of family background, Cohen's group found that in each of their twelve cases the family set itself, or was forced by others to be, apart from the general community. In some cases the separation was due to membership in a minority religion, and in others the separation was on the basis of economic differences or chronic family illness. In every case the family felt its isolation keenly and attempted to gain acceptance from neighbors. Toward this end, the children were expected to conform to a high standard of "good" behavior and to achieve in order to undo the family's alleged lower status. Cohen et al. concluded that using the child as a instrument for improving the family's social position devalues the child as a person in his own right. Even in families who thought themselves better than their neighbors, the child's accomplishments were regarded as serving to enhance the family's reputation rather than to instill a sense of achievement and self-pride in the child.

The mother was found to be the stronger parent, demanding obedience and excellence. The father, on the other hand, was often economically and socially unsuccessful. Within the home he was subjected to the mother's criticism and depreciation. The patients remembered their fathers as weak but lovable, giving them the implicit message, "Do not be like me." The mother was seen as the reliable though less accepting and loving parent. The example of the father was a dramatic reminder to the children of what might happen to them if they failed to achieve the high goals set by the mother. Cohen et al. further investigated the early childhood development of the manic-depressive and found a consistent pattern in which the mother enjoyed her relationship with the child when he was a helpless infant, but resented his individuating and independent behavior as a toddler. The mothers liked the utter dependence of an infant but could not cope with the rebelliousness of a young child, so they managed to control the unruly behavior by threats of abandonment. In contrast to Freud and Abraham, the Washington group did not find a history of a childhood loss or a childhood depressive episode (Abraham's primal parathymia); rather, they found the omnipresent threat of loss if normal, spontaneous behavior was expressed.

The later childhood development of the patients revealed that they often had held a special or favorite position within the family because of either superior endowment or greater efforts to please. This favoritism was based only on the ability to achieve and not on any true concern for the individual as separate from the family unit. As a result of this upbringing, the child grew up as a manipulator, viewing human relationships as a means of promoting his own desired ambitions. At the same time he suffered from extreme envy of others and a fear of competitiveness which manifested itself as a specious underselling of himself in order to disarm others and to obtain their needed support.

These childhood experiences were said to result in a definite adult personality structure uniformly found in the twelve manic-depressives studied. One outstanding feature was the manic-depressive's lack of appreciating another person as separate from his own needs. Other people were seen almost as pieces of property which belonged to him, and from whom he could demand continuing support. As the same time there was a fear of abandonment so that the manic-depressive shunned confrontations or direct competition. Most were diligent, hard-working, compulsive individuals (between attacks), hoping to please others in order to make dependent demands on them. Despite hard work, there was little evidence of creativity; rather, these patients tended to take on the values or opinions of authority figures in the environment.

Cohen did not find striking evidence of hostility although she and her associates describe how the patient's incessant demands and lack of empathy could create a hostile impression on those around him. In general, the Washington group felt that the most constant factor was an inner sense of emptiness and a constant need for support which external figures had to rectify. This latter demand for an external figure to meet inner needs was what predisposed the individual to clinical decompensation if the relationship with the needed other was terminated. The actual depressive episode was interpreted as the external manifestation of an attempt to win back the needed other. If hope of renewing the relationship was lost, the depression progressed to a psychotic state unless a manic denial of the needed other supervened.

The Washington group also described specific problems in the therapy of manic-depressive individuals. One obstacle is the overwhelming dependency on the therapist that eventually develops. The other is the "stereotyped response"; that is, the patient's inability to view the therapist objectively, but only as a stereotyped repetition of a parental figure. The therapist is utilized as:

1. An object to be manipulated for purposes of gaining sympathy and reassurance.
2. A moral authority who can be coerced into giving approval.
3. A critical or rejecting authority who will not give real but only token approval.

This last conceptualization is often quite accurate since these patients readily alienate their therapists with suffocating demands. These distortions of the manic-depressive are interpreted as a fixation at Klein's part-object stage, so that the manic-depressive retains an image of others as being either all good or all bad. The Washington group concluded that when such patients recognize others as separate, as being both good and bad, they experience a great deal of anxiety since this accurate view interferes with the needed idealization and dependency on others.

A last problem in therapy that is mentioned is communication. Manic-depressives were experienced as erecting barriers to true emotional interchange with others and displaying a lack of empathy. This problem appears to be a logical permutation of the patient's inordinate needs and his distortion of the other as all good and all-giving, so that the patient holds his feelings in check lest he offend the needed other. Such individuals also do not appear to want to discuss their underlying problems; rather, they utilize the sessions only to obtain reassurance. These therapeutic problems will be discussed more fully in chapters 9 and 13.

These two works of the Washington group on severely disturbed manic-depressive patients are extremely important in the psychoanalytic literature on depression. The authors objectively evaluated the family atmosphere, the early parent-child interactions, and the later experiences of the depressed individual, and related these events to the personality of the depressed patient and to his problems in treatment. They appreciated the significance of cultural and interpersonal factors as well as some of the internal dynamics of their patients and thus arrived at a more comprehensive view of the disorder.

Gibson (1958) replicated the study of the Washington group, using a questionnaire on the same patients. In comparing this group of manic-depressives with a group of schizophrenic patients, he found that the manic-depressives came from homes where there was greater pressure for achievement and prestige and a prevailing atmosphere of competitiveness and envy, and that manic-depressives showed greater concern for social acceptance. However, there is an overall paucity of family studies on depression, especially in comparison to the large number of investigations of family transactions in the genesis of schizophrenia. It appears paradoxical that while many theorists have stressed the importance of interpersonal relationships in depression, they have continued to focus on intrapsychic mechanisms in their research. On the other hand, although the pioneering studies of the Washington group are valuable, at times there seems to be an over-simplification of the depressive's inner life and a lack of appreciation of the complexity of internal psychodynamics.

The culturalist view of depression has stressed in its explanation of the disorder a reaction to social demands, the effect of the symptoms on others, and the use of depression to satisfy abnormal goals. Perhaps the first attempt at an analysis of depression from this standpoint was written by Alfred Adler as early as 1914. In a work entitled *Melancholie* (quoted in Ansbacher and Ansbacher 1956), Adler states that "Such individuals will always try to lean on others and will not scorn the use of exaggerated hints at their own inadequacy to force the support, adjustment, and submissiveness of others." Melancholics are said to suffer from an alleged "disability compensation." By this, Adler means that depressed individuals inflate the hazards of everyday life as they strive for unreachable lofty goals, and then blame others or life circumstances for the failure to achieve such goals. In the same work Adler states, "actually there is no psychological disease from which the environment suffers more and is more reminded of its unworthiness than melancholia." (Cited in Ansbacher and Ansbacher, 1956). In this manner the depressive displays both his anger at not getting his own way and his contempt for others. By debasing the world and exaggerating its perils, the depressive is said to compensate for his lack of desired yet unreasonable success.

Kurt Adler (1961) further stated the position of individual psychology (Alfred Adler's theoretical system) on depression, showing how this disorder fits into Adler's general theory of human behavior. According to the Adlerian school, psychopathology results from a striving for superiority which develops in order to compensate for feelings of inferiority. However, since these resultant grandiose aspirations rarely can be achieved, the individual develops a system of rationalizations or excuses to adjust to his imagined failures. These adopted alibis and evasions are both safeguarding maneuvers; they protect the self-esteem of the individual as well as the symptoms of a pathological mode of life. In depression, it is assumed that the individual has learned to exploit his weaknesses and complaints in order to force others to give him his way and thus to avoid life's responsibilities. By his self-bemoaning, the depressive forces others to comply with his wishes, extorting sympathy and making others sacrifice themselves for him. He is willing to go to any cost to prove to others how sick and disabled he is, and to escape from social obligations and reciprocal friendship.

The depressive's disdain for others, according to Adler, can be seen during his healthy interludes when his excessive ambition takes over and he reveals his ruthlessness and his unwillingness to exert effort to achieve results. When he fails, the depressive regularly blames others, his upbringing, ill fortune, or even his very depression.

Kurt Adler summarizes the depressive personality: "This then is the relentless effort of the depressed: To prevail with his will over others, to extort from them sacrifices, to frustrate all of their efforts to help him, to blame them—overtly or secretly—for his plight, and to be free of all social obligation and cooperations, by certifying to his sickness" (1961, p. 59).

In the current psychiatric literature, Bonime (1960, 1962, 1976) has been the most persuasive exponent of the culturalist position on depression. Bonime's contention is that depression is not simply a group of symptoms that make up a periodic illness, but that it is a *practice*, an everyday mode of interacting. Any interference with this type of functioning leads to an outward appearance of clinical depression in order to coerce the environment into letting the individual reinstate his usual interpersonal behaviors. The major pathological elements in this specific way of life are manipulativeness, aversion to influence by others, an unwillingness to give gratification, a basic sense of hostility, and the experience of anxiety.

By manipulativeness Bonime means the alleged dependency of the depressive, which is interpreted as a covert maneuver to exploit the generosity or responsibility of others. The depressive demands a response from others but gives nothing in return. In so doing, he deprives himself of true affection or fulfillment, striving only to have others do as he wishes. In proportion to his manipulativeness, the depressive is intolerant of influence from others and often misinterprets their genuine attempts to help him as the covert intention to control him. In a similar way Bonime asserts that the depressive refuses to acknowledge the responsibilities of life, subjectively sensing them as unfair demands.

Finally, Bonime interprets much of the depressive's outward behavior as disguised hostility. The depressive makes sure that others are affected by his suffering. Bonime finds themes of revenge and thus of anger to play a prominent role in the psyche of the depression-prone individual. The other major affective experience in depression is anxiety which is experienced when others are unresponsive to the patient's usual machinations. However, the depressive quite often overcomes this anxiety by shifting his manipulative style and regaining his effectiveness. This anxiety is "primarily a sense of the threat of failing to function effectively as a depressive" (1976, p. 318).

Bonime believes that the etiology of adult depression can be found in a childhood that lacked the needed nurturance and respect from parents. Instead, the child's true emotional needs were ignored or squelched so that he grew up feeling he had been cheated and solicitude was still due from others. To quote Bonime, "Despite the wide variety of depression-prone individuals, however, a constant underlying dynamic factor in their personalities is the grim pursuit of the unrealized (or incompletely realized) childhood" (1976, p. 321).

Other psychoanalytic authors such as Chodoff (1970), Salzman and Masserman (1962), and Sapirstein and Kaufman (1966) have also made contributions that stress the social rather than instinctual or libidinal roots of depression. Their emphasis has also been on the interpersonal aspects of the disorder as well as on the depressive's unrealistic yet desperately needed personal goals (and the appearance of clinical depression either when interpersonal responsiveness is not elicited or when there is a failure to achieve the grandiose goals). Becker (1964) has proposed an intriguing theory that contrasts the social consequences of depression and schizophrenia. According to Becker, schizophrenia demonstrates a disregard for social conventions, and depression represents an over-trained individual who conforms too strongly to cultural values but needs these stringent guidelines for his sense of well-being.

Becker also speculates that the depressive limits his object ties to only a few individuals, so that losing one of these object ties hits him especially hard. The depressive is conceptualized as going through a monotonous repetition of behavior for the approval of a select few. Becker writes, "In our culture we are familiar with the person who lives his life for the wishes of his parents and becomes depressed when they die and he has reached the age of forty or fifty. He has lost the only audience for whom the plot in which he was performing was valid. He is left in the hopeless despair of the actor who knows only one set of lines, and loses the one audience who wants to hear it" (1964, p. 127).

Whether Adler's thesis of depression as power through illness, or Bonime's view of depression as obstinacy and refusal to accept social responsibility, or Becker's exposition of depression as over-conformity is accepted, it cannot be doubted that the culturalist tradition has enriched the understanding of this disorder by demonstrating how it intermeshes with cultural expectations and social relationships. The culturalist sees depression as part of the fabric of sociocultural intercourse, and not as an isolated phenomenon. At the same time there is a relative lack of appreciation for depression as a personal experience, or of how the patient actually suffers in his melancholic sorrow. So much attention is given to what the depressive wishes to achieve, evade, or manipulate that one senses that the actual individual and his inner life have been overlooked. The interpersonal and culturalist orientations have served as significant correctives to the excessive concern for the internal dynamics that the early psychoanalytic writers had with depression. However, they often appear equally limited in their zeal to point out the external aspects of depression as the very "internally oriented" theorists that they criticize.

THE EXISTENTIALIST SCHOOL

This approach to psychopathology has received only limited exposure in the United States, perhaps because it utilizes its own peculiar terminology and is based largely on continental philosophical schools which are quite complex and foreign to the training of most American psychotherapists. Stated very briefly, the task of the existentialist student of psychopathology is to describe the phenomenological world of the patient without recourse to excessive nonexperiential concepts (such as unconscious dynamics) or selected causal events (such as heredity or childhood traumas). Existential or phenomenologic analysis is the examination of the world as it is grasped intuitively by an active consciousness, without any preconceived structures. Karl Jaspers (1964) has written a massive work in which he discusses all of psychopathology from this point of view. He starts by making "some representation of what is really happening in our patients, what they are actually going through, how it strikes them, how they feel." Then he progresses to the establishment of meaningful connections between experiences, and culminates in an encompassing of the patient in his total being as revealed through the patient's experience.

Minkowski (1958) reported a case of "schizophrenic depression" from this standpoint and concluded that his patient's melancholic delusions logically derived from a distorted sense of time. Arieti (1974) summarizes other existential studies by Le Mappian, Ey, and Sommer as interpreting the condition to be an arrest or insufficiency of all vital activities. There is said to be a "pathetic immobility, a suspension of existence, a syncope of time" according to Ey (cited in Arieti, 1974). These authors also stress the importance of time distortion in the experience of depression; there is an excessive concern with past events which are constantly in mind and which the individual uses to torture himself with guilty recriminations. Beck (1967) summarizes a large study by Tellenbach on the analysis of the case histories of 140 melancholics. Tellenbach found that the world of the depressive is dominated by orderliness, conscientiousness, and an overriding need to please significant others. These patients are further reported as seeking security and avoiding situations which might elicit guilt. Paradoxically, this overconscientiousness often leads the patient to feel obliged to place impossibly exacting demands on himself in order to escape guilt. When the demands simply cannot be fulfilled, clinical depression may ensue. Perhaps the most famous existential studies, however, concern not depression but mania. Binswanger (1933) investigated the inner experience of the manic patient. He concluded that logic is abandoned and difficulties diminished, and life exists only for the concrete moment. The "Ideenflucht," or flight of ideas, reveals that language ceases to be used for communication but rather becomes a source of play and fun. Distortions of time and space also are noted in the manic.

Sullivan, who was certainly not of the existential school, gives a remarkably clinical and almost phenomenologic description of depression (1940, p. 102). He mentions the stereotyped, repetitive tendency toward destructive situations, the preoccupation with a limited number of ideas, and the retardation of vital processes. He further believed that relating the onset of depression to a publicly understandable cause was merely a way of rationalizing one's suffering and of "integrating the experience into the self without loss of prestige and uncertainty about (his) social and personal future" (1940, p. 105). Thus Sullivan appears to dismiss the premise that depressions are reactions to life events.

These studies were partially a reaction to the traditional psychoanalytic neglect of the individual's actual conscious experience for the intricacies of unconscious drives and dynamics, although they also may be seen as psychiatric applications of Heidegger's basic existential philosophy.*

The existentialists allow us a more detailed and accurate picture of the subjective world of the individual. In this significant manner, existential studies complement the understanding derived by the other psychoanalytic approaches. Despite the extent to which one agrees with their basic philosophy, these studies are worth reading for their vivid and penetrating accounts of how the disorder affects the patient's conscious life.

---

* Binswanger's concise paper "Heidegger's Analytic of Existence and Its Meaning for Psychiatry" (1963) is an excellent statement of the existentialist position and is recommended as an introduction for the interested reader.

Beck's Cognitive Theory

Since the earliest description of depressive illness, distortions in cognition, such as extreme pessimism or unrealistic self-reproaches, have been noted by most authors as part of the symptom complex. The originality of Beck's view is that he considers these cognitive distortions to be the primary cause of the disorder rather than secondary elaborations. According to Beck, all forms of psychopathology (not just schizophrenia) manifest thought disorder to some degree. Obviously no one can know reality in a completely objective way, and each person's appreciation of his world is colored by his past experiences. Therefore, so-called reality testing must remain a largely subjective affair. However, there is usually consensual agreement on most experiences and, since this agreement is shared by the overwhelming majority, such perspectives are considered to be within the normal range. In psychopathology, according to Beck, characteristic distortions appear that deviate from what most individuals would consider a realistic mode of thinking or of interpreting reality.

Depression presents its own specific types of distortion which Beck has labelled the "cognitive triad" (1970). This consists of

1. negative expectations of the environment
2. a negative view of oneself
3. negative expectations of the future

Beck states that he was able to trace these core elements of depression from his patients' dreams, free associations, and reactions to external stimuli. He also presents extensive experimental data, usually obtained by depression inventory scales, to support his conclusions (Beck, 1967).

Most students of depression would agree that depressed patients often have pessimistic views regarding others, themselves, and their future. The difficulty arises when cognition is considered to be primary, and as giving rise to the affect of depression. For Beck, appropriate feelings of depression would spontaneously arise out of this cognitive stance, although he does not explain how. In a more recent work (1976) Beck relates depression to a significant loss, which in turn gives rise to the characteristic cognitive distortions. Beck writes that "the patient's experiences in living thus activate cognitive patterns revolving around the theme of loss. The various emotional, motivational, behavioral, and vegetative phenomena of depression flow from these negative self-evaluations" (1976, p. 129). Beck continues, "the patient's sadness is an inevitable consequence of his sense of deprivation, pessimism, and self-criticism" (1976, p. 129). He concludes that "after experiencing loss (either as the result of an actual, obvious event or insidious deprivations) the depression-prone person begins to appraise his experiences in a negative way" (1976, p. 129).

Beck has produced a tremendous amount of clinical and experimental work documenting his particular theory. Although it has great merit, his formulation also suffers from some drawbacks. Beck undoubtedly has done psychiatry a service by emphasizing the cognitive aspects of depression. However, he has focused on mainly conscious and simple cognitive formulations. He ignores the significant role of unconscious cognitive structures, as well as the role of conflict. For example, some depressives harbor expectations which doom them to disappointment and despair, yet these expectations are unconscious and the individual is unaware of the influence they exert on his behavior. Similarly, other depressives are ashamed of their unrealistic dependency needs or irrational ambitions and actively fight against these unpleasant aspects of the self. This area of conflict is neglected by Beck, so at times his theory of depression smacks of only "wrong thinking" and does not do justice to the complexity of the human psyche.

Beck's theory is also weak in determining why certain people become depressed following a loss and others do not. He does not really consider the interpersonal aspects of the depression-prone person and why a loss or disappointment precipitates a depressive episode. He merely relates that a loss sets off a self-reinforcing chain reaction which culminates in depression. The depressed person is described as "regarding himself as lacking some element or attribute that he considers essential for his happiness" (1976, p. 105). However, why this should lead to the "cognitive triad" is not fully explained.

Beck actually describes the results but not the cause of depression. He offers a version of depression only in cross-section, not in its longitudinal and psychodynamic unfolding. He states that upon clinical recovery the individual no longer distorts his experiences; yet the basic personality has not changed. Therefore, although Beck quite accurately describes some of the cognitive distortions seen during a depressive episode, he does not appear to go beyond these conscious beliefs to the underlying—often unconscious, conflictual, or interpersonal—patterns that make the individual vulnerable to depression in the first place.

In spite of these limitations, Beck's work is exemplary and points the way to the neglected area of cognition in psychopathology. His influence in the field is well deserved.

Seligman's Learned Helplessness Model

In experiments involving the administration of inescapable shock to dogs, Seligman and his colleagues (Seligman and Maier, 1967) discovered a reaction which they termed "learned helplessness." They found that after exposing dogs to a series of painful stimuli in a situation that prevented escape, the animals did not avoid the painful stimuli even when escape was possible. It appeared that the dogs had given up and had learned to endure helplessly the painful shocks. Seligman generalized these findings to human depression: he suggested that the depressive has been blocked from mastering adaptive techniques to deal with painful situations, instead learning helplessness. At the core of this theory is the hypothesis that the depressive sees no relationship between his responses and the reinforcement he receives from the environment. Experience with repeated trials, in which the individual eventually found that his efforts made no difference in terms of reward, caused this set of learned behaviors to become generalized and internalized into a personality trait.

Therefore Seligman asserts that the depressive has a history characterized by failure to control environmental rewards. Depression ensues when the individual feels he has lost all control over environmental responses and, due to his learned helplessness, perceives himself as unable to alter this ungratifying state of affairs. He then falls into a state of passivity, misery, and hopelessness. He believes that his behavior lacks meaning because it is so ineffective in bringing about reinforcement. It is important to stress that in contrast to Beck, Seligman differentiates overall negative expectations from learned helplessness. He states that "according to our model, depression is not generalized pessimism but pessimism specific to the effects of one's own skilled actions" (1975, p. 86). Furthermore, he does not believe that his model can account for all affective disorders but only those "in which the individual is slow to initiate responses, believes himself to be powerless and hopeless, and sees his future as bleak . . ." (1975, p. 81). Seligman's model has much to recommend it in that it is an empirical hypothesis that lends itself to direct experimental confirmation (Miller and Seligman, 1976).

While Seligman is correct in describing many depressives as feeling helpless to control environmental reinforcement, this situation is only part of the total depressive picture. Some authors such as Adler and Bonime view the actual depressive episode as the depressive's attempt to force the environment to fulfill his needs, so that he is far from helpless. According to this view, proclaimed helplessness is a devious manipulation to force others to give the depressive what he wants. Even without entertaining this concept of depression, there are some difficulties with the "learned helplessness" model. Many depressives seek to reinstate the lost sources of pleasure by hard work, self-denial, or guilt-inducing behavior. Therefore the depressive is not helpless; rather, he has learned specific ways—however inappropriate—to gain the reinforcement he requires. The vulnerability of the depressive appears to reside in his inordinate need of external reinforcement for self-esteem or well-being, rather than in his not knowing how to get the needed reinforcement. Depressives are too reliant on external sources for achieving a sense of meaning in their lives, and therefore they become very skilled at elaborating interpersonal maneuvers to keep the needed relationships in an ongoing state.

If they happen to lose the external sources of gratification, then they manifest helplessness in terms of deriving meaning from life or in their ability to derive reinforcement from self-directed activities. It is not that the depressive sees no connection between response and reinforcement, but that his system of reinforcement may be too precarious and limited.

It appears that Seligman has taken the results of a depressive episode to be its cause. During a depressive attack the individual may bemoan his fate, take no initiative on his own behalf, and appear totally helpless. However, this clinical picture may be part of the depressive's characteristic tendency to have others supply meaning and gratification for him. When these external sources are removed either through loss or through another's inability to comply with his manipulations, the depressive may indeed feel that he cannot reinstate the needed external sources of gratification by direct action. However, this pattern is not a result of learned helplessness, which assumes no perceived connection between response and reinforcement. Rather, as mentioned previously, it may be the result of an excessive reliance on external others or on the achievement of an external goal from which to derive meaning and gratification. Depressives do have self-inhibitions in certain crucial areas (to be dealt with in chapters 6 and 7), but their areas of inhibition are not a result of a lack of reward for effort, as Seligman's model suggests.

Physiological Approaches

This book is not intended to be an authoritative and detailed text on organic theories of depression, nor do I claim any firsthand experience with research on this aspect of depression. However, in order to give a more complete view of approaches to depression, some of the major physiological theories are briefly outlined below.

Before describing these theories, it should be clarified that a physiological approach to depression does not necessarily contradict a psychodynamic approach. Certainly, neurological events accompany psychological phenomena, and the experience of depression is no exception. The two views are particularly congruent if depression is conceptualized as a basic affect that automatically arises in certain situations, as exemplified in the theories of Sandler and Joffe (1965) and Bibring (1953). The more complex view of depression as being the result of complicated meta-psychological events does not lend itself so easily to concordance with biochemical approaches, since according to this conceptualization depression may be further reduced to basic drives or structures. Therefore biochemical theories favor a view of depression as a basic emotion (see chapter 7) having both psychological and physiological correlates.

The modern biochemical view of depression came about as a result of a series of serendipitous clinical observations that later were backed up with animal research studies. In the early 1950s, it was found that some hypertensive patients treated with reserpine developed episodes of depression. Reserpine has been shown to deplete the brain of norepine-phrine (NE) and serotonin or 5-hydroxytryptamine (5-HT). At the same time, in another study clinicians noted that some tubercular patients treated with isoniazid showed unexpected elevations of mood. Isoniazid has been shown to block the destruction of NE and 5-HT by inhibiting the effect of monoamine oxidase (MAO), an enzyme that metabolizes these amines. It was further discovered in animal research studies that other compounds which blocked the action of MAO could reverse the depression-like syndrome caused by reserpine. The beneficial effects of tricyclic antidepressants such as imipramine were eventually shown by Hertting (Prange, 1973) to result from a blockage of the re-uptake of NE at nerve endings. Lithium, a drug effective in decreasing mania, in contrast was believed to enhance the re-uptake of NE at the synaptic cleft.

These clinical observations and the subsequent imposing research have singled out these two compounds, NE and 5-HT, as specifically related to depression. These amines are believed to be neurotransmitters; that is, they conduct excitation from one neurone on another. It has been postulated that an excess of either one or both of these amines leads to mania, and a depletion leads to depression.

The metabolic pathways for NE and 5-HT are presented in Table 2-1 (Akiskal and McKinney, 1975) shown on page 50.

In the United States NE has been selected as the active amine, while in Europe attention has been given to serotonin (5-HT) as the neuro-transmitter implicated in depression. The success of drugs that alter the levels of these amines in the brain in treating depressive episodes has led to a great deal of study and even the hope that eventually the various subtypes of depression may be differentiated by biochemical tests alone (Schildkraut, 1975).

Support for the "indoleamine hypothesis," which implicates a decrease of 5-HT as the active compound in depressive disorders, has come from

TABLE 2-1

The metabolic pathways for NE and 5-HT

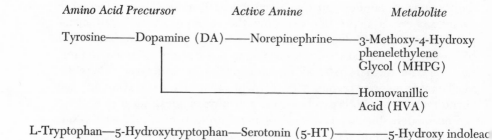

Amino Acid Precursor	Active Amine	Metabolite
Tyrosine——Dopamine (DA)——Norepinephrine——		3-Methoxy-4-Hydroxy phenelethylene Glycol (MHPG)
		Homovanillic Acid (HVA)
L-Tryptophan—5-Hydroxytryptophan—Serotonin (5-HT)———		5-Hydroxy indoleac Acid (5-HIAA)

a series of studies. The best known are those of Coppen and his colleagues (1963), in which tryptophan, a precursor of 5-HT, was shown to potentiate the antidepressant effect of an MAO inhibitor. It was reasoned that the greater antidepressant effect was due to an increased level of 5-HT. However, similar results have not been found in repeated studies (Mendels, 1974). The antidepressant effect of tryptophan alone also has not been shown uniformly (Goodwin and Bunney, 1973).

Other evidence that supports the serotonin-depletion hypothesis has been the finding of lower than normal concentrations of 5-HIAA, a metabolite of serotonin, both in the cerebrospinal fluid of depressed patients and in the brain tissue of suicide victims (Bunney et al., 1972).

Studies that do not support the role of 5-HT in affective disorders involve the failure to produce depression by drugs that block the synthesis of serotonin. Patients with carcinoid syndrome who were given the drug parachlorophenylalanine (PCPA) displayed a variety of psychic abnormalities such as anxiety, irritability, or negativism, but not depression. The same drug even at high doses also had little effect when administered to monkeys (Redmond et al., 1971). Therefore, depletion of 5-HT by itself does not appear to result in depression, although this amine still is believed to play a role in the biochemistry of affective disorders in combination with other physiological alterations.

The other major biochemical hypothesis involves the brain catecholamine NE, and its precursor, dopamine (DA). The major exponent of this hypothesis is Schildkraut, who periodically has reviewed the pertinent literature (1965, 1975; Durell and Schildkaut, 1966) in addition to contributing many research and clinical studies. As with serotonin, researchers have found decreased levels of NE in the urine of some but not all depressed patients. In one study done by Schinfecker in 1965 (cited in Schildkraut, 1975) a regular cycle of NE metabolite excretion was found to correlate with the phases of mania and depression in cyclothymic patients; high NE excretion started with the onset of a manic phase and low NE excretion reflected the depressive phase. Again, the theory postulates that a depletion of NE (as caused by reserpine) results in depression, a restoration of adequate brain NE-levels (as a result of tricyclic antidepressants or MAO inhibitors) relieves the depression, and an excess of NE is responsible for mania.

Schildkraut cites numerous studies in support of this hypothesis, but he also mentions a great deal of data that question the catecholamine theory. Among these contradictory findings are the following: (1) catecholamine excretion is not lowered in all depressed patients, but mainly in agitated or anxious individuals; (2) the concentration of plasma catecholamines was found to be much more correlated with anxiety than depression. Therefore muscular activity (in mania, anxiety states, or agitated depression) may be the cause of NE excretion levels rather than depression itself. Another difficulty is that urinary NE reflects total body reactions and may not be considered a reliable reflection of brain catecholamine metabolism.

It has recently been suggested that MHPG, a metabolite of NE that is found in the urine, may parallel the levels of brain NE and only partially reflect body levels of catecholamines (Schildkraut, 1975). Initial studies with MHPG have shown a correlation with mood, but once again, contradictory findings have also been reported. Variations in MHPG excretion in response to general stress (not just affective disorders) have been reported, so its specific relationship to depression and mania remains to be established. Finally, not all depressed patients show low excretion of MHPG. This last finding has suggested that there may be different biochemical types of depression that vary in response to certain drugs.

Mendels (1975) found no noticeable improvement in depressed patients who were given large doses of L-Dopa, the immediate precursor of DA. This L-Dopa dosage should have increased the brain levels of DA and also perhaps NE. As with sertonin, most researchers believe that catecholamines are somehow related to affective disorders but that these amines are only part of a very complex metabolic process that has yet to be elucidated.

While the beneficial effects of the tricyclic antidepressants and of the MAO inhibitors have greatly helped in the treatment of depression, attempts to correlate these clinical effects into a comprehensive biochemical theory have not been successful as yet. Reviews of experimental work (Akiskal and McKinney, 1975; Baldessarini, 1975; Goodwin and Bunney, 1973) all agree that these amines somehow are implicated in affective disorders but that there is still insufficient knowledge of brain biochemistry to make conclusive statements. That the proposed model of affective disorders entails a direct reflection of the levels of biogenic amines in the brain has been recognized as too simplistic by most investigators.

Some of the objections to this model have been discussed by Baldessarini (1975) in an excellent review article and they will be noted briefly here. Baldessarini argues that so-called animal depressions, which are induced by drugs on which much of the biochemical theories depend, actually bear little resemblance to naturally occurring depression in humans. Rather, the reserpine-induced "depression" in monkeys resembles a state of sedation. In fact, the drugs which best reverse these animal "depressions," L-Dopa and amphetamines, have the least clinical effect on human depression. Baldessarini further argues that reserpine depression may not be at all typical of human depression, for it has been found that the effects of this drug are highly variable in different individuals; some respond with lethargy, others with an organic brain syndrome, and others with no mental changes. Those individuals who became depressed after taking reserpine had a previous history of depression and thus may have been predisposed to react with depression by past experience.

Another criticism of drug research strategy is that most experiments study only the immediate biochemical effects of drugs rather than their chronic effects over time. This may be especially misleading in affective disorders since there is a considerable lag in clinical response to most antidepressant medications. The fact of therapeutic response lag after drug ingestion has led Mandell and Segal (1975) to postulate a theory of depression that is almost an exact reverse of the catecholamine hypothesis. They believe that depression may be due to an excess of brain catecholamine activity and that antidepressant drugs, by increasing the level of catecholamines, affect the enzymes and other macromolecules which synthesize catecholamines. These drugs would cause a decrease of natural production of catecholamines because the enzymes would adapt to the high levels of amines from the drugs. Since this adaptive process would require several days, they assume that their theory fits the clinical data better. The biochemical cause of affective disorders would reside in a general biochemical system that controls the levels and types of neurotransmitters in significant parts of the brain, rather than residing in the periodic excess of any catecholamine. This provocative hypothesis is far from being proven, although Mandell and Segal cite Oswald's (1972) study in which normals receiving antidepressants reported an initial discomfort, presumably due to an excess of catecholamines. However, depressed patients who receive similar drugs do not report an initial exacerbation of their symptoms.

The further significance of Mandell and Segal's work is that it points out that antidepressant drugs have many biochemical actions and may affect many systems other than biogenic amine levels. These other systems may ultimately be responsible for clinical effects of antidepressant drugs. This view is further borne out by the lack of absolute correlation between clinical response and catecholamine or indoleamine levels. The difficulties with accepting a simple model of biogenic amine levels as responsible for depression solely because antidepressants appear to affect the levels of these compounds is well summarized by Baldessarini (1975).

"There may be a risk of a *post hoc, ergo propter hoc* logical fallacy in this field, as it is often accepted uncritically that responsiveness of a behavioral disorder to a physical therapy implies not only the existence of an organic-metabolic cause, but furthermore that the cause involves metabolic changes opposite to those produced by treatment. This conclusion is no more logical than the proposition that a careful study of the pharmacology of the clinically effective preparations of Foxglove, Squill, or Mercury would have disclosed information of fundamental importance to the etiology of dropsy." (p. 1092)

While the most heuristic and prominent physiological approach to depression has involved biogenic amines, other biological systems have been investigated and may be briefly mentioned. For a long time, endocrine changes were felt to be involved with affective disorders since depression or elation may accompany some endocrinopathies. Some studies had shown a correlation between the excretion of 17-hydroxycortico-steroids and changes in affective disorders (Gibbons, 1967), while other researchers found no such relationship (Kurland, 1964). In a carefully controlled study, Sachar et al. (1972) observed that cortisol production was greatly affected by emotional arousal, anxiety, or psychotic decompensation, but not by depression itself. Apathetic depressed individuals showed no changes in adrenocortical activity during or after their depressive episodes. From this study, and from the contradictory data of other studies, it may be tentatively assumed that cortisol levels reflect the general state of upset of an individual, independent of affective disorders.

The other endocrine system implicated in depression is the thyroid–pituitary axis. Prange et al. (1969) found that 1-tri-iodothyronine enhanced the effect of imipramine in depressed females. In a later study Prange and Wilson (1972) found that thyrotropin-releasing hormone by itself may be an effective antidepressant. However, Prange relates this therapeutic result to an effect on catecholamine metabolism that is independent of thyroid functioning. In fact, although Prange has utilized thyroid-related substances in his clinical research, he is an adherent of the so-called biogenic amine "permissive hypothesis," which postulates an initial serotonin deficiency that makes an individual susceptible to depression when NE levels are low, or mania when NE levels are high (Prange, 1973). Therefore the endocrine system does not at present appear to be a promising area of research in the affective disorders.

The other major area of biochemical interest has to do with membrane transport and electrolyte balance. This line of investigation has been greatly stimulated by the success of lithium, a simple alkali metal (like sodium and potassium) used in treating acute manic attacks (Cade, 1949). Later, lithium was used as a prophylaxis for manic-depression (Baastrup and Schou, 1967) and more recently it has been tried in patients who have recurrent depression without the presence of mania (Fieve et al., 1968).

Once again the successful employment of a drug has understandably led to speculations about the nature of the illness based on the biochemical effect of the drug. In the case of lithium, it was noted that there was an initial loss of sodium which was followed after a few days by compensatory sodium retention in some patients (Tupin, 1972). It is not clear whether this effect on sodium by lithium occurs at the cellular level or through a mediating action of aldosterone (Aronoff et al., 1971).

Some investigators believe that lithium alters the ionic concentration of sodium and potassium at the cell membranes of neurones, retards neuronal transmission, and thus "slows down" the manic patient. This hypothesis is questionable since lithium also has been effective in some forms of depression. Others (Greenspan et al., 1970; Messina et al., 1970) have attempted to relate lithium administration to alterations in catecholamine metabolism. At present this area of research is too new to have crystallized a major synthesizing hypothesis. Lithium studies remain an extremely actively pursued avenue of investigation in the biochemistry of affective disorders.

This very brief review of physiological approaches to depression and mania is intended to present some basic and unfortunately limited information about this fertile approach to affective disorders which is usually ignored by psychotherapists. It was stressed at the beginning of this section that a physiological approach to depression need not contradict a psychodynamic view if depression is conceived to be a basic affect. It is unfortunate that the study of mental illness too often has become split into warring camps of organically and psychologically oriented practitioners. Obviously the clinician cannot ignore the fact that there are biological events occurring in the brain of the patient any more than the chemical researcher can ignore that the substances he is studying are affected by the life experiences of the organism.

Summary

Over the years, theories of depression have reflected the prevailing climate of psychoanalysis. It may be observed that the recent theories (with notable exceptions) have relied less on metapsychology and have grown closer to clinical experience. Modern theories of depression appear less speculative even if less imaginative. Similarly, an appreciation of cultural and interpersonal factors has become noticeable as psychoanalysis has moved away from an instinctual, mainly hydraulic model to a more en-

compassing theory that no longer seeks to reduce all behavior to unconscious transformations of energy. Certainly, the political and social milieu
as well as changes in basic scientific theory have influenced the evolution
of psychoanalytic thought, which in turn has affected the conceptualization of depression.

The psychoanalytic inquiry into depression has not been without critics
and some evaluation appears justified. In a recent review article, Chodoff
(1972) rightly mentions that in many contributions the current degree
of the patient's illness, from which observations have been generalized,
is not specified. For example, Freud clearly indicated that his formulations
were intended only to apply to very disturbed melancholics. Yet others
have applied his theory to less impaired individuals or they have not
bothered to specify the degree of impairment of the patients that they
described. Chodoff also believes that too much of the literature has been
influenced by the study of manic-depressive psychosis, with a relative
neglect of other varieties of depression.

Another criticism is that the contributors to the psychoanalytic literature on depression based their findings on the intensive analysis of only
a few individuals and the size of their sample was too small for generalizations. Unfortunately, it is one of the limitations of the psychoanalytic
method; that each practitioner can only treat a limited number of individuals on so intense a level in his lifetime. Yet this is the traditional model of
clinical medicine where a series of patients with a similar condition is
reported, and the similarities and differences noted. Larger experimental
studies may utilize a greater number of patients, but at the cost of achieving what are mainly common-sense and pedestrian findings. Chodoff
(1972) has also noted this limitation of nonpsychoanalytic studies, stating
that their level of observation is often superficial. He believes that psychoanalytic investigations are far more intensive and searching, but that in
contrast to more scientifically controlled studies, there is sometimes a
confusion between observed and inferred material. Another scientific
criticism leveled at psychodynamic reports is that there is a failure to
utilize a control group. This criticism does not appear to carry too much
weight since it is assumed that the other nondepressed patients in the
analysts' practices are sufficiently different (in that they are not included
in the description of depressed individuals) to serve as a nonreported
but nonetheless existent control group.

A more telling limitation of psychodynamic studies may be the repeated
tendency of authors to fit depression into a pre-existing general theory
of psychopathology. The more general theory at times seems like a procrustean bed that allows only those features of depression that fit the
theory to be considered, while distorting or ignoring other aspects that
may contradict the basic formulations. This does appear to be a failing
of many of the theories, and their specific biases have been mentioned
along with their positive contributions. It may be best to view the formu-

lations of each school as a different perspective on a uniform clinical problem, with each viewpoint complementing the others and highlighting important constructs that have been omitted by others. The Freudians, the Kleinians, the interpersonal theorists, and all the others we have considered here have contributed to our understanding of depression, and as much as possible their work should be considered as a totality.

While the differences in the theory may be seen as changes in the psychoanalytic Zeitgeist, it is also possible that the clinical nature of depression itself has changed over the decades. The guilty, paralyzed melancholics described in the early literature are seen infrequently to-day. Rather, most depressions appear to be milder, with less self-recriminations and more of a demanding quality motivated by thwarted aspirations. It may be that as society becomes less rigidly moralistic, and as childhood upbringing becomes more permissive, the superficial aspects of the syndrome may change. Similarly, the greater mobility between social and economic classes may promote more pressure for achievement than in a static, controlled caste society. Therefore the differences in the theories presented may accurately reflect changes in the type of patient seen.

Finally there is the real possibility that depression may result from different causes in different individuals. Depression may well be the final common pathway for various processes that alter the psychological equilibrium in different patients. Not all depressives may be alike, al-though, as with any scientific inquiry, the goal of the investigator is to search behind clinical differences to find basic, general principles at a higher level of inference from which the symptomatic picture may logi-cally be deduced. Despite the disparity of theoretical systems, it cannot have escaped the reader's attention that certain basic themes have oc-curred again and again. Therefore, even while starting from vastly differ-ent philosophical beliefs about the nature of psychopathology, most authors have noted specific core features in depressed individuals.

Before closing this chapter, it should be noted that the authors of this book have made some contributions of their own toward an understanding of depression. These works have not been included in this review because a fuller exposition of our views will be presented in later chapters. It is hoped that this cursory tour through the history of the concept of melancholia will provide a foundation for the more detailed material to follow, and help to place it in proper perspective.

[3]

THE MANIFEST SYMPTOMATOLOGY OF

DEPRESSION IN ADULTS

Introductory Remarks and Classificatory Criteria

The manifest symptomatology of the various depressive syndromes requires careful examination and evaluation. Nevertheless, even more than in the study of other psychiatric conditions, an approach confined to the observation and assessment of the manifest symptomatology of depressions leaves the clinician with an awareness of the limitation of the method. The psychotherapist senses the profundity of the syndrome with which he deals, realizes that he cannot go far with a surface investigation, and feels the need for a psychodynamic approach. This in fact will be the procedure followed in this book.

The manifest symptomatology of depression impresses the clinician as being relatively uniform, characterized at least in the majority of cases by one prevailing feature—the depressive mood. It does not present a multifaceted picture, leading to different sorts of inquiries, like that of the schizophrenic disorder. Contrary to the schizophrenic syndrome, it does not confront the therapist with an image so different from the usual one of the human being, and so distorted. However, it does have an especially powerful impact on the clinician who is struck by the intensity of the sorrow that he witnesses and to which he immediately responds with a sense of affinity, so close is that image of sorrow to a common part of the human condition. Moreover the clinical picture has a few important secondary traits which are often overlooked in the context of the mood of depression. Any description of the manifest symptomatology of the syndromes included under the category of depression implies some

This chapter was written by Silvano Arieti.

agreement on the classification of these syndromes. But such agreement has never been reached, since some aspects of these conditions are far from being clarified and several others are controversial. Some features which at our stage of knowledge seem to be fundamental marks of distinction may be proved later to be not so basic.

Any classification and description which are based on partial knowledge tend to repeat traditional ways, established by previous generations of professionals working in the field.

At the present level of our understanding the following three questions seem of pivotal importance in classificatory attempts.

Is the depression primary or secondary? A depression is called primary when it constitutes an important and/or essential component of a syndrome; for instance, in what is generally called "psychotic depression" or "severe depression."

In manic-depressive psychosis the depression is also primary. In fact, although the syndrome may have manic attacks, the depression is an important and probably necessary component. We say probably and not absolutely necessary because there are rare cases of the illness characterized only by manic attacks. In these cases, however, the presumptive evidence is that the depressive attacks occur at a subclinical or subliminal level.

A depression which occurs in the course of epilepsy or an endocrine syndrome is not considered primary because the available evidence suggests that it would not have occurred in the absence of the original syndrome.

Is the depression severe or mild? At times this question is formulated with different terminology: Is the depression endogenous or reactive; or, is the depression psychotic or neurotic? These terminologies reflect the theoretical premises of the persons who use them. An endogenous depression is based exclusively on organic, presumably hereditary factors which manifest themselves in biochemical alterations of the organism. A reactive depression would be one which is precipitated by an event perceived by the patient as harmful or unpleasant.

This dichotomy is not substantiated by any sure evidence. Any depression must ultimately be mediated by a living organism, and therefore it requires neurophysiological mechanisms and biochemical changes. On the other hand, we are not justified in claiming that no precipitating events exist just because we have not been able to determine them. In all depressions there are both psychological and biological, nonpsychological components. Moreover the biological components may not necessarily be based on anatomical pathology, but may be functional. In other words, they consist only of changes in some functions of the organism, but not of anatomical structures.

The authors of this book believe that in most cases it is possible to recognize whether a depression is psychotic or neurotic. However, these two terms have come to be used in incorrect ways by many authors and clinicians. They are wrongly used when a depression is called psychotic only if some symptoms are present which occur also in schizophrenia and are acknowledged by everybody as psychotic; for instance, hallucinations, delusions, or ideas of reference. These symptoms are not specific for any type of depression or for manic-depressive psychosis. The issue here hinges on the definition of psychosis.

As I wrote elsewhere (1973, 1974), psychosis is a term used by many to designate a severe or major psychiatric disorder. In theory and clinical practice the concept is more difficult to define because severity is not an inflexible characteristic. A certain number of cases diagnosed as psychosis may in fact be less serious from the point of view of the sufferer or of society than some cases included in other psychiatric categories. The term *psychosis* is at times indistinctly equated with insanity. The latter term, when used legally or in popular language, suggests a person who is so incompetent that he may require special control or supervision. However, psychosis indicates not only actual or potential severity, it also connotes that an unrealistic way of appreciating the self and the world is accepted and tends to be accepted by the sufferer as a normal way of living. This definition of psychosis lends itself to justified criticism because it implies that we know what is reality and what is unreality. Many philosophers would promptly indicate to us how naive we are in assuming that we have such knowledge.

In practical terms we can say that no matter what transformation the psychotic patient has undergone, that transformation becomes his way of relating to himself and to others and of interpreting the world. The organic psychotic patient has a cognitive defect but believes that the way he deals with the world is not defective. The schizophrenic undergoes predominantly a symbolic transformation, but he believes there is nothing wrong in living in accordance with that symbolic transformation.

The patient who is depressed to a psychotic degree has undergone predominantly a severe emotional transformation, but he believes that his way of feeling is appropriate to the circumstances in which he lives. Thus he does not fight his disorder, as the psychoneurotic does, but lives within it. In many cases he even seems to nourish it. In this respect he resembles persons who are affected by character neuroses and do not even know the pathological nature of their difficulties. The distortions of the character neuroses, however, are susceptible to at least partial adaptation to the demands of society, whereas in psychoses such adaptation is impossible or very difficult.

The severely depressed person may neglect feeding himself to the point of starvation; he may be so inactive as to be unable to take care of even the most elementary needs; he may think he is justified in believing that there is nothing good in life and death is preferable. He also considers any attempt to improve his life to be worthless, and in some cases he feels guilty in the absence of reasons which would make other people feel guilty. He may actually attempt suicide if he has an opportunity to implement such a plan. He considers his mood consonant with what appears to him the reality of his situation. Thus he seems to have characteristics which would make appropriate the designation "psychotic." Only in a minority of cases do delusions, especially of guilt, and hallucinations occur.

On the other hand, there are some severely depressed patients who do not accept their depression and utterly reject it. Technically, they should therefore not be considered psychotic. They are in this respect similar to the marginal schizophrenic who has at least partial insight into the pathological nature of his condition. However, both this type of severely depressed patient and schizophrenic patient can easily lose insight. If in the term psychosis we include the potential loss of insight, then they too can be called psychotic. If we do so, however, we step on unsafe ground. To obviate these difficulties, I suggest that we call a depression either mild or severe with the understanding that severe depression may be accepted by the patient as a way of living and therefore be syntonic, or unaccepted and therefore dystonic.

Our difficulties are not over. Many clinicians could correctly point out that many cases of depression cannot clearly be differentiated into mild or severe; rather, they reach an intermediate stage of intensity. Inasmuch as most cases could in their psychodynamic structure and clinical course resemble either the mild or the severe type of depression, I am inclined to classify these intermediate stages as moderate-to-mild depression and moderate-to-severe depression.

Are the age of the patient or particular contingencies in his life important to justify particular classifications? I mean, for instance, postpartum depression, adolescent depression, involutional depression, or senile depression, etc. They are justified only to the extent that they frequently have some specific clinical or psychodynamic features. It is important for the therapist to familiarize himself with them. However, the basic mechanisms are presumably the same as in other types of either mild or severe depression.

Table 3-1 demonstrates the classification adopted in this book. It also includes varieties which, although not necessary to distinguish for therapeutic reasons or for the understanding of their psychodynamics, have been recognized by several authors on account of their specific characteristics. They are reported here for the sake of clarification and to facilitate a common ground of understanding.

Before proceeding to a description of the clinical syndromes in Table 3-1, we shall briefly consider other classifications or attempts to classify depression.

TABLE 3-1
Classification of Depressions

Primary Depressions

Mild (dystonic)   a. Depressive Character or Personality
b. Reactive Depression
c. Depression with Anxiety
d. Depression with Obsessive-Compulsive Symptoms
e. Masked Depression
f. Depersonalized Depression

Severe (syntonic)   a. Pure Depression
b. Depression in Manic-Depressive Psychosis
c. Depression in Schizo-Affective Psychosis

Varieties
1. Self-blaming
2. Claiming
3. Mixed
4. Simple
5. Acute
6. Agitated
7. Paranoid
8. With stupor

Related to the Cycle of Life   a. Childhood Depression
b. Adolescent Depression
c. Postpartum Depression
d. Involutional Melancholia
e. Senile Depression

Secondary Depressions
a. Depression with Neurological Disorders or Organic Psychoses
b. Depression with Endocrine Disorders
c. Depression with Other Physical Illnesses
d. Drug-Induced Depression
e. Schizophrenic Depression

A classification based on genetic or biochemical mechanisms is not justified or possible at the present time. Frazier (1976) reminds us that

A variety of hypotheses still exists about the role of chemical transmitter systems in the biology of depression, an area which has continued to be of interest to researchers. There has been a continuing debate between British and American psychiatrists regarding the relative roles serotonin and norepinephrine play in the biology of depression.

In a very scholarly paper Akiskal and McKinney (1975) tried to integrate ten conceptual models of depression, but they failed to draw a classification based on chemistry or on theories which would explain the "leap from chemistry to behavior." They wrote that "biochemical statements that propose a causal relationship between a chemical event in the brain and a set of observable behaviors or subjective experiences present serious philosophical problems." They quote Smythies (1973) in his assertion that attempts to explain mind only in terms of brain chemistry encounter irreducible and unsurmountable elements.

The Task Force on Nomenclature and Statistics of the American Psychiatric Association has proposed the following classification of mood disorders:

Unipolar manic disorder
296.01X   Single episode
296.02X   Recurrent

Unipolar depressive disorder
296.11X   Single episode
296.12X   Recurrent

Bipolar mood disorder
296.20X   Manic
296.30X   Depressed
296.40X   Mixed

Intermittent mood disorders
301.110   Intermittent depressive disorder
301.120   Intermittent hypomanic disorder

300.410   Demoralization disorder

Other mood disorders
300.420   Other depressive disorder
296.610   Other manic disorder
296.620   Other bipolar disorder

An "X" as the sixth digit indicates that the current condition is further specified as: 1 = mild; 2 = moderate; 3 = severe, but not psychotic; 4 = psychotic; 5 = in partial remission; 6 = in full remission.

I participated in the "Working Conference to Critically Examine DSM-111 in Midstream," which took place in St. Louis, Missouri on June 10–12, 1976. During the conference many participants objected to the classification proposed by the task force. The categories "intermittent mood disorders" seemed unclear and unnecessary to several participants who thought that these conditions are only mild forms of affective disorders. Many also objected to the proposed term "demoralization disorder" intended to designate neurotic depression. Maria Kovacs of the University of Pennsylvania School of Medicine stated, "The use of the word *demoralization* seems out of place. In a sense, every patient who recognizes his illness and comes for treatment is demoralized. According to the dictionary, demoralization means loss of morale, loss of psychological well-being because one has lost one's sense of purpose and confidence in the future, or loss of task-related attitudes expected and shared by one's group. By this definition, the concept is true of practically all psychiatric patients as well as numerous other people who might not exhibit long-term, chronic low self-esteem."

I also objected to the term "demoralization disorder," as well as to the term psychotic depression as it was described in the proposed nomenclature; that is, referring only to a condition that presents delusions and hallucinations. I repeated the same objections made earlier in this chapter.

I also stated that the term "mood disorders" seemed to me less appropriate than "affective disorders." First, the word mood as commonly used in English generally refers to the usual disposition of the personality and to the usual gamut of variations found within the limits of normality. The word affective has a deeper impact, more commensurate with the depth that affective disorders can reach. Secondly, it is one of the aims of DSM-111 to preserve similarity with European nomenclatures. The word mood is very difficult to translate into foreign languages, especially those deriving from Latin. The French word *humeur* could not be used correctly. In several classifications the component *thymo*, from the Greek *thymos*, is used to mean affect. I suggested maintaining the term "affective disorders."

I also pointed out that the use of the term unipolar to specify the disorders that have only depressive or manic episodes, although increasing in popularity, is incorrect and should be discouraged. Polarity means having or showing two contrary qualities, forms, or positions. The terms for two poles, like North Pole and South Pole, are called correlational terms; like husband and wife, one cannot exist without the other. If the earth were shaped like a pear, it would have one apex but not one pole. It is true that the term unipolar is used in electricity, but for something devised artificially. We would never say that a pear is unipolar. I suggested that the terms monophasic and biphasic be used instead of unipolar and bipolar.

Primary Depressions

MILD DEPRESSIONS

Mild depressions can be classified into different types, but all or most of them share some characteristics which I shall describe here. Most conspicuous is the feeling of depression, except in those conditions called masked depressions and in syndromes of depersonalization.

Depression as a symptom is difficult to differentiate from the feeling of depression as a normal emotion, generally called sadness, which is part of the gamut of feelings of the average individual. Depression as a rule is experienced with greater intensity than sadness. It is an unpleasant feeling, difficult to overlook or shake off. It does not tend to fade away spontaneously except after a more or less prolonged period of time. As a matter of fact, the person who feels depressed often does not see how he will be able to get rid of his depressed feeling. Often it appears to him that he will remain depressed forever. Actually the opposite is true; in almost every case of mild depression the feeling sooner or later subsides or disappears completely. In many cases, however, it also recurs.

The second characteristic of mild depression is that the patient does not want to have such a despondent feeling; he rejects it, but does not know how to get rid of it. He recognizes that his symptom is unwarranted or exaggerated, and that it is a handicap and to some extent disruptive of the normal functions of life. In other words, he is aware of the dystonic nature of the symptom. The patient is generally correct in this regard: the depressive mood delays his spontaneous behavior and planned activities, requires an extra effort for concentration and work, keeps him distracted from what he would rather do or think, and leaves little room for other emotions. In some cases the patient is able to connect the depression with an event that almost everybody else also would consider unpleasant, but his reaction is nevertheless exaggerated. In Gutheil's words (1959) he is not only sad, but pessimistic. For Gutheil, pessimism is the added element that changes simple sadness into depression. We may add that this pessimism is often but not always accompanied by feelings of loneliness, unworthiness, and self-criticism.

Ideas that life is not worthwhile occur and suicidal projects present themselves, but not in an enduring fashion. Generally suicidal ideas are not carried out.

Psychosomatic and somatic symptoms accompany almost every case of depression. Appetite and eating habits change. In a large number of patients there is a noticeable but not excessive loss of weight. On the other hand, in a considerable number of patients there is a considerable increase in weight. The patient eats in an effort to assuage his depression.

Sleep dysfunction is also a frequent symptom. Many patients complain of insomnia; yet they may sleep longer than usual, either because they do not want to face the day or because they really believe, at least at a manifest level, that their sleep requirements have increased. They claim that unless they sleep longer hours they feel fatigued, but fatigue remains a common symptom even if they do sleep longer than usual. Constipation is also a common complaint. Many mildly depressed patients complain of a decrease in sexual libido, and yet some of them indulge more than usual in sexual behavior in an attempt to find solace.

In addition to all or most of these characteristics, mild depressions have other traits that permit special classification. In some cases it is impossible to ascertain to what type the depression should be ascribed. The whole issue of whether such classification is warranted also is a matter of debate.

One of these varieties can be called depressive character (Bemporad,

1976) or depressive personality. In these cases, according to Bemporad, "depression appears to be a *constant* mode of feeling lurking in the background during everyday life." It is a conscious reaction to the loss of a state of well-being. Contrary to some of the other character or personality disorders, the patient is dissatisfied with his condition and would like to change it. The unpleasant feeling often occurs after seemingly insignificant frustration. Bemporad reports that in the depressive character it is easy to find the primary triad of cognitive sets described by Beck (1967): a negative view of the world, the self, and the future.

The main feature of this variety of mild depression is its constant or almost constant character, so that the depressive mood becomes an important feature of the character. The patient is usually referred to as a depressed person. In some cases the patient does not describe himself as depressed, but as a person who is bored and has lost "la joie de vivre," or sees no possibility of joyful excitement in his life.

The variety of depression which we are going to describe now has received much more consideration in psychiatric literature—that is, reactive depression. This condition is characterized chiefly by the fact that it starts after the occurrence of an unpleasant happening in the life of the patient, or after an event which is considered by the patient to be adverse or unwelcome.

Bereavement, or loss through death of a person dear to the patient, is probably the most common precipitating factor of reactive depression. As we shall describe in greater detail in chapter 5, sadness due to mourning is a normal experience. Whereas the normal person sooner or later recovers from the experience of grief, however, the person who becomes depressed finds himself unable to shake off this unpleasant feeling. On the contrary, the anguish lingers and may become even more severe.

In my experience reactive depression connected with marital difficulties is very common. Also frequent is the depression over the end of a love relation, or over the loss of the loved person as an object of love. Loss of employment, disappointments at work, lack of promotion, financial difficulties, breaking up an important friendship, loss of status and prestige, and insults received are precipitating factors of reactive depression that can be easily understood even at a reality level.

The situation is more complex when the loss apparently does not justify the intensity of the depression; for instance, when the death of a bird, the loss of a handkerchief, or the inability to get tickets for a show provoke a depression. It seems easy to conclude in these cases that the precipitating event has a symbolic value, as we shall see in greater detail later in this book. In some cases of reactive depression other symptoms occur often, but not always: irritability, anger, an insatiable desire to get or obtain, and even a desire to alienate or manipulate others.

Another type of mild depression is "depression with anxiety." It consists of a clinical picture in which depression and anxiety occur concurrently. It is generally included under the group of depressions if the depressive mood is the prevailing one, although anxiety plays an important role in the total picture. In addition to being depressed, the patient is anxious, worried, expects something bad to happen, and is generally fearful of his own usual activities. In some instances he gives the impression of preferring to be depressed rather than anxious, and that the depression is an escape from anxiety. However, if the depression reaches great proportions, it may become more intolerable than the anxiety.

Another variety, more frequent than it would seem from cases reported in the literature, is the combination of depression and obsessive-compulsive symptoms. In addition to being depressed, the patient presents obsessions, compulsions, and rituals of the obsessive-compulsive kind. Contrary to what occurs in typical cases of obsessive-compulsive psychoneurosis, the obsessive and especially the compulsive symptoms are not very resistant. In some cases at least they are more easily overcome in obsessive-compulsive depression than in a typical obsessive-compulsive psychoneurosis.

Obsessive-compulsive depression is not uncommon in very religious persons who have learned to practice rituals in a compulsive way. Some of these cases are not mild and can be classified more properly as cases of severe depression in which obsessive-compulsive symptoms also appear.

The next two types of depression are characterized by the absence of depression as a feeling state of which the patient is aware. The first of these conditions is called masked depression. Doubts about the existence of such a clinical entity stem not only from different criteria of classification, but also from semantic and philosophical sources. In fact, can we talk of a feeling which is not felt? Can we talk of a felt experience which is not experienced? Freud too felt that an idea may become unconscious but an emotion by definition must always be felt.

In 1944 Kennedy reported that in many patients the symptomatology consists almost exclusively of somatic dysfunctions, which he called manic-depressive equivalents. Such terms as masked, hidden, or missed depression have appeared especially in the German literature. In 1937 Hempel published a paper on depression in which he characterized autonomic nervous disorders, and in 1949 Lemke wrote about depression of the vegetative system. Perhaps imitating the terminology used in reference to epilepsy, Ibor Lopes (1966) wrote about depressive equivalents and of *depressio sine depressione.*

According to Berner, Katschnig, and Pöldinger (1973) most of the authors who use the expression masked depression mean "a depression in which the physical manifestations conceal the psychopathological symptomatology." Other people mean "a depression not recognized by a previous examiner who believed it to be a somatic disease." Still others call masked depression "any depression characterized by masked physical signs and symptoms." These are circular definitions. When we say that masked depression is a depression characterized by physical symptomatology, we offer only a tautologic statement deprived of any explanatory value. In fact we would have to demonstrate that the physical symptomatology is indeed a form of depression.

Geisler (1973) made a study of patients suffering from masked depression who were diagnosed as suspected of suffering from internal diseases such as angina pectoris, autonomic nervous dystonia, cardiovascular disorders, cholecystitis, colitis, diverticulitis, food allergy, neoplasm, and pernicious anemia. Thirty-six patients suffering from masked depression complained of sleep disorders, lack of appetite, abdominal symptoms, anxiety, cardiac symptoms, constipation, and so on. According to Geisler, the most frequent combination of symptoms consisted of complaints referring to organs, sleep disorders, poor appetite, and anxiety.

According to Braceland (1966) the six most frequent symptoms of masked depression are insomnia, tiredness, gastric and epigastric discomfort, anorexia, headache, and general abdominal pain. In many of these cases the differential diagnosis from hypochondriasis or psychosomatic conditions is difficult to make. In some cases the diagnosis reflects the classificatory habits of the therapist more than the nature of the condition.

In my opinion a common form of masked depression is the condition which is generally referred to as alcoholism. A considerable number of depressed people hide their depression by making immoderate use of alcohol, and therefore they are considered alcoholic. They often reveal their depression during the alcohol-free intervals. That they are fundamentally depressed also is revealed by the fact that most of them respond satisfactorily to antidepressants like imipramine.

An uncommon type of depression without depressive feeling is one which often assumes the characteristics of the syndrome of depersonalization. The person no longer feels like himself. Sensations are dull; perceptions are changed; reality may appear modified or transformed; a sense of distance and of space seems unreal. The person's voice or part of his body seems not to belong to him. The patient is depersonalized insofar as he has the feeling that he is not the same person and he cannot think, feel, act, or be motivated as he used to be. Up to this point the picture seems unrelated to depression, but the fact is that at times the patient does feel depressed. Another characteristic that suggests the depressive nature of this syndrome is the fact that some of these patients (but not all) respond well to electric shock treatment, at least for a temporary remission. They also improve with amphetamine and amphetamine derivatives. By no means is it implied here that all or even most patients suffering from depersonalization are depressed.

There is an additional remark to be made about both masked depression and depersonalization. It is more than doubtful that if they belong to the category of depression, they should be included under the group of mild rather than severe depressions. In some of these cases the symptomatology is quite marked and incapacitating.

Severe Depression

Severe depression as a clinical entity has been known since antiquity. Its features are generally very pronounced, easily recognizable, and much more easily definable than those of mild depression.

What seems to have remained unchanged from the time of Hippocrates to the late 1950s is a picture of an intense state of depression in which one can almost always recognize a profound and overwhelming theme of self-blame, hopelessness, and self-depreciation. Although cases with this classic picture are still very common, others—with a picture which I call claiming depression—occur with increasing frequency.

We shall review the various syndromes of severe depression with the understanding that the division into types and varieties is not very well established and in many cases still a matter of controversial debate.

CLASSIC FORM OF SEVERE DEPRESSION

Severe depression is characterized by the following triad of psychological symptoms: (1) a pervasive feeling of melancholia; (2) a disorder of thought processes, characterized by retardation and unusual content; and (3) psychomotor retardation. In addition there are accessory somatic dysfunctions.

The pervasive mood of depression at times has its onset quite acutely and dramatically, at other times slowly and insidiously. The patient generally has had previous attacks of depression which, because they were mild in intensity, passed unnoticed or were considered by the patient and his family as normal variations of mood. Even an attack that will later appear severe in intensity is misunderstood at first. An unpleasant event has occurred, such as the death of a close relative or a grief of any kind, and a mood of sadness is justified. However, when a certain period of time has elapsed and the unhappy feeling should have subsided, it seems instead to become more intense. The patient complains that he cannot think freely, feels unable to work, cannot eat, and sleeps only a few hours a night.

As the symptoms increase in intensity, the patient himself may request to be taken to a physician. Often, however, the illness is advanced to such a degree that the patient no longer is able to make such a decision and he consults a physician at the initiative of family members. When the physician sees the patient, he is impressed by his unhappy, sad appearance. The patient looks older than his age, his forehead is wrinkled, and his face, although undergoing very little mimic play, reveals a despondent mood. In some cases the main fold of the upper eyelid at the edges of its inner third is contracted upward and a little backward (sign of Veraguth).

In most cases the examiner is led astray by the complaints of the patient, which consist of physical pain, a feeling of discomfort, digestive difficulties, lack of appetite, and insomnia. The physician may interpret these complaints as simple psychosomatic dysfunctions. They may persist and constitute a syndrome of severe masked depression. In the majority of cases, however, the mood of melancholia sooner or later becomes prominent and leads to an easy diagnosis.

The patient is often at a loss to describe the experience of melancholia. He says that his chest is heavy, his body is numb; he would like to sleep, but he cannot; he would like to immerse himself in activities, but he cannot; he would even like to cry, but he cannot. "The eyes have consumed all the tears." "Life is a torment." There is at the same time a desire to punish oneself by destroying oneself, which at the same time would end one's suffering. Suicidal ideas occur in about 75 percent of patients, and actual suicide attempts are made by at least 10 to 15 percent. Often the suicide attempt occurs when it is not expected, because the patient seems to have made some improvement and the depression is less pronounced. In a minority of suicide attempts, the suicidal idea was carefully concealed from the members of the family. The desire to end life applies only to the life of the patient himself, with one important exception to be kept in mind always: young mothers who undergo psychotic depression often plan to destroy not only themselves but their children, who presumably are considered by the patient to be an extension of herself. Newspaper reports about mothers who have killed themselves and their little children in most cases refer to patients suffering from unrecognized attacks of severe depression.

The other important symptom of depression concerns the content and type of thinking. As far as the content is concerned, the thoughts of the patient are characterized by gloomy, morbid ideas. In some cases, at the beginning of the attack, ideas occur that at first may not be recognized as part of the ensuing picture of psychotic depression. They may be phobic, obsessive, or obscene. They are followed by discouraging ideas which acquire more and more prominence. The patient feels that he will not be able to work, he will lose his money, something bad will happen to his family, somebody is going to get hurt, or the family is in extreme poverty. There is no great variety in the patient's thoughts. It is almost as if the patient purposely selects the thoughts that have an unpleasant content. *They are not thoughts as thoughts; they are chiefly carriers of mental pain.*

The distortion caused by the unpleasantness of the mood at times transforms these melancholic thoughts into almost delusional ideas or into definite delusions. They often represent distortions of the body image and hypochondriasis. The patient thinks he has cancer, tuberculosis, syphilis, and so on. His brain is melting, his bowels have been lost, his heart does not beat. Delusions of poverty are also common. Ideas of guilt, sin, and self-condemnation are very pronounced, especially in serious cases. At times these self-accusatory ideas are so unrealistic that the name "delusion" seems appropriate for them. "It is all my fault;" "It is all my responsibility." In some cases the tendency to blame oneself reaches the absurd; the patient blames himself for being sick or for "succumbing to the illness." In some cases, he feels that he is not really sick but he acts as if he were sick. This impression is almost the opposite of what we find in some schizophrenics, in whom there is the idea that the world is a big stage, and what happens in the world is an act or a play. The depressed patient, on the contrary, feels that he is acting the part of the sick person. Incidentally, this idea occurs generally when the patient starts to recover from his depressed attack.

These delusional ideas cannot always be traced back to an exaggeration or distortion of mood. In cases that have a mixed paranoid and melancholic symptomatology, the delusions are more inappropriate and bizarre and are in no way distinguishable from those of paranoid patients.

In a small percentage of severely depressed patients there are obsessive-compulsive thoughts, similar to those occurring in obsessive-compulsive psychoneuroses or in mild depression with obsessive features. The pervasive mood of depression prevails, however, in the context of the complex symptomatology.

In the classical or traditional type of psychotic depression, the main theme is a self-blaming attitude. In severe cases the patient seems to transmit the following message: "Do not help me. I do not deserve to be helped. I deserve to die." Together with this peculiar content of thought, there is a retardation of thinking processes. The patient complains that he cannot concentrate; he cannot focus his attention. At first he can read, but without retaining what he reads. Writing is more difficult for him and composing a letter requires tremendous effort. If the patient is a student, he cannot study any longer. Thoughts seem to follow each other at a very slow pace. Speech is also slow. In a severe state of stupor the patient cannot talk at all.

Hallucinations in severe depression are described by many authors, especially in the old textbooks. According to the experience of many psychiatrists, however, they are much less common in severe depression than they used to be. This difference is not apparent, in the sense that patients who hallucinate are now diagnosed as schizophrenics. I have found that hallucinations do occur, although rarely, in some severely depressed patients. They have the following characteristics:

1. They are very rare in comparison to their occurrence in schizophrenia.
2. They do not have the distinct perceptual and auditory quality that they have in schizophrenia. The patients often cannot repeat what the voices say; they sound indistinct. The patients describe them as "as if rocks were falling," or as "bells which ring." Often they seem more like illusions than hallucinations, or as transformations of actual perceptions.
3. They can be related to the prevailing mood of the patient much more easily than in schizophrenia. Their secondary character—that is, secondary to the overall mood—is obvious. They are generally depressive and denigratory in content, often commanding self-destruction or injury.
4. More frequently than in schizophrenic patients, they occur at night, less frequently during the day. The depressed patient, who is in contact with external reality more than the schizophrenic, possibly needs the removal of diurnal stimuli in order to become aware of these inner phenomena.

Another important sign of the classic type of depression consists of retarded hypoactivity. The actions of the patient decrease in number, and even those which are carried out are very slow. Even the perceptions are retarded. Talking is reduced to a minimum, although a minority of patients retain the tendency to be loquacious. Working at the usual daily tasks of life is postponed or retarded. The patient avoids doing many things but continues to do what is essential. Women neglect their housework and their appearance. Every change seems to require a tremendous effort. Interpersonal relations are cut off. In some less pronounced cases, however, the opposite at first seems to occur. The patient, who is prone to accuse himself and extoll others, becomes more affectionate toward the members of his family and willing to do many things for them in an unselfish manner. However, when the disorder increases in intensity later, he becomes indifferent to everybody.

The physical symptoms that accompany classic depressive attacks are reduction in sleep, decrease in appetite, and considerable loss in weight. These symptoms do not seem to be due to a specific or direct physiological mechanism, but rather are related to or are a consequence of the depression. Many patients complain of dryness of the mouth, which is to be attributed to decreased secretion of the parotid glands (Strongin and Hinsie, 1938).

Other frequent symptoms are constipation, backache, amenorrhea, and dryness of the skin. There is a definite decrease in sexual desire, often to the point of complete impotence or frigidity. In many patients sugar is found in the urine during the attack. The basal metabolism tends to be slightly lower than normal.

THE CLAIMING TYPE OF DEPRESSION

As we have already mentioned, since the late 1950s there has been a decline in the number of cases showing the classic type of depression, either as part of manic-depressive psychosis or as part of pure depression. Moreover, the cases that we do see seldom reach those severe degrees which used to be very common. Another type of depression is frequently observed now, whose symptomatology has the appearance of an appeal, a cry for help. The patient is anguished but wants people near him to become very aware of his condition. All his symptoms seem to imply the message, "Help me; pity me. It is in your power to relieve me. If I suffer, it is because you don't give me what I need." Even the suicidal attempt or prospect is an appeal of "Do not abandon me" or, "You have the power to prevent my death. I want you to know it." In other words, the symptomatology, although colored by an atmosphere of depression, is a gigantic claim. Now it is the gestalt of depression that looms in the foreground with the claim lurking behind; now it is the claim which looms, with the depression apparently receding. Poorly hidden also are feelings of hostility for people close to the patient, such as members of the family who do not give the patient as much as he would like. If anger is expressed, feelings of guilt and depression follow. Whereas the patient with the self-blaming type of depression generally wants to be left alone, the claiming type of patient is clinging, dependent, and demanding. Self-accusation and guilt feelings play a secondary role or no role at all in this type of depression.

Whereas in the self-blaming type of depression there is a decrease of appetite and insomnia, in the claiming type the appetite is not necessarily diminished and quite often there is a need and ability to sleep longer than usual. In some cases the patient does not want to get up from bed and wishes to return to it several times during the day.

OTHER CLINICAL VARIETIES OF DEPRESSION

Some authors distinguish several varieties of severe depression: the simple, the acute, the paranoid, and the depressive stupor.

Simple depression is characterized by the moderate intensity of symptoms and may make the diagnosis of psychosis difficult. Delusions and hallucinations are absent. Although there is psychomotor retardation, the patient is able to take care of his basic vital needs. Suicidal ideas and attempts also occur in this type. In recent years cases of simple depression seem to have increased in number.

In *acute depression* the symptoms are much more pronounced. Self-accusation and ideas of sin and poverty are prominent. Some depressive ideas bordering on delusion are present. The loss of weight is very marked.

In *paranoid depression*, although the prominent feature remains the depressed mood, delusional ideas play an important role. The patient feels that he is watched, spied on, or threatened. Somebody wants to hurt him. Hypochondriacal delusions with pronounced distortion of the body image may occur. As in the case of hallucinations, these delusions seem secondary to the prevailing mood of the patient. They disappear easily when the mood changes. Hallucinations may also occur.

Depressive stupor is the most pronounced form of depression. Here there is more than psychomotor retardation: the movements are definitely inhibited or suppressed. The patients are so absorbed in their own pervasive feelings of depression that they cannot focus their attention on their surroundings. They do not seem to hear; they do not respond. They are mute, with the exception of some occasional utterances. Even mimic expressions are absent and the face seems mask-like, in a way reminiscent of the faces of some post-encephalitic and Parkinsonian patients. Since the patients cannot focus on anything, they give the impression of being apathetic, whereas they are actually the prey of a deep, disturbing emotion. These patients cannot take care of themselves. Generally they lie in bed mute and have to be spoon-fed.

Unless they are successfully treated during the attack, physical health may suffer severely. Patients lose up to a hundred pounds in certain cases; they are constipated, and their circulation is enfeebled.

All the types of depression that we have so far described are also characterized by a lack of manic features or episodes during their course.

DEPRESSIVE PHASE OF MANIC-DEPRESSIVE PSYCHOSIS

All the clinical varieties of severe depression that we have described also appear as the depressive phase of manic-depressive psychosis.

In manic-depressive psychosis the classic type of depression is probably the most frequent. However, the claiming type, or mixed self-blaming and claiming type, also appears with typical or atypical symptomatology, as well as forms of simple depression, acute depression, paranoid depression, and depressive stupor.

What chiefly characterizes the depression occurring in manic-depressive psychosis is that it is followed regularly or occasionally by manic episodes. Inasmuch as the depressive picture is not dissimilar to the ones so far described, this section will be devoted to examination of the manic episode. The manic attack is not an attack of depression. Nevertheless we shall describe it here because it is a frequent component of a syndrome in which primary severe depression is an important part.

In the manic attack, as in an attack of severe depression, the symptomatology is characterized by: (1) a change in mood, which is one of elation (2) a disorder of thought processes, characterized by flight of ideas and happy content; and (3) an increased motility. Accessory body changes also occur.

It is difficult in many instances to determine the beginning of the episode. The patient is often in a lively mood. He strikes the observer as being an extrovert, active individual who likes to talk a great deal and do many things. At the time of the attack, however, the overjoyousness of the patient seems out of proportion and occasionally inappropriate; for instance, when he easily dismisses things which should make him sad and continues to be in his happy mood. The patient appears exuberant very sociable, and at times even succeeds in transmitting his happiness to the surrounding persons. This mood, however, is not constant or solid. We are not referring here to the alternations with depression, but to the fact that this euphoric mood may easily change into one of irritation or even rage and anger, especially when the patient becomes aware that the environment does not respond to his enthusiasm or does not react in accordance with the exalted opinion that he has of himself.

The thinking disorder is prominent and reveals itself in verbal productions. The patient talks very fast and cannot concentrate on any subject for more than a few seconds. Any marginal idea is expressed; any secondary, distracting stimulus affects the patient. The thoughts expressed are not disconnected but maintain some apparent ties. We can always determine that the ideas are connected by the elementary laws of association, but the talk as a whole is verbose, circumstantial, and not directed toward any goal or toward the logical demonstration of any point which is discussed. The ensemble of these thought and language alterations is called "flight of ideas."

Actually this type of verbal behavior has a goal—that of maintaining this superficial effervescent euphoria and escaping from intruding thoughts which may bring about depression. In less pronounced cases the patient realizes that he has unduly allowed details to interfere with the original goal of his conversation, and he tries to go back to it but again gets lost in many details.

In this incessant logorrhea, the patient makes jokes. The propensity toward associations leads to repeated clang associations which the patient uses to make jokes, puns, and so on (Arieti, 1950). In rare cases the lack of thought inhibition facilitates a certain artistic propensity which does not, however, lead to achievement because of the lack of concentration.

Lorenz and Cobb (1952) and Lorenz (1953), who made an accurate study of speech in manic patients, reported that in manic speech there is a quantitative change in the use of certain speech elements, namely: (1) a relative increase in the use of pronouns and verbs; (2) a relative decrease in the use of adjectives and prepositions; and (3) a high verb-adjective quotient (that is, the proportion of adjectives is decreased). These authors found no gross disorganization at the level of structural elements, and they postulated that the defect in manic speech occurs at higher integrative levels of language formulation. They concluded that,

"If the assumption of a correlation between emotional states and verb-adjective quotient is correct, the manic patient's speech gives objective evidence of a heightened degree of anxiety."

The rapid association ability that the manic possesses enables him to grasp immediately some aspects of the environment which otherwise would pass unnoticed. The patient is in the paradoxical situation in which his ability to observe and grasp environmental stimuli has increased, but he cannot make use of it because of his distractibility.

The patient's thought content often reveals an exalted opinion of himself. The patient may boast that he is very rich, a great lover, a famous actor, a prominent businessman. These statements receive flimsy support. When asked to prove them, the patient attempts to do so but soon is lost in a web of unnecessary details. He may become excitable if he is reminded of the goal of the conversation. Disturbances of the sensorium are generally of minimal intensity and are caused by the exalted mood or distractibility, not by intellectual impairment.

Motor activity is increased. Manic patients are always on the go, in a state that ranges from mild motor excitement to incessant and wild activity. They talk, sing, dance, tease, destroy, move objects. In severe states these actions or movements remain unfinished and purposeless. In spite of their constant activity, manic patients do not feel tired and have tremendous endurance.

Accessory somatic symptoms consist of loss of weight which is generally not as pronounced as in depression, decrease in appetite, and constipation. Insomnia is marked. The blood pressure is generally lowered. Menses are irregular. Sexual functions, although apparently increased in hypomanic states, are generally decreased or disturbed in various ways in manic conditions.

Manic Varieties. As with depression, many forms of manic states have been described by early authors. A brief description of them follows.

In *hypomania* the symptoms are not of a marked intensity. As mentioned before, it is difficult at times to say whether the patient is showing his usual extrovert personality or the beginning of an illness. He seems full of pep and in good humor. He wants to do many things. His verbal abilities are accentuated. Although he has always had a talent for foreign languages, he now speaks many of them without hesitation, unconcerned with the mistakes he makes. Some of these patients increase their activities to such an exaggerated degree that they show very poor judgment. They are actually compelled by their inner excitability and by their exalted mood. They may walk for miles and miles. Generally they have a goal (for instance, to reach the next village), but not a necessary one. They may send out hundreds of unnecessary letters or greeting cards and make a large number of lengthy telephone calls. They often go on spending sprees, with disastrous economic consequences. Their sexual activity is increased, and lack of control may bring about unpleasant results. Illegitimate pregnancies in hypomanic women and venereal diseases in hypomanic men and women are relatively common.

The excitability, richness of movements, and euphoric mood give a bizarre flavor to the manic's behavior. A female patient, in order to show a sore to a physician, completely undressed in front of him. Occasionally even thefts and fraudulent acts are committed. The patient retains the ability to rationalize his actions, at times to such an extent that the layman is confused and believes in the patient's sanity.

In *acute mania* the symptoms are much more pronounced. They may accelerate gradually, from a previously hypomanic state, or rapidly, from a normal condition. The patient is in such a state of extreme restlessness that his behavior may be very disturbing and difficult to control. He may disrupt theatrical audiences, sing or scream in the street, or ring bells. If an attempt is made to control him, he may become belligerent. The mood is one of such exaltation that spontaneous thoughts of self-aggrandizement are accepted immediately.

A subtype which Kraepelin differentiated from acute mania is delusional mania, characterized by an abundance of grandiose delusional ideas reminiscent of those found in the expansive type of general paresis.

Delirious mania represents an extreme stage of excitement. The patient is incoherent, disoriented, restless, and agitated. He may easily injure himself and others in his aimless activity. Restraint, chemical or physical, is an absolute necessity to avoid exhaustion which may lead to death. Hallucinations and delusions are frequent.

In addition to the types just mentioned, Kraepelin has described *mixed states* which are characterized by a combination of manic and depressive symptoms. He distinguishes the following six principal types: (1) manic stupor; (2) agitated depression; (3) unproductive mania; (4) depressive mania; (5) depression with flight of ideas; and (6) akinetic mania.

The names given to these types indicate the combination of chief symptoms for each. Of the six types, perhaps the most common is agitated depression. In this condition a motor restlessness, typical of a manic excitement, is superimposed on a markedly depressive symptomatology.

Although the types of manic-depressive psychosis have been described as if they were separate entities, all the types are related, as Kraepelin saw when he first formulated the large nosological concept of manic-depressive psychosis.

The melancholic and the manic attack, which at first seem so different, have an intrinsic similarity; the same mental functions are altered, although the alterations are in a certain way opposite. Whereas in depression the mood is one of melancholia, in the manic attack it is one of elation; whereas in depression the thought processes and motor activity are retarded, in the manic attack a flight of ideas and increased motility are found.

One of the main characteristics of manic-depressive psychosis is the recurrence of the attacks, which has conferred to the disorder the designation, often used in Europe, of intermittent psychosis.

The attack may occur in different successions, which old books of psychiatry described at great length and with many illustrations that represented the manic attack as a positive wave and the depression as a negative wave. A sequence of a depressed phase followed by a manic phase is the typical pattern of circular psychosis. We may observe, however, that the attacks of depression far outnumber those of mania. Some patients may undergo a conspicuous number of depressions without ever having a manic phase.

There seems to be no relation between the duration of the attack and of normal intervals. At times, short attacks recur several times in short succession, but occasionally the series is interrupted by a long normal interval. I have seen several cases in which an attack of depression in the patient's early twenties was not followed by a second one until the patient had reached his middle sixties or even seventies. Kraepelin illustrated that many attacks of depression occurring later in life, which many authors consider as a subtype of senile psychosis, must instead be considered to be late occurrences or relapses of manic-depressive psychosis.

According to Pollock et al. (1939) 58.1 percent of patients have only one attack, 26.1 percent have two attacks, 9.3 have three attacks, and 6.5 percent have more than three attacks. Occasionally, one finds a patient who has had 25 or even more attacks.

The age at which the first attack occurs varies. It may even happen in childhood in rare cases. By far the largest number of first attacks occur between the ages of twenty and thirty-five. Manic attacks are slightly more frequent between the ages of twenty and forty. After forty, their ratio to depressive attacks decreases further. Women are more susceptible to this psychosis than men. (About 70 percent of patients are women.)

The illness generally results in recovery as far as the individual attack is concerned. Repeated attacks usually cause very little intellectual impairment. Death, however, may occur in two instances: suicide in depression, and exhaustion or cardiac insufficiency in cases of delirious mania. Another situation which we shall discuss later is the change of the manic-depressive symptomatology into a schizophrenic one, either shortly after the onset of the illness or even after many years of hospitalization.*

* There are many psychiatrists who would deny such a statement. They feel that if a manic-depressive seems later to become schizophrenic, it is because the right diagnosis (schizophrenia) was not made. A considerable number of psychiatrists would call such a patient schizo-affective. Most psychiatrists, however, limit the diagnosis of schizo-affective psychoses to patients who present a mixed symptomatology from the beginning of the illness.

Prognostic criteria as to the future course of the condition are very difficult when the patient is examined only from the point of view of manifest symptomatology. Contrary to what happens in schizophrenia, the manifest symptomatology of manic-depressive psychosis will rarely permit prediction as to whether the patient will have only the present attack, a few, or many in his lifetime. The prognosis is almost always good as to the individual attack, but it is uncertain as to the possibility of recurrence. Rennie (1942) in an accurate statistical study found that the prognosis is worse when attacks occur after the age of forty. He found that 70 percent of all patients had a second attack; 63.5 percent a third; and 45 percent a fourth. The more frequent the attacks, the worse the prognosis is.

INVOLUTIONAL MELANCHOLIA

A common type of depression occurs during the climacterium (menopause), or shortly before or after, and is generally called involutional melancholia. This diagnosis was made more frequently in the past, before the advent of electric shock treatment, drug therapy, or psychotherapy on a large scale. Patients were admitted to psychiatric hospitals where at times they remained for very long periods of time, in some cases even for the rest of their lives. The majority of patients remained sick from one to five years. I myself while working at Pilgrim State Hospital saw many patients so diagnosed who had remained in the hospital for even more than ten years. The advent of electric shock treatment dramatically changed the picture and permitted the complete loss of symptomatology which had persisted for so long. All the mentioned types of treatment have drastically changed the course of the illness and permit a much more favorable prognosis.

Involutional melancholia is a syndrome characterized by severe depression which generally occurs for the first time during the so-called involutional age—between the ages of forty to fifty-eight in women, and fifty to sixty-five in men. It is much more common in women.

The onset may be gradual and be manifested by anxiety, apprehension, hypochondriasis, and in some cases by quasi-paranoid attitudes toward acquaintances, relatives, friends, co-workers, and so forth. Irritability and pessimism predominate at first, together with an excessive preoccupation with bodily functions and a fear of illnesses. Restlessness and frank motor agitation subsequently become the main feature in most cases. Psychomotor retardation, typical of other severe types of depression, is absent in many cases or not very pronounced. However, the patient is definitely less active than before the onset of the illness. The lack of purposeful activity at times contrasts with the motor restlessness. Female patients often are prompt to attribute their symptoms to menopause and to minimize psychological factors of any sort. In some cases that run a very acute and serious course, the examiner feels he is dealing with a person who considers his/her life already coming to an end. The remaining years are seen as a prolonged agony which it would be better to terminate with a self-imposed coup de grâce.

In the past the most pronounced forms of depression were seen in involutional melancholia even more than in the depressive phase of manic-depressive psychosis or in other types of severe depression. Prior to the introduction of three types of treatment—electric shock treatment, drug therapy, and psychotherapy—the current belief of the medical staff in psychiatric hospitals was that only "about one-third of hospitalized cases lived through their psychosis to survive" (Bigelow, 1959). We must remember that these were hospitalized cases, and that this evaluation did not include milder cases which were never hospitalized. Today the prognosis is quite different. If suicide is avoided, recovery or very marked improvement occurs in 100 percent of cases.

In early studies of this condition, the prepsychotic personality of the involutional patient was described as being characterized by rigid adherence to the ethical code, narrow range of interests, meticulousness, stubbornness, and poor sexual adjustment (Titley, 1936). Others stressed obsessional, sadomasochistic, introverted personalities (Palmer and Sherman, 1938). Rosenthal (1968, 1974), who has made recent studies of involutional melancholia, does not give much credit to the findings of Palmer and Sherman and of Titley. He states that "one is hard-pressed to find any recent studies that confirm these findings with more sophisticated statistical techniques."

In addition, all the studies that relate involutional depression to the physical changes of the menopause or to other endocrine functions have led to no conclusive results.

SENILE DEPRESSION

Senile depression must be distinguished from a depression which occurs in a predominantly organic condition, such as senile psychosis or cerebral arteriosclerosis.

Senile depression is a rather frequent form of generally moderate to severe depression, which is distinguished from the other types of severe depression because it occurs in old age in individuals who have not suffered from depression previously. It is characterized at first by psychosomatic and hypochondriacal preoccupations, followed by an overpowering feeling of depression, guilt, self-deprivation, inhibition of activity, retardation, and marked decrease in interest. At least two-thirds of the patients are women.

Some cases are relatively benign and are often diagnosed as cases of reactive depression because they occur after an unpleasant event has taken place. The most severe cases do not seem to be reactive to any specific event; rather, they seem to represent the unfavorable outcome of an entire life.

In a study reported by Charatan (1975) 52 percent of the patients who had been seen in a geriatric psychiatric outpatient clinic were diagnosed as suffering from an affective disorder—primarily psychotic depression.

In a considerable number of patients who are approaching old age, but who cannot yet really be called old—from their late fifties to middle sixties—the depression seems to be predominantly precipitated by sexual dysfunction or at least sexual preoccupations. Male patients complain that they have difficulty in erecting or that they lose the erection rapidly, ejaculate without strength or momentum, or without enough semen. Women complain of dyspareunia, complete frigidity, or even of total sexual disgust. In a minority of cases in both sexes there is also compulsive masturbation or even promiscuity in an attempt to overcome the depression. In many other cases, especially for widowers, loneliness is a much more frequent complaint than sexual dysfunction.

POSTPARTUM DEPRESSION

All kinds of affective conditions may occur after childbirth, from the so-called postpartum blues to mania and psychotic depression. Inasmuch as I consider childbirth to be a precipitating event of great psychological significance although not physically related to the depression, postpartum depression is here included among the primary depressions.

The manifest symptomatology of postpartum depression is fundamentally not different from that of other severe depressions. In most cases there is a gradual increase of depressive characteristics. In some cases the condition is recognized several weeks after childbirth and only when a full-blown depression is present.

Frequent symptoms are insomnia, restlessness, hypoactivity, and disinterest or neglect of the child. In some cases there are also phobic and obsessive symptoms, which are quite distressing: the patient is afraid of harming or even killing the child. In less severe cases the patient is afraid that she will not be able to take care of her child. She considers herself a bad or unworthy mother. She either pities the child very much or is completely indifferent to him and considers him an intruder in her life. In still other cases the anxiety about not being able to be a good mother prevails over the feeling of depression.

In the most severe cases a deep depression, often accompanied by guilt and a total feeling of hopelessness, obliterates all other sensations.

Some postpartum depressions recover quite quickly, but most of them are of longer duration than other depressions and of severe intensity, irrespective of whether the depression is monophasic or part of a biphasic manic-depressive psychosis that has been precipitated by childbirth.

A very important distinction must be made in cases of postpartum depression in regard to the safety of the baby. If the patient in an obsessive or phobic way is afraid of hurting or even killing her child, the danger is minimal or practically nonexistent. The patient has to be re-assured and told that she is suffering from a fear, not from a determination to do anything harmful. On the other hand, if the patient has no obsessive-compulsive or phobic symptoms, is very depressed, and expresses or nourishes suicidal ideas, the risk is great not only for her but also for the baby. What we mentioned before—that depressed women who commit suicide often include their children in the suicidal act and kill them too—applies especially in postpartum depressions. Twin babies are killed by depressed mothers just as easily as single children. The greatest surveillance is necessary.

Since all types of psychiatric conditions can occur after childbirth, the diagnosis may be difficult in atypical cases. The first diagnostic task consists in ascertaining whether the condition is a postpartum delirium, generally organic in nature, or any other psychiatric condition less frequently associated with organic factors. Delirium, which is characterized generally by confusion, extreme excitement, incoherent or irrelevant thinking, and a rather acute course, has become much less frequent in the last few decades probably because of improved obstetrical care and less probability of toxic conditions during pregnancy. The presence of schizophrenic symptoms such as delusions, hallucinations, or ideas of reference may lead easily to the diagnosis of schizophrenia.

However, many authors differ in their reports of the incidence of schizophrenic and affective psychoses after childbirth. According to Davidson (1936), schizophrenic and manic-depressive psychoses each constituted 30 percent of postpartum psychiatric disorders. For Boyd (1942), manic-depressive psychosis constituted 40 percent, schizophrenia 20 percent, and delirium 28.5 percent. Strecker and Ebaugh (1926) reported 34 percent delirium, 36 percent manic-depressive, and 20 percent schizophrenic. Protheroe (1969) in England reported almost twice as many cases of affective psychosis as of schizophrenic psychosis. In a review article, Herzog and Detre (1976) state that the discrepancy between English and American statistics may be due to the fact that American clinicians have tended to underdiagnose the incidence of affective disorders and overdiagnose schizophrenia. In my opinion, an additional confusion results from the inability to make a differential diagnosis between manic-depressive psychosis and a depression which is not related to manic-depressive psychosis.

It is a common belief that postpartum conditions are less common today, and as a matter of fact there are many fewer reports about these conditions in the current psychiatric literature than in the literature of a few decades ago. However, according to my clinical experience, this belief is not correct: perhaps postpartum deliriums and full-fledged psychoses are less common because prenatal care and medical assistance during labor and puerperium have improved. Although I have not been able to develop adequate statistics, my bona fide impression is that less pronounced postpartum conditions are common, and that schizophrenic and affective psychoses are not at all rare.

SUICIDE

A relatively frequent outcome of severe depression is suicide, which we have already considered in relation to the self-blaming type of depression. We shall consider it here as part of the manifest symptomatology of every severe depression. The psychodynamics of suicide will be studied in chapters 6 and 8.

The occurrence of suicide in all types of severe depression is estimated variously. Rennie (1942) gave a conservative estimate of 5 percent in patients suffering from severe depression. According to Weiss (1974) more than 20,000 suicides are recorded each year in the United States, but Dublin (1963) has estimated that the correct number is 25,000, and Choron (1972) that it is 30,000. If we add to this number the attempted suicides whose exact number cannot be evaluated, we can conclude that the problem is of vast proportions indeed.

Although people who attempt successfully or unsuccessfully to commit suicide are by no means all depressed persons, the depressed constitute by far the largest group. Feelings of helplessness, hopelessness, failure, and willingness to face death as the only way out are prominent in people who make suicidal attempts. Unfavorable prognostic signs are the seriousness of the depression, a history of previous attempts, the seriousness of intention, advanced age, and old age. The risk increases when the patient is alone and feels that nobody will oppose his plans, and when his depression has decreased in intensity to such a point that he does not feel slowed down in his motor actions or at least in his physical ability to carry out the suicide attempt. Opportunities that facilitate the attempt are also dangerous, like living on a high floor, having a large amount of sleeping pills, the possibility of drowning oneself, or the availability of guns and ropes.

Secondary Depression

DEPRESSION WITH NEUROLOGICAL OR BRAIN DISEASE

Depressions accompanying neurological disease are relatively common. Perhaps the most common is the depression occurring in various types of epilepsy. It is less common in epileptics suffering from grand mals, perhaps because the fits have antidepressant effects, like the convulsions produced by ECT. Depression is relatively common in epileptics suffering from petit mals or psychomotor equivalents, or in patients whose electro-encephalograms reveal diencephalic dysfunction or discharges from the temporal lobes.

The risk of suicide in depressed epileptics is very high because the patient has to contend not only with the depression but with the impulsive urges of the epileptic personality. Whether the depression occurring in epileptics is precipitated by the discomfort of the illness itself, or is an epileptic equivalent, or is just a depression that happens to occur in an epileptic person is difficult to determine in the majority of cases. These patients constitute serious therapeutic challenges.

In patients suffering from Huntington's chorea, depressions with suicidal attempts are quite common, especially for female patients (Whittier, 1975). Depression often is seen in postencephalitics. According to Brill (1975) these patients are characteristic for their whining voice, clinging manner, and dependent and complaining attitude. Hypochondriacal symptoms, self-accusations, and delusions of guilt are also common. Neal (1942) found that the most frequent clinical picture was similar to that described by Brill. However, in his review of 201 cases he found that pathological depression was reported nine times, psychotic depression eight times, and hypomania eight times.

Mild to moderate depression and even severe depression is common in patients suffering from Parkinson's disease. This finding, and the observation that depression often follows the use of drugs which affect the basal ganglia, have led to interesting hypotheses about the anatomical and biochemical nature of depression.

Many other chronic neurological diseases (muscular dystrophies, cerebellar atrophies) are accompanied by depression. In most cases the main therapeutic task is one of rehabilitation or adjustment to the condition. In many cases of multiple sclerosis, there is no depression in spite of the crippling features of the disease. On the contrary, the patient seems apathetic or nonchalant to his condition. Depression occurs also in mental defectives who are not so defective as to disregard their condition.

Depressed episodes occur in senile dementia and also in psychoses with cerebral arteriosclerosis. These depressive episodes do not last long and are generally not prominent in the general clinical picture. The patient feels mistreated, cries over alleged thefts of which he is a victim, and is confused.

DEPRESSION WITH ENDOCRINE AND OTHER CHRONIC DISEASES

The thyroid is the endocrine gland more frequently involved in depressions that accompany endocrine disorders. Hypothyroidism of any kind can lead to depression, especially when myxedema occurs. Hyperthyroidism (whether or not it reaches the clinical level of Graves' disease) is often complicated by depression. The patient's despondent mood is often accompanied or alternated by a mood of irritability and capriciousness.

I also have seen cases of depression in hyperparathyroidism and severe diabetes. Depression also occurs after coronary disease, although not so frequently as states of anxiety.

Many diseases, especially those running a chronic course, can be accompanied by depression. In all these cases it is difficult to determine whether the physical illness is etiologically related to depression or whether depression is merely a precipitating factor, that is, merely the patient's psychological response to the unpleasantness caused by his physical illness.

DRUG-INDUCED DEPRESSION

The following drugs induce a depressive mood in some patients: steroids, chlorpromazine (Thorazine®), the butyrophenones like haloperidol (Haldol®), and especially the rauwolfia derivatives, like reserpine (Serpasil®). The depression is generally not severe and disappears with discontinuance of the drug.

DEPRESSION OCCURRING IN THE COURSE OF SCHIZOPHRENIA

Depression may occur in the course of schizophrenia. It must be distinguished from schizo-affective psychosis, a condition in which a mixture of schizophrenic and manic-depressive symptoms takes place from the onset of the illness. Many psychiatrists, including myself, do not as a rule consider the occurrence of depression in the course of schizophrenia in negative terms but, on the contrary, as a sign of growth and good prognosis, especially if it occurs after the patient has started to respond favorably to treatment and the schizophrenic symptoms have disappeared or diminished in intensity.

DIFFERENTIAL DIAGNOSIS

The diagnosis is made in two steps. The first step consists of determining whether the patient is really suffering from a depression or from a syndrome simulating a depression. A person who seems depressed is not necessarily depressed in the clinical sense.

He may be experiencing normal sadness (see chapter 5). He may also be depressed and suffering from many psychiatric disorders, not necessarily just from a clinical form of depression. Depression, like anxiety, is found as a concomitant symptom in most psychiatric conditions. However, we are justified in calling a syndrome depression when the depressive mood constitutes the main characteristic, irrespective of whether this mood belongs to a primary or secondary form of depression.

Once we have ascertained that the patient is suffering from a real depression (and not from another syndrome), we proceed to the second step: What kind of depression is he suffering from?

An elderly person has lost a considerable amount of weight, looks depressed, and complains that he may have cancer. He may be mistaken for a person suffering from severe depression when he indeed has some kind of malignancy. If he also has depression, it may be precipitated by his appraisal of his poor physical condition. An accurate physical examination will determine the situation. In psychiatric practice, however, the opposite occurrence is more common: an elderly patient has lost weight, has many hypochondriacal complaints including a fear of cancer, and is depressed. Negative physical findings, psychomotor retardation, insomnia, and a despondent mood generally will determine that he is suffering from depression.

Some post-encephalitic patients and some parkinsonian patients are mistaken for depressed, even when their condition is not complicated by depression. The confusion is caused by the fact that patients with extra-pyramidal syndromes have symptoms and signs which are reminiscent of characteristics found in depressed patients. These symptoms include loss of accessory movements, mask-like expression on the face, slow gait, posture with stooped body and flexed head, and general psychomotor retardation. Neurological examination and the medical history of the patient will lead to the correct diagnosis.

The complete or almost complete immobility of the patient and a minimal response to external stimuli may make difficult a differential diagnosis between depressive stupor and catatonic stupor. Generally a history of depression leads to the diagnosis of depression, but not always; many catatonics have experienced some episodes of mild or severe depression before the catatonic attack. Often other concomitant symptoms such as negativism, the assumption of bizarre postures, the swelling of legs from standing, the closing of eyes, and the almost absolute absence of emotion lead to the diagnosis of catatonic stupor.

The diagnosis of schizophrenia is also to be ruled out in some cases of manic-depressive psychosis that resemble the schizophrenic syndrome, especially if manic phases occur. During the manic attack the patient's behavior may appear bizarre and there may be disorganization of thought processes. However, both behavior and thought processes are much more altered in schizophrenia. If hallucinations occur in manic-depressive psychosis, they have the differential characteristics mentioned on page 71; if paranoid ideation is present, it is only minimal. The total picture, including personality type which is cyclothymic in the case of manic-depressive psychosis, will lead to an easy diagnosis except for those cases that are usually placed in the schizo-affective category.

Once we have determined that we are dealing with a depression, we must proceed to the second step and ascertain the specific type of depression. The presence of another illness (for example, epilepsy or myxedema) will lead easily to the diagnosis of secondary depression. In the majority of cases it is not difficult to determine whether a particular case is one of mild (neurotic) or severe (psychotic) depression.

According to the *Diagnostic and Statistical Manual of Mental Disorders* of the American Psychiatric Association (DSM-11) (Committee on No-menclature, 1968), the differentiation between psychotic depression and depressive neurosis "depends on whether the reaction impairs reality testing or functional adequacy enough to be considered a psychosis."

The reality testing in this case concerns the mood of depression. Does the patient consider his depression justified; does he want to maintain it; does it drastically transform his appreciation of life? If the answers is yes, the diagnosis is bound to be one of severe depression (psychotic depression) or manic-depressive psychosis. A history of manic attacks, or at least of a cyclothymic personality, will lead to the diagnosis of manic-depressive psychosis. In mild depression we can recognize the following differential characteristics which rule out a severe depression. (1) The depression is not so intense as to affect the total personality of the patient. (2) The patient wants to get rid of the depression. (3) Suicidal ideas are not a predominant feature. (4) The patient responds, although to a moderate degree, to cheerful aspects of the environment and to attempts to comfort him. (5) The psychosomatic symptoms are different inasmuch as (a) The loss of appetite is not excessive. In some cases there is increased appetite. (b) As a rule there is no premorbid anxiety. (c) The insomnia is relatively mild. In some cases there is an increased need to sleep. (d) There is no dryness of the mouth. (e) The constipation is less marked. (f) The skin is not dry. (g) There is no hypomenorrhea or amenorrhea.

[4]

MANIFEST SYMPTOMATOLOGY OF

DEPRESSION IN CHILDREN

AND ADOLESCENTS

The conceptual status of depression in childhood is somewhat ambiguous. Some authors (Rochlin, 1959; Beres, 1966) doubt that depression is possible in children on theoretical grounds. For example, these authors believe that prior to the establishment of the superego, self-directed aggression (which for them is the *sine qua non* of depression) is not possible and therefore young children cannot become truly depressed. Others believe that children cannot sustain a prolonged dysphoric mood and will vigorously find ways of escaping from depression. From a cognitive point of view, the lack of future orientation and the "here and now" orientation make the possibility of self-perpetuating, clinical depression in children less than likely. These questions are pursued further in chapter 8. This chapter will limit itself to a phenomenological description of childhood and adolescent syndromes which have been labelled as similar to the depressive disorders seen in adults.

Depressionlike States of Infancy

In 1946 Rene Spitz published a pioneering paper on the reaction of infants to maternal separation, thus opening up an avenue of productive research that continues today. He described children who had formed a normal

This chapter was written by Jules Bemporad.

attachment to their mothers and who subsequently were separated from their mothers at six months of age. Spitz reported that such infants responded with weepy, complaining behavior that eventually gave way to withdrawal and lethargy. In this latter condition the infants would lie in their cots with their faces averted, ignoring their surroundings. If approached by strangers, the infants would begin crying and screaming. If an infant was not reunited with his mother, he gradually developed a syndrome that Spitz called "anaclitic depression" which was characterized by weight loss, insomnia, a lack of response to people, and a frozen expression with a far-away gaze. Spitz reported that if the mother and infant were reunited after three to five months, the syndrome was reversible. If the separation continued after this amount of time, however, the infant's condition consolidated and became irreversible. Later these children showed arrests in various areas of development as well as a greater susceptibility to disease.

Spitz cautioned that while the symptoms manifested by these infants are similar to adult depressions, this form of depression differs from adult episodes in that it lacks the major factor of the adult disorder, the formation of a cruel superego. Spitz did speculate, however, that the child turns his aggression on himself because he lacks an external maternal object who can both absorb his aggressive drives and elicit a strong libidinal response to neutralize the aggressive instinctual forces. A decade later Engel and Reichsman (1956) described a similar symptom picture in a socially deprived infant girl, Monica, who also had a gastric fistula. These authors were not impressed by a presence of a retroflexed anger; rather, they postulated the presence of a basic "depression–withdrawal reaction" as the infant's attempt to shut out an unpleasant environment.

These reports stimulated much thinking and research regarding the appearance of infantile depressionlike episodes subsequent to maternal separation. One of the most prolific writers on this topic is Bowlby who has carefully studied and documented the process of infantile attachment to and separation from the mother figure. Bowlby (1958) has attempted to reformulate the infant's attachment to its mother along ethological concepts such as innate responses to certain releasing stimuli. In this manner the mother elicits instinctual attachment behavior in the infant, and the infant in turn sets off innate attachment behavior in the mother. The novelty in Bowlby's approach is that he views emotional attachment as independent of oral satisfaction, and he documents the specific behaviors that play a part in the attachment process.

In addition, Bowlby has documented the steps that follow abnormal separation from the mother (1960b), and it is in this field that his work may have relevance for the study of infant depression. Bowlby proposes three stages in the separation process. First, in the stage of protest the infant is very upset and tries to reinitiate contact with the mother by crying, screaming, and thrashing about. The stage of despair follows quickly, during which the infant still seems to hope to be reunited with its mother. At this time, however, the crying is quieter and less constant. The infant gradually becomes silent, decreases its movements, and appears acutely depressed. In the final stage of defense or detachment, the child seems to have overcome his loss and will respond to other adults. He becomes cheerful and sociable once again. However, at this point the infant no longer selects out the mother and may in fact ignore her if she returns.

It would appear that Bowlby is describing the same behavior previously reported by Spitz and by Engel and Reichsman. However, Bowlby makes some crucial interpretations that differ from the previous researchers. He does not consider this behavior to represent an infantile prototype of depression, but rather to demonstrate a universal form of mourning secondary to separation. He describes a more benign prognosis than Spitz; he notes that children overcome the traumatic separation without long-range developmental retardation. In fact Bowlby speculates that such children, if they are subjected to recurrent separation, form progressively less attachment to mother figures and eventually become nonfeeling, nonempathic psychopaths—rather than depressed adults. As early as 1937 David Levy described just such an individual in the case of an eight-year-old girl who had been in a succession of foster homes and could not form a loving relationship with her adopted parents. Levy described this girl as exhibiting a lack of emotional reactiveness together with an "affect hunger," or a need to be given to by others. Since Levy's initial description other similar cases have been reported, and Bowlby has supplied these clinical data with a theoretical base.

Finally, Bowlby sees the reaction of the child as the abnormal rupture of an instinctual bond to the mother rather than a result of internalized aggression. Klaus and Kennell (1976) describe a similar "critical period" for emotional attachment in post-partum mothers and fathers. These authors believe that it is necessary for parents to have contact with their infant shortly after delivery for optimal development later. They postulate the formation of an innate bond during this period between parent and child which will continue for years. Klaus and Kennell support these speculations with animal research that demonstrates the ill effects of separating parents from neonates. The mother appears to lose interest in the infant and cannot give appropriate care if she is not present during this critical time.

In summary, depressive behavior has been observed in infants who are separated from their mothers. After a period of angry protest, these infants show unhappiness, withdrawal, and apathy. The question of whether this behavior is truly an example of depression, mourning, or a reaction to deprivation will be taken up in chapter 8.

Depression During Early Childhood

As a rule, children between the toddler years and the Oedipal phase appear to be remarkably free of depressive symptoms. In going over all the records of the outpatient department of the Children's Psychiatric Hospital at the University of Michigan Medical Center for a five-year period, Poznanski and Zrull (1970) found only one child under five years of age who could be considered as showing depressive symptoms. (Even with this child, the authors felt more confident in their diagnosis after a two-year follow-up. This child exhibited a failure to thrive, quiet withdrawal, a fear of abandonment, and according to her mother, who rejected her, would show no affection toward anyone.) Poznanski and Zrull comment on the gap in depressive symptoms between infancy and middle childhood, but conclude that they cannot account for it. They suggest that further study of the development of the preschooler's affects and drives is needed. On the other hand, the paucity of clinical reports of depression in this age group suggest to Poznanski and Zrull the question of whether it is possible for true affective disorders of clinical significance to occur in preschoolers or whether the manifestation of affective symptoms must await further maturation.

One possible explanation, which has been advanced by Anthony (1975) for the paucity of reports on childhood depression in general, is the young child's inability to verbalize how he feels. Depression must be inferred from the motor behavior of the young child and from his facial expressions, which is a difficult task. The motoric hyperactivity and general exuberance of the young child make him a poor candidate for a diagnosis of depression. Actually, as will be discussed later, the child's lack of verbal ability may lead to an overdiagnosis of depression since the examiner may tend to credit the child or infant with adult emotions and a more complex psychological make-up than is justified.

Mahler has closely observed children at this stage of development as part of her investigation of the separation-individuation process and has commented on the development of basic moods (1966) as well as on their behavioral manifestations. Mahler has not observed actual depressive symptoms in the early childhood stage, but she has noted behaviors that seem to indicate a predisposition to depression in later life. These predisposed children display excessive "separation and grief reactions marked by temper tantrums, continual attempts to woo or coerce the mother, and then giving up in despair for a while when unable to prevent separation" (1966, p. 163). Other evidence of this primary negative affective responsiveness consists of acts of impotent surrender and resignation, as well as discontentment and anger following a period of grief or sadness. In all cases Mahler found an increased clinging to the mother despite the lack of a truly satisfying relationship with her.

Mahler notes the volatility and transient nature of such moods, adding that such behaviors usually are seen only in context of the relationship with the mother and are absent when the child is alone or with others. She explains the presence of such activity by stressing the young child's disappointment in the mother and, secondarily, in the self. This disappointment prevents the full-length duration of the child's belief in the omnipotence of the mother which he requires for the development of his own sense of worth. The child shows a depletion of "confident expectation" from important others and suffers a subsequent diminution of self-esteem, which reduces the ability to neutralize aggression that later will account for the depressive symptoms. At this stage of development, however, depressive syndromes are not commonly seen, although (as will be discussed further in chapter 8) the groundwork for a predisposition to depression may be forming beneath the toddler's apparently exuberant and confident exterior.

Depression in Middle and Late Childhood

In recent years a number of articles have appeared describing depressive episodes, which phenomenologically resemble the adult syndromes, as occurring in older children (Poznanski and Zrull, 1970; Cytryn and Mc-Knew, 1972; Weinberg et al., 1973; McConville et al., 1973). In the past such children were reported occasionally (Bierman et al., 1961) but they were considered to be clinical oddities or misdiagnosed. However, these reports did present fairly large series of children with apparently depressive symptoms, although the stringency of criteria for diagnosis varied from researcher to researcher. Another difficulty in assessing the true incidence of depression, even in older children, has been the proposing of "depressive equivalents" to exemplify the clinical expression of depression in childhood (Sperling, 1959; Toolan, 1962). The line of thinking that children express depression by certain age-appropriate equivalents has led to a plethora of clinical manifestations being diagnosed as forms of childhood affective disorders.

The terms "masked depression" or "depressive equivalents" appear to be somewhat confusing or inaccurate, since they have led to all sorts of symptoms being considered as evidence of depression. What may occur in some children is a depressed mood which is not sustained because the child cannot tolerate prolonged feelings of sadness or anguish. Some chil-

dren lack the ability to bear depression and rapidly shift their attention
to more pleasant thoughts or activities. There is still a sufficient fluidity
between fantasy and reality so that harsh truths are avoided and general
behavior is still directed by immediate pleasure, so that cognitive elements
that produce depressive feelings are warded off and avoided. Therefore,
some children are very capable of defending against depression by a
variety of behaviors; however, their behaviors are not the equivalent of
depression, nor are they evidence of a masked depression. Rather, their
behaviors are adaptive attempts to deal with a situation which appears
to the examiner as capable of evoking depression in an adult. If the child
is forced to face his situation in a realistic manner, sadness may then be
elicited. However, left to his own devices, a child may skillfully deny the
realization of a depressing life situation, sometimes utilizing defenses
against such a painful confrontation. Hypomanic behaviors, hyperactivity,
delinquency, and somatic complaints have been cited as defensive opera-
tions. Toolan (1962) further notes that male children or adolescents may
feel ashamed of showing sadness or depression and cover these affects
with forced joviality. Similarly, some cultural mores may sanction aggressive outbursts and ridicule a show of despair so that the former type of
behavior is selected by the child.

This disparity in diagnostic criteria has led to highly variable reports
of the incidence of depression in childhood. Annell (1971) compared the
frequency with which different investigators made a diagnosis of depression and found that it ranged from 1.8 percent to 25 percent for all
children seen. She correctly concluded that the main explanation for this
marked variance was that different workers meant different things by
depression. In spite of this confusion about the incidence of depression in
middle childhood, an attempt will be made here to list some of the symptoms stressed by clinicians.

Weinberg et al. (1973) used a ten-symptom list to diagnose depression
tn their sample of children. In order to be so classified, a child had to
show both a dysphoric mood and self-depreciatory ideation, and at least
two of the following eight symptoms: 1. aggressive behavior, 2. sleep
disturbance, 3. a change in school performance, 4. diminished socialization, 5. change in attitude toward school, 6. somatic complaints, 7. loss
of usual energy, and 8. unusual changes in appetite or weight.

Weinberg reported that forty-five of seventy-two patients (aged six
years, six months to twelve years, eight months) attending an educational
guidance clinic met these criteria. His findings suggest a surprisingly high
incidence of depression, although it may be that Weinberg selected an
atypical group of children. He and his co-authors in fact mention that in
half of the children "depression" was considered secondary to learning
or behavior problems, and perhaps was not a primary disorder.

In contrast, Poznanski and Zrull (1970) found only 14 depressed
children of 1,788 children seen in their University of Michigan Medical

Center study. These authors found the most frequent symptom to be a negative self-image. Related symptoms were a fear of failure, the anticipation of unfair treatment, and feelings of inadequacy. A number of these children described themselves as bad. Overt signs were frequent crying and withdrawal. Sleep disturbances were less common than in nondepressed children. Aggressive behavior was evident in twelve of the fourteen depressed children, which led the authors to question the importance of inhibited, self-directed aggression as a significant psychodynamic of depression.

In an important theoretical paper, Sandler and Joffe (1965) also listed depressive symptoms they found in children undergoing psychiatric treatment: (1) The child appeared sad, unhappy, or depressed. (2) There was predominant withdrawal or lack of interest. (3) The child was discontented, with little capacity for pleasure. (4) The child communicated a sense of being unloved or rejected and turned away from disappointing others. (5) The child was not prepared to accept comfort. (6) There was a general tendency toward "oral passivity." (7) Insomnia or other sleep disturbance was noted. (8) Autoerotic or other repetitive activities were described. (9) It was difficult for the therapist to continue contact with the child. These authors were quick to point out that the children did not show these symptoms continuously and often the depressive aspect of their personalities formed part of another pathological syndrome. Other authors have not made these qualifying remarks. This difference in appreciation of the transient nature of symptoms may account for the great disparity in the reported incidence of depression in children. It is a rare child who is sad all the time and whose mood is not altered by novel situations. At the same time, almost all children show a temporary "depressed" mood in reaction to some external disappointments. Therefore, the diagnosis that is given depends on when the child is seen, whether the child is seen more than once, and whether the criteria for diagnosis require a sporadic or constant dysphoric mood.

In summarizing of the depressive symptoms of older children, the presence of a sad mood has been reported as well as a sense of withdrawal, disappointment, lack of relatedness, and overt aggression. Certain features of adult depression, however, usually are absent. There is no dread of the future, and no somatic symptoms such as psychomotor retardation or anorexia. The disorder also does not appear to be self-perpetuating or resistant to environmental variations. Children respond quickly to external changes and do not appear to sustain a prolonged sense of despair independently of life circumstances. Even among children at different stages of development, one would expect variation in the form of symptomatology which would be reflective of increasing cognitive growth.

McConville and his co-workers (1973) have noticed developmental variation in the type of depressive symptoms expressed by children of different ages. Their patient sample consisted of seventy-five children who were admitted to an inpatient psychiatric unit over a three-year period. Three types of depressive syndromes were observed. The "affectual" type was seen in children six to eight years of age and it primarily consisted of behavioral manifestations of sadness and helplessness. The "negative self-esteem" type consisted of verbalized feelings of worthlessness, of being unloved, and of being used by other people, and it was most commonly seen in the eight- to ten-year-old group. Finally a rare third type was called the "guilt" type because its prominent symptom was the child's conviction that he was wicked and should be dead or killed. This type was observed in the ten- to thirteen-year-old group. This study is significant; it demonstrates how even in middle to late childhood the normal developmental process can influence the expression of symptoms. The youngest children had difficulty verbalizing their feelings and their depression seemed to take the form of an overall sadness. The eight- to ten-year-olds could put their feelings into words and were able to identify states of self, but they did not as yet have a sense of inner evil. They continued to gauge their feelings as a response to others. Only as the children approached adolescence was there an internalization of some of the cognitive conditions for depression, the feeling of guilt and wickedness which justified the dysphoric state and perpetuated it despite environmental changes.

ILLUSTRATIVE CASE HISTORY OF DEPRESSION IN AN OLDER CHILD

The example of the following child clinically illustrates severe depression in late childhood. Jimmy, an eleven-year-old boy, was seen after he wrote a series of pathetic, demanding notes to his parents. The notes were all repetitions of the same theme: that he was worthless and a failure and undeserving of their love, yet greatly needing their love. He had also asked his mother if it was a sin to commit suicide. The family history was remarkable in that the father had suffered from chronic depression since adolescence. He was a strict Catholic who constantly read inspirational books in search of a meaning in life. At home he was frequently unavailable, although he managed to put up a "good front" at his job. The father's side of the family had a high incidence of severe mental illness.

When seen for an evaluation, Jimmy was quiet and noncommunicative. He looked sad and was able to verbalize that he did not like himself. He stated that God had let him down and he was letting God down. When he was able to elaborate on this statement, he explained that he felt he had been born a poor athlete and a poor student, but he had not done his part by trying hard enough to overcome his innate deficiencies. He was totally convinced of his basic worthlessness, and furthermore he detested his weakness in not being able to overcome his alleged liabilities. Further contact revealed that because of his poor coordination, Jimmy was tormented by his peers and his brothers. He could find no area in his life in which he felt adequate or even safe. As a result of the excessively religious atmosphere at home, he believed that much of his misery was his own doing and he was a sinful creature because he gave in to feelings of failure. He also had been taught covertly to keep his feelings to himself and to be steadfast in the face of adversity. Actually, he felt like a little boy who wanted to be nurtured by his parents but he could not allow himself to express these longings openly. He felt overwhelmed by feelings of shame and inadequacy, but could not confide in anyone. He finally managed to allow these feelings to be partially communicated in his notes to his parents, although after writing them he refused to talk about their content with his mother or his father. Little Jimmy found himself in a desperate situation; he perceived himself as failing in what he believed his parents expected, but he could not bring himself to discuss his sense of frustration because of prior training. Similarly, he could not confess his terror of bullying peers. Instead he concluded that he was inferior. The more he suffered from his frustrations, the more he wanted nurturance at home, and the more he felt ashamed of his self-perceived infantile needs. He was a failure to himself, to his parents, and ultimately to God. He gradually began avoiding peers and stayed close to home. He lost interest in school and tried not to go by feigning illness. He withdrew, while being careful to look sad at dinner or when his family was present. Finally, he fortunately evoked a sympathetic response in his parents by his notes which initiated treatment and eventual recovery.

Attempts at Classification of Childhood Depression

Despite the theoretical debate over the possibility of true depression before adolescence, a few papers have appeared which take the occurrence of childhood depression as a clinical fact and attempt to classify these dysphoric states on such empirical grounds as response to treatment, the presence of precipitating events, or associated psychopathology.

Eva Frommer (1968) maintains that depression is quite common in childhood, accounting for 20 percent of all childhood psychopathology. She describes three major subgroups and one small additional grouping which may be a juvenile form of manic-depressive disorder. The first group is designated "enuretic depressive" because of the high incidence of bladder or bowel incontinence. In addition, these children exhibited learning disabilities and social withdrawal. Complaints of depression were present in only 19 percent of this group. Frommer states that treatment is prolonged and difficult, requiring more than antidepressant medication or group therapy. Removal from the home environment is sometimes indicated.

There is some question as to whether this group of children can actually be classified as depressed. They appear to be unfortunate and unhappy children who because of a combination of factors are neurologically immature and have learning disabilities and incontinence. Such children often get into chronic power struggles with their parents which increase their frustrations, but they do not appear depressed; rather, they are perpetually angry and resort to passive-aggressive retaliation against authority figures. They lack the negative self-image, the feeling of helplessness, and the blaming of self which appears necessary for the diagnosis of depression. Such children have been described adequately in the literature on enuresis, encopresis, or learning disabilities without reference to affective disorders.

Frommer's second major group is "uncomplicated depression." It is the largest group in her sample, and the children in it manifested irritability, weakness, and tendencies to recurrent explosions of temper. Half showed some sort of sleep disturbance and roughly one-third complained of feeling depressed. There was a lack of anxiety or decreased confidence. This group does appear to describe truly depressed children. After treatment there was significant academic improvement and others noted a change in the children's demeanor.

The third group was termed "phobic depressive" because of a high incidence of anxiety and a lack of confidence. Over two-thirds of these children exhibited abdominal pain or other somatic symptoms in order to stay home from school. Girls outnumbered boys by two to one in this group. Although Frommer calls such children depressed, they seem to fit the classic pattern of "school phobia." Gittleman Klein has recently studied a large group of such children and concludes that they are impaired by an abnormal persistence of separation anxiety so that they must stay near the mother figure. If they are allowed to remain with the mother, they are happy and relaxed. If they are forcibly separated, they exhibit panic and somatic symptoms. In neither situation are they depressed.

The last group described by Frommer are children with transient outbursts of temper alternating with periods of quiet reasonableness. She speculates rather cautiously that this group may be showing early symptoms of manic and depressive mood swings.

Frommer's work suffers from a lack of psychodynamic investigation as well as from her omission of the age ranges or developmental levels of her patients. However, the greatest drawback of her study is her overinclusion of nondepressed children in the depressive categories. Clinical depression entails more than situational unhappiness brought about by family conflicts, learning disabilities, or separation from parents.

A more profound and usable classification of depression in childhood has been presented by Cytryn and McKnew (1972). These authors differentiate between a depressive affectual response and a depressive illness, in which the depression is of long duration and the sad affect is associated with disturbance of vegetative functions or impairment of scholastic or social adjustment. In more severe cases, the child's thinking is said to be affected by feelings of despair, hopelessness, general retardation, and suicidal ideation. Having established these clear criteria of depressive illness, Cytryn and McKnew delineated three types of depressive disorders in children who ranged from six to twelve years of age.

The first type was classified as "masked depressive reaction" and was characterized by hyperactivity, aggressive behavior, psychosomatic illness, or delinquency. These children also exhibited periods of overt depression as well as depressive trends on psychological testing. The families of these children were chronically disorganized but showed no history of depression. If I understand the authors' concept of masked depression correctly, it is different from so-called depressive "equivalents." Cytryn and McKnew do not speculate that nondepressed behavior such as delinquency is a childhood expression of depression; rather, this behavior is seen as a defense against feeling depressed. Occasionally the defense breaks down and the underlying depression becomes manifest.

The second type was called "acute depressive reaction" and it resulted from a clearly identifiable environmental cause, usually invoking the loss of the attention of a loved one. These children exhibited clear symptoms of depression for a short period of time and then recovered quickly. There was usually a history of good premorbid adjustment and their families demonstrated considerable strength and cohesion as well as an absence of depression. It might be difficult to separate such children from those exhibiting a grief or mourning reaction. It is speculated that the child's defenses are momentarily shaken but that reconstitution usually follows unless there are persistent environmental traumas.

Finally, they described a more severe "chronic depressive reaction" in which there was no history of a precipitating event. These children did not reconstitute rapidly and showed evidence of long-standing depression. There was a history of repeated separation from loved ones and deprivation beginning early in life. All of these children had at least one parent who suffered from recurrent depression.

This last group supports the findings of Poznanski and Zrull (1970) that the depression of the children they studied was not reactive to an immediate trauma, but part of an ongoing life process. They also found a high incidence of parental depression, frequent harsh treatment of the child, and overt parental rejection. It would appear that Poznanski and Zrull are describing the "chronic" type of child in Cytryn and McKnew's classification. The former authors may have set more stringent criteria for the diagnosis of depression and excluded those children classified as having "masked" or "acute" depression by Cytryn and McKnew. The possible merit of this more narrow definition of depression is that it allows for a study of the natural history of the disorder by excluding children whose depressive symptoms may be part of a transient grief reaction, or submerged beneath delinquent activity or other defenses. For example, in an important follow-up study Poznanski, Krahenbuhl, and Zrull (1976) found that half of their original sample (now in adolescence) was still depressed. An additional finding was that the childhood aggression had diminished and pathological dependency, common in adult depression, was more prominent. Among the patients who were still depressed, the pattern of parental rejection and deprivation had continued. It can be hypothesized that in these cases, the causes of depression became internalized and adequate coping mechanisms were prevented from crystalizing. On the other hand, it may equally be speculated that the "masked" type of depression described by Cytryn and McKnew would eventually follow a delinquent career and the "acute" type would not show pathology in adolescence.

Perhaps a follow-up study by these authors will clarify these questions as well as justify labeling children as depressed who are able to defend against depression or exhibit a transient state of grief over an environmental trauma. The theoretical problem (to be considered in chapter 8) is whether children who do not exhibit prolonged depression can be truly classified as suffering from a depressive illness. Children who exhibit equivalent or masked depressions may not be actually depressed. Rather, the examiner may infer that they should be depressed because of their difficult life circumstances. If these children can muster defenses against adverse environmental situations, then there may be a question as to whether they should be considered to be suffering from depression.

Taking these problems into consideration, Malmquist (1971) has attempted an all-encompassing diagnostic classification based simply on the predominance of depressive affect. He includes criteria of different conceptual levels, such as descriptive clinical features, age, and etiology. His classification is presented in Table 4-1 on page 99.

Malmquist arrived at this classification by an exhaustive review of the literature. His system is extremely valuable in briefly presenting all of the possible states that have been called depression in children. His classification, reproduced here as Table 4-1, can be taken as a summary of current knowledge of the symptomatic picture of childhood and adolescent depression. The reader is free to agree or disagree with the inclusion of certain subgroups, but all are essentially reported by Malmquist. The common thread of depressive affect* as the sole criterion for diagnosing depression cuts across theoretical differences but may ultimately be misleading since, as mentioned, a sad affect can be seen in numerous non-depressive conditions.

---

* Malmquist also includes "depressive equivalents."

TABLE 4-1

Classification of Childhood Depressions

I. Associated with Organic Diseases

    A. Part of Pathologic Process
        1. Leukemia
        2. Degenerative Diseases
        3. Infectious Diseases
        4. Metabolic Diseases—Pituitary Disease, Juvenile Diabetes, Thyroid Disease, etc.
        5. Nutritional or Vitamin Deficiency States
    B. Secondary (Reactive) to a Physical Process

II. Deprivation syndromes: Reality-Based Reactions to Impoverished or Non-rewarding Environment

    A. Anaclitic Depressions
    B. "Affectionless" Character Types

III. Syndromes Associated with Difficulties in Individuation

    A. Problems of Separation-Individuation
    B. School Phobias with Depressive Components
    C. Developmental Precursors of "Moral Masochism"

IV. Latency Types

    A. Associated with Object Loss
    B. Failure to Meet Unattainable Ideals
    C. "Depressive Equivalents" (Depression without Depressive Affect)
        1. Somatization (Hypochondriacal Patterns)
        2. Hyperkinesis
        3. Acting Out
        4. Delayed Depressive Reactions
            a. Mourning at Distance
            b. Overidealization Processes Postponing Reaction
            c. Denial Patterns
        5. Eating Disturbances (Obesity Syndromes)
    D. Manic-Depressive States
    E. "Affectless" Character Types (Generalized Anhedonia)
    F. Obsessional Character (Compensated Depressive)

V. Adolescent Types

    A. Mood Lability as Developmental Process
    B. Reactive to Current Loss
    C. Unresolved Mourning from Current Losses
    D. Earlier Losses ("Trauma") Now Dealt with by Ego
    E. Acting-Out Depressions
    F. Schizophrenias with Prominent Affective Components
    G. Continuation of Earlier Types (I, IV)

Source: From "Depression in Childhood and Adolescence" by C. Malmquist, *New England Journal of Medicine* 284 (1971). Reprinted by permission.

This section must end on a note of frustration and an admission of incompleteness. As yet there is no adequate classification of depression in childhood, nor are there any agreed criteria for the diagnosis of depression before adolescence. It seems almost plausible to base a classification on the developmental process as McConville (1973) tentatively attempted. Children are limited by their cognitive and affective capacities in their ability to experience and express feelings of depression. What elicits depression also obviously changes as the child matures. Young infants do not have problems of self-esteem, just as preschoolers cannot be said to be haunted by a fear of a deprived future. Ultimately the question of childhood depression may be solved as our knowledge of normal development increases.

Depression in Adolescence

In contrast to the questionable existence of depression in childhood, there is little doubt that depression definitely is experienced by adolescents. The difficulty with this stage of development is that depression may be too ubiquitous. The normal mood swings of the adolescent may give the impression of an epidemic of depressive disorders occurring after puberty. The problem is in differentiating the truly depressed youngster from the normally moody adolescent who is showing transient episodes of dysphoric affect as an overreaction to relatively trivial disappointments. Jacobson (1961) has investigated the causes for the adolescent's moodiness and she believes that emotional lability is a manifestation of a remodeling of the individual's psychic structure secondary to massive biological, social, and psychological changes. Jacobson views adolescence as a time when the individual must break with ties from the past (including old identifications with adult figures) to forge a new image of the self. The individual is pressured by both the id and the superego in the formation of a new identity, leading to alternating periods of sexual and aggressive acting out; repentant, moralistic behavior; as well as feelings of guilt, shame, and inferiority. According to Jacobson the ego does not gain sufficient stability until late adolescence so that, in the first few years following puberty, there are bound to be mood swings reflecting the dominance of id or superego forces over a relatively weak ego. Depression may be experienced as part of adolescent development for additional reasons: the relinquishing of childhood ties and pursuits, the failure to live up to unrealistic ideals, and as the result of guilt conflicts. Jacobson views adolescence as a turbulent time, with extensive psychic alterations, mood swings, and transient depression to be expected.

Other authors (Weiner, 1970) have disagreed with the view that adolescence must be a stage of turmoil and emotional lability. Disturbed adolescence is not the rule, but is the result of a disturbed childhood and the forerunner of disturbed maturity. This debate goes beyond the scope of this work but in my opinion the truth is somewhere between these two positions. The clinical literature based on severely disturbed adolescents probably has been too generously applied to all adolescents. Also, the cultural milieu may greatly affect the turbulence of adolescence. Certainly not all adolescents go through the painful traumas described by some authors. For some individuals this is not only a peaceful but a very satisfying time of life. Nevertheless, our own culture places the adolescent under a great deal of stress in terms of sexual inhibition, limitations of freedom, pressure for social and academic success, and a lack of a definable cultural role, so that disturbed behavior is not surprising.

There is also a lack of maturity of judgment that affects the adolescent, regardless of cultural milieu that may predispose him to impulsive acts and inappropriately extreme reactions. As pertaining to depression, some adolescents present such an air of urgency and total despair, as well as an alarming tendency toward self-destructive acts, that a more malignant schizophrenic process is suspected. Some adolescents become extremely agitated and others withdraw from all contact with peers. One youngster, for example, spent days alone in his room with blankets over his face while listening to records, and he refused to take meals or talk with his family. There is also an unrealistic sense of finality in the thinking of some adolescents; failure to make the school honor role means that one will be marked for life as a failure, or rejection by a peer means that one will never be acceptable to others. This lack of perspective makes the symptoms more severe and more dangerous. A related quality of cognition in some adolescents is a lack of moderation. People, society, or they themselves are all good or all bad, depending on most recent experience. One very bright fourteen-year-old boy who had been disappointed by the treatment others accorded him in his first few days of high school spent his first session on a long tirade about the innate evil of mankind and the dehumanizing effects of a materialistic society. His erudite argument was motivated by his not being given the deference he thought he deserved. Within a few weeks, after he had adjusted to his new surroundings, the world became benevolent and capitalism was now a viable system of economics. Fortunately many of these adolescent depressions are characterized by their brevity as much as by their intensity.

Other depressions, however, become chronic and no longer respond to an amelioration of external circumstances. These youngsters present depressive symptoms similar to those found in adult patients, or they may present age-specific defenses against depression. Among these defenses are restlessness, drug use, group affiliation, delinquency, or sexual promiscuity. Easson (1977) has reviewed the myriad defenses against depression in adolescence and related each to the underlying causes of a painful affect. Self-contempt may result in rebelliousness, drug use, or aggressive acts. Depression resulting from frustration of dependency needs may produce agitation, anxiety, and a desperate need to substitute new gratifying figures for the lost parents, leading to joining a gang or indiscriminate sexual unions.

ILLUSTRATIVE CASE HISTORY OF DEPRESSION IN A YOUNG ADOLESCENT

The following clinical vignette is representative of a fairly severe depressive illness in a young teenager. Betty, a fifteen-year-old girl, came for treatment after suddenly experiencing a crying spell in school. Following this outburst she refused to return to school, where she was an honor student. When seen for an evaluation Betty looked sad and lifeless with occasional tears in her eyes. She also complained of nausea and a choking sensation. She felt that she wanted to hurt herself because she was a failure, she was ugly, and she had humiliated herself in front of her schoolmates by weeping. She believed she could never become a model as she had desired to be, because she was not sufficiently pretty or poised. In actuality she was a very attractive young girl. She exuded a sense of quiet panic over being unable to control her painful feelings. There was no sleep disturbance but Betty was plagued by dreams in which she felt lost and alone or in which strange people were chasing her.

Further history revealed that Betty had not let herself enjoy anything for the past year. The reasons for her enforced anhedonia were that she felt unworthy because she sensed herself to be a disappointment to her mother as well as to herself. She began experiencing feelings of depression after she met a boy at a summer resort. She wanted the boy to pursue her but she also felt guilty about her romantic desires. The boy did not follow through and this convinced her that she was ugly and undesirable. She also hinted that this "rejection" was well deserved because she should have devoted herself only to her studies and her family. Since this episode she constantly began to evaluate both herself and the way others treated her. Mild snubs were magnified and remembered until she felt uniformly disliked. She started hating to go to school which had become a source of alleged belittling.

Betty's mother was a very disturbed woman who resented her familial role. She had pushed Betty into nursery school despite protests and later forced her to go to sleep-away camp. She was constantly critical of everyone and pictured herself as a martyr to her family. The father withdrew into his business and seemed to avoid coming home. The only praise Betty ever received was for her academic success, but even this pleasure was destroyed by the mother's use of her daughter's grades to degrade her other children.

Betty had never truly developed a sure sense of her own worth but relied excessively on her mother's opinions. She cherished normal adolescent romantic notions which she kept secret. When these dreams were dashed by her supposed "rejection," she erroneously believed that her secret desires would never be fulfilled, and she would always be unworthy and unlovable, just as her mother had covertly predicted. Only one experience appeared sufficient to convince her of the inevitability of a terrible fate. From that point on she unconsciously distorted the reactions of others to reaffirm her unworthiness and she selected only those responses that confirmed her low opinion of herself. Gradually her affective state deteriorated in step with her unconscious cognitive beliefs and culminated in a severe depression.

Juvenile Manic-Depressive Disorders

If the clinical status of depression in childhood is problematic, the occurrence of manic-depressive disorders before puberty is even more questionable. Kraeplin (1921) noted that a few of his adult manic-depressive patients reported experiencing their first episode before age ten, one patient as early as age five. Other investigators also have described adult patients who traced their illness back to early childhood; however, actual observed case reports of manic-depressive disorder before puberty are rare.

In the late nineteenth century and in the early part of this century, alleged cases of childhood mania were reported (see Anthony and Scott, 1960, for a detailed review) but it remains doubtful that these children were truly manic. Any cyclical behavior or period of excitement seems to have been diagnosed as mania. A close reading of these early reports is needed, since the present-day syndrome of minimal brain dysfunction—which predominantly consists of hyperactivity, distractibility, and emotional lability—could have been confused with manic behavior. Since these symptoms depend on the amount of external stimulation, the condition could have appeared to be episodic or cyclical. Therefore it is debatable whether these early reports were actually describing hyperactive rather than manic children. When Anthony and Scott reviewed twenty-eight such case reports, applying fairly rigorous criteria for the diagnosis of manic-depressive illness, they found only three reported children who met over five of their ten criteria, and none scored over seven. All three children were eleven years old and showed alternation of depression and mania. Anthony and Scott believe that "all the other cases were open to the charge of misdiagnosis" (1960, p. 58). This conclusion fits the earlier findings of Kasanin and Kaufman (1929) that affective psychoses do not occur in early childhood. These authors reviewed 6,000 patients and found that in only four cases an affective psychosis began before age sixteen and never before age fourteen.

Despite this somewhat uncertain position on the possibility of manic-depressive illness in childhood, some cases have been reported, especially since the discovery of the effectiveness of lithium for treating this disorder. Anthony and Scott (1960) reported the case of a twelve-year-old boy who was seen with symptoms of acute mania which subsided and then returned. This boy's history was recorded up to the time he was twenty-two years old. By then he had been hospitalized four times with a clear-cut manic-depressive disorder. The authors emphasized that the illness began before puberty. They concluded that although manic-depressive disorders are clinically rare in childhood, they are psychodynamically possible because children may utilize grandiose fantasies as a defense against feelings of sadness or disappointment.

Since the appearance of this paper, other authors have presented single case histories of manic attacks in young adolescents (Warneke, 1975; Berg, Hullin, and Allsopp, 1974). Although it is of clinical interest as well as therapeutic importance that lithium was successfully used in these cases, the articles merely call attention to a few rare cases of manic-depressive illness which began in adolescence. However, two articles have reported manic episodes in very young children, therefore tending to justify this disorder as a bona fide pediatric illness. The first article by Feinstein and Wolpert (1973) speculates that certain children may show precursors of later manic-depressive behavior. They report the case of a three-and-one-half-year-old girl with a strong family history of this disorder who began to show rapid mood alterations from the age of two. She eventually was seen because of hyperactivity and distractibility. Later she is described as reacting to an alleged disappointment with prolonged agitation and destructive behavior. (Her sister had accompanied her to the psychiatric appointment, although simply to see another psychiatrist who shared the same waiting room.) Due to the child's extreme aggressive behavior, she was tried on lithium at age five and one-half, with good effect. There was no recurrence of her agitation or destructiveness. On the basis of her family history, the episodes of hyperactivity, and her response to lithium, the authors conclude that their patient is an example of juvenile manic-depressive illness. They doubt that the hyperactivity was the consequence of minimal brain dysfunction since this form of hyperactivity is unresponsive to lithium.

Thompson and Schindler (1976) describe a five-year-old boy who was seen because of a short attention span, wandering thoughts, and disruptive classroom behavior. Past history was significant in that the child had been abandoned by his parents and spent a deprived infancy, possibly with nutritional deficiency, in an orphanage. At age three he was adopted by loving parents who showered the boy with care and attention. On evaluation there were no neurological findings, despite his distractibility. He was jovial and showed a constantly elevated mood. The authors speculate that the boy's exuberant behavior may have resulted from his sudden favorable circumstances—being placed in a loving and giving environment after having been raised in the deprivation of a poorly run orphanage. His separation from this all-rewarding environment when he started school may have set off fears of loss and a return to deprivation which, according to the authors, led to his increasing manic behavior.

These two reports are certainly provocative but they leave crucial questions unanswered. There was no alternation of so-called manic behavior with states of depression, which would have truly confirmed the diagnosis. Furthermore, the manic behavior itself consisted of hyperactivity, distractibility, grandiose fantasies, and in one case aggressive behavior. A difficulty not mentioned is that such behavior is common in many children who have variations of minimal brain dysfunction. Grandiose fantasies also are a fairly normal method of defense in all young children who confuse fantasy and reality in their attempts to compensate for being small and socially powerless. The same argument can be leveled at Anthony and Scott's claim that the psychodynamics of manic depression may be found in children. This is certainly true, for children are realistically dependent on others, have difficulty resolving ambivalence, and are prone to an omnipotent denial of reality. These psychodynamic characteristics are found in normal children who do not show features of affective disorders. Therefore the presence of such psychodynamics may be a necessary but not sufficient cause for the expression of manic-depressive behavior. The point is that these authors do not demonstrate, either on a clinical or psychodynamic basis, the specificity needed to make this diagnosis. The child who improved on lithium may be cited as showing some form of specificity in terms of drug response. However, lithium has been tried in a variety of childhood disorders, especially aggressive behavior, with reportedly good effects (Annell, 1969) so that its effects may not be that specific for manic-depressive disorders. The speculation that a childhood predisposition to manic-depressive disorders does exist nevertheless is an extremely intriguing proposition. This predisposition may take the form of excessive affective lability or impulsivity which, given a sufficiently pathological home environment and a precipitating trauma, may ultimately result in a cyclical illness. Proving the existence of such susceptibility, however, must await comparison studies of children from highly affected families, who are either raised with their natural parents or have been adopted in early infancy by normal parents so that they do not grow up subjected to their parents' cyclical moods.

Conclusion

This chapter has reviewed the clinical syndromes that have been called depression in children. There is still much controversy whether true depression can exist prior to late childhood. The reaction of infants to separation may be better conceived of as a grief reaction, and the transient unhappy moods of the young child may be considered a direct, behavioral reaction to momentary disappointments. Even when states similar to adult depression are manifested in later childhood, the symptoms are influenced by the appropriate cognitive and affective developmental level. The pendulum of psychiatric opinion has swung back and forth as to whether depression in childhood exists, but this continuing argument may ultimately center on a semantic difference: the question is not whether depression exists in childhood, but rather how the developmental process allows or limits the experience or expression of varying pathological moods and affects.

PART TWO

Psychodynamics

[5]

THE PSYCHOBIOLOGY OF

SADNESS

Introductory Remarks

Many psychiatrists warn the therapist in training not to confuse sadness, or normal unhappiness, with depression. The warning is appropriate, but certainly the confusion would not arise if there were no similarities between these two human conditions. And even if the similarities were less important than the differences, they would deserve to be studied, unless proved coincidental or casual.

In many scientific fields progress is often made when two or more conditions or things which are apparently alike can be differentiated and eventually proved dissimilar in their basic structure. But progress on many occasions is made also in the opposite way, when similarities appearing in different conditions are recognized as not being casual, adventitious, or coincidental, but indications of relatedness between the nature of the phenomena involved. As a matter of fact, in some cases one of the two similar conditions is fundamentally only a quantitative transformation of the other. For instance, fever is different from normal body temperature, but it is nevertheless a body temperature raised by some special contingencies.

I believe that a close relation exists between sadness, a normal emotion, and depression, which is a psychiatric symptom or condition. Undoubtedly I am predisposed to think so by some personal bias, but I am aware of the opposite bias held by most authors who see a completely different nature in sadness and depression. These authors interpret depression only or almost exclusively as a chemical event occurring in the brain. I do not deny that a chemical event occurs in the brain when people experience

This chapter was written by Silvano Arieti.

depression. In fact, I believe that a chemical event occurs even when they experience sadness. But the chemical event is an effect, and to some extent the medium of the psychological event, with which I—as a psychiatrist, psychologist, or therapist—am mainly concerned. The psychological event may be caused by an external event or by a previous psychological event, or a combination of the two, and it has to be studied by me, a psychotherapist, as such. Naturally I do not disregard or consider useless the study of the neuronal and biochemical events which necessarily accompany the psychological event. If in the experience of these phenomena we recognize the primacy of the psychological event, I believe it then will be easier to recognize a relation between normal sadness and abnormal depression.

When a normal person is sad or unhappy as a result of some unpleasant events which have occurred in his life, at times he calls himself depressed and melancholy. Similarly we may call our most depressed psychiatric patients sad, melancholy, anguished, unhappy. This free interchange of adjectives is based on the fact that all of them imply a similar feeling of "unpleasure." Perhaps we could bypass the study of sadness and proceed directly to the study of the syndrome called depression if we knew all there is to know about sadness, but unfortunately this is far from being the case. In the indexes of many major books on depression, I found no entry for such items as sadness and unhappiness. Sadness and unhappiness also do not appear in the psychological dictionary by English and English (1958), the psychiatric dictionary by Hinsie and Campbell (1960), and the *Dictionary of Behavioral Science* by Wolman (1973).

Normal sadness is the emotional effect on a human being when he apprehends a situation that he would have preferred not to occur, and which he considers adverse to his well-being. This definition would not pass the test of a rigorous logician. It is to some extent circular, like all definitions that refer to the subjective life of the individual, and it shows once again our difficulty in overcoming the mind–body dichotomy. Nevertheless I think we can use it as a working definition.

First we must remember that sadness presupposes the capacity to experience other normal emotions and conditions, such as affection, closeness, love, self-respect, feelings of satisfaction. In fact, the lack or loss of these positive emotions makes us vulnerable to sadness.

Sadness has many characteristics similar to other feelings and emotions, as well as some special traits of its own. Before taking sadness as the object of our study, we will review some aspects of all feelings. This is an unusual procedure in psychiatric books; but feelings do pertain to all psychiatric conditions and in particular to affective disorders. Studying them, even as they occur in nonpathological conditions, seems to me an essential prerequisite not only for psychological but also for psychiatric studies.

Feelings and Experiences of Inner Status*

In the English language the word feeling can refer to all subjective or private experiences from elementary sensations to complicated emotions.

Sensations, when they reach the level of perceptions, have two experiential aspects: they consist of a subjective apprehension of a physical state of the organism (for instance, a specific unpleasant feeling which we call pain), and they mirror an aspect of reality.

One aspect is sensory, or the transformation of a bodily change into an experience of an inner status, an experience that as a subjective event occurs within the organism. On the other side we have the function of mirroring reality, a function which generally expands into numerous ramifications that have to do with cognition.

If we examine sensory perceptions, we recognize that the importance of these two components varies tremendously. The experience of inner status is very important in the perception of pain, hunger, thirst, and temperature. It becomes less pronounced in other perceptions when the organism is of necessity in contact with some stimuli (tactile, gustatory, and, less obviously, olfactory) coming from the external world. In these perceptions the subjective alteration of the organism plays the predominant role, but the presence of the external stimulus generally also is acknowledged.

In auditory and visual perceptions, the experience of a change of inner status plays a minimal role. What is most important is the awareness these perceptions give us of what happens in the external world; thus they enable the organism to deal more appropriately with the world. They are to a great extent the foundation of cognition, they develop connections with the symbolism of language, they are elaborated to the level of apperception, and they become increasingly removed from their sensorial origin. Their importance finally no longer lies in their sensorial nature but in their meaning.

Both kinds of experience are purposeful, but the experiences of inner status have an immediate survival value and are fundamentally not symbolic, and the experiences of mirroring of reality soon acquire a symbolic function and have less immediate survival value.

I must point out that I have oversimplified this complex matter for expository reasons. No experience, especially at a human level, is ever exclusively of one type or another, but only predominantly of one type.

---

* In an article published in 1960 I described sensations and emotions as experiences of inner status, or subjective conditions of the organism. In my book *The Intrapsychic Self* (1967) I also examined in detail the main emotions. In this section I discuss this topic briefly and only in relation to the main theme of the book.

Although in this chapter we are particularly interested in the experiences of inner status, I shall make a few remarks about the general character of cognitive experiences in order to highlight their differences from the experiences of inner status.

Cognitive experiences become symbolic, that is, they acquire the property of making things stand for other things. For instance, sounds stand for words, things, and meanings. Therefore this field of cognition becomes potentially endless. It is a constantly enlarging system which must be fully evaluated as a capacity of the individual, as a social and a historical phenomenon in the spatial dimension of the community, and in the temporal dimension of the history of man. Symbols are created continuously and they become more and more detached from their original perceptual foundation. What starts as a simple perception continues as a probe of wider and wider horizons. The finitude of man seems temporarily overcome by the use of the symbolic process.

In contrast to this unlimited scope, it at first seems that the experiences of inner status play only a secondary role, at least in the human organism. They cannot expand endlessly and they seem by necessity concerned with here-and-now reality, a reality restricted to the boundaries of the organism, but one which immediately can be divided into pleasant and unpleasant experiences.

Has the organism really relegated the experiences of inner status to a secondary role? Not at all, as will be apparent if in paradigmatic fashion we take into consideration one of these experiences: an unpleasant one, pain.

When some special nerve endings are stimulated, there is a flow of stimulation which eventually reaches the thalamus and the cerebral cortex, and pain is experienced. Pain is not just a sensation and a perception. It is a warning, a signal that a discontinuity or an adverse change has occurred in the body, which may persist and increase unless the organism removes the source of pain. Pain thus translates an abnormal state of the animal organism into a subjective experience. Lower species attempt to remove pain by motor withdrawal from its source. Higher species and especially human beings generally attempt to remove the source of pain by purposeful behavior so that the regenerative potential of the organism can permit healing. If we have a toothache, we rush to the dentist.

But long before we have the capacity to understand the meaning of a toothache and to seek the help of a dentist, we have the capacity to understand pain. The baby has such a capacity in his very first day of life. Pain for him is an immediate revelation antecedent to any learning. The subjective unpleasant experience is instantaneous. It operates prior to and much faster than any cognitive experience that derives from the elaboration of the second type of sensations—perceptions. The baby does not know how to talk but he is able to express his experience of pain by crying. The fact that he cries tells us that he is already capable of attributing a negative *value* to pain. The baby seems also to convey a message to the adult: "Remove my pain by feeding me, holding me, changing my clothes."

When the child gets older, he does not cry anymore but the motivation is the same: "Remove the source of pain." This removal is attempted with the help of others or by one's own efforts. Thus the value—in this case negative—which is immediately perceived even by the infant as inherent in a particular state of awareness, corresponds to an objective value for life in general and promotes a special type of motivated behavior. In other words, the feeling of pain becomes a motivational force, and the motivation is to eliminate the source of the pain, or at least to give a warning that a method should be found to eliminate the cause of that feeling.

Of course there is no perfect correspondence between the intensity of the painful feeling, the warning implied, and the resulting behavior. A toothache can cause very distressing pain and a serious disease may produce only a dull pain. In some serious diseases the pain becomes noticeable or unbearable when the illness has reached an advanced degree which may be beyond remedy at the present stage of our therapeutic knowledge. Even if the system of feeling pain is not a precise signaling equipment or a sophisticated diagnostician, in its total effect it is of tremendous and indispensable value for the organism. It is logical to assume that pain was at first selected in evolution because the animal, unlike vegetable life, moves or changes positions and needs a sensation signal to avoid surrounding bodies having certain harmful characteristics (too hard, cutting edges, thorns, etc.). Pain is also an indicator, although an imperfect one, of certain internal harmful states and diseases of the organism. We can assume safely that pain perception has such a survival value that without it animal life would not be possible, except for the simplest species.

Elsewhere (Arieti, 1960, 1967) I have described how emotions share some of the properties of simple feelings, such as sensations and perceptions of inner status. Emotions too can be divided into those that are pleasant and unpleasant and therefore they become motivational forces: pleasant emotions motivate a behavior aimed at preserving the pleasure, and unpleasant emotions motivate a behavior aimed at ending the unpleasantness. What Freud called cathexis—that is, investment of energy or libido—is probably only the motivational value of felt experiences, as Freud himself thought before he wrote *The Ego and the Id.*

We must carefully take into consideration two important issues concerning emotions.

Many well-known psychologists (for instance, Woodworth, 1940; Munn, 1946) have considered emotions as a disorganization of the organism. It is to the merit of Leeper (1948) that he showed the fallacy of this position. I myself have independently pursued the line initiated by Leeper, and I have described the highly organized status of emotions and their motivations (Arieti, 1960, 1967). For instance, a state of tension is motivationally organized to induce a return to homeostasis and a state of satisfaction, fear warns us of a present danger and prepares us to cope with it, anxiety warns us against a future or indefinite danger, rage and anger put us in a position to fight an adverse force, and so on. The experience of emotion is indeed a change in the organism and thus may be a disturbance, but not a disorganization.

The second characteristic, which I described fully for the first time in *The Intrapsychic Self* (1967), consists of the fact that at a human level all emotions have a cognitive component, minimal in some emotions and preponderant in others.

Emotions can be divided into three orders or ranks (Arieti, 1967, 1970a, 1970b). The first rank includes the simplest emotions which I have called first-order or protoemotions. There at at least five types: (1) tension, a feeling of discomfort caused, for example, by excessive stimulation and hindered physiological or instinctual response; (2) appetite, a feeling of expectancy which accompanies a tendency to move toward, contact, grab, or incorporate an almost immediately attainable goal; (3) fear, an unpleasant subjective state which follows the perception of danger and elicits a readiness to flee; (4) rage, an emotion that follows the perception of a danger to be overcome by fighting; that is, by aggressive behavior rather than by flight; (5) satisfaction, an emotional state resulting from gratification of physical needs and relief from other emotions.

In a general sense we can say about protoemotions that: (1) They are experiences of inner status which cannot be sharply localized and which involve the whole or a large part of the organism. (2) They either include a set of bodily changes, mostly muscular and humoral, or retain some bodily characteristics. (3) They are elicited by the presence or absence of specific stimuli which are perceived by the organism to be related in a positive or negative way to its safety and comfort. (4) They become important motivational factors and to a large extent determine the type of external behavior of the subject. (5) They have an almost immediate effect; if they unchain a delayed reaction, the delay ranges from a fraction of a second to a few minutes. (6) In order to be experienced, they require a minimum of cognitive effort. For instance in fear or rage a stimulus must promptly be recognized as a sign of danger. The danger is present or imminent.

The fifth and sixth characteristics require further discussion. Protoemotions are not experienced instantaneously, like the simple sensations of pain and thirst. They require some cognitive work. However, this cognitive work is of very short duration and presymbolic, or in some cases symbolic to a rudimentary degree. Presymbolic cognition includes perception and simple learning. It also includes the sensorimotor intelligence described by Piaget in the first year and a half of life.

Protoemotions are extremely important for the survival of the species and also as motivational forces. They are important in both infrahumans and man. However, let us remember that the learning which is required at this level is very simple. It deals with messages immediately given with either direct stimuli or signals, but not with symbols. Signals or signs indicate things. Some of them may actually be parts of things. (The smell of a mouse is connected to or part of the mouse for the cat.) However, they are not necessarily so. Like the ringing of a bell for the conditioned dog, they indicate something which is forthcoming.

Organization at the protoemotional level is very simple. It does not include what is most pertinent in the field of psychiatry. In fact, we must go to the second-order emotions to find such psychological experiences as anxiety, anger, wishing, security.

Second-order emotions are not elicited by a direct or impending attack or by a threatened immediate change in homeostasis of the organism, but by cognitive symbolic processes. The prerequisite learning deals not only with immediate stimuli or signals, but also with symbols; that is, with something which represents stimuli or stands for the direct sense-data.

These symbols may vary from very simple forms to the most complicated and abstract representations. The simplest symbol is the image, a psychological phenomenon which has been badly neglected in psychology and psychiatry. We know that an image is a memory trace which assumes the form of a representation. It is an internal quasi-reproduction of a perception that does not require the corresponding external stimulus in order to be evoked. Although we cannot deny that at least rudimentary images occur in subhuman animals, there seems to be no doubt that images are predominantly a human characteristic. The child closes his eyes and visualizes his mother. The mother may not be present, but her image is with the child and it stands for her. He may lie peacefully in bed and that image will be with him until he falls asleep. By the image representing her, the mother acquires a psychic reality which is not tied to her physical presence.

Image formation is actually the basis for all higher mental processes. It enables the human being not only to re-evoke what is not present, but to retain an affective disposition for the absent object. The image thus becomes a substitute for the external object. It is actually an inner object, although it is not well organized.

Now let us see how images may increase the emotional gamut. Anxiety is the emotional reaction to the expectation of danger. The danger is not immediate, nor is it always well defined. The expectation of danger is not the result of a simple perception or signal, as it is in the case of fear. Images enable the person to anticipate a future danger and its dreaded consequences, even though he does not expect it to materialize for some time. In its simplest form anxiety is fear mediated by images or imagined fear. However, often the danger is represented by sets of symbols which are more complicated than sequences of images.

Similar remarks could be made for the other second-order emotion, anger. In its simplest form anger is imagined rage; that is, a rage elicited by the images of the stimuli which generally elicit rage. Whereas rage usually leads to immediate motor discharge directed against the stimulus that elicits it, anger tends to last longer although it retains an impelling characteristic. The prolongation of anger is possible because it is mediated by symbolic forms, just as anxiety is. If rage was useful for survival in the jungle, anger was useful for the first human communities to maintain a hostile-defensive attitude toward the enemy, even when the latter was not present.

Wishing is an emotional state which has received little consideration in psychology except when it has been confused with appetite. Whereas appetite is a feeling accompanied by a preparation of the body for approach and incorporation, wishing means a pleasant attraction toward something or somebody, or toward doing something. Contrary to appetite, wishing is made possible by the evocation of the image or other symbols of an object whose presence is pleasant. The image of an earlier pleasant experience—for instance, the satisfaction of a need—evokes an emotional disposition which motivates the individual to replace the image with the real object of satisfaction. A search for the real object thus is initiated or at least contemplated. This search may require detours, since a direct approach is often not possible.

Security is the last second-order emotion. It has played an important role in the theoretical framework of the psychiatrist Harry Stack Sullivan (1940, 1953). It is debatable whether such an emotion really exists; the term may indicate only the absence of unpleasant emotions or else be a purely hypothetical concept. We can visualize the simplest form of security as imagined satisfaction. That is, images permit the individual to visualize a state of satisfaction not only for today but also for tomorrow.

The brain, which uses images, can be compared to some extent to an analog computer. With the advent of language, the nervous system in some aspects becomes like a digital computer; a system of arbitrary signs is now capable of eliciting the emotions that earlier could be engendered only by external stimuli or images. Until now emotions seem to be only experiences of inner states which are connected with the organism itself, its immediate surroundings, or its image of the immediate surroundings. Emotions, as experiences of inner states and with some exceptions to be discussed later, are not symbolic. They stand only for themselves and they do not extend beyond the boundaries of the organism. However, when they become connected with symbolism, they are capable of partaking of the infinity of the universe.

Second-order emotions can be elicited also by a preconceptual type of cognition; that is, by primitive forms of thinking included in what Freud called the primary process. The nonhuman animal is at a level where only first-order emotions are possible and so is very limited psychologically; it remains within the boundaries of a limited reality but is indeed a realist. It is capable only of a nonsymbolic type of learning. It interprets signs but not symbols in the light of past experience. When man uses symbols, especially preconceptual symbols, he opens his mind toward the infinity of the universe but also toward an infinity of errors and the realm of unreality. For instance, the experience of anxiety may be wasted because it is based not on a realistic appreciation of danger, but on an inaccurate or arbitrary symbolism.

Third-order emotions occur with the gradual abandonment of preconceptual levels and the development of the conceptual levels of cognition. In conjunction with the first- and second-order emotions, they offer the human being a very complicated and diversified emotional repertory. Language plays an important role in third-order emotions. The temporal representation is enlarged in the direction of both the past and the future. As an experiential phenomenon emotion has only one temporal dimension, which is the present. However, because of its cognitive components it is a present experience which may have a great deal to do with past experiences and with an envisioned future. A person may be happy or unhappy now because of what happened long ago or what he thinks may happen in the future.

Third-order emotions, although capable of existing even before the occurrence of the conceptual level, expand and become much more complicated at the conceptual level. Important third-order emotions are sadness, hate, love, and joy. To discuss adequately what we know about them, which is little in comparison to what remains to be known, would fill many books. I shall take into consideration only one third-order emotion: sadness.

Sadness

Sadness is a specifically human phenomenon, although rudimentary forms of it or related emotions have been observed in other species of vertebrates. It may be referred to as a special pain which is not physical, but mental. The English word *pain* includes both physical and mental pain because they are similar as subjective experiences of suffering. If our general assumption about feeling is correct, sadness, like physical pain, must have been retained in evolution because it was useful for survival. It may have become a motivational force similar to other unpleasant feelings, whether sensations or emotions. The motivation would be an urge to remove the cause of the unpleasant feeling. This may seem hard to prove; take as examples seven situations in which a normal person is likely to feel sad or unhappy:

1. He hears the news that a person dear to him has suddenly died. He is in a state of grief and mourning.
2. A son or daughter has flunked an examination.
3. A sweetheart has openly and irrevocably declared that her love has come to an end.
4. He unexpectedly loses a position which has been held for many years with a feeling of commitment, loyalty, pleasure, and fulfillment.
5. He has been humiliated by his chief in the place of work.
6. He has been the victim of an injustice.
7. He recognizes that a basic position, a specific direction he has taken in life (for instance, allegiance to a cause, a person, a special type of work) is wrong. He has wasted time and energy, and must now change direction.

Our life experiences enable us to understand how an individual who is faced with one or more of these seven circumstances may have emotions ranging from mild sadness to despondency, anguish, unhappiness, and severe sorrow.

An individual who expects an unhappy or dangerous event to happen is in a state of anxiety. But in the seven examples, the loss has already occurred or the damage has already taken place. Because the individual realizes that the damage has already taken place, he experiences not anxiety, but sadness. It is evident that an appraisal of the situation has been a prerequisite for the sadness to occur. The individual not only realizes the impact of the undesirable event on his present life, but he is able to assess the negative effect that it will have on his future. To refer again to the seven examples, he no longer will enjoy the company of the deceased person; his son will not be promoted; he will no longer receive love from the sweetheart; he no longer will retain the coveted position; he has lost face or reputation among co-workers; he may not be able to undo the damage done to him, as people may really believe he is guilty; he has been a fool in devoting himself so much to an unworthy cause; and so on.

Some authors believe that feelings of sadness and depression are caused by a decrease of norepinephrine in certain parts of the central nervous system. It seems certain that a chemical change occurs in the brain of the individual who experiences sadness. But contrary to the position taken by Akiskal and McKinney (1975), it seems plausible that the leap is not from chemistry to psychology, but from psychology to chemistry. In other words, the cognitive appraisal of the event comes before the chemical change. If the chemical change is necessary for the subjective experience of sadness, then the chemical change must be responsible for another leap, from a chemical reaction to the psychological experience of sadness.

It is important to stress at this point how extensive the cognitive work is that prepares the ground for the feeling of sadness. To understand the meaning of the death of a person dear to us and the significance that his absence will have in our life, or to comprehend fully the meaning of a humiliation or a basic error that we have made, implies evaluating thousands of facts and their ramifications, myriads of ideas, and a plurality of feelings which are often discordant. First, billions of neurons do cognitive work in the neopallium; then sadness is experienced as the outcome of the cognitive work. The concerted functioning of all the neopallic neurons is transformed into an emotion, an experience of inner status.

In this book we shall not deal with the anatomical structures that mediate this transformation. From the classic work of Papez (1937) and those who have followed Papez's work, we know that a large number of neopallic structures must find pathways to some parts of the limbic system. But at this point already we can reflect upon a phenomenon which appears miraculous; that in as little time as a fraction of a second to a few seconds, the work of a multitude of neurons is transformed into an emotional experience. When we respond to a simple stimulus with an experience of inner status, the phenomenon may not appear impressive until we realize that the experience of inner status is the outcome of the concerted work of billions of neurons.

Similar phenomena, which include an enormous variation in the intensity or complexity of stimuli, occur throughout the nervous system. For instance, the auditory system can hear the weakest whisper and also hear and understand the meaning of an explosive sound, even though these two sound experiences vary as much as a trillionfold. The eyes can see visual images that vary a millionfold in their light intensities (Guyton, 1972). Thus some regions of the limbic system may also be capable of responding with a painful emotion to wave fronts of nervous stimulation varying enormously in size and coming from the neopallic areas.

It seems easy to establish that a cognitive work is necessary to experience normal sadness, just as we can ascertain easily that a change in the cognitive work may reverse the feeling of sadness. The following example will clarify this point. During the second World War some families were notified of a relative missing in action. The news generally provoked a great deal of sorrow and also anxiety, since the death of the missing person was not proved. When additional news arrived that confirmed the death of the soldier, any feeling of anxiety disappeared and only a profound feeling of sadness was experienced. In those rare instances, reported in the newspapers, in which the soldier who was thought to be dead was instead found to be alive and well, sadness immediately disappeared and was replaced by happiness and joy. It is thus clear that a change in the cognitive work can change the emotion. What remains to be demonstrated is how in the case of sadness the emotion becomes a motivational force.

SADNESS—AND BEREAVEMENT IN PARTICULAR—
AS A MOTIVATIONAL FORCE

If sadness is like other unpleasant feelings, it must be a promoter of behavior which will lead to the disappearance of sadness. This function is easy to understand in the case of pain, hunger, thirst, tiredness, fear, and anxiety, which all lead to behavior that tends to avoid, remove, or prevent the cause of the feeling itself. But what can we do in the case of sadness, when the harmful event or the loss has already taken place? Moreover, when we feel sad we also feel less equipped to take any action whatsoever. In contrast to persons who are angry and ready to fight, or persons who are afraid and ready to flee, we feel slowed down in our activities and thought processes. In order to understand the phenomenon, we must consider some of the seven examples listed on page 118. Let us consider in greater detail our first example of an individual who hears the news that a person he loves has unexpectedly died.

After he has understood and almost instantaneously evaluated what this death means to him, he experiences shock and then sadness; or to be exact, that particular type of normal sadness which is called bereavement, mourning, or grief. For a few days all thoughts connected with the deceased person bring about a painful, almost unbearable feeling. Any group of thoughts remotely connected with the dead person elicits sorrow. The individual cannot adjust to the idea that the loved person does not live any more. And since that person was so important to him, many of his thoughts or actions are directly or indirectly connected with the dead person and therefore elicit sad reactions. He finds himself searching for the dead person. When he sees a person who looks like the dead person, he has a fleeting impression, almost immediately corrected, that he sees the dead person. Nevertheless, after a certain period of time which varies from individual to individual, the person in mourning seems to become adjusted to the idea that the loved one is dead.

How is this change possible? If the individual is able to introspect, he will recognize that some clusters of thought have replaced the old ones which were connected with the departed. At first he had the impression at a conscious level that the painful thoughts about the departed person prevented him from thinking about anything else. But after some time he recognizes that the opposite is true: the painful thoughts attract new ones, as if they wanted to be replaced by new thoughts. This cognitive activity goes on until the grief work is completed.

At first there is an attempt to recapture the dead person, to make the deceased live again in dreams, daydreams, and fantasies. Because these attempts are doomed to fail, the individual is left with only one possibility, which is to rearrange the ideas that are connected with the departed. This rearrangement can be carried out in several ways, according to the person's mental predisposition. For example, he may come to consider the deceased no longer indispensable. He may associate the image of the dead person mainly with the qualities of that person which elicited pleasure, so that the image no longer brings mental pain but pleasure. Or he may think of the deceased's life as not really ended, but as being continued either in a different world or in this world through the lasting effects of the deceased's actions. Finally he may think that another person can replace the deceased one in his life; the deceased was not unique in every respect. Whatever the ideational rearrangement, there is no moving away from a physical source of discomfort as in pain, or from the source of danger as in fear. The moving away is only from certain chains of thought that perpetuate the feeling of sadness. It is not the passage of time that heals, but the rearrangement of ideas, which still may require a considerable amount of time.

As I wrote in *The Intrapsychic Self*,* sadness is an unpleasant emotion which has a tendency not to be extinguished rapidly, like rage, but to last. It does not have an impelling tendency toward immediate action and discharge, like rage and fear; it is neither centripetal, such as fear which is experienced as something directed from the frightening stimulus to the organism, nor centrifugal, such as rage which is experienced as being directed toward something outside of the organism. Although precipitated most of the time by certain events that occur in the external world, it is reflexive in the sense that it seems to reflect back to the organism that experiences it.

In summary, sadness slows our activities and lasts long enough in us not to evoke a prompt motor response. It favors slow mental processes which bring about a reorganization of thoughts about life directives, and eventually different purposeful behavior.

In children who are not mature enough to know that the loss is irreparable, the urge to recover the lost object is stronger than in adults, as Bowlby has described (1960a). Many authors (Anna Freud, 1960; Jacobson, 1971) doubt that the reaction of children to the loss of their mother can really be called mourning and not bereavement. At any rate, even if such a reaction is not equivalent to the mourning of adults, it is certainly a state of sadness following an unpleasant event.

Parkes (1964, 1965, 1972, 1973) has done the most extensive research on mourning. He described the effects of mourning or bereavement on sixty-six widows from several parts of England. He wrote that when a bereaved adult learns of the death of a loved person, he tends to call and search for that person. Since he knows, however, that the search is useless and painful, he denies the search. The result is a compromise, a partial expression of the search. Whereas the child cries and protests, as Bowlby described, the adult goes on searching. Parkes (1973) described a woman who was searching for her missing son. "She moves restlessly about the

* In that book I called sadness "normal depression," a term I no longer use.

likely parts of the house scanning with her eyes and thinking of the boy; she hears a creak and immediately associates it with the sound of her son's footfall on the stair; she calls out, 'John, is that you?' "

In the process of searching there is in the beginning a motor hyperactivity which, according to Parkes, has the specific aim of finding the one who has died. This hyperactivity was already described by Lindemann: "The activity throughout the day of severely bereaved persons show remarkable changes. There is no retardation of action and speech; quite to the contrary, there is a rush of speed, especially when talking about the deceased. There is restlessness, inability to sit still, moving about in an aimless fashion, continually searching for something to do. There is, however, at the same time, a painful lack of capacity to initiate and maintain normal patterns of activity" (Lindemann, 1944). According to Parkes, after hyperactivity subsequent features are preoccupation with the memory of the lost person, a scanning of perceptual stimulations to find evidence of the lost person, focusing attention on those parts of the environment that are associated with the deceased, and finally the conscious recognition of the urge to seach for the lost person.

Parkes wrote that grief is commonly described as a process by which a person detaches himself from a lost object. Yet the bereaved person acts as if he wants restoration of the object. However, Parkes (1973) adds that "with repeated failure to achieve reunion, the intensity and duration of searching diminish, habituation takes place, the 'grief work' is done. It seems that the human adult has the same need to go through the painful business of pining and searching if he is to 'unlearn' his attachment to a lost person."

I believe that Parkes focuses on an early stage of mourning, after the period of initial shock and retardation. Parkes reaffirms what I have previously described (Arieti, 1959), that the bereaved individual becomes reactivated in the search of a restoration of the lost person. There is no longer retardation, but motor and mental hyperactivity which aims at retrieving the lost person. It seems to me that by enacting this unrealistic and futile search, the individual is behaving like a person who has undergone a trauma and dreams about it again and again in order to get used to the trauma, to become desensitized to it, or to diminish its emotional impact.

I disagree with Parkes that the "grief work" is done with the completion of the activities he described. If by grief work we mean reparative work, we must recognize that Parkes has described only the first part which is preparatory for the second.

With the first part of the grief work, the patient becomes partially desensitized to the loss but, having realized the futility of his efforts, he also becomes more open to realistic alternatives. He will accept the cognitive possibilities described on page 121: he no longer considers the deceased individual to be indispensable; he thinks the deceased is still alive through his works or in another world, or that the deceased can be replaced by another person; and so forth. The grief work is done and sadness disappears only when one or more of these alternatives are accepted and they elicit in the bereaved a different type of mental and motor behavior.

Alberta Szalita (1974) wrote about bereavement: "Whenever an individual suffers a loss . . . particularly a beloved person—he normally undergoes a period of grief and mourning of varying intensity until he recovers the energy he invested in the lost object. The process of mourning is very painful. It is a travail that reconciles him to the loss and permits him to continue his life with unimpaired vigor, or even with increased vitality. A similar process takes place when one is confronted with a disappointment, failure, the loss of a love object through rejection, divorce, abandonment, and the like."

Szalita divides mourning into three stages: complete identification with the deceased, splitting of the identification, and a detailed review of the relationship. Szalita describes the third stage as "a somewhat detached appraisal of one's own conduct toward the lost object. The self-evaluation encompasses a painful working-through of myriads of minute elements and a complete scanning of one's life. There can be no glossing over in this process; shallowness is incompatible with mourning. The result of 'digging in' is that one emerges as an integrated, enriched, and revitalized person." Szalita's third stage corresponds partially to the reparatory phase that I have described.

It is useful to stress again that the slowness produced by sadness has a purpose. In sadness, the reparatory work takes a long time. Quick actions are more difficult to implement, and so are propensities to make quick escapes in completely unrelated directions.

An additional aspect of the motivational meaning of mourning has been stressed by classic psychoanalysis since Freud wrote *Mourning and Melancholia* (1917). The bereaved person feels guilty for having survived the deceased person, for not having prevented his death, or more frequently for believing that he has wished his death. Such wishing may only have been unconscious, but the sadness is an expiation for guilt. Although it is true that these complexes can be traced in some people, especially in persons who become depressed to a pathological degree after the death of a close person (see chapter 6), it is very unlikely that this mechanism explains bereavement as a universal phenomenon.*

If we review the other six situations listed on page 118 in which a normal person is likely to feel sad or unhappy, the phenomenon of sadness will appear similar and yet in some respects simpler than bereavement.

---

* For additional studies on bereavement, the reader is referred to Parkes (1972), and Schoenberg et al. (1975).

First there is a cognitive appraisal of the event and its consequences, then a state of sadness and retardation, and finally the reparative work. The reparative work of sadness is generally more realistic and consists of less unrealistic fantasies, unless pathological complications ensue. For instance, the parent of the youngster who has flunked the examination will try to convince the child to study more intensely, try again, or change vocations. The person who has been abandoned by his sweetheart will reevaluate his love or try to find a new sweetheart. The person who recognizes that he is wrong in the special direction he has given to his life or in giving his allegiance to a wrong cause, person, or work generally does not respond with sadness to any specific event, but to a realization of the pattern of his life or to a new meaning that he gives to this pattern. This is actually one of the most frequent causes of sadness and depression, as we shall study in detail in chapter 6. The reappraisal of one's life may cause sorrow but if the sorrow work is successful, the individual may reacquire normality or at least avoid depression.

What we have illustrated so far seems to indicate beyond doubt that there is a purpose in sadness. Thus we can understand why evolution has selected sadness as one of the essential feelings in the gamut of human experience.

I am aware that this type of formulation may irritate those readers in scientific research who accept an exclusively deterministic explanation without the concept of purpose or selection. I wish to remind the reader that when in biological reports we use such expressions as "evolution has selected," we follow *une faison de parler*. We do not anthropomorphize a process which has taken millions of years to happen. We use human terms to refer to the fact that mutations not suitable to the survival of the species are more likely to disappear. The unfavorable mutations therefore are not reproduced, and only those that are statistically (even if not in individual cases) favorable to survival are perpetuated. Although in some specific states sadness may lead to depression and suicide, in the total picture of the human species it has positive survival value. Moreover, the feeling of sadness may deterministically be brought about by previous causes, but in the restricted human frame of reference it has a purpose and a beneficial effect for some members of our species. When we use psychodynamic concepts, we imply normal or abnormal purposes even if the whole process of life can be reinstated in the deterministic scheme of the cosmos (Arieti, 1967, 1970).

Other Aspects of Sadness

The purpose of sadness discussed in the previous section does not exclude the possibility that this feeling has other motivations and meanings.

For instance, some thinkers are inclined to see a certain appropriateness or correspondence between an adverse cognitive appraisal and sadness which is similar to the appropriateness between a positive appraisal and happiness. What could be more appropriate than to feel sad when we learn that a friend has died or when we realize that our life has followed a wrong pattern? Would it not seem absurd to laugh in such circumstances? Thus should we not focus on the appropriateness of sadness in similar circumstances, rather than on its biological or psychodynamic function? Moreover, and notwithstanding what I have said earlier in this chapter, why should a symbolic value in sorrow and sadness not exist? Is not the unpleasantness of the sorrow a symbol (or partial reproduction) of the unpleasant event that caused it, just as joy and love are symbols of pleasant events?

On the other hand, the unpleasantness of an event may be a post hoc consideration. In other words, would we consider an event unfavorable or adverse if we did not experience sadness? Undoubtedly in a restricted human sense or at least in the adult human being, emotions can be evaluated in different ways. However, it seems almost evident in the case of sadness that the negative value of the experience appears to mirror the negative value of the event which caused it. In a certain way this appropriateness is inherent in the quality of the subjective experience, similar to what occurs in the experience of the baby who in its first day of life appreciates the negative value of pain.

Pleasantness and unpleasantness, appropriateness and inappropriateness, again may be the result of associations between stimuli and responses which have been retained because they are favorable to survival. For instance, we know of nothing that seems more favorable to procreation than to associate reproductive activities with the pleasure of sex. In other cases associations between cognitive events and emotional responses or somatic concomitants of these emotions remain obscure: we do not know why we blush when we are embarrassed, yawn when we are bored, and laugh when we hear a funny story.

Transformation of Sadness

In many cases the psyche does not tolerate more than a certain amount of sadness. These are situations in which some individuals seem to function more favorably or less unfavorably under the influence of other feelings, even if those feelings are also negative in value. Sadness thus is transformed into anxiety, rage, anger, and hypochondriacal or psychosomatic mechanisms. These outcomes will be illustrated in other chapters.

An important mechanism in the transformation of sadness has been used throughout the history of mankind, but it is available only to a few people. It consists of the attempt to project the state of sorrow into the external world and to believe it is in the external world that the sorrow work has to be done. At times the imperfection of human nature, society, history, or fate is seen as the object of sorrow. At other times it is the burden that society, religion, or our consciences compel us to bear. In other words, the sadness of the individual becomes enlarged or rationalized as a pessimistic philosophy of life, epistemology, and cosmology. Such a philosophy can always be justified, since as we can always find undesirable aspects in the world. The individual generally concludes that he must accept the ineluctably unhappy state of the world. He sees his own personal unhappiness as part of the total picture and therefore more tolerable.

Some great thinkers have been able to influence society and culture with this point of view. In its turn, culture has become pessimistic and melancholy and has facilitated a state of sadness or melancholia in society at large. Thus a vicious circle ensues and a tradition of social melancholia becomes established. This matter will be discussed in greater detail in chapter 16.

Unresolved Sadness and Depression

In some cases of psychiatric relevance the state of sadness is not resolved and becomes transformed into a more intense unhappy feeling called depression. This feeling often replaces all other feelings except those, like guilt and self-depreciation, which are associated with sorrow. In some cases anxiety remains for a long time, but eventually anxiety is also submerged by the overall feeling of depression. Any thought is negative and reinforces the depression. Thus thoughts become slow and less frequent, perhaps in an attempt to reduce the quantity of suffering that they cause. If painful thoughts could be eliminated, there would be no depression; but these thoughts are never eliminated. In some situations, as in reactive depression, painful thoughts for the most part remain conscious. In other conditions the thoughts or systems of thought which cause the depression become unconscious or submerged by a general feeling of depression. Consequently the patient is not able to say why he is depressed.

I have suggested that intense depression has (among others) the same function as repression in other psychiatric conditions. Perhaps it is a special type of repression; the cognitive part is repressed, but the painful feeling is experienced at the level of consciousness.

I am aware, however, of another frequent mechanism in people who have experienced depression in the past. They repress painful ideas in order to avert the depression. The attempt is unsuccessful; the ideas, although unconscious, continue to cause conscious depression. Some patients express themselves in this or a similar way: "I woke up this morning, and I was immediately hit by an intense feeling of depression. I don't know where it came from." Other patients attribute their depression to unhappy ideas that they have about themselves, the future, or life—the triad that Beck has described so well. What Beck does not indicate is that patients use these thoughts to justify their depression. Beck is correct to the extent that these thoughts reinforce the depression which comes from other sources. They add a secondary depression to the original, and only important, one.

In more serious cases, thinking is reduced to a minimum and retardation becomes more pronounced even to the degree of stupor. In these circumstances the retardation of mental processes becomes a self-defeating mechanism. Cognitive elements are very rare or disappear completely and the intense, agonizing feeling of depression remains almost as sole possessor of the psyche. The suffering is so intense that when a patient becomes slightly less depressed and more capable of thinking and moving, he starts to conceive suicidal plans in order to put an end to his suffering.

At this point what is perhaps the most crucial question in this book must be asked: Why do sadness or sorrow work fail in some individuals and depression ensue? At the present stage of our knowledge, no hypothesis can be verified by acceptable scientific standards. We shall examine several possibilities.

1. The biologically oriented psychiatrist is inclined to think that a faulty biochemical process is responsible. For instance, cathecolamines are not being produced in a quantity sufficient to restore the organism after the psychological event of sadness has depleted the brain's biogenic amines.
2. The neurologically inclined psychiatrist can think that the part of the limbic brain that receives the stimulation from pathways coming from the neopallic cognitive areas is particularly sensitive and responds ex-

cessively. It could also be that, for reasons so far unknown, different parts of the brain are stimulated concertedly, involving unusual neuronal pathways which lead to depression. Unfortunately this hypothesis has not received the consideration that it deserves, presumably because it is very difficult to investigate experimentally. Incidentally, this hypothesis does not exclude an altered biochemical mechanism. The neurological alteration may lead to a biochemical disorder.

3. The reparative process (sorrow work) cannot take place because the person is not psychologically equipped for it. Life circumstances, as well as psychological patterns followed by the patient, have not prepared him for the sorrow work. He has no choice; he is not able to solve psychologically his sorrow or sadness, and pathological depression results.

A psychodynamic approach to depression studies this third possibility. Incidentally, this possibility does not exclude that some biological variables may make the psychological repair work more difficult. In these cases a combination of psychological and neurochemical factors are the determinants of the depression.

A frequent criticism of the psychodynamic explanation for depression is that there is no failure of the sorrow work, no preceding sadness. Many patients have become depressed immediately, without any antecedent and external precipitating factor. If this is the case, we have to attribute the phenomenon exclusively to a faulty neurological or biochemical endogenous mechanism.

In my experience, patients whose depressions do not seem to be precipitated by psychological factors have been unaware of these factors. They have followed life patterns, sustained by cognitive components whose depressogenic value was kept in a state of unconsciousness or dim consciousness. Moreover, these rigid and static life patterns have prevented any alternative directions and any reparative work. The study of these life patterns constitutes the major part of the psychodynamic approach of this book.

It is true that many depressed patients—and, incidentally, many people who experience normal sorrow—can be relieved with ingestion of certain drugs. This possibility does not disprove the psychological origin of the feeling. It proves only that whatever physiological or biochemical intermediary exists between the psychological factors and the subjective experience can be altered. Exclusive concern with the biochemical intermediary stage is a reductionist approach. Nature has equipped us to respond to adverse aspects of life not only with biological changes but also with our sorrow—that is, with psychological participation. When sorrow is not solved and depression ensues, we must help the person to acquire a different pattern of psychological participation.

[6]

PSYCHODYNAMICS

OF SEVERE DEPRESSION

In the previous chapter we have seen that an unsolved state of sorrow tends to develop into a state of depression. Because they are most suitable to didactical examination, we predominantly have taken into consideration states of sorrow that unfold rather quickly as the result of specific, mostly sudden events. In practice we find that many states of sadness leading to severe depression have a long course, either chronic or subchronic, liminal or subliminal. We also find that in many cases in which a specific occurrence was the obvious and major precipitating factor, a subliminal state of sadness resulting from previous contingencies preexisted. Thus it is important to study the longitudinal psychodynamic history of each patient. A psychodynamic history is not just a sequence of events from birth to the present time, but an unfolding of psychological forces which derive from the interplay between external and internal events.

As mentioned in chapter 1, every human being is in a fundamental state of receptivity; that is, ready and capable of being influenced by the environment. But human beings are not to be defined only in terms of this state of receptivity. Every human being even in early childhood has another basic function which is integrative activity (Arieti, 1977). Just as the transactions with the world not only inform but transform the individual, the individual transforms these transactions with his integrative activity and in turn he is informed and transformed by these transformations. No influence is received like a direct and immutable message. Multiple processes involving interpersonal and intrapsychic dimensions go back and forth.

The object of this chapter is to describe the way the environment in-

This chapter was written by Silvano Arieti.

fluences the future severely depressed patient and the way he integrates these influences. It will become apparent that these ways are quite different from those of the normal person or the typical schizophrenic patient.

Childhood

As a rule, the childhood of a person who as an adult suffers from a form of severe depression has not been so traumatic as the childhoods of people who become schizophrenic or even seriously neurotic.

The parents of the patient generally give a picture of cohesiveness and stability. Only in a minority of cases is there serious talk of divorce. The family gives the appearance of having stable foundations and adhering to the conventions of society. The family conflicts, schisms, and special constellations described for families of schizophrenics are not seen as frequently in the families of patients suffering from affective disorders. When they exist, they are less pronounced than in the families of schizophrenics.

The future severely depressed patient generally is born in a home which is willing to accept him and to care for him. The word accept has a special meaning in this context; the mother is duty-bound and willing to administer to the baby as much care as he requires, and she is willing to provide everything for him that he needs. This willingness of the mother is in turn accepted by the child, who is willing to accept everything he is offered; that is, early in life the child is very receptive to the influence (or giving) of the significant adult (parent). There are no manifestations of resistance toward accepting this influence, such as autistic manifestations or attempts to prevent or retard socialization that one finds in schizophrenia (Arieti, 1974). If we use Martin Buber's terminology (1937), we may say that the "Thou" or the other is immediately accepted and introjected. The "Thou" is at first the mother, but this receptivity to the mother enhances a receptivity for both parents and all other important surrounding adults, and promotes a willingness to accept them with their symbols and values. It also promotes a certain readiness to accept their food (either the milk of the mother or regular food) and thus predisposes some people (but by no means all) to overeating, obesity, and the seeking of compensation from food when other satisfactions are not available.

This receptivity to others and willingness to introject the favors of others at this early age promotes special personality traits in the future patient. He tends to become an extrovert and also a conformist, willing to accept what he is given by his surroundings not only in material things, but also in terms of habits and values, and to rely less than the average person on his autonomous resources. This readiness to accept—this psychological receptivity—will predispose him also to pathological or exaggerated introjection; that is, he tends to depend excessively on others for certain aspects of life which will be considered later.

In the second year of life (or earlier, according to some authors) a new attitude on the part of the mother drastically changes the environment in which the child is growing. At times the sudden change is experienced as a severe trauma. The mother continues to take care of the child but considerably less so than before, and now she makes many demands on him. The child receives care and affection provided that he accepts the expectations his parents have for him and he tries to live up to them.

This brusque change in the parents' attitude is generally the result of many factors. Predominantly, their attitude toward life in general tends to evoke in the child an early sense of duty and responsibility: what is to be obtained must be deserved. The parents are generally dissatisfied with their own lives and at times harbor resentment toward the children who represent increased work and responsibility. However, this hostility is seldom manifested openly; it generally is manifested by the fact that the parents overly increase their expectations.

Thus the child finds his environment changed from one which predisposed him to great receptivity, to one of great expectation. These dissimilar environments actually are determined by a common factor; the strong sense of duty that compelled the mother to do so much for her baby is now transmitted at an early age to the child himself. Frequently in families of depressed patients there are many children. When the future patient is in his second year of life, a sibling often is already born and the mother lavishes her care on the newborn with the same duty-bound generosity that she previously had for the patient. This of course makes the change in the environment more marked for the patient.

This displacement by a younger sibling seems to be important in the dynamics of many cases of manic-depressive psychosis and other forms of severe depression, although no statistical proof of it can be given. Statistical studies so far have concerned themselves more with the order of birth (that is, whether the patient is the first-born child, second-born, etc.).*

In many cases the brusque change had to occur because of unexpected events: the child had to be abandoned by the mother because of illness,

---

* Some statistical works, however, seem to indicate that the first-born child is more liable to manic-depressive psychosis. Of course the first-born child also is more liable to be displaced. Berman (1933) in a study of 100 manic-depressives found that 48 were first-born, 15 second, 10 each third and fourth, and 17 fifth or later. Pollock and co-workers (1939) found that 39.7 percent were first-born and 29.7 percent were second-born. Malzberg (1937) and Katz (1934) could not find any relationship between birth order and manic-depressive psychosis.

economic setback, forced emigration, or political persecution. The child then was left in the custody of an aunt, grandmother, cousin, stranger, or orphan asylum and was subjected to a violent and unmitigated experience of loss.

For some patients the abrupt change that we have described has already taken place at the time of weaning. Future affective patients are generally breast-fed in their infancy and then suddenly deprived of mother's milk. No bottles, rubber nipples, or pacifiers are used. There is a sharp transition from the breast to the glass. In a minority of patients this loss of the breast plays an important role.

In many other patients the abrupt change occurs later, generally in the preschool years but at times even in grammar-school years. (See the case of Mrs. Fullman in chapter 10.) In other cases specific events take place which make the child feel threatened in his main love relationship. The change may be in the composition of the family, in the attitude of the parents, or on account of some unusual event. When the patient gives to the therapist an account of this change as he remembers it much later, the threat seems in some cases at least to have been experienced in an exaggerated manner. However, in many other cases there seems to have been a justification for an intensely unpleasant feeling. In still other cases the child does not remember the experience of having been threatened, but he remembers acting as if he had been threatened, and indeed at times he remembers facts which should have threatened him. The word threat and not loss is used here, although the child in many instances has sustained a loss (of mother, maternal maid, love, etc.). If the child experiences the disturbing event as a loss, he tends to become immediately depressed. But the person who becomes depressed only in adult life, somehow in childhood was able to compensate partially for this traumatic experience, or to experience it as a threat for which he had to find coping devices.

Freud (1917) suggested that the withdrawal of love, approval, and support on the part of the parent or parent surrogate during an important stage of development predisposes a person to depression in life. Abraham (1916) felt that depression occurring later in life was predisposed by a withdrawal of love in very early childhood and fixation at the oral stage. No matter how devastating these events have been in some cases, patients who become depressed only in adult life have had throughout their childhood a capacity to muster defenses which somewhat diminished the sense of loss. The loss was transformed into a threat with which the child had to learn to deal. Some stability and feeling of hope was maintained.

How does the child try to adjust to the new threatening situation? The child who later is likely to develop an affective disorder tends to adopt special mechanisms. A common one (although as we shall see later, it is decreasing in frequency) is to find security by accepting parental expectations no matter how onerous they are. The child does not reject the parents emotionally, or avoid them as the schizoid often does, but he consciously accepts them. He must live up to their expectations no matter how heavy the burden. It is only by complying, obeying, and working hard that he will recapture the love or state of bliss which he used to have as a baby; or at the very least he will maintain that moderate love which he is receiving now. Love is still available, but not as a steady flow. The flow is intermittent and conditioned, and therefore it does not confer security. The child feels that he will be punished if he does not do what he is supposed to, and mother may withdraw her love totally. At the same time that the anxiety of losing the mother's love occurs, the child is given hope that he will be able to retain this love or recapture it if and when it is lost. The child thus feels he has a choice, or the freedom, to retain the parental love. No matter what he chooses, however, he has a hard price to pay: submission or rejection. He also feels that mother is not bad in spite of her appearance; on the contrary, she is good. She is good even in punishing him, because by punishing him she wants to redeem him, make him worthy again of her love. Thus the mechanism is different from what occurs in many preschizophrenics; although the future affective patient has an image of himself as being bad, he does not feel that he is beyond the possibility of redemption as the preschizophrenic often does. The anxiety about being unable to fulfill parental expectations changes into guilt feelings. If affection or forgiveness is not forthcoming, the child feels that it is his own fault; he has not lived up to what was expected of him, and he feels guilty. When he feels guilty he again expects punishment. He wants to be punished because punishment is the lesser of the evils; he would rather be punished than lose his mother's love. If he is not punished, he often works harder in order to punish himself.

A little later, but at a very early age, many of these children assume responsibilities such as the support of the family. If they engage in a career, it is often in order to bring honor and prestige to the family. In a certain number of cases, the family belongs to a marginal group of society because of religious or ethnic minority status or other reasons, and the child feels that it is his duty to rescue the family with his own achievement. In all these cases we can recognize a pattern of compliance, submission, and self-imposed hard discipline.

In some patients incestuous wishes toward parents and, as frequently, toward siblings of the opposite sex further elicit strong guilt feelings for which the patient feels he must atone by making even more rigid the pattern of relating that we have described.

Other findings make the picture more complicated and difficult to understand. For instance, the parents of some patients appear to be not strict, but overindulgent. This is possible because in this second stage of childhood the parents do not need to enforce any rules with their actions. The rules, the principles, have already been incorporated by the child.

As a matter of fact, some of the parents now regret that the children take rules with such seriousness.

Before proceeding to describe other possibilities in the early family life of the depressed adult, we must make some theoretical considerations which take as a paradigm the situation of compliance and submission that we have described. (We shall analyze variants later.) This interpersonal relation based on compliance and placation has predisposed the child to select and adopt specific ways of facing the world, others, and himself. We do not refer exclusively or predominantly to enduring patterns of behavior, but to ways of thinking and choosing that are related to the integrative activity of the child. At times this integrative activity remains only a predisposition to live according to some schemata. At other times the integrative activity leads to the organization of patterns as rigid as imprintings which last the whole life, especially if they are reinforced by repetition of the same events. These patterns of living do not consist only of movements, or of specific external behaviors. They are cognitive-affective structures which have been built as a result of learning, in the act of facing the early interpersonal situation. To be specific, they are built on the appraisal of external events, the ability to choose some actions instead of others, and the capacity to anticipate the effect that these actions will have on the interpersonal environment.

A theory based on the prevalence of certain cognitive constructs is at variance with psychological and psychiatric conceptions that exclusively see patterns of living as reactions to environmental situations. The concept of reaction which is derived from a behavioristic frame of reference implies almost total passivity in regard to the influence of the environment, and deterministic ineluctability. According to the interpretation offered in this book, the patient sizes up a particular environment and relates to it in the best possible way or, rather, interrelates in the roles of both subject and object. The cognitive construct which receives our major consideration in this book has to do with a person who is very important to the individual in question. I have called this person the *significant other*. The significant other, generally the mother, is the adult from whom the child expects nourishment, acceptance, recognition, love, and respect.

In the interpersonal relation that we have described, the child develops an attitude of excessive compliance in dealing with the significant other. Each individual relates to more than one person and also to groups; for instance, to the family in its totality. Nevertheless, I have referred to the significant other in the singular because at this stage of development the dyadic relation is by far the prevailing one. The interpersonal pattern of behavior that the child displays in relation to the mother and which he later generalizes to his dealings with other people can be seen to derive from the interpersonal branch of the basic construct that we are considering. However, the original construct has another branch, the intrapersonal, which is expanding rapidly. It has to do mainly with the child's self-image; how the child sees himself in consequence of the way he believes other people think of him, and the way he evaluates himself as a consequence of the way he deals with people.

Each important construct can be seen as having a psychological bifurcation, with one intrapersonal branch and the other interpersonal. Both branches are intrapsychic—even the interpersonal one. They are internal structures that lead to certain external behavior and inner elaboration of this behavior. In the construct based on the relation of excessive receptivity and compliance that we have described, we can recognize a structure, a choice, a purpose—the realization of loss or threat and the attempt to cope with it.

We will now describe other situations and inner constructs and show how they predispose the patient to consequent patterns that make it difficult for him to do sorrow work, and thus make him likely to become depressed sometime in his adult life. In many instances we find that as a child the patient believed that he could reacquire love, approval, and consideration not just by complying, obeying, and working hard, but by converging all or almost all of his efforts toward a goal—for instance, toward becoming an outstanding man, a leader, an actor, or a great lover. In late childhood and early adolescence these aims were fantasized in terms of becoming a great scientist, writer, industrialist, winner of the Nobel prize, and so forth. In other cases the aim was to find a great love or a mission. Although early in life this pattern was developed in order to please or placate the significant other, it soon became an aim in itself. The significant other lost significance and was replaced gradually by a significant goal. The patient came to live for that goal exclusively. His whole self-esteem and reason for living were based on reaching the goal.

To have goals and life aspirations is a common occurrence in normal children and adolescents. As a matter of fact, it is a desirable trait for the young individual to conceive of some directions for his life and even to have fantasies and daydreams about them. However, in the person who later becomes seriously depressed, the significant goal occupies the major part of the psyche and leaves no room for other goals, or for flexibility toward other possibilities. Unless the trend is later corrected, these children become not only achievement-oriented to the exclusion of other aspects of life, but oriented toward achieving only in a given way.

Unless they shift their orientation—and fortunately many of them do —already at a young age they appear self-centered and selfish, at times even oblivious of the needs and feelings of others, including those close to them. Whereas the individual who is concerned with pleasing the significant other maintains an important interpersonal relation, even one of dubious value, the person who lives for the significant goal tends to be aloof and self-involved.

A third important pattern with which the child tries to cope with the sudden change in environmental circumstances is the attempt to make himself more babyish, more in need of the significant other. He develops a pattern of dependency. If the child makes himself aggressively dependent, the mother or other important adults are forced to reestablish an atmosphere of babyhood or young childhood, that is, of early bliss. The child and later the adult will develop a very demanding and at the same time clinging, dependent type of personality.

Since the 1950s this last pattern of living has become much more common at least in the United States. The increased frequency may be related to different fashions of raising children. The child senses permissiveness in the family environment and believes that by making claims and being demanding, he will reestablish the previous position of blissful dependency.

We must clarify the fact that in spite of these predominant patterns being established in childhood, secondary patterns coexist in all patients who later develop an affective disorder. The child develops a strong resentment toward the significant other who in the first type of mechanism imposes so much, or who in the third type does not give enough. Such resentment manifests itself in attacks of rage, anger, rebellion, or even violence. When such anger becomes manifest, it is often enough to dispel an oncoming feeling of sadness. For this reason, some therapists believe that any depression hides an underlying anger. This is true only to a limited extent: the anger is consequent to a situation which already existed and was unacceptable to the child. Anger alone is not a solution to the conflict-laden situation, although it may be a temporary defense against depression.

Feelings of anger in many cases are promptly checked and repressed, not only in childhood but throughout the life of the patient. Sadistic thoughts and impulses are at times very pronounced but seldom acted out. Consequent guilt feelings are brought about by these impulses, as well as feelings of unworthiness. The patient soon learns that rebellion does not pay: on the contrary, it increases the atonement he must undergo later. The stronger his sadistic impulses, the stronger the masochistic tendencies become. He soon desires peace at any cost, so that any compromise is worthy of peace. The mechanism which permits him to maintain a certain equilibrium is the repression of this resentment. However, the resentment is retained unconsciously, and it appears in dreams and occasional outbursts which do reach consciousness. In children and adolescents who have adopted the second pattern, there are also episodes of anger and rebellion. They do not want to sacrifice everything for the sake of the significant goal. They go on sprees of indolence, effervescence, or erratic behavior. These sprees, however, remain eposodic and do not become prominent features.

There is an additional dynamic mechanism which is found in some

cases of manic-depressive psychosis. The child senses that the acceptance or introjection of parents is too much of a burden and, without
realizing it, shifts the direction of his incorporations to other adults in
the environment (much older siblings, uncles, aunts, grandparents,
friends, etc.) whom he internalizes instead of parents. Not only does the
common tendency of children to introject adults become exaggerated,
but peripheral adults become parentlike figures. The child unconsciously
resorts to this mechanism in order to decrease the burden of the parental
introjection, but in many cases this defense does not prove useful. As
Fromm-Reichmann (1949) remarked, there will be no single significant
adult to whom the patient can relate in a meaningful way. The relationship with these other grownups is again determined by a utilitarian purpose, duty, or role. The introjection of such adults eventually fails to
provide what the child needs and may end by confusing him (how can
he satisfy all the adults?) and increasing his burden and feeling of guilt.

Predepressive Personality

The personality of the patient who develops an affective disorder is partially determined by one of the three main inner constructs and related
patterns of living described in the previous section, and also by what
has been accrued or brought about with these patterns. Even after a
pattern has become prevalent, the individual is capable of dealing with
the environment in a relatively large variety of ways. However, a certain
rigidity of personality can be detected, and his future actions are more
easily predicted. Finally the prevailing pattern becomes almost exclusively used.

First I will describe the personality of patients who have tried to adapt
to their initial traumatic environment by adopting a pattern of placation.
The first question which comes to mind is whether this type of personality corresponds to types already described in the psychiatric literature—
for instance, to the compliant or moving-toward-people personality described by Karen Horney (1945, 1950).

This type of personality certainly has some characteristics in common
with Horney's compliant personality, and perhaps it is a special variety
of it. However, it has some characteristics of its own. Horney's compliant person manifests this attitude toward life in general and in many
interpersonal exchanges, but the future severely depressed patient is
more restrictive or discriminating. His placating attitude is manifested
not toward life in general, but exclusively or at least in much more accentuated forms toward a person, the parents, or an institution. He generally

converges the majority of his dealings on a person or institution. However, if we take into consideration a large number of these people, we find in them strong feelings of patriotism, religiosity, and loyalty to a political party or to their family. These people often wish to have a military or an ecclesiastic career. These institutions and organizations are unconsciously or subconsciously experienced as parents to be placated.

Group loyalty and *esprit de corps* play an important part in the psychological constellation of this personality type. Under the pretense of belonging to a group, a close-knit family, or an organization, the individual hides his loneliness.

In many cases we find a self-conscious individual, always motivated by duty, with the type of personality Riesman et al. (1950) called inner-directed. Often this devotion to duty assumes the form of devotion to order. Abraham (1924) described the rigid need for order, cleanliness, and stubborness of the predepressed person. He mentions also his perseverence and solidity.

Shimoda (1961), a Japanese author who has studied depression deeply, refers to the tendency of the predepressed to certain thoughts and feelings. These persons appear to Shimoda to have integrity and to inspire a feeling of reliance.

Tellenbach (1974), a German author who has studied melancholia from different angles, also describes how the predepressed person craves order, cleanliness, and regularity. He expects a great deal from himself and tries to do even more. Tellenbach reports accurate clinical descriptions of patients who throughout their lives were ruled by this need to search for order and regularity, and to work as much as possible. Tellenbach does not try to explain, however, how this tendency originated.

According to my own experience, this type of predepressed person occasionally succeeds in overcoming some of his difficulties. He may even be able to channel them in original ways and become creative in special fields; but if he does not overcome his difficulties and spends all his energies to placate others, he does not unfold his creative possibilities and remains an imitator. However, what he tries to do, he does well. He has deep convictions and his life is motivated by principles. He must be a dedicated person. He is generally efficient and people who do not know him well have the impression that he is a well-adjusted, untroubled individual.

On the contrary, he is not a happy man.* He selects a mate not because he loves her, but because she "needs" him. He will never divorce the

* As is customary in English, I refer to the general patient as *he* and consider him in his male role. However, as I shall mention later in this chapter, women with this type of personality are more numerous than men. In some special situations which are described later, in which women outnumber men by far—at least in the ratio of two to one—I shall refer to the patient by using the feminine gender.

mate because she is in terrible need of him. At the same time he blames himself for being so egotistical as to think that he is indispensable. The necessity to please others and to act in accordance with their expectations, or in accordance with the principles that he has accepted, makes him unable to get really in touch with himself. He does not listen to his own wishes; he does not know what it means to be himself. He works incessantly and yet has feelings of futility and emptiness. At times he conceals his unhappiness by considering what he has accomplished, just as he conceals his loneliness by thinking of the group to which he belongs. But when he allows himself to experience these feelings of unhappiness, futility, and unfulfillment, he misinterprets them again. He tends to believe that he is to be blamed for them. If he is unhappy or finds no purpose in life, it must be his fault, or he must not be worthy of anything else. A vicious circle is established which repeats itself and increases in intensity, often throughout the life of the patient, unless fortunate circumstances or psychotherapy intervene. Thus the inner construct that was described in the previous section becomes more entrenched and more and more acquires the originally conceptualized feelings of duty and guilt.

The patient often has partial insight into his own mechanisms but he does not know how to solve them. For instance, he is willing to accept the role in the family and in society which has been assigned to him, and yet later he scolds himself for playing this role, for not being spontaneous. But if he tries to refuse the role, he has guilt feelings. His conclusion is that no matter how he tries to solve his problems, he will feel he has made the wrong choice. A patient told me that she "felt like a little girl who pretends to be grown-up but is not. I am acting." But she must live in that way; that was her duty. It was her fault that she "acted" and did not accept social behavior as being spontaneous or real-life.

The patient also tends to put his superiors or teachers in a parental, authoritarian role. Quite often he feels angry at them as they seem to expect too much, or because they themselves have been found to be at fault. The patient does not know how to act: Should he continue to accept the authority of these people and the burden that acceptance implies, or should he remove them from the pedestal? But if he removes them, there will be a void. His authorities are part of him, his values, and the symbolic world upon which he sustains himself, and to do without them is impossible. Furthermore, he would feel very guilty. The patient often realizes (as Cohen and his co-workers illustrated, 1954) that he tends to underestimate himself. It is his duty to undersell himself. On the other hand, he tends to blame himself for underestimating himself and giving himself no chance to develop his own talents and potential abilities. The patient is becoming more rigid: what used to be a defense, or a practical way to get along sufficiently well with people in everyday living, becomes a character armor. At times the rigidity of thinking and acting slips into obsessive-compulsive symptoms. Some patients are often diagnosed, with with some justification, as obsessive-compulsive.

In spite of the characteristics so far described, in many cases the patient succeeds in giving the impression that he is able to live independently or be really involved in his work. In many cases, however, he eventually becomes anchored to a person whom he needs to please, follow, and receive approval from. At this point we recognize that the equilibrium he has been able to maintain is precarious and sustained mainly or exclusively in relation to the person whom he must please. This person is no longer the significant other; at this point he is what I have called the *dominant other* (Arieti, 1962). The relation between the patient and the dominant other is not just one of submission on the part of the patient and domination on the part of the other. With this attitude are feelings of affection, attachment, love, friendship, respect, and dependency, so that the relationship is a very complicated one. The dominant other is experienced by the patient not only as a person who demands a great deal, but also as a person who gives a great deal. And as a matter of fact, he either does give a great deal or is put by the patient into a giving role. The patient can no longer accept himself unless the dominant other accepts him, and he is unable to praise himself unless the dominant other praises him or is interpreted by the patient as praising him. As Bemporad wrote (1970), the patient is incapable of autonomous gratification. The fundamental characteristics in the relationship are the inequality in the two roles and the fact that the patient is so anchored to the dominant other that he cannot establish a deep or complete relation to any other person. Although this state of affairs was tolerable when the significant other was the mother and the patient was the child, it is no longer so and becomes maladaptive. The same construct that was applied to the childhood situation is used, and in some respects it has become more inflexible than it was then.

The dominant other provides the patient with the evidence, either real or illusory—or at least the hope—that acceptance, love, respect, and recognition of his human worth and meaning of his life are acknowledged by at least one other person. The dominant other is represented most often by the spouse. In the predominantly patriarchal structure of our society the dominant other is often the male and the submissive partner is the female. We shall return to this aspect of the problem in greater detail later.

Far less often in the role of the dominant other are, in order of frequency, the mother, a person to whom the patient was romantically attached, an adult child, a sister, the father. The dominant other also frequently is represented, through anthropopathy, by the firm where the patient works or a social institution to which he belongs such as the church, a political party, the army, a club, and so forth. All these dominant others are symbolic of the depriving mother, or to be more accurate, of the once-giving and later depriving mother. If the real mother is still living and is the dominant other, she acts in two ways; her role is actual in the present and also symbolic of her old role. If the dominant other dies, he becomes even more powerful through the meanings attached to his death.

The second type of predepressed person, who is characterized by the pursuit of a significant goal, gradually becomes haunted by a dominant goal. The dominant goal is omnipresent, always lurking about; it determines most actions of the patient and excludes many others. The goal as a rule is grandiose, like winning the Nobel prize or becoming the chief of the firm, and the actions of the patient can be interpreted as being motivated by the attempt to attain what his grandiose self-image demands. However, I do not believe that the dominant goal is exactly the same as the grandiose image described by Karen Horney (1945). Again, perhaps it is a variety of her concept, the variety which occurs in people prone to develop a severe depression.

The dominant goal is conscious, although the patient is not aware of the magnitude of its role and all its ramifications. The dominant goal seems more plausible and more realistic than Horney's idealized image: some people do reach their dominant goal. The patient certainly works hard and does his best to reach it. Although he is a daydreamer, his investment in achievement is used not only in daydreaming, but in acting as efficiently as he can. He does not postpone. The attainment of the dominant goal seems to be motivated by a thirst for glory. In most cases, however, it is more than that; it is a search for love. Unconsciously the patient feels that he will be worthy of love from others or from himself only if he succeeds in achieving the dominant goal. Often at a conscious level too, the search for the dominant goal coincides with the search for a perfect love.

Not so subtle as in the other types of predepressed personality is a relationship of dependency in which the mechanism of obviously leaning on mother and maternal substitutes has been adopted after the initial trauma in childhood. Contrary to the types previously described, this third type includes people who even at a superficial examination appear maladjusted. These patients have never forgotten the bliss of their first year of life and still expect or demand a continuation of it. They demand and expect gratification from others, and feel deprived and sad when they do not get what they expect. They are demanding but not aggressive in the usual sense of the word, because they do not try to get what they want through their own efforts: they expect it from others. They have not developed that complex of duty and hard work typical of the complying, introjecting patient.

These patients alternate between feeling guilty and having the desire to make other people feel guilty. They generally find one person on whom to depend, and they make this other person feel guilty if he does not do what they want. The sustaining person (generally the spouse) is empowered with the capacity to make the patient happy or unhappy and is supposed to be responsible for the patient's despair and helplessness. He also plays a dominant role in the life of the patient, but only because the patient expects a great deal from him, not because he makes demands on the patient. Relatively often in this group we find women who depend entirely on their husbands, who are generally much older. In these cases the dominant other is not only the person who is supposed to accept, love, respect the patient, but also the person who protects and gives material things. At times the request is immense: the patient almost seems to request, metaphorically, milk or blood.

In some cases there is an apparent variation in the picture when the patient tries desperately to submerge himself in work and activities, hoping that eventually he will find something to do which will make him worthy of recognition from other people. Whereas the first two types of predepressed persons looked inward for a solution to their conflicts, the third type looks externally for the solution.

A fourth type is observed in some patients who develop manic-depressive psychosis. It is manifested either as the prevailing type of personality or as a temporary characterological structure which from time to time replaces one of the three pictures previously described. This fourth type, the forerunner of the manic, is lively, active, hearty, and friendly. On closer scrutiny the person's apparent health and liveliness are found to be superficial. In a certain way the patient actually escapes into actions or reality, but he remains shallow and dissatisfied. If he happens to be engaged in work in which action is required rather than concentration, he may do well and maintain a satisfactory level of adjustment; otherwise he may sooner or later get into trouble. He claims that he has many friends and the interpersonal relations seem warm and sincere, but they are superficial and lack real kinship. One patient said, "I joke, I laugh, I pretend; I appear radiant and alive, but deep down I am lonely and empty." This type of person is only in certain respects the opposite of the duty-bound individual. He tries to escape from his inner-directedness, but he does not correspond to what Riesman called the "other directed" person. Imitating Riesman's terminology, we could call this hypomaniclike person outer-directed but not other-directed. He does not escape into others; he escapes from his inner self, because the inner self has incorporated the burdening others. He escapes into the world of superficial reality where meditations, reflections, or deep emotions are unnecessary. His main attitude can be interpreted as a great denial of everything which, if admitted, could lead to depression.

Such an individual may at times seem so free as to be considered psychopathic. Actually, it is his deep concern with conventional morality that often leads to this pseudopsychopathic escape. Some of the pseudopsychopathic hypomanics have demonstrated asocial behavior since childhood when, for example, in order to escape from inner and external restrictions, they ran away from home or school.

These affective, prepsychotic personality types are seldom seen in pure culture. When the patient changes or alternates from one of the first three types of personality to the fourth, he presents the so-called cyclothymic personality.

The Development of the Severe Attack

The types of personality described in the previous section lead not to a stable equilibrium, but to an almost constant state of dissatisfaction and sadness (or, in some cases, hypomanic denial of sadness). If we closely examine the period of time that precedes the depression—and this period may vary from a few days or months to decades—we see a crescendo of maladjustment which is contained only by the defenses that have been described. In this unstable background, obvious and realistic factors often bring about a full-fledged attack of severe depression. These specific precipitating factors are distinct events in the life of the patient, and are not necessary in any absolute sense. However, since they occur in the most typical cases and clarify the psychodynamics of severe depression in general, I shall discuss their occurrence and import. Later we will examine the cases in which precipitating factors cannot be individuated.

The main precipitating situations may be classified into three categories: (1) the patient's realization that his relationship with the dominant other has failed; (2) the death of the dominant other; and (3) the patient's realization of having failed in his attempt to reach a dominant goal, and his subsequent negative reevaluation of the self-image.

These situations are considered separately for didactic reasons, but they have a single and common basis: the loss of something very valuable. This "something," even if represented by a concrete situation, transcends the reality of the concrete situation. At times the loss has not yet occurred, but the knowledge that it is impending seems so certain to the patient that he experiences depression instead of anxiety. The precipitating event causes a great deal of anguish or psychological pain, which is felt very intensely for these reasons:

1. The patient's cognitive appraisal of the event leads him to realize that it will cause a disorganization of his life structure and self-image.
2. His main cognitive construct and pattern of living will no longer enable him to cope with the situation. This realization reevokes what can be

pictured as a distant but resounding echo of the pain sustained early in life, when the patient felt he had lost the love of his mother or the mother substitute. The present loss has the same value as the loss of the mother's love.

3. The patient realizes that all the methods which he used to prevent the catastrophe have failed.

4. He also believes that the methods he used were the only ones he could use or knew how to use. Thus he finds himself in a situation of helplessness. He cannot put into practice the methods used by the normal person recovering from normal sadness. For the patient, using alternative courses is an impossibility. Thus he cannot do sorrow work.

5. Instead, his sadness becomes depression, which continues to increase in intensity.

The development of these psychological events will be described in greater detail in the following sections.

DEPRESSION FOLLOWING DETERIORATION OF THE MAIN INTERPERSONAL RELATION

The situation in which the patient realizes the failure of his main interpersonal relation (the relation with the dominant other) is in my opinion the most typical of those which lead to severe depression. Thus it will be described in detail, the other situations, which will be examined later in this chapter, will be described only or predominantly in those aspects which differ from the situation we are now examining. Depression following deterioration of the main interpersonal relation occurs much more often in women, so I shall refer to the patient in the feminine gender. It is to be understood that the same situation takes place in a considerable number of male patients.

Events that have drastically affected the life of the patient may have occurred recently. The husband may have asked for a divorce, or may have been discovered as having an extramarital affair. Often, however, a few disparate happenings, certain decisions which have been made, or a review of one's life have induced the patient to reexamine her marital situation. At times the effect of the precipitating event was unforeseeable: reading a book, or seeing a play or a movie which revealed itself full of psychological significance for the patient. The marital partner—whom the patient considered a protector, a pillar on whom she depended entirely, a distributor of love, sex, affect, approval, food, and money—is now seen as an authoritarian person who imposes his rule at times in a subtle, hardly recognizable fashion, at other times in an obvious way. The patient's life, believed to be devoted to affection, family care, doing hard work, or the nourishment and reaffirmation of love, is now seen as a nongenuine life. The patient has denied many aspects of living because she wanted peace and approval at any cost. She has been excessively compliant, submissive, and accommodating. By always doing what the husband wanted and by denying her wishes, she has not been true to herself; as a matter of fact, she has betrayed herself. In some cases the patient may exaggerate and see the authoritarian husband as a tyrant, somebody who deserves not love but hate, somebody who wants to enslave her and change her real nature. In most cases she does not realize that she also has played a role in establishing this type of interpersonal relation. She has done so with her submissiveness and ingratiating attitude, by accepting the patriarchal model of society, or by making the dominant other believe that she was perfectly contented or even happy with this state of living. She has indeed submitted herself, bent her head, and allowed herself to be transformed against her real wishes. There is nothing wrong, of course, in adopting the husband's ways of living if the wife really wishes to do so or because she genuinely believes they are better or more adequate than her own. But if she accepts them only to placate the spouse, and if she deceives herself into thinking that she likes these changes in her way of living when she really does not, she injures herself.

The new evaluation of her husband—the kind of dominating person he really is—is not easily accepted. A normal person would accept the new appraisal, no matter how painful it was, and try to do her best with what remained of her life (separation, divorce, other affections.) But the patient cannot. She cannot bring herself to conclude that she has wasted her life. She still needs the same dominant other to praise her, approve of her, and make her feel worthwhile. How could he continue to play that role if she expressed hate, rebellion, or in some cases even self-assertion?

Thus the patient finds herself in a situation in which she cannot change her cognitive structures. She has reached a critical point at which a realignment of psychodynamic forces and a new pattern of interpersonal relationships are due, but she is not able to implement them; and this is her predicament. Often she denies her negative appraisal of the dominant other and of her life—that is, she represses her ideas—but the feeling of sadness remains conscious and is intensely experienced. Inasmuch as she cannot organize alternative structures, such as new plans for her life and new ways of evaluating herself as a person, she feels helpless. She cannot do what normal people resort to in order to solve their sorrow.

The anguish is experienced and retained, and as a rule becomes more and more pronounced. The sorrow is replaced by an overpowering wave of depression which submerges every idea. A few very painful thoughts remain. Eventually almost all ideas become unconscious and the patient is only aware of an overpowering feeling of depression. The slowing down of thought processes is also responsible for the decrease in mobility that the patient shows at this point. Movements and actions, in order to be implemented, must be preceded by ideomotor activity which is now greatly decreased. The slowing down of thought processes is, however, a self-defeating mechanism. At this point, constellations of thought continue to activate the depression even if they are unconscious. If we ask the patient why she is depressed, often she does not know.

At times a few thoughts remain as conscious, cognitive islands in the ocean of the depressive feeling. The patient may feel very guilty. The guilt is caused by emerging thoughts that offer a new evaluation of the dominant other. The patient feels guilty for seeing him in so bad a light when she used to see him as a saint to be revered and respected. In her depressed condition, she is generally not able to trace the guilt feeling; she just feels guilty and may give absurd explanations for her guilt. She has done "terrible things," and so forth. In many instances hate for the husband is not repressed to such a degree that the patient cannot feel guilty about it. On the other hand, if she were able to deal with this hate at a fully conscious level, she would be able to change the situation less inadequately. As a matter of fact, she could even realize in certain cases that her hate was too strong a feeling, and not congruous with the circumstances. But she cannot face what she believes would undermine the foundation of her life and prove the futility of all her past efforts. Thus she represses her hate and she continues to follow a pattern of silent submission. Even when she was not so sick, she did not reveal or admit to her friends the hostile feelings for her husband.

The guilt feeling to which we have referred often assumes such a predominant role as to confer to the symptomatology the picture of self-blaming depression, the manifest aspect of which was described in chapter 3. Special characteristics of the environment either facilitate or make less probable the occurrence of guilt feelings, as will be described in chapter 16. The self-blaming picture is much less frequent now than it was until the middle 1940s. Nevertheless, even at present this picture is observed quite frequently.

The guilt feelings continue in these patients a trend started in childhood, that no matter how much the patient does to remedy the situation, it is not enough. Later she feel that it is her fault that the relationship with the dominant other has not worked out. Finally, she feels guilty, as has been described, for feeling in such a negative way toward her husband. When the patient reaches the state of severe despair and blames herself, suicidal ideas occur with progressive frequency.

The number of suicidal patients is greater in men. Thus I shall refer again to the patient in the male gender.

The patient who blames himself seems to send a message: "I do not deserve any pity, any help. I deserve to die. I should do to myself what you should do to me, but you are too good to do it."

As the suicidal ideas recur, the patient may make a suicidal attempt which in a considerable percentage of cases is successful.

At this point we must try to understand the significance of the suicidal attempt. Several hypotheses have been advanced.

1. The patient wants to punish himself.
2. He wants relief from suffering or an end to a worthless life.
3. He wants to kill symbolically the dominant other.
4. The suicide has no meaning. It is just an indication of the worsening of the biochemical alteration which brought about the depression.

In accordance with the general character of this book, we shall consider only 1, 2, and 3. The first two possibilities are self-contradictory or self-exclusive until seen from the standpoint of the emotional state of the patient. The feeling that it is better to die than to suffer so much is certainly experienced. The patient would not carry out the suicidal ideas, however, if they were not reinforced or sustained by the other idea that he deserves to die and he must inflict the supreme punishment on himself. In some cases it is possible to retrace in the patient who has attempted suicide the notion that he was making a desperate effort to redeem himself by punishing himself. Probably in a subconscious, non-verbalized way the patient feels, "Punish yourself and you will be accepted again. You are acceptable but not accepted. Forgiveness is eventually available. The intermittent love will be given again." Of course, if the patient is dead he cannot receive love, but this is a realistic consideration which he cannot conceive of at the present time. Or perhaps he believes that he will be forgiven and loved in the memory of the survivors. Thus two or more logically self-contradictory motivations coexist and reinforce one another.

The orthodox Freudian interpretation holds that suicide represents the attempt to kill the detested person who has been incorporated—in the terminology used here, the dominant other.

As I mentioned in a previous section, the individual who is prone to this type of psychotic depression has totally accepted the Thou since his early infancy. At times he lets the Thou suffocate or smother the I. In this light, the suicidal attempt is the culmination of the process; it is the Thou who finally kills the I, not the I who kills the Thou. If the I killed the Thou, there would be a complete and sudden reversal of the previous and constant trend of self-denial. Rado (1951) ingeniously tried to solve the problem by assuming that the superego (the Thou) is divided into two parts, one which the patient wants to love and another which he wants to kill. However, I am convinced that, at least in my clinical experience, the patient really wanted to kill himself. But by killing himself he would achieve a complete acceptance or introjection of a distorted image of the Thou.

There are several other factors that support this point of view. First, many cases of suicide seem to occur not when the state of melancholia is at its peak but at an early stage of remission, when the worst is over.

This characteristic may of course be interpreted in various ways. The first explanation is simple and mechanical: when the patient is very depressed, he is in or almost in a stupor; he cannot act, he is extremely slow or immobile, he cannot move or think coordinatedly, and therefore he cannot carry out his intentions. When he becomes less retarded and more capable of coordinating his thoughts, he goes ahead with his destructive intention. The alternative possibility is that the patient who has gone through terrible experiences at the acme of his depression is afraid that these experiences may recur and, rather than face them again, he prefers to die. (This of course corresponds to the first possibility mentioned.)

Another interpretation is possible: the patient who has a great deal of guilt feels that even the most severe depth of depression has not been enough; it has not succeeded in relieving him entirely of his guilt, and only by killing himself will he entirely redeem himself.

This last interpretation is supported by other factors. Significantly, there is almost complete relief after the suicide attempt. The Freudian interpretation would lead one to expect an increase in guilt feeling (for having attempted but not actually succeeded in killing the superego) and a consequent increase in depression. As Weiss (1957, 1974) and others have emphasized, in the attempt itself—that is, in gambling with death—the patient feels that he has been punished adequately. He has done what the Thou wanted and now he can live peacefully. Often there is no need for the suicide attempt; after having gone through the acme of his depression, the patient feels suddenly relieved, and a marked improvement occurs.

According to Kolb (1959), "The suicidal maneuver is often determined by family-indicated permission for acting out." In his clinical experience, the psychodynamic explanation of acting out which has been given for other antisocial acts is also valid for suicide: in families where suicide has occurred, the likelihood of suicide for the manic-depressive patient is much higher than otherwise. Where suicide has not occurred, one usually finds threats of suicide or intimidating actions suggesting suicide on the part of the parents.

Through many years of practice I have found, however, an increasing number of patients who did not feel guilty and yet had decided to put an end to their "worthless" lives. In several cases there was a confusion about whether the patient considered life, at least his own, or himself to be worthless. The only certainty was the horrible mental pain which had to be terminated at any cost.

The relief experienced by the patient after an acute attack of depression is remarkable. The patient feels guilt-free and accepted, and wants to settle down in his own life. Even reality seems pleasant, and he does not want to be alone; he wants to be close to the mate. This attempt, however, will not work out unless successful therapy intervenes. The patient who improves after the nadir of depression, whether or not this nadir led to a suicidal attempt, eventually will feel depressed again. The relatively free interval may last a few hours, days, weeks, months, or longer.

The improvement or depression-free interval is susceptible to several hypothetical interpretations. One is that the patient feels he has expiated his guilt. However, another one seems to me more plausible and consonant with what several patients in psychotherapy have told me. An idea presents itself which somehow succeeds in cutting the main line of depressogenic cognition and flashing a lesser, more hopeful, but secondary cognitive structure. This lesser structure may have always existed or, more seldom, have been provided by an unexpected external event. The secondary cognitive structure in some cases may be organized and increased to the point of offering considerable relief. In many cases, however, the predominant depressogenic structure tends to acquire the upper hand and the patient becomes depressed again.

In some untreated cases the depression may become chronic and severe; in others it remains chronic but less severe; and finally, it may alternate between being severe and mild. At the present stage of knowledge we cannot be absolutely sure why some untreated cases of severe depression become intermittent, improve, or even recover. For some unpredictable reasons they eventually become capable of escaping from the rigid cognitive construct and finding alternative patterns.

Some patients, especially those who could be classified as suffering from manic-depressive psychosis, are able to change the depression into a manic, hypomanic, or mini-manic attack.

In the manic attack the Thou is not eliminated or projected to the external world; it is only disregarded. The patient must continue to force himself into a distracted and frenzied mood which shuts out not only introspection, but any well-organized thinking. In the manic state there is no elimination of the Freudian superego, as perhaps there is in some psychopaths. The superego is very much present, and the manic frenzy is a method of dealing with it.

But neither the depression nor the manic attack actually bring about a solution to the deeply rooted conflicts. Even after having paid the penalty of the severe attack, many patients (but not all) will have a more or less free interval and then tend to be affected again by the same difficulty, which will be channeled into the same pattern—with the cycle likely to repeat itself. Moreover we must realize that this type of depression, as well as all the others that shall be discussed in this book, becomes the fundamental and habitual mode of living. As we shall discuss later, the patient selects depressive thoughts (Beck's depressive triad) to sustain the familiar mood. Little disappointments, losses, or accidental happenings that lead the patient to self-accusation, guilt, or severe depression are actually symbolic of an earlier and greater disappointment, or of lifelong disappointment. Kraepelin (1921), to show the relative unimportance of psychogenic factors, reported a woman who had three attacks of depression: the first after the death of her husband, the second after the death of her dog, and the third after the death of her dove. From what has been discussed so far, it is apparent that each of these deaths was not necessarily traumatic per se. One may guess that the death of the dove reactivated the sorrow the patient had experienced at the previous deaths, and it was also symbolic of a much greater loss, perhaps of the meaning or purpose in her life.

So far I have interpreted psychodynamically attacks of severe depression caused by the realization of the failure of an important interpersonal relation, as in the case of a patient who follows a pattern of submission and placation in her relation with a dominant other. The patient who instead follows a pattern of dependency and eventually develops a symptomatology of the claiming type, at a certain point in her life realizes that she no longer can depend on this interpersonal relationship. Without being aware of it, to a considerable extent she still is claiming the lost paradise or the bliss of the early life when she was completely dependent on the duty-bound mother or mother substitute. As the patient makes herself dependent on the dominant other and becomes more demanding, she feels more deprived. Any unfulfilled demand is experienced as a wound, a serious deprivation, an insult, or an irreparable loss, and it brings about an unpleasant feeling of sadness which cannot be solved and is followed by depression.

The new way of experiencing the relationship with the dominant other is based on the fact that the affect or love which reassured her and in whose name she expected a great deal is now recognized as uncertain, insincere, unreliable, about to finish, or finished already. She too does not love the husband anymore, and therefore she feels she cannot expect much from him. The sad reality, however, is that she depends on him psychologically, economically, and socially, and she cannot do without him. Like the previous type of patient that I described, she finds herself in a trap from which she cannot escape. She becomes more and more depressed and suicidal. In these cases the suicide attempt seems to convey the message, "Do not abandon me. You have the power to prevent my death. You will feel guilty if you don't give me what I need and let me die." However, there is a feeling of hopelessness, the feeling that the dominant other will not listen to this appeal and will let her down. For a certain number of patients in this category the dominant other is not the spouse, but one or both parents. Many patients have always remained dependent on their parents. Although they would like to be free of them to go on their own, be self-supporting, and get married, they cannot. They are caught again in a vicious cycle from which they cannot escape (dependency and resentment or hate for the persons on whom they depend). Perhaps more than any other patients, they represent those described by Abraham who, as a consequence of early love deprivation, remain fixated at oral erotism and maintain a general dependency on people.

DEPRESSION FOLLOWING DEATH, LOSS, OR
DISAPPEARANCE OF THE DOMINANT OTHER

In these cases depression occurs when the dominant other is no longer available. The most common cause is death. Cases involving divorce will not be considered here because the separation was caused by a failure of the interpersonal relation, and these cases are therefore included in the previously described category. However, some cases in which one spouse suddenly abandons the other, gives ultimatums, or unexpectedly declares his intention to dissolve the marriage may represent a mixture of the two categories.

Less common precipitating factors of severe depression are loss of friendship, companionship, affection, or approval because a person close to the patient moved away or got married and had to exclude the patient or relegate him to a minor role.

Contrary to the typical cases in the first category, the patient at a conscious level does not feel abandoned by the dominant other on account of failure in the relationship; rather, it is because of circumstances beyond his control such as death or moving to a distant location for reasons of work. Whether the patient considers these causes legitimate is debatable: in most cases there is no doubt that at least unconsciously the patient considers the dominant other responsible for leaving, even if he left because he died. He should not have allowed himself to die. There is also no doubt that some patients feel, even at a conscious level, responsible for the disappearance or death of the dominant other. If they had treated him better, he would not have died. Instead the bad behavior of the patient has made the dominant other unhappy and sick or more likely to die. Thus the patient has "killed" him or her.

In other cases the patient feels guilty because in moments of reemerging resentment he recognizes that he wished the death of the lost person. The wish has now become reality: to the wish is attributed the primitive power of engendering reality. The patient accuses himself of having entertained the murderous desire.

All these interpretations connected with guilt are derivatives of Freud's concept that guilt and self-depreciation are diverted anger which was directed originally toward the love object (our dominant other). As I have already mentioned, however, guilt does not seem to play such an important role as it did once. Perhaps it will reacquire importance in the future.

Bemporad (1970) has advanced another explanation. The patient, who was totally dependent on the dominant other for self-esteem, acceptance, approval, and appreciation, realizes that he cannot depend on him any more. And yet he is incapable of "autonomous gratification," of supplying what he needs to himself. He becomes sad and then depressed because of being deprived of this gratification. In other words, the depression is the result of deprivation (emotional and cognitive). Bemporad's interpretation is valid in some cases of severe depression, as well, but with support from other factors that complicate the picture. First, I must stress that for the reasons illustrated earlier in this chapter, the patient is incapable of finding cognitive-affective alternatives to what was provided by the former dominant other. Second, the patient does not want to believe that the dominant other could be substituted. He rejects the possibility because to admit it would be tantamount to conceding that the dominant other was not indispensable in the first place. This conclusion, if accepted, would require a reassessment of the patient's whole life and might induce a state of panic that the patient cannot even contemplate. Thus he is still motivated to think that the dominant other was indispensable and irreplaceable. Whenever reality indicates the opposite—that life can be worthwhile even without the dominant other —such possibility is assessed in a distorted way, appears threatening, and may bring about further depression.

DEPRESSION FOLLOWING REALIZATION OF FAILING
TO REACH THE DOMINANT GOAL

This type of depression occurs among men more frequently than depressions which follow other patterns, but in terms of absolute incidence this depression too is more frequent among women. The goal most frequently experienced by women as not achieved or not-to-be-achieved is romantic love. Being unloved for them means being unlovable. Thus what is disturbing is not only the lack of the joy of love, but the injury to the self-image. However, the cultural and social changes which are rapidly taking place in the status of women have already diminished the frequency of unachieved love as the precipitating factor of severe depression. To be exact, love does remain an important precipitating factor when it is lost, as described in the previous category. It is less frequently the precipitating factor of severe depression in the role of a dominant goal which has not been achieved.

In men the dominant goal which most frequently precipitates a severe depression, because it is experienced as not achieved or not to be achieved, has to do with work and career. Here too, the most traumatic part of this realization is in what it does to the self-image. Certainly the patient is very interested in his career and work, but the depressive elements are his cognitive ramifications—mostly unconscious or only dimly conscious—that associate work and career with what he and others think of him, and with his being a worthwhile person and deserving love. Now he has come to the realization that he is not going to be a great lawyer, doctor, politician, actor, writer, lover, industrialist, inventor, musician, and so forth. He cannot go into another field or give up his ambition because his whole life has been centered on the achievement of this particular goal. Nothing else counts: after this dramatic realization, life seems worthless to him; as a matter of fact, it seems painful and hard to endure.

If he wanted to be a great conductor—a Toscanini—now he has to face the fact that he is not a Toscanini; he is himself, John Doe. But he has no respect for John Doe, and he believes John Doe is nothing. There is some justification in the patient's assessment of himself in this negative way because he spent so much of his thoughts and daydreams in being a Toscanini, and his psychological life without this overpowering fantasy seems empty. Thus we must realize that the depression is not only a mourning of a fantasy; it is the mourning of a large part of one's life spent at the service of a fantasy. This explains why the depression can reach such depth and be so persistent.

This sequence of thought processes and accompanying negative feelings is made possible by the limitations of the patient, by his inability to find solutions. At times the patient may visualize alternatives, but they seem to him either unsurmountable or not worthwhile. The inability to shift to different ways of living is not due to congenital defect or to lack of intelligence, but is only the result of a life history characterized by rigid adherence to those life patterns that were described earlier in this chapter. This inability of which the patient is often unconscious can be overcome totally or to a large extent by proper psychotherapy.

In some cases the psychodynamic picture is more complicated. The patient feels that he has not been true to himself, or he has not run after the goal in the right way. For instance, he wanted to be a great conductor like Toscanini, but instead he pursued business, money, women, and so on. Now he finds himself trapped: his sadness has become a severe depression from which he does not know how to rescue himself.

SPECIAL CASES AND CONCLUSIONS

Cases that do not fit exactly into the previously mentioned categories but which partake of some of their characteristics are very frequent. I shall mention the most common combinations. The depression may occur after the patient has been dismissed from an institution, organization, or company to which he devoted the prime of his life. This disappointment is often experienced as due to the loss of employment. As a matter of fact, Malzberg (1940) found that during the economic depression of 1929 to 1937 the effect of loss of employment or financial loss was statistically evident in manic-depressive patients. In 1933, for instance, 26.2 percent of first admission patients in New York state hospitals who were diagnosed as manic-depressive presented loss of employment or financial loss as the precipitating factor, whereas in the same year only 9.6 percent of first admission patients with the diagnosis of dementia praecox (schizophrenia) presented financial loss as a precipitating factor.

In some cases, not dismissal but failure to obtain a promotion is the precipitating factor. In these cases the trauma is sustained partially as a loss of a nonpersonal dominant other, and partially as failure to reach or retain the dominant goal. The source of gratification is lost as well as a gratifying self-image that the patient could maintain only through his association with that particular organization.

Depression, often leading to suicide, occurs quite frequently in unmarried men after retirement. They feel suddenly deprived of their only aspect of gratification. In women, depressions occur frequently, but not as frequently as they used to, during or about the time of the menopause, as we shall see in greater detail in chapter 12.

Depressions occur relatively frequently in twins, especially female identical twins. Although my statistics are very limited, I can say that I have found nothing specific in these cases except the psychological picture derived from being a twin. Generally one of the twins assumes the role of the dominant other and the other takes on the submissive or dependent role. The dominant other plays the role of leader, teacher, and mentor; the submissive twin plays the role of the follower, pupil, and child. In these cases the parents have played a secondary role because of their advanced age, detachment, illness, or geographical distance; and they have always remained pale figures, thus permitting one twin to acquire a parental or dominant role. When the dominant twin withdraws his support, or gets married, or separates from the submissive twin, the latter undergoes a severe trauma, experiences a feeling of helplessness, and often becomes depressed.

Less typical but more frequent, especially among females, are cases in which two siblings, not twins but close in age, live in the same dyad of dominant-dominated. In these cases the parents also have played a parental role which has been less effective than usual and which has been assumed in quite an inappropriate manner by the dominant sibling. The submissive sibling tends to become depressed whenever there is a disruption in his relation with the dominant sibling or whenever he has to revise the image of the sibling which he has incorporated.

In some patients an attack apparently is precipitated not by a loss, but by what may even seem a pleasant event. For instance, women in their forties or fifties who may have undergone previous subliminal attacks of depression can develop a severe attack shortly after the marriage of an only son or daughter. Here the event is experienced by the patient not as something pleasant but as a loss. The child whom the mother needed so much, and who was her only purpose and satisfaction in life, is now abandoning her.

In other cases an attack occurs after a promotion, which is interpreted by the patient as a new imposition that he is unable to cope with. The patient is tired of new duties and, furthermore, the new position with its added responsibility removes the security the patient had established with painstaking effort. In other cases the individual who is faced with promotion dreads the expected envy and rage of previous associates to whom he is closely bound. The expectation of such emotions in others separates him from them and thus leads to feelings of loneliness and depression. In all these cases there is difficulty in abandoning the old patterns of living which conferred security to the patient, and inability to find alternatives suitable to the new conditions.

If we now try to abstract from all the human conditions that we have described in this chapter what leads to a severe depression, we can say that it is the experience of a loss of what seems to the patient the most valuable or meaningful aspect of his life. Even more crucial is the feeling of being unable to retrieve or substitute what has been lost.

At times the severe sorrow of the depressed person acts also as a representation of what was lost, because as long as the sorrow remains, the loss is not complete. In these cases the sorrow is like the faint image of a lost hope, the shadow of the absent, the echo of a voice heard repeatedly—perhaps with ambiguous resonance, but also with some affection, respect, and love.

At other times, implicit in the experience of loss, is the feeling that life has become unworthy or meaningless. At still other times the patient realizes that the meaning he has given to his life is inappropriate or unworthy, but if he renounces that meaning his life sustains the greatest possible loss: it becomes meaningless. His pain bespeaks his refusal to see life in that way.

[7]

PSYCHODYNAMICS

OF MILD DEPRESSION

In contrast to the individuals described in the previous chapter, those to be considered in this chapter are not so impaired that the affect of depression overwhelms all other psychic contents. They actively want to be rid of their feelings of depression and try to fight them off. These patients attempt to reestablish the pathological equilibrium that they had achieved prior to being depressed. They do not collapse in the face of overwhelming despair so that their psychic life is devoid of all content except for the repetitive painful ruminations which enhance the misery of their affliction. These individuals, while depressed, manage to function in their everyday lives, albeit often in a reduced capacity. They are capable of reasoning and normal cognitive abilities, and an insight-oriented approach to therapy may rapidly be initiated. Some somatic symptoms such as anorexia or insomnia may be present but are not pronounced. Psychomotor retardation and constipation are not seen, but loss of libido is not uncommon. Most significant, perhaps, is that these less severely depressed individuals maintain their relationships to others: in fact, they may frantically search for comfort and support from other people. They do not withdraw from interpersonal relationships into a silent world of solitary suffering.

Such individuals are typified by the presence of the affect of depression which may be constant or fluctuate in intensity. As will be further discussed, this sense of mental anguish may take a variety of forms—from an agonizing awareness of loss to a despairing conclusion that life is pointless and lacks any form, purpose, or meaning. Regardless of the cognitive variations, the basic mood of depression is definitely present. Before proceeding with an analysis of such individuals, it may be worth-

This chapter was written by Jules Bemporad.

while to consider the conceptual status of depression as an affect as I view it, since this view naturally will influence the interpretation of depressed patients.

As described in chapter 2, the psychodynamic interpretation of depression has undergone numerous transformations in the history of psychoanalytic thought. Some authors have attempted to explain the experience of depression as a complex metapsychological phenomenon, such as an aggressive cathexis of the self-representation, or as a conflict between the punishing superego and the helpless ego.

Others have presented the less complicated position that depression is actually a primary affect that cannot further be reduced to more basic constructs. I definitely lean toward this latter conceptualization and agree with Sandler and Joffe's (1965) statement that "if depression is viewed as an affect, if we allot to it the same conceptual status as the affect of anxiety, then much of the literature on depression in childhood (and this could be extended to adults) can be integrated in a meaningful way" (p. 90).*

However, considering depression as a primary affect does not automatically imply that it is a simple emotion devoid of complex cognitive components. As indicated by Arieti in chapter 5, different emotions presuppose a greater or lesser cognitive maturity and intellectual understanding. Depression appears to be a third-order emotion necessitating some awareness of the past and the future, some linguistic ability, and some recognition of the effects of human beings on one another. This particular painful feeling automatically arises whenever the individual "senses" that he has either irrevocably lost or never will achieve a needed state of well-being of the self. I have put the word senses in quotes because this awareness is not necessarily explicit; rather, it is the unconscious cognitive system that seems to give rise to emotion. By unconscious cognitive system I mean a structure of aspirations, fears, and general expectations from the self and from others that guide the individual's behavior but of which he may not be explicitly aware. These systems of belief are postulated to be at a different level of consciousness than the superficial pessimistic distortions which occur subsequent to the onset of a depressive episode. These deeper cognitive systems are the cause rather than the result of the manifest experience of depression and are not so readily available to being clearly spelled out in conscious awareness.

---

* Some confirmatory evidence for considering depression (as a primary feeling state and not as a clinical syndrome) as a basic psychobiological response is that it can be produced by physiological means. Mild depressions can be observed following viral illnesses or in states of fatigue. Depression also can accompany hypothyrodism or pancreatic disease or be produced by drugs such as reserpine. All this seems to indicate that depression, while most frequently caused by psychological events, is closely tied to basic neurochemical alterations and thus appears to be a fundamental mode of reaction which is similiar to other emotions.

For example, an individual may become depressed after a loss but remain unclear as to the manner in which the loss has affected him. Similarly, other individuals may become depressed without any precipitating environmental trauma or without knowing why they should experience a sense of dysphoria at this particular time of their lives. Freud (1917) astutely noted this lack of awareness: he observed that even when the melancholic relates his plight as resulting from the loss of someone, "he knows whom he has lost but not *what* it is he has lost in them." What has been lost is an environmental prop that allowed the perpetuation of a needed state of self. The depressive does not appear to grieve for the other; rather, he grieves for himself—for being deprived of what the other had supplied. He grieves over his state of self without the other or without his all-important goal (as seen in so-called reactive depressions). Or the individual may grieve over a state of self that finds no meaning or gratification in life, unaware that his unconscious cognitive system has forced him to inhibit himself so that he shuns meaningful achievement or pleasurable activities (as seen in so-called characterological depressions).

The philosopher Kierkegaard was well aware that the true cause of despair is despair about one's own self, regardless of the apparently precipitating events. He wrote that "when the ambitious man whose watchword as 'either Caesar or nothing' does not become Caesar, he is in despair thereat. But this signifies something else, namely, that precisely because he did not become Caesar he cannot endure to be himself" (1954, p. 152). In describing depression resulting from an environmental loss, Kierkegaard observed:

A young girl is in despair over love and so she despairs over her lover, because he died, or because he was unfaithful to her . . . . No, she is in despair over herself. This self of hers, if it had become "his" beloved, she would have been rid of in the most blissful way, or would have lost, this self is now a torment to her when it has to be a self without "him" (1954, p. 153).

Kierkegaard beautifully and concisely revealed the self-centered aspect of depression as well as its cause that ultimately resides in the deprivation of something which is needed to transform the self and to give the self a sense of worth and well-being, whether this something is the achievement of an ambition, a continued relationship with a needed other, or the maintenance of a particular mode of life.

Therefore depression may be conceptualized as a complex emotion that arises when an individual is deprived (or deprives himself) of an element of life that is necessary for a satisfactory state of self. However, most if not all mature individuals experience such episodes of mental pain during their lives without becoming clinically depressed. Some marshall their inner resources and continue to press on for fulfillment with renewed hope. Others tolerate the shattering of their wished-for state of self and readjust their aspirations or seek other avenues of meaning. Still others do not give in to their depression but defend against it by various external or internal means: external defenses are usually drugs or alcohol, and internal means are commonly states of depersonalization or an obsession with hypocondriacal concerns. Many individuals, however, progress from the initial depressive psychobiological reaction as described by Sandler and Joffe (1965) to a true clinical depression. These individuals are predisposed to depressive attacks; that is, they have a particular premorbid personality which leaves them vulnerable to repeated bouts of depression. These pathological personality patterns are always present; so that depression has been described by some authors, such a Bonime (1962), as a practice, a way of life, rather than a periodic illness with healthy intervals. According to this view, Bonime has further implied that the predisposed individual decompensates when his maladaptive interpersonal transactions are no longer effective in bolstering a specious sense of self. This position can be widened to include the role of one's concept of self and others in the role of depression. When such a concept either obviates the possibility of meaning or is transformed by a loss or frustration so that meaning is no longer possible, depression ensues.

Types of Mild Depression

As previously indicated, mild (or dystonic) forms of depression may be classified into three major types: reactive, characterological, and masked. The symptoms of these varieties have been described in chapter 3. Here the discussion will focus on the underlying psychodynamics of these varieties first. The reactive and characterological depressions will be considered. The major clinical differentiation between these two types is that the former occurs after an identifiable and subjectively severe trauma in the individual's life and the latter is exhibited in a chronically ungratifying form of existence.

The reactive forms of depression have already been described in detail and their exposition will not be repeated here. The differences between individuals who develop a severe depression following the loss of a dominant other or frustration in the attainment of a dominant goal, and those who respond to such subjective traumas with only mild or moderate feelings of depression, may lie in the quality and relative quantity of pathological beliefs.

Most, but by no means all severe depressives appear to have utilized the dominant other or dominant goal in order somehow to absolve themselves from a sense of inner evil or badness. In contrast, the individual who suffers from a milder form of depression does not uniformly see himself as evil, but utilizes the dominant other or goal to obtain pleasure and meaning. The search is not to eradicate a negative; rather, it is to add a positive aspect to life. Obviously each situation is more complicated, consisting of a mixture of relative absolution and satisfaction to be derived from others. However, in my experience, individuals suffering from milder forms of depression do not give protestations of personal malevolence or baseness. They may see themselves as deprived, lazy, helpless, or at fault for their loss, but the malignant undercurrent of true self-vilification (not a specious self-blame in order to manipulate others) is usually absent.

Another difference is the degree to which the dominant other or goal has completely monopolized the person's life. Severe depressives appear to derive their total sense of self from some external agency. Less afflicted individuals, while showing an inordinate need for the other or for the goal to serve vital psychic functions, are able to develop other—albeit embryonic—forms of obtaining self-esteem. In terms of cognitive beliefs, mildly depressed individuals appear to be better able to discover alternatives in their modes of thought. They are less rigidly bound to one set of ideas which govern all validations of the self. For example, these individuals are able to shift their attention rapidly to the therapist in the hope of reestablishing a pathological relationship. In contrast to severe depressives, they are not bound to so limited a cast of characters from whom to derive meaning. (Other differences between these two groups are presented at the end of this chapter.)

The term chronic depression is meant to describe two general types of patients. One group has a similiar psychic structure to the reactive group but differs in that the relationship with a dominant other or the pursuit of a goal does not consistently or adequately dissipate feelings of depression. The other group is chronically depressed as a result of unrealistic standards that result from irrational beliefs of the self and others and which prevent satisfaction or pleasure in life. Both groups share a consistent lack of joyfulness in life, a low estimate of self, and an oversensitivity to minor environmental frustrations or to trivial negative reactions of others. Most significantly, both groups endure periods of depression of varying intensity. This painful affect is a constant undertone to daily existence, during which it is at times more or less pronounced. This sense of depression, joylessness, and at times even of despair is multidetermined but most immediately results from a stifling self-inhibition of pleasurable activities and a fear of other people's reactions which the depressive often distorts or magnifies.

The first group appears to inhibit normal pleasurable activities for fear of losing the dominant other or because such activities may interfere with the attainment of a dominant goal. In this former case, the cause of inhibition may appear to be initiated externally. However, there is actually an internal restriction of activities since the individual will project all sorts of prohibitions on others in the environment. His fantasied restrictions are often more severe than the dominant other would impose. Similarly, in the latter case the individual erroneously believes that, as if by some sort of malevolent magic, any momentary diversion or pleasure will threaten his quest for the all-embracing goal. Such individuals are in a precarious situation since any sign of disapproval (real or imagined) from a glorified other or any subjectively believed impasse to obtaining a significant goal will result in prolonged periods of depression.

The second, or inhibited, group does not appear to experience depression directly as a result of environmental events. Rather, these individuals suffer from a chronic sense of futility and hopelessness because they do not allow themselves to become actively involved in rewarding activities. They often superficially exhibit a sense of prideful and moralistic superiority that covers a quite infantile personality which is scrupulously hidden from others. Evidences of this underlying pathology are the almost paranoid belief that others watch their every move, and their secret wishes to be passively taken care of by powerful others. These individuals dread the exposure of their dependency needs or the public expression of free, spontaneous behavior. They live ascetic, unfulfilled lives, imagine that others are keeping track of their behavior (as their parents had done), and suppress healthy desires for closeness and mutuality. The mode of existence that such structures impose becomes chronically dissatisfying and eventually devoid of meaning. These individuals may gradually become so removed from true involvement in life that their unsatisfied needs become forgotten and they simply feel an inner emptiness or feel cut off from the world. In some depressives this inner emptiness may be temporarily abated by alcohol or drugs which can offer only short-term relief.

From afar, these individuals appear to be paragons of success and proper adjustment as well as of psychological maturity. It is in the course of therapy that they begin to recognize and reveal not only the extent of their depression, but also the well of unsatisfied yearnings that they have shunned since childhood. They also demonstrate the presence of rigid, inflexible beliefs about themselves and others which prevent fulfillment in life. This strict code of conduct exacts its price in terms of closeness, pleasure, and meaning. In later life they may see through the irrationality of their behavior but be unable to bring themselves to change without the aid of therapy. They see themselves caught in a way of life that no longer brings even the bogus self-satisfaction of alleged moral superiority. Yet there is no awareness of how they can alter their beliefs by themselves. The old parental "shoulds" have lost their former rationality but not their tyrannical power.

Masked depression presents somewhat of an enigma since the concept implies a diagnosis of depression without the major symptom of this disorder—a conscious feeling of depression. However, as described in chapter 3, various authors have maintained that patients who are addicts, have psychosomatic disorders, are accident-prone, or have other behavioral abnormalities are actually hiding an underlying depression. Lesse (1974, 1977), who has contributed extensively on this condition, wrote that "usually the depressive core surfaces spontaneously with the passage of time in a manner comparable to an iceberg that may rise to the surface under certain climactic conditions" (1977, p. 186). He believes that masked depression is a common condition that is often missed by the untrained clinician. He found that over 30 percent of depressives whom he saw as consultant to a medical unit had masked depression. Others, including myself, have found this condition to be rather rare. The frequency with which masked depressions are encountered may depend on the sample of patients seen, whether in a private psychiatric office or on the wards of medical services.

Part of the disparity in the reported frequency of masked depression also may reflect the definition of depression as well as diagnostic criteria. For example, I believe a depressed person who drinks or takes drugs should not be considered to be a masked depressive. Such a patient's depression is quite conscious and is being reduced by external factors. In contrast, an individual with an incapacitating medical illness or a serious psychiatric problem who experiences an understandable state of depression secondarily, as a reaction to his predicament, would not be classified as primarily depressed. In fact, most patients who request therapy for a variety of complaints are unhappy because their defenses or character adaptations are no longer effective. However, these individuals also would not be called depressed. In therapy such individuals describe different psychodynamics, life histories, modes of interaction, and cognitive distortions. An additional note of caution may be warranted: a large number of patients may become transiently depressed in the course of therapy as they become aware of some disagreeable aspect of themselves or have to relinquish gratifying yet neurotic behavior patterns. For example, an hysterical patient may suffer a temporary feeling of depression when he stops utilizing denial to a massive extent and takes a realistic look at his life. This does not mean that a hidden, masked depression was present all along; rather, the affect corresponds to a new and possibly healthier way of seeing reality. The process of working through may sometimes be quite painful.

With these provisos in mind, it cannot be doubted that cases of masked depression do exist. In my experience these are truly depressed patients who utilize certain defenses against the unpleasant affect just as other patients evolve methods of eliminating the experience of anxiety. These patients usually present hypochondriacal complaints which absorb their every waking moment. They are so involved with their physical state of health that they apparently manage to fight off feelings of depression. Yet even in these patients some of the familiar depressive symptomatology is present: they are sure they will never get well, they are fearful of novelty and enjoyment, they utilize symptoms to greatly inhibit their behavior, and they manipulate others by their alleged ill health.

Another type of true masked depression I have seen is the rare instance of depersonalization. In these patients the affect of depression is so painful that they cut off all feelings as a way of avoiding experiencing it. As noted in chapter 3, these patients often experience rather severe and incapacitating depression when they do not depersonalize, and it may be questioned whether they should be considered mild depressives. On the other hand, they do try to fight off the affect of depression and do not realign their cognitions so that the depression is seen as justified. They pay a great price for this defensive warding off of depression but the toll becomes understandable when they reveal the depth of their despair in the safety of the therapeutic situation. I have treated one such patient over a period of about five years. She initially had episodes of feeling empty, during which her body did not seem normal and she sensed herself as apart from the rest of the world. This woman had recurrent dreams of a terribly misshapen child whom no one could ever help. The affect in these dreams was extreme despair. In addition, she gave a history that was typical of depressed patients. As she became stronger in therapy, she was able to see the dream image as a distorted childhood estimation of herself and to confront the depressive affect related to this cognitive construct.

The status of masked depression is still unsettled since clear-cut diagnostic criteria have not been delineated and different authors may use this diagnosis liberally or very conservatively. While I lean toward the latter direction, such individuals do exist and successful treatment depends on recognizing the depressive core of their illness.

All types of mild depression share certain psychodynamic and cognitive features beyond the manifest experience of a dysphoric affect which links them together as variations of a basic disorder. These underlying characteristics will be elaborated in the following sections in order to define the basis for the spectrum of clinical phenotypes of depression. Each factor may be relatively more or less prominent in different individuals, but the totality of these characteristics form a multifactorial network of beliefs and attitudes that predispose an individual to depressive episodes.

RESTRICTION OF SOURCES OF SELF-ESTEEM

Pathologic dependency is perhaps the one characteristic of the depressive that has been unanimously emphasized in the psychiatric literature. It was most probably this tenacious, demanding quality of melancholics that suggested to Abraham, in his pioneering work on depression, the existence of a libidinal regression to the oral stage. Although many authors have subsequently disregarded Abraham's formulations of unconscious dynamics, there has been a uniform acceptance of his excellent descriptions of the depressive's mode of object relations and character structure. Later authors have echoed the theme of dependency as central in depression, although they consider this characteristic from vastly different theoretical positions. Arieti (1962) has especially stressed the role of dependency in the etiology of depression. He noted that in his experience, decompensation of the depressive often occurs following the failure to maintain an ongoing relationship with a significant environmental figure. In contrast to the schizophrenic, in whom the psychotic transformation is in reaction to a failure of "cosmic magnitude involving the relation with the whole interpersonal world" (p. 401), depression seems to result from the loss of a relationship with one highly esteemed person in the immediate environment. Arieti calls this idealized figure the "dominant other." who regardless of substitution in adult life is symbolic of the depriving mother.

Jacobson (1971) described a similar interpersonal situation, although she utilized a different terminology in recounting her treatment of a young woman who had been subject to recurrent depressions. In formulating the dynamics of this case, Jacobson observed:

Hence her love objects represented glorified parental images with which she identified through participation in their superiority. To be loved and to find recognition by them served the purpose of supporting her self-esteem, which was forever threatened by the overstrictness of her standards and the intensity of her ambitions. It is significant that Peggy (i.e. the patient) did not "borrow" the ego or superego of her love objects, as certain schizophrenics will do. What she needed was respect for them, and love, praise, and emotional support from them (1971, p. 224).

This last point is extremely important in that the depressive does not "merge" with the dominant other; he retains his own identity. However, the depressive will misuse the dominant other in order to maintain self-esteem. The dominant other structures the life of the depressive in the areas of gratification and self-worth but not so globally as in the symbiosis seen in schizophrenia.

Becker (1964) called attention to limited areas of esteem as being a significant determinant of depression. In comparing depression with schizophrenia, Becker wrote, "The depressed person, on the other hand, suffers instead from a too uncritical participation in a limited range of monopolizing interpersonal experiences" (1964, p. 131).

Becker cited Volkart's (1957) study of bereavement which showed that pathological mourning seems to occur when the bereft has limited his sources of gratification to too few objects:

Any culture which, in the name of mental health, encourages extreme and exclusive emotional investments by one person in a selected few others, but does not provide suitable outlets and alternatives for the inevitable bereavement, is simply altering the conditions of, and perhaps postponing, severe mental illness. It may, in the vernacular, be building persons up for a big let-down by exacerbating vulnerability (Volkart, 1957, p. 304).

Certain individuals by virtue of their upbringing appear to develop too narrow a range of activities that can supply self-esteem and thus they are vulnerable to depression if their limited number of objectives are not realized. As mentioned in chapter 6, for some the objective is the achievement of a dominant goal; for others the objective is to receive love and praise from a dominant other.

It may be noted that, contrary to the early classical formulation of depression, the predisposed individual does not create an ego introject of the mother following a loss in infancy. The internalization of parental values does not mean the incorporation of a lost love object as initially intended by Freud. Certainly all children adopt certain values and attitudes of their parents in the course of normal development without becoming depressives in adult life. The difficulty with the different meanings of internalization may be the result of a lack of reconciliation between the Freudian theory of depression and the later conceptualization of the superego. In the former, the infant incorporates the parent; in the latter, the child identifies with the parent as a solution to the Oedipal conflict. However, it is possible that internalization of parental values occurs as a gradual process throughout childhood and the concept of an introject is an unnecessary reification. More recent psychoanalytic contributions that stress infantile superego precursors seem to postulate just this preoedipal acceptance of parental attitudes without having to hypothesize the formation of a pathological introject.

Further clarification of the process of internalization also may be needed. The difference between imitative learning, whereby the child models himself after the parent, and reactive learning, whereby the child is coerced to become an idealized model desired by the parent, should be specified in reference to such terms as self-image and superego. In the case of imitative learning, the self is automatically modeled after an esteemed environmental figure, often without any underlying conflict. Reactive learning as intended here is the process whereby the child is made to become a desired ideal which does not necessarily resemble the parent, in order to win love or escape punishment. The attainment of this parental ideal leads to a sense of satisfaction not because of any inherent gratifying quality, but because it ensures parental favor.

The depressive appears to be the product of excessive reactive learning and to have developed a reactive identity; that is, he functions best in a role that reflects the dictates of dominant other rather than any independent standards. These individuals require the presence of an external agency in order to derive satisfaction, and they are unable to gain pleasure from independent achievement.

FEAR OF AUTONOMOUS GRATIFICATION

Patients often exhibit a marked inability and even dread of obtaining self-esteem or pleasure through their own efforts rather than by means of a dominant other. I have found this type of pathological functioning, which may be called the fear of autonomous gratification, to be a consistent feature of depressives. This characteristic may not always be immediately apparent, especially in view of the impressive achievements of some depressives. However, on further investigation it is found that social or professional accomplishment bring the depressive little pleasure in themselves: they are sought in an attempt to win love and acceptance from an external agency or to affirm an irrational sense of self that still follows parental dictates.

Nancy, a highly successful executive who began psychotherapy after years of visiting internists with vague pains and insomnia, exemplified this fear of autonomous gratification. Although she held a position of considerable importance and made an attractive salary, she could not bring herself to furnish her apartment comfortably or live in a manner commensurate with her income. She considered anything spent on herself to be a shameful extravagance, but would buy inordinately expensive gifts for her parents. Nancy was equally self-sacrificing with her free time and canceled social engagements if her boss asked her to work late or if her father asked to see her. In actuality Nancy was unable to enjoy a social evening unless she could somehow relate it to her work, just as she had to justify buying clothes by saying that she had to dress well for work. She found it difficult to date and dreaded sexual confrontation. When she did go out, she tried to structure the evening so that she would be part of a group and thus escape being alone with a man. Even then she had to drink a good deal in order to fight feelings of guilt and degradation. Eventually Nancy confessed that even her work, which seemed to be her major concern in life, brought her no pleasure in itself but only served as a means of pleasing her boss. Whenever she gained recognition from him or when she was praised by her father, Nancy became ecstatic with a great sense of well-being and felt vibrant and alive.

Although she had been subject to mild depressive episodes for most of her life, Nancy became clinically depressed when her boss decided to retire. She felt betrayed by his leaving after her many years of self-sacrifice. This sense of desertion was intensified by her parents' coincidental plan to take an extended vacation overseas. Nancy felt that her only means of gratification and meaning were abandoning her, and the prospect of life without them was unbearable. Never having been able to gain a sense of self-esteem from her own efforts, but only through the presence of a dominant other, her life now seemed empty and pointless.

Nancy's early history can be briefly outlined. Her mother was described as a shy, helpless woman living in fear of her husband, who tyrannically ruled the household. Nancy was not allowed to form extrafamilial attachments, but was coerced to work hard and study arduously in order to bring honor to the family. She was sent to strict parochial schools and her work was closely supervised by her father, who made her feel guilty and ashamed if she did not perform according to his aspirations. She was repeatedly told how her parents were sacrificing themselves for her and how she frivolously squandered their hard-earned savings by not studying enough or by wanting to enjoy herself with school friends. Nancy grew up determined to win her father's admiration and to redeem herself against his accusations. She reacted to any activities that were not directed toward this goal with apprehension and anxiety, although she superficially disparaged them as childish and immoral. In keeping with this "pleasure anxiety," Spiegel (1959) commented that the depressive fears the experience of happiness and pleasure as much as the experience of anger. The only thing that matters is to be passively gratified by the dominant other, to be reassured of one's own worth, and to be freed of the burden of guilt. Even patients who strive toward a dominant goal will shun any activity that does not eventually lead toward their overriding objective. Any involvement that is simply fun is carefully avoided because it induces guilt or shame.

A general characteristic of all types of depression-prone individuals which is apparent throughout their lives and not only during clinical episodes is an almost paranoid feeling that others are overly conscious of their behavior. They uniformly see themselves as the center of other people's attention and thus pursue what they believe is model behavior. This characteristic is closely linked with the fear of autonomous gratification in that such individuals can never actively have fun because they are sure that others will deem them foolish or wasteful. Such individuals live highly restricted and hypermoral lives, not from any superior inner ethical code, but because they feel themselves to be constantly observed by others. These individuals also tend to be obsessive and to find safety in conformity and rituals. They constantly speak about one's duty and obligations and are quick to point out the trivial failings of others in a superior, haughty manner. In actuality, these individuals who go by the book often make life miserable for those around them, reproaching them for not living up to some imagined set of standards and constantly accusing those close to them of having humiliated them in public.

In therapy such individuals reveal that as children they were constantly observed by overly critical parents who expected model behavior from them in order to bring honor or acceptance to the family. As described by Cohen et al. (1954), the childhood behavior of some future depressives was exploited by the parents in the search for upward social mobility. Such individuals soon learn to see their behavior as the constant object of public and parental attention. They also do to their children what had been done to them. As therapy progresses, they often reveal a secret desire to be just the opposite of what they pretend to be. All sorts of sexual, antisocial, and romantic desires emerge which had been strongly suppressed for fear of criticism from parents and later from society at large.

This fear of autonomous gratification appears to play a very significant role in depression and may be primarily responsible for the eventual precipitation of a clinical depressive episode that does not involve an environmental loss. Some depressives decompensate when they realize after years of self-deprivation that they will not receive some special reward which they believed would be granted to them. Others become depressed as a result of the joyless life that they have imposed on themselves; they gain no pleasure from life and yet feel unable to alter their way of living. One woman who presented a variety of psychosomatic complaints gradually became depressed when she saw herself trapped in an ungratifying mode of existence. She described her life as going through the motions of the role of an upper-class suburban wife and mother. She admitted that she detested her fund-raising activities, her husband's business associates, her clubs, and the usual daily routine to which she nevertheless strictly adhered. Her feeling of being trapped in an apparently successful and enviable life had been the prevalent mode of seeing herself for many years. She had grown up in a wealthy midwestern suburb, but due to the Depression her family had lost most of their capital. However, they continued to live as if they were wealthy, though everyone knew they could not really afford their lifestyle. The parents insisted on carrying out this economic sham and were careful to instruct their children on proper behavior, pointing out to them that others would be observing them to see if their loss of wealth had affected their "breeding." Throughout her life this woman made choices that would ensure social approval at the expense of personal satisfaction. When she reached middle age, she began to realize that it was too late to do the things she had really wanted to do. She confessed that even if she had been younger she could not have allowed herself to go against a harsh code of conformity which she expected from herself, even though it brought her only misery, Her anger at having to live according to her self-imposed restrictions seemed to result in violent headaches, and her fear that she might act out her secret desires accounted for other bodily symptoms. Her current life, dismal as it seemed to her, at least offered a structured and secure code of behavior. Without it she believed that she would feel not only sinful but alone, abandoned, and without a set course to follow.

Other patients could be presented who throughout their lives have always made the same, if ungratifying, choices. These choices appear to be predicated on the original dictates of the dominant parent and on the later transference of parental authority to current life relationships. Such individuals distort others to fill the role of the demanding, critical parent and then act according to these transferential distortions, culminating in an existence which does not allow pleasure and predisposes them to chronic depression with definite paranoid and obsessive features.

BARGAIN RELATIONSHIP

Implicit in the depressive's dependency and inhibition is what may be called the bargain relationship, which typifies some depressives' mode of interpersonal relations. The bargain is simply that the depressive will deny himself autonomous satisfaction in return for nurturance from the dominant other. This relationship is initiated by the parent, but the depressive reestablishes it on unwitting transference objects. This *quid pro quo* relationship ensures that gratification and acceptance will be forthcoming if willingness for self-sacrifice is properly demonstrated.

This pathological mode of relating was hinted at by Cohen et al. in their study of manic-depressives (1954). They mentioned the patient's use of splitting a significant other into an all-good partial object and repressing the other's bad characteristics in order to idealize the important other. This other has to be inflated and seen as totally good so that the patient can then depend on and utilize the other for his own needs. Jacobson also implied a similar relationship, employing orthodox terminology: "The libidinal cathexis of their self-representations thus depends on the maintenance of a continuous libidinal hypercathexis of the love object, designed to prevent its aggressive devaluation in which their self is bound to participate" (1971, p. 259). Therefore, according to Jacobson the depressive must idealize the dominant other if he is to prevent a devaluation of the self which would precipitate a depressive episode. Actually, in some cases the other may be overvalued so that he can give structure to the depressive. In other cases the dominant other is utilized to absolve guilt, and in still other cases he is needed as a source of constant applause and selfless love.

An example of the first type of bargain relationship, in which structure is given by the significant other, is a brilliant graduate student who did extremely well under the tutelage of his professor. The student had a godlike reverence for the senior man and would consult him about all of his life decisions. He felt himself to be safe and secure as long as the professor approved of his work, and he subtly used the older colleague to structure his day and to plan his lectures and research. While he was fawning in regard to the professor, this student was indifferent to his wife, competitive and suspicious with his fellow students, and generally terrified of life outside the university. However, he managed well until the time came to do his dissertation. His professor found the student a prestigious job in a physics think tank where he could support himself while doing his thesis. The young man took the job without questioning his elder's choice, though it entailed moving to a nearby suburb and essentially cutting himself off from all regular contact with the university.

In his new job the student felt immediately uncomfortable; there was no academic hierarchy, people did their own jobs without competing, and the atmosphere was loose and egalitarian. Worst of all, the director of the institute was a quiet and benevolent figure who did not interfere in the lives of his employees, all of whom were expected to be mature self-directed scientists. The student gradually became depressed in these new surroundings. He could not work unless he felt he was being observed and supervised by an esteemed superior, and the director simply refused to take on the role that the former professor had filled. Without the secure sense that a dominant other was watching and directing him, this promising scientist lost all interest in physics. He began to bother his co-workers with elementary questions in order to gain attention and developed a great dislike for the director for not fulfilling his inappropriate needs. When he was deprived of the structure supplied by the dominant other, all activities became meaningless. The student gradually started staying in bed, complaining to his wife, and having difficulty sleeping. His dreams of being empty and lost reflected his waking psychological state.

In this case the positive or gratifying aspects of the bargain relationship are illustrated rather than the more painful type of bond in which coercion by guilt is prominent and usually results in a more severe form of depression. In the latter case, the dominant other is needed to reassure against feelings of inherent evil and badness. In addition to an air of helpless resignation and a sense of worthlessness, these patients believe themselves to be inordinately vile and malicious and they are convinced that only the dominant other can free them this self-image. One such patient who required brief hospitalization described herself in the most derogatory terms imaginable, whereas in reality she seemed to have led an exemplary life. Her mother was a selfish woman who resented any responsibility and detested the mothering role. When her husband left her, she blamed the patient and repeatedly told her that if she had never been born the father would have remained. The mother continued to blame her for her later misfortunes and in addition projected all sorts of sexual desires onto the patient, eventually making her believe that her incestuous desires had driven her father from the house. This woman accepted the blame for her mother's unhappiness and dedicated her life to seeking forgiveness. She could not tolerate her mother's being cross or angry, and she did everything she could to soothe or please her. For more than twenty years this woman forced her husband and children to visit the mother weekly in another city where the patient would fuss over her and try to win her praise. The patient's mood for the following week depended on the success of these Sunday outings.

This woman became severely depressed when she developed intimate feelings for her employer. She could not tolerate her desires, which proved to her that her mother had been right in the estimation that she was wanton and base. All her previous efforts to redeem herself were now without meaning. She would never change; she had always been and always would be evil and worthless. She succumbed to the image of herself that she despised and which disgusted her.

A third example of the bargain relationship can be illustrated by a businessman who demanded to be adulated and nurtured by his wife. However, his needs appeared insatiable; he had to be told constantly that he was loved and that he was appreciated. If the wife dared to express interest in any topic that did not concern him, he would become hurt and begin to pout or to berate his wife for not realizing how hard he worked for her welfare. At times he would threaten to leave her just so she could beg him to stay. On the rare occasions when his wife told him that she felt "sucked dry" by his demands, he punished her by crying and going through his speech of being unappreciated. The wife eventually unconsciously evolved her own defensive maneuvers by developing (and on occasion feigning) illness so that he could not ask her for nurturance.

This man feared that his wife would abandon him at any moment and his manipulations were pathological attempts to continue his needed relationship with her. At times he was also convinced that he was unlovable and so had to put his wife to the test to see if she really loved him, which meant he was worthy of love. While his behavior might appear controlling and even sadistic, as Rado (1928) described the depressive and his love object, this man truly believed that he was only trying to get the love he so desperately desired. His pathological needs blinded him to the destructive effect he had on his spouse. When she was sick and therefore not in danger of leaving him, he became solicitous and kind, only to revert again when she appeared healthy. This man had a long history of depressions following emotional abandonments throughout his life. He had married a submissive and frightened women in order to ensure that she would stay with him, and he continued to fight off his neurotic fear of abandonment by his machinations. It must be mentioned that her effect on him was totally out of proportion: if she smiled and told him she loved him at breakfast, he felt sure of himself the entire day; if she were sleepy and quiet, he felt depressed and neglected.

This bargain relationship demonstrates the depressive's excessive reliance on a dominant other for maintenance of self-worth and a sense of meaning. It may take various forms, but basically it is a revival of a real or fantasied childhood relationship in which the parent was able to grant the child a needed state of self in return for appropriate behavior.

Finally it should be stressed that what predisposes one to depression in the bargain relationship is not only the exclusivity but also the quality of the relationship. For example, Lewinsohn (1969) suggested that depressives tend to limit their range of personal interactions. This conclusion seems valid but incomplete. An individual may lead a happy, productive life with only a few mutual, sharing relationships and not become depressed upon termination of these relationships. It is only when the relationship serves pathological needs, prevents autonomous gratification, and enforces the inhibition of independent self-worth that a predisposition to depression exists.

FELT HELPLESSNESS TO ALTER THE ENVIRONMENT

As a result of this excessive reliance on external agents for gratification, and in certain cases for structure, the depressive displays a glaring lack of mastery over self-rewarding functions. Some are so constricted by strong inhibitions that they simply cannot overcome the guilt and shame that accompanies simple enjoyment. Every act that might be perceived as pleasurable must be rationalized and disguised as leading to a productive or serious goal. These individuals experience intense anxiety at even the dim prospect of enjoyment, so that they strongly shun such activities. Therefore they complain that they are helpless to alter their depression and they feel overwhelmed and weak. Other depressed individuals who depended on a dominant other for gratification feel similarly hopeless and helpless if this other is lost. However, these individuals are not really helpless but they would rather be depressed than break the taboos that they impose on themselves. Obviously this is not true of all depressed states: some people face situations which they are indeed helpless to alter. However, these individuals usually do not totally collapse in their efforts; they may feel frustrated, cheated, and angry, but not uniformly depressed. In addition, nondepressives do not display the undue emphasis on moral issues which are so often seen in individuals with recurrent depressions who must see everything as someone's fault—usually their own. Healthier individuals also do not show the characteristic maneuvers of involving others to relieve their suffering through manipulation and guilt-inducing behavior that is seen in neurotic depression. To repeat what Sandler and Joffe (1965) elaborated in detail: we are all susceptible to the initial psychobiological response of depression which carries with it a transient sense of helplessness, but only selected individuals will progress to a clinical episode of depression in which the sense of helplessness is magnified and utilized to control others to reinstate the lost sense of well-being.

Seligman (as mentioned in chapter 2) proposed a theory of learned helplessness to account for some forms of depression. Seligman essentially postulated that the depression-prone individual has learned that action does not result in reinforcement of needs, and so he gives up and gradually lapses into a state of depression. Actually, the depressive is far from helpless in that he is adept at manipulating others and also is capable of impressive accomplishments when required to gain love or approval. Rather, the depressive's apparent helplessness results from a disruption in his usual mode of behaving and gaining esteem through pathological means. The sense of helplessness is both an automatic and pathological attempt to induce others to supply the needed reassurance, and it is a result of training that one must act in reaction to others in order to win the desired acknowledgment. Therefore learned helplessness does account for some aspects of depression, but it is limited to the areas of assertion and pleasure without guilt or shame. It is understandable how the depressive might superficially appear to demonstrate that effort and reward are unrelated, yet on closer inspection it becomes evident that his efforts are just more surreptitious and devious in achieving their reinforcements.

Two depressed patients will be briefly described who had an overwhelming sense of helplessness. It is of interest that while both had histories of only mild depression, both had received electroconvulsive therapy (which effected only temporary relief). Their air of helplessness may have resulted in their being given this form of treatment since they refused to take any responsibility for their own therapy once they became depressed. In retrospect, they appeared to derive some pleasure out of being thought of by loved ones as severely incapacitated and requiring hospital care and shock treatment.

One of these patients was a woman of thirty-five who had suffered her first depressive episode fifteen years earlier when she was in college. Her mother was a teacher and had essentially ordered the patient to attend a local teacher's college while continuing to live at home. Throughout her childhood this woman had been trained to gauge her own worth by the amount of approval she received from her mother. She was restricted from playing with others and her nonscholastic pursuits were severely criticized. However, she was allowed—indeed strongly encouraged—to achieve in school. This woman remembered that as a child whenever she excelled in some scholastic activity, she would immediately think of her mother and hoped that the latter would be pleased. The woman's father was a pleasant but weak figure in the household. His role was to earn money (which was never enough for the mother) and to appease his wife. Another clear message that the mother gave to the patient was that the world was a very dangerous place where others would trick you and take advantage of you. The mother further implied that the patient was no match for such a world and could only survive with the mother's protection.

As the patient reached adolescence, she began to rebel mildly against the mother, mostly in her fantasies. Boys started to show an interest in her and she was starting to derive pleasure outside the maternal orbit. She made secret plans to leave her local teacher's college and to go to an out-of-town university where she could live on her own and study what she herself chose. At this point her father suffered a severe heart attack which necessitated giving up his job. As a result, they shortly experienced financial problems and her hopes of leaving home were thwarted. With their dwindling income the mother became even more critical of the father, whom she berated in the cruelest terms. The patient found it impossible to live at home with her mother, who appeared to have been continually angry, yet she did not see how she could afford to live on her own. Her one escape was to marry a young local businessman who did not fit her romantic ideal although he did offer a haven from the unhappy situation at home.

These were the circumstances in which she suffered her first attack of depression. The reasons for her decompensation appear fairly clear. She could no longer please her mother, who had become obsessed with money and filled with venom against the world. Furthermore, the mother had changed in the patient's own eyes; the patient now saw her as uniformly punishing and abusive. The patient wanted to defend her father who, after all, had supported the household until his illness, but she dared not assert herself against the mother. She also was not assertive or adventurous enough to move out on her own and support herself. Instead she chose the security of a marriage which rapidly revealed that it would not satisfy her needs.

After recovering from her initial depression she returned to school, received her teaching degree, and from then on felt herself locked in a profession and a marital union which were both ungratifying. Her husband futhered her sense of helplessness by discouraging any social or personal activities that she might independently enjoy. Throughout the remainder of her life and until she entered psychotherapy, she succumbed to a semiparasitic and largely childish existence. Whenever external pressures, such as having a child, put additional demands on her, she became depressed.

It is noteworthy that in her dreams during therapy, she repeatedly returned to the original situation in college. Another telling incident about this patient was that as she began showing signs of assertion, her husband tried to get her to discontinue therapy in spite of her history of frequent hospitalizations. It is to her credit that she refused his demands and decided to pay for her therapy herself. At the beginning of her therapy, this woman exuded a sense of helplessness, of everything being too much trouble, of being incapable of any independent action. She wanted things done for her, and to be taken care of by others or to be told what to do by others. She did not dare to make any decisions on her own. However, she had been far from helpless in other areas; she was a competent teacher, housewife, and mother. Her area of helplessness centered on assertion of her beliefs and independence from the evaluations of others.

The second patient was in his late twenties but already had been given two courses of electroconvulsive therapy. Initially, he constantly complained of being ineffectual and of being mistreated by others. Actually, he was very adept at indirectly getting his own way by manipulating those around him. He never considered the numerous times when other people tried to help him or treated him fairly. He focused only on those incidents when others had not lived up to his own idiosyncratic code of honor and had not accorded him special treatment. His two depressions had occurred when he could not get what he wanted, namely, the approval or special attention from esteemed others through his usual machinations. This patient believed he was helpless, but what actually occurred was that his usual mode of controlling others had failed.

This young man had been raised in an atmosphere of deception, secret deals, and obligating behavior and he could not at first consider any other mode of conduct. This form of interaction had become automatic and unconscious. What remained in consciousness was a highly exaggerated response to the slightest rebuff and a feeling that everyone should go out of their way for him. The following excerpt is from a note he brought to one of his early sessions in order to convey his plight:

My heart is so affected by things, it cries. I am sad and I can't stop it and say "be happy." It just doesn't seem to do any good. But what else can I do— do it myself or have it done for me. What can I do. Something has to be done before one day I jump off a bridge or at least seriously want to. Will it pass? I pray, but if God exists I don't even know if he cares—look at the world we live in. I am lost.

On the surface, this pathetic passage may illustrate the helplessness this patient felt in terms of improving his condition; others had to do it for him. However, during the time he wrote this passage he reluctantly worked at his job and even gloated over making some especially good business deals. His despair actually related to being unable to attain the special recognition he felt he deserved from his father, who was also his boss.

There is no doubt that even mild depression can be an incapacitating illness which not only involves a felt sense of helplessness but also may affect an individual's level of performance. However, when the origin of this feeling of helplessness is traced psychotherapeutically what usually emerges is that the individual first felt helpless in achieving meaning or gratification either as praise from a dominant other or in pursuit of a dominant goal. Having failed in these pursuits, the individual finds little meaning in any of life's other activities and his sense of helplessness generalizes to his entire social space. In other depressed individuals, such as the woman just described, the individual has made choices throughout life that lock him into an ungratifying existence. Here again the individual lacks the courage to break his self-imposed taboos and thus despairs of his helplessness first to gain pleasure and eventually to accomplish even the most rudimentary tasks.

The Cognitive Avoidance of Overt Anger

In a recent paper on depression, Coyne (1976) related a strange cure for depression practiced by a Dr. Williams of London in the early nineteenth century. When a depressed individual consulted Dr. Williams, he informed the patient that he should seek out a certain doctor in Scotland who was famous for his ability to cure the disorder. The patient obediently journeyed to Scotland only to find that the highly able physician did not exist. After this fruitless search, the patient found that "a desire to upbraid (Dr. Williams) had engaged his entire thoughts on his way home, to the complete exclusion of his original complaint cited" (Coyne, 1976, p. 38). This anecdote suggests what has been almost universally found by authors on depression: the affect of depression is incompatible with the overt expression of anger. This finding has led to specific behavior modification techniques (although less circuitous than those of Dr. Williams) to evoke anger in depressed patients by assigning them to monotonous, repetitive, and ungratifying tasks until the patient "blows up" and anger replaces depression (Taulbee and Wright, 1971). On the other hand, the incompatibility of overt anger and depression has also led to the notion that depression is a result of repressed rage. Indeed, as described in chapter 2, some have seen it as misdirected anger which torments the ego or the self-image.

The fact that clinical depression appears to decrease as the ability to directly express anger is displayed, however, does not prove this "repressed rage" hypothesis. Brenner (1975) reviewed a number of contributions which assert that enjoyment is also incompatible with the affect of depression. Does this prove then that enjoyment is repressed during depression and therapy should induce the patient to "get the enjoyment out"? It gradually becomes evident that direct repression of an affect is a complicated affair, if such a process can occur at all. What actually appears to be the case is that an individual's unconscious cognitive system structures a situation to produce a specific effect. Therefore the depressive does not overtly display anger because he automatically structures his view of himself and others so that anger is not produced. Rather, the depressive appears to respond to what most individuals call anger-producing situations with self-blame, feelings of hurt, or some sort of excusing the other. Rather than simply assuming that the depressive represses anger or directs it at himself, a search for the cognitive distortions which fail to elicit an aggressive response may be more productive.

The depressive's lack of overt anger recently has been interpreted in terms of his tenuous object relations. The expression of anger may antagonize the dominant other and jeopardize the depressive's sources of gratification. For example, Arieti (1974) described that anger in depressives ultimately leads to more depression; it creates the fear that the dominant other will abandon the individual, which leads to an increased sense of loss and hopelessness. Anger is seen as a highly dangerous affect which must be concealed and suppressed. Klein's classic formulation of the depressive position emphasizes the infant's fear of losing his inner good objects through his aggressive wishes. She interpreted the infant as attributing the pain and frustration of loss to his own angry behavior with a subsequent suppression of overt hostility. If Klein's basic formulations are extended to the interpersonal sphere, the depressive's plight of being angry while in a state of need for nurturance from the other, and the resultant fear of the manifestation of that anger, becomes more understandable. To express anger directly means to lose the all-important other who supplies the incorporated good objects, that is, gratification and self-esteem. The depressive eventually believes that any expression of anger will catastrophically result in the loss of gratification.

The depressive's lack of overt hostility can also be due to his distortion of relationships. Some depressives idealize the dominant other and so implicitly trust the other's judgment that they see no reason for resentment or anger. If they fail to obtain the other's acceptance, it is because they have not tried hard enough to be worthy, and not because the other is stingy or unjust. They feel they have only themselves to blame and thus have no cause to become angry. A middle-aged depressed woman, describing the failure of her considerable attempts to win praise and love from her father, exclaimed, "What is wrong with me that he doesn't love me?" This woman could not conceive of her father as ungiving or unloving; it was her fault that she could not please him. Although married and the mother of three children, she still believed that her chief role in life was to please her father and devote herself to him. As in her childhood, her father was the only one who could make her happy and give meaning to her life. To alter her view of her father would have required an alteration of her entire mode of being.

Another possible reason for the depressive's inability to express anger is that the capacity to feel angry and to use anger as a direct mode of achieving an objective implies a sense of autonomy and independence that is just the ability the depressive lacks. These individuals are tuned to the reactions of others rather than to the expression of self, regardless of consequences. To become angry means to satisfy one's impulse without considering the effect on others, and it requires exactly the sense of self that the depressive has not developed. Thus he resorts to more reliable manifestations of displeasure such as pouting or suffering, which produce the appropriate impact on others—guilt and forgiveness. Some depressives that Bonime (1967) so aptly described are stubbornly uncooperative in therapy; they spitefully refuse to take their share of responsibility and take pride in their resistance to change. Manipulation and control of others seem to be the cardinal features of their activity. This type of depressive, which is similar to Arieti's claiming type, may be understood as rebelling against the disappointments in past bargain relationships. These individuals feel themselves cheated by past dominant others who did not fulfill their promise, real or imagined, in return for self-sacrifice. These patients then resolve never to show any signs of true mutuality or cooperation as a way of punishing the dominant other, whose role the therapist has transferentially assumed. They will demand all sorts of favoritism and support while refusing to take any initiative in therapy and ultimately want to frustrate the therapist by not becoming what they believe he would wish them to be.

However, such patients never show anger overtly but punish the therapist by continually reminding him of their lack of improvement in therapy —that is, of the therapist's inability to change them. In this manner they make the therapist feel powerless and frustrated, but never give him cause to terminate the relationship. Thus they defeat the dominant other without losing him. Yet these patients continue to center their existence around the therapist and in reality defeat themselves in order allegedly to control the other. Their activity continues to be judged in terms of the effect it will have on the therapist and the reaction it will elicit. Living in a world of reflective gratification, the depressive cannot conceive of himself as acting simply for himself. His every thought and act implicates the other and includes the other's reaction.

A talented college student who began experiencing episodes of anxiety and depression as she approached graduation described this type of other-dependent relatedness. She became immediately attracted to any man who showed her attention and would rush into a close relationship without adequately evaluating the other person. Her main concern was that he be pleased with her, and she devoted herself to fitting into her boyfriends' preferences. Despite her efforts to hold onto the relationship and placate the other, she was often exploited and treated with little consideration. When this occurred, she persistently blamed herself for having been rejected. She believed that she had somehow offended the other or that she had not been sufficiently perceptive of the other's needs. The other was right even in mistreating her. Each failure to maintain a relationship proved to her that she would be an old maid and condemned to a life of solitude. She believed that the only way she might escape abandonment would be to surrender autonomy and spontaneity. Any display of assertiveness, especially of anger or disagreement, would surely drive the other away. This young woman did occasionally get angry, but always after the fact: in the presence of esteemed others, she was overcome with the desire to please and to endear herself. Even her considerable gifts were at the mercy of others, and a project that had taken her months to prepare became worthless if mildy criticized by a teacher. The teacher's judgment was never in question: if she had only worked harder, she might have pleased him.

A specific confirmation of the lack of repressed anger in mildly depressed patients comes from studies of their dreams. If they were bursting with unexpressed rage rather than distorting their view of the world in order to avoid anger, their dreams should reveal the repressed hostility. Beck and his colleagues examined the dreams of 218 patients who were independently rated by two judges as nondepressed, moderately depressed, and severely depressed. The major characteristics of the dreams of the depressed groups was a consistent masochistic trend. The dreams of the depressed patients revealed themes of disappointment, rejection, humiliation, or other similar unpleasant experiences, but the dreams did not exhibit notable anger.

Hauri (1976) reviewed some of the literature on the dreams of depressed patients as well as reporting his own study on eleven patients remitted from depression and who were matched with eleven control subjects. Past studies had shown that several depressed individuals report dreams that are bland, barren, and involve mainly family members. As depression lifts the dreams become more conflictual, although masochistic and dependency themes persist even after clinical improvement.

Hauri's own study is noteworthy in that patients who had recovered from a depressive episode were selected and therefore their dreams reflected basic personality structure rather than the possible distortions of an acute depressive state. In addition, Hauri utilized all-night EEG tracings and awakened each subject to report dreams in order to reduce selective recall of only pleasant or socially acceptable dreams. In comparing recovered depressives with control subjects, Hauri found a number of significant differences in their dreams. Dreams of remitted depressive patients showed more past than present or future events, more unhappy than happy emotions, and more action exerted by nonhuman entities (storms, motors, bullets, and so on). Equally important was the finding that depressives did not show more hostility toward others or hostility toward the self in the dreams. Hauri commented that this may be the most important result of his study. Hauri concluded that on the basis of dream content, the depressive may see the world as dangerous or ungiving or even hostile, but this hostility neither emanates from the dreamer nor is directed against him.

Even Bonime, who believes that much neurotic depressive behavior is a distorted manifestation of anger, does not report excessive aggression in the dreams of depressed patients presented in his book, *The Clinical Use of Dreams* (1968). His work as well as that of Beck does not support the repressed rage hypothesis.

Overt anger may occasionally be seen in some mildly depressed individuals when they view their situation more realistically. This may occur through therapeutic effort, or in some individuals before change through treatment. They can experience periods of insight when they are not blinded by their needs and distortions. This is usually not the case with severe depressives for whom reality has become completely transformed in its meaning. However, even in mildly depressed patients these periods are short-lived and the patients return to their accustomed mode of cognitive interpretation of events.

On the few occasions that I have observed depressive openly express anger, their expression was consistently clothed in moralistic terms with great attempts to justify the outburst. Even then the show of anger was not a simple expression of self, but a calculated attempt to coerce another to do something or to justify the feeling of depression by showing how they had been mistreated. Cohen and her co-workers (1954) also were not impressed with the importance of anger in their study of manic-depressive patients. The conclusions they reached are:

> We have said little in this report about the manic-depressive's hostility. We feel that it has been considerably over-stressed as a dynamic factor in the illness. Certainly, a great deal of the patient's behavior leaves a hostile impression upon those around him, but we feel that the driving motivation in the patient is the one we have stressed—the feeling of need and emptiness. The hostility we would relegate to a secondary position; we see hostile feelings arising in the patient as the result of frustration of his manipulative and exploitative needs. We conceive of such subsequent behavior—demandingness toward the other or self-injury—as being an attempt to restore the previous dependent situation (1954, p. 252).

The Washington group further adds "that much of the hostility that has been imputed to the patient has been the result of his annoying impact on others rather than of a primary motivation to do injury to them."

Perhaps much of the confusion of the role of anger in depressed states owes its origin to differences of opinion regarding both the nature of depression and of anger. As Mendelson (1974) accurately observed, there is no uniform consensus about the definition of either affect. Some psychoanalysts require the presence of aggression in some form or other as necessary for the diagnosis of depression. These manifestations can be self-recriminations (self-directed anger), low self-esteem (aggressive cathexis of the self-representation), or manipulativeness (controlling others by anger). This difference of opinion shows the equal lack of agreement on the nature of aggression. When Jacobson writes about an aggressive cathexis, she is describing a highly abstract metapsychological process that does not coincide with the overt, conscious expression of anger as known to the layman. The same is true of the intersystemic conflict between ego and superego. However, Bonime (1960) conceives of aggression as the covert motive of the depressive's behavior in his lack of cooperation in therapy or his control of others. Here aggression is implied from nonaggressive behavior by its end result or by its alleged motive. Still other psychiatrists describe anger or aggression as a felt state of self—of being angry. Therefore it appears that there is a discrepancy in the psychiatric literature as to whether aggression should be seen as a primary instinct or form of psychic energy (that cannot by definition be directly experienced), as a motive force behind behavior which is not phenomenologically felt as anger, or as a primary feeling state.

Despite this confusion over the conceptual status of aggression, it is clinically evident that the depressive shuns the direct expression and even the experience of anger. He does not use overt anger in the service of his needs; rather, he utilizes manipulativeness to control others. If this manipulativeness is termed a form of anger or aggression, then this special use of the term should be made explicit.

The extreme emphasis on the role of hostility in depression may be a lingering influence of Freud's original theories stated in *Mourning and Melancholia*, which described a good deal of depressive symptomatology as misdirected aggression. As Mendelson (1974) wisely observed: "Freud's explanation of the melancholic's self-reproaches and Abraham's description of the manic-depressive's ambivalence became universally and, it is feared, uncritically and uniformly applied to all depressive phenomena. And later authors frequently sought to justify these constructions rather than to investigate their applicability" (p. 194).

Family Background of Mild Depressives

As mentioned in chapter 2, there is a paucity of studies on family transactions in depression as compared with schizophrenia. The few studies that have attempted to determine the childhood roots of adult depression mainly have centered on the experience of parental loss. This interest in childhood bereavement appears stimulated by the hypotheses that adult depression is the reawakening of a childhood trauma, or that object loss is the basic problem in depressive disorders. Most studies have compared the frequency of the death of a parent during the childhood years of adult depressed patients and of matched controls. The results of these studies have been contradictory except for the finding that childhood loss (through death of a parent, divorce, or some other form of separation) is more common in all forms of psychiatric disorders, especially delinquency. Brown (1968) made an additional intriguing observation: 55 percent of the poets listed in the *Oxford Book of English Verse* and the *Dictionary of National Biography* (in England) lost a father or mother before the age of fifteen. This is a higher rate of parental death than is found in depressive (or delinquent) samples. Brown speculated that these poets turned to internal sources of gratification through fantasy to soften the blow of the parental loss, and their native genius later allowed these fantasies to be expressed poetically.

The rate of parental loss may not be the significant factor for later disturbance if it is taken in isolation. The effect of the loss on the surviving parent, the subsequent disruption of the family, the availability of substitutes, the child's age at the time of the loss, and his conception of the loss must all be taken into account in retrospective studies. Loss of a parent through death or other misfortune is certainly a significant childhood trauma but it does not appear specifically to predispose one to depression as an adult. To view the adult depressive as the recapitulation of an actual childhood loss is somewhat simplistic. Freud, who originated this concept of reactivated childhood trauma, did not intend the actual loss of the parent but the loss of the parent's love, which is a totally different matter. This loss of love may then represent an unconscious decathexis of the object representation and thus an unconscious object loss, but it is not meant to imply a loss of the parent in reality. Here again a metapsychological hypothesis and clinical data become confused. Sandler and Joffe (1965) tried to clarify the matter by stressing that depression is not the result of the loss of an object but a state of well-being of the self supplied by the object.

Cohen et al. (1954) did attempt a retrospective reconstruction of the childhoods of their twelve manic-depressive cases. They did not find evidence of early object loss or of a childhood depressive reaction equivalent to Abraham's "primal parathymia" (1924). Rather, these investigators noted that the families felt isolated or ostracized from the mainstream of society, the mothers blamed the fathers for the alleged social failure, and the child was expected to redeem the family's honor or prestige. In terms of more specific child rearing, this group found that the mother accepted the child when he was a helpless infant but began to reject him when he displayed the normal willfullness of a toddler. These findings are confirmed by Arieti in chapter 6: in the early childhood of severe depressives the mother is initially giving and loving but quickly begins to make stringent demands on the child so that continued nurturance is contingent on the child's fulfillment of expectations. The important aspect of this interpersonal relationship for the child is the realization that love can be abruptly withdrawn if parental expectations are not met. It may not be an actual loss that predisposes the individual to depression, but the constant fear that a loss can occur if the proper behavior is not forthcoming.

A later development noted both by Cohen et al. (1954) and Arieti is that the parent assumes the power to redeem the child, to make him feel worthy. The child is convinced that it is his own fault if he does not achieve this redemption: if he had tried harder he could have obtained the needed support of the parent. This interchange sets up the process by which the adult depressive attempts to attain love by obedience and hard work, blaming himself if he does not achieve his objective. Much of this aspect of the future depressive already has been covered in chapter 6 and will not be repeated here. It is sufficient to note that the child's failure to fulfill parental expectations is experienced as guilt and worthlessness.

Slipp (1976) studied the family setting that produces a depressive individual. He found that the child is given a contradictory message from the parents: the child is expected to succeed socially and at the same time expected to fail, so as not to become too independent of the parents. Slipp described the parents as expecting achievement and yet simultaneously rewarding failure. The child learns to succeed but fears that this success will bring abandonment. According to Slipp:

> The depressive evolves an oppositional form of symbiosis as a compromise solution to this double bind. By partial compliance to both succeed and fail messages, he does not risk abandonment by either parent; yet by rebelling sufficiently against these injunctives, he preserves some autonomy. Through halfhearted performances to his parents' wishes, he can play off both pressures and avoid being either strong or totally helpless. By partially defeating himself and losing he can claim to be a victim of external circumstances, and he does not have to take responsibility (1976, p. 398).

Therefore Slipp traces the pathological behavior of the adult depressive to the childhood solution of a double message: succeed for the family but fail lest you become independent of the family.

While I do not agree with every aspect of Slipp's analysis, the observations presented by him are important in demonstrating how the experience of independent success is perverted in the childhood of future depressives. In my experience, some future depressives have been given a clear message to succeed, but the success later was robbed of its meaning; rather, it was presented as rightful repayment to the parent, as simply keeping up with the alleged superiority of the family, or as a way to get love from the parent. The child was told to succeed but that he should not enjoy his success.

The disparities between the childhoods of severe and mild depressives appear to be more a function of the amount of this thwarting of development than a function of qualitative differences. As a rule, the childhood of mild depressives was not so blunted by moralistic blaming and early threats of abandonment. Often the patients were made to feel weak or lazy rather than evil. They also did not have to work as hard or to distort their perceptions as much to gain parental approval. They often were the family favorites and were able to maintain this role by compliance. Therefore their inducements for buying the parental distortions were positive (favoritism, praise) rather than negative (guilty recriminations, threats of abandonment). Finally, for most but not all mild depressives, the father rather than the mother was the dominant parent. This finding was also reported by Slipp (1976). While such individuals soon became imbued with the family distortions that everyone owed everything to the father and their task was to insure the father's benevolence, they managed to continue a close relationship with a loving though weak and submissive mother. The threat of abandonment also came at a later stage of development and so had less impact on the personality. It was not until such individuals could bring social value to the family by model behavior or excellent grades that the father became interested in them. Before this time they were treated as unimportant charges of the mother.

Nevertheless, in these individuals as well as in the severe melancholics there is a basic instability of self-esteem. They also have been unable to internalize sources of worth and must constantly derive their meaning as individuals from external agencies. They remain forever excessively vulnerable to the disappointments and losses which, for better or worse, form part of human destiny.

[8]

PSYCHODYNAMICS OF DEPRESSION

AND SUICIDE IN CHILDREN

AND ADOLESCENTS

Chapter 4 was concerned with an exposition of the clinical syndromes of depressionlike disorders in children and adolescents. This chapter will attempt a deeper look at the phenomenon of childhood depression, going beyond clinical descriptions to theoretical issues.

For decades the classical psychoanalytic position on the possibility of depression in childhood was firm and unanimous: it could not exist. Rochlin (1959) plainly stated that depression, by definition, is a result of an inward deflection of aggression mediated by a strong superego. Since the superego does not exist in young children, neither could depression. Beres (1966) also expressed the belief that depression, as a primary superego phenomenon involving intersystemic conflict, must be manifested by predominant sustained guilt which is absent in children.

Even psychoanalysts who did not emphasize the older retroflected anger hypothesis of depression expressed grave doubts over the possibility of this affect or its development into the clinical syndrome before adolescence. Rie (1966) in an excellent review of the theoretical literature argues that even if depression is conceptualized as low self-esteem resulting from a discrepancy between the ego ideal and the actual self, there is great difficulty in applying this model to children. The difficulty is that a stable self-representation is not expected to develop, on theoretical grounds, until adolescence. Rie concludes, "Hence, the major dynamic elements of depression, perhaps not inappropriately regarded as the essence of depression, and indeed some of their structural antecedents, seem not to be generated in toto until the end of latency age" (p. 679).

This chapter was written by Jules Bemporad.

Mahler (1961) also sums up the matter quite unequivocably: "We know that the systematized affective disorders are unknown in childhood. It has been conclusively established that the immature personality structure of the infant or older child is not capable of producing a state of depression as that seen in the adult" (p. 342).

Despite this unanimity of distinguished opinion, depressionlike states do appear in children, theory notwithstanding. Mendelson (1974) has taken the theorists to task over their lack of clinical familiarity with the subject matter that they have so elegantly discussed and dismissed. He writes of the theoretical literature on childhood depression: "It would seem that in no other area of the psychoanalytic literature on depressives are the theoretical papers so far removed from the observations that any clinician can make in the course of his daily practice" (p. 165).

The conflict between theory and observation is far from new in the history of thought (Kuhn, 1962). When such a clash occurs, either the observations are in error or the theory needs revision. As documented in chapter 4, more clinicians are reporting depressionlike states in children; thus we must turn to the underlying theory in our search for error. Indeed, most of the authors who make the claim that depression in childhood is *a priori* impossible subscribe to the orthodox Freudian view of melancholia. If a different theoretical framework is adopted, then a more workable and harmonious interrelation between deduction and observation may evolve. What appears to be most sorely needed is a system of childhood development that stays within the general boundaries of psychoanalytic thought and modifies certain postulates to be more in line with clinical observations and experimental research. Unfortunately, much classical psychoanalytic thought has ignored findings from allied disciplines, and due to this insularity it has become limited in dealing with various clinical problems. The growth or true evaluation of any explanatory system appears to require a healthy interchange between observation and inference.

Even on a strictly theoretical level, the classical psychoanalytic formulations can be found wanting in certain considerations of the development of affect in children. There does not appear to be a sufficient acknowledgement of the gradual accretion of abilities or the gradual consolidation of internal psychic structures over a period of years. Even if the usefulness (one cannot say validity) of such concepts as the superego or the self-representation is agreed upon and accepted, the consolidation of these structures must be thought of as a very gradual process. However, a more evident failing of classical theory is its almost total disregard of cognitive factors in the affective development of the child. The ability to experience certain affects and the advancement of cognitive structures are continuously intertwined throughout development. As indicated by Piaget (1951) cognition and affect are but two aspects of the same evolving unity of the child's psyche.

Without the ability to cognitively appreciate certain aspects of experience, specific affects can not be experienced. Therefore a consideration of cognitive development must go hand in hand with any attempt to understand the development of affect. This does not necessarily mean that the processes of understanding that give rise to emotions must be conscious, any more than Piaget's cognitive schemata are explicitly conscious. Rather, these schemata are unconscious principles that organize experience and give the experience its meaning and thus its emotional content.

This concomitant aspect of cognitive and affective development has been described by Arieti (1967), who postulates that there are various levels of emotions which develop during ontogenesis. This view is founded on a good deal of theoretical logic as well as experimental evidence. Werner (1948) definitively showed that one of the major processes of development is differentiation. He conceived of the child as proceeding from a relatively global "syncretic" state to an articulated, differentiated mode of being. Therefore, the global positive experiences of the young infant gradually become separated into bodily pleasure, mastery, love, joy, or quiet satisfaction. Similarly, global negative experiences differentiate into the adult states of pain, fear, anxiety, depression, or despair. Although somewhat corrected by the recent developments of ego psychology, classical psychoanalysis has been guilty of a double error: ascribing an excessively precocious cognitive system to the child and an excessively immature motivational structure to adults. Just as young children cannot grasp the realities of the world as seen by the adult and therefore cannot experience the exact emotions of adults, mature individuals—by virture of their developed cognitive state—are motivated by more highly differentiated feeling states than children. Experimental studies which partially support this view have been performed by Kohlberg (1969) in the area of moral development and by Loevinger (1976) in regard to overall ego development. These studies are extremely relevant to the study of the individual's affective experience at different stages of development, since they reveal a progression of the predominant modes of thought through ontogenesis. These studies have found that it is not until relatively late in childhood that the individual proceeds beyond a conformist point of view which simply accepts social rules without a great deal of self-awareness or freedom to reflect on multiple possibilities in situations. Loevinger states that many individuals never advance beyond this level and their inner life remains filled with banal clichés, shallow emotions, and simplistic moralizing. While it is possible that adults at this level of psychic development can experience depression, it appears certain that children who have not reached this level are incapable of depressed feelings, according to Loevinger's system.

Therefore, when conceptual systems other than classical psychoanalysis are considered, the question of depression in childhood becomes transformed. As stated in chapter 4, the problem is not whether adultlike depression can occur in childhood, but how the cognitive and affective limitations at different stages of childhood modify the experience and expression of emotions in general. Therefore the most fruitful approach to a theoretical discussion of childhood depression might begin from a developmental standpoint, although our current knowledge of the inner life of children is still very far from adequate. The implicit assumption in this discussion is that any affect necessitates the presence of unconscious cognitive structures which develop through childhood.

Another assumption is that depression is a direct affect much like anxiety (see Sandler and Joffe, 1965), free from complicated metapsychological events that are automatically experienced in certain situations by susceptible individuals. At the same time, depression is seen as a complex affect (see Arieti, 1967) which presupposes a good deal of cognitive maturation. Thus a more realistic search for the vicissitudes of depression would focus on ego development rather than the previous psychoanalytic emphasis on the evolution of the superego.

Depression and Development

INFANCY

Syndromes which are phenomenologically comparable to adult depression have been described by Spitz (1946) and by Engel and Reichsman (1956). Spitz delineated the well-known entity of "anaclitic depression" described in chapter 4. Engel and Reichsman reported a thirteen-month-old girl who withdrew into a state of sleep when strangers approached. From their observation of this young child, Engel and Reichsman postulated an innate "conservation withdrawal" reaction which they believed to be an infantile prototype of the "giving up" attitude in adult depression.

Although Spitz's observations included crying, withdrawal, and sad faces, he did not believe that this infantile behavior was the result of the same intrapsychic situation manifested by adult depressives, because the infants lacked the formation of a tyrannical superego which would direct aggressive drives toward the ego. However, Spitz speculated that self-directed aggression did play a role in these infants' symptoms since they lacked an external love object (the mother) who would both absorb the released aggression and stimulate the expression of libido, which would neutralize the aggression. Being deprived of a maternal figure, these infants directed their instinctual drives on themselves. In this manner Spitz appeared to maintain the concept of self-directed aggression as basic to depression while bypassing the theoretical problem that the infants had not yet formed a superego. However, even if Spitz's formulations are tentatively accepted, the problem remains as to who is the ultimate recipient of these aggressive drives. Jacobson (1971) postulates an aggressive cathexis of the self-representation in adult depression, but can we ascribe self-representation to a six-month-old infant? Can we equally postulate a pathognomonic introject as the recipient of the aggression?

Herein lies the problem that arises when we consider Spitz's model of "anaclitic depression" as a form of depression at all. It appears that the young infant is simply too immature and his psyche too unformed actually to experience depression. There is certainly grave doubt whether infants of this age have any awareness of themselves, or what type of mentation actually exists. Piaget (1952) has in fact called the first eighteen to twenty-four months of life the sensory-motor stage, emphasizing his belief that at this early age mental life consists mainly of innate reactions, habit sequences, and possibly physical discomfort.

However, infants do appear distressed by separation from their mothers and after some time withdraw into a sort of detached, defensive state that Bowlby (1960) described. Thus there is a great temptation to ascribe feelings of depression to the infants' experiential state. This is a dangerous undertaking, for in so doing we may be projecting our own adult affects on the minds of infants. Anna Freud (1970) warned of this danger, writing that "some psychoanalysts credit the newborn already with complex mental processes, with a variety of affects which accompany the action of the various drives and, moreover, with complex reactions to these drives and actions, such as for instance guilt feelings."

We shall probably never exactly know what the infant who has been separated from his mother actually feels, but we can safely assume that he does not experience the same range or depth of emotion that are part of the adult's inner life. The abandoned infant has served as the prototype of adult depression, but such a relationship must be taken as metaphorical at best.

The dissimilarity between these infantile states and adult depression becomes more striking when we learn that lack of cognitive stimulation (Dennis and Najarian, 1957) or even malnutrition (Malmquist, 1971) can produce the same behavioral result. Yet these findings are not so surprising, since the mother serves the infant in countless ways. To use Piaget's terminology, she is the primary "aliment" for the infant's budding schemata. Her deprivation results in stunting psychic development, whether it is affective, cognitive, or motor. Probably all of these discrete functions may be syncretically intermeshed at this early age (Werner, 1948). Therefore loss of the mother may represent the same thing as losing stimulation or tangible nourishment. The mother allows the infant's mind to develop. Through her, the infant forms a sense of self and can begin to anchor himself in reality. The absence of proper mothering, because of its significant role in maturation, thus can result in such long-range deviations as described by Spitz and Bowlby. Early deprivation, if prolonged, does not lead to later depression, but to either retardation or psychopathy.

In this light, it might be more correct to classify the reactions of the infant as development deprivations that are unpleasant but which may be as globally experienced by the immature psyche as persistent non-specific pain or the absence of external stimulation. Since mental development may well begin with emotion and the infant may be capable of suffering long before it can think, there is no doubt that these states are painful, but there can be little relationship to the later pain of depression.

Even in later infancy, such as in the cases described by Engel and Reichsman (1956) and Bowlby (1960), it seems that turning away from the environment represents a possibly innate withdrawal reaction from an ungratifying world rather than true depression. In Bowlby's experience, after a period of time infants eventually will come out of their withdrawal and begin to interact with strangers.

EARLY CHILDHOOD

This developmental stage may be defined arbitrarily as beginning with the infant's psychological individuation from the mother. During this time there is a shift in the child's gratification processes; he now delights in actively doing rather than in being given to and passively nurtured (Mahler, 1968). This is the era of normal oppositionalism and the embryonic testing of the will. There is a delightful "love affair with the world," in which normal fears, apprehensions, or inhibitions are overruled by a constant curiosity about the external world. Clinical reports of depressionlike symptoms at this exuberant age are conspicuously absent. Yet this may be a crucial period for laying the initial groundwork of later depressive episodes.

At this stage the child appears to be faced with a critical choice: to satisfy his own pleasure in the exercise of his will and risk the censure of the parent, or to inhibit his spontaneity and insure the love of the parent. Silverberg (1952) has beautifully called this the conflict between the "heroic" and "unheroic" solution to childhood. Obviously, the eventual decision depends on the temperament of the child, the personality of the parent, the presence of siblings, the economic standard of the family, and an infinity of other factors. However, the initial battle between self-gratification and the surrender of the burgeoning self for the insurance of love leaves its scars long after the war is over. If the parent insists on perfect behavior or is threatened by the willfulness of the child, then a sense of self-inhibition will gradually crystalize and sow the seeds of later self-denial and fear of personal fulfillment. If there is as an additional complication a depressed parent who cannot participate in the joyous excitement of the child's discovery of the world, then a certain sense of deadness and lack of spontaneity may also evolve.

In retrospective studies, Cohen and her co-workers (1954) found that the mothers of later depressives were uncomfortable with their child's emergence from a passive infant into a willfull toddler. Green (1946) in another context indicated that middle-class mothers create an exorbitant need for love in their children and then utilize the threat of withdrawal of love as a disciplinary measure. It may be just this form of sabotaging of the will not through physical punishment but through threats of abandonment or through shaming that causes the child to begin to associate free expression with loss of love or with causing harm in needed others. Mahler (1966) contended that the origins of a depressive mood state lie in the abrupt and simultaneous collapse of the young child's belief in his own omnipotence as well as that of his parents. This view also appears to ascribe psychological processes which are too sophisticated to the young child. Although the preschooler may act as if the world is his oyster and show an alarming lack of fear in dangerous situations, we cannot therefore assume that he believes himself (or others) to be omnipotent. Rather, the young child derives a primitive sense of pleasure in doing, what Freud termed *funktionlust* and Mahler herself described so well as part of the practicing subphase of the separation-individuation process. The roots of depression appear to reside in parental punishment and lack of response to the child's normal exploratory and mastery behavior, which leads to an automatic and unconscious inhibition of activities necessary for later development of an independent sense of worth through individual accomplisment.

Such children present a clinical picture of seriousness, a lack of spontaneity, and often a clinging relation to the parent. While displaying precocious self-control, they are immature in terms of venturing away from the needed parent. These children are being trained to inhibit and distrust their natural inclination toward mastery and autonomous gratification. They are already substituting their parent's pleasure for their own in order to continue the needed security of the parental relationship. To use Sullivanian terms, they are foregoing satisfaction needs for the insurance of security needs.

These children cannot be called depressed, although they may appear sad, frightened, and unduly serious. We do not know their feeling state; although they are able to verbalize, they cannot yet identify or describe emotions through language. We may diagnose these children as overly inhibited and at risk for later depression. Because they still inhabit an age-appropriate action world, they express their pathology through overt behavior. Even then they can alter their mood state readily as the situation demands. Thus if they are fortunate enough to attend a nursery school or be with adults who appreciate their spontaneity, they quickly become fun-loving active youngsters. As Mahler (1966) aptly observed, they tend to show their symptoms in the presence of the parent, possibly because it is the parent who demands the submissive, controlled reaction. They do not as yet generalize these patterns and have not yet fully internalized the parental controls. Their behavior is normally tuned to the rewards and punishments that arise from the environment and not from within.

MIDDLE CHILDHOOD

As the child grows to school age, longer periods of genuine sadness have been observed. These children are clearly unhappy although they are usually unable to give reasons for their plight. As this age, the child simply responds to his surroundings without much thought about who he is or how good or bad he is. Being good is what brings external reward and being bad is whatever provokes external punishment (Piaget, 1932). The child cannot form a stable sense of self in terms of worth and quite appropriately confuses fantasy with reality in his thoughts about himself. He does not have the capacity to sustain a consistent and continued low estimation of himself if any true estimation of self is indeed possible. Nevertheless, depreciation from others can adversely affect the child's mood. As Anna Freud (1970) remarked:

> Neurotic symptom formation waits until the ego has divided itself off from the id, but does not need to wait until ego and superego also have become two independent agencies. The first id–ego conflicts, and with them the first neurotic symptoms as conflict solutions, are produced with the ego under pressure from the environment, i.e., threatened not by guilt feelings arising internally from the superego but by dangers arising from the object world such as loss of love, rejection, punishment (p. 25).

Therefore the child can easily react with sadness to a chronically depriving environment or to an acute loss of needed sources of gratification. He may appear sad but this does not automatically imply an internal conflict. However, reports of such children (Sandler and Joffe, 1965; Poznanski and Zrull, 1970) do report some evidence of a cognitive transformation toward depression; these children are described as expecting bad treatment from others. Although they do not demean themselves, these children can generalize from their past frustrations with their parents to an intuitive attitude toward the rest of humanity.

Another reported finding is a tendency to give up when disappointed, which sets up a future predisposition toward hopelessness and helplessness after a blow to one's sense of self. It may well be that this early form of resignation results from accumulated experiences in which mastery was prevented and failure was insured by the responses of significant others. Therefore rejection or inflated, unrealistic demands by parents can lead to a sense that the child cannot win, that trying makes no sense. These findings tend to support Seligman's (1975) "learned helplessness" model as the root of depression. However, the actual situation is not so clear-cut. What seems to occur is that the parents reward certain behavior and show love, but only for activities that undermine the child's individuation and self-gratification. At this age the child's sense of worth is normally dependent on the responses of parental figures, so that their disapproval or rejection will have devastating effects and will inhibit the behavior that brought disapproval. As Sandler and Joffe remark, "It not infrequently happens that the child's parents are in unconscious opposition to progressive individuation, and the influence of the parents may be perpetuated in their successor, the superego" (1965, p. 54). At this age the child has not internalized a view of himself or a set of prohibitions, but he begins to automatically inhibit those behaviors that threaten to cut off the needed flow of approval from the parents.

We can perhaps define two types of dysphoric states in children of this age—one in which the parents gradually inhibit responses that would yield a sense of satisfaction or pleasure, and another in which the child directly responds to the deprivation of gratification in his environment. The former type can be seen in families in which the parents set up unrealistic ideals, use shame as a form of punishment, and are threatened by the child's individuation. The latter type is seen in homes where the parents are consistently rejecting or where they are themselves depressed. However, such dysphoric states frequenty can be observed in children who are physically ill and whose illness interrupts their normal, everyday enjoyable activities.

The most extreme illustration of this latter form of dysphoria is a six-year-old boy reported by Bierman, Silverstein, and Finesinger (1958). This child had been hospitalized because of poliomyelitis. After two months of illness he manifested symptoms reminiscent of adult depression. He seemed to give up hope and lapse into a depressionlike withdrawal as he experienced day after day of frustration, confinement, and inability to participate in his usual gratifying activities. However, there is no record of self-recriminations, feelings of guilt, or low self-esteem. He was simply very unhappy at having lost the use of his legs. This was a true loss of enormous magnitude, and the child's response seems completely understandable and appropriate. His mother visited him regularly but her presence was insufficient in relieving the child's quite realistic sense of chronic deprivation. With clinical recovery of the primary illness, his mood returned to normal. This case is instructive since it demonstrates that children of this age are capable of extreme sadness under chronically frustrating circumstances, but these moods are reactive to the environment and the child does not perpetuate a depressive mood in the absence of an external cause. However, one need not go to the extreme of a crippling illness and prolonged hospitalization to produce these moods; a chaotic family or a disapproving parent usually suffices.

Even in such instances the sadness is relatively short-lived. This short duration may be due to two major underlying characteristics of children of this age group: they are still creatures of the moment, and they will readily defend themselves against unpleasant feelings. The latter trait may account for conditions described as "depressive equivalents" or "masked depression" in children. Feelings of sadness often are defended against purely by distraction. The child simply attends to other more pleasant matters rather than to the environmental conditions that are causing him pain. If his attention is focused on these conditions, he will display the appropriate affect. However, this does not prove that an underlying or unconscious depression was present all along, seething beneath a seemingly happy exterior. The child maintains an amazing capacity to forget about things when not confronted by them. When this trait is coupled with normal childhood hedonism, it becomes clear why depressionlike symptoms should be rare and fleeting in this age group. It is only when the behavior appears to be excessive in its denial of an ever-present frustrating reality or the behavior is extremely maladaptive, that one should suspect a pathologic defensive denial of unpleasant affects, similar to what is seen in some adult hysterics.

The problem of "depressive equivalents" is more complex and at times confusing. Toolan (1962) lists eating and sleeping disorders, colic, and head-banging as depressive equivalents in infants, and temper tantrums, truancy, running away from home, and accident proneness as similar states in older children. Sperling (1959) suggests that sleep and gastrointestinal disorders in children may be equivalent to depression. These authors speculate that children cannot express depressive affect in an adult form, and these symptoms represent a childhood form of the disorder. This concept of symptom expression is clearly different from the "masked depression" described by Cytryn and McKnew (1972), who emphasize it as a childhood form of defense against feelings of depression.

Rie (1966) has written a thoughtful and thorough critique of the concepts of depressive equivalents in children. Briefly, Rie's major arguments are that: (1) There is no logical connection between the equivalent symptom and the alleged underlying depression. (2) There is no proof that any feeling of depression exists for which the symptom is taken as an equivalent. (3) Depression is inferred on the basis of theory only, so that any child who does not manifest depression directly after a loss must be expressing this painful affect in some other form. (4) Any symptom that can be interpreted as symbolic of oral deprivation (i.e., an eating disorder) has been mistakenly termed a psychodynamic equivalent to depression. Once again clinicians have projected their own expected reactions onto the psyche of a cognitively immature organism. Rather than assuming that depression must be present but expressed differently from adults, the possibility of the experience of adult forms of depression in a young child should be investigated more rigorously. This "adultomorphic" distortion perhaps has been utilized more in the study of childhood depression than in any other pediatric psychiatric problem. The concept of depressive equivalents has done much to confuse the diagnostic status of childhood depression by allowing almost any symptom to be so classified. Until we know more about the inner life of children, it might be best to refrain from using this questionable concept.

In summary, children of early school age do display periods of prolonged unhappiness in response to chronic environmental stress. They are increasingly sensitive to the rejection of others as well as to deprivation of gratifications. However, these moods are rarely sustained and respond readily to external changes. Even in these states of sadness, there is no evidence of guilt or lowered self-regard. What may be present is an abnormal pressure to make the parent happy or to thwart personal satisfaction to obtain favor with the parent.

LATE CHILDHOOD

At this stage of development, the child's cognitive abilities appear to allow for a system of thought that includes the sense of responsibility toward others, the internalization of values and rules, and a budding sense of one's self. Children of this age are normally less concerned with their families and more with the judgments of peers and society. However, they carry within themselves and into the community the internalized family belief systems that have been learned from the parents. Depending on the particulars of this belief system, the child will face frustration in a variety of ways* and derive different coping mechanisms. It is at this age that Sandler and Joffe's (1965) theoretical differentiation between depression as a psychobiological response and a clinical illness may assume particular importance. Children of this age not only react to disappointment or the loss of well-being with an initial depressive affective reaction, but they may continue to evolve a more chronic depressionlike illness. At this time the consolidation of adaptive processes takes place, so that the child will respond to stress in a repeated and characteristic manner. One such response, described by Sandler and Joffe (1965) and others, is to capitulate in the face of frustration and to develop a sense of overwhelming loss, a feeling of personal impotence, and shame.

The cognitive growth of the preadolescent years also allows for a recognition of the self which can be morally evaluated. The child may believe himself to be unworthy or unsatisfactory in the face of life's demands. Therefore, reports of dysphoric states at this stage do mention lowered self-regard. For example, McConville et al. (1973) described a subgroup of depressed children from eight to ten years old who expressed fixed ideas of negative self-esteem. Similarly, Poznanski and Zrull (1970) observed that older depressed children expressed disappointment in themselves rather than simply reacting to an external unpleasant situation.

Much of the deprivation of this age group appears to result from the child's thinking about his predicament and arriving at certain conclusions.

---

* The Freudian concept of the superego does not entirely do justice to the internalized cognitive system. The superego seems to be limited to punishment and idealization while the internalized cognitive system assumes many of the functions normally ascribed to the ego, such as modes of adaptation, self-assessment, and relationships with others.

The affect state is not an automatic consequence of experience, as in younger children; rather, it is a personal logical evaluation of the experience. Children of this age who cannot attain the parental ideal become depressed because they perceive this circumstance to be a personal failure and not simply that the parents are themselves unhappy. Similarly, older, repeatedly rejected children are reacting to their own belief that they are unlovable rather than only to the immediate pain of the rejection. Therefore, depression at this stage takes on a more cognitive, evaluative characteristic and in this sense is no longer the immediate, stimulus-bound sadness of the younger child. The younger child might directly seek dependency gratification or openly regress to infantile needs in the face of frustration, but these preadolescent children inhibit expression of these desires of which—like the adult—they feel ashamed. Behavior is scrutinized and evaluated in terms of the self. This cognitive aspect causes older children to remain depressed regardless of changes in external circumstances. Because of these self-perpetuating and self-evaluative aspects of the child's dysphoria, it may be correct to speak of actual depressive illness at this age. The point is that the depression results from cognitive conclusions which may be erroneous but are one step removed from the immediate environment.

Anthony and Scott (1960) reported a twelve-year-old child who manifested a depressive episode which may illustrate some of the features of depression in late childhood arising from pathological needs. Although this child's symptoms were much more severe than normally seen at this age, the underlying psychodynamics are not uncommon. This boy developed a severe depressive illness with manic interludes after his parents decided to adopt a ten-year-old boy to act as his companion. The patient suffered neither the loss of a love object nor the loss of gratifying activities, but was described as succumbing to depression as a result of the imagined loss of his favored status with his mother. His premorbid history was significant in many aspects: he was always overly close to his mother, he was timid and self-conscious, he rarely played with peers, he was unhappy at school (although he did well academically), and he generally solved his problems by giving up or by running to his mother. The authors described this patient as deriving a sense of omnipotence from being the "only fruit" of his mother's womb and the most precious thing in her world. The thought of sharing his mother with another child meant the loss of his inappropriate sense of self-meaning and an end to his pathological tie with her.

This child clearly suffered a depressive illness not only on the basis of his symptoms, but because his reaction was not in concert with the realistic stress; it evolved from his own distortions of the situation. His need for his mother was so great, and he had been so prevented from normal individuation and deprived of self-reliant sources of meaning and gratification, that at age twelve the prospect of another child entering the charmed mother–son circle was sufficient to cause a depressive decompensation.

Even in children who are this cognitively mature, however, the depression is not the same as in adults. The older child's self-evaluation is still more malleable than the adult's and more readily responds to positive environmental experiences. The negative sense of self is not so crystalized as to automatically devalue all successes or shun all gratifications. However, the major difference between depression at this stage and the adult variant is a lack of future orientation. The child during latency cannot truly relate his present state on a continuum with his future experience. Rather than denying the future defensively, he simply does not think of it. Rie (1966) made the pertinent observation that one of the crucial differ-ences between adult and child depression may be the absence of hopelessness in the latter. Rie cited numerous definitions of adult depression and stressed that they all contain some reference to a time perspective that includes a representation of the future. He further argued that if the individual before adolescence cannot comprehend concepts such as long-range goals and their relationship to present strivings, the meaning of infinity, and the absolute permanence of loss or disappointment, then such an individual could not experience hopelessness and despair, two cardinal features of adult depression.*

Rie's arguments appear to be theoretically sound since Piaget (1952) also concluded that until early adolescence the child is wedded to the "concrete" and not capable of abstractions that would be involved in projecting himself into the future. Rie's conclusions also concur with clinical observations. Children do not complain of being unable to face tomorrow or that they will remain eternally depressed. They do not deny the prospect of an unbearable future; they simply do not think of it.

ADOLESCENCE

It is not until the end of childhood that depressive episodes truly comparable to adult states are seen clinically. The depressions of adolescence equal the adult forms in severity, surpass them in self-destructiveness, and still betray a characteristic developmental stamp. As mentioned before, the child does not appear able to conceive of his future; however, the adolescent seems capable of little else. The concept of time looms large is adolescent thought and in adolescent depression. There is the terrifying sense that all actions or experiences are irrevocable and ever-lasting, and result in eternal shame and despair. This overemphasis on the relationship of today with tomorrow is beyond the capacities of the child and is usually tempered by a greater life experience in the adult. For the adolescent, however, all seems lost and nothing can be redeemed.

* Rie's argument is equally important for showing again how depression is ultimately dependent on the development of the capacities of the ego (especially cognitive abilities) rather than simply on the formation of the superego.

Erikson (1959) has examined this distorted sense of time in his studies of disturbed adolescents who, from a different vantage point, can be seen as experiencing severe depressive episodes. Erikson notes: "Protests of a missed greatness and a premature and fatal loss of useful potential are common complaints among our patients as they are among adolescents in cultures which consider such protestations romantic; the implied malignancy, however, consists of a decided disbelief in the possibility that time may bring change, and yet also a fear that it might" (1959, p. 26). This fear of time and the inability to handle time appear to give adolescent depression an urgent, overwhelming quality.

Another factor that influences the expression of dysphoria in adolescence is the lack of moderation in thought. The adolescent appears to live in an all or nothing world; he gives seemingly unimportant events an inflated status and responds to them in a dramatic, all-consuming manner. Here again, the adolescent appears to lack sufficient maturity to put everyday events in proper perspective. Everything has an air of finality and, at times, of desperation.

Perhaps these attributes of adolescence are magnified by the social pressures that are exerted at this developmental phase in our own culture. In our society, youngsters are constantly reminded that they are building for their future lives—whether it is in terms of career, marriage, or social acceptance. This is also the age when many individuals are away from home for the first time, feeling unprepared for this responsibility and yet ashamed of what they perceive to be childish, dependent strivings. Such adolescents are so accustomed to living out the dictates of another that the availability of freedom leads to self-doubt and utter loneliness. They often form a tie with a new authority on whom they can depend for direction and meaning.

Other adolescents carry with them the need to reach some parental ideal only to find that either they are not able to reach it or to do so would mean giving up their own chance for individuation. Anthony (1975) uses John Stuart Mill's early difficulties to exemplify some pertinent aspects of depression in adolescence. Anthony writes that one day young Mill asked himself the crucial question: would he be happy if he accomplished all that his father had asked? Mill was forced to answer no, and of that moment Mill wrote, "At this, my heart sank in me; the whole foundation on which my life was constructed fell down . . . I seemed to have nothing to live for." Anthony explains "he fell ill when he became aware that the realization of his father's aims in life would not satisfy him, and he regained his mental health (to the degree that this was possible) when he understood that the death of the father brought with it the growth of identity, autonomy, and responsibility for the son" (1975, p. 448).

Not all adolescents are as fortunate as young Mill. Many continue to strive for the parental ideal which has become their ideal, denying life and pleasure and ultimately succumbing to depression whether or not the goal is ever reached. In adolescence one may observe the shaping of the characteristic forms of depression: the need for others, the dominant goal, and especially the ascetic self-denial that gradually erodes any experience of pleasure or meaning.

Conclusion

The foregoing sections have attempted to apply a developmental approach to depressive phenomena in childhood. If depression is conceived of as a sophisticated affective experience that necessitates extensive cognitive maturation, then the dysphoric states that precede the experience of depression may be seen as continuous with, but not equal to, depression. The deprivation of the infant, the inhibition of the toddler, the stimulus-bound sadness of the young child, the limited depression of the older child, and the exaggerated yet acutely felt despair of the adolescent may all be understood best against a framework of the developmental process.

The types of reaction, the causes for their manifestation, and the underlying structural elements are presented in Table 8-1 with a parallel schema of ego development adapted from Loevinger (1976). Although obviously incomplete, such an attempt at synthesis may help in delineating the causes and types of depressionlike experience in childhood.

Suicide in Children and Adolescents

Attempted or completed suicide in children appears to differ markedly from the self-destructive behavior of adults. There are differences in frequency, sex distribution, effect of socio-cultural upheavels, and most significantly, in the motives underlying suicide in adults and children. As will be discussed further, there is some question whether the self-destructive behavior of young children can be considered truly suicidal since they may have little appreciation of the meaning of death. There is even more question about a uniform association of suicide and depression in childhood. However, a sufficient number of depressed children and adolescents ultimately attempt suicide so that this topic may be considered here.

TABLE 8-1
Symptoms and Causes of Depression at Various Stages of Development

Developmental Stage	Symptoms	Major Psychodynamics
Infancy	Withdrawal after crying and protest	Loss of stimulation, security, and well-being supplied by the mother
Early childhood	Inhibition, clinging behavior	Disapproval by parents
Middle childhood	Sadness as automatically responsive to the immediate situation	Rejection by parents, loss of gratifying activities (i.e., chronic illness)
Late childhood	Depression with low self-esteem	Unable to meet parental ideal, unable to sustain threat to parental relationship
Adolescence	Depression with exaggerated urgency, time distortion, and impulsivity	Unable to fulfill internalized parental ideal, inability to separate from family.

STATISTICAL DATA

Demographic reports (Seiden, 1969) suggest that the rate of suicide for children under fifteen years of age has changed little in this century. The general rate of 0.5 deaths per 100,000 population (for children under fifteen) (Seiden 1969) seems to have remained stable since 1900. This rate was unaffected by both World Wars (which decreased the total suicide rate) and by the Great Depression (which increased the total suicide rate). However, it is notoriously difficult to determine accurately the true rate of suicide in young children since such deaths may be greatly underreported. The suicides of young children are obviously tinged with shame, guilt, and embarrassment for the survivors so that the true nature of the death is concealed. Also, children do not leave suicide notes and there is greater opportunity for their deaths to be termed accidental.

In those cases where suicide cannot be doubted as the cause of death, it has been found that males outnumber females in actual suicides (Shaffer, 1974) although females may threaten suicide or make suicidal gestures more frequently (Mattsson et al., 1969). Cultural beliefs also greatly influence the rate of suicide, especially in adolescents and young adults. Catholic countries such as Ireland, where suicide is considered a sin, have a low rate. In countries such as Japan, where suicide is considered an honorable way to die, self-destruction is the most common cause of death for individuals under thirty (Seiden, 1969). There is also some debate over hidden suicides in ghetto youths or among American Indians. "Hidden suicide" refers to youngsters who do not literally kill

Type of Dysphoria	Loevinger Ego Development Stages*
Deprivation of needed stimulation	Presocial, symbiotic
Inhibition of gratification of emerging sense of will	Impulsive, self-protective, fear of being caught, externalizing blame, opportunistic
Sadness, unsustained crying directly related to frustrating or depriving situation	Conformist: conformity to external rules, shame and guilt for breaking rules, superficial niceness
Depression with a cognitive component in terms of affect resulting from deduction about circumstances	Conscientious: conformist, differentiation of norms and goals, awareness of self in relation to group, helping
Accentuation of depression by cognitive distortions about the finality of events	Conscientious: self-evaluated standards, guilt for consequences, long-term goals and ideals

* Adapted from Loevinger, J. 1976. *Ego development.* San Francisco: Jossey-Bass.

themselves (which would be considered cowardly) but force others to kill them through acts of delinquency or bravado. Wolfgang (1959) studied the Philadelphia police records and found a high number of such victim-precipitated homicides among black youths. Finally, while suicide is very rare in young children, its incidence increases rapidly with age and it is among the leading causes of death in older adolescents and young adults. Seiden quotes the Vital Statistics of the United States as recording the following rate of suicide by age group per 100,000 population in 1964: age five to nine, 0.05; age ten to fourteen, 0.4; age fifteen to nineteen, 4.6; and age twenty to twenty-four, 10.8. We can glean from these figures that there is a draamtic rise in the suicide rate as children grow toward maturity.

MOTIVATION

Any attempt to deal with the motives behind the suicidal behavior of children must consider their concept of death. As stated by Seiden, many children want to kill themselves but they do not wish to die. This paradoxical statement becomes clear if we understand that many children do not consider death to be irreversible or perceive suicide as a grave act. Seiden cites the work of Winn and Halla, who found that young children attach as much significance to stealing from their mother's purse as they do to threatening to kill themselves.

The gradual development of the child's concept of death was studied by Schilder and Wechsler (1934) and later by Nagy (1959). The former investigators found that the young child does not believe in death as a natural termination of life but sees it as an event which can be caused only by violence or illness. Young children also do not believe in their own self-destruction. Death is seen as a temporary, reversible state.

On the basis of projective materials such as drawings, written compositions, and verbal responses to questions asked of 378 children, Nagy described the development of the concept of death in children. She delineated three conceptual stages: children under age five conceive of death as a temporary, reversible state in which the individual is still alive but deprived of action, as in sleep. Between the ages of five and nine, the child begins to appreciate death as a fearful state in which one is separated from loved ones. Death is personified as a "skeleton man" who carries off children at night, and is thought of as a fortuitous external event and not as a certain eventuality. Children at this stage also identify death with physical changes (i.e., a dead person is all bones) rather than with a possible obliteration or transformation of consciousness. Around age nine, children begin to exhibit an adult view of death as the termination of life and as universal. As one boy of nine years, 11 months put it, "Death is something that no one can escape."

Anthony (1967) postulated an "eight-year anxiety" in the child which consists of a preoccupation with ideas of death or dying, either about himself or his parents. In agreement with Nagy, he found that around this age the child realizes death is irreversible and also feels helpless in the face of its inevitability, since everyone is in the same predicament. This phase passes quickly and a sense of personal immunity soon reasserts itself. However, if traumatic events occur during this phase, there may be an additional challenge to the child's defenses and pathology may result.

On the basis of these studies, it is questionable if self-destructive acts before age nine or ten can be truly considered suicidal. In many cases, even after this age (and also in some adults) the individual appears to momentarily deny the extreme gravity of death in order to escape an intolerable situation or to punish others by a suicidal act. Such extreme measures, however, only can occur against a background of a lack of compassion and care. As to why very young children do not appear to kill themselves since they deny the permanence of death and are impulsive, a logical possibility is Shaffer's suggestion (1974) that they lack the cognitive maturity to carefully plan suicide or even the knowledge of how to carry out the act.

In rare instances in which a childhood death by suicide can be substantiated, researchers have found a few predominant themes which seem to underlie most of these acts. As early as 1855, Durand-Fardel reviewed all suicides by persons under sixteen years of age in France between 1835 and 1844. Of the 192 childhood suicides reported, he was able to study 22 such incidents in detail. Of these, ten children drowned themselves, ten hanged themselves, and two burned themselves. There is no mention of death by ingestion of toxic substances or by overdose of drugs, which today is the most prevalent form of self-destruction. However, the motives behind childhood suicide have remained essentially the same over a century. Durand-Fardel mentions fear of impending punishment, reproach for a misdeed, an attempt to punish the parents, or the wish to join a dead loved one as reasons for suicide. Overall, he makes an impassioned plea for better treatment of children. He also observes that it is the deprivation of love rather than material goods that predisposes childhood suicide: "In the poorhouse of farmers as well as in the houses of workers and educated people, one finds children that cannot take the absence of tenderness. They cannot cope with brutality and injustice."

Later studies have echoed these themes. Bender and Schilder in 1937 studied eighteen children under thirteen years of age who were admitted to the Bellevue psychiatric ward with manifested suicidal preoccupations. They found that these children came from backgrounds of emotional deprivation in which they did not receive the amount of love they desired or needed. This deprivation was said to arouse feelings of aggression against the parents but, because of concomitant guilt, the aggression was allegedly turned against the self, resulting in suicidal wishes. Bender and Schilder also noted other suicidal motives in their sample such as the children's wish to punish those around them, to attain the desired love by coercion, and to be reunited with a departed love object. Despert (1952) came to similar conclusions fifteen years later, in studying a group of children who had unsuccessfully attempted suicide.

Shaffer (1974) recently investigated contemporaneous data on children who actually committed suicide. He reports detailed information on thirty-one children under the age of fifteen who killed themselves in England and Wales between the years 1962 and 1968. In over one-third of the cases, the precipitating event was a disciplinary crisis of some sort— usually the anticipation of punishment. Other precipitants in order of frequency were problems with peers, disputes with parents, being dropped from a school team, interaction with a psychotic parent, and imitation of a "fantasy model," meaning that the child was copying the act of a well-publicized suicide. The personality descriptions of these children were: (1) children who felt that others didn't like them, (2) children who were quiet and uncommunicative, and (3) children who were perfectionist and self-critical. The first of these descriptions overlapped with the others, and a fourth type of personality found in six cases, that of being impulsive and erratic, did not coincide at all. Shaffer concludes that suicidal children may conform to two stereotypes: children of superior intellect who were isolated from peers and possibly became depressed; and children who were impetuous, prone to aggressive outbursts, and overly sensitive to criticism. While such stereotypes may be familiar to psychiatric profiles, the propensity to suicide is believed to reside in their familiarity with the phenomenon of suicide itself. Shaffer backs up this supposition with the finding that the families of these children showed a high incidence of attempted suicide and depression (with possible talk of suicide).

Shaffer concludes that childhood suicide is the end result of many factors, not the least of which is a certain cognitive maturity both in terms of what death actually means and in terms of being able to plan and execute a suicidal plan. Other significant variables were a disturbed family background, a depressed mental state, a precipitating incident (often of a humiliating kind), access to a means of suicide, and close experience with suicidal behavior. Out of respect for the family's sensibilities, Shaffer did not directly interview the surviving family members and thus does not stress the emotional deprivation so strongly emphasized by other investigators.

The following case example may help in giving an idea of the familial atmosphere so often found in the evaluation of suicidal children.

ILLUSTRATIVE CASE STUDY OF SUICIDAL CHILD

Donna was an eleven-year-old girl who told her teacher that she was planning to kill herself and had been contemplating suicide for some time. This "confession" did not appear to be a manipulative gesture but was divulged in the context of a personal talk with the teacher whom Donna preferred to her own mother. Donna was the oldest of four children and was expected to be responsible for her younger sibs. They would tease her but she could not retaliate for fear of being punished by her parents. Donna had been raped by a relative when she was six years old, and apparently had borne the brunt of blame for this incident. Her mother continually accused Donna of being promiscuous and of having secret liaisons with boys despite the fact that the girl was only eleven years of age. The mother kept a close watch over Donna and did not allow her any significant extrafamilial relationships. She had to be home directly after school and she frequently was beaten by both parents. One week prior to her "confession" to the teacher, Donna's mother in a fit of rage said she would kill her and Donna believed her. She decided it would be better to take her own life instead. When the mother was seen, she denied any history of child abuse (despite documented evidence to the contrary). It was learned that the father probably had had a series of affairs which infuriated the mother. Both parents seemed to utilize Donna as a scapegoat for their own frustrations. If she had not found some comforting outsider and revealed her plan, she may well have killed herself.

SUICIDAL BEHAVIOR IN ADOLESCENCE

A totally different picture emerges when adolescent suicide is considered. Suicide among adolescents is not rare, and gestures or attempts are very frequent. Suicide ranks as a leading cause of death among the fifteen- to nineteen-year age group and 12 percent of all suicide attempts are made by teenagers (of these, 90 percent are female) (Seiden, 1969). The reasons for this high rate of self-destructive behavior are not completely understood. Some authors believe that depression is a significant predisposition and others believe anger toward others is the major determinant. Here again, semantics confuses the issue since some authors will classify depression only when there is clear evidence of anger turned toward the self, ignoring responses to loss or frustration and often labelling these latter states as grief reactions. Therefore the prevalence of depression among teenagers who attempt suicide remains largely a matter of how the particular author defines depression.

Mattson et al. (1969) distinguished six groups of child and adolescent suicide attempters in their study of seventy-five patients at a psychiatric clinic. The motivations for each group were: (1) Loss of a love object: these patients sustained the death or desertion of a parent or peer of the opposite sex. They were depressed and wished to die in order to join the deceased person. Although lonely and sad, they did not exhibit guilt or self-recriminations (three boys, fourteen girls). (2) "The bad me," that is, markedly self-depreciating patients: these patients hated themselves and felt they deserved to die. They viewed death as a solution and possible rebirth as a more worthy person (nine boys, eleven girls). (3) The final "cry for help" directed beyond the immediate family: these patients appeared worn out by chronic overwhelming external stress such as physical illness or family disruption (one boy, fourteen girls). (4) The revengeful, angry teenager: these adolescents clearly stated the coercive, manipulative aspects of their suicidal gestures and did not actually intend to kill themselves (three boys, ten girls). (5) The psychotic adolescent: these patients made repeated suicide threats, and suicide seemed to be a desperate solution to inner tension and confusion rather than an acting out of delusional belief (two boys, five girls). (6) "The suicide game": these patients flirted with death in order to get peer approval and to experience a thrill. They exhibited denial of death and questionable suicidal intent (one boy, two girls).

This breakdown of a large sample of suicidal children, mostly teenagers, demonstrates the variety of motivations for self-destructive behavior. It is significant that girls outnumbered boys over two to one in suicidal threats and gestures, while the actual suicides committed in the same geographic area for the same time period were all committed by adolescent boys using firearms.

From these and other data, it may be concluded that although adolescent girls more frequently attempt suicide, more adolescent boys actually kill themselves. The main feature which seems to differentiate true suicidal intent from suicidal gestures is social isolation (Seiden, 1969). As long as there is someone to whom the teenager can turn for help or against whom he can vent his rage, true suicide may be averted. If the youngster believes no one who will care if he lives or dies, then suicide becomes a real possibility. Many of the attempts or gestures may be seen as desperate communications to others, but true suicides are well planned with no chance of survival. Two difficulties that obviously attend gestures are that the attempt may misfire and the individual die unintentionally; or if this desperate gesture is not taken seriously by loved ones, the youngster may be convinced that no one really does care and then attempt a true suicidal act.

A subgroup which has received considerable attention is the suicidal college student. Students attending Harvard or Yale showed twice the suicide rate as nonstudents of the same age (Seiden, 1969). Similar findings were obtained from studying the suicide rates at Oxford and Cambridge in England (cited in Seiden). Investigations of the differences between suicidal and nonsuicidal classmates revealed that the former group was older, did better academically, and showed more indications of emotional disturbance. There was also a greater number of foreign students among the suicidal group, which may indicate separation from the usual social support systems and a greater sense of isolation. Some authors have mentioned fear of academic failure, extreme scholastic pressure, or shame over feelings of inadequacy and dependency as major suicidal motives in the college student. Again, there is no uniform motivation that can account of all suicidal behavior. On the other hand, Hendin (1975) proposed some common characteristics among students who attempt suicide. He eloquently wrote that some individuals are drawn to death as a way of life: they are so inhibited and tied to a past familial atmosphere of gloom and despair that they cannot tolerate the opportunities for pleasure and involvement which college life offers them.

These students see their relationships with their parents as dependent on their emotional if not physical death and become tied to their parents in a death knot. Coming to college, graduating, becoming seriously involved with another person, and enjoying an independent existence have the power to free them. In fact, the meaning of suicide and depression lies in their encounter with the forces that might unleash their own possibilities for freedom (pp. 238–239).

For such individuals, numbness is a sort of protection and the possibility of gratifications arouses guilt over betraying a secret bond with the parent. This guilt and the understanding that it blocks pleasure leaves the individual frozen in a state of inhibition; he cannot break through the old sanctions and yet cannot endure living in accordance with them. Suicide becomes a possible solution to this conflict. Death has always held a special fascination for these individuals who, according to Hendin, by their own self-destruction appear to fulfill the parental command not to dare to live.

Hendin's work draws attention to some of the potent forces for suicide in all age groups: a lack of being appreciated for what one is, a failure of parents to instill a sense of joy and approval of life in the child, and finally, a prevailing sense in the individual that his enjoyment of other relationships or other activities is a guilty betrayal. Suicide, like depression, may ultimately result from a self-induced elimination of satisfactory and satisfying life alternatives that are not tied to omnipotent others or dominating goals. This lack of freedom to form new interests or relationships—that is, a lack of freedom to enjoy life—results in depression and ultimately in some suicides. If the adolescent can achieve some wholly personal aspect of life, free from the deadening burden of guilt and parental "shoulds," he may escape the premature termination of his own potential. Some adolescents find solace in a relationship, a cause, or an academic interest which may lead them to liberation and away from their heritage of obligation and self-denial.

In his autobiography Bertrand Russell recalls the cold and unloving atmosphere in which he grew up. Throughout his teens he often considered doing away with himself, but he survived to live a long and productive life. He wrote, looking back at the time he was fifteen, "There was a footpath leading across fields to New Southgate, and I used to go there alone to watch the sunset and contemplate suicide. I did not, however, commit suicide, because I wished to know more of mathematics" (1967, p. 45).

PART THREE

Psychotherapy

[9]

PSYCHOTHERAPY

OF SEVERE DEPRESSION

Choice of Treatment

Four major therapeutic approaches or combinations of them are presently available for the treatment of severe depression: psychotherapy, drug therapy, shock therapy, and hospitalization and milieu therapy.

The therapist must have a knowledge of their range of applicability in order to decide which one or which combination to use with a specific patient. Because of the special scope of this book, a discussion of methods other than psychotherapy will be limited to a few remarks.

In the last several years, drug therapy for the treatment of depression has received a great deal of attention even in the press. Often it is the patient himself who asks to be treated pharmacologically. Generally it is easy for him to accept the idea that a pill can relieve him of depression just as a codeine pill can relieve him of a toothache. However, in severe cases of depression characterized by a feeling of hopelessness and the belief that everything is futile, it may be difficult to convince the patient to accept even drug therapy.

Drug therapy is generally started with administration of one of the tricyclics, the best known of which is imipramine (Tofranil®). The patient is informed that improvement will not occur overnight and that it may take two or three weeks before he notices a difference in the way he feels. As a rule, the decrease in intensity of the feeling of depression is preceded by increase in appetite and improved sleep patterns. If no sign of improvement is noticed within a month, the treatment generally is switched to a MAO inhibitor.

According to my observations, amelioration of symptoms treated with

This chapter was written by Silvano Arieti.

drug therapy occurs in many cases, but not in the most severe. Moreover even when the patient improves, he inwardly remains the person he was before starting drug therapy; that is, he retains the same psychological equipment, potentialities, and vulnerabilities unless other types of treatment are given or unexpected propitious circumstances occur. At best, drug therapy must be considered a moderately effective symptomatic treatment. Nevertheless pharmacotherapy should not be rejected or even belittled on account of its limited effect. Many cases of severe depression cause terrible suffering for the patient. Anything that can even partially relieve the mental pain is to be welcomed unless it produces undesirable collateral effects. To my experience and knowledge, drug therapy which consists of the common antidepressants (tricyclics and MAO inhibitors) does not produce damaging psychological effects or conditions which would prevent psychotherapy unless massive doses are used, at times in conjunction with neuroleptics. With the use of the MAO inhibitors, dietary restrictions must of course be imposed and careful vigilance exerted for hypertensive crises, which occur on rare occasions. Lithium therapy is effective in the treatment of manic episodes, but only rarely helps depressed patients or prevents recurrence of attacks.

In conclusion, antidepressant drugs are effective in the treatment of severe depressions, but only to a moderate degree. They seem less effective than neuroleptics are in the symptomatic treatment of schizophrenia.

Whenever drug therapy is completely ineffectual and psychotherapy cannot be obtained, or whenever there are urgent reasons for bringing about an immediate change (in such contingencies as concomitant physical illness, high suicidal risk, or extreme suffering), electric shock treatment is indicated. Whereas ECT has practically no effect on mild (or reactive) depressions, it is quite effective in many cases of primary severe depression. The treatment may be beneficial even if the patient has been sick for many years, as demonstrated by successfully treated cases of involutional melancholia. However, not all patients respond to ECT, and many refuse to undergo this type of treatment. In manic patients ECT is less effective than lithium.

In my experience, ECT treatment does not make a patient less accessible to psychotherapy. However, many patients who are quickly relieved of their suffering with ECT unfortunately no longer feel motivated to embark upon long psychotherapy which necessitates reconsidering aspects of their life that they wish to forget. They generally do not accept any additional treatment until another attack ensues.

Hospitalization must be considered especially when there is danger of suicide. However, we must realize that a suicidal risk exists in practically every patient suffering from a severe form of depression. It is up to the psychiatrist to assess whether the risk is great, moderate, or minimal, and there are no infallible methods for making such a distinction. The danger is generally greater in people who are single, widowed, separated, or divorced, for two reasons. First, their life history more easily leads them into a feeling of hopelessness and helplessness. Second, surveillance is less available; often they live alone and therefore, if seized by sudden destructive impulses, are much less likely to be prevented by others from carrying out these impulses.

If the danger is deemed great and the patient cannot be kept under proper surveillance at home, hospitalization becomes necessary. Often it is more difficult to convince the relatives than the patient that he should be hospitalized. The very depressed patient, perhaps in a masochistic spirit, at times is ready to enter the hospital whereas the relatives would prefer to send him on vacation. It is more difficult to hospitalize a manic, as he himself prefers to take trips and to escape into action. When the risk is moderate or minimal, the decision is more difficult. At times the risk is worth taking in view of the fact that long psychodynamic psychotherapy is not available in many hospitals, and also because the possibility of suicide is not completely eliminated even in a hospital setting. Moreover, in some cases a certain amount of risk remains for an indefinite but prolonged period of time because the patient does not benefit from therapy even in a hospital milieu. Thus he would have to be hospitalized for an indefinite period of time, with great damage to his self-image and increased feelings of hopelessness. All these possibilities should be discussed openly with the members of the family. The responsibility for the decision must be made in a spirit of collaboration and, if possible, unanimity among patient, family, and therapist.

Contrary to what can be said in reference to schizophrenia or other psychiatric conditions, hospitalization is not a good milieu therapy for most depressed patients. The main and often the only advantage of hospitalization lies in decreasing the danger of suicide and in making certain that the patient will receive adequate drug therapy or electric shock treatment. Hospitalization also may be advisable for severely depressed, but nonsuicidal patients who live alone, have no relatives or friends, and are unable to take care of themselves.

Although I recognize that my theoretical inclination and my personal clinical experience are influencing me, I think that I can make the following statements with a fair degree of objectivity.

1. Indications for psychotherapy exist in every case of primary severe depression.
2. The intensity of the depression should not deter the therapist from making psychotherapeutic attempts.
3. Concomitant or prior drug therapy does not make the patient less accessible to psychotherapy, except in cases in which antidepressants or a combination of antidepressants and neuroleptics are used in massive doses.
4. Drug therapy may have much more rapid action than psychotherapy in

ameliorating the distressing symptoms, but it does not modify the basic structures of the personality which render the patient highly vulnerable to depression.

5. Prior use of electric shock treatment does not make the patient less accessible to psychotherapy. However, during the period of forgetfulness, mild confusion, and other organic effects which follow ECT treatment, psychotherapy cannot and should not go beyond a superficial supportive role.

6. Psychotherapy is strongly recommended in patients who are hospitalized.

7. Psychotherapy becomes a necessity when drug therapy and electric shock therapy have been ineffective, when the syndrome keeps recurring in spite of these treatments, or when the patient refuses to try physical therapies again.

8. Psychotherapy also should be instituted in patients whose acute attacks have ended spontaneously. In these cases the aim is to make recurrence of the attacks less likely.

In spite of a great increase of interest in depression, the literature on the psychotherapy of severe cases is still in the pioneer stage. Many recent books on depression either omit this topic entirely or offer only a few and cursory indications. There are several reasons for this relative neglect. Mild depressions are easier to treat with psychotherapy and have received the focus of attention by psychotherapists. On the other hand, the lure of quick results has converged the interest of many therapists onto drug therapy, even in cases of severe depression. Although it is true that, unlike cases of schizophrenia, patients with severe affective disorders have been treated psychoanalytically since early in the history of psychoanalysis, it is also true that these patients have been very few and as a rule were treated in the intervals between depressive attacks. Important books on depression by distinguished authors have taken into consideration only special problems resulting from the psychoanalytic treatment of specific cases.

Beginning of Psychotherapy

The initial stage of the treatment is the most difficult and the most crucial. As a matter of fact, we can say generally that unless an immediate and intense rapport is established at the beginning of the treatment, the likelihood of having a successful therapy is considerably reduced. At the beginning of treatment verbal contacts are hard to make, not because the patient is withdrawn as many schizophrenics are, but because he is absorbed in his seemingly everlasting mood. The patient is retarded in every action and does not always succeed in finding words which express his feelings. The effort he has to make in order to communicate appears enormous to him and, what is more important, futile. He seems possessed and overwhelmed by feelings of futility, helplessness, and desperation.

The therapist assumes an active role from the beginning. He is a firm person who makes clear and sure statements and asks very few questions or none. He is compassionate, but not in a way that can be interpreted by the patient as an acknowledgment of his helplessness. Unless the patient voluntarily explains why he is depressed, no effort should be made to compel him to justify his depression. If he is severely depressed, he is not able to answer and the renewed awareness of this inability would make him even more discouraged and depressed. On the contrary, the therapist may initiate the conversation by saying, "Most probably you do not know why you are depressed. But in my professional work I have found without exception that there are reasons for every depression. The depression does not come out of the blue. The anguish and the suffering stem from sources that a person like you, at a certain period of life, cannot find out by himself. He needs help."

When the therapist succeeds in establishing rapport and proves his genuine desire to reach, nourish, and offer hope, he will often be accepted by the patient, but only as a dominant third—a third entity or person in addition to the patient and the dominant other (or goal). Immediate relief may be obtained because the patient sees in the therapist a new and reliable love object.

Although this immediate relief may be so pronounced as to be mistaken for a real cure, it is only a temporary expedient. It may be followed by another attack of depression if and when the patient realizes the nature and limitation of this relation. The procedure of leaning on a dominant third may arouse objections on theoretical grounds as well. In fact, we have seen how often the difficulty of the depressed patient stems from his dependence on a dominant other. And now we would encourage him to substitute for the dominant other a dominant third; in other words, we would not encourage him to assume an independent role. However, we must be aware that—similar to what we do in the treatment of schizophrenia—at the beginning of therapy of the severely depressed, the therapist cannot disregard the demands of the illness and act as if it did not exist. The first meaningful rapport with the patient must be made only through the mechanisms that the illness puts at our disposal. To do otherwise would not only be useless, it also would be likely to increase the pathology of the patient. Treatment would be immediately experienced by the patient as dangerous and would therefore be rejected before meaningful therapeutic relatedness had been established.

After the first stage of treatment, however, the therapeutic approach must be characterized by a therapeutic relation in which the therapist is no longer a dominant third, but a *significant third,* a third person with a firm, sincere, and unambiguous type of personality who wants to help the patient without making threatening demands or requesting a continuation of the patient's usual patterns of living. Whereas the dominant other was experienced as a rigid and static person, the significant third will change rapidly and will appear eventually as a person who shares life experiences without aiming to control and dominate. He may indicate alternative possibilities but he does not demand their implementation.

The only demand the therapist makes is that the patient become part of a *search team,* a group of two people committed to finding the cause of the depression and to altering or making it harmless. I personally use the term search team rather than therapeutic alliance, which to my ears smacks of militarism. We are together in the search, but of course we have different roles. The nebulosity, uncertainty, hesitation, and discouragement of the patient are compensated by the guidance that the therapist gives with a sense of assurance. When the patient realizes that the therapist is oriented in the right direction, he acquires hope. The more the obscurity diminishes, the more faith increases. The patient will tend again to lean on the therapist and make him a dominant third. Sooner or later, however, the patient will trust the therapist fully and see him as an accepting, not disapproving, and basically undemanding person. The therapist will only demand that if the patient wants understanding and possible guidance, he must give information about his past and present life.

How can the therapist offer guidance and interpretation which, by being recognized as accurate, will reassure the patient that he can trust the effect of therapy? The therapist will be able to orient the patient in the right direction if he has mastered the psychodynamic development illustrated in chapters 5 and 6. For expository reasons its salient features are summarized here.

1. The range of life possibilities has undergone a gradual narrowing throughout the history of the patient, who has come to follow a rather rigid pattern of living with specific attitudes toward himself and others, and set ideas and aims.
2. A rupture of the pattern occurs because of either some inner reevaluation or given events and contingencies which externally impinge upon the patient. This rupture is experienced as a loss of vital importance, a loss which may reactivate the feelings experienced from a loss sustained early in life.
3. This rupture produces sadness, but sorrow work is not possible. The patient feels helpless and hopeless, and depression ensues.

When the therapist has established a good rapport with the depressed patient, he must aim at a quick discovery and understanding of the patient's basic drama. What is really the loss that the patient has experienced and which has threatened him so much? Has the loss disrupted a life pattern so that the patient no longer is able to sustain himself on habits, attitudes, ideas, feelings on which he had always relied? The loss may not consist of actual things or be connected with definite events, but may pertain to the symbolic values attributed to these things and events. The event may seem insignificant to others and yet the patient may have attached to it the meaning of loss of a hope or a fantasy, nourished consciously or unconsciously, that had filled a great part of his psychological life.

Many therapists who are convinced that so-called endogenous depressions are the result only of biochemical disorders are not attuned to detecting the occurrence of previously stressful events or, if they are, they look only for facts and not for symbols. On the other hand, we must realize that even when a stressful event has taken place, the event becomes important only in the context of the patient's background, history, and special psychological picture. This point must be emphasized: just as there are a large number of therapists and patients who deny the importance or occurrence of precipitating events, there are also a conspicuous number of therapists and patients who give exclusive importance to them. They focus on the precipitating event and do not investigate adequately the course of life as it unfolded prior to the occurrence of the specific event. The death of a person very important to the patient (generally the death of the dominant other) may seem sufficient in itself to cause a depression. However, even in these cases we must explain to the patient—in terms that he will easily understand and at a time when he seems receptive to explanations—that the sorrow, although justified, is different from depression and not the only cause of it. Whereas sorrow and sadness are appropriate, consonant with the situation, and even adaptive, depression is inappropriate and maladaptive.

The therapist must be aware that the crucial problem is in the inability of the patient to sustain sorrow work after the event. For understanding this crucial inability, a longitudinal study of the patient's life is required.

The recognition of the specific precipitating event generally will indicate to the therapist the kind of depression from which the patient most likely suffers. For instance, depression following the death of the spouse points to a depression based on the relation with the dominant other. When depression follows the loss of a position or the failure to satisfy a particular ambition, it will suggest that most probably we are dealing with a depression based on the relation of the patient with a dominant goal.

When the therapist has determined which of the major psychodynamic patterns of living the depressed patient has followed, he will orient the treatment in specific ways, try to retrace the course of events that were illustrated in chapter 5, and offer therapeutic alternatives which will enable the patient to do successful sorrow work. First I will describe in detail the treatment of the patient who has followed a pattern of submission toward the dominant other. In the treatment of other categories of severely depressed patients, only the differential modalities will be described.

Therapy of the Patient with a Pattern of
Submission to the Dominant Other

In self-blaming types of depression, one of the first therapeutic challenges consists of ascertaining the person with whom the patient is most involved. Soon the existence of the dominant other is revealed. Often the patient will try to protect the dominant other, saying that there is nothing wrong with this person. Whatever is wrong is to be blamed on the patient himself. But once the therapist has been able to gather enough information, the relation with the dominant other must be interpreted to the patient. The recommendations which are given in this section may seem direct, quick, and incisive. This impression is due only to expository reasons. In practice the interpretations have to be given slowly and cautiously, lest they be vehemently rejected. Even when a specific precipitating event (like the discovery of a clandestine love of the spouse or the spouse's announcement that he wants a divorce) easily reveals the failure of the relation on which the patient sustained himself, the depressed patient may find reason to exonerate the other and to blame himself. What is clear to the therapist is not necessarily clear to the patient, who continues to repress feelings and facts. Our caution must be even more pronounced when the depression was precipitated by the death of the dominant other. The guilt experienced in these cases and the possible idealization of the departed make it very difficult for the patient to learn to visualize in a different way his past relation with the dominant other.

Step by step we must clarify to the patient that he does not know how to live for himself. He has never listened to himself or been inclined to assert himself, but cared only about obtaining the approval, affection, love, admiration, or care of the dominant other. For the sake of the dominant other he has conformed to the wishes of others and denied his own, and he has even led himself to believe that the wishes of the others are his own. At times the fault of the other has been transformed by the patient into his own fault or flaw. For instance, the extreme thriftiness of the dominant other has been transformed into the patient's alleged largesse; the carelessness of the other has become the patient's fastidiousness or his obsessive behavior. In cases of married couples, the dominant other's lack of sexual desire has become an exaggerated sexual appetite in the patient, or vice versa; the immoderate demands of the dominant other are interpreted in terms of the so-called frigidity or quasi-frigidity of the patient.

With the permission of the patient, in some cases it is important to discuss with the dominant other the general climate of the relationship and the possibility of some environmental changes. The dominant other may be shown by the therapist how he can relieve the patient's feeling of having to bear a heavy yoke of guilt, responsibility, or feelings of un-accomplishment and loss. The dominant other, because of repressed hos-tility or because of perfectionistic, ultramoralistic, or obsessive-compulsive attitudes, quite often unwittingly increases the patient's feeling of guilt, duty, and self-denial. Such sentences as, "You are too sick to do the house-work now," or, "For many years you took care of me; now I will take care of you," increase the guilt feeling of the patient. The patient must be guided by the therapist to become aware of his personal wishes and the meaning he wants to give to his own life. This is not easy to do because the patient has denied and repressed his own wishes for so long. In many cases we have to reevoke the daydreams, aspirations, and fantasies of childhood and adolescence in order to figure out what the patient ex-pected from his life, what his life claim was. As has already been men-tioned, the dominant other is not necessarily a person, but may be the whole family or a special group, organization, or firm. The patient's relation to them must be reevaluated and possibly changed.

After the therapist has made some headway into the patient's psyche, several developments may occur. The patient may become less depressed but angry at either the dominant other or the therapist, whom he would like to transform into a dominant third. The anger and hostility toward the dominant other (most frequently the spouse) at times is out of pro-portion. Once repressed or unconscious ideations come to the surface, the dominant other may be seen as a tyrant, a domineering person who has subjugated the patient. At this point the therapist has a difficult task in clarifying the issues involved. At times the dominant other really has been overdemanding and even domineering, taking advantage of the placating, compliant qualities of the patient. However, it is often the patient him-self who has allowed certain patterns of life to develop and persist by being unable to assert himself and by complying excessively. Now, when he wants to change these patterns, he attributes the responsibility for them to the dominant other. No real recovery is possible unless the patient understands the role that he himself has played in creating the climate and pattern of submissiveness.

I have so far referred to the patient as he or him, and shall continue to do so. However, I would again remind the reader that approximately two-thirds of the patients belonging to this category are women and, if the language required referring to the most common sex involved, I would use the pronouns she or her. Undoubtedly the improved attitude of so-ciety toward women's rights and needs will change the cultural climate or at least the frequency of certain developments. At the present time, the still-prevailing partriarchal character of society makes it easier for a woman to assume an attitude of dependency on a male dominant other, or even on a female dominant other. By tradition many more women than men have been trained overtly or in subtle ways to depend on others for support, approval, and appreciation. Some of these women actually live a vicarious life.

The fact that society and culture have facilitated these developments does not exonerate the female patient from recognizing the role she has played. By omission or commission the patient has allowed the dominant other to assume that specific position in her life. Many husbands, certainly helped by the prevailing patriarchal character of society, are not even aware of playing the role of a dominant other. When they come to such a realization, they may try to deny certain facts, become busy in defending themselves as if they stand accused, and may require psychotherapy (or family therapy with the patient). The same remarks can be made, although less frequently, for dominant others other than husbands.

The realization of these factors by the patient does not yet relieve the depression, although in most cases it is diminished. Generally the patient continues to be depressed because: (1) He broods over what he did not have. (2) He has a feeling of self-betrayal. By accommodating to the dominant other, he has not been true to himself. (3) He has some sort of realization that many of the gratifications he once desired in life were given up. (4) He has a feeling of hopelessness about remedying or retrieving what he has lost, the opportunities he did not grasp.

As mentioned in chapter 6, ideas of this type are not kept in consciousness for long. The ensuing depression covers up these cognitive components. The therapist must train the patient to catch himself in the act of having these ideas, or in an attitude in which he expects to become depressed. If the patient becomes aware of these ideas and consequently of expecting to be depressed, he can stop the depression from occurring or at least from reaching its previous intensity. Then he must discuss with the therapist these depression-prone cognitive components. If the patient understands that he had a role in this dynamic complex, he will abandon a state of helplessness and hopelessness. Both in the present and in the future he may act differently by learning to assert himself and to obtain what is really meaningful and gratifying to him. Any feeling of loss or disappointment is no longer translated into self-accusation or guilt.

With the help of the therapist, the patient must obviously change his way of living and interrelating with the dominant other. The patient cannot devote his life to the dominant other or live vicariously through him. On the other hand, the patient may be afraid of going overboard and being too hostile and angry at the dominant other. However, this stage will be outgrown when the dominant other is recognized as not what the patient consciously saw him to be in recent years, but as the early childhood situation made the patient envision him. In other words, the trauma over the alleged or real loss of love sustained in childhood, and the mechanisms adopted in an attempt to reobtain this love or its equivalents (admiration, approval, affection, care) have led to a series of events in which the patient had to create or choose as a mate a person who would fit the role of dominant other. The patient has also misperceived some attributes of the dominant other in order to see him in that role. When the patient is no longer concerned with the dominant other in his recent role, and concentrates instead on his childhood situation, treatment will be at an advanced stage. The patient realizes more and more that he has not lived for himself or even for the world, but for an audience which often has been limited to one person, the dominant other. There will be a gradual abandonment of the stereotyped way of living and a progressive enlargement and embracing of life's possibilities.

However, even at this point the patient may become easily depressed since depression has been his fundamental mode of living. Depressive thoughts should not be allowed to expand into a general mood of depression, but must retain their discrete quality and content in order to be analyzed. The patient learns that because of this pattern of depression, even innocent thoughts at times have the power to elicit a depression. Little disappointments or losses which lead the patient to self-accusation, guilt, or severe depression are actually symbolic of an earlier, greater disappointment or of lifelong disappointment. But now the early or the recurring losses are unlikely to be repeated because the patient is learning to assert and fulfill himself.

It is not possible to eliminate historically the original traumas of childhood, but it is possible to change the pattern by which the patient tries to remedy or undo the original traumas. The original traumas and these patterns finally will lose their power and the compulsive qualities that caused their persistence or recurrence.

The handling of irrational guilt feeling is important in the treatment of self-blaming cases of depression, not only at the beginning of therapy but also at advanced stages. Fits of strong guilt feeling tend to recur. The patient has learned and repeated for many years of life the following pattern: guilt feeling → atonement → attempted redemption. Guilt about what? Originally the child attributed the responsibility for the original traumatic loss to himself. He was naughty, terrible, and evil. By atonement—that is, placating, obeying, working hard, doing his duty, denying himself, wanting peace at any cost—he felt he could obtain the love, approval, or admiration that he desired. But if he did not get it, he felt guilty again for not having done enough, for not having atoned enough. If some energy is left, it must be used for self-punishment. The patient continues to feel, although in a rather vague way, that enough punishment will make him acceptable to others and will restore a self-image acceptable to himself. The cycle thus repeats itself.

The guilt feeling is often experienced for hating (consciously or unconsciously) the dominant other in a way which is reminiscent of the sadistic trends that Freud (1917) described as directed by the depressed patient against the incorporated love object. Thus the greatest relief from guilt occurs when the patient has drastically changed his relation with the dominant other. However, since this pattern of guilt is so ingrained in many patients with the self-blaming type of depression, other psychological mechanisms are often transformed to fit into this guilt complex. Often breaking habits elicits guilt. For example, the patient does not go to church on Sunday or does not accompany his child to grammar school. Now the patient has something to feel guilty about. In many instances anxiety is transformed into guilt feeling. As painful as the guilt feeling is, the patient is aware that the possibility of suffering and thus of redeeming himself is in his power, whereas with anxiety he is at a loss; he does not know what to do about it.

The obsessive-compulsive symptoms which complicate a minority of cases of severe depression are attempts to channel guilt feelings and to find measures for relieving them so that the lost love or approval will be reacquired. They actually aggravate the situation instead of solving it. For instance, the patient may be obsessed with thinking about something profane or sacrilegious, or about the coming death of a relative, and feel guilty about having such thoughts. Similarly, compulsions may obligate the patient to perform actions condemned by the rituals of his religion, and consequently he feels guilty.

In most cases it will be possible to show the patient how he tends to translate anxiety into guilt and depression. He will finally learn to face anxiety rather than to reproduce the sequence which leads to depression. He also will recognize the cognitive components which lead to anxiety. If the therapeutic climate established with the therapist is a sound one, the patient will realize that he can manifest and consequently share his anxiety with the therapist. His anxiety—that is, his negative attitude toward what is uncertain or what is about to come—will progressively change into a hopeful attitude.

The therapist eventually will learn to handle little relapses, to understand and explain little psychological vicious circles which are formed, or stumbling blocks which are encountered and tend to reestablish a mood of depression. For instance, the patient may become depressed over the fact that he so easily does become depressed by any little disappointment which triggers off the state of sadness or guilt. Again, he has to be reminded that the little disappointment is symbolic of a bigger one. Another difficulty consists of the fact that some clusters of thought seem harmless to the therapist and are allowed to recur: they actually lead to depression because of the particular connections that they have in the patient's frame of reference. Eventually, however, the emotional pitch of the therapist becomes more and more attuned to that of the patient.

We must also remember that the patient who is familiar only with the mood of depression will search for reasons to be depressed and succeed in finding seemingly plausible ones. They are negative appraisals of the self, the world, and the future, and they constitute the cognitive triad described by Beck (1967). The therapist involved in deep psychodynamic therapy should not be easily sidetracked. These negative appraisals are part of the manifest symptomatology and their significance and use must be explained to the patient. The therapist must also realize, however, that these ideas may accrue a superficial layer of depression over the deep-rooted disposition to become depressed.

The Treatment of Claiming Depression

The treatment of the claiming type of depression is also difficult. Before starting therapy the patient has become more and more demanding of the dominant other, but he also feels more deprived. Any unfulfilled demand is experienced as a wound—a loss—and increases the depression. When treatment starts, the patient wants to find in the therapist a substitute for the dominant other who has failed. To the extent that the patient's demands are plausible or realistic, the therapist should try to go along with these requests and satisfy some of the needs for affection, consideration, and companionship. Even clinging and nagging have to be accepted.

Kolb (1956, 1959), English (1949), and Cohen (1954) emphasized this excessive clinging as one of the main problems encountered in intensive psychotherapy with manic-depressives. Some patients do not want to leave at the end of the hour; they suddenly remember many things they must say, plead for help, and attempt to make the therapist feel guilty if they are not improving. As Kolb described, these patients have learned proper or apparently suitable social manners and, with pleading and tenacity, they are often capable of eliciting in the therapist the reaction they want.

Occasionally we have to prolong the session for a few minutes because at the last minute the patient feels the urge to make new demands or to ask "one more question." The recommended attitude may seem too indulgent, but especially at the beginning of treatment we cannot expect the patient to give up mechanisms he has used for a long time.

Many patients, especially at the beginning of the session, are not able to verbalize freely and should not be requested to explain their feelings in detail or to go into long series of associations. On the contrary, the therapist should take the initiative and speak freely to them even about unrelated subjects. As a patient of Thompson (1930) said, the words of the analyst are often experienced as gifts of love by the depressed person. By following the suggestions made by Spiegel (1959, 1960) the therapist will soon learn to communicate with the depressed, in spite of his lack of imagery and the poverty of his verbalizations. It is in the feeling itself, rather than in verbal symbols, that the patient often expresses himself.

When this immediate craving for acceptance is somewhat satisfied, the claiming depression will diminish considerably but will not disappear. The depression will no longer appear in the form of a sustained mood, but in isolated discrete fits. At this stage it is relatively easy to guide the patient into recognizing that the fit of depression comes as a result of the following conscious or unconscious sequence of thoughts or their symbolic equivalents: "I am not getting what I should → I am deprived → I am in a miserable state." The patient is guided to stop at the first stage of this sequence, "I am not getting what I should," because these words mean "I would like to go back to the bliss of babyhood. I do not want to be a person in my own right, with self-determination." Can the patient substitute this recurring idea and aim for another one, for instance, "What ways other than aggressive expectation and dependency are at my disposal in order to get what I want?" In other words, the patient is guided to reorganize his ways of thinking so that the usual clusters of thought will not recur and will not reproduce the old sequence automatically and tenaciously. The psychological horizon will enlarge, and new patterns of living will be sought. The patient will be able to activate these changes in himself only if the new relationship with the therapist has decreased his feeling of deprivation and suffering. More and more frequently he will make excursions into paths of self-reliance. At the same time, the therapist will put gradual limitations on the demands that the patient makes on him. Once the fits of depression have disappeared, the treatment will continue, giving special importance to the exploration of the past. The patient will learn to recognize the basic patterns of living which led him to the depression, and the special characteristics of his early interpersonal relationships which led to the organizations of these patterns. Such characteristics as superficiality, insensitivity, marked extroversion covered by depression, recurrence of clichés, and infantile attitudes such as "Love me like a baby" will be recognized as defense mechanisms and will disappear.

Treatment of Depression Following Failure to Reach the Dominant Goal, and of Depression with Mixed Patterns

When the therapist has ascertained that the depression follows the patient's realization that he has failed to reach the dominant goal or is hopelessly going to fail, the psychodynamic inquiry following the initial state of treatment is focused on why such a realization had such a strong impact. The psychological integrity of the patient has depended only on the fulfillment of a life claim. But it is only a narcissistic integrity. Deprived of it, the patient feels mortally wounded and deeply depressed.

Therapist and patient must come to a full understanding of how important the fantasied achievement was. How many conscious and unconscious ramifications did it have? How big a place did the patient allow the fantasy to occupy in his psyche? Is it true that life without that particular fantasy has no meaning? The patient must be helped to find alternative paths. Is it really necessary to be a singer, a dancer, a successful politician, or a big businessman in order to find a meaning in one's life? The patient will answer, yes, at least for him. In many other instances he will say that intellectually he knows that he should say no, but with the depth of his emotions he feels that the achievement of that particular goal is necessary in his case. From his subjective point of view he is correct, as we have seen in chapter 6. His self-esteem and self-identity have depended on the goal, and he now feels cheated of his dream. We must help him to realize that he has started with a great demand upon life. Whatever the origin, this demand has become a false pride or hubris from which he has to be relieved. But his life is certainly more valuable than an ill-founded illusion, a fantasy which has reached a stage of pathetic naïveté. The disillusionment must actually be seen as an awakening, as a recognition of unfounded values, and as the start of a search for new and stable values.

In many cases we succeed in ascertaining a specific and very important reason for which the patient gave supremacy to the achievement of a particular goal, and this reason must be explained to him. In middle childhood the patient came to envision the achievement of a particular goal as a way of recapturing the love, affection, or approval of the mother or whoever else was in the role of the significant other. Later in life the patient saw the attainment of that goal as the only occurrence which would make him worthy of love and approval and make him feel worthwhile. His life previously was experienced not beautifully, but like a long tunnel with only one exit, one commitment.

Treatment entails a call for a different integration of values and habits and for a considerable change in character. Thus it may be difficult. Just as patients belonging to the previously described categories had to enlarge their involvement with people and change their attitude toward the former dominant other, this category of patients must acquire a latitude of choice toward life claims. Many of the modalities recommended for patients with a pattern of submission or of claiming dependency also apply to patients in this category.

The same modalities also can be applied to a large number of patients who do not fit into the previously mentioned categories either because they represent a mixture of them, or because their patterns of living seem different from those which are commonly encountered. Particularly difficult are cases which had an insidious, slow course. Some of these patients at first seem to suffer from relatively severe depressive characters. Eventually they are recognized as being affected by severe depression. No single episode can be recognized as a precipitating factor. The patient lives in the mood of an existence whose only meaning seems to be suffering. Conversely, in some cases a single and in itself not important episode is recognized as the precipitating factor, but only because the patient has given it an unusual interpretation. For instance, for a person who previously appeared well-adjusted, an illness which is not serious at all becomes the signal that life is going to end, and that life has been wasted.

Many of these cases eventually can be understood as the acute or slow realization by the patient that he has never developed a meaningful interpersonal bond based on love or affection and neither has he achieved any meaningful goal. We must help the patient to reevaluate his life and find alternatives, in the same manner as with the previous categories of patients.

As was mentioned at the end of chapter 6, the patient may feel that the meaning he has given to his life is inappropriate or unworthy but if he renounces that meaning, his life becomes meaningless. We must help the patient understand that his sorrow over the loss of meaning in his life actually indicates how much life means to him. In other words, implicit in his sorrow is the affirmation that his life—a human life—is very meaningful, as something that transcends its mere factual circumstances. If the patient's sorrow is real and meaningful, life is too. If his sorrow is authentic then life can be authentic too, but up to now he has lived an unauthentic life in pursuit of an unauthentic goal.

The therapist helps the patient become aware that his great sorrow implicitly reaffirms the authenticity and value of life. The therapist also helps him to make authentic choices and to retrieve a sense of purpose. Even if life has not delivered what it promised, it is not meaningless. The patient feels helpless and hopeless because his patterns of living have prevented him from switching to alternative behaviors. As we do with the other categories of severe depressions, we help the patient become aware again of the cognitive structures that have caused his sorrow and to look again at the array of life's infinite possibilities. The task will be made easier if the patient understands the meaning of his sorrow, that it implicitly asserts how much he attributes to life.

Advanced Stage of Treatment

At an advanced stage of treatment with any type of depression, therapy consists of repeatedly going over the patient's life patterns and explaining how his present dealings with life situations are often in accordance with the old psychogenetic mechanisms. Sooner or later the patient, who by now has understood the psychodynamics of his life history, learns to avoid the old ways because he recognizes them to be pseudosolutions, futile defenses, and vicious circles. In some patients the old mechanisms tend to recur even after they have been completely understood. As a matter of fact, even discussion of them may evoke strong emotions which are not congruous with the gained insight, but which demonstrate the usual affective components of the original symptoms. Even after the patient has understood the meaning of his symptoms and behavior patterns, it is sometimes much easier for him to repeat the old patterns.

For example, it must constantly be pointed out to the patient that he should learn to ask himself what he wants, what he really wishes. Quite often his attempted answer will be only a pseudo-answer. He may say, "First of all, I wish peace. Then I wish the happiness of my children." He must learn—and relearn—that peace at any cost implies satisfying others before himself and that even the happiness of children, although a natural wish of every parent, is not a wish predominantly related to the individual himself.

In other words, the patient must learn to listen to himself and to reduce the overpowering role of the "Thou." At the same time he must make a voluntary effort to develop inner resources. In the attempt to imitate others or even to surpass others in proficiency and technique, some patients do not rely on their own individuality. They cannot be alone (unless they are depressed), and when alone they cannot do anything that gives them satisfaction: they must work for the benefit of others or escape into common actions. They must learn that they too may have artistic talents. As a matter of fact, some very depressed persons have become able to transform their conflicts into high forms of creativity. Creative upsurges in apparently uncreative, conventional depressive personalities are a good prognostic sign. Transient feelings of depression will be tolerated at this point, indicating as Zetzel (1965) put it, a measure of the ego strength.

As has already been mentioned, the therapist must be alert to spot early signs of depressions which at times are precipitated even by trivial disappointments or chance associations of ideas. Jacobson (1954) and Kolb (1959) emphasize that the recurring depression must immediately be related by the therapist to its precipitating cause.

At the same time the patient must learn new patterns of living which will lead to his own independence, individual growth, and self-fulfillment. Learning new patterns will reduce the tendency of the old ones to recur.

Other secondary recommendations may be useful in the treatment of the depressed. Except during the time when the depression is very severe, the patient must be encouraged to be active. Inactivity fosters depressive trends. He must assign himself graded tasks. A daily program can be structured with the therapist until the patient is able to structure one by himself. He must often be reminded that, contrary to what he believed at the beginning of his illness, life changes, the depression lifts, and gusto for life comes back. He must be told that the worst moment is generally in the morning when he wakes up and the depressogenic thoughts tend to emerge fully, soon to be repressed and replaced by a general depressive mood.

Another characteristic which occurs quite frequently is the acquisition of a personality characteristic or trait opposite to the one that the patient has relinquished. For instance, a formerly submissive patient is now assertive to a degree which is beyond the tolerance not only of family members but of what social customs require. With the new fervor and zest with which he tries not to be submissive anymore, the formerly depressed patient may become somewhat obtrusive, abrasive, and quite angry. At times he is prone to give too much importance to events that should not make him as angry as he is. This anger is often misplaced anger which has accumulated through years of submission or frustration in attempts to attain impossible goals. It is often exaggerated, at times inappropriate, and likely to put distance between the patient and others. When the patient becomes aware of these mechanisms, he will be in a better position to control them. On some occasions the members of the family who do not adjust well to the new self-assertive personality of the patient become angry at him and in their turn arouse his anger.

In other cases a very dependent, clinging patient tends to assume a degree of independence which is unrealistic. Again, with therapeutic intervention this trait is easily changed.

Orthodox psychoanalytic procedure with the use of the couch and free association is not indicated in the treatment of severe depression even during the interval periods. Many failures in the treatment of these patients have been due to the adoption of the classical psychoanalytic technique. Today many therapists feel that retarded and hyperactive patients generally should be treated with less frequent sessions—from one to three a week. Many patients, especially elderly ones, seem to do well with one session a week. The therapist must play a relatively active role, not one that conveys to the patient the feeling that he is being pushed or under pressure, but not one in which the passivity of the therapist is too much in contrast with the natural extroversion of the patient. Whenever the therapist feels that he has succeeded in reaching some conclusions or in understanding the feelings of the patient, he should express them freely. Often the patient prefers to keep quiet, not because he is unable to put things together as in the case of the neurotic or the schizophrenic, but because he feels guilty or ashamed to express his feelings of rage, hostility, and—paradoxically—even guilt and depression. Dream interpretations are very useful and portray the major conflicts of the patient as well as the general mood of pessimism. Many severely depressed patients have great difficulty in recalling dreams.

The treatment of hypomanic episodes is far more difficult, as the flight of ideas prevents any significant contact. An opposite procedure is to be followed: the patient is asked to cut out details, so that irritation and rage are purposely engendered; or he is reminded that he must talk about certain subjects—the subjects that are liable to induce depression. Conversion to a mild depression is therapeutically desirable.

Treatment of the severely depressed patient requires a change in his psychological make-up which is substantial and difficult to implement. Of course we do not ask him to give up his identity; rather, whatever lie or impossible value has become connected with an unauthentic identity. We do not help a human being to lose a sense of commitment, but only the commitment that seduces and saps the self.

Although difficult, the treatment may be successful and rewarding for both patient and therapist. It is hard to imagine something more gratifying than the fading of a seemingly endless sorrow and the dissolution of a pattern of living which had drastically narrowed a human existence, or to imagine something more uplifting than the restored ability to look with hope at the array of life's infinite possibilities.

[10]

PSYCHOTHERAPY

OF SEVERE DEPRESSION:

CASE REPORTS

In this chapter the case of Doris Fullman* is reported in detail. The other cases are described briefly and only in their essential aspects. All these patients have been treated exclusively with psychotherapy from the time they started office treatment. Although described in detail, the case of Doris Fullman is not examined in all its possible aspects. Some inferences have been omitted because they are relatively easy to make, and their omission may give the therapist in training an opportunity to fill the gaps. Other inferences have been omitted because they are so difficult to make and they are uncertain: their omission will stimulate the reader to venture his own interpretation.

Doris Fullman

The last day of March 1967, Mr. Andrew Fullman came to my office, having requested a consultation by phone. He promptly told me that it was not for himself that he came, but on behalf of Doris, his wife. Doris, a fifty-eight year-old Jewish woman, had been in a psychiatric hospital and was not getting better. The hospital staff did not know what to do.

This chapter was written by Silvano Arieti.
   * All names of patients in this book are fictitious and identifying data have been altered. Homonyms are purely coincidental.

All types of treatment, drug therapy, shock therapy, psychotherapy, and milieu therapy had been tried with no appreciable result. His wife was still very depressed and suicidal ideas persisted.

Mr. Fullman added that this depression was not the first in his wife's life. Although she had been depressed several times, the first time she became seriously depressed was after the birth of the first of their three children. He was told at the time that probably his wife's depression was related to the fact that during her pregnancy she had developed high blood pressure. A second very severe depression developed much more recently, after the mother of the patient died. I inquired about the relations between Doris and her mother, and Mr. Fullman said that the mother had been rather authoritarian, overcritical, and demanding, and she had never approved of Doris. The mother had been a "son of a bitch." Upon my probing, Mr. Fullman told me that his marriage was a happy one, although Doris had felt somewhat deprived sexually. He did not elaborate on this topic. He stressed the point that Doris wanted to go home, but the hospital would only discharge her against medical advice because of her suicidal tendencies, and he did not know what to do.

I told him that I would call the hospital, talk to the doctors in charge, and then we would make some decisions. He said that he would wait for my call. He hoped I would call very soon. It was now his vacation time and he had decided to go on a cruise, although sorry to go alone and without his wife.

I called the hospital and got a most pessimistic report. The patient was suffering from a severe depression and was in a group of patients constantly watched for the possibility of suicide. The fact that the depression had not lifted after such a long time made several members of the staff suspect that an underlying schizophrenic disorder was probably at the basis of her condition, although hallucinations, delusions, and ideas of reference were never elicited. From the beginning of her hospitalization, Mrs. Fullman had received high doses of Tofranil® with no result, but recently her medication had been changed to Thorazine® (200 mg q.i.d.), Stelazine® (2 mg b.i.d.), and Artane® (2 mg b.i.d.). This change was put into effect when doubts arose about the diagnosis. I asked whether the hospital could send the patient to my office for a consultation, accompanied by an attendant. I was told that this could be done.

When I saw Doris for the first time (April 15, 1967), I observed her face, posture, and attitude and exchanged a few words with her. I felt I was already in a position to make some early assessment, to be convalidated later of course, because although these early assessments are useful, they may be drastically wrong. I could immediately exclude schizophrenia, confirm the diagnosis of severe depression, and feel that the patient could relate to me well and probably I could to her.

She told me that she had heard about me and was eager to see me, but she was very depressed and probably unable to talk. Two days before she had gotten up with the idea that she would never get well. She had definite suicidal ideas: life was not worth living. However, she believed she would never commit suicide. I told her that I felt we could talk to each other, and that I certainly wanted to see her again. I was seeing her that day because her husband had come to consult me and I had made the arrangements for her visit in my office. She told me that her husband's vacation time had come up and he had already gone on a cruise. Somewhat surprised, I asked, "How do you feel about your husband going on a cruise without you?" She replied, "Angry, because the *Aurora*, the ship my husband is on, is a ship I like very much. I am not angry at him, but at my illness, which prevents me from going with him." She had difficulty in talking and was quite slow in her speech. In an attempt to sustain the dialogue I became more friendly, and in a somewhat joking tone I told her she was the only woman I knew who allowed her husband to go alone on a cruise. She replied that she recognized he was entitled to a vacation. She had been in the hospital for almost three years and he did not have anybody to go with. She said that she was not at all angry at her husband. If she was angry at somebody, it was at her mother, who had recently died at the age of seventy-nine. Her mother was a person whom she could never please in spite of trying very hard.

When I explored the relation with her mother a little more, the patient told me that her mother used to make constant requests and tell Doris how to behave, even when Doris was in her fifties. The patient felt she had to go along with her mother in order not to incur her disapproval. To be approved of by her mother was absolutely essential, especially when the patient was very young. Since her marriage, her dependency on her mother had sharply decreased. However, after the mother died she felt very guilty for having put her into a home for the aged instead of caring for her. She felt that her guilt had probably contributed to the depression. She also said that she was eager to leave the hospital and go home, and yet she told Dr. B., her doctor in the hospital, strange things; for instance, that she hated her home and wanted to set it on fire.

At the end of the session I told her that I felt we were communicating well, and that I would make arrangements with the hospital to have her regularly accompanied to my office by an attendant for the session. When I knew her better I would tell her when I thought she could leave the hospital. She was attentive, yet incredulous. I felt I had reached her. And indeed, at the end of that very first session I felt I already knew a great deal about her. She seemed to be a very submissive person and unable to assert herself. When Doris left, the idea of her husband going on a cruise alone came back to my mind as something which was nagging at me. And yet I dismissed the idea, and thought that I had been unwise to make a little joke about it. The patient was probably right in saying that after all, she had been in the hospital almost three years and Mr. Fullman was entitled to go on a vacation. But then I said to myself that Mrs.

Fullman had been able to influence me: she had been persuasive enough to make even me accept her general orientation of submission. After all, it was true that he was entitled to a vacation. but did he have to go on a cruise especially on the *Aurora*, which Doris liked so much? Wasn't he rather insensitive? It is because I think it is important to retrace the marginal thoughts which come to the therapist's mind even during the very first session that I include these details. It was already obvious that the patient had made an impact on me, and I hoped I had on her.

So far I have stressed only the exchange of ideas. It was evident to me, however, that her slow movements and her austere and rather stiff face— although capable of a little emotion and of a tiny smile when I was trying to cheer her—as well as the look of melancholy that she seemed to wear, constituted an intense picture of depression which elicited in me an eagerness to penetrate into her secret anguish and to help her. Her sub-missiveness and placating ways were already giving me precious clues. The idea came to me that her case seemed to fit some of my theories. The mother had been the patient's dominant other, and further analysis would have to confirm or deny the hypothesis. "Beware," I said to myself, "not to force the case into your favorite preconceived schemata."

Between the first and the second session, I continued to get reports from the hospital that the patient was very depressed, inactive, and suicidal.

When she again came to see me, accompanied by an attendant, the second session was as revealing as the first. Doris started by saying that she was very depressed. She had the feeling that she would never get well, and she was very discouraged. After all, before going to the hospital, she had been in treatment with Dr. N., a psychotherapist, for fourteen years and had not gotten well. And the first serious depression had occurred at the age of thirty-two, after the birth of her first child. I asked her to tell me something about her childhood. She told me that she had two brothers and she used to compete with them for her mother's affection, without ever being sure of getting it.

Then she told me that when she was eight years old an incident had occurred, but perhaps she would lose precious time in recounting the episode to me. I encouraged her to tell me what happened, and she told me that one day she and her brother Richard were playing together. They started to fight. In a fit of anger she threw a pen at him and the pen hit Richard in the eye. Richard was rushed to the hospital, but he lost the eye. Doris told me that she always felt guilty about what she had done then. I asked her whether she was scolded or punished by her parents, and she told me no. The parents were very nice, and realized that what she had done to her brother was unintentional. Not only was she not punished, but the whole incident was never mentioned to prevent her from feeling guilty. After all, she was only a child, and she was playing when the accident occurred. I thought that the patient felt more guilty than she admitted, and that this matter should not be so easily dismissed without even touching on the possible implications; but it was obvious that she was not ready to discuss that episode further, and I did not insist. I told her that what she had said to me was important and that eventually we would discuss the event in greater depth. I told her that I wanted to see her regularly once a week as long as she was in the hospital, and probably three times a week when she was discharged. She came regularly once a week, accompanied by an attendant.

The third session was also important. She told me that she was afraid she would not get well because she did not want to get well. She felt hopelessly depressed with no desire to live. She said she had no feeling for anybody, not even her husband and children. As a matter of fact, she had felt depressed when Walter, her son, was born twenty-six years previously. She believed that every woman would be happy to have a son, but she was depressed when she gave birth to him. She was so depressed that she felt she could not take care of him. At the same time she felt guilty for not being able to be a good mother. She had always felt guilty toward Walter for the way she reacted to his birth. When her twin daughters Elsie and Roberta were born, she tried to make up for the poor mothering she had displayed toward Walter. But again, what she had done for Elsie and Roberta was only because she felt she had to do it, and not out of love.

The next time she came, she said again that she was very depressed. There was nothing in her which pushed her toward getting well. The idea had come to her that I had called her husband who had returned from the cruise, and I had told him to put her away for good, maybe in a state hospital. She had a feeling of hopelessness. She said that her family life was also like an emotional vacuum. Nothing could push her back into her home. She had no love for her husband and children. She had never accepted them, and they never accepted her. Even her sex life with her husband was no good. Apparently he found her undesirable; since they were married, Andrew never approached her or showed any desire to make love unless she made overtures.

At this point I started to talk to her, and I explained that from what she had told me so far I could conclude that she was a person who had never followed her own wishes. As a matter of fact, she would not even listen to her wishes; she did not even know what they were. She lived for others with resentment, and therefore with the feeling that she did not love the others. She lived only for doing what she felt the others expected from her. Thus she had the feeling that the others did not love her, because they expected so much from her. From now on she must listen to her inner self, to her secret desires, and I would help her to do so. Although I spoke with conviction, my interpretations appeared to me somewhat pat; perhaps psychiatrically correct, but lacking some additional important dimensions specific to the case. The patient added, "But if I listen to my wishes, I feel guilty. I always felt guilty, guilty, guilty! I was five and told my mother a boy had pulled up my skirt and kissed my knees. My mother looked at me with contempt and said, 'I know what kind of woman you will grow up to be.' But," the patient added, "I did not feel guilty when the boy kissed my knees. I would have forgotten all about it. I knew nothing at all about sex. I felt guilty later about everything, and about what my mother had previously told me about this boy, and about everything which smacked of sex."

"You said you started to feel guilty later. When?" I asked. The patient said, "I don't know." I said, "I have the feeling you know." The patient, paused, pensive, and then said, "I know you know. Everybody knows; but nobody has ever admitted the truth." She started to cry and said in a rather loud voice, "My brother! My brother's eye! I made him lose an eye! I had not told you before how it happened. We were playing, but soon he started to torment me. I told him, I'll throw this pen in your eye. And I did it. The pen did hit his eye. It was intentional, doctor. I remember that after the accident I thought: Why didn't they punish me? They didn't; nobody even scolded me. But I expected they would. I still do. Even today I say to myself: Why don't they punish me? When I look at others, I expect them to punish me."

"And you feel you must atone, and be submissive and obey. You are still carrying a heavy burden for what you did when, as a little child, you were playing with your brother. You told him that you were going to hit him in the eye, and it happened that you did. That's why it is so easy for you to accept this role of the guilty one. When this accident occurred, you even thought of what you possibly had done wrong before, and you remembered the episode of the boy who kissed your knees and what your mother said."

The following session, Doris told me that for the first time in years she felt better. She smiled at me. I had really helped her, she said. Now she felt hopeful again. What I had said had made sense to her. I reminded her that she had done most of the talking during the previous session, but I had helped her to see the significance of what she told me.

In the rest of that session and in others which followed at that time (Spring, 1967) she disclosed several things to me which were preying on her mind. Her husband was a very successful businessman, but she was not a successful woman, mother, or wife. In reality the brother of her husband had started the business in which her husband was still involved, but her brother-in-law died and her husband, who was his partner, took his place. After the death of her brother-in-law she felt sorry for her husband, who was depressed, and therefore, to console and please him, she became pregnant at the age of thirty-two; that is, five years after she got married. She actually felt more depressed than her husband about the death of his brother.

In the following sessions she became alternatively more depressed and less depressed. She dreamt that her husband was marrying a very young woman and divorcing her. In the sessions which took place over the span of a month, she gave me a detailed account of how she had become the depository of guilt feelings: guilt when the brother-in-law died, because she had not taken care of him; guilt about the way she felt about her son when he was born; guilt when Dorothy, the sister of her husband, died and left her money to the patient's husband. Doris enjoyed Dorothy's money, but she had wished Dorothy's death because she was very bossy and had acted as a mother-in-law. Even when Doris married her husband, she was not sure that she loved him. It happened that her husband had been in love with another woman to whom he had been engaged. This woman suddenly broke the engagement and married her boss. Mr. Fullman had been very depressed. Doris felt that perhaps she had to compensate for what another woman had done to him. I told her, "You had to atone for what another woman had done. Your mission was to make your husband happy, not so much to make yourself happy." The following session she said that she could not face what I had told her about her marriage, but yes, it was true that she had to atone; she felt guilty about many things. I told her that she was depicting her situation accurately. She had assumed not only an attitude of submission but one of responsibility and guilt for the whole family.

The following session, she said she felt much better. She had not needed pills to fall asleep at night. Then she looked at me and said firmly, "Did you know, doctor, if I had wanted to hit my brother in the eye with that pen, I could have tried a thousand times and not succeeded. It was an accident that I hit that spot." She looked at me and smiled. Then she added, "This was told to me before, and I did not believe it. But now I do. I was not good at all at aiming, but I happened to hit the spot." I rose and said, "Mrs. Fullman, you have made a major breakthrough. You are on the way to getting rid of the burden of guilt, the main origin of your depression. I predict that in the beginning of June you will be able to leave the hospital."

And indeed, at the beginning of June Mrs. Fullman left the hospital after almost three years of confinement.

In the following months there was a gradual but steady improvement, and a quick readjustment to life. The patient reported much more information about her marriage. On the wedding night her husband did not show any intentions of having sexual relations with her. When she asked Andrew why he was not interested in making love, he replied, "We are going to be married for the rest of our lives. Why rush?" She was convinced that Andrew was right and she felt that there was something wrong with her for expecting so much. Since her childhood, her mother had been able to convince her that she was much too interested in sex and that sex was dirty. We have already seen that her guilt feelings about her brother's accident and her assumption of the guilty role made her rekindle previous episodes in her life for which she could have felt guilty, especially the episode of the boy who kissed her knees.

Throughout almost thirty years of marriage, her husband had very seldom made sexual overtures. She had to take the initiative, and then he would go along. Therefore she felt undesirable and unattractive. However, in pictures taken early in her married life which she brought in to show me, she appeared quite attractive. As the treatment proceeded, she became able to express complaints about her husband. According to her, he was bereft of romantic feelings and never indulged in affectionate gestures. He would never use endearing terms like "sweetheart" or "honey." He would not hold her hand in the movies, would not buy her a bouquet of flowers, would not hug her before going to sleep. She knew that the members of her husband's family were rather cold and not given to expressions of warmth. They never kissed and embraced, but who knows? Perhaps Andrew was so cold because he did not love her.

Andrew belonged to a well-to-do family, whereas she came from a poor family of immigrants who lived in the slums. Her parents came from Russia when she was eleven. She still remembered an uncle who remained in Russia; he loved her very much and did not make demands on her like her mother. The memory of this uncle had remained with her as something to revere.

When she got married, she thought she would liberate herself from her mother's yoke. Instead she assumed new yokes. First, she felt that all the members of her husband's family and especially Dorothy, the wealthy sister-in-law, considered her inferior because of the social class from which she came. She always had to placate, to accommodate, to follow, and to attune her tastes and her ways to those of the Fullmans. Second, she felt that her husband also was superior to her and everything had to be done for his sake. After all, he was an important businessman and had an unusual social position. He had to be well dressed, respected, and catered to. According to the patient her husband had a very pleasant personality and everybody admired him and paid respect to him, but not to her. She was a doormat: a doormat which, if not stepped on, acted as if she would say to the passerby, "you have forgotten to step on me."

At this point we are in a position to attempt a profile of Doris before going into a few other interesting aspects of the case. Much more clearly than in the majority of cases of depression, a single episode in childhood played a crucial role, with its aftermath affecting the patient for the rest of her life. The accident which caused the loss of her brother's eye crystallized in Doris an attitude of guilt, expiation, and submission. Most probably it would have been better to punish Doris immediately after the occurrence of the accident, not severely, but in a firm and clear disciplinary manner. Lack of punishment left her with a suspended feeling of guilt and unworthiness for which she entered an interminable pattern of expiation. Nobody spoke about her guilt, but a sense of guilt was in the air, and she felt that it was expected of her to be very good, obsequious, and obedient. Without admitting this feeling to herself, she felt she had the obligation to expiate for the terrible thing she had done. Doris's mother was a very demanding, rigid, perfectionistic woman, never satisfied about the state of the world or about the way things were done, especially by Doris. Because of her mother's personality, Doris most probably would have manifested these depressive traits even if the accident had not occurred. However, Doris made an unconscious connection between the accident and the way her mother treated her, and later between the accident and the way the world was treating her.

Her life became a way to prove that she was able to atone for what she had done and an effort to be accepted by a nonaccepting mother. This feeling was often changed into equivalent cognitive constructs. For instance, at times in her young life she felt she was born for the single purpose of pleasing her mother because her mother needed her. Very early in the patient's life the mother became the dominant other. When she got married, she thought she would liberate herself from this dominant other, but soon the husband was put in the position of being a dominant other. He could never do anything wrong. Again and again Doris tried to please him and his family. She never dared to make her wishes prevail. This state of affairs occurred in spite of the fact that with her industrious and alert personality and ability to grasp new situations quickly, unless depressed, she helped her husband very much in his career, by making business decisions and proceeding successfully toward a higher socio-economic status.

It is interesting to point out how even certain weaknesses or neurotic traits of her husband were transformed by her into her own faults or shortcomings. Like all persons prone to depression, she had the tendency to introject, which is the opposite of projecting. For instance, although she felt frustrated sexually, she thought that she was too libidinous and therefore vulgar and cheap. Her husband's reluctance to make love on the wedding night was interpreted by her as cogent proof of her lack of charm and sex appeal. It never occurred to her that a husband who acts in that way on the wedding night might have sexual problems of his own. That Mr. Fullman had sexual problems was confirmed to me later when I learned that he could never become aroused unless Doris took the initiative. And yet Doris interpreted his lack of interest in sex as proof that there was something wrong with her rather than with him. Of course there was something wrong with her too, for accepting the situation.

When her first child was born, she had a post-partum depression—the first severe depression in her life. She felt guilty for not being a good mother, and her depression increased. The birth of her child made her realize that she had to accept a life which consisted of pleasing others. She had become pregnant to console her husband, who was depressed at that time about the death of his brother. Having a child meant to Doris accepting irrevocably the life of a submissive housewife who had to take care of an unwanted child. Nobody was there to explain psychodynamically her post-partum psychosis, or to tell her to accept the fact that she did not accept the child; that the day would come when she would accept him and love him. Nobody was there to relieve her guilt for what she could not prevent. (See chapter 11.)

Mrs. Fullman leaned on me as a dominant third, and I told her that for a while she had to accept that type of relation. She understood more and more the role she herself had played in denying herself, in putting herself in the role of the sinner who had to atone. I explained that her husband, although somewhat inconsiderate, was not so domineering or demanding as she had assumed. She herself had put him in the dominant position to replace her mother. It was true that her husband inflicted suffering on her with his sexual detachment, but instead of suggesting treatment to him, she was ready to assume that there was something wrong with her in the sexual area too. I helped Doris to listen to her wishes and to dare to assert herself and depend less on the approval of others. Of course she needed my approval now, but I succeeded in changing my role from dominant third to significant third (as described in chapter 9). Mrs. Fullman underwent the typical changes which occur in persons who emerge from a deep depression. She became too self-assertive at times, and even angry. Occasionally she would express opinions rather strongly and hurt the feelings of people who were shocked at the change in her personality. They felt that she had been more considerate when she was depressed. In some cases it was difficult to determine whether her anger was justified, due to misconstructions, or due to an inability to reevaluate the new family climate now that an important member had changed so drastically. An important episode will illustrate this point.

When Doris came back from the hospital, everybody tried to cheer her up and her daughter Roberta, in a joking mood, once made a passing reference to a woman named Eloise who had pursued father while he was cruising on the *Aurora*. This woman had lent him a handkerchief to dry his perspiration, and with that excuse she called up once and asked to speak to him. Doris became very upset and jealous, expressing her indignation to the children and to her husband who insisted that she made too much of it. This woman was described by Andrew as an unattractive spinster who had noticed a man alone on the boat and had tried to attach herself to him. He perhaps had liked to receive some attention, but nothing had happened. A few days later when she was dusting her husband's desk, Doris saw some pictures taken on the *Aurora*, and in several snapshots Andrew was always next to the same woman in the group of passengers. She asked whether the woman was Eloise, and he said yes. He reiterated that her jealousy was absurd. Nothing had really happened. Doris reluctantly accepted his version of the facts. Knowing how conservative her husband was, she was sure that no sexual encounters had occurred on the ship, but all the attention that Eloise apparently had bestowed on Andrew, and Andrew on Eloise, infuriated her. She no longer felt depressed, but very angry.

A sort of bombshell exploded a few days later. The phone rang. Doris did not know that her husband had picked up the extension in another room, and she picked up the phone. She heard the jubilant voice of a woman saying, "Hello, Andrew, do you remember the *Aurora*?" That was all. Doris dropped the phone and went into the other room where Andrew, embarrassed, tried to terminate the conversation as soon as possible. The Fullman's phone was unlisted. Why had Andrew given the number to Eloise? Andrew said that in a moment of weakness or thoughtlessness while he was on the cruise, he had done so. He reaffirmed again and again that nothing had occurred between him and Eloise. Walter, Elsie, and Roberta sided with their father. They felt their mother was making too much out of nothing. This Eloise was a poor woman desperately seeking a companion on the cruise. Father loved only mother. Walter, Elsie, and especially Roberta tried to reassure her that he had always been faithful to her in spite of her illness. Their words "in spite of her illness" infuriated Doris. She thought, "I have been in the hospital for about three years, and nobody thought I would ever return. Who knows what would have happened if I had not come back soon? Had Dr. Arieti not made that announcement that I would leave in June, and if he had not helped me to leave, what then? Eloise would be living here."

I joined the children in pointing out that she was making much too much out of this episode. I must admit that at times I am too prone to believe people's affirmations and on a few sporadic occasions I have been sorry about it, but in this case I was and still am inclined to believe that nothing sexual or of any spiritual significance occurred between Eloise and Andrew. Perhaps Andrew responded to the attention of another woman, but to what extent he responded is hard to say. Knowing his extreme unaggressive attitude, it is probable that nothing intimate occurred; but that is what irritated Doris even more. If at least something sexual had happened! But Andrew was his old self, interested only in platonic love and companionship. And another woman could easily replace Doris in what she meant to her husband; not sex and love, but companionship. The episode was disturbing to Doris because it gave a new perspective to her whole marriage and compelled her to do some serious thinking. What could she do now, at the edge of old age, if she could not trust Andrew? She could do a lot, I told her. At the same time that she should try to improve her marriage, she should become less dependent on her husband and rely on her own inner resources. She did: after she left the hospital, she did not use tranquilizers or antidepressants of any kind. She won other battles. For instance, from the chain smoker that she used to be, she stopped smoking entirely.

As I have already mentioned, at times she became too self-assertive. On some occasions her remarks, although correct and always to the point, were too strong and irritated people. Whereas she used to appear weak and frail to the members of her family, now she seemed a "rock of Gibraltar" and they resented her new attitude. Roberta would often tell her that she had been "too psychoanalyzed." But Doris did not any longer need the approval of everybody. She was capable of autonomous gratification.

Doris's treatment continued mostly for the purpose of preventing her from slipping back into a mood of depression when small disappointments occurred. After all, it is easy to reacquire a mood which has been so basic to one's life. Doris, however, became capable of distinguishing disappointments from sadness and depression. Her attitude toward her marriage changed. She realized that she herself had easily assumed a submissive role, put her husband in the position of being a dominant other, and accommodated herself to a patriarchal type of society. She had been prepared to do this by the events of her early life. Her husband was not a tyrant, but a nice man who had become insensitive to her needs, to some extent because she herself had not revealed them to him. It is true that her husband was not as sexually adequate as the patient would have wanted; however, his inadequacy was not due to lack of interest in her, but to his own sexual patterns. Doris even started to teach him some romantic habits like holding hands, and he proved accessible to the new ways. She learned to accept taking the initiative sexually, without feeling guilty or inappropriate. Once she took the initiative, Andrew was able to function.

Although this state of affairs was not ideal, it proved to be a satisfactory compromise. I was always aware in the treatment with Doris that, because of her age when she started treatment with me and her almost constant state of depression since the age of thirty-two, it would be almost impossible to eradicate all the problems, or to erase all the early ferocious imprintings that had caused so much suffering. I also was aware that in some areas we would be able to obtain only satisfactory compromises.

Nevertheless the treatment seemed to exceed the expectations. She became proud of having been a mother of three nice and successful children, now themselves expecting to be parents. Once the serious period of depression lifted and Doris became able to be self-assertive, she could also show the brilliancy of her intellect, her sensitivity to psychological nuances, and her deep understanding of human relations and life in general. She had a practical knowledge of many subjects, ranging from real estate to antiques, which she put to good use. She won several bridge tournaments. Her way of talking acquired an incisive quality which was striking both for the originality of her remarks and for her occasional, surprising touches of humor. Here is a verbatim example. "I can say my life has been unusually interesting. I have witnessed three things which were beyond my wildest imagination: the first, the foundation of the state of Israel after a span of two thousand years; second, with my own eyes I saw on television human beings walking on the moon; and third, one day I picked up the phone and I heard the voice of a woman saying to my husband, on another extension, 'Hello, Andrew, do you remember the *Aurora?*' "

When I started to collect the notes for this report, I thought the case would end here. For nine years Doris was totally free of depression. She participated more and more in the various activities of life and appeared happy and industrious. After nine years she developed a severe case of herpes zoster, with excruciating pain. Shortly afterwards she started to bleed frequently during defecation. Cancer of the colon seemed certain. She underwent all possible physical examinations and the experts concluded that she was suffering from a rare but benign condition which does not require treatment, but which occasionally produces bleeding. Doris became depressed again. Treatment had to be resumed and had to be even more intense than it was originally. In the beginning, she believed that the doctors were lying to her and did not want to tell her her real illness. She eventually was convinced that her illness was benign, but she remained terribly depressed for a few months.

It was eventually found out that when she became ill, she thought her life had come to an end and she felt she had not fully lived. Actually, she had had a premonitory depression of only a few seconds' duration a year earlier when she went on a cruise with her husband and she realized that the ship was not so beautiful as the *Aurora*. She said to herself, "Is this what life is for?" and she became unhappy. She was able to overcome the few moments of depression, but when she became physically ill, she could no longer resist. The old feelings began submerging her again. She believed she was lost and incapable of doing anything. She was like a dead body. All her complexes or cognitive constructs, which I hoped had been weakened to the point of not disturbing her again, came back. We had to reexamine again her whole past, the relation with the mother, the burden of guilt originating with the accident of the brother, her marriage, the difficulties she still had in believing her husband cared for her, and so on. All her pathogenetic cognitive constructs proved not to have been extinguished by the previous treatment, but only weakened, and potentially capable of reemerging in situations of psychological stress. Although her relationship with me as her therapist was fundamentally good, I at first had greater difficulty in assuming the role of a significant third. Doris in a certain way felt disappointed in me because she had believed me, and yet after nine years she had become ill again. Sessions were very frequent. A tape recorder was used so the patient could hear the session a second time during the day.

Finally all the cognitive constructs which had to be reexamined were eventually altered and deprived of their pathogenetic effect. Although approximately sixty-nine years old, Doris again became able to trust life and to believe that even at her age living could be worthwhile. She understood that in her inner self she did not really believe life was worthless. She would not be depressed if she thought life was worthless. Life was very important to her. She became depressed when she thought she was very sick and would die without having fully accepted the essence of her life. The cruise ship, not as beautiful as the *Aurora*, stood for an unattractive, worthless life; but every life can be attractive if the person cultivates it. I told her that she had to accept being dependent on me again for a few months. When we again explored her past, she came to the realization that her adult life, although difficult, had proved not only her weaknesses but her strength and values. When we discussed her problems, we also stressed that she had been able to master her problems. She had been able to become a very good mother and grandmother, had helped her husband immeasurably in his business, and had become proficient in many aspects of life which she cultivated exclusively for her own sake. Instead of concentrating on how unhappy she had been, she focused on the little progress she made every day. Thus in the treatment of this last attack we concentrated not just on reexamination of the past from different points of view, but also on a detailed reconstruction of her present life.

I frankly told Doris that at the end of her first treatment with me I should have been more cautious and prepared her for the possibility of a recurrence. However, I explained that her physical illnesses did play an important and unpredictable role. Again, they were interpreted as meaning retribution for her alleged guilt. It meant dying without achieving any worthwhile goal, and without the fulfillment of an intense love.

Doris has recovered again. Her husband, who incidentally also has learned a great deal by listening to the recorded sessions as Doris advised him to do, has become capable of communicating fully with her and of being more expansive. He also seems to have lost some of his inhibitions. It is never too late. Doris and her husband plan to go on a cruise around the world. The *Aurora* does not exist any more; it has been dismantled. They will go on another ship.

If I may conclude this case with my own free associations, I wish to say that *Aurora* means dawn, but a sunset is often more beautiful than the dawn. The sunset of the Fullmans' life promises to be beautiful and serene.

Henry Tusdori

Dr. Henry Tusdori, a forty-seven-year-old physician, requested treatment on account of a depression which had already lasted seven years. Being a physician, he had been able to prescribe all sorts of antidepressants for himself, but there was no improvement. Recently the depression had become worse and he was wondering whether he should be hospitalized. The exacerbation of his depression had occurred after his divorce. He said that Phyllis, his former wife, had become unable to accept him because he was a discouraged and beaten man. After the divorce he felt abandoned and without love. In reality he had already found a girl friend named Peggy who was very devoted to him, but he did not appreciate her love very much. He felt that if she cared for him it was only because he was a physician and she considered herself intellectually and economically inferior to him. He was still mourning the loss of Phyllis, who had become tired of him and had abandoned him. Phyllis knew how to love, he didn't; Phyllis knew how to assert herself, and he didn't. On the other hand, it was true that he had wanted Phyllis to submit to all his wishes, but she would not.

Although considered by others to be exceptionally competent in dermatology, the specialty in which he had made noteworthy contributions, Henry Tusdori said that he disliked medical work. As a matter of fact, in the last two or three years his work had become less satisfactory, he had lost patients, and he felt ready to give up his profession. He felt tremendously frustrated, dissatisfied, and unwilling to continue any of his undertakings. He did not know whether life was worthwhile.

Relatively soon in the treatment he disclosed that he did not want to be a dermatologist, but always had aspirations of being a great writer. Since his adolescence he had devoted several hours every day to writing fiction and poetry, but the publishers rejected all his work. He did have a considerable talent for writing but, since he was involved with his medical work, he could not cultivate his literary ambitions. Still he had daydreams of winning the Nobel prize for literature.

He actually lived for the dominant goal of becoming a world-renowned writer. Everything else in his life was subordinate to this goal. Not only did he neglect some aspects of his clinical work, but his relations with women left much to be desired. They counted in his life only inasmuch as they enhanced his writing aspirations. First Phyllis and then Peggy had to listen to his poetry recitals until very late at night. They constantly had to reassure him that he would succeed at writing. When they protested or would not accede to his taxing requests, he would become angry. He never became violent but, according to his own account, on a few occasions he had a hard time controlling his aggressive impulses.

Suicidal ideas occurred every time he concluded that he was a failure both as a writer and as a physician.

Henry was born in Italy. When he was four, his parents sent him to live with friends in a distant city. His father had been a notorious antifascist and the parents felt persecuted by the fascists. They wanted to be sure that their child was safe. Henry could not understand all this very well and felt that he was being punished; that they were sending him away because he was bad. The family reunited later, and Henry always tried to do his best so that his mother and father would never again "reject" him. Mother, and especially father, always stimulated him to become a "great man," commented on his intelligence, and incited great ambitions in him.

Because Henry had to divide himself between his literary and medical work, he never achieved the high goals to which he aspired. Although he and his family emigrated to the U.S. when he was twenty, no linguistic difficulties interfered with his literary ambitions. He knew English well, but he could not fulfill his literary aims. As a doctor he was always found to be more than satisfactory. Still, he felt that only if he became great in the literary field would he deserve his parents' love, or the loves that later replaced parental love. Although he very much needed the love of a woman, the dominant goal of his literary aims actually prevented him from attaining a genuine intimate relation with a woman. Until the conflicts were discussed and to a large extent solved, Henry continued to suffer frustrations and to nourish hatred for the medical profession.

Eventually he decreased his literary ambitions. He accepted himself as a worthwhile person even if it did not mean becoming a Dostoevsky. More and more he came to value being a competent physician, capable of helping many people. He also became able to apply his unusually high intelligence and inner resources to many other aspects of life. His relations with Peggy improved greatly as he started to consider her as a person in her own right, as a person who loved him dearly but who did not want to be treated as an object for the sake of being loved. Henry continued to write for his own pleasure. He recognized that the medical profession had not been imposed on him; he had chosen it, and not just in order to make a living. Actually it was the literary work that lost some importance because he came to recognize the role it had played in his life. In other words, he understood that he used the fantasy of becoming a great writer in order to recapture the loss that in childhood he imagined he had sustained. Suicidal ideations disappeared and there was no longer any thought about hospitalization. Occasionally, however, he continued to experience mild fits of unhappiness when the idea presented itself again that he had to abandon his life's great ambition. This dominant goal was so ingrained in the fabric of his psyche that some of its effects could not be totally erased.

Sandra Carquois

Sandra was a 24-year-old married woman who, three months earlier, on awakening one morning felt that she could not get up from bed. Her husband, whom she had married a year and a half previously, urged her to get dressed but she insisted that she couldn't. She felt miserable and wanted to die. And yet the night before when she retired she felt everything was all right. During the night she felt restless, but she did not remember having unpleasant dreams. At the suggestion of the family physician, she sought psychiatric treatment.

Sandra was quite an attractive young woman, spoke without hesitation, and repeatedly said that she felt depressed to the point of having no desire to live. She did not know why she had become depressed all of a sudden. She loved her husband George, whom she had known for three years before deciding to marry him. All this she told me during the initial interview.

During a few of the following sessions, she repeatedly described an interesting phenomenon which she did not know how to explain. It was still very difficult for her to get up in the morning. Everybody knew that she was ill and her mother came from a nearby city to help her. Sandra was an only child. In reality the parents had had another child, a boy, who died a few days after his birth. Sandra's mother became fully devoted to her after her birth and would do anything for her. But in the presence of her mother, Sandra became even more helpless. She acted like a child; or rather, like a baby. She did not want to do anything. She had no energy to move, and she needed help to get dressed. When her mother went away she felt helpless, lonely, and a complete invalid. But if the mother was around, she underwent complete infantilization and wanted to be treated like a baby. If her mother refused to do anything for her, even giving her a glass of water, she felt resentful, rejected, and angry. Thus there was no way for her to get out of this predicament. She felt hopeless and wanted to die. This behavior in front of the mother lasted several weeks. Later it continued to be difficult for her to get up from bed and to come for the sessions, but nevertheless with the help of George she managed to do it. Once she was up, getting out of the house was relatively easy.

A brief history of the patient follows. The mother was described as an extremely overprotective person, an overloving mother who would do everything for the patient. She actually lived through the patient in a vicarious way. Mother was an extremely anxious person and Sandra seemed to have "inherited" her anxiety. When Sandra was a little girl she was not allowed to practice sports for fear that she would hurt herself. She wished she could be like her father, her preferred parent. She never understood why her parents got married, because they seemed to be so poorly matched. Father was a well-to-do man who treated Sandra like a princess and provided for all her financial needs. The patient and her husband had recently moved to a rather elegant part of New York City. They used to live in a town in New England, but since her husband wanted to be a physicist and had to go to school, it was easier to live in New York. Sandra too wanted to continue to go to school for her master's degree in English literature, but recently she had dropped out.

The morning in which she felt unable to get up loomed for her like the beginning of a new era, or actually the end of another era; the very end of her life. Why did she have to get up? she felt. What for? What was it all about? What was there in life to live for?

In the beginning of treatment she said that she did not know how to explain the striking experience of that eventful morning. She was apparently happy. It was true that her husband on the one side was a dreamer who wanted to discover the secrets of the atom, and on the other side was a person who enjoyed life in a material way and did not mind being supported entirely by his rich parents-in-law. But the fact was that George and she got along well. There was absolutely nothing wrong in her life which should make her feel depressed.

Many sessions were devoted to interpreting what had happened that eventful morning. Eventually she was able to verbalize what she had never been able to say or even to think about. She insisted that even when she tried to do some serious thinking while she was alone, she was not able to say to herself the things that she could later express in the therapeutic situation.

All of a sudden life had appeared false to her. That morning even the furniture in her home became flashy, appeared *nouveau riche,* and was not to her taste. It reflected the artificiality of her life, a "pseudo-life which was filling the emptiness of her life." The night before, her husband had made love to her in a routine and meaningless manner. She herself was no longer interested in making love. Everything appeared grey, even her marriage. Even George, a man whom she had insisted on marrying against her parents' advice, appeared boring and common to her. George was not really devoted to becoming a great physicist. Now he seemed much more interested in savoring the pleasures of a mundane life. Sandra and George lived in an expensive apartment in a nice part of the city, but all that was artificial too. How much more genuine was life in the New England town where she used to live! She could not divorce her husband; he was fundamentally a nice fellow. Moreover, what would her parents say? She had insisted on marrying him against their advice. She had given up everything, even going to school. She wanted to be a child. Mother would give her everything she wanted, but then she would become a baby again. But she did not want to be a baby.

Good progress was made relatively soon. The patient came to accept the fact that she was not accepting her present life. She was praised for recognizing the false values which characterized her style of living. She understood how she grew up making claim after claim which was methodically fulfilled by her parents. By satisfying all her wishes, they actually retarded her maturity. The claims that she was making now to her husband could not be fulfilled, and certainly she would have to determine which of her claims were legitimate or illegitimate. She eventually would have to decide whether or not to continue in her marital situation. She realized that she had not continued to go to school when she sensed that her husband did not really have the devotion to become a physicist as he pretended. She did not want to be better educated than he was.

During the first few weeks of treatment the patient was almost always confined to bed, but she became quite active later. At first she became involved in philanthropic activities. Then she worked for a while in a nursery school. Soon, however, she resumed going to school in preparation for her master's degree, and did very well. Fits of depression continued, and she seemed fairly sure now that they were related to her marital situation. While she was attending school, she noticed that several teachers and often students were paying a great deal of attention to her. That did not surprise her because she had always considered herself to be very attractive. What surprised her was that for the first time since she was married she was responding to other men's attentions. After a period of a few months during which she had serious conflicts, she started to become involved with men and had a series of short love affairs. None was serious enough in her opinion to justify leaving her husband, but each of them gave new moment and zest to her life, and rekindled her desire to live. Not many months passed when she discovered that her husband too was having repeated affairs.

After a period of about a year during which there was no depression, the patient terminated treatment against advice. I felt that the patient's problems had not been solved to a sufficient degree, and that some of her solutions were questionable. On the other hand, there was no sign of depression, and depression has not reappeared since then.

José Carrar

José Carrar was a thirty-nine-year-old South American businessman who purposely came to New York to seek treatment for his deep depression. He had been diagnosed as manic-depressive and indeed he occasionally had periods of euphoria and hypomanic state. However, these euphoric periods were very mild and rare. What disturbed him and his family most were the attacks of depression, which were long and intensive. According to the patient, he had had episodes of depression since he was twenty-one but the attacks became worse since the age of thirty-five, shortly after his father's death.

The father of the patient was a self-made man who built up a successful chain of stores over his country. He started as a porter and ended up as a multimillionaire. He stimulated his six children to follow his example. The patient was the second child, looked very much like his father, was considered the most intelligent of the children, and was expected to take his father's place in the corporation. José lived for the goal of becoming the chief of the company. He got married and had six children, just as his father had. He did well in school and displayed unusual intelligence and interest in many aspects of life.

At superficial examination it appeared that José was using the attacks of depressions in a manipulative way to provoke anxiety and guilt in his wife and to avoid unpleasant situations. It also seemed as if he would use hypomanic episodes to obtain what he wanted and to request what he did not dare to ask for when he was in a normal condition. For instance, when he was hypomanic he acted as if he were already the chief of the company, and would give orders and dispositions which were not appropriate to the circumstances. Upon deeper analysis, however, it became obvious that his depressions started when he realized that his brother Pedro, the oldest of the children, was also the most qualified by temperament and business talent to take his father's place. Each attack of depression was precipitated by an event which indicated to José that Pedro would eventually become the chief. When the father died and Pedro did take his place, a very intense depression with suicidal indications occurred. At first the depression was interpreted as mourning for the death of the father. José denied that rivalry for the brother was at the base of his depression. He said that intellectually he knew that Pedro was the more qualified to take that position. Although it was true that José had intellectually accepted Pedro's access to the prominent position, emotionally he had not. Since childhood he had lived for the day when he would take his father's place. All the other aspects of his life were minimized for the sake of this ambition which now would not be fulfilled. It was quite revealing to observe how everything else in his life had lost significance.

The psychodynamics of this case were simple. However, it was very difficult to change the attitude of the patient and to help him to pursue alternatives. It was not enough for him to realize the implications of his great life's disappointment. He had to reconstruct his whole attitude toward life and find other avenues for fulfillment. This was made difficult also by the fact that he had learned to exploit the secondary gains of his illness. In other words, he could say to others but especially to himself that if Pedro was more qualified for that position it was because he, José, was ill. Within two years of treatment there was marked improvement.

Five Depressed Women

Brief reports of five female patients are presented in this section. The outcome was favorable in four cases, although in one of them divorce was necessary. Three of the patients showed striking similarities in life history, symptomatology, and successful outcome. The fifth patient contrasts sharply with the others both in her life history and because of her negative response to therapy.

Rose Farsmith, a forty-five-year-old woman, made a suicide attempt when she learned that her husband was in love with another woman and wanted to divorce her. She took an overdose of barbiturates and was miraculously saved when even her doctor had started to lose hope. She was hospitalized for a few days and on her discharge she learned that her husband had already moved out of the house.

Rose said that she had been depressed for a long time, mostly because of her husband. He was unreliable, would not pay debts, would make promises which he did not fulfill, and did not respect her.

An underlying sense of inadequacy and inability to assert herself had characterized Rose's whole life. A fear of being abandoned had existed since childhood when, after the birth of her brother, she felt her mother would cease to love her and possibly go away. During the first ten years of marriage she tried to devote herself entirely to her husband and two children. She tried to please the members of the family as well as she could. At a certain point in her life she came to the realization that her marital situation could not improve. She had several attacks of depression, but did not seek treatment. At the level of consciousness she did everything she could to cling to her husband, and to keep the marriage going. She was terrified at the idea of remaining alone. She felt unattractive and the possibility of finding another man seemed to her nonexistent. On another level—that is, without realizing the implications of her actions—she did things to antagonize her husband, to render herself unattractive, and to urge him to seek the companionship of other women. During treatment she became aware of the role she had played. She accepted the divorce without a sense of panic and started gradually to rebuild a life for herself.

Mrs. Lucille O., Frances R., and Marie P. had almost identical life histories. The three of them each developed in childhood and adolescence a relation of submissiveness and dependence on their mothers, who became the dominant other. All three married self-assertive men who were moderately successful in their business activities and were good providers, but rather callous and insensitive to family relations. The three patients put their husbands in the position of being the dominant other after they had succeeded at least partially in removing the mother from that position. In one case, the mother retained a very strong role although not quite comparable to that of the husband. The three patients gave up whatever career ambitions they had once nourished and devoted themselves entirely to the family. One of the three had been a music teacher, one a business woman, and the third a secretary. They became increasingly depressed; the former music teacher also developed suicidal ideas. Hospitalization, however, was not necessary for any of them. The three insisted that their marriages were happy and their husbands were wonderful men, good providers, and excellent fathers.

The course of treatment revealed the rancor of these patients toward their husbands, the marital situation, their condition of submission, and their frustration. The three of them responded to intensive psychotherapy with complete recovery. A large part of the treatment of these patients was devoted to the study of their marital situation. They all understood the relation between the role the mother had once played and the role the husband was playing at present. After the first stage of treatment, the husbands were invited to participate in a certain number of sessions and these marital therapy sessions had excellent results. Both spouses in each of the three couples understood the roles that they had played in assuming the respective positions of dependency and the dominant other. In one of these cases the husband was at first rigid in his ways and unwilling to change but, with the help of individual psychotherapy from another therapist, he acquired insights into his own subtle behavior and the way his wife related to him.

Quite different is the case of Louise S., a single woman and a registered nurse, who started treatment with me at the age of forty-three, after having been treated at various times by six previous therapists. Louise had had several attacks of severe depression. The first one occurred at the age of twenty-two, after her graduation. She was hospitalized then and received twenty-two electric shock treatments. At the age of thirty, she had a second hospitalization which lasted seven months. After having changed many therapists who had treated her with psychotherapy and drug therapy, she requested treatment with me.

The patient lost her father at a young age. She was brought up by her mother, a perfectionistic and rigid woman who never gave her approval or comfort. Louise left her home town and came to work in New York, but it was obvious that she was more interested in finding a husband than in pursuing a nursing career. She was told that she was an excellent nurse but this appraisal did not comfort her. As a woman she felt unattractive and unable to keep men interested in her. They only wanted to use her sexually. Every time she looked at herself in the mirror, she was horrified by her appearance. Nobody ever proposed to marry her. When she came for treatment she was very despondent. Nobody would marry her or find her desirable: she would never become a mother. Even as a nurse she was no longer good. The head nurse in her department was constantly criticizing her. The patient felt that her work was deteriorating. Occasionally a man would still sleep with her, but it was always a one-night stand.

Two events caused an exacerbation of her condition. A gynecologist whom she consulted found an enormous fibroma and recommended hysterectomy. After she consulted a second gynecologist who made the same recommendation, the operation was performed. Louise recovered very quickly but became seriously depressed and suicidal. For her, the hysterectomy was the coup de grâce to her femininity. Now it was definite that she would not become a mother. Although she was forty-three, she had always clung to the idea of becoming a mother one day, and now any last hope had dissipated. This part of her history seems typical of involutional melancholia (see chapter 12), but the history of previous attacks of depression ruled out this diagnosis.

The second event which exacerbated her depression was of an entirely different kind. In the hospital where she worked, an elderly doctor started to pay attention to her. He propositioned her and made definite proposals to her. He had an invalid, terribly crippled wife whom he could not divorce. He wanted Louise to become his girl friend, mistress, and spiritual companion. He would do anything for her except marry her. Louise's answer was a flat refusal. This was her reply to him as she reported it to me: "You offer me a piece of pie, and I am entitled to the whole pie." She became very despondent, also angry at the whole world, including me as her present therapist, and suicidal. Since she refused hospitalization, her mother had to be summoned. Louise went back to her home town with her mother, where she received another series of electric shock treatments. I heard that she did not improve.

Some Conclusions

The patients described in this chapter, and those reported in detail in chapters 11 and 12, constitute a group of twelve patients who were treated with intensive psychotherapy for a period extending from eighteen months to three years. In these cases, diagnoses other than severe depression (such as schizophrenia, organic condition, and so on) could definitely be excluded. Any patient who after the second session manifested the desire to continue psychotherapy was accepted for treatment. A preliminary report of these case studies has already appeared in the literature (1977). In that report it was stated that full recovery with no relapses was obtained in seven patients, marked improvement in four, and failure in one. That statement was to be corrected to some extent because since then one patient (Mrs. Fullman) had a relapse.

I consider the overall result to be more than satisfactory. Of course, this type of treatment has to be tried with many more patients. The treatment that we have started but not yet completed with several other patients seems also very promising. The failure in the treatment of Louise S. is not difficult to understand. The events of her life made it impossible for her, in spite of psychotherapy, to disentangle herself from the cognitive constructs which perpetuated her feeling of hopelessness.

It is worth considering the moral issues which quite often emerge in these cases of depression. The therapist must of course respect the moral decisions made by the patient even if he personally happens to disagree with them. In the case of Sandra Carquois, her decision to embark on a promiscuous life was something to which we may object. Incidentally, I have seen similar occurrences in some recovering schizophrenics, in which a promiscuous stage (at times accompanied by definite psychopathic traits) is of brief duration and by no means so disturbing or incorrigible as the asocial behavior of typical nonschizophrenic psychopaths. The limited number of similar developments in the cases of depression which have come to my attention do not permit me to draw any conclusion.

Almost opposite is the case of Louise S., who refused "the piece of pie" offered by the elderly doctor. Another person would have considered that piece of pie sweet and nourishing enough to be seen not necessarily with contempt, especially since the elderly doctor also was in a very precarious and unhappy circumstance and felt he could not offer anything more. The position Louise S. took certainly was tenable and to be respected, but unfortunately it became integrated and reinforced into a framework of hopelessness and depression.

[11]

POSTPARTUM DEPRESSION

Introductory Remarks

We have seen in chapter 3 that most types of psychiatric disorders can occur after childbirth. Many authors have stressed that there is nothing specific about these conditions: childbirth is only a precipitating factor which acts by weakening the resistance of the puerperal patient.

The birth of one's child, however, is a very significant event and cannot be considered just as an ordinary precipitating factor. It may well be an event that, because of its intrinsic characteristics, finds in the patient the most suitable ground in which to evoke a psychiatric condition. It is quite possible that no other event could have caused a similar condition in that particular period of time in the life of the patient, or in any antecedent or subsequent time.

My studies of postpartum schizophrenic psychoses have convinced me of the psychogenic importance of the birth of one's child (Arieti, 1974). The study of postpartum depressions leads me to similar conclusions.

Zilboorg (1928, 1929) was one of the first authors to consider postpartum conditions from a psychodynamic point of view. He gave, however, the most orthodox Freudian interpretations. According to him, the mother has a castration complex and sees in the child "more the value of a lost male organ than anything else." She also experiences an inadequate motherly relation to the child and for this reason turns to masculinity. In contrast with Zilboorg's observation, only rarely have I found a rekindling of dormant homosexual tendencies in women who underwent psychiatric complications after childbirth.

Zilboorg (1931) was also one of the first authors to report depressive conditions in both father and mother following the birth of a child. He mainly interpreted them as reactivations of incestuous Oedipal attach-

This chapter was written by Silvano Arieti.

ment for the parent of the opposite sex. In 1959 I reported that depression may be precipitated in either parent by the birth of a child that was ostensibly wanted. I wrote, "In some young fathers the birth of a son reactivates the trauma of replacement by a new sibling. In these cases one finds unconscious fantasies about the lost breast (for now the baby will have the breast of the mother-wife). It is interesting that, whereas the birth of the child precipitates a schizophrenic psychosis only in the mother, it precipitates an attack of depression as frequently in fathers as in mothers" (Arieti, 1959). I wish to add now that in my opinion, depressive conditions occurring in fathers following childbirth are reported less frequently than those occurring in mothers for two reasons: first, because it does not occur to many authors to make the connection between the father's depression and the birth of a child; and second, because these depressions are generally much less serious than those occurring in mothers. I can also add now that although depressions in fathers occur much more frequently after the birth of a son, they also may occur after the birth of a daughter.

In 1966 Wainwright reported ten cases of fathers with psychiatric illness after the birth of a child, in seven of those cases after the birth of a son. In 1977 Bieber and Bieber reported postpartum psychiatric conditions of various kinds in mothers and fathers. A mechanism they encountered frequently in women was that the patient was afraid of evoking competitive hostility in her mother and consequently was afraid to have as many children as her mother had. When the pregnant woman was about to reach a number of children equal to that of her mother, her anxiety increased to the point of eliciting a serious psychiatric condition.

Psychodynamic Developments

I repeat here what I wrote in a chapter devoted to postpartum schizophrenic psychoses:

The more we study each case psychodynamically, the more we realize that the experience of giving birth to a child was an episode of such magnitude as to require a complete psychological readjustment on the part of the patient. Chertok (1969) writes that maternity appears to be an integrative crisis in women's psychosexual development. The assuming of the maternal role involves the revival of the structuring conflicts that have marked the mother's personal history and molded her identifications. Chertok adds that "childbirth is the 'end'—at least a temporary one—of this crisis, and also frequently its culminating point. The way in which it is experienced depends upon the woman's whole past history; at the same time, it is exposed to the hazards of a crucial moment in time and may have a directive effect on the future." These words seem to be even more pertinent in relation to women who develop psychiatric conditions after childbirth. I believe that the revival of the structuring conflicts at times necessitates psychopathological developments. The psychopathology is the result of the interplay of the conflicts of the patient and of the psychological defenses that she can build up. Childbirth was thus an essential factor in the engendering of the disorder (Arieti, 1974).

What Chertok calls the crisis is the emergence, at a clinical and conscious level, of the instability of a certain equilibrium which had been reached previously through the adoption of certain patterns of living.

The baby—the little intruder—becomes for the vulnerable and very sensitive psyche of the mother and, as we have seen, also for the father, a big intruder who is capable of smashing the previous tenuous and precarious balance. The baby is now there, in his physical reality; he has finally arrived and cannot be sent back. Before his arrival he was experienced as something as vague as a dream, a forthcoming desirable addition to the family, or an object of love to be cherished and tended; however, now he is seen as a threat or as a smasher of an illusion, and more frequently as both.

Why does he appear that way? Let us examine the depressions occurring in fathers, which are much easier to understand. We have already mentioned that as a rule they are less serious. The father generally reexperiences the trauma that he underwent when he was a child and the birth of a sibling caused what he interpreted then to be a partial or total loss of maternal love. In the majority of cases, the patient's mother (the grandmother of the present baby) did not decrease her love for the patient (the baby's father), but the patient interpreted the arrival of the sibling in this way for reasons which have to be elucidated in the course of psychotherapy. As we have already mentioned, many of these fathers are able to reevoke scenes of the mother in the act of nursing the sibling. In conjunction with these memories, they are able to reevoke fantasies in which they visualized the sibling not just as an intruder, but as a thief who had stolen the love and the breast of the mother. These fantasies were often accompanied by anger, vindictiveness, and guilt feelings.

Now the patient is threatened in a similar way. Against the dictates of his reason, he interprets the arrival of the baby as that of a usurper who will steal his wife's love from him. But more than that, the baby will demonstrate that he, the father, is not worthy of love—something that he had always suspected. Thus the father experiences the loss of an acceptable self-image and undergoes a catastrophically negative reevaluation of himself which is totally or predominantly unconscious and quite irrational. Generally the depression is not very severe; the patient is able to verbalize freely, and with the help of the therapist he can bring back to consciousness what was repressed. He can also regain reassurance about his wife's love. There are, of course, important variables in these cases.

In some patients the original trauma, sustained at the birth of the sibling, is the major antecedent factor; in some others it is the uncertain relation with the wife.

Depressions occurring in mothers after childbirth are more complicated. Unexpectedly an intense drama unfolds. Generally there are four characters in this drama: the mother, the baby, the husband, and the patient's mother (the baby's grandmother). On rare occasions the patient's father (the baby's grandfather) plays a role. The young therapist is inclined to suspect that the baby and the husband of the patient play a great role, and indeed they do, but in the majority of cases not so great as that of the patient's mother. In most cases which have come to my attention, the dominant other was not the husband or the baby, but the the patient's mother. I have already mentioned that Bieber and Bieber (1977) found as a frequent dynamic factor the patient's fear of competition with her mother over the number of children to have. I believe that what the Biebers have described could be called the Niobe complex, from Greek mythology. Niobe, queen of Thebes and daughter of Tantalus, boasted of her fertility, saying that the goddess Leto had only two children. Apollo and Artemis, who were Leto's two children, were angry at the insult and killed all the children of Niobe. Zeus also joined in the revenge and turned Niobe into a stone image which wept perpetually— an image of depressed stupor. The patient described by the Biebers feels that she is about to show her superiority over her mother and, I would like to add, she also feels that she is already being punished in a way similar to Niobe.

In my experience, however, patients as described by Bieber and Bieber are only a small percentage of postpartum depressions. And even in their cases, the intense relation with the mother concerns many aspects of life and not just giving birth to a certain number of children.

In the majority of cases of postpartum depressions in young mothers which have come to my attention, the patient's mother—in addition to being a dominant other whom the patient had to placate and from whom she had to obtain constant approval—was a person with whom the patient identified, although reluctantly. In other words, the patient modeled herself after her mother, not because she admired her, but in order to obtain her approval and love. When the baby arrives the identification seems complete and irreversible. Now the patient is going to be a mother as her mother is, and probably the same type of mother her mother always has been. But the patient cannot accept this. Thus she must reject her mother and consequently a great deal of herself, modeled after mother, and a great deal of her connections with other people, imitated from mother's ways, and of course her relation with the baby, which confirms her as a mother. At the same time she experiences guilt feelings because she cannot accept the idea that she does not accept her maternal role.

In some instances, other constellations of thought become mixed with the one described and may even acquire prominence. The patient does not want to give up the woman she wanted to be—let us say, a scientist or a lawyer. Now she is going to be a mother and the career which was her dominant goal will not be actualized. She will be a mother in a role whose significance she now minimizes: even female animals can be mothers. Thus her whole sense of self and of life in general undergoes drastic changes.

Contrary to what one would expect, fear of losing the husband's love, which from now on may be directed only to the baby, has not played an important role in the cases of postpartum depressions that have come to my attention. This finding contrasts with what I have observed in postpartum depressions occurring in fathers. However, I must reiterate that patients treated by a single therapist cannot constitute a large number. Thus any impression about the possible incidence of a certain cluster of psychodynamic factors is likely to be corrected if a large number of cases could be assembled and correlated. In many cases of postpartum depressions, after following the initial modalities described in chapter 9, I try to determine as soon as possible whether the patient rejects the child and feels guilty about it. If she does reject the child and is willing to admit it, I rush to say, "Remember three important things: (1) You must accept the fact that you do not accept the child now but the day will come when you will accept him and love him (her). (2) Try not to feel guilty for what you cannot prevent. (3) Your child is not going to suffer. Somebody will take care of him (her) until you are in a position to do so." I have found that these words are temporarily reassuring and helpful until deeper understanding of this situation is obtained.

The rest of the chapter is devoted to a case report which illustrates the psychodynamics of postpartum depression, as well as some therapeutic modalities. This report deals with one of the most severe cases of depression that I have ever seen. Although I believe that I have brought to solution the main aspects of this case, by no means do I claim that I have understood it in entirety. The reader will certainly discover several untapped possibilities and issues which would benefit from further clarification.

Case Report

Lisette was twenty-four years old when I first saw her. She was from Australia and was in this country with her husband, who had won a scholarship to do postgraduate research in New York City. Here is a brief account of the events that brought her to me. Several months previously she had given birth to a girl. Immediately after the birth she became depressed; however, she and her family did not give too much importance to her condition, and she received no treatment. Her condition became much worse and eventually she had to be hospitalized for a few months. She was treated with drug therapy, she improved, and was discharged. A few weeks later, however, she started to be seriously depressed again. She started treatment with a psychoanalyst of classic orientation, but there was no improvement. On the contrary, the situation was deteriorating rapidly. The patient became unable to take care of the baby and was completely incapacitated. The mother-in-law, who lived in Australia, had to be summoned to New York to help the patient. When she arrived the patient resented her very much, so she returned to Australia. Then the patient's mother came and remained with her for several months. Suicidal ideas were freely expressed by the patient and suicide was an impending threat. She could not be left alone.

When I first saw her entering the waiting room of my office, she was accompanied by her mother and husband who were sustaining her on each side, almost to prevent her from falling. When I looked at her face, I saw a picture of intense sadness and abandonment, so picturesque as to give me a fleeting impression that perhaps it was not genuine, but histrionic and theatrical. I had never seen such scenes before except in Italian movies. But when Lisette was alone with me in my office, her real suffering revealed itself: it was a genuine, uncontrollable, overpowering, all-evolving, all-absorbing, all-devastating depression. The feeling of hopelessness and despair, as well as the motor retardation, prevented her from talking freely. Nevertheless she managed to tell me briefly that her therapist was not doing her any good, and she was sick and wanted to die. When I spoke to the mother and husband later, while she was closely watched in the waiting room by another person, they told me that I was supposed to be only a consultant. They wanted to know whether the patient should receive electric shock treatment; it was no longer possible to manage her at home. They were consulting me to find out whether I was firmly opposed to electric shock treatment in this case. In view of the failure of drug therapy, psychoanalytic treatment, and the seriousness and urgency of the situation, I told the husband that shock treatment should be tried, and that they should consult me again afterward.

The patient received fifteen shocks. This is a large number for depressed patients, who receive an average of five. As a matter of fact, the treatment was eventually stopped because there was no improvement. I remembered from my early experiences in Pilgrim State Hospital that depressed patients who do not improve even after such a large number of treatments have a poor prognosis. When Lisette returned to see me, she was still very depressed, suicidal, and hopeless. In spite of fifteen grand mals there was practically no memory impairment. She told me that she strongly resented going back to her analyst or for more electric shock treatment and begged me to accept her in therapy.

I wish to describe my feelings when she made such a request. This wish of mine is undoubtedly partially motivated by narcissism, but also by my belief that it is important to evaluate the feelings of the analyst at the beginning of the treatment of every seriously ill patient. I was very touched by that profound, seemingly infinite pain. I was also perplexed: I had already understood that all this had to do with the birth of the child, but how a birth could produce such devastating depression was a mystery to me. What basic construct or relation was undergoing a disintegration capable of producing such a violent and seemingly unhealing process in that young, promising, intelligent, and sensitive young woman?

Needless, to say, when I discussed the matter with the previous therapist, he did not object to terminating his treatment. So Lisette came to me. I am now going to give a brief history of the patient as it was collected during the first few months of treatment.

The patient was born in a small town which was contiguous to a big city in Australia. The parents belonged to the upper-middle class. The father was a successful divorce lawyer, blessed with a cheerful character that made him see the world with rose-colored glasses and helped him to make a brilliant career. His refined form of shallowness, with such effervescent optimism, made him navigate surely and fast but without leaving a wake. The patient felt much closer to her mother, who actually was a very demanding person. Mother had a humanistic education; would speak about art, literature, and poetry in particular; and seemed to have much more in common with the patient. She helped her with her homework while the patient was in high school and college. Mother also made many demands; and, according to Lisette, there was an almost constant expression of disapproval in her face.

Mother had been engaged to a man who died during the engagement. She often referred to this man with enthusiastic terms never used in relation to father. Although father adored mother, mother had for father only a lukewarm, amicable attitude. Lisette defined the marriage of her parents as fairly good, but not marvelous. The patient knew that sexual life between the parents was not a thrilling one; mother had told her that she obliged.

Earlier in life mother had suffered from epilepsy and also from depression. It seemed that both her epilepsy and depression had started with the birth of the patient's brother. Mother became depressed to such a point that four-year-old Lisette had to be sent to live with her grandmother for a while. Incidentally, this grandmother, the mother's mother, was the only person throughout Lisette's childhood who shone as a giver of affection, love, warmth, and care. Lisette always loved her dearly. In spite of grandmother's affection, separation from her mother was experienced as a trauma by Lisette. Mother recovered quickly from her depression but, as already mentioned, she had also developed epilepsy. There was an atmosphere of secrecy in the family about mother's epilepsy. In fact, Lisette had never seen her mother having an attack until she was twenty. On that occasion Lisette called on God to help mother, but in mother's face during the attack was God's denial of her request. The truth could no longer be concealed, and she experienced a sense of horror—moral horror—because of the denial.

The patient was always very good in school. During adolescence she felt inferior and unattractive. She had a negative attitude toward life. Everything that appeared good or likable also appeared superficial, like father. Everything that was deep and worthwhile appeared inaccessible, like mother's approval. There was no doubt in her mind that mother had always preferred her brother, for whom she had strong rivalry and jealousy. She went through a period of rebellion during which she felt people were empty, superficial, and made of plastic. She did not care how she looked and was neglectful of her appearance. Because she was not well dressed and because of her bohemian ways, she felt disapproval not only from her mother but also from the upper-middle class of the small town where she lived. And yet as much as Lisette was critical of these people, she seemed to need their approval and acceptance.

When Jack, a young man of the lower-middle class, started to pay attention to her she was grateful that somebody had noticed her presence. Soon she felt very much in love with him, admired his idealism, intelligence, and interest in research; and when Jack graduated from school, they got married. The patient stated that her marriage was a happy one from the very beginning. The only thing she resented in her marriage was her husband's family, and especially her husband's mother. Jack's mother was so different from her son, so cheap, vulgar, and materialistic. She was coarse; she ate with her fingers and sniffed tobacco. She was also narrow-minded. To the degree that Jack was desirable, his mother was undesirable. Jack won a research fellowship in the United States, and everybody was very happy. In the meantime, however, Lisette had become pregnant. The pregnancy was accidental and came at a very inopportune time. The patient was angry about it and also experienced nausea. Although the pregnancy was a complication, Lisette and her husband came to the United States in May, during her fifth month of pregnancy. (The baby was expected in September.)

Lisette told me that during her pregnancy she had a peculiar idea. I must make it clear that when I first heard about it, the idea indeed seemed so peculiar as to make me think of a schizophrenic disorder. Lisette told me that during her pregnancy she had the feeling that her mother-in-law had entered her. "What do you mean?" I asked, unwittingly approaching her with an obvious feeling of perplexity or even consternation. Lisette told me with a reassuring voice, "Don't worry. I did not mean it literally. My husband's sperm that had impregnated me contained genes inherited from his mother. I was displeased that inside of me a baby was growing that was partially a derivation of my mother-in-law."

In spite of this reassurance the idea seemed bizarre to me and, in a different context, I still would have considered the possibility of schizophrenia. In fact we know that in preschizophrenics and also schizophrenics, certain expressions used metaphorically are forerunners of delusions. In these cases the delusion eventually denotes literally what was previously meant in a metaphorical sense. However, in this case nothing else was schizophrenic or schizophreniclike. I had to rely on my clinical experience with schizophrenics to evaluate the clinical picture in its totality and exclude such a possibility. The future development of the case supported my clinical evaluation that there was no schizophrenia.

The patient gave birth in September, and the symptomatology of a depression first manifested itself in a mild and later in a very pronounced form. The childbirth represented a focal point from which the whole manifest symptomatology originated and irradiated in various directions. For a long time Lisette could not even talk about the birth of Clare in more than fleeting remarks. The episode of the birth itself, as experienced by Lisette, was painful to such a tragic degree as to prevent discussion of it until the groundwork had been prepared by treatment. However, at this point it may be useful to evaluate what we already know about Lisette's case and to delineate some basic constructs.

In the life of the patient there was a dominant other, and this person was not the husband but the mother; the mother so much needed for approval, and from whom approval was so uncertain; the mother with whom she would like to identify, but no longer could.

This dominant mother as a basic construct had, so to say, a satellite in the mother-in-law. The patient did not have to be as careful in her conceptions about the mother-in-law as she had to be in reference to her mother. Without guilt or compunction of any sort, and strengthened by some realistic facts, Lisette displaced to the mother-in-law some of the bad characteristics of her mother, and also the feeling that she had for her mother. The mother-in-law was not only vulgar and disapproving, but she herself had made Lisette become a mother. The mother-in-law became, although at a quasi-metaphorical level, the phallic mother who entered Lisette and made her pregnant. The husband was totally dismissed; the mother-in-law who had made her become a mother was a monstrous distortion of Lisette's own mother. It was almost as if, by accepting her pregnancy, Lisette had to accept her mother and her mother-in-law and what they stood for. If they stood for motherhood, it was a motherhood that she wanted to reject. Acccepting their type of motherhood would mean being as they were and giving up her self-image, a cognitive construct about herself which was cherished and gratifying. However, the fact remained that during her pregnancy Lisette was apparently all right. It was the childbirth itself that precipitated the condition; but Lisette did not want to talk about the birth for a long time.

Nevertheless, from the beginning of treatment I got the impression that Lisette could open up to me. I was immediately accepted by her as a dominant third; and when she trusted me fully and saw me as an undemanding, accepting, and not disapproving person, I became a significant third. I had the feeling that although she did not consider me to be a source of love, she saw in me a source of strength, clarity, and hope.

For several months the sessions were devoted to studying her relations with her mother, and how Lisette lived for her mother's approval. A look, a gesture of disapproval, would make her sink into a deep state of depression. To be disapproved of by mother meant utter rejection and unworthiness. She required her mother to take care of and fuss over her as grandmother had done. Grandmother was really the person to whom the patient was close. Her affection was profuse, a steady flow, without fear of interruption because of sudden disapproval. In contrast, mother's approval could always end abruptly whenever she decided that Lisette had committed an infraction, no matter how little. There was no doubt that the patient put in operation manipulations and other characteristics, as Bonime (1976) has described. However, there was in addition this constant need for mothers' approval, as Bemporad (1970) has illustrated. Not only did she want to be mothered by mother, but she wanted mother to have a good opinion of her. Mother seemed to be the only person who counted in her family constellation, and yet many actions or words of mother were interpreted in a negative way by Lisette—not with the suspicious distortion of the paranoid, but with the adverse appraisal of the depressed. For instance, when mother said that the patient had been lucky in comparison to her, she implied that the patient was spoiled and had an easy life. When mother said how wonderful Jack was, she meant that Lisette did not measure up to her husband. If mother was making a fuss about Clare and called her darling, Lisette would become very depressed, wishing mother would refer to her in that way. She resented mother terribly and yet she could not even contemplate the idea of being left alone with Clare if mother went back to Australia. Then she would be overwhelmed by her duties and feel completely lost.

Using the formulation of Bemporad (1970), I repeatedly pointed out to Lisette that at present she was incapable of autonomous gratification. Any supply of self-esteem and feeling of personal significance had to come from mother. Mother was not just a dispenser of love, but was put in a position to be almost a dispenser of oxygen and blood. By withdrawing approval, the supply would end and she would become depressed. At the least sign of forthcoming disapproval, it was as if the supply was interrupted. Disapproval brought about not only depression but also guilt feelings, because she felt she deserved disapproval. And yet a part of her wanted to be like her mother, although mother was not like her grandmother.

I explained to Lisette that she sustained a first important trauma after the birth of her brother, when she was sent away from the depressed mother and she experienced a feeling of deprivation. Moreover, she associated deprivation, loss of love, and depression with childbirth. I have found that in postpartum psychoses of both schizophrenic and depressed types, the patient makes a double identification with her mother and with her child. Inasmuch as Lisette identified with her mother, she was a mother incapable of giving love, a mother who would become depressed, a mother who would only love an intruder like Clare. Little Clare became the equivalent of Lisette's brother, who had once deprived her of mother's love: if Lisette identified with the child, she felt deprived as a child feels who is deprived of love. All these feelings were confused, and of course self-contradictory.

Lisette came to experience the treatment as a liberation from mother. Mother's disapproval gradually ceased to mean loss of love and loss of meaning of life. Indeed, treatment was a liberation from mother; not so much from mother as a physical reality, but from mother as the mental construct of the dominant other. The relation with the analyst as the significant third permitted her to stop identifying with mother without losing the sense of herself as a worthwhile human being. Moreover, anticipation of maternal disapproval no longer brought about depression or guilt feelings. At the same time that mother lost importance, the satellite constructs of the mother-in-law, as well as of the upper-middle class of the little town, lost power. During the early periods of the treatment, in fact, when Lisette talked about the people in her home town she was still worried about what they would think of her in spite of the distance of ten thousand miles. At the same time that the mother, as an inner object, and the related constructs were losing value, the husband was acquiring importance. The patient had always admired and respected her husband, but she had never put him in a position where his withdrawal of approval would be of vital importance. Now the husband could be enjoyed as a source of love. Lisette's desire for sexual relations returned. The patient also became more capable of sharing interest in Jack's professional and scientific activities. Before she had been interested only in humanistic subjects, as mother was.

Up to this point, treatment had consisted of changing the value of some basic constructs so that their loss would not be experienced as a psychological catastrophe and new, more healthy constructs could replace the disrupted and displaced ones. In other words, the patient was searching for and finding a meaning in life which was not dependent on the old constructs and not connected with pathological ideas. She was now astonished that she could have had certain thoughts and feelings. For instance, she remembered that when the newborn Clare was sucking at her breast, she would become more depressed. She did not want to nurture her; she herself wanted to be nurtured, perhaps by her mother. She also remembered that she had been angry at Jack when he would tell her to look after the baby. He should have told her to look after herself. She realized that her depression, as well as her identification with the baby and her rivalry with the baby, had made her regress to an unbelievable degree.

After several months of treatment we felt that the patient could manage her life alone and that mother could return to Australia. The patient had a mild fit of depression caused by their separation, but no catastrophe occurred. After awhile Lisette was asking herself how she could have tolerated her mother in her home for so long.

It took some time after mother left for the patient to bring herself to talk about a most important issue—the experience of childbirth. Lisette told me that when she discovered that she was pregnant, she decided to take a course for expectant mothers on natural childbirth. According to the basic principle of natural birth, the woman in labor does not succumb to the pain; she maintains her grip on herself. The woman in labor should not scream; the scream is ineffectual despair, it is being no longer on top of oneself. What happened instead? In spite of the preparation, Lisette in labor could not bear the pain and screamed. It was a prolonged, repeated, animal-like scream. While she was screaming, she wanted to kill herself because to scream meant to give up as a human being, to disintegrate. But she screamed, she screamed, she screamed! What a horror to hear herself screaming, what a loss of her human dignity.

During many sessions the patient discussed her cognitive constructs about childbirth. She resented being a biological entity, more an animal than a woman. Biology was cruel. Women were victims of nature. They became the slaves of the reproductive system. You started with the sublimity of romantic love and you ended with the ridiculous and degrading position of giving birth. While giving birth, you were in a passive, immobile position which was dehumanizing. Nurses and doctors who meant nothing to you saw you in an animal-like, degrading position. You revolted and screamed and lost your dignity. Lisette wanted her husband to be present in her moment of greatness during her childbirth, and instead he was witness to her descent to utmost degradation. Childbirth was the death of love, the death of womanhood. You were no longer you, but a female of an animal species. You became what these dominant adults made you; and what is even worse, you needed them. You were no longer yourself, you were already dead because the ideal of yourself—what you were or what you wanted to become—was no longer tenable. You gave up the promise of life; you went through a dissolution of thoughts and beliefs. The pain increased, became insurmountable.

Eventually Lisette felt not only physical pain, but also moral pain. She could not think any more. She felt depressed, and the waves of depression submerged her more and more. But at the periphery of her consciousness, some confused thoughts faintly emerged: she did not want to be a mother, she did not want to take care of the child, she would not be able to take care of the child, she could not take care of her home, she should die. It was impossible for her to accept what she had become—a mother—and the concept of mother did not have for her the sublimity that culture attributes to it, but all the mentioned negative animal-like characteristics. She felt she had probably become an animal-like mother, as her mother-in-law was.

At an advanced stage of the treatment Lisette was able to recapture all these thoughts that had occurred to her during and after the birth of Clare—thoughts which had become more indistinct, almost unconscious, as the depression occupied her consciousness more and more. In treatment the ideas emerged that had precipitated the depression and which the depression had made unconscious.

Although these thoughts appeared in an intricate confused network when they were revealed to me, it was not difficult for me to help Lisette disentangle them and to get rid of them because we had already done the preliminary work. Once we dismantled mother as the inner object of the dominant other and as an object of identification, it was easier to bring the associated ideas back to consciousness. It became easier for Lisette to understand that when she gave birth she strengthened her identification with her mother who, when she gave birth to Lisette's brother, had become depressed and epileptic. But she no longer could accept identifying with mother, at least to that extent. In order to reject that identification, she had to reject motherhood as well. But now that the treatment had helped her to remove the need to identify with her mother, she could accept motherhood and herself as she was, and as what she had become —a mother.

In the beginning of treatment Lisette gradually became aware that her suffering was partially due to her not having received approval and gratification from her mother; but later she became aware that her greater suffering was due to the twilight of her basic constructs which had not been replaced by others. Lisette realized that the depression had been so strong as to prevent her from searching for other visions of life. She understood that the physical pain which she sustained during childbirth was symbolic of the greater and more overpowering pain caused by the incoming twilight of the basic constructs. Eventually the therapy permitted her to accept the loss of these constructs without experiencing depression. Even her attitude about being a member of an animal species changed greatly. She came to accept that we are animals and procreate like animals because we can transcend our animal status. And there is beauty in our animal status, provided that we are able to fuse it with our spiritual part; and that together with our animal status, we retain our status as persons. This last point was clarified by the analysis of some dreams, as shall be seen shortly.

The analysis of her dreams was another interesting aspect of her therapy. From the very beginning of treatment, most of them had to do with childbirth. Here are a few typical ones. She was in labor and in a state of terror. She was swollen like a balloon. Somebody pricked the balloon. She felt deflated. Shame and horror continued. Discussion of the dream revolved around how pregnancy had made her a person which she did not want to be. The bodily transformation was, both in real life and in the dream, symbolic of an inner transformation which she was experiencing.

In another dream the patient realized that she was pregnant for a second time and told herself to be passive, not to fight the pregnancy. All of a sudden she found herself in prison. She looked at the street through the bars of the window and saw it full of garbage cans. There was another girl in jail, in the same cell. This other girl was courageous, not fearful like the patient. Lisette knew that she was going to be executed by hanging. She looked at her face in a mirror and thought, "How shall I look when I am dead? I want to look the same." She was wearing a beautiful nightgown, and she was concerned not with dying, but with how she would look after her death. The ensuing discussion revealed that the dream repeated how she had felt in the past and to a certain extent how she was still feeling about becoming a mother. Motherhood would make her a prisoner: her real self, the real Lisette, would die and she would become another, not authentic woman. She could not be like her cell-mate, her ideal self, brave even in adversity.

In another dream the patient saw a woman in labor. Her cheeks had become withered and wrinkled. They had actually changed in the moment in which she gave birth. A man, the husband of the woman, was smoking and talking about a party which he wanted to give to celebrate the birth. The patient thought he was hateful and cruel because he did not know what the wife was going through.

In her associations the patient said that nobody, not even a loving husband, can understand what a woman goes through in those moments. When the patient was asked to focus on the fact that the cheeks of the woman had become withered and wrinkled, she winced and in an anguished voice said, "That face had a strong resemblance to my mother's face, when I saw her during the epileptic attack. My mother became epileptic when she gave birth to my brother."

These dreams and others not only repeated the themes which were discussed earlier, but revealed other aspects which otherwise would have received only secondary consideration. The last dream I mentioned disclosed resentment not only toward a husband, but toward a male world or a patriarchal society which does not know what women go through. Male society does not know either the pain of labor or the status to which women are relegated. Pregnancy and child-rearing practices in some

Psychotherapy

respects enable society to keep women in a secondary position, stressing their biological roles and depriving them of many opportunities available to men. Pregnancy becomes a prison, as one of Lisette's dreams symbolized, and leads to the death of existence as a total person (being hanged). Although difficult for her to admit, Lisette retained a certain resentment at having left her country in order to enhance her husband's career. The resentment grew when the pregnancy, the labor, and anticipation of having to take care of the baby pointed out life's limitations for which she was not psychologically prepared.

Lisette's case obligates us to see some connection—perhaps not fundamental, but nevertheless important—between postpartum depressions (or possibly all postpartum psychiatric disorders) and the status of women in a patriarchal society. Possibly postpartum disorders occur more frequently at times and in places in which women are less willing to accept the traditional role. Pregnancy and labor may make a woman feel as if she is confined to the biological role of reproduction.

Lisette was able to reassess old meanings in a nonpathological frame of reference, and to accept new meanings. She made rapid progress in treatment. My fear that it would be difficult to change the husband's role in Lisette's life proved unfounded. Contrary to the other males, the father and brother who were not significant figures, the husband rapidly acquired importance and was fully experienced as a source of love, communion, and intimacy.

I asked Lisette whether I could publish her case report, and she said, of course. I told her then that whoever reads her story will be reminded by her that we are barely out of the jungle; we can easily resume an almost-animal status, not because we are animals—which we are—but because we are human beings with ideas. Certain ideas that we adopt can make us feel and act like animals—that is, as biological entities which have lost a personal image. The study of life circumstances is important, I told her, but her story shows that even more important is the study of our ideas about these circumstances; because it is with these ideas that we lay foundations for life which eventually may not be able to sustain the weight of our existence. I also told her—and she agreed—that her story shows we can change even basic ideas and their accompanying feelings, and thus restore the promise of life and move again toward fulfillment.

Lisette and her family have returned to their native country. In a span of ten years there have been no relapses.

[12]

PSYCHOTHERAPY OF DEPRESSION

DURING THE MIDDLE YEARS

(INVOLUTIONAL MELANCHOLIA)

Specific Psychodynamics in the Middle Years

There is a time of life when the human being is prone to reassess his past and, by virtue of this reassessment, to envision his remaining years.

In our day, with the considerable increase in length of life, most people make this reassessment at a rather advanced age of about sixty or older. But one group of people—considerable in number but smaller than it used to be—makes this reassessment much earlier, during the so-called middle years, a period of life sometimes called the involutional age or the age of menopause and the climacterium.

This early reassessment generally is evoked by a deep pessimism about one's existence which emerges in full force when youth is over and maturity takes its place. Discontentment about one's lot in life, and the belief that what is left is not going to be worthwhile, bring about this negative appraisal. To make the situation more complicated, the cognitive substratum on which the discontentment and negative appraisal are based becomes confused and either remains at the periphery of consciousness or is fully repressed. What does remain in full consciousness is a severe mood of depression. In a nutshell, this is the drama of what used to be called involutional melancholia.

Several issues are subsumed in the previous statements. In women, the first severe depression often occurs at the time of menopause or shortly afterwards. This cannot be considered accidental; but in spite of much

This chapter was written by Silvano Arieti.

research on this subject, no causal connection has been determined between the cessation of estrogen production by the ovaries, and depression. Most women do not become depressed at the time of menopause. Most women, unless seriously depressed, retain sexual desire after menopause and in quite a few women, lust is increased. If menopause is responsible for the depression, it is probably because of psychological meanings attributed to the phenomenon of menopause.

Several factors have to be considered. Although the woman retains sexual desire and may continue to have satisfactory sexual relations for the rest of her life, she knows that she can no longer bear children. In our era, very few women wish to have children at the time of the menopause. Thus we cannot consider the end of reproductive life to be a direct cause of depression. In some patients, however, the age at which it is no longer possible to bear children acquires a meaning which has very little to do with the ability to procreate. In some women menopause elicits the following constellation of thoughts: youth has ended, attractiveness is diminished, old age is approaching. I will begin to look worse and worse. Life will offer less and less. Nobody has ever really loved me in the past, and the chances of my being loved now are nonexistent. I have nothing to look forward to; I am trapped in a condition from which I cannot escape. The patient would not be inclined to think this way if her life had been a rewarding one. In the past there was the hope that life would be better. Now the woman interprets menopause as a milestone indicating that hope is no longer possible. In chapter 3 it was mentioned that many authors have described the premorbid personality of the involutional melancholic as rigid, meticulous, obsessional, and having a narrow range of interests. These descriptions point out that the patient more or less followed one of the patterns of life that were analyzed in chapter 6.

Menopause seems to remove the last ray of hope for romantic or professional fulfillment. Although lack of professional achievement plays an important role for some women, in most female patients complexes about romantic love are more common. The patient feels that she sought love, but did not find it. If she found it, it was a love with impossible strings attached, or not a worthwhile love, or a love by far inferior to the one she had fantasized in adolescence. Although the patient does not regret the fact that she no longer can have children, she regrets the fact that she did not have children; or if she did, that they did not bring the joy she expected. The depression which frequently follows hysterectomy has this meaning.

The patient broods over the idea that whatever she aspired to be did not come to pass, and whatever she did accomplish was of little import. Nobody cared for her enough, nobody considered her enough, even a deep and lasting friendship was denied to her. If she did spend most of her life for the sake of a human relationship or cause, that motivation now appears unjustified, badly conceived, disguised, distorted, masked.

Whatever compensation she obtained was ludicrous in comparison to what she expected, to the efforts she made, or to what she could have achieved if she had followed a different path. But now it is too late: there is nothing she can do about it. If she looks for a meaning in life, she will end with the conclusion that her life is meaningless. Death may be preferable.

This picture is substantially the one described in chapter 6. The major difference is that the depression is precipitated by the menopause or, more accurately, by the cognitive work of reevaluating one's existence that the end of the prime of life has urged the patient to do. I must stress that the menopause is not simply a precipitating factor; it is a special factor with meanings easily attached to it because of the particular biological effect of the cessation of menses. The patient who has been able to escape depression, in spite of more or less having followed the patterns of life described in chapter 6, is no longer able to do so when she has to face what she interprets as the twilight of her life.

In some cases an unpleasant episode occurs around the time of the menopause, it is interpreted in accordance with the climate of the involutional syndrome, and it is recognized as the precipitating factor. The patient is able to remember the episode after the period of severe depression has subsided.

Szalita (1966) reported the example of a woman who at the age of forty-nine went on a trip abroad. She had been widowed from the age of thirty-eight. From a movie, she got the idea that a trip abroad could bring her adventure. To enhance her chances she traveled first-class and took with her an entirely new wardrobe, on which she had spent a full year's income. The trip was a total failure. She felt not only ignored but avoided by everybody. Szalita continues:

At a certain point she sat down in front of a mirror in her cabin and started to meditate. She could not recall what she had been thinking about when an intense fear suddenly took hold of her. She felt that she was going to faint— to die. She ran out of her cabin and requested the ship's doctor be brought to to her. She was afraid to be on deck for fear she might throw herself into the water. She became agitated, walked restlessly in circles, and counted her steps. She could not sleep, however, was extremely restless, and decided to fly back home (1966).

Although these cases are tragic and at times devastating in their effects, the psychodynamics are seemingly easy to understand even at a manifest or conscious level. Why, then, is the treatment so difficult? No matter how simple the psychodynamics are, and how many components are retained at the level of consciousness, the patient is not aware of the totality of the picture—its effects, origin, and implications. When awareness emerges, it is rapidly submerged and replaced by the feeling of depression. Sometimes the patient claims not to know why she is depressed. Other times she finds seemingly plausible reasons to justify her melancholia. Like many depressed patients, she makes rather superficial and negative appraisals of herself, the world, and the future. In other words, she puts into operation the cognitive triad described by Beck (1967). In these cases, too, we must be aware that this triad is a cover-up, a superficial depression covering a deeper one whose cognitive counterpart originated long ago and now has become partially or totally unconscious.

Psychotherapy techniques used for patients suffering from severe depression, as described in chapter 9, can be applied to most cases of severe depression occurring in the middle years. There is a group of patients in whose dynamics we must include an additional factor. Although both males and females are found in this group, we shall refer to the patient as female, since women are much more numerous. When the middle years, menopause, or climacterium occurs, the patient starts to brood over a "lost opportunity." If she had married the man who pursued her and not her husband, or if she had pursued another career for which she had an inborn talent and not the one she finally chose, her life would have been completely different and fulfilled. The lost opportunity now becomes the trauma of the loss, and it is often relived at this particular period of life when the woman believes nothing else is left for her. The "lost opportunity," however, is not often referred to, at least at the beginning of treatment. The patient in explaining her manifest symptomatology refers to hypochondriacal symptoms, unexplainable feelings which torture her, or Beck's cognitive triad. Only at a more advanced stage of treatment does the patient start to talk about the lost opportunity. Depression largely based on the complex (or cognitive construct) of the lost opportunity may reach severe intensity, but not to the most severe degree possible. An oceanic state of depression is seldom seen in these cases. Yet the "lost opportunity" is experienced as lost forever, without any hope of retrieving it.

Why do these cases not reach the most devastating degree of depression? This is not difficult to understand if we realize that this complex is a defense. Although it causes the patient to grieve, in a certain way it permits the retention of a moderate amount of self-esteem; the patient feels that she once had a chance in life. Whether what she missed was love or self-fulfillment in a career, she feels that she could have obtained the rewards of that love or that career—she was worthy of it—but it was either her wrong choice or fate (that is, circumstances beyond her control) which determined otherwise. Regret for what one has not done or left undone is an important cause of depression, but not of the most extreme forms.

Conditions similar to those which have been described in women exist in men, too, although they are much less common.

If endocrinological factors cannot be considered important in the engendering of involutional depressions in women, they are even less important in men. Testicular hormones are produced for a much longer period of time than ovarian hormones. We also know that most men, unless physically ill or depressed, can have normal sexual relations until advanced age. Maranon (1954) reported that Pavlov found active spermatozoa in the semen of men as old as 91, and Metchnikoff in men as old as 103. Men who have reached the middle years are less concerned than women about the ability to procreate or about their physical appearance, and as a rule they do not see life as already approaching the end. Undoubtedly most of these differences between the sexes are to a large extent culturally determined and are probably bound to disappear with greater recognition of women's rights.

Szalita (1966) reported the case of a sixty-two-year-old man who connected the onset of his agitated depression to the following episode.

He met an old friend whom he had not seen in thirty years, and he barely recognized him. "I saw in front of me an old, decrepit man," he said. "It dawned on me then that I must look like him. I went home and looked at myself in the mirror and hardly recognized myself in the image I saw. From the mirror gazed at me a shrivelled-up face, with bags under the eyes. 'This is me!' I screamed, and felt like breaking the mirror."

Szalita added that this man had never married, but had had numerous love affairs and regarded himself as being successful with women. After this episode he considered himself "finished." He became hypochondriacal and developed symptoms similar to the ones his mother had had. He started to behave exactly as she had before she was sent to a psychiatric hospital. "Now I know how my mother cracked up," he explained.

Although a certain number of men feel threatened by what time has done to them physically, a larger number are disturbed by the fact that they have not kept up professionally as they should have. Some men feel threatened by younger competitors in matters of love and romantic liaisons, but many more feel threatened professionally. Some men become insecure in their work and unable to make decisions. On the other hand, they resent depending on others. Pathological states of depression occur when the patients experience themselves as being in a serious predicament from which they cannot escape.

Psychotherapy

Today not many patients suffering from typical involutionary melancholia —characterized by severe depression occurring for the first time in the so-called involutional age and by motor agitation—seek psychodynamic psychotherapy. The material reported in this chapter derives from cases which, although serious, did not reach the nadir of severity.

The reasons hard-core patients with involutional melancholia are seldom seen by psychiatrists today follow:

1. Fortunately, such cases are much rarer than they used to be. Cultural changes are responsible to a large extent for this decrease in number. Women who consider menopause to be a catastrophe or a tragic event are decreasing rapidly in number, and even those who continue to see the cessation of the menses as an undesirable occurrence respond to it in a less intense manner.*

2. Practically all severe or hard-core cases after a futile attempt with drug therapy are hospitalized and/or receive electric shock therapy. Electric shock therapy is an effective treatment in many cases. We can assume hypothetically that the organically induced changes disrupt the preconscious cognitive network.

We do see a large number of patients with severe (but not extremely severe) degrees of depression at about the time of the menopause and climacterium. They are in many respects similar to other cases of severe or moderate depression, and in many instances it is difficult to determine whether the present depression is the first in life, as a diagnosis of involutional melancholia would require. Many patients state that they were never depressed before, but it could be that earlier depressions passed unnoticed or were so mild in comparison to the present one that the patient did not even consider them as attacks of depression.

A rigidity of character at times interferes with treatment. The patient may tend either in the direction of being scrupulous, excessively moral, and motivated by high principles, or in the opposite direction, as an undisciplined person with no goals and principles. The early stages of therapy do not differ from those outlined in chapter 10. When the therapist has become a significant third, and patient and therapist are ready to form a search team, the analysis must be directed to the study of those rigid patterns of living which have led the patient to the present predicament.

What sooner or later emerges is the symbolic importance of having reached the middle years, the menopause, or the climacterium. The patient starts to talk more and more in reference to the issues that were mentioned in the previous section. A recurring theme is that life has come, or is about to come, to an end. The therapist, who by now has established a working relationship, will be able to convey the message that it is only because the patient gave excessive importance to certain aspects of this period of life that she now sees herself in a state of hopelessness. For people who are willing to search, life offers new possibilities for fulfillment during the middle years. As a matter of fact, the patient is disturbed because in spite of having reached the menopause, she feels full of life and does not want to surrender. Nobody wants *her* to surrender; only some

---

* It has already been mentioned in chapter 3 that Winokur (1973) found a 7.1 percent risk of developing an affective disorder during menopause, and a 6 percent risk during other times. He considered the difference *not* significant.

wrong and archaic conceptions she has about herself and life. Her reluctance to surrender is a healthy sign: what is unhealthy is her complex, which consists of archaic conceptions. In the second half of the twentieth century, there are very few human beings indeed who in their forties or fifties consider themselves ruins of what they used to be. The patient is told that she is just one of the few who think so. The truth is that she did not feel fulfilled in the past, but now she interprets the menopause or the onset of the middle years as the event which has given the coup de grâce to her hopes. The patterns of thinking and living that she has adopted now make her believe she has no alternatives. These patterns have to be explored in accordance with the procedures described in chapter 9.

Although some patients suffering from involutional melancholia have followed a pattern of submission to a dominant other, or mourn for what they previously thought was a good relationship with the dominant other, most belong to the category of patients who have experienced failure in their attempts to reach the dominant goal. But the dominant goal, especially for female patients, is to find a suitable love object—preferably a husband, but also other reliable romantic liaisons. Like the heroine of some novel, the patient always longed for and searched for a monogamous romantic relationship that would satisfy all her needs. Now she feels that her goal is unattainable. With this dominant goal, the patient often retains the traditional role of the passive, possibly masochistic woman who at times is even willing to be brutalized by a man in order to be accepted, loved, or desired sexually. At other times, with the passivity there is resentment and even the tendency to see the men with whom she comes into contact in a much worse light than they deserve to be in.

When a good relation has been established with the patient, a resolution of these complexes occurs, alternatives are found, and depression recedes, as illustrated by the following two cases. The first one is reported in detail; in the second one only the fundamental aspects are outlined.

CASE REPORTS

Mrs. Marie Carls

Mrs. Marie Carls was in her middle fifties when she came for the first interview. She appeared distinguished in her manner, with an almost aristocratic demeanor. A college graduate, she spoke in a beautiful literary style which was characteristic of the well-educated, upper-middle class family in which she was brought up. She had been born and had lived in Europe until a few years prior to the onset of treatment.

During the first interview she made several statements, some of which appeared self-contradictory. She said that ten years earlier she had had a hysterectomy which was necessitated by a very large fibroma. There were no sequelae to the hysterectomy, but unpleasant symptoms had started a few months before she came to see me. She felt depressed and in a constant state of tension or agitation. Her mouth was dry. Since she became depressed, she had slept no more than three hours per night. She stated that her life had been serene and without problems. Why she should feel depressed was a mystery to her. She lived happily with Julius, her husband, and she was happy to be in the United States for a few years, as required by her husband's occupation. When her husband was ready, she would happily return to her country. It was true that in the past she and her husband each had had an infatuation for another person, but neither affair had amounted to anything. Both affairs were now relegated to the buried memories which nobody wanted to resurrect.

All her complaints were somatic in nature. She tired easily, to the point of exhaustion. She knew she was melancholy, but she thought that it was because she did not feel well. She was very religious and had been brought up in an environment in which there was strict adherence to Catholicism. She went to confession very often.

A few sessions after the beginning of the treatment, she started to define her various complaints and general state of malaise as "an obscure force" which would take possession of her. She knew that this obscure force was a psychological experience. It was something which would come suddenly and make her depressed, tired, and often cause cramps in her stomach. Asked whether she had experienced something similar in her past life, she said that when she had given birth to her first child, at age twenty-four, she felt depressed in a way vaguely reminiscent of what she was experiencing now, but at a much less intense level and not to be compared with her present condition.

During much of her treatment, which lasted three years, the patient spoke repeatedly about the obscure force. At times she felt well, and then suddenly she would become depressed. The psychosomatic symptoms—the tiredness, the general malaise, the cramps—would completely possess her. She felt as if she were being invaded by a black cloud or fog.

Marie Carls was the youngest of three children. Her mother was described as a woman of whose presence everyone was immediately and intensely aware. She had a "volcanic" temper and was passionate and emotional, but also obsessive-compulsive. There were some drawers in the house that only she was allowed to open. Once, when the patient's father opened them, the mother became hysterical and threatened to throw herself out of the window. The father slapped her face. The father was very conventional and was described as a loving person and a devoted family man. He had always confided in the patient. As a matter of fact, when he was seventy-eight years old and a widower, he confided to her that he was still disturbed by sexual desires and did not know what to do about it. Did she have any advice to offer? She didn't.

The patient had always felt very attached to her mother. As a matter of fact, they used to call her "Stamp" because she stuck to her mother as a stamp to a letter. She always tried to placate her volcanic mother, to please her in every possible way. The mother, however, did not fulfill her maternal role very well. The patient remembered that when she started to menstruate at the age of thirteen, she did not know anything about it. She went to her mother, who explained, "It is a natural thing, but a dirty one." The subject of menstruation was never brought up again; it was taboo. The patient described herself as being naive for a long time. She remembered hearing from a girl friend that a thirteen-year-old girl had found out that she was pregnant and had not known how this could happen. In a state of desperation the girl killed herself.

The patient remembered that her menses were often late, and until the age of nineteen she was always afraid that she was pregnant, although she had had no contacts with men. When she got married at the age of twenty-three, she was a virgin. However, when she had intercourse with her husband on the wedding night, she did not bleed. The husband said to her, "Perhaps when you are seventy years old, you will have to confess a little sin." But she was a virgin, and the husband did believe her because he never spoke about this matter again. She, on the other hand, thought from time to time about the "little sin", and what came to mind was the beautiful garden of the home where she had spent her childhood and adolescence. Two boys also came to mind, the sons of the gardener; but the patient was sure that she had never had any physical contact with them, nor had she wished to. She admitted, however, that she might have repressed fantasies of that type. No: she was proud of having been a virgin when she got married. She came from a family where religious precepts, traditions, rules, and laws had to be respected. She had an aunt, however, who had challenged the world with her free behavior. Everybody ostensibly criticized her; almost everybody secretly admired her. Unlike her aunt, the patient did not challenge the world or any human being. She submitted to and obeyed the wishes of society.

When the man who became her husband revealed his intention to marry her, she shared the unanimous opinion of her family that he was an excellent match. Although she was not enthusiastic about this man, she could find no fault in one who appeared so honest, reliable, a good provider, and a good Catholic. After the marriage she continued her pattern of submission and compliance. Before her marriage she had difficulty in complying with a volcanic mother, and after her marriage she almost automatically assumed a submissive role. Actually, she described her husband as very considerate, egalitarian, and not domineering at all. His only fault was that he did not have a volcanic or dynamic personality. He was too placid, too good, and rather boring.

The first few months of treatment were devoted to describing the placidity of her life, the goodness and the considerate attitude of her husband, her great respect for him, the boredom of life and of her marriage, and her lack of any desires—including sex. Only two things were prominent in her life, and they were repeatedly mentioned in her sessions: her profound religious devotion; and the obscure force which came from an unknown place to possess her, make her feel depressed, or fill her with psychosomatic symptoms.

Her dreams contrasted with the placidity and uneventfulness of her life. After reading Dostoevsky's *Crime and Punishment*, she dreamed of having committed a crime with one of her brothers. In another dream a girl had been found killed. Many dreams repeated the motif of guilt and retribution.

Several months after beginning treatment, the patient reported a dream. Ignatius and she had decided not to see each other again. She would have to leave him forever. I asked who Ignatius was, because I had not heard the name until then. The patient replied almost with surprise, "But the first time I came to see you, I told you that in the past I had had an infatuation." She then told me that when she was thirty years old, in the middle of the Second World War, she lived at the periphery of a city which was frequently bombed. Ignatius, a friend of the family, had had his home completely demolished by bombs. The patient and her husband invited Ignatius, who was single, to come and live with them. Ignatius and the patient soon discovered that they had an attraction for each other. They both tried to fight that feeling; but when Julius had to go to another city for a few days, the so-called infatuation became much more than that. There were a few physical contacts, but the patient had no complete orgasm. However, there was an intense spiritual affinity. Ignatius understood her: he spoke her language, liked what she liked, and gave her the feeling of being alive. She remembered that before she married Julius, she had invented a slogan which she often emphatically repeated, "Long live life"; but only with Ignatius could she believe in that slogan again. Ignatius suggested that they elope, but she did not take him seriously. A few months later everybody had to leave the city. Ignatius and Marie promised to keep in touch, but both of them were full of hesitation because of Julius, a devoted husband to Marie and a devoted friend to Ignatius. Nothing was done to maintain contacts. Two years later, approximately a year after the end of the war, Marie heard that Ignatius had married. She felt terribly alone and despondent.

For several sessions Marie spoke almost exclusively about Ignatius, and in this period the so-called obscure force acquired prominence. She described this force as "a feeling which grows to gigantic proportions; an internal sensation, physical and psychological, occasionally accompanied by thoughts. It is a malaise which first spreads through the whole organism, and then becomes localized in the stomach or in the whole abdomen." On one occasion she said, "The obscure force is a faceless entity which often strikes me with a terrible violence. It leaves either physical illness or deep depression. It comes suddenly, at the most unexpected moments. For instance, once I was watering the geraniums and all of a sudden the force struck me."

During this stage of therapy Marie revealed that there had been a period during which she felt very guilty because of her relationship with Ignatius, and she decided to confess the whole thing to Julius, ready to accept whatever decision Julius made. Julius' reaction was unexpected on more than one count. First, he did not become at all incensed or punitive. Second, he said "Marie, I must tell you something I never told you before. I, too, had a brief affair with a woman during the war. Let's forgive each other entirely, forget the whole thing, and continue to love each other." At first Marie felt injured that her husband had had an affair, but then she was relieved, and accepted her husband's "supreme wisdom and maturity." Moreover, after her husband found out about Ignatius he seemed to become more intensely interested in her sexually.

Many years passed, during which she lived a comfortable and uneventful life. She had two children, who married at a young age. To further Mr. Carls' career, the couple emigrated to the United States after the war. She became enthusiastic about the United States; she had what other people would call a happy life; and yet, in spite of it, she became depressed.

In a subsequent stage of therapy Marie concentrated on her marriage. Had she really accepted her husband's proposal to forgive and forget? Only ostensibly. The pact with her husband partially relieved her guilt, but not her loneliness and her thirst for life. The obscure force stood for the suffering that she wanted to repress. Her suffering had become more acute as she realized that old age was approaching and she had lost all her chances. Ignatius remained as the memory of lost opportunities. Yes, Ignatius had wanted her to go with him, but she wouldn't, because she felt that her husband and God would never forgive her. Even that beautiful short relationship was spoiled by her feeling of guilt. Her life of compliance and obedience had not permitted her to reach her goal. An Ignatius existed in the world, but she had lost him forever. She had never loved her husband, and that was what was wrong with her marriage.

For many years she had tried to forget Ignatius, to minimize her encounter with him as her husband had suggested. But how could she? The encounter with Ignatius was the most beautiful episode of her life, and she was happy it had happened, although she should prefer that it had never happened. The rest of her life did not seem to count. Eventually the obscure force struck her.

For many years she had hoped she could make up for the loss of

Ignatius, but now she could no longer do so. She could no longer scream, "Long live life!" She would rather think, "Down with life without Ignatius, a life which has lost its meaning."

When she became aware of these ideas, she felt even more depressed. She was complaining less and less about the obscure force, and more and more about her marriage. She felt that everything she had built in her life was false or based on a false premise. In a certain way her husband was not so compliant, permissive, and tolerant as she had seen him; but possessive because she had to live by his way of living, with all its placidity and the boredom. But this was impossible to do when she really did not love the man.

A few sessions later she said that there was only an empty space in her life. She had utterly and irrevocably failed. She had made terrible and irreparable mistakes. It was better to contend with the obscure force than with the truth; better not to know than to know. At times the ideas of the past were forgotten and the obscure force returned, but not for long, because it was not possible to suppress the truth any more. Had the therapist really helped her? Why didn't he leave her alone in her blessed obscurity, less painful than the enlightenment?

At this point we have to take stock of what is known about this woman before proceeding to illustrate the subsequent course of treatment. It was obvious that her life had not been a happy one from childhood to the present time. When she was a young girl, she was brought up to believe that her happiness would eventually come as a result of a romantic encounter. An ideal husband would fulfill all her needs and would give a complete meaning to her life. Both the family's influence and the general contemporary culture, especially fiction and the cinema, nourished such expectations. Even in her daydreams she, like many contemporary women, assumed a role of dependence on a man. The man would be the fulfiller of her dreams.

The finding of such a love became the dominant goal. But this goal was not reached in marrying her husband, who fell so short of her ideals. Ignatius appeared on the scene and was immediately invested with all the attributes of the dominant goal. He came and then went away, becoming a dominant goal which could no longer be achieved. It was difficult to suffocate and suppress gigantic feelings and to adjust to a pale, conventional marriage. To some extent Marie succeeded with the help of her religious beliefs. As a matter of fact, during confession she made two promises to the priest: she would no longer look for Ignatius, and would no longer pray for him. But it was obvious that she always looked for him and she always had a rock-bottom hope that she would find Ignatius, or another Ignatius, or what Ignatius stood for. When she realized that Ignatius was no longer likely to appear, the ideas and feelings which she had suppressed—or actually repressed—threatened to reemerge. She tried to suppress them again and again, but the depression and the so-called obscure force were conscious. Part of the depression was psychosomatically transformed into the effects of this obscure force.

When the patient became able to verbalize what she had kept within herself for a long time, her conscious ideation increasingly assumed the form of mourning for the "lost opportunity." She could have decided to elope with Ignatius, and her life would have been a beautiful realization of a love dream. But she had spoiled everything because of her guilt and conventional habits. As much as she could stick to the idea that her goal had had the possibility of being realized, she preserved some self-esteem and sustenance, and her depression never reached a stage close to stupor or to the point of having serious suicidal intentions. She had an ambivalent feeling toward her feelings of guilt: at times the guilt feeling had spoiled her life; at other times it was the redeeming feature which had protected her from total catastrophe.

A therapist could easily pick out what was wrong with Marie Carls's cognitive structure and formulate a therapeutic strategy. She could be helped to demolish the dominant goal, with all its accessory constructs, and be guided to find alternative patterns of living. But it was not easy to do so in practice.

When the patient had established a good rapport with the therapist, had started to relate to him as to a significant third, and had revealed a large part of her history and its implications which she had repressed or suppressed, the cognitive structure was at first challenged in its more superficial and common-sense aspects. Was Ignatius really the ideal man she had envisioned? What was so wonderful about him? Even sexual life with him had not been completely satisfactory. Why did he go away so easily and not return after the war? Evaluation of past events was complicated by her strong feelings that she had done what God demanded. The patient attributed these feelings to herself and to Ignatius. She continued to defend Ignatius and to keep him on a pedestal, but with less and less strength. Eventually the patient asked herself whether in real life Ignatius corresponded to her image of Ignatius, or whether he was a mythical figure. She became more and more inclined to think that Ignatius was a myth. But when she thought of him as a myth, the depression—unless replaced by the obscure force—became more pronounced; obviously because she needed the myth of Ignatius, the myth of the "lost opportunity." As mentioned, these interpretations remained at a rather common-sense level.

But a much more profound blow to the cognitive structure of the dominant goal was struck when she was asked whether, before Ignatius entered her life, she had ever daydreamed about a man who would one day appear and be like Ignatius. And indeed she said yes, she had often daydreamed about such a man; and when Ignatius appeared, he was the exact embodiment of what she had been expecting. When the patient reached this conclusion, she rose from her chair and said with a profound melancholia which was full of strength, not weakness: "The myth of Ignatius existed before Ignatius." She paused awhile, and then added, "Three myths. The myth of the expectation of Ignatius, the myth of having lost a wonderful Ignatius, the myth of the return of Ignatius." This was indeed a great revelation. The cognitive trap started to be dismantled. What I and my pupils call the dominant goal was more poetically called a myth, and a myth generating a series of myths. I told her that I thought she was quite right, but could she explain why the myth of the Ignatius-to-be, or the expectation of an Ignatius, was a myth? By making such a request, I obviously intended to make her work on restructuring the cognitive substratum of her problems.

She told me again the many reasons which throughout her youth had made her focus on the expectancy of this ideal man. First, her grandmother had been a writer of romantic novels, which the patient had avidly absorbed. In those novels the woman was a passive entity whose main job was to wait for some male to acknowledge her existence and finally discover her secret virtues. But the few who do notice her are not worthwhile. The man who is worthwhile is either a sadist or a marvelous man who for various reasons is unattainable. These themes recur even in contemporary American novels, the patient added, novels written not only by women but by men as well. The patient wanted to stress that the origin of her trouble did not reside in her grandmother. Her grandmother was only representative of a culture which fostered a false goal in women. The goal was false in that it was the only one, or one of the very few, that a woman in her social environment could have. In subsequent sessions the patient made connections between this goal and the predominantly patriarchal, male chauvinistic society which seduces women into accepting such a goal. Her original desires to placate her volcanic mother and to please her father, for whom she had an Oedipal attachment, were channeled toward the aim of being the lady that she had believed she was expected to become.

Mrs. Carls explained that after the termination of the Ignatius episode she herself had done some reconstructive cognitive work, but it had been wrong and led nowhere. Once she realized that Ignatius was lost, she tried to improve her marriage, but she also made this attempt in an erroneous way; she was still searching for the perfect life or the ideal goal in a relationship in which she again could assume a dependent role. But every time Julius showed his human weaknesses—or rather, his human dimensions—they appeared very small. If she could not have the ecstatic, voracious flame of love she had for Ignatius, she thought she could have a solid, profound, spiritual relationship with Julius based on commitment, loyalty, companionship, and shared experiences. But she still depended on Julius, and Julius could not share life's experiences with a strength equal to hers. She had what she called a thirst for the absolute, which she was trying to find in her marriage. Occasionally she would refer to a thirst for perfection which cannot be found on earth, for it belongs only to heaven. As a matter of fact, at times during the night she would wake up with a sense of anxiety or what she called religious terror. But it was interesting that one of the nights when she woke up with a "religious terror" she had been having a dream in which she was kissing Ignatius. During the dream she experienced an intense pleasure whose sweetness was impossible to express in words.

Thus there was no doubt that searching for the absolute was really a substitute for searching for Ignatius. She was still searching for Ignatius; but with her religion, sense of loyalty, and the pact made with her husband (to forget the past and to love each other) she also was trying to suppress Ignatius, or whatever myth was a derivative of the Ignatius myth.

I have already mentioned that while Marie was trying to demolish the myth of Ignatius, she was at times experiencing very intensely both the obscure force and wave after wave of depression. The depression at times became very severe, and I was under pressure from the family doctor to give her antidepressants. I resisted the pressure. With some patients I consider it advisable to prescribe antidepressants, but not for patients with whom I feel that I am about to make psychological progress. In the case of Marie we had reached a psychological understanding of why the dominant goal had had a chance to develop, but we did not know why it was still so necessary for it to exist. Eventually we came to understand that this dominant goal has a special flavor or nuance: loss of Ignatius represented the lovelessness of life, and lovelessness of life was equated with death. The dominant cognitive constructs in her mind thus could be summarized as, "I have discovered the lovelessness of my life. Lovelessness equals death. My life is a living death. Real death would be preferable."

A psychiatrist must agree that love is important, and a life without love is an impoverished life. But love means many things, just as there are many types of love. For Marie it meant only romantic love, all passion and flame, like the one she had imagined with Ignatius. Life without that type of love is not at all a life characterized by lovelessness, and by no means to be equated with death: but it was so for her. There are many strong and pleasant feelings that one can feel for family members, career, friends, humanity, cultural interests, and so on. They are different loves, but they count too. A life without the type of love she imagined with Ignatius can be a rich and rewarding life. In summary, the meaning of Marie's life did not have to be found in the actualization of the Ignatius myth. A long time was devoted to the discussion of these basic issues.

In many cases of involutional depression occurring in married women, we find a picture simpler than the one presented by Marie. The woman was led to believe in her youth that she should want to have a nice companionable husband who would be a good provider, with a house in the suburbs. She has to depend on her husband, become his appendix or satellite, live for him. At a certain time in life she wakes up, realizing that those goals which indeed she has attained are not what she intended to live for. Depression then ensues. In the case of Marie Carls, she did not reach her goal, and her unattainable goal was transformed into the myth of the lost opportunity.

In spite of the differences that I have mentioned, Marie's pathogenetic complexes had several characteristics in common with those of many other depressed women: total reliance on a man for fulfillment of life aspirations, and belittlement and finally impoverishment of all other aspects of life for the sake of reliance on a man.

Marie Carls gradually understood all the complicated ramifications of her complexes or cognitive constructs. Many of these components had to be disentangled, rectified, and put into the proper perspective. She came to see her life as not wasted, and she came to recognize that her good qualities and potentialities were worthwhile when not put at the service of lost opportunity. She became active in many cultural directions and found fulfillment in life. Her relations with her husband improved; the marital situation was given an important but not all-inclusive role among the array of life's possibilities. The patient, of course, always had been able to distinguish the periods of depression and anguish from those which were apparently asymptomatic. But now she became able to distinguish apparent calm which is only a tacit resignation and a forceful repression of rancor from the serenity which reflects real acceptance of oneself and one's life.

There were many ups and downs during the first half of the treatment, because the patient had fits of depression when old constructs or subcomplexes had to be given up; but the main upward trend was discernible from the beginning of the second year of treatment. Treatment lasted three years and ended with complete recovery. At this time six years have passed, and there has been no relapse.

Before concluding this report, two points deserve further discussion. If we use Freudian terminology, we can say that one of them deals with the patient's id psychology and the other with her superego psychology.

A psychoanalyst of orthodox orientation would have put more stress on the Oedipal fixation of this patient and on other sexual connotations of the case. There is no doubt that the patient had a strong attachment to her father, and her father possibly had some counter-Oedipal attachments, which may be subsumed from some remarks made by the patient. This Oedipal attachment could have strengthened the patient's desire for the unattainable man, since one's father is unattainable. It is also very possible that sexual desires for the gardner's sons, which had been repressed from consciousness, were once very strong and made her feel very guilty. They came back to her mind, during the wedding night, when the husband spoke of her "little sin" that she eventually would have to confess. What was once an imagined or fantasied little sin in childhood was transposed in time, and became the sin with Ignatius which she did confess.

The second point has to do with the role that the patient's religious devotion played: Did it do more harm than good? Love of God protected her from experiencing the "lovelessness" of her life even more deeply. On the other hand, it increased her guilt; when she felt that she could not accept life without a sinful love, she believed she would lose even God's love. We have seen in chapter 6 that some depressed patients, especially those who live in a very religious culture or subculture, can make a dominant other of God. The loving attributes of God are minimized, and the demanding and exacting attributes are stressed. In these cases the patient can experience more or less toward God the conflicts or ambivalence that are experienced toward a human dominant other. Mrs. Carls's attitude toward God did not reach such a pronounced involvement. When she became able to dismantle her myth of romantic love, the practice of religion and love of God resumed an important place among the several loves of her life. Love for children, husband, work, and culture—together with love for God—helped her find rewarding and rich aspects in life. These loves bestowed serenity and optimism on what had been an anguished existence.

The word "anguished" elicits a final comment. Were there sufficient and irreversible causes in this case that would ineluctably confer anguish to Marie's life? The answer seems to be no. Her mother was as temperamental as a volcano, but not cruel or hostile. Her father was not tryrannical or seductive, and only when senility approached did his behavior seem somewhat inappropriate. The family was on the whole a loving one, although dominated by restrictions, conventions, and a strong sense of duty. One gets the impression that if an atmosphere of spontaneity had prevailed in which it would have been possible for the patient to build less rigid patterns of thinking, feeling, and behavior, then she never would have known a deep depression. This is another case that shows how ideas chosen by the culture, the family, and the patient himself can entrap the human being into rigid patterns and absurd myths, and confine him in a desperate position to which he feels ineluctably tied. The alternative left to the patient is generally to submerge all his perceptions of life in a mood of depression; or at other times, as in the case of Marie, to experience something strange that comes from the obscurity of the inner self and possesses one entirely—an obscure force.

This case also shows that no matter how intricate the labyrinth of the cognitive structure may be, psychodynamic therapy can disentangle it, lift the depression even when it presents itself as an obscure force, and make the human being feel receptive again to the array of life's aims and loves.

Mr. Rafgaf

Mr. Paul Rafgaf asked for a consultation at the suggestion of his sister, who realized that he was terribly depressed. He was forty-nine years old and had worked for twenty-four years in a travel agency. Several months earlier he noticed that he could not keep up with his work because he was becoming slower and slower. His company agreed to give him a prolonged leave of absence. They did not want to dismiss him because of his prolonged, effective, and loyal work. When he left, they told him that he could come back whenever he felt well. Several months had passed, however; and instead of feeling better, Mr. Rafgaf felt he was getting worse. The idea of going back to work terrified him. He thought he would never have the courage to call his boss and ask to be reinstated. Why should they reinstate him? He was not good.

When asked why work terrified him, he replied that the company had computerized most of what had to be done in the various offices. He believed that he could not learn how to use those terrible machines, those computers which were supposed to be very simple, but appeared to him so complicated. The idea of using computers was enough to put him into a state of panic. He felt he could not survive in the business world. He would like to fall asleep and never wake up. He had contemplated committing himself to an insane asylum, but had decided against it. Perhaps the best thing would be to commit suicide.

The patient was living alone. I told him to call his sister and me every day. These telephone calls would make him feel less alone and would alert us for the real possibility of suicidal attempts. When he was asked why he lived alone, he said that he was not married; he was a homosexual. For twelve years he had had a relationship with George, three years his senior, but now even that relationship was fading. It had not kept up its initial momentum and had become purely platonic. The patient had the most negative appraisal of what this relation had been for twelve years. He was suffering from premature ejaculation in his homosexual relations, and sexual encounters had always lasted only a few seconds. He was a lost man, unable to love, unable to work. There had been only one important homosexual relationship in his life, and that was now extinguished without the possibility of being replaced by another one. He did not feel up to finding a new one.

The patient was reassured about the possibility of treating the depression with psychotherapy. A therapeutic team was established, and he became able to talk about his past life. He was brought up in a very religious Catholic environment. When the patient was seven, his father lost his job and the family had to split up for economic reasons. Mother, father, and sister went to live with the paternal grandparents. The patient went to live with his maternal grandmother and aunt. After a few years the family was reunited, but the parents did not get along. They could live neither together nor apart. The patient admired his father, who was a hard-working man, but never loved him. Father could not communicate with him, and the patient felt distant or not considered enough by him. Nevertheless the patient had frequent crushes on father figures from an early age. He remembers that when he was eight he had a crush on the priest. He became an altar boy to please the priest. Later he experienced pain when he had to leave the young priest. He felt abandoned by the priest, as he had when mother and father left.

The patient became aware of his homosexual orientation very early in life and he felt very guilty about it. His father called him "sissy" from the age of six or seven. Later the patient tried to enter the heterosexual world, but without success. When he left high school, he thought of joining a religious order. Perhaps religion would cure him of his homosexuality: priesthood would make him forget sex and avoid sin. However, he indulged in masturbation with homosexual fantasies.

Mr. Rafgaf described his youth as marked by constant self-depreciation and disappointments. He had to leave college after two years for lack of funds. He had acne and felt ugly and unwanted by both women and men. Nevertheless, through hard work and discipline he managed to make some kind of adjustment. His work with the travel agency gave him some satisfaction, and his long relation with George gave him the feeling that there was somebody who cared for him. He tended, however, to comply and have a submissive role toward George.

Now at the age of forty-nine he realized that the relationship with George was fading and no longer sexual, and he would not be able to find another partner. He had been "abandoned" by George as he once was by father and mother and later by the priest. The use of computers by his firm was the culminating point of his desperation. It was a symbol of the fact that life always confronts one with new challenges, but he was not up to it. The little security he had found in his job and in the relation with George was now crumbling, and he felt open to the hostility of the world. He also felt more and more inadequate now that old age was approaching.

Establishment of a therapeutic team was easy. Attitudes that the patient had repressed or suppressed reemerged to full consciousness. Explanations of basic facts were accepted and decreased the intensity of the depression. The patient understood the significance of childhood events and the original feeling of inadequacy that reemerged when his citadel of security seemed to be crumbling. He understood how the fear of being abandoned again, which he experienced early in life, had reacquired supremacy in his mind.

The difficulties of homosexuals in establishing new relations in the middle years were explained to him so that he would not consider his situation to be a personal defeat. He was encouraged to find new liaisons. He understood that his age status required some readjustments, but it did not indicate the end of life or a state of hopelessness. The patient gradually reacquired the feeling that he was wanted in the travel agency, they would accept him again, and he would be able to work with the computers. I encouraged him to call his boss and to ask to be reinstated. The boss was happy to have him back. Mr. Rafgaf started work again with no difficulty or trace of depression. Treatment lasted eighteen months, although depression had subsided a few months earlier. Three years have passed with no recurrence.

[13]

PSYCHOTHERAPY

OF MILD DEPRESSION

Brief Survey of the Literature

Historically, the first papers to appear on the psychotherapeutic approach to depression dealt with the treatment of severely impaired individuals. The early contributions of Abraham (1911) and Freud (1917) concerned themselves with psychotic depressions or with manic-depressive disorders. Descriptions of the psychoanalytic therapy of mild depression, which today is perhaps the condition most frequently encountered by psychiatrists, did not appear until the late 1930s. In 1936 Gero published a comprehensive report on the psychoanalytic psychotherapy of two nonpsychotic depressed individuals. The following year, Lorand (1937) published a more general paper on the dynamics and therapy of mild depressive states. Since the appearance of these two important contributions, a great number of pertinent articles have been written on the psychotherapy of mild forms of depression. However, some have been flawed by slavish adherence to the formulations set forth in *Mourning and Melancholia* which were not meant to be particularly applicable to mild depression. This chapter outlines a fairly detailed program for the psychotherapy of mild depression which I have found to be fairly effective. This program is by no means original, and my debt to prior excellent contributions is evident by the frequent citing of previous workers in this field. One conviction that I share with most of the writers on the psychotherapy of mild depressions is that a psychodynamic approach is the treatment of choice for these conditions.

Some objections may be raised to this last statement, one being that

This chapter was written by Jules Bemporad.

the efficacy of psychotherapy is impossible to prove, since mild depressions improve even without treatment and the "cure" may be only a spurious coincidence. It is true that most depressive episodes clear up eventually, but the problem is that they also recur. Therefore the psychotherapy of mild depression should not aim simply at recovery of the presenting condition, but at protecting the patient from future depressions, barring extreme life circumstances. Furthermore, while acute depressive attacks may pass with time, some patients present a specific character structure that results in their being continuously depressed to a mild degree. In these individuals, strong inhibitions prevent them from finding meaning or enjoyment in life so that they are constantly on the brink of despair, leading unsatisfying and fruitless lives. Other individuals, because of their extreme dependence on external agents for self-esteem and worth, are constantly vulnerable to depressive attacks and only show improvement with prolonged psychotherapy which alters their sources of meaning and lifts their self-imposed inhibitions. Another reason for stressing the use of psychotherapy for mild depressions is that physical agents have not been shown to be very helpful for this form of depressive disorder.

A review of studies on the effectiveness of antidepressant drugs (Smith, Troganza, and Harrison, 1969) concluded that, "In well-designed studies, the differences between the effectiveness of antidepressant drugs and placebo are not impressive" (p. 19). Another difficulty is that some researchers (Kurland, 1976) claim equally successful result in the treatment of mild depression using either a major tranquilizer such as thioridazine (Mellaril®) or a minor tranquilizer such as diazepam (Valium®). Therefore there is some question regarding the specificity of antidepressant drugs, and their efficacy in mild depression.

Klein (1974) has devised his own classification of depressive disorders into three groups: "endogenomorphic," reactive, and chronic neurotic. The first type is manifested by anhedonia, inhibited psychomotor mechanisms, and somatic symptoms; and the latter two types are characterized by low self-esteem. On the basis of this classification, Klein believes that tricyclic antidepressants would be effective against the endogenomorphic and reactive types but not against the chronic neurotic type of depression. While this typology of depression is hypothetical and not uniformly accepted, Klein does review a good deal of the literature on drug treatment in reaching his conclusions, and his work is worthy of consideration.

Other researchers, such as Klerman et al. (1974) and Weissman et al. (1974), believe that antidepressive agents are effective in depressive disorders but these drugs affect mainly the somatic symptoms of depression such as anorexia, insomnia, and psychomotor retardation. However, these physical complaints are not a predominant part of the symptom picture of mild depression. In contrast, Klerman finds psychotherapy to be more effective than medication in altering the individual's social competence and self-perceptions: disturbances in these areas of functioning do form a large part of the problems of patients with mild depression.

In my own experience, I have tried tricyclic antidepressants with mildly depressed patients and with characterological depressives, usually with poor results. Not only was there little symptomatic improvement, but most patients complained of side effects—mainly sedation and dryness of the mouth. Raskin (1974) has noted that mild depressives show less tolerance for the adverse effects of antidepressants, and medication in this group often has to be terminated because of severe side effects.

There is as yet no report of a well-designed study comparing the efficacy of psychoanalytic psychotherapy and chemotherapy in mild depressive disorders. The work of the Boston–New Haven Collaborative Depression Project (Weissman et al., 1975) most closely approximates such an ideal study but it falls short in many significant areas. This group compared the therapeutic results of a large number of depressed individuals treated with amitriptyline (Elavil®), a placebo, or no medication, both with and without psychotherapy. They found that psychotherapy had a significant effect in enhancing social adjustment (which only became apparent after six to eight months of therapy), but it had no effect on actual symptoms of depression. In contrast, amitriptyline had a marked, quick effect on symptons and prevented relapses, but it did not affect social functioning. However, the psychotherapy utilized in this study consisted of one session per week with a social worker in which the patient discussed here-and-now problems, with no effort made to help the patient gain insight or grasp the deeper reasons for the depression. Therefore, a true trial of psychodynamic psychotherapy was not instituted and the study actually compared drug treatment with minimal supportive therapy. It is unforunate that this group called the brief therapeutic contact "psychotherapy": although literally correct, the term is misleading for the therapy did not consist of an analysis of character defenses, unconscious cognitive contents, or tranference manifestations. Covi et al. (1974) found that drug treatment was superior to either weekly group therapy or biweekly supportive psychotherapy for the treatment of "neurotic" depression. However, his conclusions are open to the same criticism as those of the Boston–New Haven group.

The value of drug therapy versus psychotherapy in mild depression is still an open question. The one fact that these studies reaffirm is that the two treatment modalities do not interfere with each other's effectiveness. There is even some indication that drugs and psychotherapy affect different aspects of the depressive symptom complex. Drugs appear to ameliorate vegetative and somatic symptoms while psychotherapy is most effective in helping the patient to relate better socially, to adjust to his environment, and to raise his self-esteem.

The present state of knowledge has been aptly presented by the Group for the Advancement of Psychiatry in their report on pharmacotherapy and psychotherapy (1975), ". . . despite our quite substantial information about the psychology and biology of depression, we still lack those integrative concepts needed before pharmacotherapy and psychotherapy can be combined in rational treatment programs which are demonstrably more effective than treatment regimens based on one or the other" (p. 346).

Electroconvulsive therapy is generally not recommended for mild depression (Prange, 1973). I have seen a small number of mildly depressed individuals who had received ECT with questionable improvement. Usually they again succumbed to depression after the organic brain syndrome caused by ECT had cleared. In addition, the amnesia induced by ECT added to their feeling of deficiency and may have increased their depression. Hospitalization is rarely required for mild depression since individuals are not suicidal nor are they severely incapacitated. Hospitalization might help mild depression in the short run, in that the individual is able to get the dependent nurturance and attention from others that he so desperately desires. However, in the long run hospitalization would increase the depressive's resistance to doing things for himself and further hinder the needed realization that he must solve his problems by his own efforts.

Therefore, in my opinion psychotherapy remains the most effective treatment for mild depression with or without adjunct drug therapy. Yet these depressives are very difficult patients to treat; by the very nature of their disorder, they strongly resist change and utilize their symptoms to manipulate the course of therapy. The depressed individual, as a result of his dependency, also is often caught in a network of pathological relationships with others who will attempt to prevent his altering of personality. Thus there are also formidable obstacles to change beyond the patient's own personality. These internal and external forces combine to produce an often long and laborious course of therapy. Therefore, while amelioration of the presenting depression is quite rapid and simple, change in the basic personality structure is lengthy and difficult. As Lorand (1937) wrote: "The constant unhappiness of depressive patients, their fundamental distrust caused by the sufferings of early environmental influences, combine to make the therapy extremely difficult" (p. 333). Yet if therapy is to have a lasting effect, this more arduous and radical path should be attempted, especially since the final result is ultimately quite rewarding.

The therapeutic approach to mild depression centers on three basic parameters: the characterological defenses, the underlying unconscious cognitive structures (in terms of evaluation of self and others), and the transference situation, which is the major therapeutic factor.

Initial Stage: Setting the Proper Course of Therapy

Most depressives come for treatment only when they are in an acute state and after they have reconstituted their self-appraisals and expectations from the environment subsequent to a loss of a meaningful role or relationship. While the patient may appear agitated, confused, or retarded, underlying his behavior is a persistent demand for magical relief. It is at this initial stage that the therapist must be wary of being trapped into promising too much to the suffering human being before him who seems to be so appreciative of reassurance. At this stage the patient will praise the therapist and inflate his importance. The therapist must be careful not to become a new dominant other on whom the patient then will depend for nurturance and reflected gratification. The acceptance of this role by the therapist, narcissistically gratifying as it may be to one's professional image, is doomed to failure. Eventually the patient will demand more and more from the therapist. When the therapist finds himself in an unrealistic situation in which the whole burden of the patient's life rests on his shoulders, his attempts to reinstate a more constructive therapeutic relationship will be met with a response of sullen anger and a sense of betrayal by the patient, who has already formed a bargain relationship with the therapist in his mind.

Coyne (1975) cited an unfortunate instance in which a depressed patient seduced the therapist into promising more than could possibly be fulfilled:

> The present author became aware of a dramatic example of this when a student therapist showed up at a Florida suicide prevention center with a recent client. The therapist had attempted to meet her client's complaints of worthlessness and rejection with explicit reassurances that she more than understood her and cared for her, she loved her! After weeks of such reassurance and increasingly frequent sessions, the client finally confronted the therapist with the suggestion that if the therapist really cared for her as she said, that they should spend the night together. The therapist panicked and terminated the case, suggesting that the client begin applying her newly acquired insights to her daily life. The client continued to appear for previously scheduled appointments and made vague suicidal gestures, at which time her therapist brought her to the suicide prevention center. When it was suggested that the therapist should honestly confront her client with what had happened in the relationship, the therapist angrily refused to speak to her, stating that she truly loved her client and would do nothing to hurt her (p. 32).

In this case, the therapist reacted with continued overprotectiveness and nurturance. In other instances, the therapist may become angry at the patient for covertly reducing his therapeutic effectiveness and forcing him into an unrealistic all-giving relationship.

The subtle manipulativeness of mildly depressed or characterologically depressed individuals has been described astutely by Bonime (1960, 1976). He has repeatedly commented on this type of depressed patient who coerces others to do things for him while refusing to join in a truly collaborative therapeutic effort. For Bonime, much of depression is angry behavior that results from a failure to modify directly the actions of others. As alluded to here, this anger may well be the result of a betrayal of a bond that existed only in the patient's psyche. I have seen a depressive who formerly had been in therapy, on and off, for nineteen years without any real change of his underlying personality. He utilized his former therapist to give him direction in life, to protect him magically from the vicissitudes of life, and to allow him to proceed with quasi-legal business deals (which he disguised in order to get the therapist's approval). This patient would try to wear a different outfit for each session and to look "nice" for his therapist. The therapist was constantly with him in the manner of a mental protective amulet which would keep him from harm. Eventually (after nineteen years), the therapist refused to take him on again for regular therapy and the patient became quite severely depressed. This patient provides blatant evidence that giving in to the depressive's demands may relieve the symptomatic superstructure but leave the underlying patterns untouched.

Jacobson (1971) also commented on the difficulties of setting a proper course of the therapy with depressives who have learned to see their every move as calculated to provide a desired response from a dominant other. She wrote about the therapy of one of her patients: "There followed a long, typical period during which the patient lived only in the aura of the analyst and withdrew from other personal relationships to a dangerous extent. The transference was characterized by very dependent, masochistic attitudes toward the analyst, but also by growing demands that I display self-sacrificing devotion in return" (p. 289). Kolb (1956) also noted that the initial relationship with the depressed individual "bears up on the therapist heavily because of the clinging dependency of the patient. The depressed patient demands that he be gratified. He attempts to extract or force the gratification from the therapist by his pleas for help, by exposure of his misery, and by suggesting that the therapist is responsible for leaving him in his unfortunate condition."

These individuals will insist on calling the therapist repeatedly between appointments or will request extra sessions. One man called me after an initial consultation during which he appeared only mildly depressed. After profusely apologizing for calling, he stated that he had had some suicidal ideas, and then fell silent awaiting a response. When I told him I was with another patient and would return his call later, he replied in a bewildered manner that his previous therapist had always taken time, even during sessions with other patients, to talk to him when he felt "blue." The silence that followed this initial statement is an example of the depressive's expectation that another person will solve his problems. While this man had been seen only once, he immediately expected to get special preference and nurturance on demand. The initial sessions should impart a definite set of limits for therapy, although such treatment may seem harsh, and is certainly not applicable to severely depressed individuals. The therapist's personal regime regarding phone calls, missed appointments, and so on must be spelled out in great detail and not left to an assumption of mutual common-sense judgment. Even under these circumstances, some depressives will try to bend the rules with proclamations of suffering. There is no question in my mind that the suffering is real, and there is a great natural inclination to do all one can to help a fellow human being in distress. However, breaking the agreed-upon rules then will determine the remainder of the course of therapy. The depressive must be aware from the beginning that he has the power to help himself, the therapist will help him achieve this goal through confrontation and interpretation, but ultimately the task of therapy rests on the patient.

Ultimately, the patient must widen the horizons of his consciousness which had been narrowed in childhood to distort patterns of relating and a sad neglect of much that is joyful and meaningful in life. He must be made aware of his own resources for pleasure, previously unknown areas of satisfaction, and relief from the relentless feeling of guilt that accompanies each attempt at gratification. As will be discussed, this entails a cognitive restructuring in which old experiences are brought to consciousness and given new meanings. In the therapeutic relationship behavior is elicited, examined, and utilized for an alteration in the estimation of self and others.

THE THERAPIST'S REACTION TO THE PATIENT

Much has been written about the beneficial roles of a positive attitude and reassurance in the therapy of depression. Exaggerated reassurances may be detrimental rather than beneficial in allowing the patient to believe that the therapist shares his own estimation of his helplessness and terribly impaired state. As Bonime (1962) aptly wrote, "False reassurance at almost any time is harmful, and probably never more harmful than when a patient is depressed; he believes he is powerless, and false reassurance obscures his genuine resources instead of mobilizing them." Actually this therapeutic stance may be relaxed in the later stages of treatment as the patient learns to share his activities and mutually participates in the therapeutic effort. However, from the very beginning the patient must understand that amelioration is his therapeutic task and not an obligation of the therapist.

On the other hand, the therapist cannot maintain a silent analytic posture; nor is the use of the couch advisable in the early sessions. To remain silent and let the patient recount his miserable state is to further the transference distortion of an omnipotent other. Rather, the therapist should be active and forthright. Depressed patients, when they begin therapy, often want to talk only of their depressed feelings. Spiegel (1965) described how some depressed patients wear out the therapist with an initial repetitiveness consisting of complaint after complaint and a restriction of cognitive processes. She accurately observed that free association at this stage is impossible and the therapist must actively elicit information. Levine (1965) also described the "broken-record response" in which a depressed patient goes on and on about his complaints. Levine believes that the therapist must actively break this circle of complaints in order for the patient to consider other pertinent issues and widen the horizons of his consciousness. The therapist may initiate discussion of other topics and prevent the reiteration of symptoms. Most important, as Kolb (1956) indicated, is for the therapist to be open and honest about his own limitations and feelings. Depressives are reared in an atmosphere of deceit and secret obligations, and they must be shown how to be direct and forthright. In addition the therapist should treat such individuals with dignity and give them the expectation of adult behavior. Interpretations should never be phrased in a pejorative manner, but in a way of sharing an insight with a mature individual. Regression in therapy is definitely to be avoided; rather, the attitude of the therapist must reinforce the mature parts of the depressive's personality. Furthermore, the individual should be helped to understand that he is important as a human being in his own right, and not for what he may do for the therapist. I have found it best to interpret evidences of transference immediately, especially since they reveal the depressive's desire to reinstate a bargain relationship and be taken care of by a dominant other by demonstrating good behavior. Jacobson (1975) also recommends immediate transference confrontation in the early stages of treatment: "the early interpretation of such a patient's tendency first to aggrandize and idealize the analyst and then to feel disappointed in him is of great value for their futher analysis because it prepares them for the negative transference that will make its appearance in the future" (pp. 434–5). This negative transference can be avoided if the patient's distortions of the therapist are made clear early in treatment.

The problem of eliciting a negative therapeutic reaction in which the patient's condition worsens after accurate interpretations attracted Gero's early interest (1936) in the treatment of nonpsychotic depression. The major contribution of his excellent paper is in his stressing that the therapist must work through the depressive's character resistance before successful analytic work can take place. Gero at this time was influenced by Wilhelm Reich's technique of character analysis, and he used it to good effect. His paper is still valuable; it shows that only after one has interpreted the patient's mode of dealing with others, including the therapist, can therapeutic results be achieved. Therefore the patient's demandingness, dependency, hypersensitivity, and manipulativeness should all be made clear in the treatment so that the roots of the disorder can be unearthed and analyzed.

At this beginning stage of therapy, the patient may show a rapid symptomatic improvement because he believes that he has found a new dominant other to minister to his inordinate needs. When the therapist refuses to comply with these demands for nurturance, however, the patient may complain that the therapist is aloof and unsympathetic, therapy is not helping him, it is not worth the cost, and he wishes to discontinue therapy. It is during this stage that the content of the sessions is relatively unimportant; the patient's primary objective is to set up the therapist as a new dominant other and to reestablish a bargain relationship. These attempts should be the focus of therapy, in showing the patient through the transference how all of his significant human relationships have been characterized by pathological dependency.

Eventually a picture of an extremely inhibited and anhedonic individual materializes, who despite considerable public achievement has never enjoyed his successes. This image can be made apparent to the patient and he will realize that he has never allowed himself to be free or spontaneous, but always has had to attune his behavior to the reactions of others. This fear of self-assertion has displayed itself not only in a lack of satisfaction, but also in some cases in work inhibition, so that the depressive has rarely achieved his true potential.

The therapist must be careful not to accept the depressive's estimation of himself as helpless, inept, or overwhelmed. These self-recriminations result from a multiplicity of causes and are over-determined. They are partially manipulative interpersonal techniques to insure the other's support and to evade responsibility, and they define the depressive's characterological defenses in terms of dealing with others. However, as indicated by Gero, considering only the interpersonal affects of the depressive's behavior is to appreciate only part of the total situation. The inner cognitive systems that form the core of the depressive's personality must also be considered. Inwardly the depressive believes in his inferiority and truly feels incapable of facing life's demands. In childhood the depressive was made to feel weak and dependent, with each attempt at independent assertion bringing a rebuke of ingratitude or disloyalty. What emerges from the retrospective accounts of depressives, as carefully documented by Cohen and her co-workers (1954), is that they were pressed to achieve in order to insure the continuation of a needed relationship. Yet at the same time, too much achievement was threatening to the needed other so that real-life accomplishments were treated as "repayments" for love given, or as expected behavior for upholding the family honor. In every case, the achievement was somehow perverted so as to rob the individual of joy in his efforts and from obtaining a sense of independent competence. Work and effort were utilized in the hope of pleasing the powerful parent rather than in the gradual development of self-esteem or the sense of mastery. One patient, for example, remembered how as a girl she made remarkably good grades and even came in first on state examinations on two occasions, eventually winning a university scholarship. Her mother seem to take these impressive accomplishments for granted while criticizing her daughter for lacking social grace or being without boy-friends. On the other hand, if this woman ever made less than outstanding grades, her mother gave her long guilt-producing scoldings.

This lack of self-confidence, and the need of an external other to give meaning to life as well as to absolute guilt, may partially explain the depressive's difficulties in functioning in positions of command or leader-ship. They are excellent in "number two" positions, following directions without question and working hard in order to obtain the praise of their superior. Often this excellent performance promotes them into a leader-ship position and this sudden loss of a relationship with an esteemed supe-rior may precipitate a severe clinical depression. In such situations the depressive finds himself forced to make independent decisions that he is never sure are correct, but which he feels must be always correct. He longs for the reflected cues from a dominant other, the constant reassur-ance that he is doing a good job, and relief from independent assertion.

All this is to confirm that depressives do have an unrealistically low picture of their capabilities. Joffe and Sandler (1965), Jacobson (1971), and others have, in fact, described depression as partially resulting from the discrepancy between an unrealistic ego ideal and the real self. From a Kleinian point of view, Slipp (1976) noted that in families of depres-sives, the child's effort is to alter the bad parental introject into a good parental introject so that the child can feel worthwhile. Slipp described how the parents bind a child to themselves by creating an impossible achievement situation. The point to be appreciated here is that the unrealistic ego ideal is not desired for its own sake, but only in order to retain the nurturance of others. This self-sacrifice of a personal sense of achievement, as well as the hopelessly unrealistic expectations, are to be pointed out repeatedly to the patient. It can be shown that beneath the self-recriminations are unrealistic expectations, the patient's erroneous feeling that he himself is responsible for everything that happens to him —if he has failed, it is his fault for not having tried hard enough. The therapist must not reward conspicuous achievement unduly, but encour-age a sense of inner satisfaction regardless of life's vicissitudes. This can be done through both interpretations and by transferentially showing the patient how he inflates the power of the therapist and overly regards the therapist's opinions. Here again, an open, frank attitude in which the therapist admits his own limitations and past failures helps the patient to see supposedly perfect others as merely human. Sometimes patients will become angry with the therapist for not fitting their ideal of omnipotence and this is useful material for interpretation.

The establishment of this specific therapeutic relationship, in which the patient can view the therapist as an interested, understanding, but neither nurturing nor idealized individual; the gradual realization of the depressive's inordinate need for others' approval; and the inappropriateness of his demands, can be seen as roughly comprising the first stage of treatment.

Middle Stage of Therapy: Working Through

The next stage of therapy appears to center on the depressive's reaction (and reluctance) to relinquishing the dominant other. This is often the major struggle of therapy, for it invokes a cognitive and interpersonal restructuring of the individual. The patient will regress to prior modes of behavior and even become angry with the therapist for causing him to give up the older and secure, if ultimately disappointing, sources of self-esteem. One patient, for example, reported a dream in which she was being forced to do dangerous acts by an insistent man. The man had a curious aspect in the dream, in that he wrote upside down. She immediately realized that from where she sat in the office, my writing was upside down. In the dream she had a sense of apprehension, confirming her fear of the possibility of altering her behavior, as had been discussed in therapy. A frequently encountered dream at this stage of therapy is of the death of a parent. Freud (1900) described such dreams as typical and used them to elaborate his concept of the Oepidal conflict by stating that they represented revived childhood death wishes against the parent. He felt further evidence for this interpretation was in the fact that often the parent who was dreamt of already had been dead for many years and therefore the death in the dream could not represent a current wish. Another confirming point, for Freud, was the inappropriate affect experienced in these dreams.

In depressives, these dreams seem to have a different meaning. They appear to represent the relinquishing by the patient of that part of themselves that the parent represents. It is an attempt to give up the original dominant other and the part of the self that still adheres to the original dictates. The affective component of these dreams is often a clue as to how the patient feels about relinquishing an ingrained mode of behavior that is characterized by a response to authority. Contrary to the Oepidal interpretation of such dreams is the clinical finding that patients may dream of the death of either parent, the choice seemingly related to which parent was the dominant other rather than to sexual rivalry.

For example, a woman who had been chronically depressed reported the following dream prior to taking a trip by herself for the first time in her life. She dreamt that her father had died, yet she could not believe it. Other people were trying to convince her of his death and her feeling was one of bewilderment. Then she was in a drugstore with her brother, trying to get a death certificate to prove that her father was dead, and the druggist refused to sign the certificate. This woman's father had died twenty years before the dream but remained in her memory as a despotic autocrat who favored the brother and severely intimidated the patient through fear and guilt. Although the dream cannot be explored fully here, it might be helpful to add that the patient was going to visit her brother in a distant city and was eager to show him how she had matured in therapy. The ambivalence in the dream over her father's death can be seen as her own insecurity over relinquishing her dependent mode of life and her anxiety about renewing close contact with her brother. The druggist in the dream may well have represented the therapist who refuses to reassure the patient that she is truly free of her father's influence.

Another patient reported a dream in which he was at his father's gravesite, in which his dead father was lying. In the dream the patient was crying and others were trying to comfort him. He had the feeling that everyone close to him was sick. He woke from the dream crying. In his associations this patient remembered the actual death of his father, stating that at the time, "I felt as if my purpose in life had been extinguished." The patient had had a quasi-symbiotic relationship with his father who had preferred him over the other children. He followed his father's orders to the letter, in return for which his father lavished praise on him and gave him substantial sums of money. He never dared to cross his father since he had the experience of witnessing what had occurred to his brothers when they disagreed even slightly with the father. This patient had grown up in a rural area where the father, a wealthy and influential businessman, had ruled over a large estate like a small monarch. Although he had slavishly followed his father's instructions, the patient often had been irresponsible in his own affairs, and had lost moderate sums of money because of his naiveté. He had the dream after losing a considerable sum of money at cards. The dream may have represented an awareness that he was now on his own, yet there remained within him a desperate desire to be taken care of once again by a powerful other. The dream showed his characteristic turning to others to make things right, as his father had done in the past whenever he was in trouble.

Another patient reported a dream of his father's death after having been at a family reunion during which he reailzed that he could no longer maintain the bargain relationship which had existed for years. He humored his father during the day but did not feel the old need to gain his approval or nurturance. That night he dreamt that he was attending his father's funeral, but he felt no emotion. It was as if the death were a neutral statement of fact.

As seen from these examples, the parental figure that is killed off in dreams is usually but not exclusively the father, for both male and female depressives. This finding may be accounted for by the peculiar childhood history that many of these patients are able to reconstruct. It appears that the mother had been quite loving and adequate when the patient was an infant but as the patient grew into the oppositional toddler stage, he became part of the family system in which the father was the sole authority to be placated, with the mother relinquishing her care of the child to meet paternal demands. As soon as the child became an independent and willful being, he or she seemed to threaten the mother who then withdrew from parental responsibilities. Often such individuals were exploited as go-betweens or mediators between the weak mother and the powerful father because the mother could not directly confront her overwhelming spouse. Soon these children internalized the familial belief system that the purpose of life was to please and mollify the omnipotent father by exemplary behavior. Gradually the paternal reactions became the barometer of one's worth, rather than the evolution of independent agencies with which to assess self-esteem.

The point to be emphasized regarding these "death dreams" is that the affect in the dream appears to be the key to the patient's progress. These dreams also may represent punishment for behavior that had been forbidden and thus would cause abandonment. In such instances, the patient feels a desperate feeling of loneliness and helplessness in the dream. In instances where the part of the self that still adheres to the dominant other's belief system is weakening, the effect is one of relief or resigned determination.

CHARACTERISTIC RESISTANCE OF DEPRESSIVES

At this stage in therapy, a surprising regression and resistance is sometimes encountered. While the patient is resolved to change and makes realistic efforts in this direction, he begins to experience a different form of depression which for lack of a better term may be called deprivation depression. The depressive now sees no point in life whatsoever, having given up the mode of doing for the reward of a dominant other, or at least seeing the futility in such a mode of life. He is terrified by the sense of loneliness that results from his realistic assessment that others are not watching his every move and he is of little consequence to most individuals. Although he feels relieved of the burden of living for the reflected praise of others, he cannot conceive of living without praise.

In a previous article (1973), I described a young doctor who preferred to believe that he was being evaluated by authorities who scrutinized his every move than to feel that no one supervised (or in his terms, cared about) his work. He was so programmed to calculate his actions and their consequences on others, that his appreciation of others as primarily concerned with their own lives and welfare destroyed his reason for being.

He became clinically depressed when his training was coming to an end and he realized that he would soon be on his own, without the structure as well as confinement of an authoritarian academic structure. In therapy he had a somewhat irritating quality of having to explain in great detail his every action as if to convince the listener of the justification for his behavior. This habit had been initiated by his mother, who in her intrusive way had demanded to know everything he did and the reasons for it. It became apparent that he had no means by which to measure his own worth, and he was completely at the mercy of the judgments of those around him. As therapy progressed and he was able to acknowledge his dependency on others for his self-esteem, he also became aware of his covert demands and calculated self-sacrifice which were used for continuing to receive the needed feedback from others whom he considered important. As a young attending physician, he understood with great distress that others at the hospital were primarily involved in their own lives and beyond friendly concern, essentially wished to pursue their own careers. He desperately wanted someone to take care of him, to worry about him, and to advise and instruct him in the way his mother had done throughout childhood. Without this external source of care, he felt totally unimportant and devoid of worth. For a while he began to invent dominant others in an almost paranoid fashion, but his reality testing was sufficiently strong for him to realize that he was merely fulfilling a wish in fantasy.

During this difficult time, he dreamt that he was running by himself on an open, exposed track and he was conscious of having to pace himself. In the dream he felt he was making "good time" and woke up in an optimistic state of mind. This dream was significant in that it was the first dream in which he portrayed himself alone; in former dreams he was always involved with others, usually his mother, his superiors at the hospital, or occasionally his wife. His associations to the dream were a mixture of progressive and regressive tendencies: he immediately stated that now he had to go it alone but then remarked that his current life was like running on a treadmill, without goal or purpose. He elaborated on still longing for the excitement that praise from a superior had given him, although he simultaneously realized that the absence of praise formerly had devastated him for days and caused him self-recriminations for not being able to please powerful others. He also commented on being exposed in the dream (a common feeling in dreams of such patients at this stage of therapy), in that he could no longer use his usual subterfuge to get what he wanted from people. The dream also may have indicated (although he did not associate this) that he still required a track on which to run (external structure), and he had to be careful to pace himself, again exhibiting a sense of inhibition and lack of spontaneity.

During this period of "emptiness," the patient began—to his surprise —to read novels for the first time since college, to spend time playing with his children, and to enjoy sex with his wife to a much greater extent. As with other patients, as the need for external or reflective gratification decreases, inner sources of pleasure automatically arise despite the pro-testations of a barren, purposeless life. As these new avenues of pleasure were pointed out and reinforced in therapy, along with the interpreta-tion that as an adult he no longer needed to attune his waking life to the imagined wishes of others, he reported another dream. In this dream, he was back in college but now the dorm was coed and he felt hopeful about establishing a sexual relationship. His associations to the dream revolved around his actual college years when, because of his preoccu-pation to get into medical school, he shunned social contacts and re-mained rather isolated. He also remembered his fear of rejection and humiliation from girls and that in mixed company he had sensed himself to be in a dangerous, hostile world. Finally he brought up the repetitive theme of really having gone to medical school to please his mother and not out of any true desire to become a physician. The dream appeared to symbolize his new attitude toward life; that life promised the oppor-tunity for pleasure, and others would respond warmly without his having to employ his usual manipulations. Finally, this dream is fairly typical of depressive patients when they are resolving their fear of aloneness and freedom; in it are reawakened memories of a time of life, usually adolescence, when the patient could have rebelled against the dominat-ing parent and followed a more gratifying path in life. In most cases the path was not taken and any attempt at autonomy was short-lived, quickly being curtailed as a result of parental objections.

Eventually this man was able to live a satisfying life without the imagined protection of powerful others who transferentially served as mother substitutes. He gave up his mode of reflective gratification and the use of others to serve as external measures of self-worth. However, as briefly indicated, he was able to do so only after a long period of feel-ing lost and empty.

This basic reaction to relinquishing a former mode of gratification was also exemplified by a middle-aged housewife who experienced depression, headaches, and transient anxiety attacks. She was referred for treatment after a prolonged medical work-up (at her insistence) for a brain tumor had proved negative. In this case, her depression did not result from an environmental loss, but from a persistent realization that she was trapped in a life that offered her no pleasure. In therapy she confided that she had always had a desire to lead a free bohemian existence but she had kept this horrible side of her personality hidden, for fear of being criticized or rejected. Instead she carefully did what she believed others expected of her, although she resented her activities which she perceived as being the result of obligations and unfair restrictions. This woman also believed that others continuously observed her every move, and she lived in fear that they might discover her secret, romanticized self. She constantly complained about her life's being nothing but drudgery, but made every effort to add new responsibilities (which she perceived as onerous) to her daily routine. She was stuck in what she perceived to be an existence devoid of gratification by her own volition and by her need to believe herself at the center of everyone's concern. The satisfaction that her life did afford was in seeing herself as a burdened martyr, and she utilized this self-image to allow herself to feel superior to her "frivolous" friends and to extract support from her family for her alleged sacrifices. When the expected praise and appreciation were not forthcoming, she would lapse into depression.

Obviously there was a secret satisfaction in her unsatisfying life, but at tremendous cost to herself and those around her. Needless to say, there were potent reasons for her neurotic behavior; in childhood, her mother had constantly criticized her and unfavorably compared her to an older brother; she had grown up in an upwardly mobile family and subculture in which she had to achieve and always be on her good behavior; any sign of normal childhood oppositionalism had been treated as a sign of ingratitude and disloyalty; and her family members had utilized guilt as the main form of control over one another. However, what is to be emphasized here is not so much the distortion of her adult life to fit childhood patterns, nor the genetic aspects of her neurosis, but the deep need that this woman felt for the constant reassurance that she was acting out a certain role, ungratifying as it might ultimately prove. In one session she painfully admitted that without this role she would not know what to do. She was indeed frozen in a pleasureless fishbowl, supposedly observable to everyone. Yet this was preferable to the possible lack of structure and meaning that giving up this role would entail. Here again, one of her major resistances to cure was her reluctance to realize that freedom was possible; that her "role" was her own doing, and others really did not measure her every move as her mother had done. She tenaciously continued to distort others—especially her husband—to fit the model of her mother, and she carried on an entire secret game of pleasing and then spiting him without his even being aware of it, except for bewilderment by her inexplicable mood swings.

During this phase of therapy, the patient complains of feeling empty and lifeless, often blaming the therapist for his condition. Interpretations relating this feeling to the gradual renunciation of a previous narcissistic mode can counter some of the patient's discomfort. Simultaneously, it may be pointed out that this new aloneness also permits freedom from imagined obligations to others and a possibility for real involvement in life. Here again, a review of lost opportunities in the patient's past may help him view this transient period of alleged emptiness as a healthy although painful step. Finally, this cognitive restructuring of his own abilities and his relationship with others will help in preventing future depressive episodes. The relinquishing of the dominant-other orientation can be seen as a liberation and not a loss. With the therapist's encouragement, feeble and later more significant attempts at autonomous methods of gratification will be attempted.

Sometimes an actual attempt will be preceded by a trial attempt in fantasy or a dream. For example, a woman in this phase of therapy reported a dream in which she was intensely involved in a political argument. She recalled that in her life she had always been afraid of becoming involved in anything on her own, so she had followed the dictates of others and as a result found most of her activities to be devoid of joy or real pleasure. The one exception to this pattern occurred during her early college years when she became very interested in politics and considered majoring in political science. She secretly joined radical political groups and intensely enjoyed long discussions about social issues. Then she met her future husband who forbade her to associate with radicals, and she dutifully obeyed. This brief rebellion was forgotten for twenty years until, through therapy, she again dared to feel committed although only in a dream. She remarked on how good it felt in the dream to be involved in something. The fact that she used the metaphor of an argument may have represented the resistance that not only she herself but others would have to her changing.

It was mentioned that depressives rarely have hobbies or interests that are not means to win approval from others. The patient will shy away from pleasurable activities, deriding these behaviors as childish or impractical. However, what he is actually avoiding is the risk of attempting anything without the sanction of a dominant other. There is an intense feeling of guilt over enjoyment as well as a fear that pleasure will bring abandonment. This is to be interpreted as a remnant of the patient's childhood experience in which he was punished—usually by threats of separation or by being made to feel selfish—if he dared to enjoy independent behavior. One depressed man, during this phase of treatment, confided a secret desire to learn how to fly an airplane which he had kept to himself since he was seven years old. He always had told himself that he could not afford the lessons (he easily could) or that such an activity woud take time away from business. He eventually divulged this secret intention to his wife, who innocently told some friends. The patient became very upset at this, feeling that the friends would think him frivolous and wasteful. This example shows that depressives can have interests or hobbies, but wishes in this direction have been stifled for fear of criticism. Once the patient drops his self-inhibitions, old discarded sources of pleasure automatically come to the surface.

This conflict over daring to experience pleasure is clearly illustrated in a dream of a depressed woman. On the day preceding the dream, we discussed how she had inhibited herself in childhood and especially in adolescence when she had felt uneasy because boys were attracted to her. She remembered that she had been flattered by their attentions, but

at the same time felt guilty about feeling so flirtatious and worried that
her interest in boys would detract from her studies and anger her father.
In the dream there was a beautiful room with two women in it. One was
"thin and sallow with a childish body, who is downcast" while the other
was "voluptuous with shiny brown hair and beautiful intricate tattoos
on her body." The voluptuous woman was saying, "Use my body and I'm
happy." Then she went into a magnificent and luxurious bathroom, exuding a great sensual aura. Suddenly this beautiful woman did something
"disgusting" which the patient could not exactly specify. The scene immediately changed to a hospital room where the patient learned from a
teenage boyfriend who had been mentioned in the session that her father
was dying. The patient felt "sad and horrible" as well as guilty and abandoned, but was helpless to prevent the death. The boyfriend tried to
console her and finally said "I've always loved you" to the patient,
whereupon she awakened in a state of anxiety.

This dream is complicated by reference to childhood masturbation as
well as by the fact that the body had special importance to this woman
because she had been anorexic in her late teens. Nevertheless the conflict
between sensual pleasure and self-denial is clear in her visualization of
the two contrasting women, and in the sequence of the dream where
pleasure gives rise to loss of the father (which is then fortunately recon-
ciled by the love of an old boyfriend). In this dream, as in many others,
the area of conflict is over sexual pleasure; however, this conflict ultimately represents a defiance of the dominant other for one's own gratification, regardless of the mode in which the gratification is obtained.
Similar dreams could be reported involving other modalities of pleasure
with the ever-present sequelae of loss and abandonment.*

The patient should be encouraged to venture into new avenues of
satisfaction, no matter how trivial or slight such activities may appear. As
Levine (1965) stressed, "Depression may diminish when a patient gains
new sources of satisfaction in physical activity such as golf or dancing,
which led to a career and largely prevented depression in an adolescent
patient of mine. It is especially helpful to direct the depressed patient into
satisfying activity; in fact one should be wary of doing anything to dis-
courage activity in the depressed patient even if some of it is clearly
symptomatic. As long as the patient is not destructive to himself or to
others, his activity may give him purpose and narcissistic satisfaction."

It is during the psychotherapeutic attack on this pleasure anxiety that
the therapist may offer himself as a model to the patient as an individual
who is able to enjoy life and independent interests. If a good working
alliance has been formed, the patient will understand that even esteemed

---

* In terms of therapeutic progress, it is obviously important that the dream resolves
itself with the patient's being loved by a nonfamilial individual. The patient may have
realized that the death of the dominant other, painful as it might be, would allow her
to experience closeness and love, as well as pleasure.

doctors do not have to be deadly serious all the time but take time for nonproductive activity that is simply fun.

It is hoped that, concomitant with this shift from other-rewarded to self-rewarded activity, a transformation in human relationships will emerge. The depressive has had a narcissistic, need-fulfilling involvement with others so that people have been important only to the extent that they could give praise or absolve guilt. There never has been an attempt to appreciate others as people in their own right. It is amazing that these individuals who are so adept at manipulating the desired response from others are so unknowledgeable about significant aspects of the inner life of the other individuals. They do not seem to appreciate the core of a man, but only his superficialities. As such, depressives often appear psychopathic in their subtle control and seeming disregard for the independent welfare of others. Yet all their efforts are directed at the effect it will produce in others.

Cohen and her co-workers (1954) remarked on what they called "the stereotyped response" in depressed patient; meaning that other individuals, the therapist included, can only be viewed as stereotyped repetitions of parental figures rather than as different, specific human beings. Other people are not conceived as being complex, both bad and good, and ultimately existing outside the orbit of the depressive's needs. Cohen and her colleagues believe that this stereotyping is a defensive maneuver, in that the depressive is afraid to acknowledge unpleasant traits in significant others, and they trace this defect to a childhood failure to integrate part-objects into a whole good and bad object. This stereotyping appears to be a manipulative estimation of others as to whether they can become surrogate sources of self-esteem; that is, whether they can fulfill an intrapsychic need.*

The depressive in adult life searches for a suitable individual on whom he can project the role of dominant other so that he can function in terms of obtaining esteem and escaping guilt over everyday behavior. This other is bestowed with all sorts of magical powers and directives. The depressive then distorts this other to fulfill his inner needs, and he simultaneously modifies his own behavior to meet what he believes the other desires. Freud (1921) was well aware of this pathological form of ego-object relationship and described it in detail in *Group Psychology and the Analysis of the Ego*. In this work Freud demonstrated how in certain circumstances the object is put in the place of the ego ideal so that an external other serves the purpose of a normally internal agency. As for the effect of this process on the ego, Freud commented, "It [the ego] is

---

* However, the excellent work of Cohen et al. may not be directly applicable here, in that they based their interpretations on hospitalized manic-depressives who were much more impaired than these patients. Furthermore, it is again questionable how much of this stereotyping was the result of being severely depressed, and how much pertained to the individual's premorbid mode of interrelating.

impoverished, it has surrendered itself to the object, it has substituted the object for its most important constituent." It is for the therapist to resist the patient's distortions, to interpret the transference, and to restore this most important constituent with an independent, intrapsychic agency.

Succinctly stated, what appears to be the basic problem of the depressive is that he has remained a child in the area of obtaining self-esteem; and he needs others to determine his worth. As Arieti has indicated in another context, the original interpersonal relationship of parent and child has not been transformed into an intrapsychic situation of various mental agencies. Therefore the depressive continues to make parents of others, using them as external consciences and restricting his own behavior to obedience or rebellion. Here, then, is the interface between the interpersonal and intrapsychic aspects in depression: *Others are used in the place of internal agencies within the self and the individual projects upon others distorted images from the past.* It is an alteration of this dual process that forms the basis of therapy with depressives, and to which the various manifestations of the character defenses may be traced. In short, the depressive has failed to develop internal regulators of self-esteem.

In order for the change to occur during this middle phase of treatment, a cognitive restructuring in various areas must occur; that is, an alteration of the meaning that the patient assigns to his usual experiences and anticipations. In terms of self, a decrease in expectancies and an ability to derive pleasure from one's activities is basic. New meanings are given to the usual everyday experiences with others, as well as to events in the past. Other people and their behavior are viewed differently and therefore evoke different emotions than they had previously. This cognitive restructuring does not apply only to interpersonal experiences. The individual is able to acknowledge thoughts and feelings which in the past he had to repress. There is an overall enlargement of consciousness in that the self is able to deal with intrapsychic material without fear of guilt. Fantasy life becomes richer and independent of the previously recurring themes of dependency and manipulation.

Therefore, the encouragment of independent activities, the resolution of the deprivation depression, and an alteration in the mode of interpersonal behavior form the bulk of the second stage of treatment. As the patient actually becomes freer with others, he may be surprised that they do not reject or punish him. A young woman reported the following dream in the initial stages of therapy, which in a different way states the same theme. She dreamt that she was disguised as a specific character on a daytime TV soap opera who was intensely loved by her husband and other men. In the dream, the TV husband is kissing and embracing the disguised patient, who enjoys the experience but at the same time realizes that she can only obtain love by being someone else. If she were discovered to be who she really is, no one would love her. Here again is the theme of having to pretend to be someone else in order to win love. The patient felt that if she were to act according to her own desires and not in order to please others, she would be abandoned. A crucial step is to truly trust others without having to coerce their support through emotional bribery or threats. The individual may feel for the first time that he can be liked or loved without his usual machinations.

At the same time, behavior toward the therapist changes; he is no longer the center of the patient's world. At this stage new material emerges which the patient previously feared would alienate the therapist. Therapy is no longer a game to win the therapist's love, but a mutual endeavor in which a new mode of being is explored and solidified.

This is the time of working through, in which current behavior is examined, related to the past or to possible transference, and either encouraged or discouraged through interpretation. Beck's (1976) cognitive style of therapy may be useful in correcting the patient's distortions and identifying the stimuli that elicit erroneous modes of reacting. While this type of analysis is done throughout the therapeutic process, at this time it can be done explicitly with the patient's consent as a joint endeavor. During this stage of treatment, dreams are especially crucial since they often betray old patterns of functioning despite surface improvement. At this point the patient can begin to adequately scrutinize his own thoughts and feelings and search out possible areas of regression as well as areas of healthy change. He can accept more of the therapeutic task and function pretty much as a typically neurotic individual in therapy.

Final Stage of Therapy

The last stage of therapy deals mainly with external rather than internal obstacles to change when the patient needs the therapist's support to continue his newly acquired mode of functioning. Realistic problems that arise during this time are the result of the patient's having altered his way of relating and his way of seeing himself. This is true in most instances of psychotherapeutic change, but perhaps more so in the case of depressives, since so much of their former pathology involved specific relationships. Parents, spouses, friends, and employers will try to prevent changes in what had been for them a comfortable relationship with the patient. Usually their obstructions will take the form of inducing guilt or shame in the patient over his new independence from them. For example, one patient's mother threatened suicide because the patient wished to move out on her own.

However, the strongest external obstacles to change have been the spouses of older married depressives. The patient's change in behavior usually threatens the spouse who, while despairing over the repeated episodes of depression, actually wants the depressive spouse to remain dependent, inhibited, or simply easily controllable. This is especially true in instances in which the depressed patient is a woman married to a domineering male who is frightened of his own emotions. These husbands do not perceive their own role in the perpetuation of their spouse's depression; in fact, they are often skeptical of psychotherapy and believe the depression to be purely metabolic in origin. They are threatened by the gradual appearance of autonomy and independent satisfaction that result from therapy but they cannot openly admit these fears; for to do so would be to admit their own dependency needs, which they consider signs of weakness. Instead they subtly attempt to sabotage change by recriminations or self-righteous complaints that the patient is somehow failing in her marital obligations. Such husbands satisfy their own dependency needs by having others become dependent on them and so are able to exert their control.

A familiar pattern for married male depressives is to have a spouse who is chronically unsatisfied and belittling, who arouses old inferiority feelings originally experienced with an overdemanding mother. Here again, these wives consciously do not wish the patient to become depressed, yet they constantly complain or find ways of deflating their husband's self-esteem.

When the therapist is faced with such a reality situation which impedes therapeutic progress, the spouse may be referred for therapy. However, another tactic which is occasionally effective is for the primary therapist to see the patient and spouse together. In these joint sessions the therapist must guard against becoming the patient's advocate, but must allow the patient to assert him or herself openly in an effort to establish a new marital equilibrium that will no longer perpetuate the interlocking psychopathology.*

Obviously, not all spouses will resist change in the depressed patient. Some gradually will accommodate themselves to the emergence of new reactions and activities. Others genuinely will welcome these changes, finding their own lives much more satisfying with a partner who is not only no longer depressed but also no longer guilt-provoking, manipulative, sexually inhibited, and emotionally unavailable.

Regardless of the external forces that mitigate against continued change, the patient needs the therapist to fortify his resolve to break old patterns of behavior. Setbacks are to be expected, as are frequent angry denunciations of others' manipulative behavior with which the patient

---

* Forrest (1969) has also been impressed by the perpetuation of depression in some patients by pathological marital interactions, and the obstacles to cure that these obstacles represent. She advocates combining marital therapy with individual therapy from the start and reports good results with this therapeutic regimen.

had formerly complied, but of which he was unaware. Thus the final stage of treatment for depressives is similar to that for other neurotic disorders. A consistent new pattern of behavior emerges and is consolidated over time despite obstacles from within and without.

Some features which I have found to be of value in ascertaining the success of this stage of therapy are the emergence of specific characteristics that were previously absent. Almost all revolve around a fundamental sense of freedom from the reactions of others and the crystallization of the capability to assess one's self-esteem independently. Creativity is sometimes evidenced toward this stage of treatment, in a field of the arts or by applying original ideas in work. It must be realized that every creative attempt carries with it the risk of being not only inadequate but rejected. The patient's freedom to experiment and try something new bespeaks a trust in himself and others. Related to creativity is a sense of fun and humor lacking in previous interchanges. To be joyful or exuberant previously was seen as dangerous, since the old authorities insisted on serious work and diligent performance. As mentioned, there is an expansion of interest in others and learning from the experience of others. This new mode of relating is based on a widening sense of empathy in which the patient can identify with others and see them as separate but similar individuals. Previously, the depressive had a psychopathic type of empathy; he knew how to obtain a reaction, but he could never truly place himself in the role of another and share that person's experiences. An ability to show anger over realistic situations will indicate that the patient feels secure enough to assert himself.

Coming to terms with the ghosts of the past is also necessary: the transition is often from one of overestimation of past dominant others to angry recriminations against them. Before termination of therapy, the past must be accepted without excessive rancor. Similarly the relationship with the therapist takes on the attitude of friendship, with neither too much gratitude nor admiration. A sharing of experiences helps in allowing the patient to feel more like a partner and less like a patient. The door should be left open, for the patient will need the therapist as the one individual with whom he can be genuine and open, until he establishes other such relationships in everyday life.

While depressive patients can often be most difficult, anger-provoking, and even boring, ultimately they may also be the most rewarding; through therapy, they can begin to utilize their considerable talents in the service of selfless endeavors, rather than in forcing others to grant them infantile devotion.

[14]

CASE ILLUSTRATION:

THE PSYCHOTHERAPY OF

MILD DEPRESSION

This chapter presents the history and psychotherapy of a mildly depressed young adult as a way of concretely illustrating the concepts discussed in chapters 7 and 13 on the psychodynamics and treatment of this form of affective disorder. This young man's depression can be categorized as characterological with acute exacerbations. However, at no time was his symptomatology so severe that his powers of reasoning and reality testing were threatened. Also, despite his repeated protestations of despair, medication did not appear indicated; medication might have been detrimental, since the reliance on drugs could have worked against the necessary realization that relief had to result from personality change in the long run.

A further prefatory note may be warranted before presenting the actual case material, concerning the frequent analogy between femininity and weakness. This analogy was presented in therapy by the patient and not by the therapist, who does not adhere to such an equation as universally valid. However, the patient grew up in an Italian-American subculture in which women were devalued, and he utilized the symbol of a woman in dreams and associations in accordance with the unfortunate prejudices of his ethnic roots at a particular point in time. Obviously individuals from other cultures would select different symbols as well as view heterosexual relationships differently. In therapy one must initially follow the lead of the patient in accepting the specific symbolism which he uses to describe parts of the self, even if one does not agree with these obvi-

This chapter was written by Jules Bemporad.

ously biased productions. It was satisfying to note that as the patient improved, he dropped his male chauvinist attitudes and was able to form a close and mutually respectful relationship with a woman.

Initial Presentation

When first seen in August 1964, Fred was twenty-three years old. He was a good-looking, powerfully built young man neatly dressed in a dark suit and tie. His behavior and mannerisms, however, were a marked contrast to his appearance. Fred was painfully apprehensive and awkward. Perspiration soaked through his suit and he found it difficult to sit still. He had trouble explaining why he was seeking treatment, although he seemed to be making every attempt to be cooperative and agreeable. He said that he felt completely inadequate, he was afraid of people, he felt incapable of doing anything, and he was a pathetic failure. His only regular activity at that time was to work in his father's grocery store for a few hours a day so that his father could rest and have lunch at home. Even this limited amount of work seemed an unbearable ordeal; he had difficulty concentrating, he was distractable, and he continually feared making mistakes. The rest of the time Fred stayed home and watched TV, occasionally running errands for his mother. During these periods of inactivity, he felt a sense of emptiness and despair, yet he lacked the motivation to fill his time with pleasurable pursuits. About once or twice a week he would go with a friend or a cousin to a local community center dance, where he would stand around trying to work up the courage to ask a girl to dance. As soon as he did ask someone to dance, however, he became terribly anxious and found it difficult to carry on a conversation. As a result, he never really made contact with anyone and would return home depressed, convinced that he would never really be able to have a girl friend.

Fred described having felt anxious and depressed, as well as having had an "inferiority complex" for many years, but in the past few months he had gotten much worse and new symptoms had appeared. He dated their onset to the time his father had suffered a heart attack. There was never any question of mortality and his father quickly came out of any danger, but did have to remain in the hospital for a period of convalescence. Fred had been concerned about his father but was quickly reassured by the latter's improvement. Rather, Fred felt that with his father convalescing in the hospital, he would have to run the family store. He saw a chance to prove his ability and to take on manly responsibilities. Instead, the father rapidly made it clear that he would control the business from his bed and he treated Fred in what Fred felt was a disparaging manner. Fred increased his hours at the store but worked in a semi-servile capacity with an uncle temporarily running things. This situation was very degrading to Fred and he sensed that his father did not think enough of him to carry on the family business. This confirmed his own negative view of himself and resulted in increased feelings of depression and low self-regard. Fred never openly contested his father's decision, justifying his silence by saying that he had not wanted to upset his father because of the latter's precarious physical condition.

As soon as his father was discharged, he immediately went back to his usual work schedule despite medical advice to the contrary. He used Fred only to relieve him for lunch and a short nap, a period of about two hours, and the rest of the time Fred was essentially free. Since his father's return home, Fred had begun to awake at night in a state of terror, finding it difficult to return to sleep. Although unaware of having been dreaming, he felt that these anxiety attacks might somehow be related to his father, who got up at 5 A.M. daily to go to various fish and meat markets. Another new symptom was what Fred described as freezing, which usually occurred at the store or in social situations. During these episodes Fred felt his surroundings becoming distant and quiet, and he felt himself becoming disengaged from the concrete world. These states of depersonalization, although frightening at first, had become rather peaceful and pleasant—and thus all the more frightening.

The predominant symptomatology was, however, an overwhelming sense of hopelessness and futility. Everything seemed to have a feeling of doom and pessimism about it, of being unsurmountable or else menacing and frightening.

Two days later Fred returned for his second session. He seemed much less blocked and anxious and better able to communicate. He again talked about his current life situation, describing an excessive dependency on his father whom he idolized. Fred described his few happy moments as those in which his father praised him for doing some chore. He was extremely tied to his family circle and spent almost all his time with his parents, a cousin, or some other relative.

During this session Fred paused to look at me after each statement, as if waiting to get some sort of feedback. He asked repeatedly if he had made himself clear, or if I understood what he meant. He was also polite to the point of obsequiousness.

Following this session Fred had his first dream during treatment. He dreamt that he was in the waiting room of my office. He walked to the door of my office and to his surprise saw himself dressed as a nun whispering to me at the desk. He felt both relieved and disappointed by what he saw and quietly, so as not to be noticed, backed away from the door and left.

Fred reported this dream with some embarrassment. He stated that it showed him wanting to escape from therapy and he was afraid that I might be angry with him. Throughout the session he continued to be apologetic and placating. The dream was not interpreted, although Fred seemed to comprehend a good part of it without help. In retrospect, the dream was pregnant with multiple meanings and prophetic of the entire analysis. His presentation of himself as a pure, nonthreatening female was to recur often as Fred's defensive social facade; while his true self, full of mistrust and suspicion, silently retreated down the stairs refusing to be acknowledged or exposed.

Clinical History

Fred had spent his entire life in an Italian section of New York. Although both of his parents were American-born, they retained many of the familial and cultural values of their own immigrant parents. The family lived an almost secluded existence, visiting only other Italian Americans who were usually relatives.

Fred's father had grown up in poverty and began contributing to the family income when still a child. Despite his lack of schooling, he showed a good deal of native ability and managed to reach a position of moderate affluence as the owner of a successful grocery store. He had a suspicious, almost paranoid view of society. He described everyone as self-seeking and dishonest and the world in general as a jungle in which the unsuspecting and the unfit could not survive. He repeatedly gave the family lectures on how, as a result of his labors, they now enjoyed a position of wealth that he had never known in his own youth, adding that, were it not for him, the entire family would quickly revert to a state of helplessness and poverty. His exaggerations of the hostility of the extra-familial world served to enhance his self-proclaimed superiority and heroism.

Although extremely stubborn and unyielding when crossed, Fred's father was generous and even tender when others acquiesced to his demands. When his wishes were carried out—that is, when he was allowed to be in a position of control and authority—he lavished praise and gifts on his relatives. If contradicted, however, on even so trivial a topic as the particular ability of some baseball player, he became argumentative and sullen, often flying into a rage and then keeping a grudge for weeks. Within the immediate family, the father rarely had to go to such measures; a hard look, a mild comment of dissatisfaction, was sufficient to stop any opposition. Actually, he seemed to intimidate his family more through guilt than fear. It was generally believed that they all owed their very existence to him, and to make him upset or unhappy was a sign of disloyalty. During the first few sessions Fred described his father as "wonderful, very intelligent, logical, a real man."

In contrast, Fred described his mother as "an Italian Gracie Allen," or as the "family pet." He spoke of her as if she were completely scatter-brained although good-natured and nondemanding. She seemed to be completely overshadowed by her husband and never dared to contradict him. Fred remembered her reprimanding him as a child by saying, "what will daddy think"; as though she herself could offer no objections to his behavior, but that his actions were bad because they might offend or disturb his father. After twenty-five years of marriage, she still smoked in secret because her husband thought it improper for a woman to smoke.

In the course of therapy, Fred altered this original estimation of his mother. He confessed that beneath this superficial joviality and simple agreeability, he found her puzzling and distant. He could never "really get hold of her," or somehow elicit a meaningful response from her. She seemed to flutter from one thing to another, never divulging her true feelings and becoming embarrassed by attempts at genuine closeness or mutuality. She eventually emerged as a somewhat withdrawn and depressed woman with an almost hysterical defense against feelings of closeness.

Fred's destiny seemed to have been decided prior to his birth. The father greatly desired a son to serve as the final evidence of his worldly success. He took an avid interest in Fred's upbringing and actually directed his wife in her behavior toward *his* son. During infancy, however, Fred was completely cared for by his mother. Although unable to cope with a self-willed, independent toddler, she fortunately could be giving and maternal to a nonthreatening infant. Fred was breast-fed, reached all the developmental milestones at the appropriate age, and seems to have experienced a happy infancy.

When he was eighteen months old, his sister Susan was born. We may speculate that this event was traumatic for a number of reasons. A new pregnancy and a new baby must have removed the mother and reduced the time that she could spend with Fred. The withdrawal of the mother may have been magnified since he soon became his father's boy while Susan became his mother's girl. The father's overbearing concern for Fred, and the mother's relatively greater comfort with a neonate than a young child, may have caused the mother to withdraw more than ordinarily might be expected. The long-term effects of this primary loss of object were influenced by the timing of the sister's birth which corresponded to Fred's initiation into the oppositional-individuation phase. Whether the withdrawal of the mother became correlated in Fred's mind with his rudimentary attempts at self-assertion can only be speculated; however, he rapidly became a compliant model child who rarely rebelled against parental demands. Toilet training, for example, was quickly and effortlessly established.

Fred's sister was hardly considered by his father; as mentioned, she was primarily the mother's concern. Fred, in contrast, was coddled and fussed over by the father. Soon Fred's favored position was being exploited by his mother, who utilized him as a mediator and go-between with her husband. Fred remembered that at an early age he was told he was the only one who could talk to his father. Thus Fred was further pushed into a dependent relationship with his father by his mother, who misrepresented her husband's power and greatly inflated Fred's sense of self-importance. Fred's earliest memory dates back to this time (age 3 to 4): "I was hiding under the table and everyone was looking at me. I might have been playing at hiding, but I was uncomfortable." At this same time Fred began having recurrent nightmares of being squashed and smothered by a huge tree that was slowly falling upon him. Fred was continuously on display for his father; he was the apple of his eye. Although praised and pampered, he was rarely permitted to express himself directly or openly in being groomed for a sort of crown prince role. As such, he also was discouraged from playing with children in the neighborhood and instead was steered toward cousins of his own age. Since the parents of these children were often financially obligated to his father, they accorded to Fred an inappropriate respect and deference. The major method of punishment for the usual childhood misbehavior was to make Fred feel guilty for worrying his parents, or to make him feel that he had caused them to be ashamed of him and that he had brought dishonor to his father.

In school Fred was an above-average student. He was liked by his teachers for his self-control and precocious politeness. He worked hard and was very eager to please. Fred remembers feeling that he had to get good grades so as not to let his father down. He made a few friends in school and was a pretty good athlete, spending most of his afternoons playing baseball. He was generally well-liked, although a bit shy and aloof. His years in elementary school stood out in Fred's memory as particularly happy. As long as he made good grades and behaved himself, his parents did not make strenuous demands on him. He felt accepted by others, and even a bit superior to them. He completely dominated his sister and his cousins and, as a result of his father's praises and glorious predictions for the future, Fred was pretty full of himself.

Then at age thirteen, Fred was challenged by another boy at school and got into a scuffle. The other boy pulled a knife and stabbed him. When the bell for the next class rang, the fight broke up and Fred, although aware that he was bleeding, tried to hide his wound and went to class because he was afraid of getting in trouble. When his teacher discovered that he was hurt she rushed him to a nearby hospital. He remembered his parents arriving and making a huge, embarrassing scene in the hospital. Fred developed secondary pneumonia and had to remain in the hospital for two months. The psychic sequelae of his injury were more serious. Upon his return to school, Fred was singled out as "the kid who got stabbed" and he felt himself humiliated and ashamed. He felt he should have somehow beaten the other boy and not allowed himself to be hurt. He also believed that the incident proved his father's view of society to be correct and he was foolish to have been so trusting, believing the other boy would fight fairly. A drawn-out court case instigated by the father failed to convict the assailant, who merely got a suspended sentence. This so infuriated the father that he created a scene in court, ranting about how his defenseless son had nearly been killed by hoodlums. As far as Fred was concerned, however, the gist of his speech was that Fred had been belittled in public. After the trial, in fact, his father angrily told him, "If anybody tried to stab me, I'd tear them up alive." Fred felt himself to be a weakling and a coward, and a failure in his father's eyes.

The most damaging result of the incident was that the father decided Fred should come to help in the store after school and on Saturdays. Ostensibly, the reasons given were that he was old enough to learn the business and his father needed him, but it was an open secret that the father wanted to keep an eye on Fred and did not trust him to play with other youngsters after school. Fred did little more at the store than sit around and deliver a few packages, but he was cut off from contact with people his own age and was forced to be continually with his father. Fred did put up a short-lived resistance to this arrangement but eventually was won over by promises and intimidations. He was told that this was merely a temporary situation and he was destined for greater things. Ten years later when Fred entered therapy, he was still his father's helper in the family store.

From this point on, Fred was never really outside the family circle. He made no real friends and his only true peer relationships were with his cousins. He gave up trying to rebel against any parental demands and he accepted the role that was created for him, asserting himself exclusively in fantasy. His daydreams fell into two categories: seeing himself as powerful and successful, with other men looking up to him; or picturing himself having relations with beautiful women who threw themselves on him, with this type of fantasy frequently accompanied by masturbation. Fred's attempts at self-stimulation were not always successful and were often accompanied by shame and guilt. The family attitudes toward sexuality were quite prudish and the subject was never discussed. The only times that Fred remembered any mention of sexuality were when his father refused to let Susan go out at night, or demanded to know where she had been. In the course of therapy, Fred recalled having been caught at some time when he was very young doing something with his sister. The memory was vague and he was not sure of what had really happened, except that he had felt very ashamed and embarrassed.

One evening when Fred was sixteen, he went to visit one of his cousins, and to his horror found him hanging dead from the ceiling. Despite his initial shock Fred managed to cut down the body and attempted artificial respiration. When this failed he called his father to come over. In recalling this incident at various times during therapy, Fred expressed different attitudes: he was genuinely horrified at his cousin's suicide, yet at times this reaction became obscured by more egocentric motives. His ability to act in a situation of tragedy gave him a sense of heroism and excitement. However, when the police arrived his father took over and sent him away, thus depriving him of his glory and belittling him. The family seemed to have settled its own guilt by repeating to Fred that he could have saved his cousin by going to see him earlier that evening. They also felt that since he was Fred's friend, Fred should have been able to detect signs of unhappiness and thus avert the suicide. Fred accepted their interpretations partially because they made him feel important in that he could have prevented the tragedy. In later years the tragic death of his cousin became a painful reminder of the transitory nature of existence and the finality of death, adding to his own feeling of futility and hopelessness. Finally Fred identified with his cousin, equating the latter's extreme act as an outgrowth of their similar backgrounds and resulting unhappiness.

One year later Fred's father underwent a hernia repair and spent a prolonged convalescence at home. To his surprise, Fred found his father to be cowardly toward pain and surgery, and to behave in a demanding and infantile manner. He had trouble integrating the experience of his father crying and moaning with the former view of him as a stoic hero. Fred finally rationalized that his father was delirious or simply not himself and promptly forgot these events until the memory was revived in therapy.

Fred completed high school at age eighteen and went to a New York City college, primarily because his father wanted him to go. Fred had little desire to get a college education and had no special interests in scholarship. From the first day at the university, he felt terribly afraid and apprehensive but could not share his feelings at home for fear of ridicule. He had trouble concentrating and studying, and had to reread his assignments many times. In class he feared being called upon and facing ridicule. Even when he knew the correct answers, he never volunteered them for fear of blurting out something he did not mean to say. He also became afraid of his teachers, who were predominantly male and did not approach the class in the solicitous way his high school teachers had done; they were more businesslike and detached, and Fred simply could not win them over with good behavior.

He made no friends in college, nor did he try to. After classes Fred returned home immediately, feeling anxious and exhausted. Usually he slept through the day and at night struggled with his homework. University life was a terrible ordeal from which he retreated at every opportunity.

His one outlet during these years was that he began dating the daughter of family friends. It was significant that Fred did not especially like her or even attempt to get close to her, but she did go out with him weekly for about two years. The fact of having a girl friend for social appearances at least, and the security of having a date each weekend, were an important boost to his self-esteem. It became apparent in therapy that Fred actually knew very little about this girl and had never tried to see her as an autonomous person. Their dates consisted of going to the movies where there could be little communication, or going out in a group which also prevented any real contact. In retrospect Fred described her as being equally cold and uninterested. Very possibly she had used Fred for similar social reasons. She eventually stopped going out with him.

Other attempts at social life consisted of going to local dances with his cousins and friends in an effort to pick up some girls. They never did, and merely spent the evening standing around making comments to each other, winding up criticizing the dance and the girls over a soda. One night they were accosted by a prostitute who offered to perform fellatio on them for payment. Fred went along with his friends and was able to reach orgasm. However, he was so worried about his performance that he felt almost nothing and was relieved when it was over. The prostitute seemed to take a liking to Fred; she asked him to return by himself and she would offer her services gratis. After a great deal of deliberation, Fred did return but was impotent. This time he talked to her for a while, and the more he got to know her, the less aroused he felt. He also wished that his friends were there, sudenly feeling shy and withdrawn being alone with a sexual partner. The previous time he had seen himself as proving his masculinity and simply being one of the boys. The idea of an individual relationship seemed to prevent sexual performance. Although greatly embarrassed by his failure, Fred rationalized it by alternately telling himself that he had felt sorry for the poor woman, or that she was "just a dirty whore" who for that reason had turned him off.

In his senior year at school, Fred went to see the university clinic psychiatrist. He could no longer rationalize his limitations: classes were more and more terrifying, his grades were barely average, his girl friend had stopped seeing him, he was continuously paralyzed by anxiety, and he suffered periods of depression and hopelessness. Fred was very disappointed by this first therapeutic encounter. He found the therapist to be cold and aloof, and either bored or eager to get rid of him; Fred was convinced that the therapist didn't like him. In any event, the therapist did not treat Fred the way he wanted to be treated and after two months Fred discontinued therapy.

The final year of college was one of the worst times of Fred's life. He did very poorly scholastically and barely graduated with a C average.

He had selected psychology as his major in the hope of getting some insight into himself but actually found himself developing the symptoms he read about, eventually deciding that he was schizophrenic. This diagnosis was certified by his failure in therapy: he believed that the therapist had brushed him aside because he was incurably sick and beyond help.

Although there was much family fanfare when Fred graduated, he felt little elation and realized that he had no idea about what he wanted to do with his life. His father suggested that he try for junior executive training in a department store and Fred did manage to get through an interview for the job. The actual work proved too anxiety-provoking and he quit after a few weeks. He found work to be a repetition of his college experience; he was frightened of his boss, rarely spoke to anyone, and had difficulty concentrating. He tried another store and resolved to stick it out, but he was so incompetent because of his anxiety that they had to let him go. Fred then decided to join the Marines as a solution to all his problems. He felt that they would make a man of him and teach him how to be tough. His family of course refused to let him enlist and suggested that he wait and try another job. It was signifiacnt that the father seemed content to let his son do very little and merely play the college graduate. It may have been that Fred had fulfilled his role as far as the father was concerned; or that the father, who was far from stupid, realized his son's problems and did not want to push him.

Fred was relieved of making his decision to join the Marines when his father suffered his heart attack and Fred had to work full-time in the store. As stated previously, he was allowed no true responsibility and neither did he ask for any. When the father returned to work, Fred found himself performing the identical duties as he had when he was thirteen years old.

This was the current situation when Fred presented himself for treatment five months later. In that time, he had become increasingly depressed and anxious, feeling himself trapped and helpless. Fred resentfully spent his few hours a day in the store and then retreated to his room where he lost himself either in fantasies or in watching TV.

Treatment

With the exception of specific interruptions which will be noted, Fred was seen two to three times weekly for three years. During the three years of therapy, Fred never missed an appointment without giving advance notice and a good excuse. Lateness or financial arrangements never were a problem. He was seen sitting up rather than on the couch. The first few sessions consisted of obtaining a detailed history, following which the basic analytic rules were explained.

The initial history taking in itself proved difficult, because Fred would take every opportunity to dwell on his numerous complaints. He obsessively ruminated on every area of his functioning which was slightly impaired—his memory blocks, his poor concentration, his insomnia, and his minor physical symptoms. Following each mention of his suffering, he regularly apologized for complaining and stated that he detested himself for being such an "old woman." These barrages of self-centered misery were communicated with an air of urgency and despair, as if to elicit immediate reassurances. He asked if I had seen other patients with similar symptoms and whether they had recovered. He seemed upset by my failure to be impressed with his symptomatology and for the next few sessions he went into long explanations of his feelings of helplessness and inadequacy. He described his pitiful social condition—lack of friends, lack of dates, lack of a career—with the same urgent and pleading quality, often pausing as if waiting for me to say something. However, I made no comment other than to ask what he was thinking of during silences and showing him customary politeness. My attitude was friendly and respectful but neither indulgent nor reassuring. During this time Fred also would stare at my face, perhaps attempting to get a clue from my reactions as to what to say. He was overly polite and considerate, saying that he must be boring and depressing me; and he often commented on how I must be feeling or what I must be thinking about him.

At this time Fred reported a dream in which he was on a cold, barren road which offered no protection and where he felt himself to be on exhibition. I interpreted the dream as symbolic of the therapy, that he felt exposed and without support. However, I also indicated that the dream appeared to indicate he could not utilize his usual manipulations, which was fine, since all that was asked of him in therapy at this time was that he be open and honest and not resort to his usual subterfuges. Furthermore, the dream seemed to indicate that he saw himself as helpless in a cold, barren world, a view which was a distortion of both his own abilities and the nature of society. This distorted view coincided with his father's own perspective which Fred had learned to duplicate for himself. I also mentioned that being without his usual machinations allowed him a rare opportunity to be truly free and genuine. Fred countered that I was cold and indifferent and he had trouble expressing himself to someone who was so unsympathetic. I got the feeling that he wanted me to react in the same manner as his overprotective father. When I refused to comply with this request, he reported a series of dreams whose manifest symbols were taken from TV programs and consisted of being pursued by Gestapo officers or Mafia gangsters. I interpreted these dreams to have reference to me as the pursuer and asked why he felt I was after him when in reality I had simply kept silent. He then complained that I must dislike him because I had not shown him the concern he expected from a doctor. He made associations to his father and continued talking about his involvement with his father, a theme which recurred again and again. He essentially blamed his father for his present state. Fred believed that his father had not kept his promise of giving him a pleasant life. At other times he stated that if his father had not gotten sick and he had been allowed to join the Marine Corps, he would have been all right. His condemnation of his father had a demanding, expectant quality as if to enlist my support against the father. It became obvious that Fred could in no way conceive of himself as actively changing his life situation and he somehow expected his fate to be altered by someone else. It seemed as though he had no conception of himself as capable of assertive action; rather, he hoped that by passive cajoling he could induce someone who would take over control of his life by replacing the father.

In the third month of therapy, Fred reported a surprising experience: on the way to a dance where he hoped to meet some girls, he inadvertently got into an accident and slightly damaged his father's car. He suddenly felt jubilant and managed to ask a girl to dance without the usual anxiety. In the subsequent session he related his euphoria to damaging something of his father's with bewilderment, but then he remembered an incident in which he had gone to park with his old girl friend one night, determined to try and neck with her. Unexpectedly his father came by in his truck and ordered the patient to take the girl home and then return home himself immediately. Apparently Fred's parents had become worried when he didn't return at a customary hour and his father had gone out looking for him. Fred felt furious and embarrassed, but obediently took the girl home. His rage turned into guilt, however, when his parents reproached him with having worried them and the girl's parents by staying out so late. In the session his anger returned and was freely expressed when he saw the incident in a more realistic perspective. I suggested that damaging the car in some way made him feel he was striking back at his father and thus made him feel vindicated and assertive. Unfortunately, Fred utilized this interpretation in the service of submitting to what he felt were my wishes rather than toward any real attempt at autonomy. He began to praise me and the analysis for "freeing" him, and in future sessions he continued to compare me favorably with his father. He reported feeling better and became even more courteous, but in an inappropriately chummy way. I then interpreted that he was angry with me for not being able to establish the type of relationship that he desired. Fred disagreed, stating that he was perfectly happy with therapy and that he could "take" any sort of treatment. He felt that even by rejecting him, I was merely testing him.

I then began interpreting bits of behavior as they appeared in the sessions as his attempt to gain reassurance from me. This tactic produced the following dream, which unfortunately I did not properly appreciate at the time. Fred dreamt that he was standing on the street with another man who was known to be a ladies' man. An attractive girl walked by and Fred pleasantly anticipated that the man would say something admiring and clever. Instead the man ignored the girl, causing Fred to feel letdown and depressed.

In retrospect this dream indicates Fred's wish to attract the therapist by posing as a seductive woman, and his anticipation of some pleasing comment from me. Thus in the dream Fred has the girl pass by, but I do not take the bait and he feels letdown, much as his waking reaction during the sessions. The dream also shows the deceptive aspect of the passive-feminine persona, in that the real Fred is standing aside waiting to see what happens. A probable confirmation of this interpretation, also appreciated only in retrospect, was that Fred's associations to the dream centered on his father's ideas of women, thus suggesting the origin of the passive-feminine facade. In the dream he may have been saying, "This is the way my father likes me; how would Dr. Bemporad like me to be? I see I cannot please him by being feminine (passive)."

Instead of pursuing this line of inquiry, however, I asked Fred how he felt about girls. This question provoked visible anxiety and caught him off-guard. He offered a standard reply that he liked girls, and blamed his symptoms for preventing him from having an adequate sexual life. He spoke of his symptoms as if they were completely alien and not related to him in any way. This led to a discussion of the nature of his symptoms, stressing the following points: his symptoms were a part of his personality and thus an essential aspect of himself, and they often occurred when he was about to do something on his own or when he was close to someone of the opposite sex. Thus, despite his assurances that he desired autonomy and sexuality, part of him found such enterprises unpleasant or dangerous. This interchange was geared to impress on Fred that he had a role in the development of his problems and the solution for them resided within himself. These interpretations provoked the following dream:

I am in a house. There is a monster threatening everyone and everyone is afraid. The monster looks like a blob in a science fiction movie. I am running away but feel there is no defense against it. Then the monster comes up to the window and I see it is a huge bed mattress that is ripping apart and growing enormously. I feel I have to sew it up. I get a needle and thread and start sewing it up. My family looks at me proudly.

On the day of the dream Fred had seen an ad for the movie, *The Conjugal Bed*, which was probably the stimulus for the mattress symbol. Another association was "sew up your fly," which he remembered from childhood. The dream was interpreted as Fred's fear of his own sexuality which he saw as a monster, and which he kept in control to the applause of his family by somewhat feminine behavior (that is, sewing brought to mind "women's work"). It was during this session that Fred related the incident when he was impotent with the prostitute. This gave me the opportunity to stress further that his restraint and inhibition were within him, and could not be blamed on his situation or environment. Fred confirmed his understanding of this by confessing that he often became anxious even while masturbating, when obviously there was no one else involved.

I believe that this session was pivotal in the analysis because Fred finally begin to realize that he had something to do with his symptoms and the responsibility for improvement was his own. He realized that his sexual problems could be resolved only by a change within himself rather than by altering his relationship with his father or pleasing me. He was beginning to be "engaged" in therapy.

Fred had a mixed reaction to this feeling of self-determination. He was elated that he actually could do something to help himself, but he was equally frightened of the possibility of acting on his own or of asserting himself merely for himself. The latter feeling went beyond a simple fear of action; Fred had trouble conceptualizing himself as a separate entity that existed for himself and not for someone else. His entire life had been directed at obtaining gratification and meaning from others; and the fact that he could be self-sufficient was frightening, especially since he was totally unable to achieve satisfaction autonomously. He believed it safer to remain passive and lead a reactive life to some dominant father figure who would guarantee gratification. To my suggestions that he begin to see himself as a separate person, which in retrospect were probably premature, Fred responded with dreams in which a car got demolished (loss of control) or of being on a beach and wanting to go swimming, but fearing the presence of sharks in the water (fear of retaliation for pleasure). As a result of my prodding, he became anxious during and before the sessions. Again he began complaining of his numerous symptoms, and he accused me of not understanding his terrible position in life as well as of making him upset by being unsympathetic and cold. I countered that I was making him anxious by confronting him with the possibility for change and action; I suggested that we examine the reasons why change was so fearful to him. He replied that he was too helpless and inadequate. He told me that he recently had gone back to his university campus and while there had become depressed because he realized he had wasted his college years and now it was too late to do anything. I countered this pessimism with my feeling that he almost enjoyed a romanticized fatalism because it was a most convenient facade for hiding other wishes which he did not want to acknowledge, and I used his elation at damaging his father's car as a concrete example. I interpreted his self-imposed abstinence as a defense to sexual strivings, and his innocence and passivity as a reaction formation to powerful and unpleasant desires for vindictive behavior. Fred denied any underlying motives beyond his feeling of having been cheated by life.

In the ensuing sessions, however, he began to degrade his father brutally for having crippled him and prevented his individuation. This hostility, however, was expressed with vehemence and pressure of speech, and it seemed more genuine than manipulative. I agreed that he had developed a hostile-dependent relationship with his father but also confronted him with his wanting to reestablish the same sort of relationship with me and most probably with others, again in an effort to point out his own role in his neurosis. Although sympathetic with his past helplessness as a child, I could not encourage the perpetuation of this infantile relationship in a mature individual. I again suggested that he had learned to present himself in a harmlessly passive manner in order to hide his true feelings from others which, if expressed, could have resulted in punishment. Fred then recounted his worries about his father which perhaps were motivated by an inadmissible wish for the father's destruction. Some of his concern seemed reasonable in that his father had suffered a heart attack, but some of it was clearly irrational. The dynamics at the time seemed to be:

1. a wish to destroy the father as a means to freedom and gratification,
2. a simultaneous fear that the wish might be realized and thus leave Fred helpless and alone, leading to
3. overconcern as well as resentment toward the father.

The hated figure was also the needed figure, which gave rise to the ambivalent relationship with his father and all subsequent authorities. He needed their support and yet felt suffocated by them. Intertwined with these dynamics was his overestimation of individual assertion, believing that any action on his part would result in the destruction of himself and others.

This last point was clearly illustrated in a dream reported at this stage of the analysis. Fred dreamt that he was in an airplane that was about to take off. Fred felt terrified and wanted the plane to remain on the ground, but it took off anyway. He then feared that the plane would crash into his father's store; but he discovered that if he concentrated with great effort, he could keep the plane floating in mid-air. This work of concentrating was terribly exhausting but he had to keep it up in order to avert the crash. He awoke feeling depressed and exhausted. The dream revived many childhood memories centering on Fred's fear of upsetting his father or of somehow doing something which his father would disparage and thus make him feel ashamed. He related how his every move as a child seemed to be crucial to his father. Fred complained that even now he could not look sad or unhappy at home without his father's immediately asking him what the matter was, and Fred having to assure his father that everything was all right. As a result of his father's overconcern, to which his mother also contributed by reprimanding him with "That will break your father's heart," he developed a greatly exaggerated picture of his own power to affect others and a fear of acting spontaneously lest he destroy them with alleged inflated aggression. The hostility in the dream could not be ignored. Fred wished to destroy the suffocating father but was equally terrified of doing so. I further interpreted the dream as expressing his anger at the father's dictates within him, rather than at the flesh-and-blood father. I stressed that it was the introjected values of the father, and thus Fred himself, which was the true cause of his present inhibitions. To blame his father at this time would be simply another denial of his own responsibility for change.

This was the status of the analysis in February 1965, when Fred called me unexpectedly and told me that his father had suffered a second myocardial infarction and had been taken to the hospital. I expected the worst and feared that Fred might break down upon seeing his hostile wishes fulfilled in reality. However, Fred took his father's illness rather well, probably as a result of two factors: his father was soon out of any real danger; and Fred was forced by circumstances to take complete charge of the store, which necessitated working ten to twelve hours a day. In this time of emergency he felt himself useful and equal to his father for the first time in his life. This schedule continued for about three months because his father suffered the complication of a pulmonary embolus which prolonged his hospital stay. During this time Fred was unable to come for regular sessions and I saw him infrequently. No real analytic work was attempted, and we talked predominantly about reality problems.

Fred at first felt very proud of being able to take over the business, but rapidly began complaining of being overworked and exploited. There was little chance of his quitting, however, in that he quite realistically was keeping the business going with the help of his uncles. During this period of real need his symptoms diminished, and he did not complain of decreased concentration or confusion. As his father recovered, the old status quo resumed: the father once again ran the store from his bedside and Fred followed orders. This time Fred was allowed to wait on customers but his father refused to let him take any responsibility regarding the financial aspects of the business. Fred found himself being a ten-hour-a day unpaid clerk, and his burst of enthusiasm at his initial responsibility turned to resentment and depression. An important change in Fred's attitude at this time was his realization that being a clerk was as far as his father was willing to allow him to go, and that his father, despite his earlier promises, would never tolerate a competitive, egalitarian relationship.

It was during the absence of his father that Fred reported his first manifestly sexual dream: "My sister fell into the water from some high place. I dove in after her and gave her artificial respiration. But I found myself overdoing it." The day of the dream he had walked in on his sister while she was changing clothes. He realized the sexual overtones of the dream and equated resuscitation with intercourse. I suggested that he had taken advantage of his father's absence to allow himself to experience some sexual feelings and perhaps also some revived sexual wishes toward his sister which had been repressed for fear of being punished by the father. This was the extent of the interpretation at the time, except to point out again that he had numerous feelings and wishes which he did not like to acknowledge but which were part of him nonetheless.

The father returned home in April and in a month's time was able to work part-time. Regular twice-weekly sessions were resumed in May 1965. At the first session, Fred came in openly angry. He had gotten into an argument with a customer and during the argument his father came into the store and sent Fred away. He felt humiliated, especially since his father was not supposed to get excited due to his cardiac status. Nevertheless Fred left and quietly went home. Later he pouted around his father, who sort of apologized but told Fred that he simply didn't know customers as well as he did, implying that Fred could not hold his own in the store. I utilized this episode and Fred's current mode to revive the whole discussion of his self-inhibition and his fear of his father, as well as of his desire to compete and assert himself against his father. Fred confessed that a few years previously he would have decided that his father was correct, and in fact would have been secretly relieved to get out of an unpleasant situation. Now Fred vowed with much dramatic bravado never again to be submissive. He reported the following dream in the next session: "I am with a girl and we are looking for a place to have intercourse. We find a room in a hospital and I draw a curtain so that we can be alone. I feel that someone is watching us and I become frightened. It all seems very new to me. Then the fear changes to pleasure and I feel aroused." The hospital brought to mind his fathers' hospitalization. Fred remembered being momentarily aroused by seeing some semi-clad female patients when he went to visit his father. The fear of being observed revived the memory of some sort of sexual play with his sister, mentioned earlier. He further associated to this memory the crystallization of his present attitudes toward sex as something shameful and repugnant. He felt that his father would be more disappointed than angry if he caught Fred having relations with a woman. Sex was somehow related to exploitation of women and was repugnant with someone for whom one cared. Fred realized that his beliefs were irrational, but he believed them nonetheless.

I tentatively suggested that his views of sexuality might be colored by incest wishes, noting the dream in which he was giving artificial respiration to his sister and the recent memory of childhood sex play; but Fred felt that even if his experience with his sister was the genesis of his feelings, it was his father's prudish attitude which had been really decisive.

He then related his father's tirades against his sister when she wanted to go out and his almost paranoid suspicion that someone would take advantage of her. The session ended with a discussion of the following themes: sibling sexual wishes are not uncommon; especially in view of his past and present restrictions in terms of extra-familial contact, he would be more prone to be aroused by family members since he didn't really know anyone else; and the dream represented his wish to show his father that he could have sexual relations as well as his fear that his father would discover Fred as a "genital" male.

The theme of sexuality was continued to the next session in which Fred reported the following dream: "A woman came into the store. I tried to sell her apples but she walked out. I said to my helper that I was going to sell her apples anyway and I go out after her. I catch up to her on the street and she coldly tells me she doesn't want any apples. I get furious and explode. I say, 'What kind of gratitude is this.'" Fred's associations were concerned with his fear of sexuality, and his terror of being ridiculed by a woman if he approached her sexually. He related that on dates he would try to blot out sexual feelings, and when he did kiss a girl he would find his mind wandering and thinking about something else. On the day of the dream a woman had come into the store and flirted with Fred. The helper started teasing him after she left, saying that he had missed a golden opportunity. That night Fred fantasied having sexual relations with the woman and became depressed because he felt that in real life he was too cowardly ever to attempt anything. The apples reminded him of opportunity, but also of "Adam and Eve, the snake with the apple, something deceptive and sexy, feminine deception." He then talked about how some women were coy and flirtatious and that "you never know where you stand with them."

At this point I believed that the woman in the dream represented Fred's feminine facade, especially since apples brought feminine deception to mind. The dream thus would mean that his passive-feminine role was not paying off, despite all he had sacrificed in becoming that facade. However, Fred then began talking about how many older women who were widowed or divorced came to the store, and how his helper would joke about their having "hot pants" and that Fred should "set himself up with one," because older women were "grateful."

I remarked that in his dream the woman was not grateful, that somehow she should have appreciated his deception (apples). I asked Fred what woman in his life he felt should be grateful to him. He uneasily replied that no one should be grateful to him since he had done everything for his father. Then he reflected, and said that possibly his mother had used him against his father and he had often protected her by mollifying his father. He immediately retracted this suspicion, saying that his mother was completely innocent and really too simple to be of any significance. He said she was the family pet and said that her nickname was "cutie" although he never called her that. I asked why he never did and Fred self-righteously added, "Because she's my mother . . . it wouldn't be right . . . especially when other people are around." I asked if there was something about his feelings regarding his mother that he didn't want other people to know. Fred replied again self-righteously that he had no feelings to be ashamed of and he always had felt very positively toward her. He seemed to imply that by insinuating he had mixed feeling about his mother, I was guilty of some sort of sacrilege. Nevertheless I interpreted his dream as representing anger at his mother for not having appreciated his "sacrifice" of assertiveness in order to protect her from his father. He had in the dream expected some sort of quasi-sexual reward from the woman, but instead she wants no part of the apples. Thus the dream, stimulated by his frustration over his supposed inferiority with women as well as by the sexual content of the previous sessions, may be interpreted as follows: Fred originally adopted a feminine facade in an attempt to please and obtain love from his mother, but this adaptation backfired and Fred found that his mother—and women in general—wanted no part of his passive-feminine personality. The dream ends with the assertion that older women, like his mother, are not really grateful.

The dream may also be interpreted along more classical themes, and be seen as Fred's attempt to tell the therapist that he was really not capable of attracting women and so should not be punished by the therapist father. Flirting with his customer and the teasing of his helper may have revived Oedipal fears against which Fred needed to reassure himself by proving his unattractiveness.

According to either interpretation, the moment seemed opportune to explore Fred's feelings toward his mother. I tried to do just that and met implacable resistance. In the next series of sessions Fred again began complaining about his work at the store and even brought up his symptoms again. I repeatedly tried to discuss his feelings about his mother but he dismissed them by giving the usual noncommittal response that he had already told me all there was to say about her.

The therapeutic relationship at this time could be described as my insistence that he was resisting and refusing to acknowledge feelings, with Fred sensing that he was disappointing me and becoming anxious about displeasing me. For example, he attempted to "please me" during this time by making some realistic gains, such as insisting that his father give him a regular salary after he had procrastinated about this for months. Although this action was a decided step forward, it was done in the spirit of placating me rather than for healthy motives. He also began criticizing his father again with the definite implication that he preferred me to him.

Having encountered stubborn resistance, I decided to try and examine the transference again in the hope of stimulating new material. Therefore I brought up the subject of his feelings about therapy. He responded enthusiastically, saying that therapy was helping him and he felt he had made great strides. I frankly pointed out that aside from some sympto- matic relief, his problems had changed little after a year of therapy and possibly he was obtaining some gratification by keeping things at the status quo. Fred responded by telling me his troubles were so severe that treatment would take a long time and he was very content with his progress. He added that he looked forward to his sessions and they were the high points of his week. Rather than responding with gratitude, I commented that the purpose of therapy was to improve his life *outside* the office, and I bluntly suggested that he liked therapy not because he was getting any better, but because he had found someone who could replace his father in directing his life and offer him the feeling that he was loved and significant.

During the next few weeks, I continued to examine the therapeutic relationship and to attack the transference directly. The picture that evolved can be characterized as a bargain relationship in which Fred agreed to do whatever he felt I wanted him to do, if in return I would praise him and offer him nurturance, or at any rate continue the relation- ship. What impressed me at this time was Fred's pathetic dependence on others for gratification and meaning. As mentioned, he was totally unable to achieve satisfaction from his own actions but had to rely on someone else whom he clothed with unrealistic importance to supply his life with significance. He was terrified of any type of autonomous pleasure or asser- tion and only knew how to put himself passively in a situation in which he could win the praise of a significant other. I carefully interpreted this to Fred and told him that in reality he did not want to change but merely to perpetuate in therapy the dependent relationship he had formed with his father.

Following this interpretation, Fred had a dream in which I was giving and supportive, and in which I repeated almost verbatim what I had said during the session. Although supposedly a confirmation of my interpre- tation, I felt that the dream was a gift; that is, further evidence of his submissive acceptance rather than any real conviction for change on his part. I believed that the dream was a smoke screen intended to reassure me and to prevent him from doing anything for himself.

A few sessions later Fred confessed to having had the fantasy that I would secretly call his father and arrange things with him so he would change in regard to Fred, and together we would help Fred start on a career and even get him a girl friend. Fred had hoped to make this wish a reality by his constant complaints about his father, feeling that this would provoke me to action. With this fantasy, Fred's resistance to change and his fear of responsibility and activity were fully out in the open and became the central theme of many subsequent sessions.

During this examination of the transference and resistance, Fred ad- mitted that he actively sought out clues at the beginning of each session as to what he should talk about so that I would be satisfied with the session. He said that he felt depressed and frustrated when he was unable to get me to respond in a happy, reassuring manner. The genesis of the transference was again related to his relationship with his father. I tried to impress upon him that he was now independent and responsible only to himself. At this point Fred bought himself a tape recorder. This was actually a notable event, being the first thing he had ever purhcased for himself.

The next few months of therapy were spent on working through aspects of Fred's self-inhibitions and restrictions. Fred would attempt some change in his everyday life which then aroused feelings which in turn were discussed in therapy, resulting in further motivation for change and more material for analysis. For example, Fred tried to get dates through his sister and friends and even attended a party or two. He found himself becoming very anxious at social occasions and brought this up in therapy, where his feelings of competition and his desires to dominate others were explored. He then attended another party and sensed that he wanted to be the center of attention and at the same time he was afraid to be noticed. At another time he found himself trying to copy his father's authoritarian manner with others, and in therapy realized that his was one way of reassuring himself against feelings of inferiority and inadequacy. Out of these interchanges evolved Fred's secret ideal of being a replica of his father, which he had hidden beneath his passive-submissive facade. I tried to show him that either role—superman or infant—was bound to result in frustration and illness.

Eventually Fred started dating sporadically. He went through a period of deconditioning and had to withstand much anxiety before finally feeling somewhat comfortable with women. Around January 1966, he reported having met a girl, Frances, whom he "really liked." He was hesitant about asking her out, however, because he feared that she would reject him or that if she began to like him he would dominate her the way his father had dominated his mother. Despite his hesitations Fred did ask the girl out and continued to date her, although he often felt apprehensive. During this same time Fred continued to complain about the store and his irritation with his father. In the midst of a tirade against the father, he blurted out, "I resent my mother too. Why the hell doesn't she stand up to him for once. Why do I always have to be in the middle." I felt that this was an opportunity to revive the whole theme of his feelings toward his mother which he had resisted the summer before, and I mentioned that this was the first time I had ever heard him say anything derogatory about his mother. Fred replied that recently he had noticed that whenever he was about to go out on a date his mother would pull him aside and begin complaining to him about her life with her husband. This did not occur every time but frequently enough to make him suspicious that somehow his mother wanted to ruin his evening out by making him feel guilty. Her complaining had been so successful that on a few occasions Fred was tempted to return home, feeling he should be there in order to protect her from his father or at least to make her happy. When I asked why his mother should suddenly start acting in such a manner, Fred speculated that in recent weeks, between the store and going out at night, he was rarely home and his mother missed talking and confiding in him. He then commented, as if it were a sudden realization, that over the years he had spent most of his time at home with his mother and she had confided in him and somehow used him to "get things off her chest." I reminded Fred of the "gratitude" dream and his reluctance to talk about his mother, suggesting that he must have many feelings about her that he did not wish to acknowledge. I hoped that the therapeutic relationship had been sufficiently clarified and that his recent social improvement might encourage him to start exploring his feelings about his mother, but Fred still felt empty and uncommunicative about her.

A few weeks later Fred double-dated with friends and was sitting in the back seat of their car necking with Frances, when he became very anxious and felt himself depersonalizing. He returned home depressed and angry with himself and had the following dream: "I am in the back seat of a car driven by a chauffeur with a very made-up and pretty girl. We are looking for a place to park but every place is crowded. In the dream I am also a girl and we are anxious to touch each other. She touches my breasts and I enjoy it very much, but feel it's wrong." He reluctantly admitted that the girl reminded him of his mother when she got dressed up. He also felt embarrassed that he was a girl in the dream. The chauffeur seemed surprisingly silent but knew where he was going and Fred felt he trusted him. The dream seemed to take place at night and everything was lit up as in Times Square. This reminded Fred of lurid, forbidden sex. The most vivid aspects of the dream were the pleasure he felt and his confusion: "I was anxious for her to touch me but knew it was wrong: I kept saying to myself, 'How come I'm a woman?' but felt good while she was touching me but confused because I wasn't supposed to be a woman. I felt like how did I get this body, how come I have breasts?" Fred continued, saying that he often felt like a woman in real life, being unmanly and passive. In the dream it seemed important for him to be that way in order to get the woman to fondle him. I interpreted this to mean Fred had accepted a passive, castrated role in order to get love from his mother, and that perhaps she had seduced him into being daddy's little boy. I reiterated the earlier session in which he had talked about having to stay home to protect his mother from his father. His passivity was evident in that he would protect her not by standing up to his father, but by pleading her case, offering himself to his father and thereby renewing the neurotic bargain relationship. Fred responded by remembering episodes in which he wished he could have been a girl like his sister so that he also could have been left alone the way she was: "She never had to do anything, she could just be herself."

The interpretation of this dream continued over to the next session and the additional themes may be summarized here. The chauffeur stimulated a memory from age six or seven. Fred was in the back seat of the family car with his mother, and his father was driving. They were going to some family gathering and Fred had some schoolwork to do which he had brought along. He was trying to study but his father kept singing or shouting and he couldn't concentrate. Fred appealed to his mother to ask him to be quiet but she told him to study later and not to disturb his father. She gave him a hug as if to show him that she understood his frustration but she had resigned herself to submitting to her husband. In the dream the chauffeur was "strangely silent," meaning that as long as Fred kept up his feminine facade, his father would not interfere: Fred could form an alliance with the mother and enjoy forbidden gratification. On the other hand, the chauffeur also may have been the analyst who was guiding Fred through therapy. This interpretation of the dream allowed for a reexamination of the transference. Fred still was in the back seat, pretending to be a woman and not accepting an active role in his own treatment.

The stimulus for the dream appeared to be in my reviving his feeling about his mother and the experience with Frances, when he found himself confronted by a woman whom he liked and who was eager to have him take the initiative sexually. His inability to perform without depersonalizing aroused the whole Oedipal conflict, as well as his particular solution.

This dream is presented in detail because it illustrates some of the dynamics behind Fred's problems and indicates how his present personality evolved. A good part of the spring of 1966 was spent applying the general themes revealed in this dream to Fred's everyday behavior. For example, his reluctance to expose his Oedipal wishes in therapy the previous summer may have indicated that he saw me as possibly adopting the role of the punitive father who had to be constantly mollified by submission and dependence. Similarly, Fred's fear of assertion and exposure could be traced to being forced by both parents into a role which best suited their interests rather than his welfare.

Here is an apt example of the depressive's self-imposed anhedonia. He will forego pleasure, sexual or otherwise, in the hope of winning the love of the all-important other. Fred not only feared sexual gratification; he lived an all-encompassing ascetic life. He rarely bought anything for himself, had no hobbies or interests, and took no notice of national events. His curiosity and talents, as well as his ability to derive autonomous gratification, had been severely thwarted in the quest for parental approval.

It is just this childhood blockage of all those things that make life inter-esting and worthwhile that so often leads to the truly barren existence of the adult depressive, and his justified lack of meaning and pleasure in that existence.

Another trait that was examined was Fred's extreme passivity which prevented him from seeing himself as self-determined and capable of actively changing his life. He continued to be guarded and to keep his feelings to himself, afraid to offend others. I attempted to encourage his expression of anger or annoyance in treatment and he eventually man-aged to verbalize some criticism of me and the analysis. This was utilized to work through his great fear of retaliation and his overinflated concept of his effect on others. His continuing relationship with Frances produced a great deal of material for therapy. He still felt himself closing up, he demanded certain reactions from her, he felt he was just playing a role with her. As a result of his experiences with Frances, Fred acknowledged feelings of futility and frustration that he remembered having felt toward his mother, in that he had never really been able to relate to her. Although she was sweet and maternal, she seemed shallow and self-involved. In the course of therapy it became apparent that although she was affectionate, the mother appeared to be threatened by true close involvements and often denied her own feelings towards others. She would confide in Fred and appear to want to get close but when he began to mention his own feelings, she either got silly or suddenly found something else to do.

It took a tremendous effort on Fred's part to establish an honest rela-tionship with Frances. He was afraid that she would respond much as his mother had done and so he resisted showing any weakness or depend-ence. Gradually Fred did tell her about his problems at the store, about his difficulties in college, and eventually about being in therapy. Frances reacted in a supportive yet matter-of-fact manner, as if she understood that people generally have problems and try to overcome them. Her prag-matic attitude, in contrast to Fred's extreme shame and self-pity, was definitely salutary and helped Fred gain some perspective with reference to his past orientation.

Throughout the session, the theme of the father reappeared in various forms. At first Fred had been afraid to do anything lest it displease his father; now with each gain in his everyday life, he experienced not fear but guilt. Once when he was out with Frances and having a good time, he suddenly got the feeling that his father had suffered another heart attack and he should call home immediately. The more Fred asserted or enjoyed himself, the more he believed that something was going to hap-pen to his father: thus he prevented himself from finding gratification in his own activities. The idea of Fred's destroying his father by doing some-thing on his own was illustrated by our discussions about Fred's career choice and future plans. Fred still could not conceive of doing things apart from his father, and he wanted him to share in his eventual success. Any achievement without his father's participation was seen as a betrayal and provoked feelings of guilt and selfishness.

Originally Fred had no idea of what he wanted to do with his life. He knew that he did not want to remain in the store, but the anxiety which was aroused when he thought of leaving caused him to put the whole issue out of his mind. In his fantasies he had often thought of being a policeman, but he knew that this was a neurotic choice which would allow him to express his retaliatory and domineering impulses under the guise of respectability and self-righteousness. He eventually expressed a desire to go into social work or probation work. This choice might have evolved out of an indentification with the therapist, but it was also stimulated by a discussion about his having been stabbed in grade school. He rightly felt that if he and his family had been able to get counseling at that time, much of his present dilemma could have been averted. In the summer of 1966 he took the civil service examination without too much anxiety, and received a passing mark. Shortly after receiving notification of his eligibility for social-service training, he began having fantasies that his father was dying. On one occasion he awoke at night in terror, having dreamt of seeing his father dead in a coffin. Fred realized the irrationality of his feelings but he suffered their impact nonetheless. Some clues as to the underlying causes of this behavior was given in a dream reported at the time.

In the dream, Fred was walking between two women on a beach. They approached a virile-looking man. Fred wanted very much to be admired by the man and was afraid that the man would ignore him and concentrate on the women. Fred felt ashamed of wanting to attract the man but felt equally lost and depressed at not being able to attract him. The man probably represented Fred's father, and the two women were his mother and sister. The conflict in the dream seemed to be whether or not to relinquish the father as a source of gratification. As Fred became more and more independent in his behavior, he felt that he would lose his privileged place in his father's affections, and this revived his old rivalry with his mother and sister. Fred's fantasies of his father's death could be interpreted as the giving up of his father—not as a real person, but as the fulfillment of neurotic desires. The father had become so important in Fred's life as a means to pleasure and satisfaction that he found it difficult to outgrow this avenue of gratification. Fred wanted to be both assertive and independent while still being able to enjoy his father's support and coddling. To give up the father meant to give up a whole approach to pleasure that had taken years to formulate. Thus the psychic death of the father was terrifying.

The fantasy of his father's death had other causes to which I have alluded, such as his overestimation of his effect on others and the growing awareness of his competition with his father. However, the major dynamic at this time seemed to be his reluctance to break off the bargain relationship. Over the course of the next few months, this general theme recurred again and again. Here Fred experienced the deprivation depression discussed in chapter 13. By being forced to relinquish his mode of being for others, Fred felt lost and unhappy. He experienced a revival of his depression although he knew he had to extricate himself from his pathological ties, whatever the emotional cost. He was truly miserable, unable to find a meaning for his activities or a purpose in his life. This transitional period reflected the abandonment of the dominant other before the self could begin to take over the functions formerly fulfilled by the dominant other. He felt that he alone was responsible for his father's well-being and happiness, and this feeling paralyzed his efforts to do anything for himself. Fred actually experienced a sort of mourning process for the loss of his psychic relationship with his father. He complained of feeling isolated and alone, that there was no purpose in life and nothing to look forward to. The following quotes from various sessions at this time illustrate his depression over giving up the father as a source of gratification and meaning:

I have to keep trying to keep it in my head that he's gone. I get the feeling of being all alone but I don't feel afraid, just very sad.

I know that it won't be so terrible and I'll survive. I'll manage. I know we have to split, that I have to leave him but it's upsetting . . . a large part of me doesn't want to.

I must leave him emotionally. I must change. One day I'll really be without him. I don't like the idea of it.

I actually see him dead in the funeral parlor. It's like in order for me to get well he has to die. I have to lose him. I have to give him up. Not do everything his way.

I keep feeling like I'll never see him again, like when he was on the critical list. I feel like I'm leaving a wounded man in the street. I keep feeling I'm betraying him.

I interpreted quite plainly that he wished to have both his freedom and his dependence but in reality had to choose between them. I interpreted his new depression as due to the loss of dependent gratification and stressed that he had to give up this source of pleasure if he were ever to achieve a sense of emotional freedom.

Fred renewed his efforts to do things despite a good deal of guilt and anxiety. At first he was not too successful, and he was frequently frightened and apprehensive although apparently determined to follow through. His frustration was revealed in a dream about a cat, a type of animal that he considered to be parasitic and lazy. In the dream, he found the cat in his house and gave it some milk, but the cat was not satisfied and demanded more and more. The cat became affectionate in a sneaky and manipulative manner (which reminded him of his old self), but Fred didn't trust him and threw him out of the house. Fred then went back into the house, proud of his accomplishment, only to find the cat there as before. This dream epitomizes the struggle that the patient must go through in order to change. Fred realizes in the dream that he must alter his prior personality patterns. Yet these patterns are so ingrained, so imprinted, that it appears a hopeless task. The patient requires the full support of the therapist at this stage, for a sense that he is not alone in the battle against pathological modes of being.

Over a period of many months, with my encouragement and with support from Frances, Fred did manage to free himself from the image of his father and to find satisfaction in his own efforts. In retrospect, Fred described this time as "having to convince myself that it was all right to be free." Part of his change derived from remembering that his father had exploited the family into feeling responsible for his behavior. The father seems to have blamed the family if anything went wrong, saying that they made him do it. In this manner Fred's whole area of initiative became tinged with doubt and guilt so that it was safer to be rewarded passively and be directed by someone else than to attempt something independently.

Another part of Fred's progress came from his realization that he was not as helpless as he made out, and his supposed inadequacy was a good defense against risk as well as a consequence of his great ambition and expectations. Compared to his secret aspirations, any actual accomplishment was meager and inconsequential. This competitive view of human relations was crystallized in a fragmentary dream of a terrifying totem pole. He could only conceive of society as a hierarchical pecking order in which one was either a master or slave. This vision of the competitive strivings within himself was so horrifying that he preferred to attempt nothing and remain daddy's boy. These tendencies were interpreted in regard to his father, society in general, and the therapeutic situation in which Fred had hoped to reestablish a dependent relationship that would satisfy him and thus relieve him of having to accept responsibility for himself. I was supposed to assure him that he was sick; thus he would not have to do anything.

Fred did not always accept these interpretations gracefully and often accused me of being too rough with him, and of not appreciating his delicate state of mind and unpreparedness for life. However, as he moved out of his secluded family environment and was confronted with people his own age, his competitive strivings as well as his defense against them could no longer be denied. The whole area of social relationships was reviewed again with emphasis on his competitiveness and hostility. This time I related these feelings to the treatment situation, and eventually he was able to verbalize his competitive feelings toward me. In a sense, he no longer needed me as a gratifying father and so was free to express negative feelings.

The factor of experiencing, in the session, feelings that previously he had only been able to describe objectively as happening outside the office was beneficial, especially since I did not retaliate but rather simply tried to clarify his motives and confront him with his behavior. He proudly reported a short time later that when his sister had started getting into a disagreement with their father, Fred had believed she was right and to his own surprise took her side against the father. Fred slowly was able to experience his feelings of anger without anxiety over losing control, or the fear of massive retaliation. In the sessions he became more assertive and less concerned with my reactions. He occasionally was able to free-associate and to give vent to his feelings regardless of their content. This newly developed ability to express anger and disapproval openly was partially due to his realization that he had a right to such feelings, as well as to a lessening of his need to gain constant approval from others. At the same time, this ability reflected that he perceived and evaluated situations more realistically so he no longer had to distort situations in such a way as to minimize the need for anger. Therefore the appearance of anger at this time appears to have resulted from a gradual cognitive restructuring rather than from the redirection of an unconscious affect.

He seemed to be motivated for change and was eager to explore his reactions as they arose. He discussed with his father the possibility of leaving the store, and they agreed that if Fred would work until the summer of 1967, the father could either find a partner or replace him. Fred then made arrangements to be employed by the city at that time. He seemed quite happy and proud about these accomplishments.

Intertwined with the exploration of Fred's competitiveness was the theme of his relationship with Frances which, for the sake of simplification, is presented separately. Frances was a few years Fred's junior and also of Italian descent. She was the third of six siblings and thus, in contrast to Fred's pampered childhood, she grew up as one of several children. She graduated high school and then took a secretarial job.

Fred's relationship with Frances initially was characterized by his attempt to validate himself through her, seeing how she would respond to him, if he could be attractive to her, and so on. At this point he appeared almost unaware of her individuality and she might have represented women in general. Later, Fred continued to have only a narcissistic interest in her. He wanted to see if he could manipulate her into giving him the nurturance and adulation that he desired. At this stage he wanted Frances to be happy not for her own sake, but in order to prove his adequacy: he wanted to give her the pleasure that he felt unable to give his mother and then enjoy her feedback. Throughout this time I never got a real feeling for Frances as a person from Fred. She may well have been simply a mother transference object, or a transitional object in Winnicott's sense (1953).

Once Frances responded warmly to him, his feeings toward her slowly changed. It was as if he had proved himself and now she was no longer a challenge or threat. Fred began talking about her with tenderness and sensitivity as a unique human being. As mentioned previously, she was pragmatic and not excitable. She encouraged Fred to loosen up and she was not frightened of expressing herself. Eventually Fred began comparing her with his sister, Susan, and he expressed guilt over his preferential treatment in childhood. He felt his father had driven Susan out of the house by his lack of consideration and that he himself had totally ignored her. He felt that somehow he wanted to make things up to Susan. The significant factor in this comparison of Frances with his sister was that Fred finally saw women as people with feelings and rights. He opened up to Frances and tried to be as genuine and honest with her as he could, being very careful not to repeat his father's manipulations, which included degrading and dominating women as a way of denying his own dependency needs.

Sexuality presented special problems. In addition to Oedipal fears, Fred had trouble unifying sexuality with tenderness. Much of this conflict was a result of strong cultural attitudes, but much also seemed to have developed as a defense against sexual feelings toward his sister. As this theme was being discussed in therapy, Fred mentioned many of his father's attitudes about sex which the father considered dirty and wicked, representing the typical madonna-prostitute dichotomy of women. Much of this material had been covered previously in therapy but this time Fred was actively involved in a relationship and his experiences were immediate and confirmatory.

In the spring of 1967 they made plans to marry when Fred achieved some financial security, but then they decided not to wait and set a date in June. By then Fred possibly would have a job and they both had put money away. The whole idea of being on his own with responsibilities caused Fred to be both proud and apprehensive. We discussed at length his going with Frances to look at furniture and apartments from the point of view of sharing and mutuality.

At this time he spoke little about his parents and seemed to be free from his family, although he still lived at home and worked in the store. His resentment toward both his parents gradually diminished. When he talked about them, it was with resignation that they would remain the way they were, but they no longer had a great affect on him. At times the father would try and engage Fred in long conversations and Fred would go along with him out of consideration rather than fear. Fred looked forward to the day he would be on his own and with this goal in mind he tried to make his remaining days with his family as smooth as possible.

As his wedding date approached, we talked about separation and responsibility. Fred was interviewed and accepted for training in a career that he desired and he was very pleased that he felt no anxiety during the interview.

He was married in June and when I saw him after his honeymoon, he seemed quite satisfied with his life. After returning home to a small family reception he had the following dream. "The whole family was at a party. We were talking about this big watchdog that died. I felt relieved and felt like who needed him anyway."

The remainder of Fred's therapy concerned itself with discussions of career choice, his ability to decide what he wanted to do with his life, and the responsibility of marriage. Fred became much more determined, self-motivated, and conscientious. He continued his job but also took graduate courses leading to a professional degree. Toward the end of therapy he was more confident and yet open and honest about his limitations. He continued a cordial and undemanding relationship with his parents. To my knowledge, he has not had another depressive episode since his therapy ended over ten years ago.

Discussion

In considering Fred's psychopathology, initial consideration should be given to the social milieu in which his family participated and formed its particular values and distortations. As will be more fully explored in chapter 16, cultural mores influence family values which in turn affect child rearing.

Fred's father was a reaction to his own early poverty and inferiority, and, in time, Fred became a reaction to him. The father needed to have his son succeed as a proof of his own adequacy yet never to allow his son to reach that point of success which could engender independence and open competition. In a sense Fred was to be his father's vindication on what he considered to be a hostile culture. Fred was predestined to become the evidence of his father's worldly success.

Fortunately there is not much in the way of worldly success that can be demanded from a vegetating neonate, and thus Fred's early infancy appears to have been non-traumatic. The mother, who saw herself predominantly as a nurturing mother and dutiful wife, seems to have been able to give generously to a non-threatening infant. She resembled the mothers of depressives described by Cohen et al. (1954) as having "found the child more acceptable and lovable as infants than as children, when the manifold problems of training and acculturation became important."

It was during the emergence from the stage of baby to child, when the organism acquires human rather than animal qualities, that troubles began. The withdrawal of the mother, which might have occurred simply as a result of her own personal vulnerability, was greatly enhanced by the birth of Susan. As alluded to above, the neonate seemed to have elicited greater response from the mother than a semi-autonomous toddler, but the fact that the second-born was a girl caused a family rift that was never really healed: Fred became his father's son and Susan became her mother's daughter. The father's interest was in his heir, while his wife appears to have been willing to relinquish her son but not her daughter. It may be assumed that much of Fred's later pathology was the result of his being "deserted" by his mother and his being taken over by the father. The "car dream" previously described in which Fred is coddled by the mother while playing the role of a woman may indicate his solution to his feeling of deprivation. He may have believed that if he succumbed to his father's wishes and willingly denied himself, he would regain the mother's love. On another level, the dream may represent his envy of his sister who was able to get the mother's affections by simply being a girl. Some of Fred's later resentment may have arisen from a sort of Silverberg's "pattern of the broken promise" (1952), in that despite his sacrifices Fred never really felt reunited with the mother. These early experiences may have accounted, as well, for his later distrust of women and his fear that he could not really satisfy them.

In any event, Fred, at that time, entered into his chronically dependent relationship with his father. He was both pushed by the mother, and drawn by the father who felt that Fred had reached the age when he could begin to fulfill his potential. From that time on Fred was given the role of the family "crown prince" and his every move and behavior carefully scrutinized. It is significant that Fred's autonomy was undermined not by force but by shame and guilt. He was made to feel ashamed of his attempts at gratification rather than simply afraid. In contrast to severely depressed individuals, however, Fred was never told by his parents that he was evil or the cause of their misfortunes. While he required the father's approval for feeling worthwhile, he did not need it to absolve himself of a basic sense of inner badness. Throughout Fred's mild depressions, he felt weak, lazy, hopeless but never vile or malicious, which is usually a manifestation of more severe pathology. In addition, the parents, while misguided and limited, appeared well-meaning and tried to do what they felt was best for their children. They did not openly reject them or degrade them. While inhibiting Fred's sense of effectiveness in the extra familial world, the parents bestowed affection and care (even if in stifling doses) on him. Again, in contrast to severe depressives, Fred never felt himself a burden to his parents in childhood. He was even placed in the role of a favorite although maintenance of this role meant a sacrifice of vital aspects of the self and was also exploited by the mother.

In treatment Fred immediately tried to re-establish passive bargain relationship which rather than allowing him to get well would have afforded him the security of being passively gratified by the therapist.

The working through of this transference relationship and the clarifying of the misconceptions which had originally given rise to it were the major tasks of therapy. Related to this relationship were Fred's fears of self-gratification and his refusal to see himself as self-determined and capable of change. Until he could free himself from his dependency relationship, he could really make little gain toward a more satisfactory way of life. I refused to see him as "someone special," nor did I consider his symptoms or past experiences sufficient to excuse him from responsibility and choice. This process of deconditioning was accompanied, as much as possible, by confrontations of his behavior so that Fred could appreciate his impact on others as well as understand the causes of his present problems as perpetuations of earlier reaction patterns. His life history was utilized in illustrating the origin of his misconceptions as well as defining the genesis of his transference reactions.

In view of the length of this report, I will only briefly mention one additional theme which I have purposely omitted before: the question of Fred's homosexuality. Fred's dreams and his relationship with his father suggest a homosexual identification. Similarly, I have described him as adopting a passive-feminine facade. Despite these data and my terminology, Fred at no time appeared overtly homosexual nor did he ever express an erotic attraction for someone of his sex. He considered women as the only possible object choice and his masturbation fantasies were exclusively heterosexual. Fred *was* extremely passive and dependent on his father. However, passivity and dependence may be insufficient to create homosexuality on any level. It is difficult to determine where passive gratification ends and actual homosexuality begins.

Fred's history illustrates how, through specific childhood experiences, selected unconscious cognitive structures are crystalized and later give rise to psychopathology. Fred's early rejection by the mother, his bargain relationship with the father, his punishment for autonomous gratification, all set the stage for the need of a dominant other and the self-inhibition that predisposes to depression. His ideas of himself, of others, and of the way life should be led caused him to become stagnant in an unhappy circumstance which he felt himself unable to alter. Through psychotherapy these structures were somewhat modified with resultant change in Fred's values and behavior, ultimately leading to an overcoming of his depression and, hopefully, some protection from later depressive episodes in the future.

[15]

PSYCHOTHERAPY OF DEPRESSION

IN CHILDREN AND ADOLESCENTS

The treatment of depression in the pediatric age group must consider the psychopathological symptoms against a framework of the developmental process. The clinical manifestations, causes, and therapeutic options vary greatly with age and one has to be flexible both in terms of understanding the disorder and in the therapeutic course of action. As outlined in chapters 4 and 8, true depression is not seen before late childhood, and even then it is quite rare. In over a dozen years of private practice of child psychiatry as well as of directing a psychiatric division in a large pediatric hospital, I have seen only a handful of prepubertal children who were truly depressed. Many children appeared sad or unhappy, but each was reacting to a readily discernable stress in the environment and had not as yet crystallized modes of interaction or ideas of the self which would perpetuate this sense of unhappiness. In every case, the unpleasant affect responded proportionally to ameliorating the environmental situation. Children with chronic illnesses which have prevented the attainment of age-appropriate satisfaction, or children with chronically punishing and depriving home situations, regularly react with sadness but rarely feel badly about themselves as well. They are upset over having an illness or over being criticized and ignored by parental figures.

Even when there is a sense of self-blame, it is not the same as in the adult depressive. The lowering of self-regard shifts from situation to situation and responds readily to happier surroundings. For example, I have found that many children with learning disabilities believe they are basically inadequate and may be chronically unhappy if they are in a situation in which academic achievement is highly prized. Parents and

This chapter was written by Jules Bemporad.

teachers unconsciously convey the message that they could do better if they only tried harder. Competitive peers also may select these children for teasing and taunting, adding to their sense of being different and inferior. However, these children respond well to a more understanding environment which appreciates their other abilities, and their non-academic capabilities can be utilized therapeutically to build a better sense of self. Often such children are excellent artists, able athletes, or adept mechanics, and these assets are enhanced to balance their frustrations in the academic area. Children with learning disabilities usually find compensatory areas of achievement on their own, without therapy, although all too often these achievements are in the area of delinquency.

This digression into learning disabilities may serve to stress the difference between a child who is unhappy because of some current problem and a child who is depressed. Depression—in my opinion—involves a self-perpetuating pathologic mode of interaction fostered by unconscious cognitive distortions. These distortions are the result of child-parent interactions and result in an excessive need of others for maintaining self-esteem, a self-inhibition from achieving gratification independently of the dictates of significant others, and an unrealistic self-regard in terms of effectiveness. It is not until late childhood that the individual can distort his interrelations so as to repeat older patterns. Before this time, the child simply reacts with unhappiness to a reality situation which is perceived according to age-appropriate cognitive modes. Therapy aims at removing or diminishing the source of frustration, on the one hand, and building or maximizing areas of gratification and esteem, on the other. Therefore, with young children a certain amount of environmental manipulation and family involvement is necessary.

As the child approaches puberty, however, these therapeutic efforts are no longer effective; the child carries within himself the sources of his dissatisfaction and imposes a distorted view of himself and others on his activities. In general parlance, one speaks of problems having been "internalized" and no longer "reactive." Changes in the behavior of others, especially parents, is still of benefit but now individual psychotherapy becomes the treatment of choice. The child should be made aware of his distortions, his tendency to repeat the past, and his own responsibility for his problems within the context of the relationship with the therapist.

In many respects the therapy of depression at this age is similar to that of adult depressives. However, there are some significant differences which should be emphasized. First is the limitation on abstract thinking. In contrast to the adult, the child finds it difficult to utilize verbal interpretations of a general nature and apply these to various areas of his life. Interpretations have to be concrete, specific, and practical. Everything must be put in such a way as to be immediately usable and comprehensible to the child. Similarly, interpretations may not carry over from one session to the next, and much repetition and patience is necessary.

Second, therapy with children should aim at being a developmental experience in itself. There is less reconstructive work than with adults and more of a shared process of growth. Therapy sessions are not considered as separate from other life experiences by children and so the relationship to the therapist is very reality-bound and influential in promoting growth in itself, aside from the content of the sessions. In brief, therapy with children is much less artificial than with adults; for the child, it is a living relationship with another adult and is treated as part of the totality of experience. This implies that the therapist does not spend a great deal of time correcting the child's distortions by verbal interpretations; rather, the therapist demonstrates by his very behavior that he does not accept the child's mistaken estimation of himself and others.

For example, one depressed eleven-year-old boy felt he had to make grades that were beyond his academic capabilities, and he was surprised that the therapist was not dissatisfied when he did not earn an A on his report card. In this manner the child learned that a significant person in his life did not react with anger to his alleged lack of achievement. This utilization of the relationship is much more effective than a verbal interpretation such as "you expect too much of yourself" which might be appropriate for an adult. Children treat therapy as part of life, and respond to actions rather than words.

Since the child is still in a fluid state of development, therapy is often easier and shorter than with adults who have already consolidated modes of thinking about themselves and others. Children change more rapidly once they have begun to trust the therapist and to allow therapy to influence their lives. Therapy is partially a transferential repetition of an earlier child-parent relationship, and partially a new experience which will shape the future psyche of the patient.

However, this advantage is balanced by a strong limitation. Children have less control over their everyday lives and continue to be greatly influenced by other significant adults. In this sense, therapy is rarely effective if the home environment continues to be detrimental to change. The child cannot move out, switch jobs, or make radical changes in his day-to-day life. He is still realistically dependent on the whims of others, and those powerful others quickly can undermine the changes that are laboriously achieved in the office. In undertaking therapy with a child, therefore, one really must deal with the resistances of the family as well as those of the patient. A good working alliance with the parents is needed as well as a therapeutic relationship with the child. Often the parents are well-intentioned but still unconsciously sabotage progress toward health. These automatic reaction patterns must be pointed out so that the parents realize their contribution to the continuation of psychopathology.

One of the potent contributors to child psychopathology, which is rarely mentioned in the clinical literature, is the home atmosphere. This is a vague concept and is difficult to describe accurately, yet it must be considered in the formulation of the factors that influence behavior. The atmosphere in the homes of depressed children is, quite simply, depressing. Sometimes there is a depressed parents or a chronically ill relative. There is a general solemnity and a lack of spontaneity, joy, and laughter. There is a deadly seriousness that contaminates the inner life of all the family members. There is also a stifling network of extreme interdependence in which the psychic welfare of others inordinately becomes the emotional burden of the child. The child feels a sense of disloyalty if he enjoys himself while his parents are so unhappy. He sets himself the task of brightening their lives, a task at which he can never succeed. At other times the child is made to feel that he must devote all his energies to pleasing the parent who withholds love or rewards except for acts of obedience and servitude. Independent behavior or external influences threaten the domination of the parent and are met with guilt-provoking rebukes or belittlement. These families were accurately described by Cohen and her co-workers (1954) in their retrospective studies of adult manic-depressives. (This work has been summarized in chapter 2.) In general, the common thread that runs through families with a depressed child is that the child has been unfairly burdened, at too early an age, to feel responsibility for either the happiness or the aspirations of the family unit.

This situation is most inopportune, for one of the major tasks of late childhood is for the child to establish a sense of worth in the community, apart from his family. If the parents contaminate this autonomous sense of esteem with guilt, or pervert it so that esteem is desired for the family instead of the self, then not only depression but also a significant developmental stasis may result. It is in this sense that developmental tasks must be kept in mind when doing therapy with children. One must constantly be alert not only to the present symptoms, but to the blocks to normal growth that the current situation may be creating within the child. In the older child, a gradual devaluation of the prior inflated importance of the parent as well as turning to extrafamilial figures for self-validation are necessary for normal development. These crucial processes are all too often sabotaged in the life of the depressed child, as well as in the life of the later depressed adult.

This lack of individuation is also prominent in depressed adolescents who, in contrast to children, are not at all rare in clinical practice. These youngsters are bound to the family by ties of guilt and obligation and they are unable to participate fully in activities outside the family circle. While they may do well academically or even socially, they are basically achieving for the family and not for themselves. Hendin (1975) described a group of severely depressed college students who had attempted or contemplated suicide. Hendin found that a close tie to the parent was a central feature of the problems of these individuals. They saw their relationship to their parents as predicated on relinquishing all personal pleasure or freedom. In college they encountered the potential to become free but were threatened by it, for it would sever the needed emotional tie with the parent. Hendin described these students as having been raised to be quiet drones who never showed excitement or pleasure, but who grimly strived for the parental ideal, the achievement of which they felt was their sole purpose in life.

Other adolescents may rebel against the dictates of the parents, often doing themselves harm in the process. They wish to make the parent feel guilty for what he has done to them and so they try to hurt the parent by hurting themselves. In this way they are using the same indirect manner of coercion through guilt that the parents used on them. Despite their self-proclaimed freedom, they are still tied to the parent in an ambivalent and yet needed relationship.

Still others replace the parent with another dominant other and establish a new bargain relationship outside the family circle. These youngsters appear to do well on a superficial level, and it is only after the relationship has either ended or failed to satisfy them that the pathological aspects of the bond become apparent.

Finally, some adolescents experienced childhoods in which they were overly sheltered and not really allowed to develop independent competence in any area. Their sole task was to gratify the dominant parent who expected little beyond obedience. While secure at home, these adolescents feel—and in some aspects are—incapable of facing the demands of life outside the family circle. They collapse in the face of expectations they feel they cannot fulfill, and recoil from strangers who do not accord them the special treatment they believe they deserve.

In doing therapy with depressed adolescents, developmental tasks again must be kept in mind. This is a time of testing the self in society. This process usually starts in late childhood with the child's participation in peer-oriented activities, but it really comes to fruition in adolescence. At this time the youngster encounters intimate relationship with nonfamily members. He begins cognitively to consider alternate systems of values and different life styles than those to which he was exposed in the family unit. At the same time he cannot rely on family status or backing for his place in society, and he is essentially on his own for the first time. Acceptance or rejection by peers or by esteemed adults depends on his own abilities and personality. Thus there should be a gradual weaning from the family and a looking toward society for sources of meaning and gratification. Much has been written about the pressures of this weaning process in contemporary middle-class culture. This is a troubled time for most individuals and a good deal of floundering as well as unrealistic optimism and pessimism is to be expected. However, the process is even more difficult for youngsters who cannot feel free from their families or who believe that they must redeem the family's honor in society's marketplace. These are often the adolescents who become depressed, and treatment aims at both altering the cognitive distortions that predispose one to depression and insuring that the individual can master the specific developmental tasks of adolescence.

JOAN: A CASE OF MILD DEPRESSION

A clinical example of an adolescent who believed she could not face life outside the family unit was Joan, a fifteen-year-old girl who had had mild feelings of depression for about six months. She described herself as unable to enjoy anything and not caring about anything anymore. She admitted some suicidal thoughts but felt she was too cowardly to act on them. She felt markedly uncomfortable outside of her home and so stayed with her family a great deal, but found that she was bored by the company of her parents. Even going out to dinner with her father, which had been a special treat in former years, was no longer enjoyable. Her grades had dropped and she remarked that she saw school as a waste of time. She had gone to a few dances and parties but left after feeling herself too uninvolved and preoccupied with her own thoughts.

Her history was significant in that Joan had suffered from extreme separation anxiety throughout childhood. She resisted going to nursery school and later developed stomachaches on school mornings in the third and fourth grades. Her mother believed that these somatic symptoms began after an unpleasant experience with a second-grade teacher who was a perfectionist and intimidated Joan in class. This experience was undoubtedly detrimental but it also became clear that Joan's mother was an anxious, depressed woman who was overly occupied with her own problems and could not devote herself to her children. Later in therapy Joan reproached her mother for never having taken the time with her or her sister Nancy to stimulate interests or to teach them activities in order to bolster a sense of adequacy. In contrast to the mother's aloofness, the father made Joan his "little princess" and showered affection upon her, but only for being a helpless and pretty little girl. He never encouraged her to achieve for herself, but he used Joan to comfort him. The younger sister, Nancy, was rejected by both parents and in her teens turned to delinquent activities for recognition from peers. Joan's role was the good girl while Nancy was clearly the bad, rebellious child.

The home atmosphere was consistently gloomy and tense. Although the family was affluent, there was always talk of a shortage of money and long discussions about the family business, in which one member was always accusing the others of cheating him of his proper share. The parents argued frequently about money, and it was possible that the mother overspent in an effort to hurt the father and also to fill an empty life with material possessions. The father was quite status conscious, but under his well-groomed facade he was actually stingy and controlled the family by carefully doling out money as a reward for obedience. Joan was indulged by him as long as she was "good," meaning that she was never to assert herself or rebel against his authority. There was a clear, unspoken rivalry between Joan and her mother which neither of them openly acknowledged.

The effect of this type of family constellation on Joan was that she never learned how to fare for herself. She expected the world to respond to her much as her father did. She thought she would be special to others just by wearing pretty clothes or by passively appeasing them. In her late childhood years, she made few close friends although she did enjoy going shopping with other girls. Aside from her sophisticated knowledge of clothes and cosmetics, she had no interests and had developed almost no talents. She had started piano lessons and dancing classes, but had been allowed to quit when she had to put forth effort in these pursuits. Her parents never demanded good grades and she was able to be an average student with very little work.

In therapy it became apparent that no one had ever considered Joan as a separate human being. Her mother treated her as an obstacle to her own vague ambitions, while her father used her for his own purposes —as a source of affection in a barren household. When Joan reached puberty, she expected to live a romantic life similar to the heroines of the soap operas she religiously watched. Instead, no one paid any attention to her. She was not particularly pretty or really socially adept. Because she was not given special attention, she retreated more and more to her home. However, the mother was rarely home, having embarked on a career; and the father no longer babied her and even turned away from her, possibly as a result of being threatened by seeing her as a sexual stimulus.

As a result of being tied to the home and lacking any personal initiative or independent avenues of esteem, Joan could not cope with the task of individuation required at adolescence by her social class. She had been reared to become a princess but now no one acknowledged her as such. She tried to rescue her sense of importance by choosing a boy who was her senior by a few years. Joan hoped that he would respond to her in the same manner as her father had when she was a child. She expected him to salvage her sense of importance and desirability. This young man at first politely told Joan that he was not interested in her. When she persisted, he was fairly brutal in his rejection of her, telling her exactly how he saw her. At this confrontation, Joan's world collapsed. She saw herself as inadequate in every way and she was filled with shame and despair. Her father tried to comfort her but she realized that his attentions no longer sufficed to make her happy. She wanted to be recognized and needed outside the home, but felt she could never achieve this aim.

Therapy lasted for three years in which Joan gradually was able to alter her expectations of herself and others. At first she wanted everything done for her, including the diminishing of her depression. An early dream demonstrates this lack of personal initiative and her reliance on others. In the dream Joan announced to her parents that she was going to kill herself. They offered no protest and did not react. Joan then started crying loudly, causing her mother to call a doctor. The doctor arrived and made her feel better. This dream implied that the therapist should take over the nurturing role of the parents, that the therapist should make her feel better since her parents could not. There was no effort on Joan's part in the dream except to cry loudly. On a positive side, the dream may have indicated that the therapist, in contrast to the parents, appreciated the seriousness of her despair.

In working with youngsters like Joan, I have found that better results are obtained if one is active and direct, making concrete suggestions and offering avenues for change. These youngsters have an urgent need for relief and change, so that they do not respond well to the prolonged, introspective, and reconstructive aspects of therapy that form so great a part of the treatment of adults. In view of these special aspects of therapy, specific suggestions for new activities were discussed with Joan. There was also an open discussion about having to learn to do things for herself and not being able to rely on her parents any longer. These sessions were followed by a somewhat encouraging dream: Joan realized that a building she was in had caught fire, she ran to an elevator, and was able to save herself by fleeing the building. This dream may have demonstrated Joan's beginning awareness that she had to rely on herself to overcome her depression.

Joan's depression lifted in the course of a few months. She realized that the social reality of her life was neither as effortless as she had expected it to be as a child nor as hopelessly unattainable as she had felt after her rejection. Despite this improvement in her clinical condition, therapy was continued to correct other distortions about herself and others which could have led to problems in the future. Also, while she was rid of her feelings of depression, she was far from emancipating herself from her family or feeling comfortable among her peers. She continued to worry about being an old maid and of never being loved. She read the popular novel *Sheila Levine is Dead and Living in New York*, which recounts a depressed woman's unhappy love affairs in a most self-deprecatory way, and she closely identified with the heroine. The recitation of these worries were countered by the therapist suggesting that she leave the future alone and concentrate on living a gratifying life in the present.

Toward this end, Joan attempted to socialize without the expectation of special treatment, immediate acceptance, or the fear of eternal rejection when others just treated her neutrally. She eventually formed some relationships with other girls and was able to confide in them and obtain a sense of closeness. It was important for her to see herself as neither privileged nor deficient, but on an equal status with others. In time, her group of friends met some boys and started going out as a group. While there were no one-to-one relationships, they accepted each other and enjoyed doing things together.

As a result of extrafamilial involvements, Joan became more sure of herself and of her place in adolescent society. She then was able to cross a line she had never dared to even imagine in previous years: she was able to get angry with her father. Her father had blown up at Nancy and struck her. In the ensuing family argument, Joan took Nancy's side and critically attacked the father. This was a big step for her; it showed that Joan could realistically evaluate her father and her need of his praise no longer blinded her to his faults.

The recounting of this episode in therapy was utilized as an opportunity to begin to review with Joan her past experiences and the reasons for her current problems. A good deal of reconstructive work was accomplished and Joan was able to understand how she was tied to her family by a distant mother and an indulgent, yet controlling, father.

The remainder of therapy dealt with applying insights to everyday life, and with stressing the need for independent activities and autonomous avenues of meaning. Joan did find a boyfriend, and proved to be capable of emotional intimacy and of giving love and affection. She never achieved her academic potential but did decide on a business career which pleased her. She was never able to form a truly good relationship with her mother, who could have helped her greatly in her growth toward maturity, but this failure at closeness seems to have been more a result of the mother's resistance than a reluctance on the part of the patient. In other respects Joan was able to enjoy herself, had an accurate image of herself, felt comfortable on her own, and did not force others to give her the special deference she had been accustomed to receiving from her father.

PAUL: A CASE OF SEVERE DEPRESSION

Joan's depression can be considered mild. However, adolescents also present melancholic episodes as severe as those seen in adult patients. One such patient's treatment is briefly presented here as a contrast to Joan's relatively benign course.

Paul was an eighteen-year-old college dropout who was seen following a bona fide suicide attempt. Paul had taken a large number of assorted pills after breaking off with a girl friend. He intended to die, but the mixture of pills was fortunately not lethal. Paul's history revealed evidence of psychopathology dating back to early childhood: he always had been shy and seclusive, he had had difficulty separating from his mother, he was afraid of peers, and his school performance was erratic despite a superior intellectual endowment. He also found it difficult to express his feelings and suffered severe stomach cramps in times of stress. (His sister had developed an ulcer in childhood and their mother was plagued with migraine headaches.)

When first seen, Paul could hardly carry on a conversation. He was in extreme mental torment and repeatedly stated that he wished he were dead. All of his brilliance and mental abilities were paralyzed by an overwhelming sense of pain and despair. He paced up and down the office, often bursting into tears. He complained of severe abdominal cramps. At times he was silent, as if in a stupor; at other times he could not sit still, but had to resume pacing. He could not bear to speak of his lost love without breaking down into tears. He could neither eat nor sleep but spent his nights pacing in his room. Paul was seen daily, with frequent telephone contacts between sessions. The aid of the family was enlisted for fear of another suicide attempt. Hospitalization was considered but Paul expressed a terror of being away from home at this time. He seemed to gain some solace from having his father with him. In view of the extensive somatic symptoms (and the remote possibility of an underlying schizophrenic process) he was started on Stellazine®. The initial sessions were spent in simply being with Paul and inducing him to talk about the thoughts that were eliciting his depression. Paul repeated that without Carrie—his former girl friend—his world was empty, his life was no longer worth living, and he felt himself to be incomplete and deprived of any hope of happiness.

The picture which gradually emerged was that Paul had been depressed for years, but recently his involvement with Carrie had relieved him of his feeling of inner deadness and had given him a reason for living. Her loss had plunged Paul into a state of total despair and hopelessness.

Paul's history is similar to those of depressives described elsewhere in this book. In his case, the dominant other was his mother. Paul's mother had grown up with wealthy parents in an exclusive suburb. She was given much in terms of material comforts, but little in the way of love or warmth. Her parents were greatly concerned with social standing and outward appearances, rewarding financial success and upward mobility. Paul's father also came from a prominent family, but he had chosen music as a career, much to the dismay of his parents. As an aspiring musician he had achieved moderate success, but was unable to support his own family in the manner of his own or his wife's childhood households. Although Paul's parents truly loved each other, financial limitations created a constant undercurrent of resentment from Paul's mother and a sense of failure from Paul's father. Both parents hid these feelings from other people, and in fact they carried on as if they were still very wealthy, despite having to exist on a middle-class income.

Paul's mother seemed to have developed a sense of inferiority over her limited financial state, partially because she was snobbishly treated as a poor relation by her siblings who had married into wealthy families. Urged by a desire for vindication, she attempted to regain her status by forcing her children to succeed so as to justify her choice of marital partner. Both Paul and his sister were blessed with superior intelligence and the mother utilized this gift by insisting that they excel in academics. She was a loving and giving mother as long as her children behaved in an overly polite, exemplary manner and made top grades. If either faltered, however, she would become furious or subject the children to long lectures. She honestly believed that she was doing what was best for them, unaware of the pressures she was putting on her offspring.

Paul's father was a more relaxed, fun-loving individual who lived for "Art" and seemed satisfied with his accomplishments. However, he felt ashamed that he could not give more to his family and this shame had forced him into a secondary role from which he rarely interfered with household matters. His work forced him to travel a great deal so that he absented himself from parental responsibilities, and even when home he did not contradict his wife in her dealings with the children.

Under his mother's tutelage, Paul grew up as a superior student but also very naive about crucial aspects of life. His sole responsibility was to make good grades, and he was discouraged from assuming other tasks which would prepare him for adult life. As he reached puberty he sensed himself to be different and weak in comparison with his peers. He attempted to compensate for these feelings by weight lifting or with tests of endurance, such as walking barefoot in the snow or camping out in bad weather. Despite these efforts, he continued to see himself as unmanly and inadequate.

He felt a great deal of anger toward his mother but was afraid to express any of his feelings. The home atmosphere was one of false gaiety, where everything was supposed to be lovely and yet all the family members realized this to be a sham. However, no one dared to question this pretense and so each suppressed feelings, which may explain all the psychosomatic illnesses.

In his early teens Paul became truly depressed when he compared himself with other boys. He felt himself an outcast, unable to relate to most of them. He was painfully shy in social situations, often developing stomachaches at parties or dances. He did not divulge his painful feelings to anyone, but tried to find solace in solitary hobbies and in continuing to build up his body. He feebly rebelled against his mother by keeping his room a mess or by dressing in a shabby fashion, but he still needed her to direct his life and give him structure. He had difficulty being with her and even more difficulty in being without her. His happy times during this period were rare outings with his father, who also loved nature. However, the two would rarely talk when together. Both were shy, quiet people with a great deal of sensitivity, but neither could open up to the other.

When Paul started at an out-of-town college, he was totally bewildered, lacking any previous experience in caring for himself. As a result of poor planning, he had to quit college to avoid failing in his first year. This near-failure took him by surprise; it seemed as though he did not fully comprehend what was happening to him at school. Paul returned home feeling totally disgraced. He had not succeeded in his one area of achievement. It was at this time of self-devaluation that he met Carrie, and she transformed his view of himself. She accepted him as he was, without conditions, and despite his alleged failures. Carrie allowed him to feel that he was worthwhile and deserving of love. Paul felt absolutely in love and made Carrie the fulcrum of his existence. His relationship with her represented the only truly happy time of his life. He became so involved with her that when he started college again he could not attend to his studies because she was constantly in his thoughts, and he yet again dropped out to avoid failing. After about a year of intense involvement, Carrie tearfully decided that she was too young to bind herself to one person and broke off the relationship. Shortly afterward, Paul attempted suicide.

It took a long time until Paul was able to view himself without Carrie. He had not only loved her, he had also depended on her for seeing himself as valid, important, and worthwhile. He had utilized her to fight off a former sense of self that resulted in chronic depression and low self-esteem. He could not mention her in therapy, but continued to dwell on his symptoms. At this time Paul was incapable of any analytic work, but he could still communicate about day-to-day events and not utilize his therapeutic time merely to complain. We initially discussed ways he could attempt to fight off his feelings of despair, as well as the daily transactions of his life. From these concrete, matter-of-fact sessions, a recurrent theme emerged—Paul's inability to express anger openly. From the content of his productions it could be assumed that he was angry at Carrie for leaving him, at his mother for her former treatment of him, and even toward his therapist for not helping him more. However, he never alluded to a sense of resentment toward anyone.

In one early session, Paul described how his sister had lost patience with him and "chewed him out." He took her criticism in silence but later suffered stomach cramps. His denial of anger was interpreted, to which Paul replied that he considered himself a special sort of person who did not need to get angry. This interchange opened up the whole area of his defensive facade of stoicism which served to cover deeper feelings of inferiority.

With this session began an investigation into his blocking of feelings and his fear of the effects of expressing his feelings to others. He began to talk more freely and to be more introspective in terms of trying to find causes for his current predicament. He recalled his mother making schedules for him as a child and his bitter resentment toward her which he had not dared to reveal. He also recalled the sense of being overwhelmed by his mother and of being all alone with no one to help him. This feeling of isolation had persisted into the present and he continued to feel that he was apart and different from others. Only Carrie had understood him and now she was gone. Paul was not yet ready to appreciate how he had used his relationship with Carrie to fulfill narcissistic needs, but he could understand that his restriction of social contacts, his denial of hostile feelings, and his fear of his openness hurting others had predisposed him to becoming depressed. He was also ready to acknowledge that his special view of himself was only a rationalization.

After six weeks of therapy Paul's somatic symptoms had sufficiently subsided so that medication could be discontinued and the sessions reduced to three times a week. Therapy focused on his ambivalent relationship with his mother and how this all-important tie had shaped his personality. It would have been simple to blame the mother for all of Paul's problems, but this conclusion would have been both erroneous and antitherapeutic. Paul had to see his own participation in his problems and the fact that he continued to function in a pathological manner despite the freedom to change. Paul continued to conceive of himself and others according to childhood cognitive patterns in which he was helpless and passive and others were overly powerful and dominating. As this self-concept was explored in therapy, it helped to explain Paul's numerous self-defeating actions such as the refusal to take responsibility for himself in college, his various passive-aggressive maneuvers by which he got even with his mother, and finally his expectation that someone else would transform his life—a role which Carrie had temporarily assumed.

A striking aspect of Paul's failure to master the developmental tasks of adolescence was his inability to let experiences from everyday life alter the unconscious cognitive beliefs which he had learned in early childhood. Part of the adolescent experience is an exposure to novel ideas or ideologies, often in direct contrast to familial belief systems. Paul had totally insulated himself against change or a reevaluation of his world view. He had missed out on the necessary psychic readjustment that takes place as one leaves home and begins to broaden life experiences in day-to-day interchanges with the world. Carrie had not really widened Paul's psychological horizons. It became clear that she had fit into his expectations in an almost delusional way; she had not been truly appreciated as a separate person, but only as a flesh-and-blood embodiment of a fantasied good mother. Paul actually knew very little about her—she existed to fulfill his nonchanging needs, just as his own existence was based on the fulfillment of his mother's unconscious needs.

Much of Paul's therapy consisted of allowing him to feel secure enough to open himself up to new experiences and to form a new cognitive equilibrium based on more realistic data. Many sessions were spent on discussions of his perceptions of actual events rather than on the extensive reconstruction that would have been appropriate with an adult patient.

Past scars and their resulting distortions were not avoided, but therapy was given a much larger function as a process for stimulating developmentally appropriate growth outside the office.

The relationship to the therapist was also important in correcting distortions. Initially Paul projected on the therapist the role of omnipotent healer who, like his mother, would magically make everything better. At the same time he distrusted this needed other and had to guard against what he said or how he behaved in the office. He learned that the therapist was quite limited in offering magical relief and that essentially he had to cure himself. At the same time, he encountered an adult authority figure who encouraged freedom rather than control and who accepted feelings as important. Transference was not directly interpreted because his changing relationship with the therapist was considered to be part of a more general adolescent growth of the self.

Paul has remained free of depression for over eight years. It is perhaps more important that he was able to move away from home, embark on a career of his own choosing, and enjoy mutually beneficial relationships with others.*

SUMMARY

The cases presented in this chapter may not differ significantly from adult depressives in terms of family history, basic psychodynamics, or unconscious beliefs. Modifications in the therapeutic approach are necessary, however, when the therapist considers the developmental tasks that are appropriate for the age of the patient. The need for alteration of the therapeutic process becomes apparent if the actual phenomenological world of the child or adolescent is appreciated. Young patients learn more from action than from words, more from concrete experience than from sophisticated interpretations. Therapy must not only be an experience that corrects past misfortunes, but a situation that frees the individual so he can utilize his new experiences for continued psychological growth.

---

* After this section of the manuscript was completed, I was delighted to receive from Paul (now in his late twenties) an invitation to his wedding and a communication that he continues to feel gratified by his life and his work.

PART FOUR

Sociological and Literary

Aspects of Depression

[16]

PART ONE: SOCIOCULTURAL FACTORS,

SOCIOLOGY OF KNOWLEDGE,

AND DEPRESSION

Introduction

It is a well-established fact that sociological and cultural factors are relevant to the study of psychiatric conditions. Here are some of the questions commonly asked. Are these factors political, religious, economic, dietary, ideological, related to the culture in its totality, or to some of its specific, salient, or secondary characteristics? Are they etiologically essential for the particular disorder which is being considered? Do they facilitate its occurrence or make its occurrence more difficult? What does historical inquiry reveal to us when we study the incidence of a psychiatric condition over a long period of time? And what does anthropology add to our understanding?

This field of research is vast indeed, even when it is confined to the psychiatric syndromes of depression.

Bemporad and I had our training in psychiatry and psychoanalysis, and we do not claim professional expertise in the other fields which I have just mentioned. Therefore we have limited ourselves to discussing in this chapter the few areas which we could investigate with a certain depth. Although our selection of topics is arbitrary, we hope to demonstrate that the issues raised are all very relevant. We are fully aware that much more work has to be done in these areas and we hope that other authors will continue this type of inquiry.

At this point I wish to indicate that a cognitive approach lends itself

Part one of this chapter was written by Silvano Arieti.

better than any other to the integration of psychiatry and sociocultural studies. A cognitive approach stresses the importance of ideas, and most of a person's ideas derive from the sociocultural environment. Although a large number of thoughts and habits of thinking are acquired in childhood from the members of one's family, the family members are carriers of the culture to which they belong. Later the individual continues to acquire ideas and systems of ideas from different people in his sociocultural milieu and from the various institutions and media which the culture provides.

The branch of sociology called sociology of knowledge is of particular relevance to a cognitive approach. It is the branch of sociology that studies the relation between thinking and society. Since the Greek classical era, it has been known that social circumstances shape the psyche of the human being. In the early eighteenth century Giambattista Vico was the first great writer to demonstrate that every phase of history has its own mode of thought. In much more recent times Emile Durkheim, Karl Mannheim, and Max Scheler have made important contributions which are beyond the scope of this book to review. What is important to stress, because it is more closely related to the theme of this book, is that the human psyche is never concerned with more than a sector of reality. This sector is to a large extent chosen by society. A society is attuned to certain ideas and values which consequently predispose or inhibit other feelings, ideas, and actions. Here it is important to study how a special sector of social awareness and concern is related to the occurrence of depression.

Before proceeding, it is appropriate to mention that some sociologists and philosophers attribute a less important role to ideas in the shaping of human life. One of the major sociologists, and an exponent of the non-cognitive point of view, is Vilfredo Pareto: according to him, the human being acts first and thinks of reasons for his actions afterwards. He calls these reasons "derivations," that is, they are derived from the instincts or quasi-instincts which determine modes of human behavior, and through them, human modes of thought. This position is not distant from the Freudian stance. That a considerable part of human life consists of simple actions, quasi-instinctive in origin, is undeniable, but to see the whole or most of human life as a derivation of these simple actions and physiological functions is a reductionistic approach which does not do justice to man's infinite symbolic possibilities. It is true, as Pareto says, that man acts first and thinks of plausible reasons to justify his actions and feelings only afterwards, but these "reasons" are only rationalizations. At a human level the real reason or motivation is not necessarily instinctual but is very often the result of complicated cognitive constructs which have become unconscious. Pareto is thus correct only to the extent that he considers some levels of the psyche, but not others. In other words, in analyzing this phenomenon Pareto goes much further than the man in the street inasmuch as he realizes that the "reason" is an *a posteriori* (after-the-fact) rationalization. However, he does not go far enough because, like the man in the street, he is unaware of the unconscious cognitive constructs which determine many human actions and feelings.

When we take feelings rather than actions into consideration, we find that many authors have made similar errors. As an example, I shall mention the philosopher Miguel De Unamuno who, in his book *The Tragic Sense of Life,* rightly explains how human life is predominantly emotional. Man is said to be a reasoning animal but he should be defined as an affective or feeling animal. Unamuno is right but, like the many authors who have made similar statements since ancient times, he does not understand the psychological origin of most human emotions. Unamuno tells us, for instance, that it is not "usually our ideas that make us optimists or pessimists, but it is our optimism or our pessimism, of physiological or perhaps pathological origin, as much the one as the other, that makes our ideas." In other words, the mood of sadness or elation selects our ideas and our conclusions. Any observer who remains at this level of investigation would agree with Unamuno. In our psychiatric practice we see many examples which at first seem to confirm this philosopher's point of view.

The following report seems a joke; actually it is a vignette similar to many others encountered in a psychiatrist's daily dealings with depressed patients. A depressed woman reported to me that she felt very melancholy, especially since she had seen a very depressing movie full of misery, unhappy events, and a tragic ending which reminded her of what her life had been and probably would continue to be. She vowed never to see an unhappy movie again. A few days later she reported that she had gone to see a very frivolous and happy movie, full of jokes and laughter. When I asked her whether that movie had made her feel better, she replied, "On the contrary, I left the movie more miserable than ever. The movie reminded me of how life could be; it made me see that there are people who laugh and are happy. How different all that is from my personal situation!" This vignette seems to confirm Unamuno's point of view. The patient's a priori pessimism (an emotional state) made her interpret all external events in a pessimistic way. Like Pareto, however, the Unamuno type of interpretation remains at the level of consciousness. Although it is true that the patient's pessimism (or basic emotional tonality) made her think in a negative way, irrespective of the nature of the external event, it is also true that her pessimism was based on a cognitive substratum, perhaps a very large constellation of thoughts and memories, of which she was totally or almost totally unconscious.

One could argue that even an unconscious cognitive substratum is a derivative of a primitive emotional, quasi-intuitive state, or in a Freudian sense, derivative of a purely instinctual life. Again, our basic assumption is that the appearance of the cognitive–symbolic level in the human mind makes such a revolutionary transformation into animal psychology as to change life itself in the most drastic way.

Returning to our major topic, the relation between sociocultural factors and depression, the following issues will be discussed in the first part of chapter 16:

1. The greater incidence of depression in women.
2. Affective psychoses, and inner-directed or other-directed society.
3. Depression and literature, with special emphasis on tragedy.
4. Our contemporary period as an era of depression.
5. Socio-philosophical premises of the psychotherapist of depression.

In the second part of this chapter Bemporad discusses methods of child-rearing in relation to depression.

Greater Incidence of Depression in Women

There is no doubt that depression, especially in its severe forms, occurs much more frequently in women than in men. Statistics collected in several parts of the world confirm this marked difference. In the United States, Winokur and his collaborators (1971) found a greater incidence of depression in women in relatives of 129 probands. Helgason (1966) in Iceland found a much greater risk of affective psychoses in women. McCabe (1975) in Denmark found that women admitted to hospitals for affective psychoses were much more numerous than men (male to female ratio was 0.64). In an excellent article, Weissman and Klerman (1977) reviewed the evidence for the different rates of depression between the sexes in the United States and elsewhere during the last forty years. In the United States they consistently found a 2:1 female-to-male ratio for depression, and in all the other industrialized Western countries the ratio was about the same. Among highly industrialized countries, only in Finland and Norway was the preponderance of female depressives, although still present, not as marked. In a small number of developing countries (India, Iraq, New Guinea, and Rhodesia) there seems to be a preponderance of male depressives.

Weissman and Klerman (1977) asked the pertinent question of whether the reported preponderance of female depressives was an artifact. According to this hypothesis, women perceive, acknowledge, report, and seek help for depressive stress and symptoms more than men. This attitude and habit would account for the sex ratio findings. Reviewing data from the pertinent literature, the authors were able to exclude the importance of these attitudes, and they reached the conclusion that the female preponderance is real and not due to an artifact. Weissman and Klerman reaffirmed the possibility of a genetic factor in the etiology of depression, but concluded that "currently the evidence from genetic studies is insufficient to draw conclusions about the mode of transmission or to explain the sex differences."

Weissman and Klerman (1977) proceeded to examine whether the longstanding disadvantaged social status of women has had psychological consequences that lead to depression. Two main hypotheses have been proposed. The first, which the authors call the "social status hypothesis," refers to social discrimination against women. Social discrimination and inequities would lead to legal and economic helplessness, dependency on others, low self-esteem, low aspirations, and eventually clinical depression. The second hypothesis, which the authors call "learned helplessness," states that "socially conditioned, stereotypical images produce in women a cognitive set against assertion, which is reinforced by societal expectations . . . . The classic 'femininity' values are redefined as a variant of 'learned helplessness', characteristic of depression."

Weissman and Klerman (1977) discuss marriage in relation to depression. They quote many authors and in particular Gove (1972, 1973), who concluded that whereas being married has a protective effect for men, it has a detrimental effect for women. In each of the following categories women have a lower relative rate of mental illness than men: single, divorced, widowed. Only married women have a higher incidence than married men. Weissman and Klerman's paper offers other data which leave no doubt about the preponderance of depression in women. (The authors also summarize other interpretations which cannot be reported here: the reader is referred to the original source.)

According to prevailing concepts of modern psychiatry, psychiatric conditions are multi-determined. Thus the presence or absence of specific social factors may be the decisive factor in the adoption or avoidance of specific pathogenetic patterns. It seems plausible to me that most of the important psychodynamic patterns leading to depression which have been illustrated in the previous chapters, especially in chapters 6, 9, 11, and 12, are for sociocultural reasons much more likely to occur in women. Let us examine, for instance, the following mechanisms: the experience of having sustained a loss or been threatened by loss, with the consequent adoption of a pattern of submissiveness to a dominant other; the pattern of living for the sake of the dominant other, or for obtaining approval and gratification from the dominant other; the pattern of dependency; the pattern of living in which romantic love is a dominant goal; and so on.

The first important mechanism is the childhood experience of loss, which is generally interpreted as loss of mother's love or threat of such loss, and it seems to occur equally in boys and girls. If there is a difference, it has so far received no reliable confirming evidence from available data. I can only postulate in the most hypothetical way that in families which practice gender prejudice, and in which a girl has already been born, the birth of a boy is experienced with great joy and leads to neglect of the older girl. A great deal of attention is devoted to the newborn boy and the girl experiences the trauma of the loss of love. Although this hypothesis may be purely speculative, it is not at all speculative that cultural factors predispose more strongly in girls than boys all the other mechanisms and interpersonal relations that lead to depression. In many environments it is possible to recognize a relation of transmitted duty between mothers and daughters. Daughters feel the transmitted sense of obligation more strongly than sons, and consequently tend to become duty-bound. Submissiveness to a male-dominant other is also favored by the patriarchal character of our society. It seems natural to a woman to affiliate herself with a male-dominant other. Jean Baker Miller (1976) and other writers have illustrated how it is commonly expected that a woman will serve others' needs and to be tied to the destiny of a man, and how much more difficult it is for her than for a man to become an authentic self.

I could say that culture at large enters into a conspiracy with the woman's private conflicts, so that it is easier for her than for the male partner to give up self-determination and personal power, and to indulge in masochism. The conspiracy on the part of the culture consists in diverting the woman from becoming aware of the abnormality of her situation. As I had the opportunity to say elsewhere (Arieti, 1974b), it is not only the patient who represses the abnormality of some interpersonal relations and the accompanying cognitive constructs, but society as well. In *The Will To Be Human* (1972), I wrote:

> The individual has a double burden to repress: his (her) own and that of society. How does society repress? By teaching the individual not to pay attention to many facts (selective inattention); by masking the real value of certain things; by giving an appearance of legality and legitimacy to unfair practices; by transmitting ideas and ideals as absolute truths without any challenge or search for the evidence on which they are supposed to be based; by teaching certain habits of living, etc. The defense against objectionable wishes which Freud described in the individual (for instance, repression, reaction formation, isolation, and rationalization) can be found in society, too. (Pp. 45–407).

In a patriarchal society the woman often represses the sorrow, the anger, and the frustration which accompany her subordinate way of living. The repression, however, in the best circumstances leads to neurotic defenses; in the worst, to facilitating serious mental disorders, especially depression. Although it is true that the very beginning of a pattern of female dependency can be traced back to the first two or three years of life, it is also true that this pattern would not persist and become ingrained in many cases if society at large did not promote it.

Femininity in some social classes becomes confused with being dependent. Self-assertiveness substitutes for reliance in a "strong" man. The man often depicts himself as the pillar, the ruler, or the direction-maker to the point of fostering a state of helplessness in the woman in his life. And yet later this very state of helplessness which has been fostered by men becomes bitterly criticized by them. As a rule, only in the areas of motherhood and homemaking is the woman allowed to assert herself fully. Homemaking, however, is decreasing in value in modern society, and many functions which in a preindustrial society were entrusted to the woman are now relegated to other agencies. The nursery school, the kindergarten, the grammar school, the church, the restaurant, the laundry, the clothing store, and many other institutions are taking over the functions of the home. Many wives feel relieved, but the problem remains that the woman has very little to do which she can consider stimulating. Therefore she feels dissatisfied. Society has prevented her from developing according to the male model. If she decides at a certain point to pursue a career, she feels left behind by contemporary men. Thus it becomes difficult for her to muster enough courage to pursue a career with initial disadvantages.

The acquired state of dependency and submission makes the woman more prone to the developments described in chapter 6. Her dependency also makes her less able to help herself and more vulnerable to certain events which become precipitating factors to psychopathology. A person who relies more on his/her own inner resources and ability is less intensely affected by adverse circumstances. The feeling of helplessness and the inability to find alternative paths may evoke the return of an original experience of irreparable loss or impending loss.

One would expect that the depression which follows the realization of not having achieved the dominant goal is very common in women. We know in fact that especially in the past, but even in our own time, women have had fewer opportunities than men to become part of the high-level hierarchy of political parties, government institutions, churches, corporations, universities, industry, hospitals, and so forth. Undoubtedly many women suffer on account of this discrimination. However, as far as I can determine from my personal experiences, this discrimination does not lead to severe depression as frequently as one would expect.

In chapter 6 it was shown that in absolute figures even the type of depression which is connected with the realization of not having achieved the dominant goal is more common in women than men. We must remember, however, that it is because the dominant goal of many women is connected not with a career but with the pursuit of love. It is in the area of love that many women feel disappointed. Thus, often it is difficult to categorize their depression, that is, if it is connected with the relation with a dominant other, or with the dominant goal of love achievement. It is not difficult to understand why this is so. Many women since early in life have not been encouraged to pursue a career, but have been subtly or openly directed toward the aims of motherhood and housekeeping. This prospect was made to appear very desirable to them because it was connected with the realization of dreams of romantic love. Love is of course very important and has to be pursued by everybody, men and women, but when romantic love becomes the only concern or aim in life and takes the place of any other aim including the pursuit of other types of love, then life becomes unduly restricted in rigid patterns for which it will be difficult to find alternatives later.

In men, depression caused by the realization of failure to achieve the dominant goal generally concerns a career. Inasmuch as a larger number of women are now diverting their aim from the traditional one to that of pursuing a career, it is possible to predict that a larger number of woman will become frustrated as a consequence of not achieving this aim, especially if discrimination against working women persists. It is more probable, however, that society will move more and more toward giving equal opportunities to women, and consequently this type of depression in women will decrease. Up to now the depression which follows the realization of not having achieved the dominant goal has put women in a state of double jeopardy. Inasmuch as many women become affiliated with a male dominant other through marriage, they feel unfulfilled not only when they themselves do not achieve the dominant goal, but also when their husbands do not. Unfortunately, and purely for sociological reasons, the married woman's happiness depends more on her husband's feeling of fulfillment than the husband's happiness depends on his wife's sense of fulfillment.

At this point it is worthwhile to reconsider the theory which from time to time has appeared in classic psychoanalytic literature, that a castration complex can explain the greater occurrence of depression in women. I think it is easier to affirm that depressed women are more likely to mourn not for the castration of their penis, which would be pure fantasy on their part, but because they really have been castrated—although in a metaphorical sense. The symbolic penis of which they have been deprived is the male role in the world, including all opportunities connected with that role, from becoming president of the United States to being the director of a small bank. In *Creativity: The Magic Synthesis* (1976) I explained how the fact that women have played a less important role than men in various fields of creativity is the result of social conditions rather than of different biological endowments. Here I wish to add that in addition to being hindered in cultivating the great fields of creativity, women have found it more difficult to grow in several aspects of life because only the husbands have had access to a large number of stimuli such as intellectual exchange with others, the practice of special occupations, trades, and so on.

Being denied the possibility of growth in many areas, some women have found it easy to regain power through functions which wrongly have been considered to pertain more to femininity than masculinity: sex appeal, the art of seduction, love. Many women who are afraid to lose these functions at the time of menopause are easy candidates for involutional melancholia. Fortunately, these tendencies are now being rapidly reversed.

Although society has made progress in changing the conditions which make it more likely for a woman to become depressed, the present situation is far from satisfactory. First, abolition of double standards and unequal opportunities has not taken place as much as would be desirable. Second, even though some changes have occurred at a behavioral level, the old cognitive constructs and accompanying feelings still operate in contemporary people. Moulton (1973) wrote, " . . . the unconscious of modern woman contains many remnants of the conscious misconceptions of her grandmother . . . . [The human being's] adaptive powers are remarkable for their ultimate versatility, but rarely for their speed. A culture in flux offers an apparent breadth of choices, but effects are unpredictable . . ." We could add that the unconscious of modern man also contains many remnants of the conscious misconceptions of his grandfather. Moreover at the level of consciousness old and new concepts and guidelines are mixed, and the result is confusion.

In the last third of the twentieth century, many people are still under the influence of ideas which prevailed in the nineteenth century and at the beginning of this century. I have found it interesting to draw conclusions on the conceptions about women which prevailed in these historical periods by focusing on a form of art from that period which continues to affect us. I am referring to operas, and specifically to how women are represented in them. Although works of art generally accentuate certain traits and special characters are selected as heroes and heroines, this accentuation and choice are not haphazard but represent the ideas of the time in which these works appeared. My conclusion (which I will illustrate) is that if women were in situations as depicted in the lyric operas or if they were conceived of as they were in operas, they had good reason to be sad and were certainly facilitated in a trend toward depression. To the extent that these ideas continue in our conscious or unconscious, women are still affected in this way.

Before I proceed with my exposition, I wish to inform the reader that I believe I have no prejudice against operas. I have loved them since my childhood, and for decades I have had a regular subscription at the Metropolitan Opera House. Nevertheless, I must reluctantly admit that in our day quite often we must make a strong effort to reconcile sublime overtures, melodious arias, and enrapturing intermezzos with the absurd ideological contents of the librettos. As to the way women are represented in most librettos, I can differentiate six major categories.

1. Women are victimized, exploited, insulted, and brutalized by men; and they are prevented by society from redeeming themselves.
2. Women are sick or frail.
3. Women are infantile, vain, and dependent.
4. Women are loose and promiscuous.
5. Women are mechanical, insincere, and untrustworthy.
6. Women are beautiful and lovely when young, but their youth is of brief duration.

Often the woman is in a situation in which she fulfills several of these categories at the same time.

The first category is the most common and states that men are brutal toward women, and the conclusion is a very pessimistic one from the point of view of the woman. If we consider all six categories, we can conclude that either woman's life is made miserable by men and therefore she is right in being depressed, or she is regarded by men in such a negative way as to justify being in a state of despondency. A few significant examples will illustrate the points made. I shall start with the sixth category, which fosters the belief that youth is very important and at the age of the menopause a woman is finished. In Puccini's *Madama Butterfly* the heroine is fifteen when she develops a love which becomes tragically unattainable. In Strauss's *Der Rosenkavalier* the most touching point concerns the Marschallin, who at the age of thirty-two mourns her past youth. In the magnificent mirror aria she laments that she is no longer the beautiful young girl she used to be. Thinking about the inexorable flow of time, she prophetically concludes that her lover Octavian will leave her for a much younger girl.

The list of heroines to be included in the first category is long indeed. Madama Butterfly is abandoned by her husband, and she kills herself. In Donizetti's *Lucia di Lammermoor*, Lucia is victimized by her brother who forces her to marry Arturo, a man she detests. Edgardo, with whom Lucia is in love, rushes in just after the ceremony and curses her for betraying him. Lucia becomes insane, kills Arturo, and then sings the beautiful "mad scene."

In Tchiakovsky's *Eugene Onegin*, the heroine Tatiana dares to do the inconceivable for a Russian woman. She writes a letter to Onegin, revealing her love for him. This action brings about a series of misfortunes. And yet in writing the letter, Tatiana asks for mercy and understanding. In Verdi's *Rigoletto* the heroine Gilda is victimized by the Duke of Mantua who seduces her, and by her father Rigoletto who keeps her in a state of dependency and infantilization. Rigoletto tells the housekeeper to watch Gilda and take care of her as if she were a beautiful flower. After Gilda's seduction, revengeful Rigoletto hires a man to kill the Duke, but Gilda offers herself in place of the Duke and is killed by her father's hired assassin. In Verdi's *La Traviata* Violetta, a high-class courtesan, finally finds real love and attempts to revise her life drastically. But society cannot forget her past, and she is doomed. The libretto, taken from Dumas's *La Dame Aux Camelias*, portrays a familiar theme in French literature: the *demi-mondaine* or loose woman who, in the French bourgeois environment, is not given a chance to redeem herself.

Loose women appear quite often in operas as main characters (for instance, Thaïs, Manon) or as foils to the heroine (Musetta in Puccini's *La Bohème*, Maddalena in *Rigoletto*, and Lola in *Cavalleria Rusticana* by Mascagni). Sick women appear just as frequently, for instance, Violetta in *La Traviata*, Mimi in *La Bohème*, and Antonia in *The Tales of Hoffmann*.

It is true that in some rare operas there are women who do not belong to the six categories that have been mentioned, but who are rather strong and active promoters of a good outcome. This is the case with Minnie in *La Fanciulla del West* by Puccini. It is worth mentioning, however, that Puccini had the least success with this female character. Although Puccini was a master at depicting the woman as victim (Butterfly, Tosca, Suor Angelica, Liù), sick (Mimi), or sexually loose (Musetta, Manon), he did not do such a good job with Minnie.

The most comprehensive picture of how women are portrayed in the world of opera probably appears in *The Tales of Hoffmann* by Offenbach. Hoffmann, a poet, offers to tell the story of his life's three great loves to a group of students. The first woman he loves is Olympia, the daughter of the great scientist Spalanzani. But alas! He discovers that she is not a real woman but a mechanical doll, an automaton which is finally smashed to pieces. The second of Hoffmann's loves is the Venetian high-class prostitute Giulietta, who causes a lot of trouble to others and to herself. Hoffmann's third love is Antonia, the daughter of a musician. Antonia is also in love with Hoffmann, but she loves her musical career more. She is warned not to sing because of her frail health, but she does sing, and dies. Hoffmann is disappointed again. In the end he decides that neither human love nor earthly woman is for him; his real love is for the Muse of poetry.

This unusual libretto cannot be taken literally. It has obvious symbolic meanings. We can easily agree with Hoffmann that he had better stick to the ivory tower of poetry since he is so maladroit in practical life and in his choice of women. However, he professes to demonstrate something philosophical, perhaps that love in unattainable on earth. Love may inspire human beings, as the notes of Olympia's waltz do, and as the famous barcarolle sung by Giulietta and Antonia make us envision, but all this is not to be trusted; it is only illusion. Love is really impossible to find. Although as psychiatrists we cannot adhere to this point of view, we can respect it as a philosophical conception. Even the great Schopenhauer thought so. But what is objectionable to our modern ears, in spite of the beautiful melodies, is the way women are depicted. The three loves of Hoffmann are prototypes of women described in many operas and in other works of art from the nineteenth century and even later. Olympia is not a real human being, but a mechanical creature, made by men and very fragile. Giulietta is a high-class prostitute, and Antonia is a very frail human being.

In summary, in a world which sees women in the role of victim, or as sick, gullible, and naive, or loose, as a prostitute, it is no wonder women are bound to feel despondent about their lot and more inclined than men to become melancholic. One could argue that the melodrama represents special cases which are in fact selected because they are special. But special cases attract attention only because they accentuate or exaggerate common views. Most of the librettos derive from popular novels or plays which reflected the prevailing views of society at the time they were written. It could also be said that the librettos present the prevailing views only of the nineteenth and early twentieth centuries, views which are no longer shared in our time. It is true that these views are rapidly disappearing, but not so extensively as one would hope. There is still a great deal of the cognitive structure (sociology of knowledge) of the nineteenth and early twentieth centuries in our own time. Moreover, many of our patients of today were brought up when these ideas were still accepted, especially in certain milieus. Mrs. Fullman (described in chapter 10) and Mrs. Carls (described in chapter 12) retained many features of the operatic heroine.

Although the present attitude of society toward women is still short of our desires, the future seems promising. We can hope in the years to come that there will be less discrepancy in the incidence of depression between women and men. And yet we cannot make predictions with strong convictions. New and unexpected social factors may develop, causing the same discrepancy to persist, to be altered in the reverse order, or to increase in incidence for both sexes.

Affective Psychoses and Inner-Directed
or Other-Directed Society

From the time of Kraepelin to the early 1930s, affective psychoses (manic-depressive psychosis, psychotic depression, involutional melancholia) received an amount of consideration equal or almost equal to that of schizophrenia (dementia praecox). However, from the thirties to the beginning of the seventies there has been a progressive disinterest in these conditions.

As I reported elsewhere (1959, 1976) the decline of interest seems due to a decline in the frequency of serious affective disorders. The present revival of interest in manic conditions is probably connected to the enthusiasm with which lithium has been recently used in the treatment of manic states. Actually, Cade's introduction of lithium in the treatment of manic patients goes back to 1949 but at the time of its introduction it was considered dangerous, and only in the 1960s did it become a popular form of treatment. The recent interest in depression or in manic states does not rule out the persistence of a low incidence of the typical biphasic manic-depressive psychoses, characterized by full-fledged manic episodes and severe attacks of the self-blaming type of depression.

In 1928, in New York state there were 10 new hospital admissions of manic-depressive patients per 100,000 inhabitants, and in 1947 this incidence had decreased to 3.7 per 100,000. The percentage of first admissions of manic-depressive patients in 1928 was 13.5 percent of all admissions, and in 1947 the percentage was reduced to 3.8. Thus in a period of twenty years, the incidence of manic-depressive patients admitted to New York state hospitals decreased to approximately one-third, and has shown no tendency to increase since then. Similar statistical trends are obtained in most of the other states. The statistics point out that a definite decrease of this psychosis has taken place. However, interpretating the statistics is difficult because, as in all cases of psychiatric vital statistics, there are many variables involved. Bellak (1952) offered three possible explanations: an actual lessening of the relative frequency of this disease; greater toleration by the healthy population of milder cases of manic-depressive psychosis; and changing diagnostic trends.

To these three hypotheses a fourth and a fifth can be added. The fourth hypothesis is that new therapeutic methods administered at the beginning of the illness produce such improvement or recovery that the patients do not need to be hospitalized. One thinks in particular of electric shock treatment which is capable of rapidly ending a manic-depressive attack, especially in the depressive phase. But this hypothesis does not withstand close examination. The first reports on electric shock by Cerletti and Bini appeared in 1938. Electric shock was introduced into the United States in 1939, but it did not receive wide application, especially in private offices with nonhospitalized patients, until the year 1942–43. On the other hand the statistics indicate that the decline in first admissions of manic-depressive patients started in 1928. What I have said in reference to electric shock treatment can be reported with even more emphasis for antidepressant drug therapy or lithium therapy in manic cases. These therapies were introduced long after a marked decrease in the incidence of affective psychoses had taken place. Before examining a fifth hypothesis, it is worthwhile to discuss in detail Ballak's three hypotheses.

Bellak's third hypothesis, that changing diagnostic trends are completely responsible for this decrease, is difficult to sustain. It is correct that many patients with a mixed symptomatology have been classified since the 1930s not as cases of manic-depressive psychosis, but as cases of reactive depression, senile depression, schizophrenia, schizo-affective psychosis, obsessive-compulsive psychoneuroses, etc. The pertinent question here is: Why has the diagnosis of manic-depressive psychosis been made with great reluctance?

It can be argued justifiably that this reluctance is not merely due to caprice, but has been determined by the fact that for a long time the typical or severe manic-depressive features played only a secondary role in many cases which needed hospitalization, whereas in the past they played a predominant role. I have also mentioned (chapter 3) that in the last few years an increase of cases has been noticed in which depression follows a typical initial schizophrenic symptomatology. In these cases preference obviously is given to the initial, and much more marked, symptomatology. Moreover, schizophrenic residues are often detectable in these cases even when the depressive features prevail.

Relevant information has been gathered in other parts of the world. Gold (1951) found a relatively larger incidence of manic-depressive psychoses than schizophrenic psychoses in the lands of the Mediterranean basin, as well as in Ireland. He reported that in Oriental countries, especially where Hinduism and Buddhism prevail, manic-depressive psychosis is much less common, but in the Fiji Islands manic-depressive patients are numerous. He added that whereas in India, where the incidence of manic-depressive psychosis is low and schizophrenia is higher, the reverse is true for the Indians who have emigrated to Fiji. Immediately after the Second World War classical or pure manic-depressive patients were more numerous in Italy than in the United States. In 1949, in the United States the rate of admissions was 4.7 for manic-depressives and 16.1 for schizophrenics; In Italy it was 10.0 for manic-depressives and 8.2 for schizophrenics.* Italian psychiatrists, however, state that since the late 1940s, in Italy the incidence of the classical type of manic-depressive psychosis also has decreased approximately as much as in the United States.

Another important point to consider concerning diagnostic trends is whether the differentiation of such categories as involutional paranoid state and involutional melancholia, used in the last few decades, is responsible for the statistical differences. In other words, patients previously diagnosed as manic-depressive might have been diagnosed as suffering from the involutional syndromes. Here again it is difficult to evaluate all the factors. Involutional patients previously might have been diagnosed as having paranoid conditions or paraphrenia, for example. It is only in cases of pure involutional melancholia that competition with the diagnosis of manic-depressive psychosis exists. It is doubtful whether the

---

* Italian statistics were kindly provided by Professor Francesco Bonfiglio of Rome. To be exact, first admissions of schizophrenics in Italy were 3,541 in the year 1947, 3,780 in the year 1948, and 3,854 in 1949. First admissions of manic-depressives were 4,298 in 1947, 4,562 in 1948, and 4,791 in 1949. The rate of admission per 100,000 citizens represents the annual average of the triennial period 1947–1949.

cases of pure involutional melancholia, if added to the official figures of manic-depressive cases, would reverse the decline or explain the difference between the rate of first admissions of schizophrenia and of manic-depressive psychosis. Again the trend is shown sharply by the statistics. Bellak reported that of first admissions to New York civil state hospitals for the year ending March 1947, 27.7 percent were diagnosed as dementia praecox, 7.0 percent as involutional psychosis, and 3.8 percent as manic-depressive psychosis. (Involutional and manic-depressive combined were 10.8 percent.)

Bellak's second hypothesis is that the healthy population has more tolerance for milder cases. Bellak states that the "full of pep and energy" salesman type of person has become an accepted type. He is correct, but—in spite of some similarities—this person corresponds not to the cyclothymic hypomanic who is liable to become manic-depressive, but to the "marketing personality" of Fromm (1947) and the "other-directed" personality of Riesman (1950). This second hypothesis of Bellak, however, implies a corollary: milder cases have been much more common in recent decades. I believe this to be the case. But an explanation for the difference will be discussed when the fifth hypothesis is examined.

These observations and considerations seem to lead to the conclusion offered by Bellak's first hypothesis: the decline in the number of manic-depressive patients, at least of those who are so seriously ill as to require hospitalization, is real and not apparent. Although this decline is not universal, it seems to affect many countries and especially Western countries, but not with the same speed.

It would appear that understanding the reasons for this decline in number or the lessening of the symptomatology of manic-depressive psychosis could lead to conclusions relevant to the field of mental hygiene in particular, and of psychiatry in general.

What David Riesman called the inner-directed personality and culture may be related to typical manic-depressive psychosis with the self-blaming type of depression. When this type of personality and culture tend to disappear, this psychosis tends also to disappear.

Riesman explained that the establishment of the inner-directed society is the result of demographic and political changes. At certain times in history, a rapid growth of population determines a diminution of material goods and a psychology of scarcity. This type of society has occurred several times in history. The society with direct relevance for us had its beginning at the time of the Renaissance and developed during the Reformation. Fromm (1941) wrote that in this period of history, the security that the individual had enjoyed in the Middle Ages by virtue of membership in his closed class system was lost, and he was left alone to rely on his own efforts. The religious doctrines of Luther, and indirectly those of Calvin, gave the individual the feeling that everything depended on his own efforts. Deeply felt concepts of responsibility, duty, guilt, and punishment, which had existed in the early Middle Ages but became confined to a few religious men, reacquired general acceptance and tremendous significance and came to color every manifestation of life. This type of culture, which originated during the Renaissance and developed during the Reformation, sooner or later permeated all Western countries: only in the third or fourth decade of this century has it faced replacement by another type of culture, the other-directed.* In some countries such as the United States, this replacement has taken place at a rapid rate; in others, it is still taking place but at a slower pace.

In the inner-directed society, the parent is duty-bound and very concerned with the care of the newborn child. It is this duty-bound care, and later burdening the child with responsibilities and a sense of duty and guilt, which may permit the child to develop the strong introjective tendencies that play such a prominent role in the development of manic-depressive psychosis.

The typical manic-depressive and the typical inner-directed person have the following characteristics in common:

1. Very early in the life of the child, the duty-bound parent gives such tremendous care to the child as to determine strong introjective tendencies in him.
2. A drastic change occurs later, when the child is burdened with responsibility. This change produces the trauma of the paradise lost.
3. The individual feels responsible for any possible loss. He reacts by becoming compliant, working hard, and harboring strong feelings of guilt. Life becomes a purgatory.†
4. This tremendously burdened life leads to depressive trends, or to inactivity, which leads to guilt feelings, or as a reaction to activity which appears futile. These negative states and feelings are misinterpreted as proof of one's unworthiness, and they reactivate the expectancy of losing the paradise again, this time forever. A vicious circle is thus formed.

Other social studies point out a relation which is more than coincidental between manic-depressive psychosis and inner-directed society. The research by Eaton and Weil on the Hutterites (1955a, b) may throw additional light on this hypothesis, although these authors did not use the term inner-directed society. The Hutterites are a group of people of German ancestry who settled in the Dakotas, Montana, and the prairie provinces of Canada. Their life is very concerned with religion and their birth rate is very high, with the average family having ten children. This society seems to be typically inner-directed. In a population of 8,542

---

* Do not confuse the other-directed culture and personality, described by Riesman, with what I have described as outer-directed personality. The outer-directed personality is a hypomaniclike defense against, or a reaction formation to, the inner-directed personality. Riesman's other-directed personality is basically a different type of personality, occurring predominantly in an other-directed society.

† At this point many manic-depressive patients deviate from the inner-directed personality; instead they develop an excessively dependent or hypomaniclike outer-directed personality.

people Eaton and Weil found only 9 persons who at some time in their life had suffered from schizophrenia, and 39 who suffered from manic-depressive psychosis. In other words, manic-depressive psychosis among the Hutterites was 4.33 times more frequent than schizophrenia, whereas in the general population of the United States, the incidence of schizophrenia by far exceeded that of manic-depressive psychosis. In the second part of this chapter Bemporad discusses child-rearing among the Hutterites and its relevance to the incidence of affective disorders.

Other historical facts point to a relation between inner-directed society and manic-depressive psychosis, but these facts although suggestive are by no means reliable or scientifically proved. For instance, among the physicians of the pre-Christian era, Hippocrates in particular seemed concerned with cases of mania and melancholia. It is possible to assume that his experience with such cases was extensive, making it probable that their incidence was high. Significantly, Riesman's theories postulated that Athenian culture at that time was inner-directed.

What has been discussed in this section should not be interpreted as if I were suggesting that inner-directed culture is "the cause of" manic-depressive psychosis. I only advance the hypothesis that this type of culture tends to elicit family configurations and interpersonal conflicts which generally lead to severe forms of manic-depressive psychosis with the self-blaming type of depression.

A fifth hypothesis concerns the possibility of a change in the symptomatology of many cases of depression, including the depressions which are part of manic-depressive psychosis. This change would result in a different symptomatology of milder intensity which often does not require hospitalization. That a change has occurred has already been seen in chapter 3, when the manifest symptomatology was discussed, and in subsequent chapters. I have described the claiming type of depression, which as a rule is less severe than the self-blaming type.

The relation that has just been illustrated between inner-directed culture and a self-blaming type of depression cannot be repeated for the claiming type. A person who tends to rely on others for autonomous gratification has since early childhood resorted to the external environment for most kinds of stimulation and has been less prone to internalize or conceive distant values and goals. He is likely to be other-directed. In Reisman's conception (1950), the other-directed person uses peers as models rather than the older generation. A person whose major orientation is not inward or toward himself but toward the external world is more inclined to claim from others than to expect from himself. He also has less inclination to blame himself.

Again, according to Riesman, the other-directed types of culture and personality have increasingly replaced the inner-directed types. It can thus be postulated that at present a larger proportion of the claiming type of depressions tend to occur. Although the claiming type is less severe than the self-blaming type and does not require hospitalization as frequently, it is still to be considered a rather serious type of disorder and should not be confused with what is called neurotic or reactive depression.

Literature and Depression: Tragedy

Since sadness and depression are such common states, it is no wonder that these emotions have been described in the literature since ancient times. In some particular historical eras, however, the literary involvement with melancholy has been much more intense than in others. It is difficult to say whether the culture has stimulated accounts of melancholy in the literature or whether the literature has contributed to create a cultural climate of sadness by giving particular stress to this emotional state. Probably a vicious circle often is established between what is called the *Weltschmerz* (melancholy pessimism of some authors) and the *Weltanschauung*, or sadness of some eras. It is also important for us to evaluate whether the general cultural climate of sadness or the literary trends of melancholy favor the onset of individual depression.

A rapid excursion from the world of antiquity to our day will reveal various representations of sadness and depression in the literature. The field is immense, and any selection is certainly arbitrary.

According to Koerner (1929), the earliest record of depression in Indo-Germanic cultures is the melancholia of Bellerophon in the *Iliad*. In the Bible (Samuel I) the depression of King Saul, terminating with his suicide, is dramatically reported. In the classical Greek era we have the writings of Aristotle, who followed the Hippocratic school in believing that melancholia was due to an abnormal mixture of the black bile. In *Problemata*, Aristotle asks a question which is said to have inspired the painter Dürer to make his famous painting of Melancholia First nineteen centuries later. Aristotle asks: "Why are all men who excel in philosophy, politics, poetry, or arts definitely melancholy, and some of them in such a way as to be really affected by the morbid manifestations which derive from the black bile?" Thus Aristotle implies that many creative people are not just melancholy, but morbidly so.

Joannes Cassianus was a fourth-century monk who spent some years as an ascetic in the Egyptian deserts. In his long book *De institutio coenobiorum* he describes two types of depression: the rational, to be accepted; and the irrational, to be rejected. The Spaniard Isidore of Seville (560–636), who for over forty years was bishop of Seville and eventually was sanctified by the Catholic church, wrote that hopelessness and depression derive from sinfulness. He advised that confession and atonement would help. Alcuin, originally Ealhwine or Albinus (735–804), an advisor of Charlemagne, wrote *The Vices and Virtues* in which he anticipates some modern views of depression. He considers melancholia to be a loss of hope of salvation. He also describes the depressed person as one who hates himself and wishes his own death.

Throughout the Middle Ages depression was seen as something negative, probably associated with sinfulness or with some kind of disease, as Hippocrates and Aristotle had thought.

The medieval literature does not portray a pervasive atmosphere of sadness, as what we know about Dark Ages would lead us to expect. It is fair to assume that people were indeed saddened by the state of the world then, but they either were not allowed to express or were incapable of expressing their negative feelings. To do so would have been interpreted as a rebellion or revolt against the divine order. People were allowed to express discontent only when they could do so in theological terms. Actually, it is safe to assume that in a cultural atmosphere where despotic feudalistic power prevailed, where the concepts of sinfulness and atonement reigned, and where contempt was preached for earthly life, sadness and depression should have been rampant, unless neutralized by fanatic faith.

Some historians who have studied the Middle Ages used to believe that a large percentage of people living in that period had interpreted the New Testament as predicting the world would perish in the year 1000. Thus they stopped being active, and literature, arts, and works of any kind languished and were reduced to a minimum. After the year 1000, when people realized that the world had survived that fatidic date, hope for the future was renewed and people moved toward the innovating spirit of the Renaissance. This theory was later discarded by historians. The fact remains, however, that the Middle Ages contributed much less to Western civilization than the classic world of antiquity and the period of time which started with the Renaissance. Undoubtedly, complex historical, political, and sociocultural factors are responsible but they are beyond the scope of this book to investigate. However, I would like to suggest another hypothesis for consideration: at a cultural level a climate of depression prevailed during the several centuries of the Middle Ages that slowed the activities of entire generations of men. Relatively little was accomplished in literature, art, and science.

Melancholy makes its official entrance into the philosophy and literature of the modern world with Marsilio Ficino, a Platonist-humanist (1434–1499). Developing a trend which had already entered the Christian literature with St. Augustine, and the Italian literature with Petrarch, Ficino rehabilitated melancholia. Melancholia was no longer considered to be exclusively a negative state, as it had been since Aristotle. According to Ficino the human being lives in exile, in a world to which he does not belong, since he still retains a divine spark. Melancholia is the emblem of the Christian. Love stimulates in the human being a state of perennial dissatisfaction, a constant craving and anxiety, a thirst of knowledge which is never quenched. Thus love leads to disappointment, fatigue, and consequently to melancholia. But melancholia will rekindle the desire for love.

According to Ficino, melancholia is a restless and uneasy state of mind which typifies inner experience. It is not a paralyzing sadness that leads to renunciation, but a desire to lift oneself from a vulgar existence; it is the pain of the soul which aspires toward higher and immaterial places. If I understand Ficino correctly, it is the sorrow of the human being for being human, and for being so distant from the divine to which he aspires.

Ficino retained the conception that melancholia derives from one of the four humors of the organism. According to him it has an astrological meaning, too: those who are subjected to the influence of Saturn tend to be melancholy.

Lorenzo the Magnificent (1449–1492), the Florentine prince, statesman, and poet, was very much influenced by Ficino. He was both a man of action and a man given to contemplative life. In a celebrated sonnet he describes how Death is the teacher who shows how any hope is vain, any plan is futile, and the world of men is full of ignorance. Lorenzo does not have the faith in a better world which animated Ficino. For him, death is the end. Thus in the most celebrated of his poems he reminds people of the beauty of youth which ever flies; there is no certainty in tomorrow; let him be glad who will be.

A more complete literary rendition of melancholia is provided in the Italian literature by the poet Iacopo Sannazzaro (1456–1540). He mourns for Arcadia, the world he has lost. Here is a passage from one of his descriptions.

Our Muses are extinct; withered are our laurels. Our Parnassus is ruined. The woods are mute, and pain has deafened the valleys and the mountains. No longer are nymphs or satyrs to be found in the forest; the shepherds have lost their songs and the flock hardly grazes the grass . . . . Everything is lost, every hope has failed, every comfort is dead. [Translation mine.]

The climate of melancholia spread from Italy to the rest of Europe. It is found in Albrecht Dürer (1471–1528), the painter who portrayed the concept of melancholia in fine art. In England *The Anatomy of Melancholy* by Robert Burton appeared in 1621 under the author's pseudonym, Democrites Junior. Burton repeated the idea that melancholia is a state of the organism resulting from the perturbation of one of the four primary humors. The work is preceded by a prologue which explains and justifies the selection of the topics and the system of exposition. The book is divided into three parts: two deal with melancholia in general; the last with melancholia as related to love and religion. This work is a huge compilation and a strange conglomeration of disparate quotations. It offers hardly anything original about melancholia from a philosophical, psychological, and psychiatric point of view. However, it had some influence in English literature—especially on Milton, Sterne, Byron, and Lamb.

It is beyond the purpose of this book to discuss the complex problem of how melancholia gained ground in the European literature and finally emerged in the literary movement called romanticism. Romanticism is permeated by a philosophy of pessimistic idealism. The romantic writers advocated not a practical utilitarian morality, but an absolute one which never triumphed because of either adverse fate or human flaws. Often the Romantic hero was depressed, but not so much because of the suffering inflicted on him or the defeats to which he was subjected. He was not like the religious martyr who disregards lack of success on earth because he aspires only to eternal values and superior goodness; his pain and rancor, which made him utterly depressed, came from not being understood and appreciated by other humans. His great suffering often derived from the fact that he could not in good faith respect those who were not able to recognize his value. He finds himself in a state of despair in which he must reconcile himself to the tragic fatality of human existence as it is now, in his present milieu, and as it probably always will be. Suffering and disappointment often lead the romantic hero to suicide, as in Goethe's *The Sorrows of the Young Werther*, a book imitated by many authors in various languages. This book, and its imitators, were said to have caused an epidemic of suicides in Europe.

In this depressed climate the French poet Lamartine wrote in a poem dedicated to Byron:

> *Plus je sonde l'abîme, hélas! plus je m'y perds.*
> *Ici-bas la douleur à la douleur s'enchaine,*
> *le jour succède au jour, et la peine à la peine.*
> *Borné dans sa nature, infini dans ses voeux,*
> *l'homme est un dieu tombé qui se souvient des cieux.*

> The more I plumb the abyss, alas! the more lost I become.
> Here on earth, pain is bound to pain;
> As day follows day, sorrow follows sorrow.
> Limited in his nature, infinite in his desire,
> Man remains a fallen god with memories of Heaven.
> [My translation]

Victor Hugo represents man as a blind giant who travels in the darkness of the night and sustains himself on a special cane: his sorrow. Musset, in his well-known sonnet "Tristesse," assesses his life which craves joy but is full of disappointments, and he concludes with these verses:

Dieu parle, il faut qu'on lui répond;
le seul bien qui me reste au monde
est d'avoir quelquefois pleuré.

God speaks, and I must answer;
The only wealth left to me in this world
Is that of having sometimes cried.
[My translation]

The Italian poet Giacomo Leopardi, in a poem written on the occasion of the wedding of his sister Paolina, reminds her that she will add an unhappy family to unhappy Italy.

Whether it is transformed into realism or decadence, romanticism continues to exert an influence even today, and it possibly facilitates the occurrence of depressive thoughts. For instance, the realist Thomas Hardy viewed the human being as the victim of destiny and uncontrollable forces. Disappointment and sadness pervaded the poets in the 1930s (W. H. Auden, Louis MacNeice, Stephen Spender, Cecil Day Lewis, William Empson, and many others).

I have taken examples from several literary genres, without yet taking into consideration the one which probably portrays more intensely than any other genre the oceanic feeling of despair and melancholia. I am referring to the tragic situation as portrayed in literature in the form of tragedy. This is a vast issue, and only books of literature and philosophy can deal adequately with it in its many parts. I shall only refer to what is particularly relevant in connection with the psychiatric understanding of depression.

Can the state of the tragic hero be compared to that of the severely depressed patient? In some respects, yes. The hero finds himself in a situation which is tragic insofar as it is inevitable, irreversible, and unwanted to an extreme degree, like the irreparable failure of one's mission, life plan, or lifelong hope, and the renunciation of life itself for the sake of the ideal. The hero is at the mercy of uncontrollable forces or he is responsible for deeds which he carried out without being aware of them; if he was aware of them, he was not conscious of their significance and their possible consequences. He is supposed to have no faults, like a god, but he is a human being and has flaws. Oedipus is unable to "see the truth," Othello is jealous, Lear is proud and arrogant, and Hamlet is unable to make decisions. The hero's flaws in and of themselves would not be sufficient in some instances to bring about the catastrophe if other circumstances had not worked together toward the tragic end, for instance, if Othello had not been misguided by Iago, if Macbeth had not been enticed by the witches, and so forth. Often a group of circumstances seems to conspire against the human being who, no matter how much he towers in his human dimensions, is still too little to cope with the gigantic situation which confronts him.

We can recognize a hero in our depressed patient, too, and more frequently a heroine, who lives a tragic drama. He or she is the protagonist, but often obscure circumstances have set the stage. He or she seems at the mercy of uncontrollable forces, but the patient's flaws also play determining roles: not recognizing the rigidity of the selected patterns of living; the unwillingness to change life goals and find alternatives; and the total commitment to a cause, in spite of repeated subliminal warnings that the patient should change his or her ways of thinking and feeling.

The literary tragedy is in some respects a human protest. It mirrors the terror the human being has to face at times, the injustice he has to suffer, the anguish he feels. The protest is against whoever is responsible—the gods, fate, historical or social circumstances—or the limitations of human nature. The patient's depression also is a protest, but he often seems to lack the grandeur which is inherent in the ultimate acceptance of the tragic hero. He may even seem to lose his dignity at times and to indulge in a personal melodrama. And yet we must see him or her in an even more tragic light than the tragic hero; because unless he is successfully treated, he cannot maintain his own belief in himself or in his ideas, and he has contempt even for his own depression, for his own protest.

Literary tragedy often portrays the struggle between man and fate, which ends with the defeat of man and the victory of fate. But as Schlegel wrote (1818), the moral victory is with man. The depressed patient is not concerned with moral victory; he or she does not want to be heroic or a person who challenges the power of destiny, but only a happy human being.

A common conception of tragedy was originally presented by Schiller (1796), who interpreted the tragic conflict as being between the ideal to which the human being aspires and the real world. The depressed person also sees a big discrepancy between what he aspired to in terms of human relations and life goals and what he can achieve in this meager reality. He cannot solve the conflict. What is available is not acceptable to him, and what would be acceptable he cannot grasp. He experiences the tragic situation of having no choice.

For Schopenhauer, tragedy as a literary form portrays what to him is the terrible essence of life, "the unspeakable pain, the wail of humanity, the triumph of evil, the scornful mastery of chance, and the irretrievable fall of the just and innocent" (Schopenhauer, 1961). The original sin is the sin of being born at all. Many patients at the nadir of their depression would echo Schopenhauer if they were endowed with his style and vocabulary. Other conceptions of tragedy are probably closer to those that a psychotherapist would accept. For example, Aristotle saw literary tragedy as a catharsis or purgation of the spectator through pity and fear. For Goethe (1827), the catharsis had to be understood as expiation or reconciliation on the part of the hero, rather than as purgation of the spectator. Goethe in his maturity changed the points of view he held earlier in life. I have already mentioned that young Goethe had his first hero, young Werther, commit suicide, and in the first part of *Faust* he had his protagonist sell his soul to the devil, an act which in the Christian tradition is an absolute form of suicide. But in the second part, written after a long interval, Faust undergoes purgation and obtains salvation.

Contemporary feelings of tragedy and depression, as they have occurred in the literature and other media, are discussed in another section of this chapter. A theme which has recurred in several periods of history is similar in its negativity to that of Schopenhauer. It has appeared frequently in literary forms and even in the common expressions of people. Any human being is a tragic figure: he finds himself on earth for no reasons that he initiated, coming from nobody knows where, and going toward indefinite paths. Only one thing is sure, that he will die and will have to face death. As tragic as this portrayal of man seems, the depressed patient does not experience his predicament in these terms. His protest is a personal one. He does not speak for Man or Woman, but for John Doe or Mary Smith.

The therapist who wishes to help the depressed patient must be a person who assumes that the human being could do a great deal to change the otherwise tragic circumstances of his life. Obviously our destiny is not entirely in our hands, but we ourselves are one of the major forces which mold our existence.

The therapist must admit, however, that there are tragic situations which the human being cannot change at all. What then? What can the therapist do to help? If the individual cannot change the tragic situation after having done his utmost to change it, his position becomes heroic, and he must learn to accept the heroic stand both for himself and as a spiritual example to others. Let us remember, however, that as our rapid survey may have indicated, there is not only one type of tragedy, but two, and the second is more frequent than the first. The first follows the Greek paradigm, in which the human being is the ineluctable victim of destiny and as such is ineluctably predestined to suffer and perish. Ananke—necessity or fate—which at times works in conjunction with other human beings, is the cruel puppeteer who pulls the strings. If this is the human situation, the heroic position is in seeing the heroism of the puppet.

But there is a second type of tragedy, the tragedy of the Judeo-Christian tradition. It is the tragedy of having to sacrifice one's own beloved son, Isaac, the tragedy of Joseph being sold by his own brothers, the tragedy of Job, the tragedy of Christ—wherever the tragedy leads to the triumph of the human spirit. It is the tragedy in which the heros are not *les petites marionettes*, but where they themselves pull the strings which at times move the world, not necessarily in a direct way or during their lifetime, but through their legacy. The tragedy that ends with the triumph of the spirit may be called a spiritual or divine "comedy," as it was called by those who interpreted Dante's allegoric journey.

Our Era As the Age of Depression

Depression is acknowledged as being so common in our time that some people are ready to classify our era as the age of depression.

Since I have been in the field of psychiatry, I have heard periods of time, stretching up to about a decade each, being referred to with psychiatric terms. In the 1940s we repeatedly heard that we were living in an age of anxiety; in the 1950s, in the age of alienation; in the 1960s, in an era of anger; and in the 1970s, in the age of depression. Is there any truth to these affirmations?

First of all, we must remember that these terms—anxiety (and/or fear), alienation (and/or detachment), anger (and/or hostility and violence), sadness (and/or depression)—are the basic negative emotional states that affect the human being. These basic negative feelings have existed since man made his appearance on this troubled planet. It is true, however, that one basic mood is felt more intensely than the others in particular periods of time. It is also true that periodical cultural trends make the human being as an individual and the whole society more sensitive to one particular mood than to another.

Anxiety has always been man's companion, but psychoanalysis has focused on this emotion and has made us recognize that it is a practically constant affective tonality. The popularity of psychoanalysis in the 1940s and the experiences of the Second World War have made us more aware of anxiety and more ready to respond to it. The triumph of technology, mechanization, industrialization, corporation, and bureaucracy in the 1950s made us aware of our rampant alienation and brought about a revival of theories about this human status, which were originally formulated by Hegel, Marx, and others. The revolt against the Establishment, manifested by the students' confrontation and rebellion and by the increase in crime in the 1960s, made us think of an age of anger and violence.

But what about the 1970s, and why depression? What accumulation of facts had made sadness (or depression) more common, or increased our awareness of it, or made us more responsive to it? I have already mentioned that in some psychiatric circles the hypothesis has been advanced that since Cade discovered the beneficial effect of lithium in manic-depressive psychosis, we have focused on what we are able to treat and therefore on our manic and depressive trends. So many assumptions have to be packed into this hypothesis as to put its credibility in serious doubt. Lithium is an effective symptomatic treatment in some manic patients, not in depressed patients. It is also difficult to see how the enthusiasm of a few pharmacotherapists could influence the whole culture. We have seen that eras of depression have recurred throughout history. First in the early Middle Ages and then after the Reformation it was enhanced by the prevailing concepts of sin, guilt, damnation, retribution, and unworthiness. In our time depression, at least at a cultural level, seems to be connected with the loss of traditional values and the inability to replace them with new ones. A state of meaninglessness, reminiscent of that which is experienced by the severely depressed patient, permeates contemporary culture. Our contemporary literary tragedy is best represented by the theatre of the absurd. It conveys the premise that God is dead, and with the death of God all hope is dead; life is meaningless and essentially absurd, unfit to its surroundings, disharmonious, and purposeless.

The significant writings of some authors who actually had started to write in this vein in the 1930s and 1940s has finally permeated the spirit of the culture. When the present literature—especially the novel and the theatre in their most eloquent representations—portrays the tension between the forces of growth and the forces of dissolution, it ends with the victory of the negative forces. Already in 1942 Camus in *The Myth of Sisyphus* asked why man should not commit suicide, since life has lost its meaning. Echoing with modern themes the quoted verses of Lamartine (page 381) he writes ". . . In a universe that is suddenly deprived of illusion and of light, man feels a stranger. His is an irremediable exile, because he is deprived of memory of a lost homeland as much as he lacks the hope of a promised land to come." In *Waiting for Godot,* Beckett says "Nothing happens, nobody comes, nobody goes, it's awful" [1959]. The awfulness is the state of meaninglessness in this cultural climate, in which a considerable number of people feel that they have lost their ideals and have not replaced them with new ones. Many persons no longer see themselves as part of a worthwhile whole, as part of either society or an ideological group. In some cases cynicism, distance-making, and alienation of all kinds are not strong enough antidotes to the state of meaninglessness; and despondency and depression ensue, often as a chronic, anxious sadness or as an apathetic form of depression.

Some sociologists and psychiatrists have asked themselves whether the terrible events which have happened in our century—the First World War with millions of people killed on the battlefield and the massacre of millions of civilian Armenians, the Second World War, with the Holocaust of the Jews and the atomic bombing of Hiroshima—have engendered a feeling of overwhelming hopelessness in generations of young people, culminating with a pervasive feeling of sadness and meaninglessness about mankind and life in general. Studies of this type are difficult to make on a large scale. Conclusions drawn from answers in response to questionnaires seem inadequate to the depth of the inquiry. I can only speak for myself and express the conclusions that I have reached from my studies of both depressed patients and patients belonging to other clinical categories whom I have treated since the end of the Second World War. I am fully aware that the limitation of my inquiries and my personal biases may have led me to wrong conclusions. Nevertheless, I must dare to express my tentative feelings.

None of my patients have seemed concerned at more than a superficial level with the effects and meaning of the Holocaust and Hiroshima, unless they had some relatives or friends caught in these tragic events. The massacre of the Armenians has practically been forgotten by everybody except the Armenians. I expected people to be concerned about these terrible events, but they were not. I could not conclude that the concern was deeply repressed and I did not catch it because I have included in my inquiry only people who were adequately and deeply analyzed. If repression existed, it was to an extent that could not be overcome with the usual therapeutic procedures.

Alexander and Margarete Mitscherlich (1975), two well-known German analysts, have described the inability of the German people to mourn for what their fellow citizens had done during the Second World War. But we could extend the Mitscherlichs' regret to the whole world and say that people in general have not been able to mourn adequately for the Armenian massacre, for the Holocaust, and for Hiroshima. They could not do sorrow work, nor did they fail to do adequate sorrow work as described in chapter 5 of this book because they did not feel the need to mourn. They did not experience adequate sorrow in the first place. A sad or depressed reaction would have been more adequate, and probably would have made them experience a salutary sense of tragedy. Perhaps a longer interval of time for a thoughtful appraisal of historical events is necessary. In any case I cannot attribute the present cultural mood of depression directly to the tragedies of our century or relate depression to them in a sequence of linear causality. Perhaps the lack of adequate emotional response has contributed to the feeling of lost values and meaninglessness which may be responsible for this state of aimless despondency and vulnerability to depression. Nothing matters in a world reputed to be aimless, amoral, and deprived of personal or cosmic harmony.

Instead of finding reconstructive inspiration from the historical tragedies of our time, some of which were of a magnitude never before conceived, literature has contributed to this feeling of meaninglessness and abolition of values. Unfortunately, we must subscribe to John Gardner's view when he writes of "death by art" or death by cultural influences. He says, "Some men kill you with a six-gun, some men with a pen" (1977).

In defending writers of the absurd, some critics indicate that by pointing out the meaninglessness of the world and the destructive tendencies of everything, such writers want to help people and to stimulate the emergence of constructive forces. This does not seem to me to be the case, because writers of the absurd identify very well with these negative forces, feel them very strongly, and with the greatest sincerity point out what seems to be their inevitability and irreversibility.

Socio-Philosophical Premises of the Psychotherapist of Depressed Patients

Not everything is negative, however. We have made progress in some areas, for instance, in the way women are treated.

The task of the psychotherapist of depressed patients is made more difficult in a cultural climate in which the meaninglessness of everything is advocated. I have mentioned, however, that the patient who feels very sick is seldom concerned with anything that transcends his private predicament. The therapist has to find his own identity and pave his own way, but if he shares the feeling that any waiting is a waiting for Godot, how can he help the patient to wait for recovery, and to reacquire hope in himself and life? Rather, he must think that waiting in a passive way and doing nothing else, while the earth continues to rotate on its axis, is not enough. The patient must move too, with open eyes, toward various possibilities. I cannot make generalizations which will be satisfactory for every psychotherapist, since specific issues enter into the dealings of each individual. I will nevertheless attempt to formulate guidelines which may help the therapist of depressed patients to do his work. These guidelines obviously also derive from our culture, and they can be seen as common denominators of the philosophical premises on which psychotherapy is based:

1. A psychotherapist assumes that a person does not need to become depressed if he is able to focus not on the daydreams which did not come to pass, but on those which were realized. The fewer the actualized dreams, the more valuable they are and the more they should be cherished.

2. Because of the infinite cognitive, emotional, and volitional functions of the psyche, the patient's age, sex, physical appearance, and intellectual ability may decrease but—with rare exceptions—they do not extinguish his human possibilities. It is not necessary for the individual to feel trapped in certain patterns of living as if they were indelible imprintings. He can preserve a mobility consonant with life's array of alternatives.

3. A therapist cannot adhere to the concept that life is meaningless, or therapy becomes meaningless too. Two possibilities exist: (a) the therapist feels that there is a transcendental order and consequently a meaning in the universe and in life. But this is an act of faith, and we cannot prescribe it on demand to the therapist who cannot experience it. (b) The therapist shares the idea that even if there is no preordained order in the universe, and even if man and human affairs are random and inexplicable occurrences, an order and consequently a meaning can evolve in the human environment. Thus a purpose can still be given to one's life.

PART TWO: DEPRESSION AND
METHODS OF CHILD-REARING

In attempting to delineate the etiological factors that culminate in adult depression, some information might be obtained by scrutinizing the methods of child-rearing in those societies or subcultures that produce a high number of depressed adults. As with family studies of depression in our own culture, such reports are very scarce although some data exist and will be presented here. However, child-rearing methods cannot easily be separated from the cultural context in which they occur. Cultural beliefs permeate all areas of the individual's existence, just as these beliefs influence the parents and, in particular, the ideology that they impart to their offspring. Therefore more than simple child-rearing practices are involved. The whole cultural system of beliefs which are handed down through the parents, and which continue to shape the individual after childhood, must also be considered.

The importance of cultural beliefs was highlighted in a comparative study of neighboring Ojibwa and Eskimo tribes reported by Parker (1962). He found that although these two peoples shared common ecological hardships of cold winters and poor food supply, the Ojibwa tribe

Part two of this chapter was written by Jules Bemporad.

had a high rate of depression together with anorexia, paranoid ideation, and obsessiveness; and the Eskimos demonstrated frequent hysterical attacks and some conversion reactions, but essentially no depressive disorders.

The reason for this difference may of course reflect different genetic pools, but this explanation is difficult to support in that both groups exhibited changes in symptomatology as their contact with Western culture increased. Rather, the discrepancy in types of pathology seemed to result from basic tribal beliefs which in turn affected the mode of child rearing. The Eskimos are, or were, a communal people who believed in total sharing and equality. It was difficult to discern any leadership structure, and there was no emphasis on social rank or individual accomplishment. They exhibited a confident attitude toward the supernatural, expecting their gods to grant them the necessities for survival. In times of hardship, they banded together and shared what little food could be obtained. Also, if any one member of the tribe transgressed some taboo, the community as a whole assumed responsibility so that there was essentially no concept of individual sin, or perhaps even of individual guilt. Those who came in contact with the Eskimos described them as exuding an atmosphere of joviality, friendship, camaraderie, and modesty. They openly expressed their emotions and were not ashamed to ask each other for help or to admit weakness.

In contrast, the Ojibwa Indians were described as boastful, sullen, competitive, and secretive. They were hypersensitive to criticism and nursed grudges for inordinate periods of time. In times of hardship they lived apart, in closely knit, small family units that competed and were suspicious of each other. The Ojibwa showed a masochistic attitude toward their gods; they humbled themselves and begged for pity from spiritual powers. They also tried to propitiate their gods by personal suffering. This religious attitude may have been based on their belief that impersonal causes were never the reason for misfortune. Someone was always responsible and had to mollify the gods by personal sacrifice for guilt which was not shared by the others. Their gods were appeased only by suffering and even children were required to suffer in order to insure the gods' favoritism.

As regards child-rearing, the practice of the two neighboring peoples were also different. The Eskimos believed that a child was the repository of the soul of a recently departed family member. Unless the child was treated kindly and prevented from suffering, they feared that the protective soul would leave the child's body and the child might become sick or die. Therefore the Eskimo baby was welcomed into the tribe as the return of a departed loved one. He was satisfied in every way, even being nursed on demand until four years of age. Any sign of discomfort was appeased by food, distraction, or engaging the child in a pleasurable activity. There was complete dependency gratification without the expectation that the child had to work in order to deserve the love given him. In general, there were few restrictions on behavior, with great tolerance for bowel and bladder accidents or sexual curiosity. Around puberty the child was gradually initiated in the adult role with great patience.

In marked contrast, the Ojibwa believed that the neonate was an empty vessel who was vulnerable to the myriad evil powers that filled the world. In order to protect the child from misfortune, he was disciplined early and "toughened" to prevent being seduced by evil spirits. Early in life the child was introduced to the gloomy pessimism of the Ojibwa; for example, he was regularly starved to prepare him for periods of food shortage. As with the cultural belief system, he was made to feel responsible for his misfortunes and that salvation was possible only through self-induced suffering. Finally, the child was given a goal that he had to achieve in his later life: he was expected to have a vision during an intensely painful rite of passage which would show him his future path. Therefore, he later felt obligated to achieve the goal revealed to him in his "vision."

Parker concluded that the Eskimo's need for immediate gratification and the easy reliance on the community to fulfill his every need may have predisposed him to public histrionics in times of deprivation. On the other hand, the Ojibwa's consistent shame over dependency needs, his lack of community support, his belief that gratification could be achieved only through self-induced suffering, and his need to achieve in order to feel worthy might have accounted for the selection of depression as a common expression of conflict and stress.

Another anthropological study which may shed some light on the psychogenesis of depression is Eaton and Weil's (1955b) report of the self-contained Hutterite community in the northern United States. As mentioned earlier, this is a highly puritanical and duty-oriented community which has been found to have an extremely high rate of depressive disorders. The values of this community may be summarized as follows: to deny oneself (or others), to shun (and be ashamed of) hedonistic or aggressive tendencies, to have complete loyalty to the group, and to seek rewards for self-denial and hard work in an afterlife.

Child-rearing procedures differ markedly from the neighboring American communities. For example, babies are delivered at home by natural childbirth, families have ten to twelve children (since birth control is considered sinful), and there is communal mothering after the infant is two months of age. From the age of roughly thirty months, each child spends most of the day in a nursery school, and from this point on his entire life becomes group-oriented with ever-increasing ties to the community. Eaton and Weil comment that there is a great deal of identification with the peer group and a strong need for conformity. Education is described as colored by "a continuous, uniform, but general rote form of religious indoctrination" (p. 31). Furthermore, the children are taught an absolute value system with a clear code of admissible behavior, the only justification for which is tradition. The children are told that they are superior to their decadent and spiritually contaminated neighbors and they are expected to lead exemplary lives. Competition between children is not encouraged, but everyone is expected to do his utmost and to try his hardest in any endeavor.

In Eaton and Weil's study one is struck with the lack of freedom, spontaneity, and even privacy allowed to the growing child. While there is a great deal of community support and security, these comforts appear to be achieved at the price of individuality. In addition, there appears to be a constant fear that one has failed by insufficient effort and will be liable to judgment from peers or from God.

The effects of these pressures on Hutterite children was clearly noticeable to the authors and to their non-Hutterite teachers. The Hutterite elders had remarked that there were no maladjusted children in their community, while the teachers believed that about two-thirds of the children demonstrated some degree of psychopathology. Ironically, the behavior thought to be pathological by American teachers was approved by Hutterite religious teachers, and the behavior encouraged by the American teachers was judged as bad by the Hutterites. For example, impulsive and spontaneous behavior was criticized by the Hutterites. On the other hand, extremely inhibited, submissive, obedient behavior was applauded by the Hutterites to the dismay of the American teachers.

A vignette described by Eaton and Weil epitomizes the atmosphere that surrounds the Hutterite child.

A young staff member, who was very spontaneous with children, started to play tag with a group that had gathered around him. The tagging progressed into hitting, and our field worker was soon preoccupied with warding off shouting boys and girls who were competing in the effort to get a lick at him. The staff member enjoyed the 'game' and encouraged it. Suddenly the shrill voice of an elderly lady came out of an entrance door of the communal kitchen across the courtyard: 'Gebt Heim!' (Go home). As if hit by lightning, the children froze, stopped, and dispersed. One remark from a respected adult was enough to curb them, although the woman was not the parent of any of them. Later, she and several other adults apologized profusely to the staff member for the behavior of the youngsters explaining: 'They are awfully bad.' (Pp. 132–133).

Nevertheless, while the child is highly disciplined, he is also given much love. Children are the only wealth a Hutterite may call his own and so they are prized by their parents. This counterforce may protect them from severe psychopathology in childhood, but the stern system of beliefs that is indoctrinated shows up in adult life as an inordinate propensity for depression.

For the Hutterite as for the Ojibwa child, life experience is channelled by strong taboos against spontaneity or fun. There is an ever-present sense of inhibition and a fear of letting go. Furthermore, there is an equally pervasive atmosphere of sin, accountability, and self-denial.

The world is seen as a place full of evil temptation from which the child is to be protected by stern discipline. The Hutterites temper this severity with love, but this parental love must be won by hard work. The Ojibwa seem to make a virtue of suffering and to show their love for their off-spring by preparing him for the harsh difficulties of adult life. While the Objiwa child seems to be allowed more freedom and individuality than the conformist Hutterites, he is burdened with a sense that he must accomplish his visionary goal and that others cannot be counted on to help in this endeavor. These differences might account for the variations in secondary symptoms seen in the respective depressive episodes. Finally, both cultures view outsiders with suspicion and consider themselves to be both different and superior.

These studies, while limited in number, confirm the fundamental thesis that the predisposition to adult depression results from the individual's early relationships and from cognitive structures that are internalized. In reading the accounts of child-rearing among the Objiwa or the Hutterites, one sees many areas of similarity in the accounts of the childhoods of depressives in our own society. Our cultural mores do not strengthen or amplify the family beliefs and transactional styles that predispose to later depression. However, the early learning of these beliefs or the child's early experiences (such as those described by Cohen and co-workers, 1954) appear sufficient to mold the individual's way of thinking and behaving so that he is later impervious to healthier modes of adaptation. In our society, specific subcultures do exist whose values tend to produce depression-prone individuals. However, the lack of general cohesion in current American society may allow for a pathological belief system of even one nuclear family to be sufficient to create a depressive vulnerability in childhood.

[17]

FRANZ KAFKA:

A LITERARY PROTOTYPE OF

THE DEPRESSIVE CHARACTER

> Dearest Father,
> You asked me recently why I maintain that I am afraid of you. As usual I was unable to think of any answer to your questions, partly for the very reason that I am afraid of you, and partly because an explanation of the grounds for this fear would mean going into far more details than I could even approximately keep in mind while talking.

In this dramatic manner, Franz Kafka, at the age of thirty-six began one of the great literary confessions of all time (Kafka, 1973). This "letter to his father" remains as a remarkably moving and insightful human document which reveals the intricacies, the pain, and the strength of Kafka's pathological bond to his father and the disaster that this relationship brought to Kafka's life. In this lengthy letter, Kafka analyzes with remarkable skill the causes of his depressive paralysis and the role of his childhood experiences in his difficulties in facing a responsible adult existence. The letter is both an *apologia pro vita sua* and an attempt at reconciliation with the father. Franz gave the letter to his mother for her to give to his father. Ironically and yet quite understandably, she never delivered it.

Franz Kafka has been selected as a well-known paradigm of the depressive character, since in his writings as well as in his life he exemplifies the dilemma of the depressive and writes of this dilemma with such eloquence and imagination that his works transcend the impersonal and narrow textbook descriptions of depression. In choosing Kafka to

This chapter was written by Jules Bemporad.

represent a man obsessed with the conflicts of depression, I have not been blind to his extensive contributions toward laying bare the universal problems of modern man. His existentialism is beautifully portrayed throughout his work, especially in *The Castle*, in which man repeatedly attempts to serve a god who simply will not respond and yet who appears to demand continued servitude. Georg Lukacs commented on the sinister emptiness of Kafka's castle: "If a god is present here, he is a god of religious atheism: Atheos Absconditus." (Cited in Politzer, 1966, p. 234.) Similarly, *The Trial* wearies the reader with its repeated dehumanization of man by an endless, mysterious bureaucracy. Martin Buber, who knew Kafka and published his work, sees in *The Trial* "a district delivered over to the authority of a slovenly bureaucracy without the possibility of appeal . . . Man is called into this world, he is appointed in it, but wherever he turns to fulfill his calling he comes up against the thick vapors of a mist of absurdity . . . . it is a Pauline world, except that God is removed into the impenetrable darkness and that there is no place for a mediator." (Cited in Politzer, 1966, p. 179.)

However, it is not as a commentator on life's absurdity or as a grim prophet of twentieth century civilization that Kafka will be considered here. Nor will attention be paid to his remarkable individualistic style which in a few lines creates an atmosphere of gloom and despair. His writing has been accurately described as the "objective depiction of absurdity" (Magny, 1946), and indeed Kafka meticulously details the objects of a world that makes no sense, that has no meaning. His intentional avoidance of describing scenery and locale lead to the uneasy realization that he is really writing about the landscape of the mind, and not of external space.

Cooperman (1966) accurately observes that Kafka may be appreciated on three levels: (1) the socio-materialist level, by which Kafka reflects the decay of prewar German culture, (2) the theological-mystical level, in which the meaning of the works can be seen as an existential search for grace which will not be achieved in a world without God, and (3) the psychological-rational level in which Kafka's writings reveal the struggles of a neurotic personality. One interpretation need not conflict with the others, as long as one does not try to reduce all levels to one, just as a study of his striking literary style may be taken as a separate investigation in itself. Most but by no means all students of Kafka have focused on his theological or social meaning. Two exceptions are Edmund Wilson and Charles Neider. Wilson fails to see any great philosophical depth to Kafka's work, regarding the writings as a painful "realization of an emotional cul-de-sac" (1962, p. 96).* Neider (1948) believes he has

---

* Wilson concludes: "In Kafka's case, it was he who cheated and never lived to get his own back. What he has left us is the half-expressed gasp of a self-doubting soul trampled under. I do not see how one can possibly take him for either a great artist or moral guide" (1962, p. 97).

found the key to Kafka in his discovery of alleged masculine and feminine symbols interspersed throughout the writings, and he uses these symbols to reconstruct Kafka's personality problems according to the method of early classical psychoanalysis.

It is my opinion that Kafka was acutely disturbed by existential philosophical questions and that these dilemmas are expressed in his works, especially the novels. However, for our present purposes, Kafka's gifts as a moralist and stylist will be left to students of philosophy and aesthetics. Here we shall be concerned with Kafka as a depressed, neurotic individual whose talent for writing and introspection allowed him to describe the inner world of depression with rare insight and power.

The external details of Kafka's life are relatively uneventful, except perhaps in the area of intimate relationships where the effects of his psychopathology may be discerned. As outlined in Brod's biography (1973), Franz was born in Prague on July 3, 1883. It is of psychological significance that his two younger brothers died in infancy and his younger siblings were all girls. A second son was born in 1885 and survived only two years. A third son born in 1887 survived only one year. It may be speculated that Kafka's infancy was troubled not only by the usual loss of the mother's attention when a younger sib is born, but by an additional burden of familial sadness and despair at the deaths of these younger brothers. Kafka's mother gave birth to six children in nine years, so that even without the tragedy of the deaths of Kafka's brothers, the availability of the mother may be questioned. While we do not know the actual effect of these events on Kafka as a child, his later troubled relationships with women may indicate early difficulties with his mother.

In any event, Franz became the designated heir to the family business, and his father's future successor as well as predestined rival. The father Herman Kafka, through hard work, shrewdness, and force of character had risen from the level of proletariat to become a respected middle-class wholesale merchant. He was reported to be a giant of a man who was gruff, coarse, and autocratic both at home and at work. Franz's mother, in contrast, came from a family of Jewish scholars as well as dreamers and eccentrics. She was described as an intelligent and wise woman who, however, was quietly submissive before her husband. She worked daily in her husband's business and usually spent her evenings playing cards with him. There is not much evidence that she offered much support or solace to her children when they opposed their father. In the same letter cited earlier, Kafka compares her to a beater during a hunt, forcing out the prey to be slaughtered by the powerful father. His diary entries include the following: "How furious I am with my mother. I need only begin to talk to her and I am irritated, almost scream" (written in 1913: Kafka, 1949) and, "Father from one side, mother from the other, have inevitably almost broken my spirit" (written in 1916: Kafka, 1949).

In childhood Franz was a pale, thin, sickly youngster given to scholarly pursuits. At the German University in Prague he finally decided on law although he would have preferred to study literature. According to Brod (1973), Kafka disliked the study of law but chose it because a legal degree allowed him the most options and the least dedication. He had already decided to become a writer and saw studying for the bar as eventually leading to a nondemanding way to earn a living while allowing time for literary pursuits. He duly obtained his degree of doctor juris in 1906, having already completed a number of stories and the greater part of a novel (which has been lost to posterity). Following a year's internship in the law courts, he worked briefly for an Italian insurance company and then for the Workers' Accident Insurance Institute until his retirement in 1920. Apparently he detested his work and tolerated it only because it gave him sufficient income to continue his writing. Much of the hopeless, sterile, gloomy atmosphere of his novels seems to be derived from his experience with the long, drawn-out insurance claims which he processed through endless series of bureaucratic official levels.

On August 13, 1912, at the age of twenty-nine he met Felice Bauer, a young woman from Berlin who was visiting with friends. Kafka became immediately infatuated with her and one month later began an extensive correspondence that lasted five years. He twice became engaged to Felice and twice broke off the engagement. Shortly before the termination of their relationship, he was diagnosed as suffering from tuberculosis.

In 1919 he was briefly engaged to Julia Wohryzek, whom he met at a summer resort. It was the senior Kafka's objection to this union that prompted the famous "Letter To His Father." Kafka broke off the engagement and began a long, tempestuous relationship with another woman, carried out primarily by correspondence. This woman, Milena Jesenska, was married to an unfaithful, highly exploitative man who apparently exerted an uncanny power over his wife as well as over other women. During his "affair" with Milena, Kafka was in and out of various sanatoriums for his tuberculosis, so that while he and Milena wrote each other several letters a day, they actually saw little of each other. Kafka eventually broke off their relationship because she was unwilling to leave her husband for him. Milena was willing to live with Kafka for awhile but not to permanently sever her marital union. We do not know her reasons (although in her letters to Brod, she clearly demonstrates her anguish and guilt), but it may have been that Milena was well aware that Kafka's remaining days of life were severely limited.

In the summer of 1923, while staying with his sister, Kafka met Dora Dymant, who at that time was about half Kafka's age. Dora was a rebellious and assertive girl who had escaped from a highly respected Orthodox Jewish family to support herself by servile work. Dora and Kafka moved to Berlin together, over both their families' objections. Despite Kafka's illness and their extreme poverty (due to the rampant inflation in

Germany at the time), Kafka wrote Brod that for the first time he felt happy. Gradually his tuberculosis became more severe, and after stays in various sanatoriums, Kafka died on June 3, 1924 at the age of forty-one.

An ironic and yet somehow appropriate postscript to Kafka's life was Brod's discovery in 1948 that Kafka had fathered an illegitimate son. The child had lived only seven years and died before Kafka. Brod wrote that the child's mother, identified solely as M.M., had had only a brief relationship with Kafka which was followed by a lasting hostile alienation. The tragic aspect of Kafka's ignorance of the existence of this offspring is that, according to Brod, there was nothing Kafka more fervently desired than children. Brod wrote: "Fulfillment of this desire would have seemed to him a confirmation of his worth from the highest court of appeal" (1973, p. 240). Just as in one of Kafka's own stories, redemption exists, except that he who might be redeemed is not aware of it and thus is denied it.

These are the outward events of Kafka's life, and they are somewhat unremarkable, if not barren. If we wish to encounter Kafka's genius as well as his psychopathology, we must turn to his inner world. In fact, one must consider whether Kafka was more alive in his writing than in his actual day-to-day existence as a noncommital lover and steady civil servant.

One avenue of inquiry in Kafka's inner life is an ingenious study of his dreams conducted by Hall and Lind (1970). In his *Diaries* Kafka recorded 31 dreams, and six more in his letters to Milena, which he had from the ages of twenty-three to forty. Hall and Lind subjected these to a dream content analysis which had been standardized on 500 reported dreams of 100 male college students. From this careful scrutiny of the 37 recorded dreams of Kafka, the authors elicited a series of interesting themes. They found little aggression in Kafka's dreams and a paucity of success events. This finding coincides with other studies on the dreams of depressed individuals (see chapter 7), and forms part of an overall passivity. Other themes which stood out were a preoccupation with the body and its disfigurement and an emphasis on clothing and nakedness. There was also a marked degree of scoptophilia (sexual pleasure derived from looking or observing). Finally, the authors found ambivalence toward both men and women and a preponderance of masculinized female characters. In contrast to Kafka's fictional works, there was little evidence of guilt in the dreams.

From their analysis Hall and Lind concluded that the main determinants of Kafka's adult personality were his childhood fixations on his mother and on his own body. They wrote, "Rejection by the mother meant that he could not cope with the father nor could he establish a satisfying and permanent relationship with a woman. Rejection of his body resulted in neurasthenia and hypochondria and was one of the reasons for his becoming consumptive" (1970, p. 91). These authors are probably correct in detecting the primary roots of Kafka's psychopathology, but they do not follow the development of the distortions of his personality that occurred later in childhood, namely, Kafka's relationship with his father and with his peers.

Those few individuals who were close to Kafka could not help but discern his overwhelming emotional tie to his father. His intimate friend and biographer Max Brod explicitly wrote of the impact of the father figure on Kafka's life. "In how many talks did I not try and make clear to my friend" wrote Max Brod, "how he overestimated his father, and how stupid it is to despise oneself. It was all useless, the torrent of arguments that Kafka produced (when he didn't prefer, as he frequently did, to keep quiet) could really shatter and repel me for a moment" (1973, p. 23). Brod appears constantly to have had to stimulate Kafka to write and to keep up his morale. Throughout his biography there are frequent allusions to Kafka's self-denigration, his creative paralysis, and his continuous melancholy.

Brod wrote, "Still today I feel that the fundamental question, 'What difference could his father's approval make to Kafka?' is put not from Kafka's point of view but from an outsider's. The fact that he did need it existed once and for all as an innate, irrefutable feeling, and its effects lasted to the end of his life as a general load of fear, weakness, and self-contempt" (1973, p. 23).

If we wish to penetrate Kafka's inner point of view and to understand his pathological tie to the dominant other from his internal vantage point, then we must turn to his writings where the conflict of the depressive often is so dramatically presented. From his autobiographical letter to his more symbolic works, the constant theme recurs: the realization of the brutality of authority, and, nonetheless, the hero's (or antihero's) need to grovel before and obey that authority.

In the letter to his father, Kafka realistically portrays his plight, recounting his early experiences and their lasting effect on his personality. The father is described as all-powerful and yet as critical, unfeeling, and crude. The father could tolerate no disagreement or show of strength in those around him, but then he disparaged the very weakness and submission he demanded and engendered. Kafka wrote: "From your arm chair you ruled the world. Your opinion was correct, every other was mad, wild, *meshugge*, not normal. Your self-confidence indeed was so great that you had no need to be consistent at all and yet never ceased to be in the right" (1973, p. 21). Kafka even recognizes his father's selfish interests in his relationships with others, that to him, anyone else's autonomous desires were irrelevant: ". . . and it is characteristic that even today you really only encourage me in anything when you yourself are involved in it, when what is at stake is your own sense of self-importance . . . ." (1973, p. 19). Kafka fully realized the burden of guilt that accompanied daring to act without the internalized doctrines of giving all for the honor of the family and pleasure of the father. "In all my thinking I was, after all, under the heavy pressure of your personality, even in that part of it—and particularly in that which was not in accord with yours. All these thoughts, seemingly independent of you, were from the beginning burdened with your belittling judgments" (P. 23).

More and more quotations can be cited which demonstrate Kafka's awareness of his inability to obtain his father's blessing and his constant painful need of it. He hated himself for his emotional dependency, yet he could not imagine living without it. Kafka beautifully describes this dilemma in one of his paradoxical parables. "It is as if a person were a prisoner, and he had not only the intention to escape, which would perhaps be attainable, but also, indeed simultaneously, the intention to rebuild the prison as a pleasure dome for himself. But if he escapes, he cannot rebuild, and if he rebuilds, he cannot escape" (1973, p. 113). While Kafka included this passage in a discussion of his reasons for not being able to marry Julie, it is clear that Kafka had the knowledge that he must escape his psychological prison. Yet he was simultaneously seized with the desire to reinstate himself as a prisoner, for he knew no other way to live than in relation to his father.

The long letter culminates in the reasons for Kafka's third renunciation of marriage: his father's suspicions of Kafka's intended and his ridicule of Kafka's reasons for desiring the girl, Kafka's own thoughts that marrying would mean becoming like his father and his concern that marriage would interfere with his writing. But there is more—Kafka felt that he could never face the responsibilities of marriage: "I tested myself not only when faced with marriage, but in the face of every trifle, you by your example and your method of upbringing convinced me, as I have tried to describe, of my incapacity and what turned out to be true of every trifle and proved you right, had to be fearfully true of the greatest thing of all: marriage" (1973, p. 121). Finally, Kafka alludes briefly to what may have been the most telling danger, that the father would break relations with him if he married: "I should flee him [Kafka's hypothetical son], emigrate, as you meant to do only because of my marriage" (1973, p. 117).

So much for Kafka's calm, reality-oriented recollections of his past. Perhaps a more accurate vision of his depressive conflict can be gained from his fictional creations which, although distorted, may like the distortions of dreams reveal a greater inner truth. For example, what he so persuasively and reasonably argued was his inability to marry in the letter written in 1919, was boldly foretold in a dramatic story written seven years earlier. This work, whose title may be translated as either *The Verdict* or *The Judgment*, was penned in one furious eight-hour sitting two days after he sent his first letter to Felice Bauer, to whom the story is dedicated. This work has been singled out by Politzer (1966) as signifying a breakthrough in Kafka's writing; it was here that Kafka dis-

covered his unique literary style which he continued to employ throughout all his later works.

The story opens with Georg, a young and successful merchant, who is
writing to an old friend who has emigrated to Russia. The mysterious
friend has fallen on hard times; he is sick, poor, and estranged in a foreign land without friends: "a man one could feel sorry for but not help."
In contrast, since the friend's departure Georg's fortunes have greatly increased. He has taken over his aging father's business and multiplied it
fivefold. He has even planned to marry, having become engaged a month
earlier to Frieda Brandenfeld, a girl from a well-to-do family (much
like her real life counterpart). The contrast between Georg and his
emigré friend is highlighted in a conversation that Georg recalls having
had with Frieda, in which he informs her that he cannot invite his
friend to their wedding. The friend would be hurt and discontented by
the disparity in their life circumstances, "and without being able to do
anything about his discontent he'd have to go away again alone." "Alone
—do you know what that means?" asks Georg. Finally Georg informs
his friend of the impending marriage at the end of the letter he has been
writing. Georg then enters his widowed father's darkened room. Although
the father is old and apparently ill, Georg remarks to himself, "My father
is still a giant of a man." Immediately they begin discussing the friend
in Russia. After Georg recounts his thoughts of inviting the friend to the
wedding, the father after a long preamble asks "Do you really have this
friend in St. Petersburg?" Georg reassures him with, "Never mind my
friends. A thousand friends wouldn't make up to me for my father." But
old man persists, he tells Georg that there is no such friend in Russia.
Georg again reassures the father, tenderly carries him to bed, and gently
tucks him in.

Suddenly the father springs from the bed, throwing the covers off.
"You wanted to cover me up," he shouts reproachfully, "but I'm far from
being covered up yet. And even if this is the last strength I have, it's
enough for you, too much for you. Of course I know your friend. He
would have been a son after my own heart." The father's numerous reproaches then turn to his son's ingratitude for allowing himself to plan
realistically to marry.

During this tirade, Georg begins to fantasize about his friend in
Russia, alone in a barren warehouse. "Why did he have to go so far
away?" he thinks. But the father interrupts his reverie. "Attend to me,"
he commands. He continues his attack: "Because she lifted her skirts like
this and this you made up to her, and in order to make free with her
undisturbed you disgraced your mother's memory, betrayed your friend,
and stuck your father into bed so that he can't move." Georg shrinks back
in the face of this barrage. "But your friend hasn't been betrayed after
all," cries the father, "I've been representing him here on the spot."

The tables have turned completely. The feeble old man that Georg carried to bed has risen into a giant. He brags to Georg that he could sweep Frieda from Georg's side if he so desired. Then comes the final twist: the now omnipotent father tells Georg that he has been in touch with the friend in Russia all along, and the friend prefers the father's letters to those of Georg: "In his [the friend's] left hand he crumples your letters unopened, while in his right he holds up my letters to read through," shouts the old man.

The father continues his condemnation of Georg. "So now you know what else there was in the world beside yourself, till now you've known only about yourself! An innocent child, yes, that you were truly, but still more truly have you been a devilish human being! And therefore take note: I sentence you now to death by drowning!" At these words, Georg dashes from the room, driven toward the water. Hanging from a bridge, he utters, "Dear parents, I have always loved you, all the same," and drops to his death, carrying out his father's sentence.

What is one to make of this grotesque story, especially since it was apparently written in a passionate fury after Kafka had decided to initiate his first real love affair? In his diaries Kafka wrote that the friend was the pivotal character, uniting all the others who are to be seen in relation to him (Brand, 1976). Indeed, the friend appears to be the liberated Kafka, the self that he pictured himself to be without his father. The friend is free, but he is also impoverished, sick, and a failure. Georg—the superficial Kafka—is successful, self-content, and about to be married; but as the story later makes clear, he is also a child, deluding himself about his social success. The father makes him aware of his selfish dependency and plainly states that he would have preferred the friend as a son. Finally the father after a series of rebukes sentences Kafka to death for his weakness, his self-centeredness, and his immaturity; and Kafka accepts the verdict.

The Judgment has attracted the attention of a number of students of psychology. Each finds his own particular meaning, and yet all agree on the son's overriding dependency on the father for his own self-evaluation. Becker (1969) wrote a semicommentary on the story, analyzing it almost paragraph by paragraph, and he ultimately used the story to illustrate his own thoughts on the Oedipal conflict. Becker believes that overcoming the Oedipal complex really means becoming a person in one's own right. Since George has failed in this task, Becker concludes, "he has literally not been able to be born into manhood; and so he must die" (1969, p. 68). Becker sees the father's judgment as proof of Georg's lack of personal individuation, "the parental appraisal of the child's personality is itself a command; the parent's opinion becomes the child's life will" (P. 68).

Indeed, the story seems to illustrate Kafka's inability to free himself from the father or from the family's beliefs. *The Judgment* offers Kafka a choice between two modes of life, each unsatisfactory. He cannot retain a social facade after the father has revealed the weakness, parasitism, and egotism of this role. Yet to free himself might mean to become like the friend—alone, sick, impoverished, an exile in a foreign land. Because he lacks the courage of the latter choice, he accepts the father's judgment that he does not deserve to live. Kafka's own diary entries closely support this interpretation.

The friend is the link between father and son, he is the greatest thing they have in common. Sitting alone at the window, Georg takes a sensual pleasure in rooting about in the common possession, believes he has his father in himself and, but for a fleeting, sad hesitation, considers everything is peaceful (1949).

Kafka's curious phrase about Georg having the father in himself so that everything is peaceful, may indicate Georg's belief that he has overcome the dominant other, that he has internalized his own value structure, so he is free to consider marriage, run a business, become prosperous, and—most important—attain maturity. All of this confident serenity is eventually disrupted as the father reassumes his commanding position. Kafka's diary entry continues, indicating that in reality Georg has no real identity, "and it is merely because he himself has nothing, else the sight of his father, that the verdict that shuts his father off from him completely has such a powerful effect on him." Kafka appears to be saying that the father is able to control Georg because the father is all that Georg has.

However, it should be noted that Kafka wrote this story after he had decided to initiate his first romance. *The Judgment* obviously prophesizes his inability to marry Felice, and yet he dedicated the story to her. His conflict over beginning a love affair must in some manner have served as the story's stimulus.

Brand (1976) in fact interprets the story as a renunciation of marriage and a dedication by Kafka to live the life of an ascetic, solitary artist. For Brand, the friend is the inner Kafka—the exile, the writer, and the bachelor—while Georg is Kafka's facade of bourgeois bliss and self-deceiving hypocrisy. According to Brand, in *The Judgment* Kafka kills his mundane self but gives birth to his artistic mastery. It is as if meeting Felice had upset his ideal of a bachelor purity, which the story sets right. Certainly the two characters are polar opposites and they may represent disparate aspects of Kafka's personality. What may be considered characteristically neurotic is Kafka's belief that the two aspects cannot be integrated. He must be a lonely outsider, an outcast, or he must be a self-indulgent, childlike burgher. However, it should be pointed out that Kafka chooses to have the father reveal Georg's hypocrisy, prevent his wish of marriage to materialize, and ultimately sentence him to death. Seen in this light, Kafka may be saying that his father's constant belittling, as revealed in the letter, made him feel too incapable or guilty to dare aspire to a normal, fulfilling life. Rather, Kakfa resorts to the romanticized existence of the pure artist because he cannot face the responsibilities and the pleasures of human commitment. It appears that Kafka is creating a virtue out of an inherent deficiency.

In a diary entry of July 21, 1913, Kafka listed seven points for and against marriage to Felice. The entry closes with "Miserable me!" and, "What misery" written in large letters. Briefly, the seven points consist of: his inability to live alone, yet his not understanding how to live with someone else; his becoming frightened when he hears that married men are happy; his being able to accomplish something only when alone; his fear of being tied to anyone, of overflowing into another personality; his fears that other distractions would interfere with his writing which had become his only means of open self-expression.

This list of arguments for and against marriage has been taken as evidence of Kafka's holy dedication to literature. However, it may also indicate his inability to communicate (except through his writing), his fear of responsibility, and ultimately his fear of earthly pleasure. Writing may have been Kafka's salvation, but it was salvation at the cost of an active participation in life. His self-imposed taboos against actual gratification and his fear of the responsibility and closeness of a true relationship appear to have been the limiting factors in his life, rather than his all-consuming devotion to writing. The romanticized notion of giving up marriage for art was only a rationalization. Rather, his fear of failing at marriage forced him further into art where, free of guilt and responsibility to others, he could feel himself truly liberated. Yet even in his writing he constantly returned to the same themes: the irony of life, the helplessness of the individual in the face of public humiliation, the awesome power of authority. Brilliant as it is, his work is an obsessive outpouring of inner turmoil and repeated self-hatred. As Hall and Lind (1970) observed, "Kafka's demons were purged not on the psychoanalytic couch but by the relentless, clear-eyed explorations of the nethermost limits of his being" (P. 94). It is a final irony that Kafka's one alleged area of freedom appears not to have escaped the prison of the father's early restraints. As he finally admits in his fateful letter to his father, "My writing was all about you; all I did there, after all, was to bemoan what I could not bemoan upon your breast" (1973). So much for Kafka's liberation through art.

Kafka's own realization that the perpetuation of his childhood self into his adult years prevented his fulfillment as a mature human being appears to have been the theme for a later story, *A Country Doctor*. In this brief work, a doctor is called to attend to a sick boy during a thick blizzard. At first the doctor cannot go because his horse has died of exposure, but then a mysterious groom, a gruff, burly, licentious man, appears with two powerful horses. The doctor is instantly transported to his patient ten miles away, leaving his servant girl Rose at the mercy of the amorous groom. In the sickroom the doctor examines the child and finds nothing wrong, complaining that he has once again been called out needlessly. As he is about to leave, however, the sister of the patient flutters a blood-soaked towel (as the mother bites her lips with tears in her eyes and the father sniffs a glass of rum), which convinces the doctor to take a second look at his patient. This time the doctor discovers a horrible wound full of blood-spotted worms. At this point Kafka writes: "Poor boy, you were past helping. I had discovered your great wound; this blossom in your side was destroying you. The family was pleased" (1971, p. 223). The doctor now realizes that the boy has no chance of recovery. Nevertheless, he allows the villagers to act out some ancient folk custom: the doctor is stripped and put into bed with the patient, where the two of them are left by themselves. When alone with the doctor, the young boy tells him, "Do you know, I have very little confidence in you. Why, you were only blown in here, you didn't come on your own feet. Instead of helping me, you're cramping me on my death bed. What I'd like best is to scratch your eyes out." The doctor replies: "Right, it is a shame, and yet I am a doctor. What else am I to do? Believe me, it is not easy for me either." The boy then retorts, "Am I supposed to be content with this apology? Oh I must be, I can't help it. I have always had to put up with things. A fine wound is all I brought in the world; that was my sole endowment." The doctor reassures the patient that his wound is not so bad; that many an individual offers his side to an ax and does not receive such a fine wound. But now the doctor is thinking of escape. He surreptitiously leaves, naked, unable to get into his coat. However, now the horses scarcely move through the freezing snow. The story ends with the doctor unsuccessfully trying to get home:

Never shall I reach home at this rate . . . in my house the disgusting groom is raging, Rose is his victim; I do not want to think about it anymore. Naked, exposed to the frost of the most unhappy of ages, with an earthy vehicle, unearthly horses, old man that I am, I wander astray . . . Betrayed! Betrayed! A false alarm on the night bell once answered—it cannot be made good, not ever (1971, p. 225).

A Country Doctor may partially be understood as Kafka the doctor–adult vainly attempting to cure Kafka the child–patient. All that he accomplishes by his efforts is to sacrifice Rose and to end up naked and cold in the midst of a blizzard behind two horses who refuse to move. The story ends with the prophetic words, "it cannot be made good, not ever." But what of the child patient? On first sight he seems well, but his sister knows that he is not well. On closer inspection the boy has an incurable, horrible wound which he calls his "sole endowment." The boy accepts his wound, realizes the pathetic helplessness of the doctor, and resigns himself to his fate. The only help the doctor can give is to tell the boy he should be proud of his wound. I believe that the interchange between doctor and child demonstrates Kafka's refusal of help from others (he was familiar with psychoanalysis but ridiculed it) and the turning of his psychic deformity into a badge of honor, the badge of a victim. At the same time he seems to be saying that his persistent attention to his former sick and childish self is robbing him of satisfying adult experiences. Not only is he unable to cure the child, but in the sham process of cure he loses everything.

As telling as *A Country Doctor* may be of Kafka's sense of self as a sick child and helpless adult, if we wish fully to realize Kafka's own view of his role within his family and the intensity of the self-loathing that his familial relationship engendered in him, then we should turn to his classic, *The Metamorphosis*, written in the same year as *The Judgment*. This novella opens with the startling sentence, "As Gregor Samsa awoke one morning from uneasy dreams he found himself transformed in his bed into a gigantic insect" (1971, p. 89).* By beginning the story with the metamorphosis already accomplished, Kafka gives his main protagonist no choice: he already is a repulsive bug. The story deals with how Gregor as well as others react to this transformation, which is taken as a given. As with most of Kafka's works, the narrative is a painful process of public humiliation and externally inflicted pain. The plot is fairly simple: the giant bug (which retains its prior human sensitivity and consciousness) is imprisoned in its bedroom and at first tolerated. Later, on an excursion into the family parlor, the bug is pelted with apples by the father. One of the apples sticks in his back, causing an infection. The metamorphosed Gregor gradually loses his appetite and strength, and eventually his will to live. The night before his death, Gregor hears his sister playing her violin for three boarders whom the family has been forced to take in. He approaches the group and is discovered, at which time the boarders give notice. Gregor lamely and slowly returns to his room while his family openly states that they wish they could be rid of him. The next day his body is discovered by the charwoman, who unceremoniously discards his remains. Gregor's father, mother, and sister take the day off from work to celebrate their new freedom. In contrast to the dark, interior atmosphere of the story, this last scene is filled with sunlight and joviality.

Behind the simple plot outline are an infinity of subtle and insightful revelations about the Samsa family and the psychological role of the son–insect (as well as the status of a middle-class salesman in pre-war Germany and, possibly, the alienated state of modern man). For example, Gregor's first reaction on discovering his grotesque metamorphosis is not appropriate horror, but rather concern that he will be late for work. Throughout the story Gregor appears incredibly naive about his repulsive appearance. This insistent naivete may be a key to the story's psychological meaning. It is as if Kafka were showing that his protagonist does not understand how his presence offends and disgusts others; yet

---

* Kafka never divulges what type of bug he is describing. The German word he uses is *Ungeziefer*, which may be literally translated as vermin.

by the behavior of these others, Kafka has deliberately indicated how offensive and disgusting his hero is. Gregor appears to be pleading for human acceptance, even though he has become a gigantic insect which no longer can communicate with those around him. Gregor's painful situation is made all the more pathetic in that there is never any danger from the large bug; the others recoil from him out of revulsion, not out of fear. Finally, Kafka never gives a reason for the tragic metamorphosis. It is not Gregor's fault that this disaster has befallen him. However, it is impossible for others to accept him; he is grotesque, an embarrassment to the family, and must be eradicated and forgotten. He who once supported the family has become its terrible burden. Few works in fiction convey the sense of helplessness, self-loathing, and rejection as well as *The Metamorphosis*.

Two other transformations occur concurrently with Gregor's deterioration, and both are significant for the story and for its psychological meaning. As Gregor becomes more feeble and helpless, his father gains in strength and dignity. At the beginning the father is retired, old, and weak; at the end he is employed, rejuvenated, and a tower of strength. Here, once again, is the inverse relationship between father and son: the father gains strength at the expense of the son, and ultimately destroys the son.

However, the major transformation occurs in the sister. She initially is sympathetic toward Gregor, bringing him an assortment of food and being the only one who will enter his room. The reader is also informed that prior to his metamorphosis, Gregor had a special relationship with her, "With his sister alone had he remained intimate, and it was a secret plan of his that she, who loved music . . . should be sent next year to study at the Conservatorium, despite the great expense that would entail . . . ." (1971, p. 111). As the story progresses, the sister becomes alienated and then openly hostile to Gregor, finally suggesting he be disposed of. The turning point of the story appears to be the scene in which Gregor hears his sister playing the violin and, attracted by the music, dares to approach the parlor where he is spotted by one of the lodgers. During this episode, Kafka allows Gregor to confess his feelings about his sister:

Gregor crawled a little farther and lowered his head to the ground so that it might be possible for his eyes to meet hers. Was he an animal, that music had such an effect upon him? He felt as if the way were opening before him to the unknown nourishment he craved. He was determined to push forward till he reached his sister, to pull at her skirt and so let her know that she was to come into his room with her violin, for no one here appreciated her playing as he would appreciate it. He would never let her out of his room, at least not so long as he lived; his frightful appearance would become, for the first time, useful to him; he would watch all the doors of his room at once and spit at intruders; but his sister should need no constraint, she should stay with him of her own free will, she should sit beside him on the sofa, bend down her ear to him, and hear him confide that he had the firm intention of sending her to the Conservatorium . . . . After this confession his sister would be so touched that she would burst into tears, and Gregor would raise himself to her shoulder and kiss her on the neck which, now that she went to business, she kept free of any ribbon or collar (1971, pp. 130–131).

Immediately after this last tender sentiment, Gregor is discovered by the lodger, which precipitates the final stage in the sister's transformation of feelings. It is now she who insists that Gregor be gotten rid of in some way. All this follows Gregor's ludicrous, yet poignant fantasy that his sister would allow herself to be kissed on the neck by a gigantic insect. I will not dare to venture into a discussion of the possible incestual or sexual allusions of this scene. It is sufficient to note that years later Kafka called the story an indescretion and asked facetiously, "Is it perhaps delicate and discreet to talk about the bedbugs in one's own family?" (Politzer, 1966, p. 74.)

Of greater importance is that the story was written at the time of his sister Valli's engagement in September 1912. Kafka noted this event in his diary on September 15, and added, "Love between brother and sister—the repetition of love between mother and father" (Politzer, 1966, p. 74). However, rather than seeking a sexual motive behind the story, it might be that Kafka was writing about the loss of an emotionally intimate relationship, the loss of his sister's love to her fiancé. As such, the story seems to represent Kafka's further abandonment by someone whom he hoped would care for him and, childishly, stay with him forever of her own free will. Here is juxtaposed a domineering, possessive attitude toward others as well as the knowledge that one's own repugnant qualities must drive others away. Gregor's tragedy is not simply that he has become transformed into a disgusting insect, but that he still expects others to treat him as a human being. Indeed, he has more than an ordinary human need for regard in that he expects unilateral lifelong devotion. The story may reflect Kafka's sense that the loss of his sister was a betrayal; yet at the same time he portrays his hero as being so repulsive that he cannot be loved. Here is the familiar depressive theme: one feels himself to be so base that he cannot be loved, while at the same time he naively hopes for an all-giving love that knows no bounds. Kafka artfully portrays what so many depressives describe in more pedestrian ways, that they must connive, bribe, or cheat to control the loved other because they cannot be loved for themselves. The huge, helpless, and doomed bug, wounded by the father, ignored by the mother, and rejected by the sister, may well represent Kafka's depressed self-image of a hopelessly repulsive being whose feelings were not acknowledged and who was hidden away as the family's shame.

Another illustration will be given to show Kafka's ultimate agreement with his father's low estimation of him and his willingness to go along with his father's condemnation at the expense of life itself. This time I refer to *In the Penal Colony*, perhaps the most terrifying short work in modern fiction, which Kafka wrote in 1914. This is an almost surrealistic work, taking place in some unspecified tropical prison. The entire action revolves around a specific piece of apparatus that was used to execute prisoners during the days when the recently deceased commandant of the prison was in charge. An officer is demonstrating this torture machine to some important explorer, while nostalgically reminiscing of the days when the former stern commandant was still alive and executions were staged in a grand manner with ladies, children, and the entire penal staff in attendance. The officer complains that the new commandant does not appreciate this form of execution and the machine has gradually deteriorated and is in a state of disrepair. Gradually we learn that the former commandant had personally designed the machine and this officer had been his first assistant in all penal matters. "My guiding principle is this," explains the officer, "Guilt is never to be doubted."

Interspersed with these revelations is a meticulous explanation of how the machine works. We also learn that it will be demonstrated to the explorer with an allegedly disobedient servant. The description of the machine is made all the more horrible in that its torturing and inhuman aspects are presented in a matter-of-fact, even proud manner by the officer. The lengthy description seems prophetic of the Nazis' meticulous accounting of atrocities in the extermination camps (where, in fact, Kafka's three sisters were to perish), as if the list were enumerating exchanges of merchandise for a shipping company. Briefly, the monstrous machine operates by slowly rotating its encased victim as a complicated system of innumerable needles inscribes a message on the penitent man, who is supposed to decipher the message by his wounds. When the officer tries out the machine on the condemned servant, it breaks down and in a cacaphony of needles, cogwheels, and levers seems to be falling apart. The officer removes the intended victim and, stripping himself naked, takes the victim's place in the machine. He is willing to die along with the demise of the machine, which he does, with a spike through his forehead as the machine finally collapses.

The explorer, who has been repelled by everything that has transpired, goes to the colony teahouse and he learns that the old commandant is buried there because the priest would not allow him to lie in the holy ground of the church yard. He is shown a stone which marks the grave of the commandant, and on it is inscribed, in part, "there is a prophecy that after a certain number of years the Commandant will rise again and lead his adherents from this house to recover the colony. Have faith and wait." The explorer reads the inscription, hurries to a boat to be taken off the colony, and prevents others from joining him.

Although it is written in clear, distinct, and almost journalistic prose, *In the Penal Colony* reads like a narrative of a nightmare. In this work, the characters and the objects are more symbolic than in the previously cited stories. The story is a parable of the need to obey a harsh, brutal authority and to perish with the remains of that authority (the machine) when the rigid moralistic system is jeopardized. We may speculate that the officer represents the aspect of Kafka which was tied to the autocratic dictates of his father (the former commandant) and which would heed his dictates even after the latter's death. It becomes evident that the machine, and all it stands for, is the reason for the officer's existence. Without it, life would have no purpose, and so he gruesomely sacrifices himself when the machine breaks down. Again the individual cannot escape his prison but finds meaning only in being a prisoner to the old system. Finally Kafka warns us that the old commandant is not really dead but may return. "Have faith and wait," ends the inscription.

With each story, we find Kafka going to a deeper layer of symbolism and turning further away from external reality to express his inner conflicts. Because of his ability to coalesce his primal symbolism with a clarity and sense of proportion that can be related to by others, he strikes a chord in his readers. It is in this capacity that Kafka is a literary genius rather than a nagging, complaining melancholic.

Therefore we may learn much about depression from Kafka in that he so eloquently expresses the turmoil that most patients can articulate only partially. Throughout his stories Kafka is the eternal defendant, ever on trial although always knowing that the verdict will be guilty. The judge is always the same, the father. It is as if the rest of the world did not exist, only the judge–father and the defendant–son. Here is blatant evidence of the overwhelming and pervasive power of the dominant other on the depressive. Even his writing, which some critics believe to have been his salvation against the domination of the father, did not escape the latter's influence. In the letter to his father, Kafka confesses "My writing was all about you" (1973).

Another aspect of the depressive character that Kafka's writing exemplifies is the self-hatred for not living up to the standards of the powerful other. Kafka always accepted the father's judgment that he was weak and submissive. At the same time, Kafka fully realized that to have acted otherwise, to have been assertive or independent, would have brought punishment from the same father. This is essentially a no win situation: the child is forced to be dependent and then reproached for his dependency. Eventually the individual cannot break away, even when life circumstances allow him to do so. *In the Penal Colony* horribly demonstrates how Kafka continued his self-inhibition and slavish devotion to the brutal patriarchal authority even after that authority had ceased to exist. The self-loathing for being what his father made him, yet his inability to be anything else, may account for Kafka's frequent use of death or suicide as the sole solution of his protagonists to their dilemma.

His stories are also instructive in terms of depressive psychopathology because they show how the individual later in life magnifies and distorts the childhood dominant other. It is doubtful that the senior Kafka could have been as sadistic and terrifying as the old commandant who invented the terrible death machine. Yet Kafka, like so many depressed individuals, inflated the dread and power of the dominant other. He never seemed capable of seeing the father as only another human being; rather, he retained the childhood image of the all-powerful patriarch, with the distortions of childhood cognition.

Janouch (1953) recounted an illustrative instance of Kafka's inability to alter his view of his father, even as an adult. One day Janouch and Kafka happened to walk past the father's place of business. The elder Kafka emerged and shouted to his sickly son, "Franz, go home. The air is damp!" Kafka appeared to ignore his father and commented to Janouch, "My father, he is anxious about me. Love often wears the face of violence" (P. 31). In this last phrase, Kafka exhibited his refusal to allow his father to be anything but a tyrant. It is almost as if Kafka needed this view of the father to justify his own self-imposed martyrdom—his self-pity, his self-hatred, and ultimately his self-destruction.

Brod described Kafka's everyday existence as a constant fight against depression as well as a perverse glorification in suffering. "Indeed he sometimes lived for months in a kind of lethargy, in utter despair, in my diary I find note after note on his sadness" (1973, p. 104). Yet somehow Brod believed that despite Kafka's sad heart, his spirit was so gay that he had a stimulating effect on others. His concrete examples do not bear this out, unless one considers ironic comment and sarcastic reflection to be a "gay spirit."

There is also the sense of helplessness in Kafka's works; one is caught in circumstances which he cannot control, but which he must obey because he is basically guilty—guilty for living the life of a weak parasite. Kafka's characters have no will of their own, they live an existence that is reactive to the wishes of authority. As in The Judgment, to dare to exert one's autonomy is to live a bleak, impoverished, and sickly existence. The barrenness of Russia, where the friend is in self-imposed exile, may represent the barrenness of emotional life away from the needed father. Along with the sense of helplessness is a knowledge that there is no hope of change. The character is caught in a hopeless situation as a huge insect that is unable to change on its own, and whom others refuse to help.

These elements combine to inhibit the individual continuously from leading an authentic or fulfilling life. Kafka stayed in a job he hated. He broke off engagements three times. He remained within the family orbit until shortly before his death. Even his writing did not really free him. He published little in his life and asked his closest friend, Max Brod, to burn all his manuscripts upon his death. The writings themselves are not only gloomy, they have a sense of suffocation, of endless futile repetition, in which nothing can be accomplished and nothing can be enjoyed. Everything is complex, musty, convoluted, oppressive, moralistic, stifling.

Finally, one must also appreciate the effect of Kafka on others. In his self-absorption, he appears to have been oblivious to the suffering he may have imposed on others. Brod's biography is exceptionally laudatory and in fact almost reverent, and so downplays Kafka's effects on others.* However, Kafka appears to have twice broken his engagement with Felice and kept her in a hopeless relationship for five years. Actually, she married shortly after the last break. He repeated this behavior with Julie and Milena a few years later.

Anyone who reads the tormented letters that Milena wrote to Brod following Kafka's rejection of her can appreciate his destructive effect. She was made to feel guilty because Kafka broke with her. Consider the following excerpt:

> I want to know whether I am the kind of person who has made Frank suffer the way he has suffered from every other woman, so that his sickness has grown worse, so that he has to flee from me, too, in his fear, and so that I too must get out of his life—whether I am at fault or whether it is a consequence of his own nature. Is what I am saying clear? I *must* know that (Cited in Brod: 1973, p. 232).

Here the contagion of guilt has contaminated Milena to the point that she questions her role in Kafka's consumption.

Fortunately she regained her objectivity and a while later was able to write "What his terror is, I know down to the last nerve. It existed before he met me, all the while he did not know me . . . . I know for certain that no sanatorium will succeed in curing him. He will never become well, Max, as long as he has this terror" (Cited in Brod: 1973, p. 233). Eventually Milena identifies this terror as one of the flesh, of love, and of life.

Kafka appears to have been disinterested in politics or in the actual changes of the world around him. His universe seemed restricted to himself, his suffering, and his father. As with so many depressive characters, his obsession with himself and his inner needs prevented him from fully appreciating the needs of others as well as the existence of a world beyond the circumscribed universe of his own pain. Kafka distinguishes himself by his ability to describe his plight and by showing an amazing insight into his condition and its causes. His writing may have been a catharsis and a penetrating self-analysis, but it was not a cure. At the age of thirty-six, only five years before his death, Kafka confessed the narrowness of his existence by writing to his father "And so, if the world consisted only of me and you (a notion I was much inclined to have), then this purity

---

* Neider (1948) accurately criticizes Brod's biography as failing to "understand the masochistic implications of a severe neurosis" (P. 12). Brod contradicts himself first by denying Kafka's pathology and then by excusing Kafka's behavior on the basis of his being plagued by psychological problems.

of the world came to an end with you and, by virtue of your advice, the filth began with me. In itself it was, of course, incomprehensible that you should thus condemn me, only old guilt, and profoundest contempt on your side, could explain it to me. And so I was seized in my innermost being and very hard indeed" (1973, p. 105).

One year before his death, Kafka appears to have been able to break this filial bond. He moved to Berlin with Dora Dymant and led a fairly independent and even happy existence. Perhaps it was his realization that death was near that freed Kafka from his father. Or it may have been that he found in Dora the total love that he seems to have required. While Brod (1973) portrays these final months as idyllic and happy, Kafka's last works do not entirely justify this sanguine evaluation. His final stories appear to deal with the role of the artist in society and society's acceptance of aesthetics. He must have known he was near his end and these final works represented a sort of taking stock of his life. Despite the change in theme, they still contain Kafka's irony and his bitterness, as well as his stylistic brilliance. The most important of these last stories may be *The Hunger Artist*, which can be taken as Kafka's testament and final self-assessment.

As with his earlier stories, the plot outline is extremely simple, with complex underlying psychological twists and meanings. The main character is a "hunger artist," a person who starves in public as a carnival attraction. The hunger artist is housed in a cage with relays of permanent watchers who see to it that he does not cheat (although this latter restraint is actually a formality, since any professional hunger artist would honor the code of his calling). In previous years, we are told, great crowds would gather to observe as individuals starved themselves. On the fortieth day of the fast, the flower-bedecked cage is opened, a military band plays, and doctors examine the hunger artist, relaying their findings to the enthusiastic crowd. Finally two young ladies, especially chosen for the honor, lead the frail skeleton-thin artist from the cage to a table where he has to be enticed to break his long fast amid tumultuous cheers.

Kafka wrote, "So he lived for many years, with small regular intervals of recuperation, in visible glory, honored by the world, yet in spite of that troubled in spirit, and all the more troubled because no one would take his trouble seriously" (1971, p. 272). The hunger artist is melancholic because, despite his worldly success, he is misunderstood. His art of fasting has been perverted into a commercial venture such as with the sale of photographs showing how he would appear on the fortieth day. The public did not understand that fasting was indeed an art, that he could go on beyond the forty days, and that he enjoyed it.

However, such conflicts were in the past. In recent years public interest in professional fasting had waned. People no longer appreciated self-starvation. The hunger artist, who had been cheered by thousands as a main attraction, had now hired himself to a circus where customers barely paused by his cage on their way to view the animal menagerie. In addition to his flagging public, he had to suffer the stench and sounds of the nearby animals. He was merely an impediment on the way to the menagerie. "He might fast as much as he could, and he did so, but nothing could save him now, people passed him by. Just try to explain to anyone the art of fasting! Anyone who has no feeling for it cannot be made to understand it" (1971, p. 276).

The hunger artist is gradually ignored by everyone, until he is completely forgotten by the circus-goers. Finally the circus overseer, coming upon a seemingly empty cage filled with dirty straw, discovers the dying hunger artist quite by accident. The surprised overseer asks "Are you still fasting? When on earth do you mean to stop?" The hunger artist replies in a whisper "Forgive me, everybody." The overseer, believing him crazed with hunger and fatigue, humors him and responds "We forgive you."

At this point Kafka clarifies the psychological meaning of the story, revealing the motives of the hunger artist:

"I always wanted you to admire my fasting" said the hunger artist. "We do admire it" said the overseer, affably. "But you shouldn't admire it," said the hunger artist. "Well then we don't admire it" said the overseer, "but why shouldn't we admire it?" "Because I have to fast, I can't help it" said the hunger artist. "What a fellow you are," said the overseer, "and why can't you help it?" . . . . "because I couldn't find the food I liked. If I had found it, believe me, I should have made no fuss and stuffed myself like you or anyone else." These were his last words, but in his dimming eyes remained the firm though no longer proud persuasion that he was still continuing to fast. (1971, pp. 276–277).

The story ends with a young, healthy panther taking over the hunger artist's cage and to the delight of all, eating heartily. In contrast to the self-denying artist, Kafka describes the panther as having "a noble body, furnished almost to the bursting point with all it needed." The panther "seemed to carry freedom around with it" and "the joy of life streamed" from it "with ardent passion."

The final juxtaposition of the panther, who appears to be the affirmation of life, serves to accentuate further the hunger artist's long history of self-denial. Again Kafka utilizes the theme of painful public humiliation, the futile suicide of the main character, and a harrowing examination of suffering. As in his story of *In the Penal Colony*, we are reminded that people no longer appreciate the spectre of pain or stern morality. However, in contrast to that work, the punishment here is not meted out by an external torture machine but is self-induced. Indeed, the hunger artist willingly fasts and proudly displays his self-affliction. Here it appears the older Kafka is acknowledging that the reasons for his refusal to embrace life rest within himself. He did it, says the hunger artist, for the admiration of others and yet he admonishes others from admiring him. At the end of life he seems to be saying that it wasn't really worth it. He has become the ascetic exile of *The Judgment*; he has denied himself the joy of a full existence, and it was not worth it. He ends up forgotten, an impediment on the way to the circus animals, discovered by chance.

But there is more: the hunger artist admits that he has fasted and is dying because no food was to his liking. He could find no suitable nourishment in this life and so he prefers to abstain from life. In true depressive fashion he cannot enjoy anything; he cannot allow himself to live except in self-denial. What others might have admired as a great feat of self-sacrifice or iron discipline was, for the hunger artist, actually quite easy. He could not help but fast for there was no earthly food that satisfied him. He expects more than a normal life could supply.

If we trace Kafka's fiction from *The Judgment* to *The Hunger Artist*, we see that the gradual development of the depressive is revealed. At first, he is denied life by the father who refuses to allow his son any sense of dignity or autonomy. In *The Metamorphosis*, the hero begins his social exile; and betrayed by the sister, as an insect among humans, he furthers his retreat from life. In the infernal machine of *In the Penal Colony*, he reaffirms his slavish devotion to the old harsh morality, even after the father commandant can no longer demand it. *The Country Doctor* shows us that his failure to accept the responsibilities of a full adult life is the result of his perpetuation within himself of his childhood self, described as sick, deformed, incurable. Finally, in *The Hunger Artist*, Kafka appears to look back on his life as a man who voluntarily refused to live it.

In reviewing the actual life of Kafka as reported in his biography and as revealed by himself in his writings, one finds the psychodynamic aspects of the depressive character. The relationship with the dominant other, the inhibition of autonomous gratification, the self-blame, the sense of helplessness, and the lack of effective assertion are all there. For the student of psychiatry, Kafka's works permit a rare and unforgettable glimpse into the inner world of melancholia.

PART FIVE

Further Analysis of Cognition and Depression

[18]

ADDITIONAL REMARKS ON THE

RELATION BETWEEN COGNITION

AND DEPRESSION

For decades the role of cognition in psychopathology was uniformly ignored by classical psychoanalysts. Some cognitive concepts or transformations were implied in psychoanalytic theory, such as the processes of symbolization and dream distortion, or the particular patterns of thought in schizophrenia. However, the major emphasis centered on instincts and affects, the primary motivational forces of behavior, rather than on the structural aspects of thought or the consideration of more elaborate and evolved determinants of behavior. The contributions of academic psychology to motivation were perceived by psychoanalysts as too superficial to assess the primitive forces that were thought to underlie human activity. The classical psychoanalytic position was, and largely still is, a frankly reductionistic one, in which all behavior is traced back to semibiological drives. When cognitive structures are considered, they are seen only as complex representations of more fundamental and instinctual strivings.

The philosophical reasons for the reduction of high-level psychological functions to instinctual forces already have been presented by others in detailed studies of the historical roots of Freud's thought. These authors view the early psychoanalytic formulations as representative of the particular Zeitgeist of the Victorian era and as bound by a mechanistic, deterministic, and reductionistic philosophical bias which is no longer tenable. I frankly believe that this view of man does not do justice to the creative, aesthetic, altruistic, or social aspects of human existence. I am not necessarily implying a return to a vitalistic or mystical view of

This chapter was written by Jules Bemporad.

man; these higher functions may still be encompassed by a scientific point of view that acknowledges man as partially rooted in biology. The difficulty with traditional psychoanalysis is that it has paid too much heed to the biological causes of human behavior and too little heed to the cognitive and volitional aspects of man. Actually, in more recent years psychoanalysts have tried to deal with the cognitive aspects of man, but only while still clinging to a reductionist, biological position. For example, the recent ego psychologists have considered cognitive structures in the development of the ego, but mainly in the conflict-free spheres and not as potent motivators of behavior—including neurotic conflicts. As such, cognition again has been relegated to a secondary role in everyday life problems. In the works of other psychoanalysts such as Klein and the object-relations school, cognitive constructs have been liberally implicated in psychic conflicts but never identified as such.

Arieti has been one of the first psychoanalysts to recognize the significance of cognitive factors in psychopathology and to repeatedly indicate that illness may result from conflicts between ideas, which are not reducible to more primitive or fundamental biological drives. While he does not reject the significant contributions of Freud in regard to primal urges or unconscious forces (as may be the case with some neo-Freudian or culturalist schools), Arieti considers that the more evolved aspects of man also markedly contribute to both pathology and normality. This comprehensive point of view has been called the cognitive-volitional school (Arieti, 1974) in that it underscores the importance of the highest aspects of human evolution, such as thought and will. The remainder of this chapter interprets the phenomenon of depression from this point of view, recapitulating in a highly condensed form much of the theoretical material of this book.

Unconscious Determinants in Depression

Since the inception of the psychoanalytic movement, the concept of the unconscious has been one of the central constructs of psychoanalytic explanation and one of the most important contributions to personality theory. Yet over the course of the evolution of psychoanalytic thought, the concept of what the unconscious actually encompasses has gone through many transformations. The unconscious originally was considered to be the interface between mind and body, the area where the biological instincts assumed psychic representations and affected behavior. It was thought that the unconscious consisted of primal forces, called the instincts. This was the legacy of Darwin who, through his popularizer Spencer, stressed the primacy of force—of driving biological instincts—as the major determinant of behavior.

Later Freud included not only urges and their representations in the unconscious, but also the objects that had been introjected during early childhood. These early incorporations (or identifications) continued to exert their effect well into adult life without the knowledge of the individual. This aspect of psychoanalytic theory became the nucleus of the Kleinian school. According to the Kleinians, psychological conflicts are only the representations of battles waged between good and bad internalized objects. With this innovation, it may be appreciated how the notions of the unconscious have become more cognitive and structural. The Kleinians have gone even further: they postulate the existence of highly complex, unconscious fantasies which underlie manifest behavior but are not privy to conscious awareness. These fantasies, which are proposed to constitute much of the individual's inner life, are sophisticated cognitive systems; yet this aspect of their structure has been essentially ignored. These fantasies are treated as simple force vectors which influence behavior in much the manner of the biological instincts that theoretically preceded them.

Further elaboration of the unconscious came with the revision of psychoanalysis brought about by the structural theory. With the tripartite division of the psyche into the familiar id, ego, and superego, it was postulated that the unconscious encompassed not only the instinctual forces of the id and the internalized values of the superego, but also some of the highly complex functions of the ego. In some of his last works and especially in those regarding fetishism (1927, 1938), Freud seems to have been considering a division of the psyche into two opposing world views, one conscious and the other unconscious, with both aspects being highly evolved and cognitively complex.

Thus, without directly acknowledging this trend, the psychoanalytic concept of the unconscious has become increasingly cognitive and elaborate. It becomes more and more necessary for traditional psychoanalysts to include sophisticated mental constructs among material that is considered to be repressed or denied. Yet there appears to be a strenuous effort to avoid this conclusion among classical psychoanalysts. It is to this point that Arieti's work has been innovative and allowed a more comprehensive view of motivation. Arieti agrees that man is partially driven by biological forces and primitive forms of cognition are to be found in some mental activities such as dreams or psychotic states. However, not all behavior can be reduced to mere elemental states. The unconscious also consists of highly evolved cognitive concepts which, just like more primitive strivings, are contrary to our conscious desires and so become repressed. Psychic conflicts thus may result from two opposing views of the self or others, each view equally well-formulated and structured. These repressed constructs exert a powerful effect on overt behavior, both directly and in the individual's defensive maneuvers against these constructs. Despite these motivational considerations, the essential point is that the unconscious constructs can be described as being fundamentally cognitive phenomena.

Arieti's general term for these internalized systems of ideas is "inner reality," which he defined elsewhere (1974) as follows:

> Inner reality is the result of a continuous reelaboration of past and present experiences. Its development is never completed throughout the life of man, although its greatest rate of growth occurs in childhood and adolescence. It is based on the fact that perceptions, thoughts, feelings, actions, and other psychological functions do not cease completely to exist once the neuronal mechanisms that mediated their occurrence have taken place . . . . Although they cannot be retained as they were experienced, their effects are retained as various components of the psyche (P. 879).

Therefore the unconscious—or in its broader sense, inner reality—is the accretion of past experience, which is constantly evolving and being modified by experience. Yet certain ideas or beliefs that were laid down early in life seem to resist change and to appear almost impervious to novel experiences. What often seems to occur is that experiences which might alter the childhood cognitive structures are actually distorted by the individual so as to conform to these early prejudices. These childhood misapprehensions of the self and others persist, and their distorting qualities account for the individual's seemingly inappropriate behavior, which is labelled as psychopathological.

In *Meditations* Kafka described holding on to past, outmoded ideas in a highly poetic and yet accurate way. Kafka wrote, "All these so-called diseases, pitiful as they look, are beliefs, the attempt of a human being to cast anchor in some mother soil." Unfortunately this mother soil, this bedrock of security, is all too often based on the misapprehensions and distortions of primitive cognitions of childhood. Even when these early beliefs may originally have accurately reflected the surrounding environment, the ideological system in which the future depressive was raised was so prejudiced and erroneous that it supplied a biased foundation for adult functioning. The depressive, in the same way as other psychologically maladjusted individuals, continues to process experience in a specifically pathological manner, without being aware that he is reshaping current experience to childhood beliefs. In this sense, depression as well as other psychiatric disorders may be seen as a pattern of basically pathological modes of cognition.

The individual usually continues to act out his unknown beliefs without realizing the sources of his resulting attitudes and feelings, which actually have been engendered by these systems of ideas. At other times an individual may gain a dim awareness of these beliefs about himself and others. However, these realizations are painful and at odds with the individual's expectations for himself, so he does not allow himself to formulate these beliefs accurately in consciousness. Rather, these embarrassing beliefs are repressed or defended against by more superficial sets of beliefs. These superficial concepts are never really successful, either in reassuring the patient or in directing his behavior. From a distance, it may appear that an individual is acting in accordance with mature cognitive ideation, but if his intimate relationships are scrutinized or his private thoughts divulged, the older patterns rapidly become apparent. These compensatory cognitive structures may be seen as analogous to the concept of defense or resistance in traditional psychoanalysis. In contrast to the classical view, both the defense and the unconscious content are considered to be cognitive phenomena. As such, the problem of the depressive can be understood as the perpetuation of an inaccurate mode of cognitively processing experience that was formulated in childhood and crystallized in adult life.

Childhood Cognitive Patterns in Adult Depressives

The basic beliefs that predispose one to depressive episodes concern evaluations of the self and of others important to the individual. As a result of childhood training, the depressive comes to rely to an inordinate degree on the nurturance of others in order to maintain a favorable sense of self. A dominant other or dominant goal become the individual's *raison d'être*, without which he senses himself to be devoid of meaning. Self-evaluation is not an internal capability: it is left to the whims of external events. It is just this reliance on external agencies for self-worth that predisposes the individual to repeated episodes of depression. Other people are inordinately utilized as a barometer of the individual's self-worth.

The depression-prone individual thus has a distorted cognitive view of himself and of others. He unrealistically believes himself to be basically unworthy, helpless, even malevolent, while the dominant other is greatly inflated in importance. Obtaining the nurturance of the dominant other becomes the road to redemption or gratification for some individuals, and the achievement of some spectacular goal becomes the salvation for others. Without an active pursuit of these accomplishments, the individual feels himself to be in a painful state of deprivation, having lost all meaning and self-worth.

The depressive has maintained a belief of the self and others that is typical of childhood. Indeed, the depressive persists in parentifying others and devaluing the self. This system of self-regard was so firmly entrenched in childhood that it has prevented other more realistic experiences, which might have proved corrective, from penetrating into the basic belief systems. However, adult depression represents more than the resurgence of childhood cognitive beliefs. The individual continues to elaborate these encapsulated cognitions and to magnify their contents. The self becomes more demeaned and the other becomes even more powerful, or the goal more crucial. In order to stick to accustomed life patterns and to defend against threatening alternate cognitive options, some individuals grossly exaggerate the memory of the original relationship, further perpetuating the characterological pathology within themselves. The patient's childhood recollections or transference manifestations may suggest truly horrible experiences at the hands of brutal parents. This is not always an accurate representation of the individual's past: these data contain a large kernel of truth, but this truth has been contaminated by reelaborations and exaggerations, the result of decades of psychic reworking and consolidation of early cognitive structures. As stated, this often grotesque caricature of the parents and of the self has been gradually created to insure the continuation of a maladaptive career path in the face of reality's temptations.

From this basic system of ideas, in which the self is devalued without the ministrations of a dominant other or the accomplishment of some overriding goal, secondary cognitive structures are logically derived. One such structure concerns the need to control the gratifying other somehow in order to make sure that the needed nurturance will be forthcoming. The devious maneuvers that are developed in order to maintain the needed relationship are behaviorally seen as the familiar manipulations of the depressive. These annoying and yet pathetic attempts at control of others are motivated by the more basic, inferior estimation of self.

Another aspect of the depressive personality that derives from this fundamental system of ideas is the fear of autonomous gratification. As mentioned throughout this work, the depressive eschews any chance of independent pleasure or meaning, and often he derides such activities as childish or silly. This is a perpetuation of the parental sanction against any activities which might have deterred the patient from his pursuit of the parental goal or which might have allowed the patient to have loyalties outside the household. The significance of this self-inhibition for later depression is that some patients become depressed as a result of this sterile, ascetic life pattern. Other individuals who respond to an environmental event with depression are prevented from overcoming their despair partially because of this inhibition. In either case, the individual cannot allow himself to find new avenues of meaning. He sticks to his habitual pattern of self-denial and dependence on others, so that a transient frustration or loss provokes a clinical episode of depression. These sets of beliefs regarding one's restriction of the possibility of autonomous pleasure underlie the clinical symptom of helplessness. The depressive is helpless in finding meaning in life because all of his prior meaningful activities have been sabotaged by guilt and shame. He cannot see alternate modes of meaning and therefore he feels himself to be empty and hopelessly deprived. He can only desperately seek out others to give him direction, that is, to reinstate his traditional childhood role and to confirm all of the ideas of self and others implicit in this role.

The Clinical Episode

This internal cognitive structure predisposes the individual to both repeated experiences of depression and the inability to adequately fend off this painful affect. When deprived of external supports which have maintained a satisfactory view of the self (being needed by others, pursuing some goal, or following some superior hyper-moral life pattern), the individual is faced with the painful realization that he has lost his crucial source of meaning and self-esteem. He now views himself as eternally deprived of a state of well-being. It is this realization (whether realistically justified or not) that culminates in the consciously felt emotion of depression. This affective state automatically arises as the result of an alteration in the assessment of the self in its relation to the environment. The loathed concept of the childhood self, which had been repressed, reemerges—and with it, the overwhelming sense of despair and hopelessness.

The role of self-assessment in contributing to depression was clearly observed by Freud and by Kierkegaard before him. Freud described a critical difference between mourning and depression, which centered on the locus of the loss. In the former condition, the environment is impoverished; but in depression, the self itself becomes barren and empty. It appears that without the necessary environmental props, the satisfactory image of the self cannot be maintained and a painful transformation of the self-concept occurs, leading to depression. Kierkegaard described this process in more detail. As previously quoted, he illustrates this self-transformation by reporting a vignette of a girl who has lost her lover: "A young girl is in despair over love, and so she despairs over her lover, because he died, or because he is unfaithful to her. This is not a declared despair; no, she is in despair over herself. This self of hers, which if it had become 'his' beloved, she would have been rid of in the most blissful way, or would have lost, this self is now a torment to her when it has to be a self without 'him'" (1954, p. 153). The now tormented self is perceived as being unworthy and alone, as empty and forever doomed. This alteration of the view of one's own self brings about depression.

Thus stated, depression results from a cognitive transformation. However, this is a highly sophisticated cognitive process; it involves systems of ideas about self-worth and life's meaning. Depression can be categorized as a high-order emotion in contrast to fear or rage. As described by Arieti (1967), the affect of depression necessitates the capability of assessing the self and its worth. In addition, a sense of the future appears necessary. However, the cognitive structures that predispose and underlie the experience of depression are not available to consciousness. They are the conditions for, and the forms of, this particular type of distorted awareness, but the individual is unaware of them.

Such unconscious systems of ideas in fact prolong and intensify the experience of depression. The relatively healthy individual may utilize an initial feeling of depression to mobilize his resources and alter his life so as to alleviate the causes of this painful affect. All of us are prone to momentary experiences of depression after a loss or frustration. However, as indicated by Sandler and Joffe (1965), this psychobiological reaction does not necessarily escalate into a clinical depressive episode. Most individuals can fight against depression by detaching psychic importance from the lost object or frustrated aspiration and by substituting alternate objects or goals. In time, the depression lifts because the individual can create other satisfying relationships and activities; he did not depend on the lost external agency for his total sense of worth.

The depression-prone individual, however, cannot alter his existing cognitive set and successfully defend against depression. He cannot avail himself of alternate cognitive possibilities which could lead to new sources of meaning or gratification. In an appropriate metaphor suggested by Becker (1964), the depressive is like an actor who knows a specific set of lines which are to be delivered only before a particular audience. He cannot vary his situation either in terms of what he says or to whom he speaks. He is fixed in an undeviating course in his search for meaning, and even if this course is blocked, he clings to it without flexibility. In such individuals the depressive affect increases because: (1) The loss or frustration which elicited the depression was desperately needed to fulfill a neurotic sense of self. (2) The individual cannot alter his cognitive patterns to find substitute sources of meaning. (3) The depressive continues to use learned, yet inappropriate modes of coping, such as turning to others to relieve his pain or publicly bemoaning his fate.

If the depressive episode continues unchecked, there is a coalescence of this affect so that it creates new cognitive patterns. It is at this stage that the individual may exhibit the conscious cognitive constructs described by Beck (1967). The depressed individual thinks negatively about himself, his environment, and his future. This cognitive triad may be the result of a prolonged depression which has not been relieved by either internal choices or external support. These constructs accurately represent how the individual sees his situation after becoming depressed. These negativistic attitudes serve to further increase the depth of the depression; by their pessimistic content, they prevent activity that might alleviate the sense of despair. Such beliefs are also used to justify the feeling of depression, and it becomes a self-perpetuating and self-enclosed system.

During the depressive episode, conscious cognitive constructs replace the more fundamental childhood systems of ideas that brought about the depression. In structural terms, the process is as follows: an unconscious system of cognitive constructs interacting with an environmental trauma culminate in the production of an affective state and subsequently a cognitive transformation, which in turn creates new cognitive distortions. Beck's cognitive triad disappears with the amelioration of the clinical episode, but the underlying unconscious attitudes remain, and—without extensive therapeutic intervention—leave the individual vulnerable to repeated depressive attacks.

In some cases, the depression takes on psychotic proportions; it is accepted by the individual, together with its distorted world view. The individual no longer tries to ward off his depression even by inappropriate means, and he becomes overwhelmed by this painful affect. Most cognitive processes may appear to be paralyzed by a massive sense of despair, so that there remains only the perseveration of a few painful thoughts. Other individuals may respond with a general slowing of all cognitive processes so that thinking becomes an extraordinarily laborious task. These severely impaired individuals thus may appear to have a depression without content, that is, without psychological cause. However, if patiently interviewed, the cognitive aspects of depression—both those that preceded and followed the episode—will gradually emerge. Successful therapy may not in fact be possible until the patient begins to recognize the thought processes that underlie and perpetuate his depression (Arieti, 1977).

Implications for Therapy

The conceptualization of certain forms of psychopathology such as depression as the result of a retention of childhood cognitive distortions into adult life carries with it some implications for change in psychotherapeutic technique. The primary task of the therapist is to alter these distortions and to allow the patient alternate and more appropriate conceptions of himself and others. It is in the treatment situation that these older beliefs become openly manifest, for example, in transference distortions, and thus the patient can become fully aware of the unconscious systems of ideas that have been directing his thoughts and behavior.

The first task of therapy involves the identification and formulation of the patient's unconscious beliefs as derived from dreams, transference, and general comments about other people. In the security and trust of the therapeutic relationship, the patient becomes aware of these underlying cognitive systems and begins to appreciate their effect on his life. Once out in the open, these beliefs are subject to modification and a more accurate and adult interpretation of reality is possible.

Sullivan coined the apt phrase "selective inattention" to describe the individual's defensive use of denial in order to tune out experiences that would jeopardize self-esteem. Perhaps an equally frequent mechanism is "selective distortion," or the individual's misinterpretation of events to fit into unconscious systems of ideas. These distortions are not generalized to all experiences, but they are selectively used to fulfill archaic needs of which the individual often is not aware. In depression, certain others are invested with magical, grandiose power so that they can become dominant others for the patient, who believes he can only function successfully if he lives in the good graces of such an esteemed figure. At the same time, the patient will act out a life script according to distortions about himself. For example, he will shun independent gratification, block creative potential, and unrealistically limit his life. In so doing, he still is acting in accordance with beliefs instilled in childhood by his parents. These beliefs lead to distorted interpretations of reality in terms of his effectiveness, capacity for pleasure, and often the belief that others are overly concerned with his day-to-day behavior.

These childhood distortions are revived in therapy, as they are in nontherapeutic relationships that have meaning for the patient. In the therapy situation, however, these distortions are reflected back to the patient so that he can begin to appreciate the systems of ideas which dominate his existence and cause him emotional distress. Therapy should allow the individual the opportunity to alter these childhood systems of ideas so that alternate modes of cognition will be possible.

One of the most significant aspects of this process is for the patient to allow himself to be open to extratherapeutic experiences so that life itself can alter his distortions. Depressives and also many other types of patients cling to their distorted cognitions, continue to misinterpret experience, and never change their fundamental belief systems. Therapy must encourage the patient to act and interact without his previous prejudices so that reality can penetrate to his basic distorted ideas. The recounting of these experiences in the sessions form part of the working-through process in which events are discussed and with the therapists' help are given new meanings that are free from previous misinterpretations. Despite the considerable support given by the therapist (and the analysis of transference distortions), cure is the result of the patient altering his cognition in everyday behavior outside the office. The task of therapy thus is to liberate the individual from his rigid distortions of the past and to make him receptive to the genuine novelty and flexibility of the future.

REFERENCES

Abraham, K. 1960 (orig. 1911). Notes on the psychoanalytic treatment of manic-depressive insanity and allied conditions. In *Selected papers on psychoanalysis*. New York: Basic Books. Pp. 137–156.
———. 1960 (orig. 1916). The first pregenital stage of the libido. In *Selected papers on psychoanalysis*. New York: Basic Books. Pp. 248–279.
———. 1960 (orig. 1924). A short study of the development of libido, viewed in the light of mental disorders. In *Selected papers on psychoanalysis*. New York: Basic Books. Pp. 418–501.
Adler, K. A. 1961. Depression in the light of individual psychology. *Journal of Individual Psychology* 17:56–67.
Akiskal, H. S., and McKinney, W. T. 1975. Overview of recent research in depression. Integration of ten conceptual models into a comprehensive clinical frame. *Archives of General Psychiatry* 32:285–305.
Annell, A. L. 1969. Lithium in the treatment of children and adolescents. *Acta Psychiatria Scandanavia* Suppl. 207:19–30.
Annell, A. L., ed. 1971. *Depressive states in childhood and adolescence*. New York: Halsted Press.
Ansbacher, H. L., and Ansbacher, R. R. 1956. *The Individual psychology of Alfred Adler*. New York: Harper.
Anthony, E. J. 1967. Psychoneurotic disorders. In A. M. Friedman and H. I. Kaplan, eds. *Comprehensive textbook of psychiatry*. Baltimore: Williams & Wellsing.
———. 1975*a*. Childhood depression. In E. J. Anthony and T. Benedek, eds. *Depression and human existence*. Boston: Little, Brown.
———. 1975*b*. Two contrasting types of adolescent depression and their treatment. In E. J. Anthony and T. Benedek, eds. *Depression and human existence*. Boston: Little, Brown.
Anthony, E. J., and Scott, P. 1960. Manic-depressive psychosis in childhood. *Child Psychology and Psychiatry* 1:53–72.
Arieti, S. 1950. New views on the psychology and psychopathology of wit and of the comic. *Psychiatry* 13:43–62.
———. 1959. Manic-depressive psychosis. In S. Arieti, ed. *American handbook of psychiatry*, First ed., Vol. I. New York: Basic Books. Pp. 419–454.
———. 1960. The experiences of inner states. In B. Kaplan and S. Wapner, eds. *Perspectives in psychological theory*. New York: International Universities Press. Pp. 20–46.
———. 1962. The psychotherapeutic approach to depression. *American Journal of Psychotherapy* 16:397–406.
———. 1967. *The intrapsychic self*. New York: Basic Books.
———. 1970*a*. Cognition and feeling. In A. Magda, *Feelings and emotions*. New York: Academic Press.
———. 1970*b*. The structural and psychodynamic role of cognition in the human psyche. In S. Arieti, ed. *The world biennial of psychiatry and psychotherapy*, Vol. I. New York: Basic Books, Pp. 3–33.
———. 1972. *The will to be human*. New York: Quadrangle. (Available also in paperback edition. New York: Delta Book, Dell Publishing Co., 1975.)
———. 1974*a*. *Interpretation of schizophrenia*, Second ed. New York: Basic Books.
———. 1974*b*. The cognitive-volitional school. In S. Arieti, ed. *American handbook of psychiatry*, Second ed., Vol. I. New York: Basic Books. Pp. 877–903.
———. 1974*c*. Manic-depressive psychosis and psychotic depression. In S. Arieti, ed. *American handbook of psychiatry*, Vol. III. New York: Basic Books.
———. 1976. *Creativity: the magic synthesis*. New York: Basic Books.

————. 1977. Psychotherapy of severe depression. *American Journal of Psychiatry* 134:864–868.

Aronoff, M., Evans, R., and Durell, J. 1971. Effect of lithium salts on electrolyte metabolism. *Journal of Psychiatric Research* 8:139–159.

Baastrup, P. C., and Schou, M. 1967. Lithium as a prophylactic agent against recurrent depressions and manic-depressive psychosis. *Archives of General Psychiatry* 16:162–172.

Baldessarini, R. J. 1975. The basis for the amine hypothesis in affective disorders. *Archives of General Psychiatry* 32:1087.

Beck, A. 1967. *Depression: clinical, experimental, and theoretical aspects.* New York: Paul B. Hoeber.

————. 1970. The core problem in depression: the cognitive triad. In J. Masseman, ed. *Science and Psychoanalysis* 17. New York: Grune & Stratton.

————. 1976. *Cognitive therapy and the emotional disorders.* New York: International Universities Press.

Becker, E. 1964. *The revolution in psychiatry.* New York: Free Press.

————. 1969. Kafka and the Oedipal complex. In *Angel in armor.* New York: Braziller.

Beckett, S. 1959. *Waiting for godot.* London: Faber & Faber.

Bellak, L. 1952. *Manic-depressive psychosis and allied conditions.* New York: Grune & Stratton.

Bemporad, J. R. 1970. New views on the psychodynamics of the depressive character. In S. Arieti, ed. *The world biennial of psychiatry and psychotherapy,* vol. I. New York: Basic Books.

————. 1973. The role of the other in some forms of psychopathology. *Journal of the American Academy of Psychoanalysis* 1:367–379.

————. 1976. Psychotherapy of the depressive character. *Journal of the American Academy of Psychoanalysis* 4:347–372.

Bender, L., and Schilder, P. 1937. Suicidal preoccupations and attempts in children. *American Journal of Orthopsychiatry* 7:225–243.

Beres, D. 1966. Superego and depression. In R. M. Lowenstein, L. M. Newman, M. Scherr, and A. J. Solnit, eds. *Psychoanalysis—a general psychology.* New York: International Universities Press.

Berg, J., Hullin, R., and Allsopp, M. 1974. Bipolar manic-depressive psychosis in early adolescence. *British Journal of Psychiatry* 125:416–418.

Berman, H. H. 1933. Order of birth in manic-depressive reactions. *Psychiatric Quarterly* 12:43.

Berner, P., Katschnig, H., and Pöldinger, W. 1973. What does the term "masked depression" mean? In Kielholz, P., ed. *Masked depression.* Bern:Huber.

Bertalanffy, L. von. 1956. General system theory. In Bertalanffy, L. von, and Rapaport, A., eds. *General system yearbook of the society for the advancement of general system theory.* Ann Arbor: University of Michigan Press.

Bibring, E. 1953. The mechanism of depression. In P. Greenacre, ed. *Affective disorders.* New York: International Universities Press.

Bieber, I., and Bieber, T. B. (In press.) Postpartum reactions in men and women. *Journal of the American Academy of Psychoanalysis* 6 (1978).

Bierman, J. S., Silverstein, A. B., and Finesinger, J. E. 1958. A depression in a six-year-old boy with poliomyelitis. *Psychoanalytic Study of the Child* 13:430–450.

Bigelow, N. 1959. The involutional psychosis. In S. Arieti, ed. *American handbook of psychiatry,* First ed., Vol. I. New York: Basic Books. Pp. 540–545.

Binswanger, L. 1933. *Über ideenflucht.* Orrele-Fusseler.

————. 1963. Heidegger's analytic of existence and its meaning for psychiatry. In *Being-in-the-world.* New York: Basic Books.

Bonhoeffer, K. 1910. *Die symptomatischen psychosen im gefolge von akuten infektionem und inneren erkrankungen.* Leipzig: Deuticke.

Bonime, W. 1960. Depression as a practice. *Comparative Psychiatry* 1:194–198.

————. 1962. *The clinical use of dreams.* New York: Basic Books.

————. 1962. Dynamics and psychotherapy of depression. In J. Masserman, ed. *Current psychiatric therapies.* New York: Grune & Stratton.

————. 1976. The psychodynamics of neurotic depression. *Journal of the American Academy of Psychoanalysis* 4:301–326.

Bonime, W., and Bonime, E. (In press.) Depressive personality and affect reflected in dreams: a basis for psychotherapy. In J. M. Natterson, ed. *The dream in clinical practice.* New York: Aronson.

Bowlby, J. 1958. The nature of the child's tie to his mother. *International Journal of Psycho-Analysis* 39:350–373.

————. 1960a. Grief and mourning in infancy and early childhood. *The Psycho-analytic Study of the child* 15:9–52. New York: International Universities Press.

————. 1960b. Separation anxiety. *International Journal of Psycho-Analysis* 41: 89–113.

Boyd, D. A. 1942. Mental disorders associated with child-bearing. *American Journal of Obstetrics and Gynecology* 43:148–163; 335–349.

Braceland, F. J. 1957. Kraepelin, his system and his influence. *American Journal of Psychiatry* 114:871.

————. 1966. Depressions and their treatment. In J. J. Lopez Ibor, ed. *Proceedings IV*, Part 1. Madrid: World Conference on Psychiatry. P. 467.

Brand, H. 1976. Kafka's creative crisis. *Journal of the American Academy of Psychoanalysis* 4:249–260.

Brenner, B. 1975. Enjoyment as a preventative of depressive affect. *Journal of Comparative Psychology* 3:346–357.

Brill, H. 1975. Postencephalitic states or conditions. In S. Arieti, ed. *American handbook of psychiatry*, Second ed., Vol. IV. Pp. 152–165.

Brod, M. 1973. *Franz Kafka: a biography.* New York: Schocken Books. (Paperback.)

Brown, F. 1968. Bereavement and lack of a parent in childhood. In E. Miller, ed. *Foundations of child psychiatry.* London: Pergamon.

Buber, M. 1937. *I and thou.* Edinburgh: Clark.

Bunney, W. E., Carpenter, W. T., and Engelmann, K. 1972. Brain seratonin and depressive illness. In T. A. Williams, M. M. Katz, and J. A. Shield, Jr., eds. *Recent advances in the psychobiology of the depressive illnesses.* Department of Health, Education, and Welfare: Publication No. (HSM) 70–9053.

Burton, R. 1927. *The anatomy of melancholy.* New York: Tudor.

Cade, J. F. 1949. Lithium salts in the treatment of psychotic excitement. *Medical Journal of Australia* 2:349–352.

Cadoret, R. J., and Tanna, V. L. 1977. Genetics of affective disorders. In G. Usdin, ed. *Depression.* New York: Brunner/Mazel. Pp. 104–121.

Cameron, N. 1944. The functional psychoses. In J. Mev. Hunt, ed. *Personality and behavior disorders*, Vol. 2. New York: Ronald Press.

Camus, A. 1942. *Le myth de sisyphe.* Paris: Gallimard. (Quoted in Esslin, 1969).

Carver, A. 1921. Notes on the analysis of a case of melancholia. *Journal of Neurology and Psychopathology* 1:320–324.

Cerletti, V., and Bini, L. 1938. L'elettroshock. *Archivi generali di neurologia, psichiatria e psicoanalisi* 19:266.

Charatan, F. B. 1975. Depression in old age. *New York State Journal of Medicine* 75:2505–2509.

Chertok, L. 1969. *Motherhood and personality. psychosomatic aspects of childbirth.* London: Tavistock.

Chodoff, P. 1970. The core problem in depression. In J. Masserman, ed. *Science and Psychoanalysis*, Vol. 17. New York: Grune & Stratton.

————. 1972. The depressive personality. *Archives of General Psychiatry* 27:666–677.

Choron, J. 1972. *Suicide.* New York: Scribner's.

Cohen, M. B., Blake, G., Cohen, R. A., Fromm-Reichman, F., and Weigert, E. V. 1954. An intensive study of twelve cases of manic-depressive psychosis. *Psychiatry* 17:103–38.

Committee on Nomenclature and Statistics of the American Psychiatric Association. 1968. *DSM–11: diagnostic and statistical manual of mental disorders*, Second ed. Washington: American Psychiatric Association.

Cooperman, S. 1966. Kafka's "A Country Doctor"—microcosm of symbolism. In Manheim, L. and Manheim, E., eds. *Hidden Patterns.* New York: Macmillan.

Coppen, A., Shaw, D. M., and Farrell, J. P. 1963. Potentiation of the antidepressing effect of a monoamine oxidose inhibition by tryptophan. *Lancet* 11:79–81.

Covi, L., Lipman, R. S., Derogatis, L. R., et al. 1974. Drugs and group psychotherapy in neurotic depression. *American Journal of Psychiatry* 131:191–198.
Coyne, J. C. 1976. Toward an interactional description of depression. *Psychiatry* 39:
28–40.
Cytryn, L., and McKnew, D. H., Jr. 1972. Proposed classification of childhood depression. *American Journal of Psychiatry* 129:149.
Davidson, G. M. 1936. Concerning schizophrenia and manic-depressive psychosis
associated with pregnancy and childbirth. *American Journal of Psychiatry* 92:1331.
Da Vinci, M. N. 1976. Women on women: the looking-glass novel. *Denver Quarterly*
11:1–13.
Dennis, W., and Najarian, P. 1957. Infant development under environmental handi-
cap. *Psychology Monographs* 71:1–13.
Despert, L. 1952. Suicide and depression in children. *Nervous Child* 9:378–389.
Dublin, L. I. 1963. *Suicide: a sociological and statistical study.* New York: Ronald
Press.
Durand-Fardel, M. 1855. Etude sur le suicide chez les enfants. Annals of Medicine
1:61–79.
Durell, J., and Schildkraut, J. J. 1966. Biochemical studies of the schizophrenic and
affective disorders. In S. Arieti, ed. *American handbook of psychiatry*, First ed.,
Vol. III. New York: Basic Books.
Easson, W. H. 1977. Depression in adolescence. In S. C. Feinstein and P. Giovacchini,
eds. *Adolescent psychiatry*, Vol. 5. New York: Aronson.
Eaton, J. W., and Weil, R. J. 1955a. *Culture and mental disorders.* Glencoe: Free
Press.
————. 1955b. The Mental health of the Hutterites. In A. M. Rose, ed. *Mental health
and mental disorders.* New York: Norton.
Engel, G., and Reichsman, F. 1956. Spontaneous and experimentally induced depres-
sions in an infant with gastric fistula. *Journal of the American Psychoanalytic Association* 4:428–456.
English, H. B., and English, A. C. 1958. *A comprehensive dictionary of psychological
and psychoanalytic terms.* New York, London, Toronto: Longmans, Green and Co.
English, O. S. 1949. Observations of trends in manic-depressive psychosis. *Psychiatry*
12:125.
Erikson, E. H. 1959. *Identity and the life cycle. Psychological Issues*, Vol. 1. New
York: International Universities Press.
————. 1963. *Childhood and society.* New York: Norton.
Esslin, M. 1969. *The theatre of the absurd*, rev. ed. Garden City: Anchor Books,
Doubleday.
Faris, R. E. L., and Dunham, H. W. 1939. *Mental disorders in urban areas.* Chicago:
Univ. of Chicago Press.
Feinstein, S. C., and Wolpert, E. A. 1973. Juvenile manic-depressive illness. *Journal
of the American Academy of Child Psychiatry* 12:123–136.
Fenichel, O. 1945. *The psychoanalytic theory of neurosis.* New York: Norton.
Fieve, R. R., Platman, S., and Plutchik, R. 1968. The use of lithium in affective
disorders. *American Journal of Psychiatry* 125:487–491.
Forrest, T. 1969. The combined use of marital and individual therapy in depression.
Contemporary Psychoanalysis 6:76–83.
Frazier, S. H. 1976. Changing patterns in the management of depression. *Diseases of
the Nervous System* 37:25–29.
Freud, A. 1953. Some remarks on infant observation. *The Psychoanalytic Study of
the Child* 8:9–19.
————. 1960. Discussion of Dr. J. Bowlby's paper. *The Psychoanalytic Study of the
Child* 15:53–62.
————. 1970. The symptomatology of childhood. *The Psychoanalytic Study of the
Child* 25:19–41.
Freud, S. 1957 (orig. 1900). The interpretation of dreams. *Standard Edition* 4, 5.
London: Hogarth Press.
————. 1957 (orig. 1917). Mourning and melancholia. *Standard Edition* 14:243–58.
London: Hogarth Press.

———. 1957. (orig. 1921). Group psychology and the analysis of the ego. *Standard Edition* 18. London: Hogarth Press.

———. 1957 (orig. 1923). The ego and the id. *Standard Edition* 19. London: Hogarth Press.

———. 1957 (orig. 1927). Fetishism. *Standard Edition* 21. London: Hogarth Press.

———. 1969. (orig. 1933). *New introductory lectures on psycho-analysis. Standard Edition* 22. London: Hogarth Press.

———. 1957 (orig. 1938). Splitting of the ego in the defensive process. *Standard Edition* 23. London: Hogarth Press.

Fromm E. 1941. *Escape from freedom.* New York: Rinehart.

———. 1947. *Man for himself.* New York: Rinehart.

Frommer, E. A. 1968. Depressive illness in childhood. In A. Coppen and A. Walk, eds. Recent developments in affective disorders. *British Journal of Psychiatry,* special publication no. 2. Pp. 117–136.

Fromm-Reichmann, F. 1949. Discussion of a paper by O. S. English. *Psychiatry* 12: 133.

Gardner, J. 1977. Death by art. some men kill you with a six-gun, some men with a pen. *Critical Inquiry* 3(5).

Geisler, L. S. 1973. Masked depression in patients suspected of suffering from internal diseases. In Kielholz, 1973.

Gero, G. 1936. The construction of depression. *International Journal of Psycho-Analysis* 17:423–461.

Gibbons, J. L. 1967. Cortisal secretion rate in depressive illness. *Archives of General Psychiatry* 10:572.

Gibson, R. W. 1958. The family background and early life experience of the manic-depressive patient: a comparison with the schizophrenic patient. *Psychiatry* 21: 71–90.

Goethe, W. 1827. *Nachlese zu Aristoteles Poetik.*

Gold, H. R. 1951. Observations on cultural psychiatry during a world tour of mental hospitals. *American Journal of Psychiatry* 108:462.

Goodwin, F. K., and Bunney, W. E. 1973. A psychobiological approach to affective illness. *Psychiatric Annals* 3:19.

Gove, W. R. 1972. The relationship between sex roles, marital status, and mental illness. *Social Focus* 51:36–66.

———. 1973. Sex, marital status, and mortality. *American Journal of Sociology* 79: 45–67.

Green, A. W. 1946. The middle-class male child and neurosis. *American Sociological Review* 11:31–41.

Greenspan, K., Aronoff, M., and Bogdansky, D. 1970. Effect of lithium carbonate on turnover and metabolism of norepinephrine. *Pharmacology* 3:129–136.

Group for the Advancement of Psychiatry. 1975. *Pharmacotherapy and psychotherapy: paradoxes, problems and progress,* Vol. IX. New York.

Gutheil, E. A. 1959. Reactive depressions. In Arieti, S., ed. *American handbook of psychiatry,* First ed. Vol. I. New York: Basic Books. Pp. 345–352.

Guyton, A. C. 1972. *Structure and function of the nervous system.* Philadelphia: W. B. Saunders.

Hall, C. S., and Lind, R. E. 1970. *Dreams, life, and literature: a study of Franz Kafka.* Chapel Hill: University of North Carolina Press.

Hauri, P. 1976. Dreams in patients remitted from reactive depression. *Journal of Abnormal Psychology* 85:1–10.

Helgason, T. 1964. Epidemiology of mental disorders in Iceland. *Acta Psychiatrica Scandanavia* 40.

Hempel, J. 1937. Die "vegetativ-dystone depression." *Nervenarzt* 10:22.

Hendin, M. 1975. Growing up dead: student suicide. *American Journal of Psychotherapy* 29:327–338.

Herzog, A., and Detre, T. 1976. Psychotic reactions associated with childbirth. *Diseases of the Nervous System* 37:229–235.

Hinsie, L. E., and Campbell, R. J. 1960. *Psychiatric dictionary.* New York: Oxford University Press.

Horney, K. 1945. *Our inner conflicts.* New York: Norton.
———. 1950. *Neurosis and human growth.* New York: Norton.
Jacobson, E. 1946. The effect of disappointment on ego and superego formation in normal and depressive development. *Psychoanalytic Review* 33:129–147.
———. 1954. The self and the object world. *Psychoanalytic Study of the Child* 9:75.
———. 1961. Adolescent moods and the remodeling of psychic structures in adolescence. *Psychoanalytic Study of the Child* 16:164–183.
———. 1971. *Depression.* New York: International Universities Press.
———. 1975. The psychoanalytic treatment of depressive patients. In E. J. Anthony and T. Benedek, eds. *Depression and human existence.* Boston: Little, Brown.
Janouch, G. 1953. *Conversations with Kafka.* London: Derek Verschoyle.
Jaspers, K. 1964. *General psychopathology.* Chicago: University of Chicago Press.
Jelliffe, S. E. 1931. Some historical phases of the manic-depressive synthesis. In *Manic-depressive psychosis,* Applied research in nervous and mental disease, Vol. XI. Baltimore: Williams & Wilkins.
Joffe, W. G., and Sandler, J. 1965. Notes on pain, depression, and individualism. *Psychoanalytic Study of the Child* 20:394–424.
Jones, E. 1955. *Sigmund Freud: life and work,* Vol II. New York: Basic Books.
Kafka, F. 1949. *Diaries.* Vol. 1: 1910–1913. Vol. 2: 1914–1923. New York: Schocken.
———. 1971. *The complete stories.* New York: Schocken.
———. 1973. (orig. 1919) *Letter to his father.* New York: Schocken.
Kasanin, J., and Kaufman, M. R. 1929. A study of the functional psychoses in childhood. *American Journal of Psychiatry* 9:307–384.
Katz, S. E. 1934. The family constellation as a predisposing factor in psychosis. *Psychiatric Quarterly* 8:121.
Kennedy, F. 1944. Neuroses related to manic-depressive constitutions. *Medical Clinics of North America* 28:452.
Kielholz, P., ed. 1972. *Depressive illness.* Bern: Huber.
———. ed. 1973. *Masked depression.* Bern: Huber.
Kierkegaard, S. 1954. (orig. 1843 and 1849). *Fear and trembling* and *The sickness unto death.* New York: Doubleday (Anchor).
Klaus, M. H., and Kennell, J. H. 1976. *Maternal-infant bonding.* St. Louis: Mosby.
Klein, D. F. 1974. Endogenomorphic depression. *Archives of General Psychiatry* 31:447–454.
Klein, M. 1948 (orig. 1940). Mourning and its relation to manic-depressive states. In M. Klein, ed. *Contributions to psychoanalysis, 1921–1945.* London: Hogarth Press.
Klerman, G. L., Dimascio, A., Weissman, M. et al. 1974. Treatment of depression by drugs and psychotherapy. *American Journal of Psychiatry* 131:186–191.
Koerner, O. 1929. *Die aerztliche Kenntnisse in Ilias und Odysse.* (Quoted in Jelliffe, 1931.)
Kohlberg, L. 1969. Stage and sequence: the cognitive-developmental approach to socialization. In D. A. Goslin, ed. *Handbook of socialization theory and research.* Chicago: Rand McNally.
Kolb, L. C. 1956. Psychotherapeutic evolution and its implications. *Psychiatric Quarterly* 30:1–19.
———. 1959. Personal communication
Kovacs, M. 1976. Presentation in working conference to critically examine DMS–111 in midstream. St. Louis: June 10–12.
Kraepelin, E. 1921. *Manic-depressive insanity and paranoia.* Edinburgh: Livingstone.
Kuhn, T. S. 1962. *The structure of scientific revolutions,* 2d ed. Chicago: University of Chicago Press.
Kurland, H. D. 1964. Steroid excretion in depressive disorders. *Archives of General Psychiatry* 10:554.
Kurland, M. L. 1976. Neurotic depression: an empirical guide to two specific drug treatments. *Diseases of the Nervous System* 37:424–431.
Landis, C., and Page, J. D. 1938. *Society and mental disease.* New York: Rinehart.
Laplanche, J., and Pontalis, J. B. 1973. *The language of psychoanalysis.* New York: Norton.

Leeper, R. W. 1948. A motivational theory of emotion to replace "emotion as disorganized response." *Psychiatric Review* 55:5–21.

Lemke, R. 1949. Über die vegetativ Depression. *Psychiat. Neurol. und Psychol.* 1:161.

Lesse, S., ed. 1974a. *Masked depression.* New York: Aronson.

———. 1974b. Psychotherapy in combination with antidepressant drugs in patients with severe masked depression. *American Journal of Psychotherapy* 31:185–203.

Levine, S. 1965. Some suggestions for treating the depressed patient. *Psychoanalytic Quarterly* 34:37–65.

Levy, D. 1937. Primary affect hunger. *American Journal of Psychiatry* 94:643–652.

Lewinsohn, P. M. 1969. Depression: a clinical research approach. (Unpublished manuscript, cited in Coyne, 1976.)

Lewis, A. 1934. Melancholia: a historical review. *Journal of Mental Science* 80:1.

Lindemann, E. 1944. The symptomatology and management of acute grief. *American Journal of Psychiatry* 101:141.

Loevinger, J. 1976. *Ego development.* San Francisco: Jossey-Bass.

Lopes Ibor, J. J. 1966. *Las neurosis como enfermedades del animo.* Madrid: Gedos.

———. Masked depression and depressive equivalents. (Cited in Kielholz, P. *Masked Depression* Bern: Huber 1972.)

Lorand, S. 1937. Dynamics and therapy of depressive states. *Psychoanalytic Review* 24:337–349.

Lorenz, M. 1953. Language behavior in manic patients. A qualitative study. *Archives of Neurology and Psychiatry* 69:14.

Lorenz, M., and Cobb, S. 1952. Language behavior in manic patients. *Archives of Neurology and Psychiatry* 67:763.

Luria, A. R. 1966. *Higher cortical functions in man.* New York: Basic Books.

———. 1973. *The working brain. An introduction to neuropsychology.* New York: Basic Books.

McCabe, M. S. 1975. Demographic differences in functional psychosis. *British Journal of Psychiatry* 127:320–323.

McConville, B. J., Boag, L. C., and Purohit, A. P. 1973. Three types of childhood depression. *Canadian Psychiatric Association Journal* 18:133–138.

MacLean, P. D. 1959. The limbic system with respect to two basic life principles. In M. A. B. Brazier, ed. *The central nervous system and behavior.* New York: Macy.

Magny, C. E. 1946. The objective depiction of absurdity. In A. Flores, ed. *The Kafka problem.* New York: New Directions.

Mahler, M. 1961. Sadness and grief in childhood. *Psychoanalytical study of the child* 16:332–351.

———. 1966. Notes on the development of basic moods: the depressive affect. In R. M. Lowenstein, L. M. Newman, M. Schur, and A. J. Solnit, eds. *Psychoanalysis—a general psychology.* New York: International Universities Press. Pp. 152–160.

———. 1968. *On human symbiosis and the vicissitudes of individuation.* New York: International Universities Press.

Malmquist, C. 1971. Depression in childhood and adolescence. *New England Journal of Medicine* 284:887–893; 955–961.

Malzberg, B. 1937. Is birth order related to incidence of mental disease? *American Journal of Physical Anthropology* 24:91.

———. 1940. *Social and biological aspects of mental disease.* Utica, New York: State Hospital Press.

Mandell, A. J., and Segal, D. S. 1975. Neurochemical aspects of adaptive regulation in depression: failure and treatment. In E. J. Anthony and T. Benedek, eds. *Depression and human existence.* Boston: Little, Brown.

Maranon, G. 1954. Climacteric: the critical age in the male. In A. M. Krich, ed. *Men: the variety and meaning of their sexual experiences.* New York: Dell.

Mattson, A., Sesse, L. R., and Hawkins, J. W. 1969. Suicidal behavior as a child psychiatric emergency. *Archives of General Psychiatry* 20:100–109.

Mendels, J. 1974. Biological aspects of affective illness. In S. Arieti, ed. *American handbook of psychiatry,* Second ed., Vol. III. New York: Basic Books. Pp. 491–523.

Mendels, J., Stern, S., and Frazer, A. 1976. Biological concepts of depression. In D. M. Gallant and G. M. Simpson, eds. *Depression.* New York: Spectrum Publications. Pp. 19–76.

Mendelson, M. 1974. *Psychoanalytic concepts of depression.* New York: Spectrum Publications.

Messina, F., Agallianos, D., and Clower, C. 1970. Dopamine excretion in affective states and following Li_2Co_3 therapy. *Nature* 225:868–869.

Meyer, A. 1908a. The role of the mental factors in psychiatry. *American Journal of Insanity* 65:39.

————. 1908b. The problems of mental reaction—types, mental causes and diseases. *Psychological Bulletin* 5:265.

Miller, J. B. 1976. *Toward a new psychology of women.* Boston: Beacon Press.

Miller, W. R., and Seligman, M. E. P. 1976. Learned helplessness, depression, and the perception of reinforcement. *Behavioral Research and Therapy* 14:7–17.

Minkowski, E. 1958. Findings in a case of schizophrenic depression. In R. May, ed. *Existence.* New York: Basic Books.

Mitscherlich, A., and Mitscherlich, M. 1975. *The inability to mourn.* Translated by B. R. Placzek. New York: Grove Press.

Moulton, R. 1973. Sexual conflicts of contemporary women. In E. G. Wittenberg, ed. *Interpersonal explorations in psychoanalysis.* New York: Basic Books.

Munn, N. L. 1946. *Psychology: the fundamentals of human adjustment.* New York: Houghton-Mifflin.

Murphy, H. B. M., Wittkower, E. D., and Chance, N. A. 1967. Cross-cultural inquiry into the symptomatology of depression: a preliminary report. *International Journal of Psychiatry* 3:6–15.

Nagy, M. H. 1959. The child's view of death. In H. Feifel, ed. *The meaning of death.* New York: McGraw-Hill.

Neal, J. B., ed. 1942. *Encephalitis: a clinical study.* New York: Grune & Stratton.

Neider, C. 1948. *The frozen sea: a study of Franz Kafka.* New York: Oxford University Press.

Odegard, O. 1963. The psychiatric disease entitites in the light of genetic investigation. *Acta Psychiatrica Scandanavia* (Suppl.) 169:94–104.

Olds, J., and Milner, P. 1954. Positive reinforcement produced by electrical stimulation of septal area and other regions of rat brain. *Journal of Comparative Physiology and Psychology* 47:419–427.

Oswald, I., Brezinova, J., and Dunleavy, D. L. F. 1972. On the slowness of action of tricyclic antidepressant drugs. *British Journal of Psychiatry* 120:673.

Palmer, H. D., and Sherman, S. H. 1938. The involutional melancholic process. *Archives of Neurology and Psychiatry* 40:762–788.

Papez, J. W. 1937. A proposed mechanism of emotion. *Archives of Neurology and Psychiatry* 38:725–743.

Parkes, C. M. 1964. The effects of bereavement on physical and mental health: a study of the case records of widows. *British Medical Journal* 2:276.

————. 1965. Bereavement and mental illness. *British Journal of Medical Psychology* 38:1–25.

————. 1972. *Bereavement: studies of grief in adult life.* New York: International Universities Press.

————. 1973. Separation anxiety: an aspect of the search for the lost object. In R. J. Weiss, ed. *Loneliness. The experience of emotional and social isolation.* Cambridge: MIT Press.

Parker, S. 1962. Eskimo psychopathology in the context of eskimo personality and culture. *American Anthropologist* 64:76–96.

Perris, C. 1966. A study of bipolar (manic-depressive) and unipolar recurrent depressive psychosis. *Acta Psychiatrica Scandanavia* (Suppl.) 194:42.

————. 1976. Frequency and hereditary aspects of depression. In D. M. Gallant and G. M. Simpson, eds. *Depression.* New York: Spectrum Publications.

Piaget, J. 1932. *The moral judgment of the child.* New York: Free Press.

————. 1951. *Play, dreams, and imitation in childhood.* New York: Norton.

————. 1952. *The origins of intelligence in children.* New York: International Universities Press.

Politzer, H. 1966. *Franz Kafka: parable and paradox,* Second ed. Ithaca: Cornell University Press.

Pollock, H. M., Malzberg, B., and Fuller, R. G. 1939. *Hereditary and environmental factors in the causation of manic-depressive psychosis and dementia praecox.* Utica, New York: State Hospital Press.

Poznanski, E., and Zrull, J. P. 1970. Childhood depression: clinical characteristics of overtly depressed children. *Archives of General Psychiatry* 23:8–15.

Poznanski, E. O., Krahenbuhl, V., and Zrull, P. 1976. Childhood depression: a longitudinal perspective. *Journal of the American Academy of Child Psychiatry* 15:491–501.

Prange, A. J., Jr., Wilson, I. C., and Rabon, A. M. 1969. Enhancement of imipramine antidepressant activity by thyroid hormone. *American Journal of Psychiatry* 126:457.

Prange, A. J., Jr., and Wilson, I. C. 1972. Thyrotropin Releasing Hormone (TRH) for the immediate relief of depression: a preliminary report. *Psychopharmacology* 26 (Suppl.).

Prange, A. J. Jr. 1973. The use of drugs in depression: its theoretical and practical basis. *Psychiatric Annals* 3:56.

Protheroe, C. 1969. Puerperal psychoses: a long-term study 1927–1961. *British Journal of Psychiatry* 115:9–30.

Rado, S. 1956. (orig. 1927). The problem of melancholia. In Rado S. *Collected papers,* Vol. I. New York: Grune & Stratton.

————. 1951. Psychodynamics of depression from the etiologic point of view. *Psychosomatic Medicine* 13:51–55.

Raskin, A. 1974. A guide for drug use in depressive disorders. *American Journal of Psychiatry* 131:181–185.

Redmond, D. E., Mass, J. W., and King, A. 1971. Social behavior of monkeys selectively depleted of monoamines. *Science* 174:428–431.

Rennie, T. A. L. 1942. Prognosis in manic-depressive psychosis. *American Journal of Psychiatry* 98:801.

Rie, M. E. 1966. Depression in childhood: a survey of some pertinent contributions. *Journal of the American Academy of Child Psychiatry* 5:653–685.

Riesman, D., Glazer, N., and Denney, R. 1950. *The lonely crowd.* New Haven: Yale University Press.

Rochlin, G. 1959. The loss complex. *Journal of the American Psychoanalytic Association* 7:299–316.

Rosenthal, S. H. 1968. The involutional depressive syndrome. *American Journal of Psychiatry* (Suppl.) 124:21–35.

————. 1974. Involutional depression. In S. Arieti, ed. *American handbook of psychiatry,* Second ed. Vol. III. New York: Basic Books. Pp. 694–709.

Russell, B. 1967. *The autobiography of Bertrand Russell: the early years.* New York: Bantam.

Sachar, E., Hellman, L., and Gallagher, T. F. 1972. Cortisal production in depression. In T. A. Williams, M. M. Katz, and J. A. Shield, Jr., eds. *Recent advances in the psychobiology of the depressive illnesses.* Department of Health, Education, and Welfare: Publication No. (HSM) 70-9053.

Sapirstein, S. L., and Kaufman, M. R. 1966. The higher they climb, the lower they fall. *Journal of the Canadian Psychiatric Association* 11:229–304.

Salzman, L., and Masserman, J. H. 1962. *Modern concepts of psychoanalysis.* New York: Philosophical Library.

Sandler, J., and Joffe, W. G. 1965. Notes on childhood depression. *International Journal of Psychoanalysis* 46:88–96.

Schilder, P., and Weschler, D. 1934. The attitudes of children toward death. *Journal of Genetic Psychology* 45:406–451.

Schildkraut, J. J. 1965. The catecholamine hypothesis of affective disorders: a review of supporting evidence. *American Journal of Psychiatry* 122:509–522.

————. 1975. Depression and biogenic amines. In D. Hamburg and H. K. H. Brodie, eds. *American handbook of psychiatry,* Vol. 6. New York: Basic Books.

Schlegel, F. 1818. *Lectures on the history of literature, ancient and modern.* Edinburgh.

Schoenberg, B., Gerber, I., Wiener, A., Kutscher, A. H., Peretz, D., and Carrac, eds. 1975. *Bereavement: its psychological aspects.* New York: Columbia University Press.

Schopenhauer, A. 1961. *The world as will and idea.* Translated by R. B. Haldane and J. Keint. New York: AMS Press.

Segal, Hannah. 1964. *Introduction to the work of Melanie Klein.* London: Heinemann.

Seiden, R. H. 1969. *Suicide among youth. Bulletin of Suicidology.* (Suppl.).

Seligman, M. E. P. 1975. *Helplessness.* San Francisco: W. H. Freeman.

Seligman, M., and Maier, S. 1967. Failure to escape traumatic shock. *Journal of Experimental Psychology* 74:1–9.

Shaffer, D. 1974. Suicide in childhood and early adolescence. *Journal of Child Psychology and Psychiatry* 15:275–291.

Shambaugh, B. 1961. A study of loss reactions in a seven-year-old. *Psychoanalytic Study of the Child* 16:510–522.

Shimoda, M. 1961. Über den fraaruorbideu charakter des manish-depressiven irreseius. *Psychiatria et Neurologia Japonica* 45:101.

Silverberg, W. 1952. *Childhood experience and personal destiny.* New York: Springer.

Slipp, S. 1976. An intrapsychic-interpersonal theory of depression. *Journal of the American Academy of Psychoanalysis* 4:389–410.

Smith, A., Troganza, E., and Harrison, G. 1969. Studies on the effectiveness of antidepressant drugs. *Psychopharmacology Bulletin* (Special issue).

Smythies, J. 1973. Psychiatry and neurosciences. *Psychological Medicine* 3:267–269.

Sperling, M. 1959. Equivalents of depression in children. *Journal of Hillside Hospital* 8:138–148.

Spiegel, R. 1959. Specific problems of communication in psychiatric conditions. In S. Arieti, ed. *American handbook of psychiatry,* First ed. Vol. I. New York: Basic Books. Pp. 909–949.

———. 1960. Communication in the psychoanalysis of depression. In J. Masserman, ed. *Psychoanalysis and human values.* New York: Grune & Stratton.

———. 1965. Communication with depressive patients. *Contemporary Psychoanalysis* 2:30–35.

Spitz, R. 1946. Anaclitic depression. *Psychoanalytic Study of the Child* 5:113–117.

Strecker, E. A., and Ebaugh, F. 1926. Psychoses occurring during the puerperium. *Archives of Neurology and Psychiatry* 15:239.

Strongin, E. I., and Hinsie, L. E. 1938. Parotid gland secretions in manic-depressive patients. *American Journal of Psychiatry* 96:14–59.

Sullivan, H. S. 1940. *Conceptions of modern psychiatry.* New York: Norton.

———. 1953. *The interpersonal theory of psychiatry.* New York: Norton.

Szalita, A. B. 1966. Psychodynamics of disorders of the involutional age. In S. Arieti, ed. *American handbook of psychiatry,* First ed., Vol. III. New York: Basic Books. Pp. 66–87.

———. 1974. Grief and bereavement. In S. Arieti, ed. *American handbook of psychiatry,* Second ed., Vol. I. Pp. 673–684.

Taulbee, E. S., and Wright, H. W. 1971. A psychosocial-behavioral model for therapeutic intervention. In C. D. Spielberger, ed. *Current topics in clinical and community psychology,* Vol. 3. New York: Academic Press.

Tellenbach, H. 1974. *Melancholic problemgeschichte-endogenitat-typologie-pathogenese-klinik.* Berlin: Springer-Verlag.

Thomas, A., Chess, S., and Birch, H. G. 1968. *Temperament and behavior disorders in children.* New York: New York University Press.

Thompson, C. M. 1930. Analytic observations during the course of a manic-depressive psychosis. *Psychoanalytic Review* 17:240.

Thompson, R. J., and Schindler, F. H. 1976. Embryonic mania. *Child Psychiatry and Human Development* 7:149–154.

Titley, W. B. 1936. Prepsychotic personality of involutional melancholia. *Archives of Neurology and Psychiatry* 36:19–33.

Toolan, J. M. 1962. Depression in children and adolescents. *American Journal of Orthopsychiatry* 32:404–15.

Tupin, J. P. 1972. Effect of lithium and sodium and body weight in manic-depressives and normals. In T. A. Williams, M. M. Katz, and J. A. Shield, Jr., eds. *Recent advances in the psychobiology of the depressive illnesses.* Department of Health, Education, and Welfare: Publication No. (HSM) 70-9053.

Veith, Ilza. 1970. Elizabethans on melancholia. *Journal of the American Medical Association* 212:127.

Wainwright, W. H. 1966. Fatherhood as a precipitant of mental illness. *American Journal of Psychiatry* 123:40–44.

Warneke, L. 1975. A case of manic-depressive illness in childhood. *Canadian Psychiatric Association Journal* 20:195–200.

Weinberg, W. A., Rutman, J., and Sullivan, L. 1973. Depression in children referred to an educational diagnostic center: diagnosis and treatment. *Journal of Pediatrics* 83:1065–1072.

Weiner, I. B. 1970. *Psychological disturbance in adolescence.* New York: Wiley.

Weiss, J. M. A. 1957. The gamble with death in attempted suicide. *Psychiatry* 20:17.

———. 1974. Suicide. In S. Arieti, ed. *American handbook of psychiatry,* Second ed., Vol. III. Pp. 763–765.

Weissman, M. M., and Klerman, L. 1977. Sex differences and the epidemiology of depression. *Archives of General Psychiatry* 34:98–111.

Weissman, M. M., Klerman, G. L., Payhel, E. S., et al. 1974. Treatment effects on the social adjustment of depressed patients. *Archives of General Psychiatry* 30:771–778.

Weissman, M. M., Prusoff, B. A., and Klerman, G. 1975. Drugs and psychotherapy in depression revisited. *Psychopharmacology Bulletin* 11:39–41.

Werner, H. 1948. *The comparative psychology of mental development.* New York: International Universities Press.

Whittier, J. R. 1975. Mental disorders with Huntington's chorea. Clinical aspects. In S. Arieti, ed. *American handbook of psychiatry,* Second ed., Vol. IV. New York: Basic Books. Pp. 412–417.

Wilson, E. 1962. A dissenting opinion on Kafka. In D. Gray, ed. *Kafka.* Englewood Cliffs: Prentice-Hall.

Winnicott, D. W. 1953. Transitional objects and transitional phenomena. *International Journal of Psycho-Analysis* 34.

Winokur, G. 1973. Depression in the menopause. *American Journal of Psychiatry* 130:92–93.

Winokur, G., Cadoret, R., Dorzab, J., and Baker, M. 1971. Depressive disease. A genetic study. *Archives of General Psychiatry* 25:135–144.

Wolfgang, M. E. 1959. Suicide by means of victim-precipitated homocide: *Journal of Clinical and Experimental Psychology* 20:335–349.

Wolman, B. B. 1973. *Dictionary of behavioral science.* New York: Van Nostrand.

Woodworth, R. S. 1940. *Psychology.* New York: Holt.

Zetzel, E. R. 1965. Depression and its incapacity to bear it. In M. Schur, ed. *Drives, affects, behavior,* Vol. 2. New York: International Universities Press.

Zilboorg, G. 1928. Malignant psychoses related to childbirth. *American Journal of Obstetrics and Gynecology* 15:145–158.

———. 1929. The dynamics of schizophrenic reactions related to pregnancy and childbirth. *American Journal of Psychiatry* 8:733–767.

———. 1931. Depressive reactions related to parenthood. *American Journal of Psychiatry* 87:927–962.

———. 1941. *A history of medical psychology.* New York: Norton.

———. 1944. Manic-depressive psychoses. In S. Lorand, ed. *Psychoanalysis today.* New York: International Universities Press.

NAME INDEX

SUBJECT INDEX